Your Class.
Their Career.
Everyone's Future.

PEARSON
myeducationlab

Helping today's students become the teachers of tomorrow.

"Teacher educators who are developing pedagogies for the analysis of teaching and learning contend that analyzing teaching artifacts has three advantages: it enables new teachers time for reflection while still using the real materials of practice; it provides new teachers with experience thinking about and approaching the complexity of the classroom; and in some cases, it can help new teachers and teacher educators develop a shared understanding and common language about teaching. . . ."[1]

As Linda Darling-Hammond and her colleagues point out, grounding teacher education in real classrooms—among real teachers and students and among actual examples of students' and teachers' work—is an important, and perhaps even an essential, part of training teachers for the complexities

of teaching today's students in today's classrooms. For a number of years, we have heard the same message from many of you as we sat in your offices learning about the goals of your courses and the challenges you face in teaching the next generation of educators. Working with a number of our authors and with many of you, we have created a website that provides you and your students with the context of real classrooms and artifacts that research on teacher education tells us is so important. Through authentic in-class video footage, interactive simulations, rich case studies, examples of authentic teacher and student work, and more, **MyEducationLab** offers you and your students a uniquely valuable teacher education tool.

MyEducationLab is easy to use! Wherever the **MyEducationLab** logo appears in the margins or elsewhere in the text, you and your students can follow the simple link instructions to access the **MyEducationLab** resource that corresponds with the chapter content. These include:

VIDEO ■ Authentic classroom videos show how real teachers handle actual classroom situations.

HOMEWORK & EXERCISES ■ These assignable activities give students opportunities to understand content more deeply and to practice applying content.

BUILDING TEACHING SKILLS ■ These assignments help students practice and strengthen skills that are essential to quality teaching. By analyzing and responding to real student and teacher artifacts and/or authentic classroom videos, students practice important teaching skills they will need when they enter real classrooms.

CASE STUDIES

A diverse set of robust cases drawn from some of our best-selling books further expose students to the realities of teaching and offer valuable perspectives on common issues and challenges in education.

SIMULATIONS

Created by the IRIS Center at Vanderbilt University, these interactive simulations give hands-on practice at adapting instruction for a full spectrum of learners.

STUDENT & TEACHER ARTIFACTS

Authentic student and teacher classroom artifacts are tied to course topics and offer practice in working with the actual types of materials that teachers encounter every day.

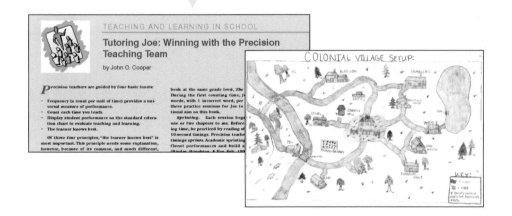

INDIVIDUALIZED STUDY PLAN

Your students have the opportunity to take pre- and post-tests before and after reading each chapter of the text. Their test results automatically generate a personalized study plan, identifying areas of the chapter they must reread to fully understand chapter concepts. They are also presented with interactive multimedia exercises to help ensure learning. The study plan is designed to help your students perform well on exams and to promote deep understanding of chapter content.

READINGS ■ Specially selected, topically relevant articles from ASCD's renowned *Educational Leadership* journal expand and enrich students' perspectives on key issues and topics.

Other Resources

LESSON & PORTFOLIO BUILDERS ■ With this effective and easy-to-use tool, you can create, update, and share standards-based lesson plans and portfolios.

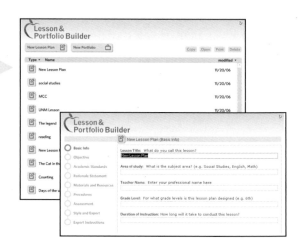

NEWS ARTICLES ■ Looking for current issues in education? Our collection offers quick access to hundreds of relevant articles from the *New York Times* Educational News Feed.

MyEducationLab is easy to assign, which is essential to providing the greatest benefit to your students. Visit www.myeducationlab.com for a demonstration of this exciting new online teaching resource.

[1] Darling-Hammond, L., & Bransford, J., Eds. (2005). *Preparing Teachers for a Changing World.* San Francisco: John Wiley & Sons.

PEARSON
myeducationlab™

An Introduction to Education

Choosing Your Teaching Path

Sara Davis Powell

Belmont Abbey College

Merrill
is an imprint of

Upper Saddle River, New Jersey
Columbus, Ohio

Library of Congress Cataloging in Publication Data

Powell, Sara Davis.
    An introduction to education : choosing your teaching path / Sara Davis Powell.
       p. cm.
    Includes bibliographical references and index.
    ISBN-13: 978-0-13-119252-2
    ISBN-10: 0-13-119252-3
    1. Teaching—Vocational guidance. I. Title.
    LB1775.P625 2009
    371.1'0023—dc22   2007035293

Vice President and Executive Publisher: Jeffery W. Johnston
Acquisitions Editor: Darcy Betts Prybella
Development Editor: Amy J. Nelson
Editorial Assistant: Nancy Holstein
Production Editor: Sheryl Glicker Langner
Photo Coordinator: Lori Whitley
Design Coordinator: Diane C. Lorenzo
Cover Design: Kristina Holmes
Production Manager: Susan Hannahs
Director of Marketing: Quinn Perkson
Marketing Coordinator: Brian Mounts

This book was set in Galliard by S4Carlisle Publishing Services. It was printed and bound by C. J. Krehbiel, Inc. The cover was printed by Phoenix Color Corp.

Photo Credits: Provided by the author, pp. 7, 10, 25 (top, middle), 38, 57, 71, 111, 131, 160, 187, 213, 214, 235 (both), 236, 247, 252 (bottom), 258 (top), 269, 271, 282, 303, 322, 327, 332, 357, 388, 395, 412, 413, 437 (top), 440 (top); Cody White, pp. 41, 294 (top); Allen Millican/Millican Art and Photography, p. 74 (top); Will Hart/PhotoEdit Inc., pp. 94, 308; Scott Cunningham/Merrill, p. 96; provided by the Kutcher family, p. 98 (all); provided by the Todd family, pp. 100 (top left, right), 292 (top left); provided by the Francis family, pp. 100 (middle left, center), 292 (top 2nd from left); provided by the Wiley family, pp. 100 (bottom left 3 images), 292 (top 2nd from right); provided by the Mancia family, pp. 101 (top left 3 images), 292 (top right); provided by the Ford family, pp. 101 (middle left 3 images), 292 (middle left); provided by the Sutton family, pp. 101 (bottom left 3 images), 292 (middle center); provided by the McBeath family, p. 102 (top left 3 images); provided by the Kutcher family, p. 102 (middle 4 images); provided by the Reyes family, pp. 102 (bottom 4 images), 292 (bottom left); provided by the Toscano family, pp. 103 (top left 4 images), 292 (middle right); provided by the Martinez family, p. 103 (middle left); provided by the Douangsavanh family, pp. 103 (bottom left 3 images), 292 (bottom right); Barbara Hairfield, pp. 125, 142, 430 (top); Jessica O'Rourke, pp. 169, 406; Corbis/Bettmann, pp. 240, 244, 246 (bottom), 256 (both); Getty Images Inc. – Hulton Archive Photos, pp. 242, 253 (middle); Corbis Digital Stock, pp. 246 (top), 253 (bottom); North Wind Picture Archives, p. 249; © Bettmann/CORBIS All Rights Reserved, p. 250 (top); courtesy of the Library of Congress, pp. 250 (bottom), 257 (middle); © CORBIS All Rights Reserved, p. 251 (top); The Schlesinger Library, p. 251 (bottom); The Prudence Crandall Museum, p. 252 (top); courtesy of Millican Art and Photography, pp. 252 (middle), 258 (bottom 5 images), 260; SCHOMBURG CENTER/Art Resource, NY, p. 257 (top); Ansel Adams/University of Chicago Library, p. 259 (top); University of Chicago Library, p. 259 (bottom); Rebecca Dunbar, p. 268; Jonathan Nourok/PhotoEdit Inc., pp. 273, 312; © Viviane Moos/CORBIS All Rights Reserved, p. 294 (bottom); Peter Byron/PhotoEdit Inc., p. 297; David Young-Wolff/PhotoEdit Inc., p. 305; Michael Newman/PhotoEdit Inc., p. 314; Philip James Corwin/CORBIS–NY, p. 333; Bob Daemmrich/The Image Works, p. 343; Valerie Berta/Journal–Courier/The Image Works, p. 350; Mark Richards/PhotoEdit Inc., p. 366; provided by Dana Boyd, p. 368; Patrick Watson/PH College, p. 375 (top); Bill Bachmann/Creative Eye/MIRA.com, p. 375 (middle); Getty Images – Stockbyte, p. 375 (bottom). All other photos by Sara Davis Powell.

Pearson Education Ltd.
Pearson Education Singapore Pte. Ltd.
Pearson Education Canada, Ltd.
Pearson Education–Japan

Pearson Education Australia Pty. Limited
Pearson Education North Asia Ltd.
Pearson Educación de Mexico, S.A. de C.V.
Pearson Education Malaysia Pte. Ltd.

Merrill
is an imprint of

PEARSON

10 9 8 7 6 5 4 3 2 1
ISBN-13: 978-0-13-119252-2
ISBN-10:   0-13-119252-3

This book is dedicated to Jesse White, a young man who has chosen to teach the middle school students who need him most. He does so with enthusiasm and creativity, with empathy and care, and with consistent commitment. The teaching profession both pushes him to grow and provides satisfaction that what he does matters. To Jesse, my son . . . and all the future teachers who will make real differences in the lives of children and adolescents, thank you.

Letter to the Instructor

■ Dear Instructor,

I'll bet you're thinking, "Why in the world do we need another intro to education text? Aren't there enough of them, in their many editions, to satisfy every professor's needs and course objectives?" Believe me, I think the same thing each time a new text is sent to me for the courses I teach. Truthfully, I rarely change texts. It's enough trouble to adjust to a new edition, much less a whole different approach.

A quick read through the table of contents will tell you it's all here—the teaching profession, student development, curriculum, instruction, assessment, the learning environment, history, law, governance, finance . . . I've included all the big pieces that need to be squeezed into one short semester. Beyond providing relevant content, my goal in writing this text was to make it one that students actually want to read. The content isn't dumbed down, but rather organized in a logical way, written in accessible language.

The most unique feature of this text is the way the experiences of 10 teachers and 12 students at 4 schools across the country are woven throughout. These people and places are authentic. It would have been much easier to make up personalities and scenarios to illustrate concepts, but I didn't. The word "real" is overused in texts when what should be said is that most scenarios are compilations of people and events the authors have experienced. That's fine and it can be effective. But it's not the case in *Choosing Your Teaching Path*. The teachers and students are from Summit Station, Ohio; Spanish Fork, Utah; Mt. Pleasant, South Carolina; and Fresno, California. I spent time with each of them. A videographer filmed them as we talked, and as they talked with each other. I took pictures while we were filming the video to help you and your students get to know the teachers and students as their lives personalize many of the text's concepts. These videos are located in the Choosing Your Teaching Path section of MyEducationLab located at www.myeducationlab.com. In addition, at the end of each chapter we direct students to the Virtual Field Experience section of MyEducationLab to watch particular segments of the video described above. Here, students can respond to questions about the video that will help them make sense of what they have read in the chapter.

I hope you'll take the time to open this book and read a few passages. Take a look at the preface to find out about the features and opportunities available for your students through the text, the accompanying MyEducationLab, and the *In the News: ABC News* DVD. I am a teacher who loves the profession—the challenges and the endless possibilities that are afforded through the classroom. Teaching is serious business; thankfully, it's also lots of fun. There's so much we want prospective teachers to know and be able to do. I hope this text will become part of the preparation of future teachers who will make positive differences in the lives of many, many children and adolescents.

Sara Davis Powell

Preface

Offering a unique experience, *An Introduction to Education: Choosing Your Teaching Path*, brings teaching to life by taking you into real schools to meet real teachers and students. Go on a journey to help you determine if teaching is for you, discover what kind of teacher you want to be, and identify what age students you would like to teach.

■ Setting the Stage

In keeping with effective lesson planning procedures, each chapter begins with an anticipatory set to help prepare readers for what's about to come. Three distinct strategies are used.

- **Teaching in Focus**
  This opening scenario centers on one of the text's 10 focus teachers and relates some of the teacher's experiences that are aligned with chapter content. A photograph of the teacher is included as a memory jogger to help readers identify the teacher as someone they have both read about and watched on the video.

Teaching in Focus

Brandi Wade teaches kindergarten at Summit Primary School in Summit Station, Ohio. We first met Brandi in Chapter 1. She has witnessed many changes at her school as families have moved into the once rural area just outside Columbus. Housing developments have sprung up all around the school, and change has been ongoing for several years. The small town of Summit Station is now surrounded by a thriving, suburban-like area, and there are no signs of the rate of growth slowing down. The Licking Heights School District continues to build bigger schools to accommodate the growth. Summit Primary is the only K–2 school in the district. This is a purposeful configuration. Principal Laura Hill says she likes the format because she has every

- **Guiding Questions**
  At the end of each *Teaching in Focus* segment, the big ideas of the chapter are presented in the form of questions to help readers understand the chapter's organization.

- **Introduction**
  Each chapter's *Introduction* provides context for the topics to be addressed.

PEARSON myeducationlab

Your Class, Your Career, Everyone's Future

"Teacher educators who are developing pedagogies for the analysis of teaching and learning contend that analyzing teaching artifacts has three advantages: it enables new teachers time for reflection while still using the real materials of practice; it provides new teachers with experience thinking about and approaching the complexity of the classroom; and in some cases, it can help new teachers and teacher educators develop a shared understanding and common language about teaching. . . ."[1] As Linda Darling-Hammond and her colleagues point out, grounding teacher education in real classrooms—among real teachers and students and among actual examples of students' and teachers' work—is an important, and perhaps even an essential, part of training teachers for the complexities of teaching today's students in today's classrooms. For a number of years, we have heard the same message from many of you as we sat in your offices learning about the goals of your courses and the challenges you face in teaching the next generation of educators. Working with a number of our authors and with many of you, we have created a website that provides you and your students with the context of real classrooms and artifacts that research on teacher education tells us is so important. Through authentic in-class video footage, interactive simulations, rich case studies, examples of authentic teacher and student work, and more, **MyEducationLab** offers you and your students a uniquely valuable teacher education tool.

MyEducationLab is easy to use! Wherever the MyEducationLab logo appears in the margins and at the end of each chapter, you and your students can follow the simple link instructions to access the Individualized Study Plan, Homework & Exercises, Choosing Your Teaching Path Video, and Virtual Field Experience sections in MyEducationLab that corresponds with the chapter content.

---

10 Chapter 1

Opportunity for a lifetime of self-growth. This is exactly what teaching offers. Few careers are as exciting or as rewarding on a daily basis. And few offer the satisfaction that teaching does of positively impacting the future of children.

Teachers experience self-growth, both personally and professionally, in many ways: through relationships, reading, attending conferences, and the wide variety of professional development opportunities available. Teaching is not a stagnant career; rather, it continually presents new experiences, all of which offer opportunities for self-growth.

  Your Teaching Fingerprint Do you enjoy personal and professional growth that's sometimes planned and sometimes spontaneous? Do you want a career that not only provides opportunities for self-growth, but also expects it of you?

We've looked at eight reasons for choosing teaching as a career. There are many more. Yet stopping with a discussion of all the benefits and rewards of teaching presents a picture that's out of balance. No career is without challenges; no career is without frustration. Teaching has its share of both, as we will discuss here and in Chapter 13. Let's examine the work of teachers.

■ What Are the Roles of Teachers?

What do teachers do every day? What's it like to be in a classroom? Most teachers are required to be in their schools for about 37 hours per week, yet almost all of them will tell you they spend many additional hours in active preparation for their work.

It would be impossible to describe all the roles that teachers fulfill. Here we'll look briefly at five of the most significant roles of teachers within their classrooms, as illustrated in Figure 1.4.

Reflective Practitioner

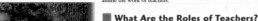

John Dewey (1933), one of the great American educators, defined reflection as "the active, persistent, and careful consideration of any belief or supposed form of knowledge in light of the grounds that support it" (p. 9). A simple definition of **reflection** with regard to teaching is thinking about what we do, how we do it, and the consequences of our actions or inactions, all with the goal of being better teachers. To be **reflective practitioners** means that we deliberately think about our practice, that is, what we do as teachers. We do this with the purpose of analysis and improvement. Sounds pretty automatic and unavoidable, doesn't it? But it's not. A teacher can repeatedly go through the motions of planning, teaching, and assessing throughout a career, yet seldom engage in reflection that results in improved practice.

So how do we become reflective practitioners who, as Dewey said, actively, persistently, and carefully think about how we teach? Here are some concepts to consider.

Derek Boucher and his family enjoy the benefits of a teacher's schedule that includes similar hours and vacations for parents and children.

- Reflective practice requires conscious effort.
- Self-knowledge is vital and can be aided by thoughtfully completing the "Writing My Own Story" and "What's My Disposition?" segments in the Homework and Exercises section of MyEducationLab.
- Reading about and researching aspects of teaching will ground our practice and provide subject matter on which to reflect.
- Talking with other educators will both inform and strengthen what we do and how we do it.

---

[1] Darling-Hammond, I., & Bransford, J., Eds. (2005). *Preparing teachers for a changing world.* San Francisco: John Wiley & Sons.

Individualized Study Plan: Your students have the opportunity to take pre- and post-tests before and after reading each chapter of the text. Their test results automatically generate a personalized study plan, identifying areas of the chapter they must reread to fully understand chapter concepts. They are also presented with interactive multimedia exercises to help ensure learning. The study plan is designed to help your students perform well on exams and to promote deep understanding of chapter content.

Video: Authentic classroom videos show how real teachers handle actual classroom situations.

Homework & Exercises: These assignable activities give students opportunities to understand content more deeply and to practice applying content. At the end of each chapter, students are encouraged to complete the following activities: *Writing My Own Story*, *What's My Disposition?*, and *Exploring Schools and Classrooms*.

Choosing Your Teaching Path: This section contains video of the text's focus schools, teachers, and students.

Virtual Field Experience: Here, students watch particular segments of the *Choosing Your Teaching Path* video. Students can respond to questions about the video that will help them make sense of what they have read in the chapter.

Case Studies: A diverse set of robust cases drawn from some of our best-selling books further expose students to the realities of teaching and offer valuable perspectives on common issues and challenges in education.

Video: Authentic classroom videos show how real teachers handle actual classroom situations.

Simulations: Created by the IRIS Center at Vanderbilt University, these interactive simulations give hands-on practice at adapting instruction for a full spectrum of learners.

Student & Teacher Artifacts: Authentic student and teacher classroom artifacts are tied to course topics and offer practice in working with the actual types of materials encountered every day by teachers.

Readings: Specially selected, topically relevant articles from ASCD's renowned *Educational Leadership* journal expand and enrich students' perspectives on key issues and topics.

Other Resources:
Lesson & Portfolio Builders: With this effective and easy-to-use tool, you can create, update, and share standards-based lesson plans and portfolios.

News Articles: Looking for current issues in education? Our collection offers quick access to hundreds of relevant articles from the New York Times Educational News Feed.

MyEducationLab is easy to assign, which is essential to providing the greatest benefit to your student. Visit www.myeducationlab.com for a demonstration of this exciting new online teaching resource.

Find Your Teaching Identity

Because *An Introduction to Education: Choosing Your Teaching Path* takes a broad, yet comprehensive look at Pre-K–12 education in the United States, readers will learn much about what's involved in being a teacher as they read the text and work through accompanying ancillary materials. This perspective will help readers decide if teaching is the profession for them.

Through this text, readers who have made the decision to be teacher candidates will begin to find their teaching identity. They will gain perspective on what it's like to teach children at early childhood and elementary levels, as well as adolescents at middle and high school levels. Readers will discover, woven throughout the text and highlighted by level icons, insights about the responsibilities and opportunities involved in teaching at various levels.

Early Childhood

Elementary

Middle School

High School

Your Teaching Fingerprint

In addition, questions are posed throughout the text to prompt teacher candidates to reflect on what they have read in the text and watched on the Choosing Your Teaching Path section of MyEducationLab. These questions are highlighted by a fingerprint icon that lets readers know they are being asked to personally interact with content and concepts. Some of the questions in each chapter are located in the "Writing My Own Story" feature of the Homework and Exercises section of MyEducationLab. After responding to reflective questions in all 14 chapters, teacher candidates will have a journal of personal history and responses to a wide variety of aspects of the teaching profession that will help reveal their teaching identity.

Focus Schools, Teachers, and Students

A unique and intriguing aspect of *An Introduction to Education: Choosing Your Teaching Path* is the personalization of the content through a focus on real schools, real teachers, and real students.

■ Focus Schools

Schools in the United States uniquely represent the rural areas, neighborhoods, towns, and cities of the country. It is impossible to determine what is typical or representative of schools in the United States because of multiple variables, many of which are discussed in this text. Four schools were chosen as focal points of discussion not because they represent four distinct areas or profiles of schools, but simply as examples of public education. In Chapter 2, the reader is presented with initial information about each school. In the Choosing Your Teaching Path section of MyEducationLab principals of each focus school talk with the author about their schools and take viewers on a tour of their facilities.

Summit Primary School, Summit Station, Ohio

Summit Primary is a school for kindergarten through second grade students. It is located just west of Columbus, Ohio, in Licking County. Once a rural farm community, Summit Station is becoming a suburban area with a growing and increasingly diverse population. Principal Laura Hill and the author talk about caring for and educating America's youngest students.

Rees Elementary School, Spanish Fork, Utah

Rees Elementary is a school for kindergarten through fifth grade students. It is located south of Salt Lake City in Utah County at the base of the Wasatch Mountains. The school has self-contained classrooms at every grade level and a multiage team as an option for third, fourth, and fifth graders. Principal Mike Larsen and the author talk about the backbone of Rees's effectiveness with students—the teachers.

Cario Middle School, Mt. Pleasant, South Carolina

Cario Middle School is a school for sixth through eighth grade students. Located in Charleston County, Mt. Pleasant is a medium size town bordering on the Atlantic Ocean and just east of the historic city of Charleston. Cario has strong interdisciplinary teacher-student teams at all three grade levels. Principal Carol Bartlett talks with the author about the qualities she looks for when hiring teachers to fill classrooms of young adolescents.

Roosevelt High School, Fresno, California

Roosevelt High School is a large urban school for ninth through twelfth grade students. It is located in Fresno County, the nation's number one agricultural county. Many of Roosevelt's students are children of migrant farm workers and others who have come to the United States seeking a better way of life. Principal Maria Romero and assistant principal John Lael talk with the author about the challenges of meeting the needs of urban teenagers, predominantly of Hispanic and Asian descent.

The four focus schools are featured throughout the text and on the Choosing Your Teaching Path and Virtual Field Experience sections on MyEducationLab at **www.myeducationlab.com.**

Focus Teachers

The readers of this text will get to know 10 focus teachers—their classroom demeanor, their areas of expertise, their teaching styles, their attitudes regarding the teaching profession, and their dispositions toward children and adolescents. Here are the teachers readers will get to know:

Kindergarten teacher BRANDI WADE and 2nd grade teacher RENEE AYERS at Summit Primary School near Colombus, Ohio

Multiage teachers TIM MENDENHALL, BRENDA BEYAL, and CHRIS ROBERTS at Rees Elementary School near Salt Lake City, Utah

7th grade math teacher TRACI PETERS and 6th-8th grade language arts teacher DEIRDRE HUGER-MCGREW at Cario Middle School near Charleston, South Carolina

10th-12th grade history and reading teachers CRAIG CLEVELAND, ANGELICA REYNOSA, and DEREK BOUCHER at Roosevelt High School in Fresno, California

The 10 focus teachers are featured throughout the text and in the Choosing Your Teaching Path and Virtual Field Experience sections on MyEducationLab at www.myeducationlab.com.

In the Text

- readers are introduced to the focus teachers through brief profiles and pictures in Chapter 1
- focus teachers' experiences are featured in the opening scenarios of each chapter in *Teaching in Focus*
- pictures of the focus teachers are used throughout to illustrate chapter concepts
- the content of Chapters 4, 6, and 7 is illustrated in early childhood, elementary, middle, and high school settings through references to the focus teachers and their classrooms
- the focus teachers give advice to teacher candidates related to the responsibilities and opportunities of teaching in Chapter 13
- personal letters are written to teacher candidates based on the experiences, and from the hearts, of the focus teachers in Chapter 14

On MyEducationLab

Choosing Your Teaching Path section
- the focus teachers respond to questions by the author in interviews
- teacher candidates tour the focus teachers' classrooms as they see and hear about appropriate use of space

- brief lesson segments illustrate the various teaching styles of the focus teachers
- the focus teachers interview the text's 12 focus students

Virtual Field Experience section
- teacher candidates learn more about each focus teacher
- virtual field experiences are provided through questions based on the video clips featuring the focus teachers

Focus Students

As with the schools and teachers, the 12 focus students are examples of students and are not intended to represent the population of all students in the United States. In particular, the focus students at Roosevelt High School (RHS), although representative of the RHS student body, are unlikely to be typical of the students with whom the teacher candidates reading this text went to school. But that's exactly why it is important to focus on these students who are the first in their families to be educated in the United States. Diversity is no longer a concept most will simply read about, but rather an increasingly prominent fact of life in the United States and in its schools. Here are the students introduced in Chapter 3 and featured throughout the text in scenarios and pictures.

DYLAN TODD
(Kindergarten)
Summit Primary School,
Ohio

SHERLONDA FRANCIS
(2nd grade)
Summit Primary School,
Ohio

AMANDA WILEY
(3rd grade)
Rees Elementary
School, Utah

HECTOR MANCIA
(4th grade)
Rees Elementary
School, Utah

JOSIE FORD
(5th grade)
Rees Elementary
School, Utah

DAVID MCBEATH
(6th grade)
Cario Middle School,
South Carolina

PATRICK SUTTON
(7th grade)
Cario Middle School,
South Carolina

TRISTA KUTCHER
former student at Cario
Middle School and currently
in (9th grade) Wando High
School, South Carolina

MAYRA REYES
(10th grade)
Roosevelt High School,
California

GUILLERMO TOSCANO
(11th grade)
Roosevelt High School,
California

HUGO MARTINEZ
(11th grade)
Roosevelt High School,
California

KHAMMANY
DOUANGSAVANH
(12th grade)
Roosevelt High School
California

Focus Schools, Teachers, and Students

 The 12 focus students are featured throughout the text and in the Choosing Your Teaching Path and Virtual Field Experience sections on MyEducationLab at **www.myeducationlab.com.**

In the Text

- brief profiles introduce each student, along with pictures of the students as they have grown, in Chapter 3.
- The students appear throughout in captioned pictures to help illustrate concepts.

On MyEducationLab

Choosing Your Teaching Path section
- each student is interviewed by a focus teacher.
- the author interviews most of the students' parents.

Virtual Field Experience section
- more information is available about each student.
- questions and prompts relate to the students in the *Virtual Field Experience* section.

Readers will enjoy exploring the schools, learning from the teachers, and envisioning ways of making the teaching and learning connection with the students.

Virtual Field Experience

In the News: ABC News

In the
News

Through the *In the News* segments on the text's DVD, we explore issues in education that have been the topic of a variety of ABC News broadcasts including *Nightline* and *World News Tonight*. Visit page xvii of this preface for a full list and description of each of the *In the News* video segments available on the DVD with this text.

Welcome to MyEducationLab
at www.myeducationlab.com

This text's MyEducationLab offers four specific sections to extend student learning. The Choosing Your Teaching Path section allows readers to get to know the 10 focus teachers, 12 focus students, and the principals of the four focus schools through engaging video footage.

The Virtual Field Experience section in MyEducationLab is organized by chapter. Before the chapter segments begin, additional information about the focus teachers and students is provided to give readers a richer sense of these important individuals.

Each chapter section includes:

- context for the Choosing Your Teaching Path video segments that are addressed in the chapter's Virtual Field Experience assignment
- guided notes to focus the virtual observation designated for the chapter
- questions and prompts to check for understanding and provide writing opportunities as readers analyze what they are observing and make sense of teacher-author interviews, classroom tours, brief lessons, teacher-student interviews, and parent-author interviews

The *Homework and Exercises* section of MyEducationLab includes features explained at the end of each chapter. Readers are provided three distinct ways to personally interact with the text as they actively participate in their own learning.

- *Writing My Own Story*—Throughout the text, when readers see a fingerprint icon, they are asked to respond to questions in individual and personal ways, the sum of which becomes their own "story" that will help them decide if teaching is their chosen profession and, if so, what their teaching identity will be.

Your Teaching
Fingerprint

- *What's My Disposition?*—Through considering their dispositions, readers will understand that teaching involves attitudes, beliefs, and values, not just content knowledge and instructional strategies, as they respond to thought-provoking questions and prompts related to each chapter.
- *Exploring Schools and Classrooms*—If the course in which this text is used includes a field experience component, readers will be directed to observe, question, and discover aspects of schools and classrooms that relate to the content of each chapter.
- *State-Specific Education Materials*—Readers in Florida, Illinois, New York, and Texas are invited to explore state-specific educational content and standards, and apply text content through state-specific activities.

The **Study Plan** section provides readers with chapter pretests and posttests aligned to chapter objectives to assess readers understanding of key chapter concepts. First readers complete the chapter pretest. Based on their results, they receive personalized study materials including interactive remediation exercises and specific text references. Finally, readers take a posttest to ensure they understand the chapter content.

Teacher Resources—Visit this section to access lists of additional web resources and publications.

■ Focus Features

Teachers' Days, Delights, and Dilemmas

Kathleen H. Thomas 2004 Delaware Teacher of the Year

Setting the tone for instruction starts on the first day of school when you begin to create a climate in your classroom. In order to establish a business-like learning community in my high school classroom, our rules are posted as "Five P's to Practice Professionalism": Be Prompt, Prepared, Polite, Productive, and Positive. These rules can be adapted to any grade level. Establishing your rules and classroom management system may be the easy part; enforcing your expectations takes time, modeling, and constant positive enforcement. As

into their cooperative teams quickly and quietly. I establish rapport with my students, but am not too familiar. I am honest, upbeat, caring, and professional. My students know that I care about them and that I believe they are capable of reaching very high standards both in terms of academics and their behavior. I purposely model and explain character traits that are important to their success in school and in life. I constantly make the real-world connections between what we are doing and how our lessons will help them in the future.

One of the keys to classroom management is lesson design. Actively involving students in engaging instruction is a teacher's best classroom management tool. Proactive teachers plan their lessons carefully, have extra activities on hand, and are flexible enough to re-adjust as needed. I often use cooperative learning to allow my students opportunities to work together and to allow me the chance to use direct instruction with each team as I constantly monitor their progress

Teachers' Days, Delights, and Dilemmas

In each chapter, a state Teacher of the Year writes about experiences and lessons learned related to the chapter content.

Letter to the Editor

This message was posted June 11, 2005, as part of the *Community Voice* of the *Tennessean*, Nashville's newspaper. The extension provides opportunities for Nashville area residents to voice their opinions, similar to traditional letters to the The letter was written by a local teacher.

JUNE 11, 2005

As a Metro public school teacher, I deplore the elimination of corporal punishment in the elementary schools. The past three years have resulted in an increase in bullying, intimidation, and threats not only to other children but to staff itself. My school (K–4) has had teachers assaulted by 5 year olds this year! The fear of not having good ADA—average daily attendance— has paralyzed administration into ignoring repeat offenses until they often turn into zero tolerance issues. If teachers aren't given tools to keep order in class, this already bad situation will worsen. . . . We have a new generation of parents who have no respect for schools, teachers, the law or anybody. And their children are entering school now! Sugarcoat it all you want; I see it

Now it's your turn. This chapter has given you information about possible consequences for misbehavior as well a sight into the controversial nature of corporal punishm These questions will help you formulate your own lett

1. Do you think there are ever instances that justify poral punishment? If not, why not? If so, what those instances be?

2. If you support the writer, what justification do you pose? If you do not support the writer, what woul say to an experienced teacher who believes in ad istering corporal punishment?

3. If you do not agree with corporal punishment, wh ternative can you suggest? If you do agree with co ral punishment, how would you explain the nee it in a public forum?

Your letter to the editor should be in response

Letter to the Editor

As readers examine relevant issues, including public responses in the form of letters in newspapers across the United States, they gain realistic perspective and have opportunities to form and express their own opinions in Chapters 1–7, and 10–12. These opinions and decisions help readers decide whether teaching is the profession for them and if so, what their teaching identities may be.

In the News

The Test

High-stakes testing has become a way of life for students in U.S. schools. The state of Florida, during the governorship of Jeb Bush, has taken the consequences of this testing to extremes, as explained in this ABC video. Large numbers of students are being required to repeat grade levels or do not graduate from high school based on the results of a snapshot of their learning taken through the lens of the Florida Comprehensive Assessment Test, the FCAT. We hear proponents of the strict use of test results acknowledge that the test won't fix the ills in the schools, but clarify how bad the problems actually are.

To view this video on *Choosing Your Teaching Path*, go to In the News, and then click on *The Test*. Think about our discussion of standardized testing, and then respond to these questions.

1. We hear a parent say of students that the FCAT and subsequent use of the results "takes the wind out of their sails." And then we hear a counselor say that the tests are "deflating." What do they mean by these statements?

2. In the Little Havana section of Miami, 98% of the children are on free or reduced lunch. Most of them

In the News

The importance of understanding national issues that reverberate in the media is emphasized in most chapters through viewing *ABC News* videos and responding to opportunities to reflect on the impact of video content on teachers, classrooms, and students. Videos are located on the text's DVD.

Balance Margin Note

The importance of casting a wide net to establish balance with regard to most issues and dilemmas in education is emphasized when readers see the balance icon throughout the text.

What Role Will Diversity Play in My Teaching Identity?

The impact of diversity as manifested in chapter content is explicitly applied to teachers and classroom practice in this feature found at the conclusion of every chapter.

> ### What Role Will Diversity Play in My Teaching Identity?
>
> A positive and productive learning environment can only be maintained if expectations, incentives, and consequences are thoughtfully established with students' similarities and differences in view. You can accomplish this through
>
> - knowing your students well—their home settings, their cultures, their abilities and disabilities
> - creating a physical space that is inviting and safe (remember that your classroom may be the most appealing place in a child's life)
> - using wall space to display posters and information from a variety of perspectives, thereby validating those perspectives in the eyes of some students
> - establishing a foundation for caring by helping students get to know each other and finding ways to encourage them to respect the viewpoints and rights of classmates

■ Professional Practice

Located at the end of every chapter, readers are able to apply chapter content to the following activities to help you become a professional educator.

Licensure Test Prep

Regardless of state licensing or certification requirements, the Licensure Test Prep scenarios, along with the short-answer and multiple-choice items, serve as checks for the understanding of chapter content as they promote critical thinking.

Standards Speak

Readers explore a variety of professional organization teaching and learning standards as they relate to chapter content and then formulate responses to questions that require application of the standards.

MyEducationLab

This web-based tool provides video of the text's 10 focus teachers and 12 focus students in the Choosing Your Teaching Path section. Also included on this website is a Virtual Field Experience section and a Homework and Exercises section. This web-based tool also includes a Study Plan for students to check their understanding of chapter content and additional resources related to chapter content. All elements will deepen the reader's grasp of important aspects of the teaching profession.

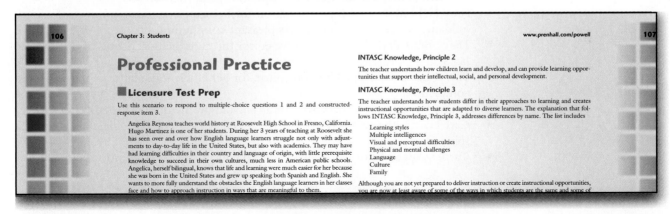

Chapter 3: Students   106   www.prenhall.com/powell   107

Professional Practice

■ Licensure Test Prep

Use this scenario to respond to multiple-choice questions 1 and 2 and constructed-response item 3.

Angelica Reynosa teaches world history at Roosevelt High School in Fresno, California. Hugo Martinez is one of her students. During her 3 years of teaching at Roosevelt she has seen over and over how English language learners struggle not only with adjustments to day-to-day life in the United States, but also with academics. They may have had learning difficulties in their country and language of origin, with little prerequisite knowledge to succeed in their own cultures, much less in American public schools. Angelica, herself bilingual, knows that life and learning were much easier for her because she was born in the United States and grew up speaking both Spanish and English. She wants to more fully understand the obstacles the English language learners in her classes face and how to approach instruction in ways that are meaningful to them.

INTASC Knowledge, Principle 2

The teacher understands how children learn and develop, and can provide learning opportunities that support their intellectual, social, and personal development.

INTASC Knowledge, Principle 3

The teacher understands how students differ in their approaches to learning and creates instructional opportunities that are adapted to diverse learners. The explanation that follows INTASC Knowledge, Principle 3, addresses differences by name. The list includes

Learning styles
Multiple intelligences
Visual and perceptual difficulties
Physical and mental challenges
Language
Culture
Family

Although you are not yet prepared to deliver instruction or create instructional opportunities, you are now at least aware of some of the ways in which students are the same and some of

Table of Concepts

This text centers on the teacher's responsibility to be professional and effective. Entire chapters are devoted to curriculum, instruction, assessment, the learning environment, and so on. In addition, important concepts that do not appear in chapter titles are approached from a variety of perspectives within the chapters. The **Table of Concepts** on page xxxiii provides an overview of some important concepts and where they are referenced in the text in substantive ways.

Instructor Support

This text has the following ancillary materials to assist instructors in their attempts to maximize learning for all students. These materials are located on the *Instructor Resource Center* at www.prenhall.com.

In the News

- *Instructor's Manual/Media Guide with Test Bank* provides chapter-by-chapter instructional material. The manual provides concrete suggestions to promote interactive teaching and actively involve students in learning.
- *Computerized Test Bank* questions give professors electronic access to the test questions printed in the *Instructor's Manual*. Instructors can manage their courses and gain insight into their students' progress and performance by creating and customizing exams.
- *PowerPoint Slides* are designed as an instructional tool. Presentations are provided for each chapter and can be used to elaborate on chapter content.
- *In the News: ABC News* DVD offers videos of current issues in education to give instructors opportunities for classroom discussion or homework.

For instructors, one-time registration at the **Instructor Resource Center** opens the door to Pearson Education's premium digital resources listed. You will not have additional forms to fill out or multiple usernames and passwords to remember to access new titles or editions. Register today, and maximize your time at every stage of your course preparation.

Acknowledgments

As a teacher and teacher educator for more than three decades, the writing of this text was a labor of love for me. I have experienced extraordinary professional development opportunities through this project as I have probed deeply the many and varied issues involved in teaching Pre-K–12 children and adolescents.

Numerous people have helped move this text from conceptualization to the college classroom. Here are some to whom I owe thanks and an outpouring of respect:

- Debbie Stollenwerk, my executive editor through much of the writing phase, for her faith in me, encouragement, inspiration, and friendship.
- Amy Nelson, my development editor, for her expertise, consistently professional guidance, creative eye, and always pleasant communication.
- Darcy Betts Prybella, my executive editor through the final phases of the text, for her skill and insight.
- Sheryl Langner, my production editor, for her efficient guidance of the project to completion.
- Jenifer Cooke, my copy editor, for all she taught me during the editing process.
- Carl Harris, the text's DVD videographer, for his considerable skills and kind spirit.
- Carol Sykes and Lori Whitley, my photo editors, for their attention to quality.

- Elizabeth Campbell, graduate assistant extraordinaire and wonderful teacher, for her help in multiple and inexhaustible ways.
- Allen Millican of Millican Art and Photography for all the time and advice he gave that helped make this text visually effective.
- Jeremy Powell of JBP Images for his assistance and creativity.
- Principals Laura Hill, Mike Larsen, Carol Bartlett, and Maria Romero, for opening their schools to me.
- Brandi Wade, Renee Ayers, Chris Roberts, Brenda Beyal, Tim Mendenhall, Traci Peters, Deirdre Huger-McGrew, Craig Cleveland, Derek Boucher, and Angelica Reynosa, the text's focus teachers, for opening their classrooms to me and sharing their wisdom with teacher candidates.
- Dylan Todd, Sherlonda Francis, Amanda Wiley, Hector Mancia, Josie Ford, Patrick Sutton, David McBeath, Trista Kutcher, Guillermo Toscano, Mayra Reyes, Khamanny Douangsavanh, and Hugo Martinez, the text's focus students, for teaching me so much.
- Linda Winburn, Denis Griner, Jeanne Gren, Kathy Rank, Kathy Heavers, Roxie Ahlbrecht, Kathleen Thomas, Burt Saxon, Karen Heath, Deb Perryman, Tessie Domangue, Dana Boyd, Louisa LaGrotto, and Denis Cruz, Teachers of the Year from their states, for their willingness to contribute valuable experiences.
- Pam Wilson, Melinda Ratchford, and Benette Sutton, my colleagues and dear friends at Belmont Abbey College, for their dedication to the preparation of future teachers that continually inspires me.
- Rus, my husband, for being my biggest supporter.

In addition, I want to thank the professors who contributed time and thought in their feedback, helping shape this text's content: Adel T. Al-Bataineh, Illinois State University; Virginia A. Batchelor, Medaille College; Erin Brumbaugh, Muskingum College; Carrie Dale, Baker College of Cadillac; Debra DeFoor, Purdue University North Central; Corey Hall, Florida Community College; Helen Harrington, The University of Michigan; Lisa A. Hazlett, University of South Dakota; Margaret Henderson-Elliott, Mary Baldwin College; Janet M. Hunt, Marygrove College; John Huss, Northern Kentucky University; David Jelinek, California State University, Sacramento; Lisa Kunkleman, Baker College–Flint; Anna Lowe, Loyola University Chicago; Raja T. Nasr, Marymount University; Ann Selleck, Lansing Community College; and Caryn S. Trapp, Slippery Rock University.

Video

In the
News

This text provides a way to get to know teachers and students in America's classrooms. Through the *In the News* segments we explore issues in education that have been the topic of a variety of ABC news broadcasts including *Nightline* and *World News Tonight*.

Additionally, the Choosing Your Teaching Path video on MyEducationLab allows us to get to know the 10 focus teachers and 12 focus students whose stories are threaded throughout the book.

In the News: ABC News Videos

Home Room: One Last Chance
In the Chapter 2 *In the News* segment, Ted Koppel introduces viewers to a unique charter school. The Seeds Public Charter School is the only public urban boarding school in the United States. Located in Washington, DC, Seeds provides housing, meals, a safe and clean environment, and an education for seventh through twelfth grade students chosen by lottery.
Running Time: 20:11

Boys in Crisis
In the Chapter 3 *In the News* segment, an *ABC World News Tonight* report raises the question of whether boys are really in crisis, both academically and in terms of motivation to succeed. Evidence and opinions are presented on both sides of the question, including interviews with young men in their teens.
Running Time: 2:36

The Test
In the Chapter 5 *In the News* segment, the controversial use of the results of high-stakes testing is explored in Florida schools. During the governorship of Jeb Bush, the consequences of standardized test scores have been taken to extremes, as explained in this ABC video.
Running Time: 19:44

Teacher Fighting Hunger: A Teacher's Mission
In the first Chapter 10 *In the News* segment, we meet teacher Kayla Brown, the originator of Backpack Buddies. Through this program, food in backpacks is given to children who eat breakfast and lunch free at school 5 days a week. The backpack food provides dinner and snacks to help families that struggle due to low paying jobs and lack of opportunity, often associated with little education and a myriad of misfortunes that beset many in the United States.
Running Time: 5:20

Lessons Learned
In the second Chapter 10 *In the News* segment, viewers see how some schools responded to the shock of the Columbine High School tragedy. Districts installed metal detectors and cameras, locked school gates and doors, hired full-time police officers, and, in general, made security a priority. The video introduces students who say the increased security leads to a better learning environment. Rather than viewing it as oppressive, they welcome the additional efforts to keep them safe.
Running Time: 1:50

No Child Left Behind

In the Chapter 11 *In the News* segment, journalist Dan Harris discusses a bipartisan report issued in 2005 that said the No Child Left Behind law is flawed in fundamental ways. The focus of the report is a boy who stayed home on the days of the Texas standardized tests that would result in him being labeled proficient or not. The child was acting on his father's belief that children "go to school to prepare for the test, not for life."
Running Time: 2:21

The Power of the Neighborhood School

In the Chapter 12 *In the News* segment, viewers are introduced to Village Academy, the first new school in Delray Beach, Florida, in 30 years. Before 2000, many of Delray's children (mostly poor, mostly minority) took long bus rides to get to schools attended primarily by White children from mostly middle- to upper-class families. Village Academy changed not only the length of the bus ride, but also the attitudes of an entire community.
Running Time: 20:14

Charles Best: Providing a Quality Education for All Students

In the Chapter 13 *In the News* segment, viewers meet Charles Best, a remarkable young man who has made it his mission in life to make a difference in the lives of kids through teaching . . . and through a web-based nonprofit organization he created called Donors Choose. This unique and growing program allows donors to personally choose the teachers and students to whom they give their money and resources.
Running Time: 19:54

Choosing Your Teaching Path

Get to know the text's focus schools, teachers, and students on the video located in the Choosing Your Teaching Path section of MyEducationLab at www.myeducationlab.com.

Filmed on location in Ohio, Utah, South Carolina, and California, the video segments profile schools, teachers, and their students in early childhood, elementary, middle school, and high school classrooms. The principals of each school give building tours and information about the schools. The teachers discuss their teaching philosophies and experiences, give tours of their classrooms, and share portions of lessons. Through the teachers viewers meet and talk with this text's focus students and their parents.

Summit Primary School, Ohio

At Summit Primary School in Ohio, Brandi Wade, a kindergarten teacher, and Renee Ayers, a second grade teacher, exemplify the joy of teaching young children. Viewers meet Renee's twin sister, Tara, a high school physics teacher, as they talk about the personal qualities that led to their career choices. Then Dylan, a precocious kindergartener, reads and retells a story. As a second grader in Renee's class, Sherlonda's personality shines through as viewers learn more about her from her parents' insightful comments.

Rees Elementary School, Utah

Three teachers form a team of multiage classrooms where third, fourth, and fifth grade students learn together at Rees Elementary School in Utah. The energy and creativity of Chris Roberts, Brenda Beyal, and Tim Mendenhall are obvious in their engaging teaching styles. Viewers meet Amanda, a third grader who is passionate about Mr. Mendenhall's class pet, Rosie the tarantula. We meet Hector, a fourth grader who is teaching his family to speak English, and is fascinated by Mr. Robert's travel experiences. We also meet Josie, a fifth grader who thrives in the multiage setting with Mrs. Beyal as her homeroom teacher.

Cario Middle School, South Carolina

The challenges of teaching young adolescents are met with care and enthusiasm by Traci Peters and Deirdre Huger-McGrew at Cario Middle School in South Carolina. In Traci's seventh grade math classroom viewers see students learning math concepts through hands-on experiences and meet Patrick, who wants to play in the NFL but will consider architecture if that doesn't work out. In Deirdre's classroom viewers watch students who struggle academically learn language arts in a small group with emphasis on reading skills. David, a 12-year-old who has difficulty reading at grade level, expresses his enjoyment of music, and his mom explains that David hummed before he spoke.

Roosevelt High School, California

Most of the students at Roosevelt High School in California are of Hispanic or Asian descent. Many in this diverse group of students speak limited English; many come from low income settings. Derek Boucher teaches reading, and Craig Cleveland and Angelica Reynosa teach history at Roosevelt. All three are grounded in philosophies that put students first, that drive them to help their students grow. Viewers meet Khammany, a conscientious young woman of Laotian descent whose mother doesn't speak English; Guillermo, an athletic young man who will be the first in his family to graduate from high school; Hugo, one of four sons of parents who crossed the U.S. border 2 years ago with their family and only the clothes on their backs; and Mayra, an engaging Hispanic girl who is determined to succeed in spite of family problems.

Brief Contents

Part I   **Teachers, Schools, and Students   1**

Chapter 1   Teachers   2
Chapter 2   Schools   36
Chapter 3   Students   66

Part II   **The Work of Teachers   109**

Chapter 4   Curriculum and Instruction   110
Chapter 5   Assessment and Accountability   142
Chapter 6   Technology in U.S. Schools   168
Chapter 7   Creating and Maintaining a Positive and Productive
                Learning Environment   202

Part III   **Foundations of Education
                in the United States   235**

Chapter 8   History of Education in the United States   236
Chapter 9   Philosophical Foundations of Education in
                the United States   268
Chapter 10 The Societal Context of Schooling in
                the United States   290
Chapter 11 Ethical and Legal Issues in U. S. Schools   322
Chapter 12 Governing and Financing Public Schools in
                the United States   356

Part IV   **Growing Toward the Teaching
                Profession   387**

Chapter 13 Teacher Responsibilities and Opportunities   388
Chapter 14 Charting My Teaching Course   420

References   **447**
Glossary   **461**
Name Index   **477**
Subject Index **480**

Contents

Part I Teachers, Schools, and Students 1

Chapter 1 Teachers 2

Teaching in Focus 3
Introduction 4
  And How Are the Children? 4
Who Teaches in the United States and Why? 4
  Teachers in the United States 4
  Deciding to Teach 6
Teachers' Days, Delights, and Dilemmas 7
What Are the Roles of Teachers? 10
  Reflective Practitioner 10
  Advocate for Students 11
  Facilitator of Learning 11
  Decision Maker 12
  Determiner of Classroom Climate 12
How Do We Prepare to Teach? 12
  Traditional Paths to Teacher Preparation 13
  Alternative Paths to Teacher Preparation 13
What Is Teacher Professionalism? 14
  Characteristics of a Profession 15
  Professional Associations 15
  Teacher Professionalism 15
What Are the Characteristics of Effective Teachers? 17
  Standards Address Effectiveness 17
  Effective Teachers Make a Difference 19
  What Students Say About Teacher Effectiveness 19
  Variety of Characteristics 19
Letter to the Editor 21
What's It Like to Teach at Various Grade Levels? 21
  What's It Like to Teach in an Early Childhood Classroom? 22
  What's It Like to Teach in an Elementary Classroom? 24
  What's It Like to Teach in a Middle School Classroom? 26
  What's It Like to Teach in a High School Classroom? 27
Concluding Thoughts 29
What Role Will Diversity Play in My Teaching Identity? 30
Chapter in Review 30
Professional Practice 31
  Licensure Test Prep 32
  Standards Speak 33
  MyEducationLab 34

Chapter 2 Schools 36

Teaching in Focus 37
Introduction 38
What Is the Culture of a School? 38
  Teachers and School Culture 38
  Changing School Culture 39

How Do the Venues of Schools Differ? 39
  Public School Venues 39
  Private School Venues 42
In the News 42
  School Choice 46
Letter to the Editor 48
What Is School Like at Different Levels? 49
  Structure and Organization of Early Childhood Education 49
  Structure and Organization of Elementary Education 51
  Structure and Organization of Middle School Education 53
  Structure and Organization of High School Education 54
What Are the Three Principle Settings of Public Schools? 56
  Rural Schools 56
Teachers' Days, Delights, and Dilemmas 57
  Suburban Schools 57
  Urban Schools 58
What Is an Effective School? 59
  Characteristics of Effective Schools 60
  We Make a Difference 60
Concluding Thoughts 61
What Role Will Diversity Play in My Teaching Identity? 61
Chapter in Review 62
Professional Practice 63
  Licensure Test Prep 63
  Standards Speak 64
  MyEducationLab 64

Chapter 3   Students   66

Teaching in Focus 67
Introduction 68
How Are We Similar? 68
  Nature and Nurture 68
  Maslow's Hierarchy of Needs 69
  Student Development 69
How Are Gender Differences Manifested? 74
  Social Aspects of Gender 77
  Achievement and Gender 77
In the News 78
  Sexual Orientation 78
  Gender Diversity: Implications for Teachers 78
How Does Cultural Diversity Impact Us? 79
  Cultural Identity 79
  Racial Component of Culture 79
  Ethnic Component of Culture 80
  Cultural Diversity: Implications for Teachers 80
How Is Language Diversity Manifested in U.S. Schools 82
  Standard English 82
  Dialects 82
  English Language Learners 82
  Services Addressing ELL 83
  Language Diversity: Implications for Teachers 84
What Impact Does Diversity in Family Structure Have on Students? 85
  Family Diversity: Implications for Teachers 85
Does Diversity of Religion Influence U.S. Schools? 85
  Religious Diversity: Implications for Teachers 86

How Does Diversity of Socioeconomic Status Affect Students? 86
    Challenges of Low SES 86
    SES Diversity: Implications for Teachers 87
Teachers' Days, Delights, and Dilemmas 87
How Are Differences in Intellectual Ability Manifested in Schools? 88
Letter to the Editor 89
    Multiple Intelligences Theory 89
    Learning Styles 90
    Differences in Intellectual Abilities: Implications for Teachers 92
Who Are Students with Exceptionalities, and How Do We Serve Them? 92
    Students with Disabilities 93
    Legal Support for Students with Disabilities 94
    Individualized Educational Programs 94
    Inclusion 95
    Assistive Technology 96
    Students Who Are Gifted and Talented 96
    Students with Exceptionalities: Implications for Teachers 97
Meet the Students 97
Getting to Know Trista 98
Concluding Thoughts 104
What Role Will Diversity Play in My Teaching Identity? 104
Chapter in Review 104
Professional Practice 106
    Licensure Test Prep 106
    Standards Speak 106
    MyEducationLab 106

Part II The Work of Teachers 109

Chapter 4 Curriculum and Instruction 110

Teaching in Focus 111
Introduction 112
What Is the Relationship Between the Learning Process and the Brain? 112
What Curriculum Do We Teach in U.S. Schools? 113
    Formal Curriculum 113
    Informal Curriculum 120
Letter to the Editor 120
    Extra Curriculum 122
    Null Curriculum 122
How Is Instruction Implemented in U.S. Schools? 123
    Big Ideas of Instruction 123
    Nine Categories of Effective Instructional Practices 127
    Instructional Strategies 128
Are We All Teachers of Reading and Writing? 130
    Reading 130
Teachers' Days, Delights, and Dilemmas 131
    Writing 132
How Do Teachers Match Instruction to School Levels? 133
    Early Childhood Instruction 133
    Elementary Instruction 133
    Middle School Instruction 134
    High School Instruction 135
Concluding Thoughts 136
What Role Will Diversity Play in My Teaching Identity? 136

Chapter in Review   137
Professional Practice   138
    Licensure Test Prep   138
    Standards Speak   138
    MyEducationLab   141

Chapter 5   Assessment and Accountability   142

Teaching in Focus   143
Introduction   144
What Is Backward Design?   144
    Understanding   145
    Content Priorities   145
What Is Involved in Classroom Assessment?   147
    Purposes of Classroom Assessment   147
    Forms of Assessment   149
    Matching Assessment to Curriculum and Instruction   150
How Do Teachers Evaluate Student Learning and Assign Grades?   150
    Evaluation   150
    Rubrics   151
    Assigning Grades   152
What Are Standardized Tests and How Are Their Results Used?   153
    Standardized Tests in the United States   154
In the News   156
    The Good, the Bad, and the Ugly of Standardized Testing   156
Letter to the Editor   158
Teachers' Days, Delights, and Dilemmas   160
Who Is Accountable for Student Learning?   160
What Are Some of the Challenges of Accountability?   161
    Adequate Yearly Progress   161
    Teachers and Accountability   162
    Assessment Drives Curriculum   162
    Test-Taking Preparation   162
Concluding Thoughts   163
What Role Will Diversity Play in My Teaching Identity?   163
Chapter in Review   164
Professional Practice   164
    Licensure Test Prep   164
    Standards Speak   165
    MyEducationLab   166

Chapter 6   Technology in U.S. Schools   168

Teaching in Focus   169
Introduction   170
What Guides the Use of Technology in U.S. Schools?   170
    Subject Area Organization Standards   170
    Grade Level Organization Standards   171
    International Society for Technology in Education   172
What Technological Tools Are Available to Enhance Curriculum,
Instruction, and Assessment?   172
    Low-Tech Teaching Tools   172
    High-Tech Teaching Tools   175
    Educational Technology Tools for Teachers   178

Does Technology Make a Difference in Student Learning? 179
    Research on the Impact of Technology 179
    Reasons for Using Technology 179
Letter to the Editor 181
How Do Teachers Use Technology in Their Classrooms? 183
    Variable: Role of Teachers 183
    Variable: Instructional Delivery and Problem-Solving Models 183
    Variable: Essential Conditions 184
    Variable: Integration of Technology 184
    Variable: Technology Use by Grade Level 184
Teachers' Days, Delights, and Dilemmas 187
What Issues Surround and Affect the Use of Technology in Schools? 191
    Equity 191
    Safety and Privacy 192
    Standards and Accountability 193
    Funding 193
    Online Plagiarism 194
    Professional Development for Teachers 194
What Does the Future Hold for Technology in Schools? 195
    Innovation: Computers for All 195
    Innovation: Wireless Technology 195
    Innovation: Software Programs 195
    Innovation: Digital Portfolios 195
    Innovation: Authentic Audiences 196
    Innovation: No More Books 196
    Innovation: Distance Learning and Virtual Schools 196
Concluding Thoughts 197
What Role Will Diversity Play in My Teaching Identity? 198
Chapter in Review 198
Professional Practice 199
    Licensure Test Prep 199
    Standards Speak 200
    MyEducationLab 201

Chapter 7 Creating and Maintaining a Positive and Productive Learning Environment 202

Teaching in Focus 203
Introduction 204
How Do Teachers Create a Positive Learning Environment? 205
    Physical Space 205
    Building Community 207
    Kounin's Philosophy 208
What Routines Contribute to Maintaining a Productive Classroom Environment? 209
    Practicing Routines 209
    Routines in the Four Levels of School 210
How Do Teachers Establish Expectations, Incentives, and Consequences? 212
    Expectations 213
Teachers' Days, Delights, and Dilemmas 214
    Incentives 215
    Consequences 218
Letter to the Editor 221
How Can I Develop a Classroom Management Plan? 222
    Prominent Theories of Classroom Management 222

Consider the Students   223
General Guidelines   228
Don't Be Part of the Problem   228
Concluding Thoughts   229
Chapter in Review   229
What Role Will Diversity Play in My Teaching Identity?   229
Professional Practice   230
Licensure Test Practice   230
Standards Speak   232
MyEducationLab   232

Part III Foundations of Education in the United States   235

Chapter 8   History of Education in the United States   236

Teaching in Focus   237
Introduction   238
What Were the Major Influences, Issues, Ideologies, and Individuals in 17th-Century American Education?   238
17th-Century American Schools   240
Teachers in Colonial America   243
What Were the Major Influences, Issues, Ideologies, and Individuals in 18th-Century American Education?   243
18th-Century American Schools   244
Education as a Priority   246
What Were the Major Influences, Issues, Ideologies, and Individuals in 19th-Century American Education?   247
19th-Century American Schools   247
Teacher Preparation   250
19th-Century Education for Children with Disabilities and Minorities   251
Higher Education   253
What Were the Major Influences, Issues, Ideologies, and Individuals in 20th-Century American Education and Beyond?   254
Progressive Education   254
Junior High and Middle School   256
Montessori Method   256
Important African American Leaders   256
The Last Five Decades   257
Teachers' Days, Delights, and Dilemmas   258
How Can I Be Aware of Education History in the Making?   261
What Role Will Diversity Play in My Teaching Identity?   261
Concluding Thoughts   263
Chapter in Review   263
Professional Practice   264
Licensure Test Prep   265
Standards Speak   266
MyEducationLab   266

Chapter 9   Philosophical Foundations of Education in the United States   268

Teaching in Focus   269
Introduction   270

What Is a Philosophy of Education?   270
> *Why Is a Philosophy of Education Important?   270*
> *Getting Started on Your Philosophy of Education   271*
Teachers' Days, Delights, and Dilemmas   271
What Are Four Branches of Philosophy?   272
> *Metaphysics   272*
> *Epistemology   272*
> *Axiology   273*
> *Logic   274*
How Do Five Prominent Philosophies of Education Affect Teaching and Learning?   274
> *Essentialism   275*
> *Perennialism   276*
> *Progressivism   277*
> *Social Reconstructionism   278*
> *Existentialism   280*
> *Other "Isms"   281*
How Do I Begin to Develop My Personal Philosophy of Education?   282
> *Revisiting the Trees   282*
> *Your Turn   283*
Concluding Thoughts   286
What Role Will Diversity Play in My Teaching Identity?   286
Chapter in Review   286
Professional Practice   287
> Licensure Test Prep   287
> Standards Speak   288
> MyEducationLab   288

Chapter 10 The Societal Context of Schooling in the United States   290

Teaching in Focus   291
Introduction   292
How Do Family, Community, and Society Impact Students in the United States?   293
> *Family   294*
> *Community   297*
> *Society   297*
How Do Socioeconomic Status and Race Affect Students in the United States?   298
> *Low Socioeconomic Status (SES)   298*
In the News   299
> *Racism   299*
> *Discrimination   300*
> *Immigration and Classroom Success   301*
Letter to the Editor   302
Teachers' Days, Delights, and Dilemmas   303
How Do Health Issues Affect Students in the United States?   304
> *Substance Abuse   304*
> *Sexuality-Related Concerns   306*
> *Childhood Obesity   307*
> *Suicide   309*
What Effects Do Bullying, Theft, and Violence Have on Students and Schools in the United States?   310
> *Bullying   311*

In the News   311
    Theft and Violence in Schools   312
How Do Truancy and Dropping Out Affect Youth in the United States?   313
    Truancy   314
    Dropping Out   315
Concluding Thoughts   317
What Role Will Diversity Play in My Teaching Identity?   317
Chapter in Review   318
Professional Practice   319
    Licensure Test Prep   319
    Standards Speak   320
    MyEducationLab   320

Chapter 11 Ethical and Legal Issues in U.S. Schools   322

Teaching in Focus   323
Introduction   324
What Does It Mean to Be an Ethical Teacher?   324
    Ethics for Teachers   324
    Professional Ethics   325
How Do Laws Affect Schools, Teachers, and Students?   325
Teachers' Days, Delights, and Dilemmas   327
    U.S. Constitution   327
    Federal Laws   328
In the News   329
    State and Local Laws and Policies   329
    Case Law   329
What Are the Legal Rights of Teachers?   330
    Employment Legalities   331
    Freedom of Expression   333
    Academic Freedom   334
    Teachers' Personal Lives   335
What Are the Legal Responsibilities of Teachers?   337
    Liability   337
    Copyright Laws   339
    Reporting Suspected Child Abuse   340
What Are the Legal Rights of Students?   340
    Freedom of Expression   340
    The Right to Be Protected   342
Letter to the Editor   345
**How Does the Law Impact the Relationship Between School
and Religion?   348**
    Religion and Compulsory Education   348
    Prayer in School   350
    Religious Organizations Meeting on School Grounds   350
    Religious Holidays   350
    Religion and Curriculum   351
Concluding Thoughts   352
What Role Will Diversity Play in My Teaching Identity?   352
Chapter in Review   352
Professional Practice   354
    Licensure Test Prep   354
    Standards Speak   355
    MyEducationLab   355

Chapter 12 Governing and Financing Public Schools in the United States 356

Teaching in Focus 357
Introduction 358
How Does the Federal Government Influence Public Education in the United States? 359
  Presidential Influence 359
  Congress and the Courts 359
  U.S. Department of Education 360
What Is the State's Role in Public Education? 360
  State Government 360
  State Board of Education 362
  State Department of Education 362
How Do School Districts Function? 363
  District School Boards 364
  District Superintendent and Staff 366
What Is the Management Structure of Individual Schools? 367
  Principals 367
Teachers' Days, Delights, and Dilemmas 368
  Assistant Principals 369
  Teacher Leaders 370
What Other Entities Impact the Governance of Public Schools in the United States? 371
  Parents 371
  Businesses 372
  Universities 372
  Special Interest Groups 372
How Are Public Schools Financed? 373
  Sources of Education Funding 373
How Are Funds for Education Spent? 377
  Expenditure per Pupil 378
  Allocation of Education Funding 381
Letter to the Editor 379
In the News 379
Concluding Thoughts 382
What Role Will Diversity Play in My Teaching Identity? 383
Chapter in Review 383
Professional Practice 384
  Licensure Test Prep 384
  Standards Speak 385
  MyEducationLab 386

Part IV Growing Toward the Teaching Profession 387

Chapter 13 Teacher Responsibilities and Opportunities 388

Teaching in Focus 389
Introduction 390
What Are a Teacher's Responsibilities and Opportunities Regarding Family Involvement? 390
  Why Parental Involvement Is Important 391
  How to Involve Parents 391
  Barriers to Parent and Teacher Partnering 394

What Are a Teacher's Responsibilities and Opportunities Regarding the Community? 399

What Are a Teacher's Responsibilities and Opportunities Regarding Colleagues? 400
    Basic Relationships Among Teachers 401
    Relationships with Paraprofessionals 403
In the News 403

What Are a Teacher's Responsibilities and Opportunities Regarding Systemic Involvement? 404
    Teacher Involvement in the School 404
    Teacher Involvement in the District 405
    Teacher Involvement at State and National Levels 405

What Are a Teacher's Responsibilities and Opportunities Regarding the Teaching Profession? 407
    Teacher Involvement in Professional Organizations 407
    Contributions to the Professional Knowledge Base 407

What Are a Teacher's Responsibilities and Opportunities Regarding Self-Growth? 408
    Professional Self-Growth 408
    Personal Self-Growth 409

What Are a Teacher's Responsibilities and Opportunities Regarding Students? 411
    Taking Responsibility for Student Learning 412
    Unconditional Teaching 412
Teachers' Days, Delights, and Dilemmas 413
    High Expectations 413
Concluding Thoughts 413
What Role Will Diversity Play in My Teaching Identity? 414
Chapter in Review 414
Professional Practice 416
    Licensure Test Prep 416
    Standards Speak 417
    MyEducationLab 419

Chapter 14 Charting My Teaching Course 420

Introduction 422
How Can I Make the Most of Teacher Preparation? 422
    Taking Full Advantage of Coursework 422
    Taking Full Advantage of Field Experiences 425
    Taking Full Advantage of Clinical Practice 429
How Can I Make the Most of Searching for a Teaching Position? 430
How Can I Thrive, Not Merely Survive, During My First Year of Teaching? 436
Teachers' Days, Delights, and Dilemmas 437
Concluding Thoughts 442
What Role Will Diversity Play in My Teaching Identity? 443
Chapter in Review 443
Professional Practice 444
    Licensure Test Practice 444
    Standards Speak 445
    MyEducationLab 445

References 447

Glossary 461

Name Index 477

Subject Index 480

Table of Concepts

This text centers on teachers' responsibility to be professional and effective. Entire chapters are devoted to curriculum, instruction, assessment, the learning environment, and other topics. These are all major concepts that are addressed in depth. In addition, important concepts that do not appear in chapter titles are addressed from a variety of perspectives within the chapters. The listed pages in this Table of Concepts are not the only ones in which the concepts are mentioned. The index provides a complete listing. This unique feature, however, allows you to quickly reference some important concepts as they are threaded throughout the text in substantive ways.

Concept	Where it is addressed
early childhood education	Chapter 1 (pp. 22–23)
	Chapter 2 (pp. 49–51)
	Chapter 3 (pp. 69–76)
	Chapter 4 (p. 133)
	Chapter 6 (pp. 185–187)
	Chapter 7 (p. 210; pp. 224–225)
elementary education	Chapter 1 (pp. 24–26)
	Chapter 2 (pp. 51–53)
	Chapter 3 (pp. 69–76)
	Chapter 4 (pp. 133–134)
	Chapter 6 (pp. 187–189)
	Chapter 7 (p. 211; p. 225)
middle school education	Chapter 1 (pp. 26–27)
	Chapter 2 (pp. 53–54)
	Chapter 3 (pp. 69–76)
	Chapter 4 (pp. 134–135)
	Chapter 6 (pp. 189–190)
	Chapter 7 (pp. 211–212; p. 225)
high school education	Chapter 1 (pp. 27–29)
	Chapter 2 (pp. 54–55)
	Chapter 3 (pp. 69–76)
	Chapter 4 (pp. 135–136)
	Chapter 6 (pp. 190–191)
	Chapter 7 (p. 212; pp. 225–226)
No Child Left Behind Act of 2001	Chapter 1 (p. 18)
	Chapter 2 (p. 47)
	Chapter 5 (p. 155; pp. 161–162)
	Chapter 8 (pp. 260–261)
	Chapter 11 (pp. 328–329)
	Chapter 12 (p. 363)
family/parents	Chapter 3 (p. 85)
	Chapter 7 (pp. 221–222)
	Chapter 10 (pp. 292–294)
	Chapter 12 (p. 371)
	Chapter 13 (pp. 392–401)

Concept	Where it is addressed
standards	Chapter 1 (pp. 17–18; p. 22; p. 24; p. 26) Chapter 4 (pp. 114–120) Chapter 5 (p. 144; pp. 153–156; p. 162) Chapter 6 (pp. 170–173; p. 186; p. 188; p. 189; p. 191)
students with exceptionalities	Chapter 3 (pp. 92–97) Chapter 6 (p. 182) Chapter 7 (pp. 223–224) Chapter 8 (p. 259)
multicultural teaching	Chapter 3 (pp. 80–81) Chapter 4 (p. 119)
arts integration	Chapter 1 (pp. 24–25) Chapter 4 (p. 119)
students from low income settings	Chapter 2 (p. 40; p. 47; p. 60) Chapter 3 (pp. 86–88) Chapter 6 (pp. 191–192) Chapter 10 (pp. 296–297)
academic rigor and developmental appropriateness	Chapter 1 (pp. 11–12; p. 26) Chapter 4 (all)
integrated curriculum	Chapter 1 (pp. 24–25) Chapter 4 (p. 118; pp. 133–134)
racial/ethnic/cultural diversity	Chapter 2 (p. 37; p. 46) Chapter 3 (pp. 79–81) Chapter 6 (pp. 191–192) Chapter 8 (pp. 251–253) Chapter 10 (pp. 297–302)

Special Features

▪ Letter to the Editor

Looking closely at important issues that affect schools and those who teach and learn in them will help guide prospective teachers in their decisions about whether teaching is the profession for them and, if so, what their teaching identity may be. In this feature, an actual letter to the editor from a newspaper is presented. The context is set by the chapter content, along with background information about the particular topic or issue involved. Following each letter are questions and prompts to help readers form their own opinions. They are then asked to write letters that support the writer's views, add additional information, or refute the writer's stance. A rubric similar to the one used by ETS to assess the writing portions of the Praxis™ II exams is provided to make clear the quality expectations of this assignment.

Chapter	Newspaper	Excerpt	Page
1	*The Charleston Post and Courier* (SC)	". . . quit blaming the teachers and devise programs to overcome the real dilemma."	21
2	*Milwaukee Journal Sentinel* (WI)	"If taxpayers are funding schools then they should see the results of their spending."	48
3	*The Fresno Bee* (CA)	"I am a teacher trying to pull, push, drag and even carry 75 seniors to their high school graduation."	89
4	*Dallas Morning News* (TX)	"The debate about intelligent design and Darwin is not about science but about philosophy."	120
5	*The Denver Post* (CO)	"The performance gap between students of different races, ethnicities or genders is not attributable solely to such stereotyping . . ."	158
6	*Portland Press Herald* (ME)	"I believe that Maine schools should continue the laptop program because . . ."	181
7	*Tennessean Community Voice* (TN)	"As a Metro public school teacher, I deplore the elimination of corporal punishment . . ."	221
10	*The Portland Tribune* (OR)	"But I don't believe that more minority teachers will solve the achievement gap."	302
11	*Pittsburgh Post-Gazette* (PA)	". . . young men from a highly rated school district find nothing wrong in objectifying young women . . ."	345
12	*The Charlotte Observer* (NC)	"I am reminded why I am so eager to leave this circus of a school system."	379

Teachers' Days, Delights, and Dilemmas

This feature highlights the words of state Teachers of the Year. Each chapter includes an honored teacher writing about experiences and lessons learned that pertain to chapter topics. The teachers, states, and topics include:

Chapter	Teacher of the Year State and Year	Topic	Page
1	Linda Winburn, high school South Carolina, 2005	Roles and responsibilities of teachers	7
2	Dennis Griner, high school Washington, 2004	Education in a rural area	57
3	Jeanne Gren, early childhood West Virginia, 2002	Children in poverty	87
4	Kathy Rank, elementary Ohio, 2005	Communicating and connecting with learners	131
5	Kathy Heavers, high school Colorado, 2005	Dilemmas posed by standardized testing	160
6	Roxie Ahlbrecht, elementary South Dakota, 2004	Technology in the elementary classroom	187
7	Kathleen Thomas, high school Delaware, 2004	Setting the tone for classroom instruction	214
8	Burt Saxon, high school Connecticut, 2005	Making history come alive	258
9	Karen Heath, elementary Vermont, 2005	The value of composing and reflecting on a philosophy of education	271
10	Deb Perryman, high school Illinois, 2004	Advocating for immigrant students	303
11	Tessie Domangue, elementary Louisiana, 2005	Caring for children and their families in times of need	327
12	Dana Boyd, elementary Texas, 2007	Teacher involvement in education issues inside and outside the classroom	368
13	Louisa LaGrotto, middle school Indiana, 2006	We teach who we are	412
14	Denis Cruz, middle school California, 2006	Student success is the greatest reward of teaching	437

In the News: ABC News Videos

Chapter	Title	Topic	Page
2	*One Last Chance*	The only public urban boarding school in the U.S. is viewed as the best chance of success for some Washington, D.C., 7th- through 12th-grade students.	42
3	*Boys in Crisis*	Evidence is presented on both sides of the debate concerning whether boys are in academic and motivational crisis.	78
5	*The Test*	Harsh consequences of low standardized test results are controversial and constitute a growing trend across the country.	156
10	*A Teacher's Mission*	Backpack Buddies is a program that provides dinner and snacks for children and families in low-income settings.	299
10	*Lessons Learned*	In the wake of the Columbine High and other school-related violent tragedies, some schools respond with increased security that is generally welcomed by students.	311
11	*No Child Left Behind*	A bipartisan report issued in 2005 that said the No Child Left Behind act is fundamentally flawed is explored through one family's story.	329
12	*The Power of the Neighborhood School*	Village Academy offers educational advantages in a neighborhood school for students who were previously bussed to locations far away from their homes.	379
13	*Charles Best: Providing a Quality Education for All Students*	Donors Choose, a web-based nonprofit organization, allows donors to personally choose the teachers and students to whom they give their money and resources.	403

What Role Will Diversity Play in My Teaching Identity?

Chapter	Focus	Page
1	There is a need for more minority and male teachers in all levels of classrooms in the United States.	30
2	Effective schools for the diverse student population of the U.S. require options, all of which must be high quality.	61
3	Diversity among students should be recognized as an asset. Teachers should also realize that some elements of diversity contribute to an achievement gap.	104
4	Multicultural curriculum brings the world into classrooms and encourages acceptance and appreciation among students.	136
5	Classroom assessments should allow students to show what they know and can do in a variety of ways that align with the different ways they learn.	163
6	One way to span the digital divide is to design assignments that involve all students in the possibilities high tech brings to life.	198
7	Teachers should look at students through eyes that see possibility, not just past performance, and set high expectations for all.	230
8	Overt segregation and more subtle forms of discrimination are realities that teachers must continually work to remedy.	261
9	Student-centered philosophies of education recognize and plan for diversity in the classroom.	286
10	Students may be at risk due to a variety of societal issues. Teachers need to provide safe havens where encouragement prompts growth.	317
11	Teachers have the responsibility to recognize student diversity and make sure all are treated fairly and afforded the same rights.	352
12	The distinct lack of diversity among school leadership makes it even more imperative for teachers to implement multicultural curriculum.	383
13	Teachers are responsible for recognizing diversity in its many forms and addressing students as individuals.	414
14	It is vital to create an atmosphere that encourages honest dialogue about differences.	443

Letter to the Reader

■ Dear Reader,

Welcome to the world of teaching! We are about to begin a lengthy conversation. Through this text I am speaking to you from the collective wisdom of numerous educators, from my experience, and from my heart. Speak back to me through your involvement in the text, your reflections, class discussions, and your open mind.

This text and accompanying MyEducationLab videos are uniquely personalized through the actual lives of 10 teachers at four schools and 12 of their students, ages 5–18. You will meet these teachers and students in their school settings and follow their stories through scenarios that are not made up to emphasize a point, but rather are the real experiences of these individuals. They bring life to the content. You'll enjoy getting to know them!

The first goal of this text is to help you answer the question—**Is teaching for me?** Serious question; it's not for everyone. The second question is—**What will my teaching identity be?** While some of us have the interest and temperament to spend our days with seven-year-olds, we would be much less effective with seventh graders. Others may be ideally suited to teach physics to high school seniors, but would crash and burn with 26 third graders day in and day out. We need committed, effective teachers at all levels, each requiring specific preparation and expertise.

Another part of finding your teaching identity revolves around whether or not you want to be a teacher of general subjects to more or less mainstream students. Alternatives include becoming special educators who teach students with disabilities, or becoming related arts teachers, those who teach music, art, languages, physical education, and so on.

Life in our country is full of dichotomies: the haves and the have-nots, the altruistic and the selfish, the powerful and the weak. Whatever the United States is, U.S. schools are a microcosm of it. Children and adolescents come to us prepared and unprepared, satisfied and hungry, motivated and resistant. They delight us; they break our hearts. Someone has said that a broken heart has more room in it . . . a larger place for more students. As teachers have always known, even something perceived as negative can actually be positive.

I'm confident you are beginning a journey of discovery. Somewhere along the way you'll recognize why teachers are my heroes. Are you ready for our conversation? Welcome to the adventure!

Part 1

Teachers, Schools, and Students

Chapter 1   Teachers

Chapter 2   Schools

Chapter 3   Students

Chapter 1

Teachers

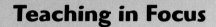

Teaching in Focus

Traci Peters teaches seventh grade math at Cario Middle School in South Carolina. By all accounts she's an excellent teacher—just ask her principal, her colleagues, and, most importantly, her students. Outside school Traci enjoys a very happy home life with husband Dwayne and 2-year-old son Robert. The seventh graders in Traci's classes know all about these two very important men in her life, and that's the way Traci wants it. While math is the subject she has chosen to teach, she is conscious of the fact that her responsibilities go well beyond fractions and equations. She views each student as an individual with relationships and often complex growing-up issues. Traci reveals herself to them, and they, in turn, feel comfortable enough to share with her.

In a prominent place in the classroom Traci has a "Mrs. Peters" bulletin board on which she displays, among other things, family photos (from her childhood to the present), her favorite poems and book titles, her own seventh grade report card, and her 5-by-7 inch middle school picture. Traci says her students spend lots of time examining the board's contents, laughing and asking questions.

Traci sees herself as a role model of a healthy, positive adult who makes good choices and tries to make a difference in other people's lives. When asked if she would just as freely share with students the not-so-positive aspects of her life, she replies yes. When she's not feeling well, she lets her students know. If Robert is sick and she needs to stay home to care for him, she tells her students.

Traci attends her students' basketball games, concerts, spelling bees, Odyssey of the Mind competitions—the typical year-long parade of events. She views this as a tangible way to show her students she is interested in them, their growth, and their lives.

At the end of this chapter you'll learn more about Traci. You will also meet nine other teachers from kindergarten through high school who will be featured in scenarios and pictures throughout this book. Throughout the text you will read about the focus schools, teachers, and students. You will often be directed to watch the Choosing Your Teaching Path videos that pertain to each. These videos are located in the Choosing Your Teaching Path section of MyEducationLab located at www.myeducationlab.com. Getting to know these teachers will help you explore how accomplished lifelong learners approach the classroom. Think about with whom you identify and which level appeals to you most. This experience will help you decide if teaching is the profession for you. Considering the teaching world of each focus teacher also will help you discover what and who you may want to teach.

This chapter is all about teachers in the United States. Among the many questions to consider in this context, here are some we'll address:

- **Who teaches in the United States and why?**
- **What are the roles of teachers?**
- **How do we prepare to teach?**
- **What is teacher professionalism?**
- **What are the characteristics of effective teachers?**
- **What's it like to teach at various grade levels?**

■ Introduction

After being a student for more than 13 years, you are very familiar with school and its routines: bus or car ride, attendance, morning announcements, work, lunch, break/recess, work, packing up, bus or car ride. Your days were planned. It all seemed very automatic, didn't it? You may have often thought, at least in middle and high school, "If I were the teacher, I'd . . ." In a couple of years you may be exactly that—the teacher!

You are considering possibly the most wonderfully challenging and exhilarating career anyone can have. Before we ask and answer this chapter's major questions about teachers and teaching, let's think about the most important question of all.

And How Are the Children?

No African tribe is considered to have warriors more fearsome or more intelligent than the Masai. It is perhaps surprising, then, to discover that the traditional greeting between Masai warriors is *Kasserian ingera,* which means "And how are the children?"

This traditional tribal greeting acknowledges the high value the Masai place on their children's well-being. Even warriors with no children of their own give the traditional answer, "All the children are well," meaning, of course, that peace and safety prevail, that the priorities of protecting the young, the powerless, are in place, that Masai society has not forgotten its proper function and responsibility, its reason for being. "All the children are well" means that life is good. The daily struggle for existence does not preclude proper care of the Masai young.

If we took to greeting each other with this same daily question, "And how are the children?" how might it affect our awareness of children's welfare in the United States? If we asked this question of each other a dozen times a day, would it begin to make a difference in the reality of how children are thought of and cared for in the United States?

If everyone among us, teacher and nonteacher, parent and nonparent, came to feel a shared sense of responsibility for the daily care and protection of all the children in our community, in our town, in our state, in our country, we might truly be able to answer without any hesitation, "The children are well, yes, all the children are well."

As you read about teachers and the teaching profession in the United States, pause occasionally to consider how what you're reading might impact the answer to "And how are the children? Are they all well?"

■ Who Teaches in the United States and Why?

Teaching is the largest profession in the United States, with almost 3 and a half million teachers in both public and private schools (National Center for Education Statistics [NCES], 2003). Figure 1.1 illustrates actual and projected teacher population growth since 1988. Notice the relatively modest increase in the total number of teachers from 2005 to 2014 compared to the 17-year period between 1988 and 2005. Although the overall number of teachers will rise moderately from 2005 to 2014, this increase will not meet the need for more than 2 million new teachers, resulting in part from the high numbers of teachers nearing retirement. In 1976 only 16% of the teacher workforce was over 50 years old. By 2001 that percentage had more than doubled, to 37% (National Education Association [NEA], 2003). Consider also the issue of changing career patterns in today's teacher workforce. Like other young professionals, many new teachers anticipate having several careers over the course of their working lives. In one study, only about 10% of new teachers predicted that they would teach until full retirement (Johnson & Kardos, 2005). Factor in an increasing number of students, as well as the continuing call for smaller classes, and it becomes obvious that you are needed more than ever!

Teachers in the United States

Examine Figure 1.2 and you'll see that teachers are better educated than ever—more than 50% hold master's degrees. About 75% of U.S. teachers are married, 15% are single,

Figure 1.1 Total number of elementary and secondary school teachers, both public and private (2014 projection)

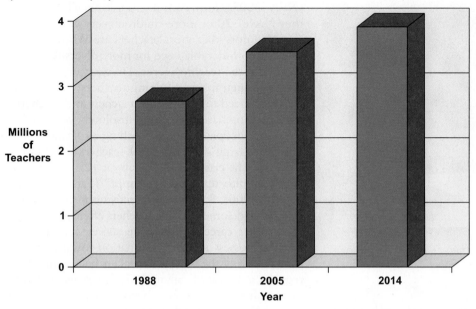

Source: Information from *Digest of Education Statistics 2005,* National Center for Education Statistics, 2005. Retrieved March 25, 2007, from http://nces.ed.gov/programs/digest/d05/tables/dt05_063.asp

Figure 1.2 U.S. teachers, 2001

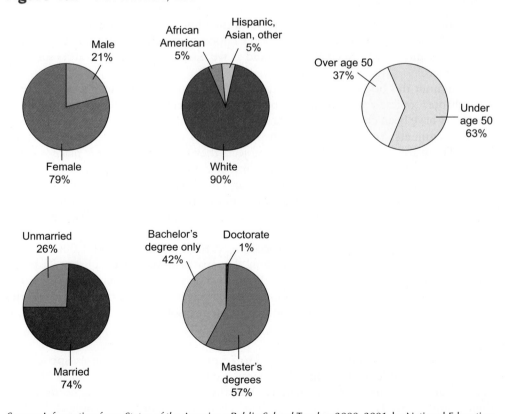

Source: Information from *Status of the American Public School Teacher 2000–2001,* by National Education Association, 2003. Retrieved May 15, 2005, from http://www.nea.org/edstats/images/status.pdf

There is a definite need for more men and people of color in the teaching profession.

and 11% are widowed, divorced, or separated. About one third of teachers have school-age children themselves (NEA, 2003). However, if you ask, they'll likely tell you they "have" 20 or more children every year!

Also note that most teachers are White and female. There is considerable need for more diversity and gender balance in the teaching force. Do we want to discourage White women from becoming teachers? Absolutely not. Is there a need for more male teachers and teachers from minority population groups? Absolutely yes.

Most people join the teaching profession purposefully. In a large-scale survey of teachers with fewer than 5 years in the classroom, only about 12% said they somehow "fell into teaching by chance" (Farkas, Johnson, & Felono, 2000). Some enter directly upon graduation from college, and some become teachers after pursuing one or more other careers. This same survey found that most teachers possess a strong inclination toward their career choice: 86% of the surveyed teachers believe that teaching requires a "sense of calling." The inference is that teaching requires a commitment beyond that required by many other careers. Once in the profession, relatively new teachers overwhelmingly view teaching in positive ways.

Now that you have an overview of the U.S. teacher population, let's look at why people choose to become teachers.

Deciding to Teach

Helping you first make the decision to teach and then find your teaching identity is at the heart of this book. Exploring why other people choose to teach can help you clarify your own thoughts and desires. Keep an open mind as we discuss possible motivators for making this choice.

Throughout this book you will read the words of some special teachers that relate to various chapter topics. The men and women in the Teachers' Days, Delights, and Dilemmas features have been chosen by their states as Teachers of the Year, a great honor. Don't skip these segments. You will find seasoned wisdom in the words of these experienced teachers. Think about the grade levels and subjects they teach and mentally place yourself in their classrooms. Doing so will help you consider your own teaching identity.

The 2005 South Carolina Teacher of the Year, Linda Winburn, says, "To teach is to answer a call to change the world—one student at a time. It is a call to make a difference . . . for a lifetime." Read more about Linda's choice to teach in this chapter's Teachers' Days, Delights, and Dilemmas.

In 2001 the National Education Association (NEA) surveyed almost 1,000 teachers asking why they chose the teaching profession. The teachers were given a list of 21 possible reasons and asked to choose their top 3. Figure 1.3 lists the respondents' top 8 reasons.

Our discussion of the reasons for choosing to teach is organized around the categories in the NEA survey. As you read, think about your own reasons for considering teaching as your career.

Desire to work with young people. Because 6 to 7 hours of a teacher's day are spent in direct contact with students, enjoying their company is a must. Getting to know the students we teach allows us to become familiar with their emotional and social needs as well as their cognitive needs. You may hear teachers talk about teaching the whole child. This simply means attending to all their developmental stages and needs (which we will explore in Chapter 3). When we view the whole child, we realize the depth of our responsibilities as classroom teachers. Is a desire to work with children or adolescents part of

Teachers' Days, Delights, and Dilemmas

Linda "Cookie"
Winburn
2005 South Carolina
Teacher of the Year

To teach is to answer a call to change the world—one student at a time. It is a call to make a difference in a life for a lifetime. It is what drives us to our classrooms each day—not to work—but to students who deserve to be empowered to meet the challenges of an ever-changing world with the skills necessary to succeed. The call can be overwhelming as we face educational challenges from budget cuts, poverty, school violence, and complacency. More powerful than any educational challenge, though, is the call to keep our focus on children. Our message must be one of hope, confidence, and inspiration.

The message of hope and confidence begins as we recognize that educators are leaders. To accept this responsibility, we must take an active role in both our schools and communities. Our policymakers must hear our voices and be invited into our classrooms. We also need to actively involve parents in their children's learning, offering parenting tips and strategies for helping their children grow and improve.

Teachers must take this leadership role to a community meeting or to a line at the grocery store with a confident message of inspiration about what we do every day as professionals. We must also become teacher leaders in our schools, researching and sharing best practices, encouraging each other through the difficulties, and celebrating our successes. We must also become teacher leaders in mentoring induction teachers—working to prevent the more than 20% of teachers who leave the profession during the first three years of teaching. Teacher retention is our responsibility.

We must also share a message of teachers being the strongest advocates for teacher recruitment. How exciting it is to hear from a former student who is now inspiring young minds in her own classroom! What a thrill it is to see my own daughter major in education and say, "I want to teach like my mom!" We need to be in the business of recruiting the brightest and best students into future classrooms!

In a world where the media celebrates violence, complacency, and corruption, our classrooms must instill character, impart knowledge, and make a connection to students' lives in a positive way. A teacher's classroom must be a place of empowerment, a place for students to feel successful. As we meet our students, parents, and the community on their playing fields of life, we will shape our world one student at a time.

Figure 1.3 Why teachers choose to teach, 2001

Desire to work with young people
Value of education to society
Influence of teacher
Long summer vacation
Influence of family
Never considered anything else
Job security
Opportunity for a lifetime of self-growth

Source: Information from *Status of the American Public School Teacher 2000–2001,* by National Education Association, 2003, Washington, DC: Author. Retrieved June 15, 2007, from http://www.nea.org/edstats/images/status.pdf

your motivation for choosing to teach? Throughout this book you will be asked to respond to ideas and questions. These mental exercises will involve you in an extended conversation about teaching. Considering your beliefs and experiences will prompt you to think about whether teaching is for you and what your teaching identity may be. When you see a fingerprint in the margin it means that you will be asked to respond to questions based on your experiences and opinions. These questions are included in "Writing My Own Story" in Chapter 1 of the Homework and Exercises section of MyEducationLab.

Your Teaching
Fingerprint

Value of education to society. Education is widely viewed as the great equalizer. This means that differences in opportunity and privilege diminish as children reach their potential. In other words, the achievement gap narrows with the increased educational success of the students who historically underachieve. An **achievement gap** is a disparity among students, with some excelling while others languish with respect to learning and academic success. Through teaching you will make a difference in the lives of individuals and thereby benefit society as a whole. Is this a major motivator for you?

Interest in subject matter. According to the National Education Association (2003), high school teachers choose "interest in subject matter" more often than elementary teachers. An intense interest in a subject area is important if you are going to teach that subject all day. Middle school is a happy compromise for people who have both a strong desire to work with students and a passion for a specific subject. Most middle school teachers teach one or possibly two subjects all day to students whose development is challenging and intriguing. Are you considering majoring in a subject area? Is interest in that subject a motivating factor as you consider teaching as a career?

Influence of teacher. Can you name the last five vice presidents of the United States? How about the current Miss America? Who represents your home district in the state legislature? Who was your fifth grade teacher? Who taught your favorite class when you were a freshman in high school? The last two questions are the easiest, aren't they? Thought so.

Teachers influence us. They are uniquely positioned to shape students' thoughts and interests during the formative years of childhood and adolescence. Are you still in touch with one or more of your teachers? Are there particular teachers you want to emulate in your teaching career?

Long summer vacation. A joke that's been around for a long time goes like this: "What are the three best things about teaching?" Answer: "June, July, August." Here's another. "What's the best time to be a teacher?" Answer: "Friday at 4." Within our ranks we smile at these harmless jokes.

Those who have not taught, or don't understand the pressure of having 15 or 25 or even 100 students dependent on them for at least part of each day, may view the schedule of a teacher as excessively punctuated with days off. The stresses of being a teacher necessitate downtime to rejuvenate. The time away from school is well-deserved, even if it is used to catch up with teaching-related tasks. The change of pace is refreshing, allowing opportunities for revitalization.

Aside from summer vacation and days off, there are other aspects of scheduling that make teaching a desirable choice for many. During the school year most teachers do not have students after about 3:30 in the afternoon. To people who work 8:00–5:00 jobs, 3:30 seems like a luxury. However, most teachers spend many additional hours either at school or at home planning for the next day and completing necessary administrative tasks. The teaching schedule allows for this kind of flexibility. A teacher's schedule is also ideal for families with school-age children. Having a daily routine similar to that of your family has definite benefits. Does this kind of schedule and flexibility appeal to you?

Influence of family. Most of us have grown up in families that value education and respect teachers. Such an upbringing can definitely affect our choices. If there are teachers in your family who are energetic and enthusiastic about their careers, they may influence you to follow in their footsteps. Do you have family members who teach? Did you grow up with encouragement to do well in school and to revere your teachers?

Job security. We will always need teachers. Those who are competent are generally assured of positions even in poor economic times. Other benefits related to job security include health insurance and a reasonable retirement plan.

Table 1.1 Average teacher salaries, 2004–2005

Rank	State	Salary	Rank	State	Salary
1	District of Columbia	$58,456	26	N. Carolina	$43,348
2	California	$57,876	27	Arizona	$42,905
3	Connecticut	$57,737	28	Virginia	$42,768
4	Michigan	$56,973	29	S. Carolina	$42,189
5	New Jersey	$56,682	30	Idaho	$42,122
6	New York	$56,200	31	Tennessee	$42,076
7	Illinois	$55,421	32	Florida	$41,590
8	Massachusetts	$54,679	33	Texas	$41,011
9	Rhode Island	$53,473	34	Kentucky	$40,522
10	Pennsylvania	$53,258	35	Wyoming	$40,497
11	Alaska	$52,424	36	Arkansas	$40,495
12	Maryland	$52,331	37	Maine	$39,610
13	Delaware	$50,595	38	Nebraska	$39,456
14	Ohio	$48,692	39	Utah	$39,456
15	Oregon	$48,330	40	New Mexico	$39,391
16	Minnesota	$46,906	41	Kansas	$39,345
17	Indiana	$46,583	42	Iowa	$39,284
18	Georgia	$46,526	43	Missouri	$39,067
19	Hawaii	$46,149	44	Louisiana	$39,022
20	Washington	$45,718	45	Montana	$38,485
21	Vermont	$44,535	46	West Virginia	$38,360
22	Wisconsin	$44,299	47	Alabama	$38,186
23	Colorado	$43,949	48	Oklahoma	$37,879
24	New Hampshire	$43,941	49	North Dakota	$36,695
25	Nevada	$43,394	50	Mississippi	$36,590
			51	South Dakota	$34,040
	U.S. average	**$47,674**			

Source: Information from *Education Statistics: Rankings & Estimates,* National Education Association, 2006. Retrieved March 21, 2007, from www.nea.org/edstats/index.html

It's unlikely that a career in teaching is chosen because of salary, although some districts and states are making progress in raising teachers' pay to be competitive with other fields that require a bachelor's degree. Table 1.1 shows average teacher salaries by state.

When considering salary, investigate the cost of living where you want to live. For example, in 2005, thousands of experienced teachers in the suburbs outside New York City made more than $100,000 a year (Fessenden & Barbanel, 2005). However, an examination of the cost of living in such places as Westchester County, New York, shows that $100,000 there is equivalent to a much lower salary in most of small-town America.

Have you researched starting and average salaries in an area where you might want to teach? Have you considered the financial benefits and constraints that a teaching position might entail?

Your Teaching
Fingerprint

Opportunity for a lifetime of self-growth. This is exactly what teaching offers. Few careers are as exciting or as rewarding on a daily basis. And few offer the satisfaction that teaching does of positively impacting the future of children.

Teachers experience self-growth, both personally and professionally, in many ways: through relationships, reading, attending conferences, and the wide variety of professional development opportunities available. Teaching is not a stagnant career; rather, it continually presents new experiences, all of which offer opportunities for self-growth.

Do you enjoy personal and professional growth that's sometimes planned and sometimes spontaneous? Do you want a career that not only provides opportunities for self-growth, but also expects it of you?

We've looked at eight reasons for choosing teaching as a career. There are many more. Yet stopping with a discussion of all the benefits and rewards of teaching presents a picture that's out of balance. No career is without challenges; no career is without frustration. Teaching has its share of both, as we will discuss here and in Chapter 13. Let's examine the work of teachers.

■ What Are the Roles of Teachers?

What do teachers do every day? What's it like to be in a classroom? Most teachers are required to be in their schools for about 37 hours per week, yet almost all of them will tell you they spend many additional hours in active preparation for their work.

It would be impossible to describe all the roles that teachers fulfill. Here we'll look briefly at five of the most significant roles of teachers within their classrooms, as illustrated in Figure 1.4.

Reflective Practitioner

John Dewey (1933), one of the great American educators, defined reflection as "the active, persistent, and careful consideration of any belief or supposed form of knowledge in light of the grounds that support it" (p. 9). A simple definition of **reflection** with regard to teaching is thinking about what we do, how we do it, and the consequences of our actions or inactions, all with the goal of being better teachers. To be **reflective practitioners** means that we deliberately think about our practice, that is, what we do as teachers. We do this with the purpose of analysis and improvement. Sounds pretty automatic and unavoidable, doesn't it? But it's not. A teacher can repeatedly go through the motions of planning, teaching, and assessing throughout a career, yet seldom engage in reflection that results in improved practice.

So how do we become reflective practitioners who, as Dewey said, actively, persistently, and carefully think about how we teach? Here are some concepts to consider.

- Reflective practice requires conscious effort.
- Self-knowledge is vital and can be aided by thoughtfully completing the "Writing My Own Story" and "What's My Disposition?" segments in the Homework and Exercises section of MyEducationLab.
- Reading about and researching aspects of teaching will ground our practice and provide subject matter on which to reflect.
- Talking with other educators will both inform and strengthen what we do and how we do it.
- Being deliberate—doing what we do for a reason—will result in better decisions based on reflection.

As reflective practitioners we become better equipped and more capable of doing what's best for students as we ask, "And how are the children? Are they all well?"

Derek Boucher and his family enjoy the benefits of a teacher's schedule that includes similar hours and vacations for parents and children.

Your Teaching Fingerprint

Figure 1.4 Roles of teachers

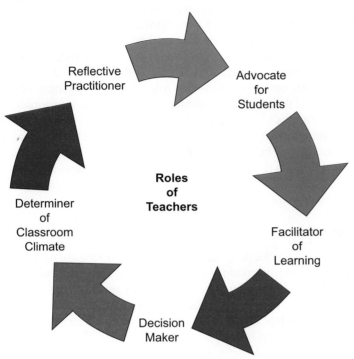

Advocate for Students

To be an **advocate for students** is to support and defend them, always putting their needs first. For teachers it means asking, "And how are the children? Are they all well?" before, during, and after every act of teaching. How do we become advocates for our students? Here are some components of advocacy.

- Understand that advocacy takes multiple forms with individuals, groups, or causes, in both large endeavors and small actions.
- In all conversations, with educators and noneducators alike, keep the focus on what's best for students.
- Take an informed stance on issues that affect children. Actively promote that stance in order to have widespread impact.
- Support families in every way possible.

Reflection leads to improvement in what we do and how we do it, while advocacy guides our best efforts directly toward the goal—improving students' learning, which, ultimately, improves students' lives.

Facilitator of Learning

Making the teaching and learning connection is the primary role of a teacher. Learning is why students are in school, and teaching is how we guide and facilitate learning. Our effectiveness as teachers should be measured by how much and how thoroughly students learn.

Advocating for students is important at all grade levels. Renee, a second grade teacher, and her twin sister, Tara, a high school physics teacher, both advocate for their students in developmentally appropriate ways.

We can categorize the responsibilities involved in facilitating learning in a number of valid ways. Perhaps none is more important than evaluating each of our actions in terms of its contribution to academic rigor and developmental appropriateness. **Academic rigor** refers both to teaching meaningful content and to having demanding expectations for student learning. **Developmental appropriateness** means that our teaching matches students' physical, cognitive, social, emotional, and character development. Academic rigor without developmental appropriateness will result in frustration for teachers and foster discouragement and defeatism in students. Developmental appropriateness without academic rigor will accomplish little in terms of student learning. Neither concept is mutually exclusive. In fact, they shouldn't be exclusive at all, but should interact in supportive ways and balance one another as they guide our decision making. When you see the balance scale in this book, you will know that two or more concepts being discussed may be incomplete or less effective if implemented in isolation. Balance is a valuable concept that is beneficial in most educational circumstances.

Decision Maker

As teachers we continually make decisions. Some of the decisions are made on autopilot, especially those that have to do with routines in the classroom. The quality of other decisions often rests on common sense and maturity, characteristics that are enhanced by preparation and experience. It's important to remember that our decisions have consequences and require reflection to make sure we are advocating for our students and maintaining a classroom climate that is conducive to learning.

Determiner of Classroom Climate

Our classrooms can be respectful environments that promote learning, or not. The sobering words of Haim Ginott (1993) reproduced in Figure 1.5 will be repeated in Chapter 7 when we consider the creation and maintenance of the learning environment. Ginott's message should occupy a prominent position in both your classroom and your consciousness.

How do we prepare to fill the many roles of a teacher? How do we turn the motivation to be a teacher into the skills necessary to be effective? Let's explore teacher preparation.

■ How Do We Prepare to Teach?

We've all had lots of experience as both students and teacher watchers. Chances are we've spent almost as many waking hours with teachers as we have with our families. So if watching somebody do something is the way to learn, we should all be experts at teaching. What else is there to know? Plenty!

You may have heard it said of someone, "He's just a natural-born teacher," and there may have been some truth in that statement. But to effectively make the teaching and learning connection, those nature-given attributes must be enhanced by the skills gained through reading, observation, practice, and reflection.

Each state has its own preparation requirements for those who teach in public school classrooms. The state issues a teaching certificate or license when a teacher candidate is

Figure 1.5 Classroom climate

> I've come to the frightening conclusion that I am the decisive element in the classroom. It's my personal approach that creates the climate. It's my daily mood that makes the weather. As a teacher, I possess a tremendous power to make a child's life miserable or joyous. I can be a tool of torture or an instrument of inspiration. I can humiliate or humor, hurt or heal. In all situations, it is my response that decides whether a crisis will be escalated or de-escalated, a child humanized or de-humanized

Source: From *Teacher and Child* (p. 15), by H. G. Ginott, 1993, New York: Collier Books/MacMillan.

determined to be sufficiently qualified. In addition, most states require a prospective teacher to pass a test before they grant certification or licensure. The most widely used tests are part of the **Praxis Series** published by the Educational Testing Service (ETS). Since all states have teacher preparation requirements, we'll look at the two major paths to initial teacher preparation, traditional and alternative.

Traditional Paths to Teacher Preparation

The traditional path to initial teacher preparation comes through a university department of education. National and state organizations carefully scrutinize university programs and evaluate how teacher candidates are prepared. About two thirds of states require university teacher education programs to be accredited (authorized to prepare teachers) through the **National Council for the Accreditation of Teacher Education (NCATE).**

All three of the basic initial teacher preparation paths include one or two semesters of **student teaching,** also called **clinical internship.** During this extended fieldwork, teacher candidates teach lessons and, for a designated time frame, take over all classroom duties. A classroom teacher serves as the **cooperating teacher** (host and mentor), while a university instructor supervises the experience. You will learn more about student teaching, or clinical internship, in Chapter 14.

Bachelor's degree. A 4-year undergraduate teacher preparation program consists of a combination of general education courses, education major courses, and field experiences. Most early childhood and elementary teacher preparation programs result in a degree with a major in education. Many programs in middle level education result in a degree with a major in education and two subject area concentrations. To teach in high school, most programs require a major in a content area and a minor, or the equivalent of a minor, in education coursework.

Fifth-year program. Some universities offer a fifth-year program. Teacher candidates complete a major other than education and stay for a fifth year for more education coursework plus student teaching. Some of these programs include a master of arts in teaching rather than an extended bachelor's degree.

Master of Arts in Teaching. People who have a bachelor's degree in an area other than teacher certification may pursue teacher preparation through a master of arts in teaching (MAT) degree. Most early childhood and elementary MAT programs consist of all teacher education courses and fieldwork, while middle level MAT programs typically require 18 to 24 hours of subject area coursework in addition to education courses. These content courses, if not completed as part of the bachelor's degree, may become part of the MAT coursework. High school MAT programs generally require a degree in a content area or the accumulation of enough content hours (usually 24) to be considered a concentration.

Alternative Paths to Teacher Preparation

There is a growing movement toward alternative paths to teacher preparation. Between 1983 and 2005, the number of states offering or sanctioning alternative preparation programs grew from 8 to 47. Currently, about 35,000 individuals enter the teaching force through alternative paths each year (Feistritzer, 2005).

Many alternative programs grow out of specific needs and are developed and coordinated through partnerships among state departments of education, school districts, and university teacher education programs (Feistritzer, 2005). Their structures vary widely, and they tend to be controversial. Some

Preparing to teach requires reflection on the many roles involved in the profession.

people doubt that teacher preparation is as effective outside the realm of university-based programs.

Teach for America (TFA) is perhaps the most widely known alternative program. TFA's goal is to increase the number of teachers willing to tackle the challenges of classrooms in low-income areas. TFA recruits individuals who are college seniors or recent graduates and who agree to teach in high-needs rural or urban schools for at least 2 years. In 2006 there were about 2,400 TFA teachers. The organization's goal is to have 7,500 Teach for America teachers in classrooms in 2010 (Teach for America, 2006).

This text has referred to teaching as the *teaching profession*. Issues such as nonstandard preparation (alternative paths) cause some people to question this status. Let's examine teaching as a profession and teacher professionalism.

What Is Teacher Professionalism?

Professionalism is a way of being. It involves attitudes and actions that convey respect, uphold high standards, and demonstrate commitment to those served. Regardless of their occupation, people can display professionalism. Whether a particular job or career qualifies as a profession is another matter.

Characteristics of a Profession

Basically, a **profession** is an occupation that meets certain criteria, among them (1) extensive training before entering, (2) a code of ethics, and (3) service as the primary product. For decades authors have delineated characteristics of a "full" profession. For equally as long, educators and others have debated whether teaching is indeed a profession. This debate is healthy because as we consider the characteristics of a profession and measure teaching by them, we see what teaching is and is not, what teachers have evolved into, and what teachers may still need to become. A summary of a full profession's characteristics, from both a historical perspective and a modern one, is presented in Figure 1.6. Let's look briefly at each of these 10 characteristics and think about whether they apply to teaching.

Considering that in the United States children ages 5 through 16 are required to receive a formal education, and that most do this through public schools, a dedicated teaching workforce can collectively deliver this *essential service* (1). Members of this teaching workforce agree that teaching requires *unique knowledge and skills* (2), whether acquired through traditional or alternative paths. Certification requirements vary from state to state with no national consensus. On-the-job *training* and *ongoing study* (2) and development are encouraged, but not necessarily required in all districts or states, although most teachers must renew their teaching certification every 5 years or so by completing graduate coursework or participating in other forms of professional development.

Figure 1.6 Characteristics of a full profession

1. Provides an essential service no other group can provide
2. Requires unique knowledge and skills acquired through extensive initial and ongoing study/training
3. Involves intellectual work in the performance of duties
4. Individual practitioners are committed to service and continual competence
5. Identified performance standards guide practice
6. Self-governance (association) admits, polices, and excludes members
7. Allows for a considerable amount of autonomy and decision-making authority
8. Members accept individual responsibility for actions and decisions
9. Enjoys prestige, public trust
10. Granted higher-than-average financial rewards

Sources: Howsam, Corrigan, Denemark, & Nash (1976), Ingersoll (1997), Rowan (1994), Webb, Metha, & Jordan (2007).

Teaching definitely *involves intellectual work* (3). Teachers pass along intellectual concepts and skills—this is the very heart of what teachers do. To enter and remain in a teaching career requires a *commitment to service* (4) and, hopefully, *continual competence* (4) as guided and measured by *performance standards* (5). The word *hopefully* is included because teachers rarely *police their own ranks* (6) to the point of excluding someone who does not live up to accepted teacher standards. If policing occurs, it is generally accomplished by administrators.

When the classroom door closes, teachers have a great deal of *autonomy* (7), sometimes approaching isolation. However, public school teachers must accept any student placed in their classrooms and must teach a set curriculum over which they have little or no control. We have already seen that one of the major roles of a teacher is that of *decision maker* (7). Even with certain restrictions, many decisions are ours to make, and we must *accept individual responsibility* (8) for them.

A great level of *trust* (9) is placed in teachers. After all, for 7 to 10 hours a day families allow teachers to have almost exclusive control over their children. In most communities, teachers enjoy a degree of positional *prestige* (9), but they are rarely *granted higher-than-average financial rewards* (10).

As you can see, not all 10 characteristics of a full profession apply to teaching. Teachers should continue to work together to incorporate each of these characteristics as part of teaching. Many associations and organizations are helping facilitate the elevation of teaching to a full profession by allowing teachers through collaborative efforts to set common goals, speak with a collective voice, and build research-based foundations to support what we do and how we do it.

Professional Associations

Hundreds of national and regional professional associations provide leadership and support for teachers. Some serve the general teacher population, while others are specific to a grade level or subject area. Most associations solicit members, hold annual conferences, publish materials, provide information, and advocate for the teaching and learning process, for both those who teach and those who learn. Participating in professional organizations is a positive step toward growing as a professional.

The **National Education Association (NEA)** and the **American Federation of Teachers (AFT)** are the largest professional education associations in the United States, with a total of more than 5 million members, including teachers, administrators, professors, counselors, and other educators. Both organizations are unions and represent their members in **collective bargaining,** or negotiating with employers and states to gain additional benefits for their members. Other large nonunion professional organizations serve a wide spectrum of educators, for example, the Association for Supervision and Curriculum Development (ASCD), Kappa Delta Pi (KDP), and the Council for Exceptional Children (CEC). Most national organizations have regional and state affiliate associations. These more local groups provide easily accessible, face-to-face opportunities for interaction among members.

Each subject area has a professional organization that provides guidelines for what to teach, sponsors annual conferences, publishes relevant books and journals, represents subject areas in education and political arenas, and encourages and disseminates research on teaching and learning. We'll take a closer look at these organizations in Chapter 4. This chapter will discuss organizations that are level-specific for early childhood, elementary, middle, and high school educators. These organizations provide information and support for teachers, addressing academic concepts from age-specific developmental perspectives. Table 1.2 lists some of the professional associations available to teachers to assist with their professionalism.

Teacher Professionalism

Fulfilling responsibilities and making the most of growth opportunities are core aspects of teacher professionalism (more on teacher responsibilities and opportunities in Chapter 13). Patricia Phelps, former academic editor of the *Kappa Delta Pi Record*

Table 1.2 Professional organizations

Teacher Unions		
AFT	American Federation of Teachers	www.aft.org
NEA	National Education Association	www.nea.org
Subject-Area Organizations		
AAHPERD	American Alliance for Health, Physical Education, Recreation and Dance	www.aahperd.org
ACTFL	American Council on the Teaching of Foreign Languages	www.actfl.org
IRA	International Reading Association	www.reading.org
MTNA	Music Teachers National Association	www.mtna.org
NAEA	National Art Education Association	www.naea-reston.org
NATIE	National Association for Trade and Industrial Education	www.skillsusa.org/NATIE/
NBEA	National Business Education Association	www.nbea.org
NCSS	National Council for the Social Studies	www.ncss.org
NCTE	National Council of Teachers of English	www.ncte.org
NCTM	National Council of Teachers of Mathematics	www.nctm.org
NSTA	National Science Teachers Association	www.nsta.org/
RIF	Reading Is Fundamental	www.rif.org
Level-Specific Organizations		
ACEI	Association for Childhood Education International	www.acei.org
NAEYC	National Association for the Education of Young Children	www.naeyc.org
NMSA	National Middle School Association	www.nmsa.org
Need-Specific Organizations		
CEC	Council for Exceptional Children	www.cec.sped.org
NAGC	National Association for Gifted Children	www.nagc.org
SCA	Speech Communication Association	www.isca-speech.org
TESOL	Teachers of English to Speakers of Other Languages	www.tesol.org
General Associations		
ASCD	Association for Supervision and Curriculum Development	www.ascd.org
KDP	Kappa Delta Pi	www.kdp.org
PDK	Phi Delta Kappa	www.pdkintl.org

(a publication of KDP), has written a philosophical framework within which to place characteristics of teacher professionalism. Phelps (2003) states that teachers achieve greater levels of professionalism when they are willing to do what it takes, to do what must be done. In other words, professionalism involves hard work. This hard work requires commitment in three broad areas.

1. The initial commitment is to *make students our first priority*. Student welfare and learning must be paramount. Remember our focus question: "And how are the children? Are they all well?"
2. The second commitment is to *quality*. Quality should characterize our relationships and interactions with students, colleagues, administrators, and families. Phelps (2003)

tells us that "modeling quality is the most significant way to motivate others to put forth the same effort" (p. 10).

3. The third commitment is to *continual growth*. Teacher effectiveness is enhanced when a lifelong learning orientation is in place. A commitment to continual growth provides a powerful model for students.

This text will continue to refer to a career in teaching as the teaching profession. Commitment to students, quality, and growth—everything a professional teacher does can be placed within this framework. Remember these three commitments as we examine what it means to be an effective teacher.

What Are the Characteristics of Effective Teachers?

Many definitions of what it means to be an effective teacher, along with lists of characteristics of effectiveness, have been written over the years. Some definitions focus on the personal traits of teachers; others focus on teaching methods. More current models of teacher effectiveness are based on standards set by professional organizations that give guidance concerning the knowledge, **dispositions** (attitudes and beliefs), and performances that lead to, and exemplify, effective teaching. Simply stated, **standards** for teachers are expectations for what they should know and be able to do.

Standards Address Effectiveness

All teacher education standards address teacher effectiveness. The 10 standards of the **Interstate New Teacher Assessment and Support Consortium (INTASC)** describe what effective teachers should know and be able to do (Figure 1.7). The five principles of the

Figure 1.7 INTASC standards

1. The teacher understands the central concepts, tools of inquiry, and structures of the discipline(s) he or she teaches and can create learning experiences that make these aspects of subject matter meaningful for students.
2. The teacher understands how children learn and develop and can provide learning opportunities that support their intellectual, social, and personal development.
3. The teacher understands how students differ in their approaches to learning and creates instructional opportunities that are adapted to diverse learners.
4. The teacher understands and uses a variety of instructional strategies to encourage students' development of critical thinking, problem solving, and performance skills.
5. The teacher uses an understanding of individual and group motivation and behavior to create a learning environment that encourages positive social interaction, active engagement in learning, and self-motivation.
6. The teacher uses knowledge of effective verbal, nonverbal, and media communication techniques to foster active inquiry, collaboration, and supportive interaction in the classroom.
7. The teacher plans instruction based upon knowledge of subject matter, students, the community, and curriculum goals.
8. The teacher understands and uses formal and informal assessment strategies to evaluate and ensure the continuous intellectual and social development of the learner.
9. The teacher is a reflective practitioner who continually evaluates the effects of his/her choices and actions on others (students, parents, and other professionals in the learning community) and who actively seeks out opportunities to grow professionally.
10. The teacher fosters relationships with school colleagues, parents, and agencies in the larger community to support students' learning and well-being.

Source: From *Interstate New Teacher Assessment and Support Consortium Model Standards for Beginning Teacher Licensing and Development.* Retrieved June 10, 2005, from http://www.ccsso.org/content/pdfs/corestrd.pdf

National Board of Professional Teaching Standards (NBPTS), listed in Figure 1.8, also address teacher effectiveness. We'll examine what it means to be certified through NBPTS in Chapter 13.

The **No Child Left Behind Act of 2001 (NCLB),** the most sweeping school legislation in decades, was enacted during the first term of George W. Bush's presidency and has far-reaching ramifications that will be discussed throughout this text. One of the major aspects of NCLB is the requirement that teachers be **highly qualified.** The government has set guidelines for the quality of teachers in public schools, but each state determines its own policy for what teachers must do to be considered highly qualified. Experienced teachers have options in terms of how to meet the "highly qualified" stipulations. New teachers are expected at a minimum to meet the requirements shown in Figure 1.9.

Your Teaching Fingerprint

One thing's for sure: effective teachers make a difference in the lives of students. Think about the teachers you have had. What made some effective and others relatively ineffective?

Figure 1.8 NBPTS principles of effective teachers

1. Teachers are committed to students and their learning.
2. Teachers know the subjects they teach and how to teach those subjects to students.
3. Teachers are responsible for managing and monitoring student learning.
4. Teachers think systematically about their practice and learn from experience.
5. Teachers are members of learning communities.

Source: From *The Five Core Propositions,* by National Board for Professional Teaching Standards. Retrieved June 10, 2005, from http://www.nbpts.org/the_standards/the_five_core_propositio

Figure 1.9 No Child Left Behind minimum requirements for new teachers

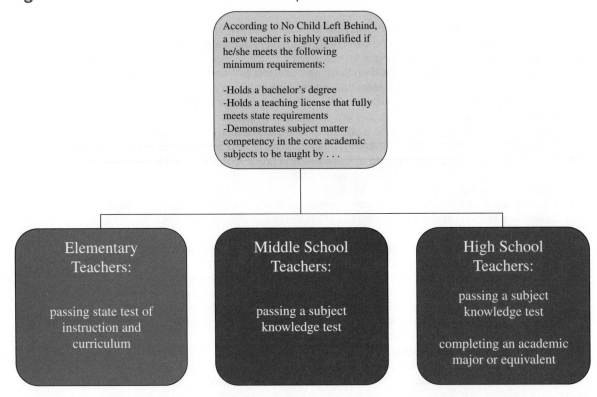

According to No Child Left Behind, a new teacher is highly qualified if he/she meets the following minimum requirements:

-Holds a bachelor's degree
-Holds a teaching license that fully meets state requirements
-Demonstrates subject matter competency in the core academic subjects to be taught by . . .

Elementary Teachers:

passing state test of instruction and curriculum

Middle School Teachers:

passing a subject knowledge test

High School Teachers:

passing a subject knowledge test

completing an academic major or equivalent

Source: From *Key Policy Letters Signed by the Education Secretary or Deputy Secretary,* U.S. Department of Education, 2005. Retrieved March 18, 2007, from http://www.ed.gov/policy/elsec/guid/secletter/051021.html

Effective Teachers Make a Difference

"Substantial research evidence suggests that well-prepared, capable teachers have the largest impact on student learning" (Darling-Hammond, 2003, p. 7). This is not to say that other factors we will discuss throughout this book do not significantly influence student learning. However, Linda Darling-Hammond and others contend that an effective teacher can overcome many of the circumstances in students' lives and positively impact student learning. When the outside influences on student learning result in an achievement gap, Kati Haycock (2003), director of the Education Trust, tells us, "If we insist on quality teachers for every student, we can dramatically improve the achievement of poor and minority students and substantially narrow the achievement gap" (p. 11). Reiterating the need for effective teachers, James Stronge (2002) writes, "Teachers have a powerful, long-lasting influence on their students. They directly affect how students learn, what they learn, how much they learn, and the ways they interact with one another, and the world around them" (p. vii).

Recently, emphasis has shifted from the teacher to the pupil as the focal point for defining teacher effectiveness. Very simply stated, the "ultimate proof of teacher effectiveness is student results" (Stronge, 2002, p. 65). But what results? What seems like a simple statement has complicated nuances because accurately assessing student learning is itself complex. Do we judge the effectiveness of a teacher solely by the standardized test scores of students? That would be easy if standardized test scores told the whole story. We'll look closely at assessment in Chapter 5. Because student success is considered the primary measure of teacher effectiveness, let's consider a few student opinions.

A disposition associated with effective teachers is respect for students and determination to foster positive interactions.

What Students Say About Teacher Effectiveness

A section on teacher effectiveness wouldn't be complete without considering what students say. In a survey of about 400 urban, low-income middle and high school students conducted by Corbett and Wilson (2002), all of them identified their teachers as the main factor in determining how much they learned. They listed a variety of characteristics of the diverse teachers most effective in helping them learn, all of which fit into the following six categories. Effective teachers

1. push students to learn
2. maintain order
3. are willing to help
4. explain until everyone understands
5. vary classroom activities
6. try to understand students (pp. 19–20)

Variety of Characteristics

Teachers can be effective with very different approaches. You can probably name two teachers in your own experience who were effective but who had different traits. Stronge (2002) tells us ". . . teaching effectiveness draws on a multitude of skills and attributes in different combinations and in different contexts to produce the results that define effectiveness" (p. 64).

Some of the chapters in this text include a feature called Letter to the Editor, in which we will explore a current events topic. Information is presented about a concept or issue to provide context for the Letter to the Editor. Following each letter are questions and prompts. You are asked to write your own letter that supports the writer's views, adds additional

Students say that teachers influence what they learn, and how quickly they learn it, more than any other factor.

information, or refutes the writer's stance. Your letter may be assessed using the guidelines in Figure 1.10. Looking closely at important issues that affect schools and those who teach and learn in them will help guide your decision about whether teaching is the profession for you. In this chapter's Letter to the Editor we read a citizen's opinion that he feels supports teachers but that at the same time portrays teachers as somewhat powerless. Think carefully as you read and respond.

An important factor to understand when it comes to the characteristics of effective teachers and teaching is that much of what makes teachers effective comes through experience in the classroom. This is not to say that new teachers can't be effective. Of course they can! But think about this. Teaching is a profession that expects a brand new teacher to do the same job as an experienced veteran (Johnson & Kardos, 2005). Don't count on someone saying, "Hey, it's okay if only half your kids learn about half of what you attempt to teach. After all, you're new." David Berliner (2000), a noted leader in teacher education, estimates that it takes about 5 years to "get smart about teaching" (p. 360). Some of the characteristics of effectiveness take time to develop: it takes time to be able to make decisions with automaticity and to draw on experience to supplement formal training.

Throughout this text you are urged to ask repeatedly, as the Masai do, "And how are the children? Are they all well?" However, when you are a novice teacher, your primary question may often be "How am I doing?" In *Educating Esme: Diary of a Teacher's First Year*, Esme Codell (1999) says that her mentor told her that with experience the question "How am I doing?" increasingly becomes "How are the children doing?"

Figure 1.10   General scoring guide for Letter to the Editor features

The following scoring guide may be used to assess the response letters you write. It is the same guide (or rubric, as we will learn in Chapter 5) that the Educational Testing Service uses to assess the writing portion of the *Praxis II Principles of Learning and Teaching* exam many states require for either initial certification or at the completion of the first year of teaching. You will refer to this page in subsequent chapters as you write additional letters to the editor.

A response that receives a score of 2:
- Demonstrates a thorough understanding of the aspects of the case that are relevant to the question
- Responds appropriately to all parts of the question
- If an explanation is required, provides a strong explanation that is well supported by relevant evidence
- Demonstrates a strong knowledge of pedagogical concepts, theories, facts, procedures, or methodologies relevant to the question

A response that receives a score of 1:
- Demonstrates a basic understanding of the aspects of the case that are relevant to the question
- Responds appropriately to one portion of the question
- If an explanation is required, provides a weak explanation that is supported by relevant evidence
- Demonstrates some knowledge of pedagogical concepts, theories, facts, procedures, or methodologies relevant to the question

A response that receives a score of 0:
- Demonstrates misunderstanding of the aspects of the case that are relevant to the question
- Fails to respond appropriately to the question
- Is not supported by relevant evidence
- Demonstrates little knowledge of pedagogical concepts, theories, facts, procedures, or methodologies relevant to the question

No credit is given for a blank or off-topic response.

Letter to the Editor

This letter to the editor appeared in the Charleston, South Carolina, newspaper, *The Post and Courier*. It was written by a concerned citizen in support of teachers. The writer is adding his opinion to the kind of blame game that commonly takes place throughout the United States when children are not successful in school.

LETTER TO THE EDITOR
MAY 6, 2005

It's not the teachers. It's the students. It's their parents and grandparents who dropped out of school. If a study was done on the disruptive, trouble-making students, I would bet that 90 percent of their parents and grandparents either dropped out of school or were socially promoted and today cannot read on an eighth-grade level.

With this in mind, how can a student with this type of background get the help at home necessary to excel in school?

Administration, school boards and others know it. All need to quit blaming the teachers and devise programs to overcome the real dilemma or it will continue to grow every generation.

Bill Pearson
Mount Pleasant

Now it's your turn. After reading about the characteristics of effective teachers in this chapter, have your opinions changed concerning responsibility for student success? These questions will help you write your own letter to the editor.

1. Linda Darling-Hammond expresses very strong belief in the power of an effective teacher. Do you agree?
2. Is it possible to break the chain of generational illiteracy?
3. Is it necessary to change the socioeconomic status of children to improve their academic success?
4. How do you feel about being in a profession (teaching) that many think is powerless to make a difference?
5. Does the concept of balance have a place in this discussion?

Your letter to the editor should be in response to the *Post and Courier* letter—supporting it, adding information, or refuting it. Write your letter in understandable terminology, remembering that readers of newspaper letters to the editor are citizens who may have limited knowledge of school practices and policies. Your letter may be written in your course notebook and shared with classmates as directed by your instructor. Remember to refer to the letter assessment rubric in Figure 1.10, page 20.

Effective teachers, regardless of whom or what they teach, share many common characteristics. Teacher professionalism is a thread that binds them all. But while there are many similarities, the day-to-day responsibilities may vary in many ways. Teachers of students with special needs; teachers who specialize in art, music, or physical education; teachers who teach all or most subjects to one group of students; and teachers who teach the same content area each day to several groups of students—all have specific preparation requirements and position responsibilities.

A valid way to categorize teachers is by the grade levels they teach. Let's turn our attention now to what's involved in teaching early childhood, elementary, middle, and high school students.

What's It Like to Teach at Various Grade Levels?

Schools in the United States offer sequential educational opportunities to students from prekindergarten (pre-K) through high school, or roughly ages 3 through 18. These opportunities progress from early childhood through elementary to middle and high school. The grade configurations of schools vary widely. Many school districts offer what are considered the traditional grade levels, including early childhood and elementary settings of prekindergarten or kindergarten through fifth grade in one building, middle level settings from sixth through eighth grade, and high schools with ninth through twelfth grade. Other districts may offer early childhood education in what are often called primary schools, consisting of prekindergarten or kindergarten through second grade, and elementary education, sometimes called intermediate schools, for third through fifth or sixth grade. Still others may offer kindergarten through eighth grade settings with ninth through twelfth grade in a high school setting.

Throughout this text your attention will be drawn to these basic levels: early childhood, elementary, middle, and high school. Regardless of the school grade configuration, student growth and learning generally move along a continuum that we will address within these four broad levels. A first grade teacher in a primary school setting and a first grade teacher in an elementary setting both teach children in the phase of early childhood. Similarly, sixth grade students in an elementary setting and sixth grade students in a middle school setting are all young adolescents in the middle school phase. As you read about each level and meet real teachers who have chosen to teach at these levels, think about your own experiences with children and adolescents. Can you see yourself in one or more of the typical grade spans? You will notice that each time a particular level is addressed you will see an icon of our cover photo with the students representing that level in color and the others in black and white. Before you read each section, take another look at the faces of the students representing the level.

Your Teaching Fingerprint

What's It Like to Teach in an Early Childhood Classroom?

The care and education of the youngest students in the United States is what **early childhood education** is all about. The wisdom of establishing an early foundation for success has made early childhood education a growing focus. The **National Association for the Education of Young Children (NAEYC)** defines early childhood as birth through age 8, or roughly through third grade. The mission of NAEYC is to lead and consolidate the efforts of individuals and groups that work to achieve healthy development and constructive education for all young children (NAEYC, 2001). To achieve its goals, NAEYC has established standards for early childhood teachers, found in Figure 1.11.

The settings for early childhood education vary more than those of the other three levels. Care and education from birth to age 5 may take place exclusively within the home, or in a combination of both home and a day-care setting outside the home. In some communities, formal school settings begin with kindergarten and 5-year-olds. In other communities, 4-year-olds have the option of attending public prekindergarten schools, often with 3-year-olds accommodated through programs that are federally funded to address the needs of

Figure 1.11   NAEYC standards for teachers

> Well-prepared early childhood professionals . . .
>
> 1. understand what young children are like; understand what influences their development; and use this understanding to create great environments where all children can thrive.
> 2. understand and value children's families and communities; create respectful, reciprocal relationships; and involve all families in their children's development and learning.
> 3. understand the purposes of assessment; use effective assessment strategies; and use assessment responsibly to positively influence children's development and learning.
> 4. build close relationships with children and families; use developmentally effective teaching and learning strategies; understand content areas and academic subjects; and use their knowledge to give all children the experiences that promote comprehensive development and learning.
> 5. identify themselves with the early childhood profession; use ethical, professional standards; demonstrate self-motivated, ongoing learning; collaborate; think reflectively and critically; and advocate for children, families, and the profession

Source: Information from *NAEYC Standards for Early Childhood Professional Preparation: Initial Licensure Programs,* by National Association for the Education of Young Children 2001, at http://www. naeyc.org/faculty/pdf/2001.pdf

low-income families. In some communities, opportunities for care and education are offered from birth. We'll look more closely at the structures of early childhood education in Chapter 2.

Now you will meet two teachers at Summit Primary School, Ohio, to help you put a face on teaching in early childhood classrooms.

Summit Primary School, Ohio. Summit Primary School does not have a preschool program. Children must be 5 years old to enter one of Summit's three levels of kindergarten. The Boost class is for children who need more basic guidance and instruction. The Average class is for most of the children. The Enrichment class is for children who have already mastered some of the typical kindergarten skills, such as recognizing and writing the alphabet, reading one syllable and often-used sight words, recalling a story orally in correct sequence, counting to 100, and making and explaining simple graphs. Some children go directly from one level of kindergarten to first grade, while others have the opportunity to stay in kindergarten for another year to build a stronger foundation for first grade. In addition to kindergarten, Summit Primary offers first and second grade.

Let's meet two Summit Primary teachers, Brandi Wade and Renee Ayers. Brandi teaches kindergarten and Renee teaches second grade. These two teachers portray joy in teaching and exemplify expertise in early childhood education. After reading about Brandi and Renee here, watch an interview, a room tour, and a brief lesson in each of their classrooms in the Choosing Your Teaching Path section of MyEducationLab. Click on Summit Primary, and then each of their names.

As you get to know Brandi and Renee, consider what you are learning about early childhood education in light of your experiences and desire to be a teacher. Does an early childhood setting appeal to you? Can you envision spending your days with young children, concentrating on literacy skills and fundamental math concepts?

Your Teaching Fingerprint

Brandi says she has found her "place" in life. Her family, her friends, her teaching career—all contribute to Brandi's exuberance. One look around her classroom and one brief conversation are enough to know . . . Read more about Brandi in MyEducationLab.

BRANDI WADE
Kindergarten teacher
Summit Primary, Ohio

Education:
BS, Elementary Ed.

Teaching Experience:
grades 5–6 (2 yrs.)
preschool and K (14 yrs.)

Renee exudes enthusiasm for life. From her experiences on the soccer field to the energy she puts into teaching second grade, her personality shines through. She says summers as a camp counselor influenced her teaching philosophy of infusing fun into instruction. Renee is a reflective teacher who . . . Read more about Renee in MyEducationLab.

RENEE AYERS
2nd-grade teacher
Summit Primary, Ohio

Education:
BA, Elementary Ed.
MS, Early Childhood Ed.

Teaching Experience:
reading teacher (2 yrs.)
1st grade (3 yrs.)
2nd grade (4 yrs.)

Now that we have briefly considered teaching in an early childhood classroom, let's explore the elementary setting.

What's It Like to Teach in an Elementary Classroom?

An elementary school is likely to serve kindergarten through grade 5 or 6. When K–3 is part of an elementary setting, these grade levels are considered **primary grades** or early childhood, and grades 4 and 5 are considered **intermediate grades**. The focus of primary grades is the acquisition of basic skills, generally in a **self-contained classroom** where a teacher spends the majority of the day with a specific group of children emphasizing literacy and reading skills and fundamental math concepts. Ideally, science and social studies are taught through projects and activities that actively involve students. Classrooms in grades 4 and 5 may also be self-contained. In many elementary settings, however, teachers specialize in two of the four **core subjects** of language arts, math, science, and social studies. For instance, a teacher may have a group of students in homeroom and be their teacher for language arts and social studies; another teacher would teach this group of students math and science. With this arrangement, two teachers are responsible for two classrooms of students.

Both primary and intermediate elementary students may have daily or weekly class sessions with other teachers who specialize in art, physical education, health, music, and other noncore subjects. You will read more about teachers who specialize in these areas in Chapter 4. Have you considered a career as a teacher of specialty area classes? Do you enjoy or have talent in art, music, physical education, or areas other than the four core subjects?

Your Teaching Fingerprint

The **Association for Childhood Education International (ACEI)** provides standards for the preparation of elementary teachers, including the recommendations shown in Figure 1.12 regarding knowledge and skills.

Now you will meet three elementary teachers at Rees Elementary School to help you envision teaching in an elementary classroom.

Rees Elementary School, Utah. Three teachers at Rees Elementary School, Utah, have **multiage,** or multigrade, **classrooms,** where children in three grade levels learn together. Chris Roberts, Brenda Beyal, and Tim Mendenhall each have homeroom classes made up of third, fourth, and fifth graders. They teach all four core subjects to their own classes, but each specializes in a fine arts area. Chris teaches dance, Brenda teaches visual arts, and Tim teaches theater to all three classes. Let's consider Brenda's class as an example of a multiage classroom. In the beginning of the school year, she has third graders who are new to her class, fourth graders who have already been in her class 1 year, and fifth graders who

Figure 1.12 ACEI elementary teacher preparation guidelines

Elementary teachers should . . .

1. learn how to provide optimal learning experiences that will support children's intellectual, emotional, social, physical, and aesthetic development
2. keep abreast of changing theories and practices, and view the teacher's role as one of a lifelong learner
3. understand that they have a responsibility to use a variety of developmentally appropriate activities
4. select methods of assessment appropriate to each of the disciplines and to the age, development, and characteristics of children
5. interpret and communicate results accurately and ethically
6. integrate information gained from assessment into instructional plans
7. be prepared to organize and implement a variety of proven instructional strategies

Source: Information from *Preparation of Elementary Teachers* (Position paper), Association for Childhood Education International. Retrieved June 12, 2005, from http://www.acei.org/prepel.htm

have already been in her class 2 years. At the end of the school year, the fifth graders move on to middle school after having been in Brenda's class for 3 years, and a new group of children who have finished second grade will be assigned to their first year with Brenda. One third of her class will be new each school year.

Chris, Brenda, and Tim bring unique interests and skills to Rees. Enjoy getting to know them in their profiles here and in the Choosing Your Teaching Path section on MyEducationLab. Go to Rees Elementary, and then on each of their names.

Tim's ready laugh sets the tone for his classroom where third, fourth, and fifth-grade students enjoy being actively involved in their own learning. Tim's comfortable manner allows his students to get to know him and each other as they . . . Read more about Tim in MyEducationLab.

TIM MENDENHALL
Multiage teacher
Rees Elementary, Utah

Education:
BS, Elementary Ed.
MEd, Math Ed.

Teaching Experience:
grades 5–8 science
(4 yrs.)
multiage, gr. 3–5 (11 yrs.)

Chris Roberts's adventurous spirit and active lifestyle permeate both his personal and his professional life. Chris has climbed Mt. Kilimanjaro, rafted his way through the rapids of the Grand Canyon, and explored the shores of remote islands. All of these rich experiences are infused in his classroom as he . . . Read more about Chris in MyEducationLab.

CHRIS ROBERTS
Multiage teacher
Rees Elementary, Utah

Education:
BS, Special Ed.
MA, Educational
Psychology &
Gifted/Talented

Teaching Experience:
special ed (14 yrs.)
multiage, gr. 3–5 (13 yrs.)

Brenda says it's not so much that she chose teaching, but that teaching chose her. The profession is very personal to her and she approaches it with a sense of calling that she feels is important in her Native American heritage. The wisdom of generations of her ancestors . . . Read more about Brenda in MyEducationLab.

BRENDA BEYAL
Multiage teacher
Rees Elementary, Utah

Education:
BS, Elementary Ed.
MA, Reading Instruction

Teaching Experience:
grade 3 (8 yrs.)
multiage, gr. 3–5 (13 yrs.)

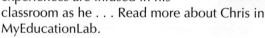

As you get to know Tim, Chris, and Brenda, consider what you are learning about elementary education in light of your experiences and desire to be a teacher. Does an elementary setting appeal to you? Elementary schools provide opportunities for professionals who are guidance counselors, media specialists, and teachers of students with special needs. Do these fields interest you?

Now that we have briefly explored elementary school, let's focus on middle school.

What's It Like to Teach in a Middle School Classroom?

A **middle school** most often includes grades 6 through 8, but may include any combination of grades 5 through 9. In the 1980s and 1990s most schools serving students between the ages of about 10 to 15 changed their names from "Junior High" to "Middle School." This new name may have accompanied a change from the traditional grade 7–9 configuration of junior highs to the grade 6–8 configuration commonly found in today's middle schools. This shift in grade levels may have been in response to facility needs, growing elementary populations, or philosophical shifts toward the philosophy of the **National Middle School Association (NMSA).**

The mission of NMSA is the establishment of developmentally appropriate settings for 10–15-year-olds, where academic rigor is in place through relevant, challenging, integrative, and exploratory curricula (NMSA, 2003). This means that NMSA wants everything that happens in middle schools to be intentionally designed for students ages 10 through 15, referred to as **young adolescents.** The balance of academic rigor and developmental appropriateness is essential in middle school education.

To ensure that teachers are prepared to achieve this balance, many states require a specialized teacher certification for middle level education that includes concentrations in one or two core subject areas. The demand for specially trained teachers in middle level grades grew out of a realization that early adolescence is a unique developmental phase of life. Given the physical, intellectual, emotional, social, and character development of young adolescents, which we will address in Chapter 3, teachers need knowledge and skills that differ from those needed by teachers trained in either elementary or high school. Categories of middle level standards for teachers are listed in Figure 1.13.

Now you will meet two teachers at Cario Middle School, South Carolina, to help you understand more about teaching in middle school classrooms.

Cario Middle School, South Carolina. Cario Middle School includes students in grades 6 through 8. Each grade level occupies its own long hallway. We'll discuss middle school organizational structures in Chapter 2. Let's personalize middle school by learning more about Traci Peters, the teacher we met in the beginning of the chapter. Let's also get to know Deirdre Huger-McGrew, a teacher in Cario's C.A.R.E. program (Cario Academic Recovery and Enrichment). Deirdre teaches English language arts and social studies to stu-

Figure 1.13   National Middle School Association Standards for Teachers

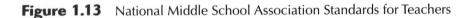

Middle level teacher candidates understand

1. young adolescent development
2. middle level philosophy and school organization
3. middle level curriculum and assessment
4. the subjects they teach
5. middle level instruction and assessment
6. how to encourage family and community involvement
7. their professional roles

Source: Information from *National Middle School Association Initial Middle Level Teacher Preparation Standards,* 2005. Retrieved May 12, 2007, from http://www.nmsa.org/portals/0/doc/preparation/standards/NMSA_Initial_Standards_July_2005.doc

dents who struggle academically. After reading about Traci and Deidre here, watch their interviews, classroom tours, and lesson segment in the Choosing Your Teaching Path section of MyEducationLab. Go to Cario, and then on each teacher's name.

Traci's classroom is filled with math—on the shelves, the walls, the tables—math is everywhere. The seventh graders in her classes know they'll be actively involved in tasks that help them understand concepts. One of Traci's primary goals is to . . . Read more about Traci in MyEducationLab.

TRACI PETERS
Grade 7 math teacher
Cario Middle School,
South Carolina

Education:
BS, Elementary Ed.
MEd, Elementary Ed.

Teaching Experience:
Grade 7 math/science
(6 yrs.)
Grade 7 math (2 yrs).

Deirdre has taught a variety of grade levels and subjects. She says each one is interesting and challenging, but none so much as her current assignment on a two-person team charged with implementing a new program designed to . . . Read more about Deirdre in MyEducationLab.

DEIRDRE HUGER-MCGREW

Grades 6–8 language
arts/social studies teacher
Cario Middle School,
South Carolina

Education:
BS, Elementary Ed.

Teaching Experience:
Grades 1,4,5 (7 yrs.)
Grades 6–8 (4 yrs.)

As you get to know Traci and Deirdre, consider what you are learning about middle school education in light of your experiences and desire to be a teacher. Does a middle school setting appeal to you? Can you envision spending your days with young adolescents? Would you enjoy teaching a core subject area or perhaps a special area such as a foreign language, band, or choral music? There are also opportunities to be guidance counselors, media specialists, and teachers of students with special needs.

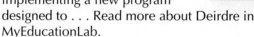
Your Teaching
Fingerprint

Now that we have considered teaching in a middle school, let's take a look at what it's like to teach in high school.

What's It Like to Teach in a High School Classroom?

High schools most often encompass grades 9 through 12. Most are comprehensive, meaning they attempt to meet the educational needs of all adolescents on a single campus. A **comprehensive high school** offers a variety of courses within the four core areas of language arts, math, science, and social studies. In addition, high schools may offer vocational arts, technology, physical education, and other classes in response to local needs and resources. A comprehensive high school generally tracks students depending on what they plan to do after high school. Student plans may be dictated by previous academic success or lack of it, or by interest and motivation. Chapter 2 will look at several different types of high schools and some of the ways high school days may be configured.

High school teachers typically teach variations within a content area. For instance, a math teacher may teach two algebra II classes, one trigonometry class, and a geometry class. He or she may see freshmen, sophomores, juniors, and seniors during the course of a day. Many high schools present opportunities for specially prepared teachers to teach art, music, health, physical education, technology, vocational arts, and so on.

Now you will meet three high school teachers at Roosevelt High School, California, who will help you understand the complexities of teaching adolescents.

Roosevelt High School, California. As an urban high school, Roosevelt is actually two high schools in one. The majority of the students (about 2,100) attend the comprehensive program, and about 500 students attend the arts magnet school, Roosevelt School of the Arts. A **magnet school** is a public school designed to cater to a specific population of students. In the case of Roosevelt School of the Arts, the students demonstrate talent in one or more performance arts.

The student population of Roosevelt High School, primarily Hispanic and Asian, is not typical of most high schools in the United States, but is more common in California, Texas, and Florida. Most of you did not attend high schools that mirror Roosevelt. Most of you will not teach in high schools like Roosevelt, but some of you will. The majority of Roosevelt's students are from low-income homes. The majority of you are not. So why is Roosevelt our focus high school? There are several reasons. First, you need to see that effective teachers engage students in interesting and relevant lessons in all schools, regardless of the student profile or school setting. Second, because the high school so fresh in many of your memories is most likely a rural or suburban high school with families in middle- to upper-income brackets, you need to be exposed to a high school that's outside most of your zones of awareness and comfort. And, perhaps most important, adolescents are adolescents. We all know that similarities outweigh elements of diversity.

You are about to get to know three excellent teachers. Their styles are different, but they share a mission: involve students in the content and process of learning and help each find his or her own voice. Read about Craig Cleveland, Derek Boucher, and Angelica Reynosa in their brief profiles here and then watch their room tours, interviews, and video segments in the Choosing Your Teaching Path section of MyEducationLab. Go to Roosevelt, then click on each teacher's name.

During lunch and during the 5-minute passing periods between classes, students gather in Craig's classroom to play a tune on his piano or strum a chord or two on his guitar. This doesn't happen by accident. It happens because . . . Read more about Craig in MyEducationLab.

CRAIG CLEVELAND
Grades 10–12 social science teacher
Roosevelt High School, California

Education:
BS, History
MS, Language Development
MS, Administration

Teaching Experience:
Grades 10–12 history, government, economics
(18 yrs.)

Your Teaching Fingerprint

As you learn more about these three teachers, consider how you might relate to adolescents. Is there a particular content area that draws your interest? Are you majoring in a content area? Have you considered majoring in or teaching art, music, or business? There are also opportunities to be guidance counselors, media specialists, and teachers of students with special needs.

Derek Boucher is an intense teacher whose conscientious involvement in the teaching profession sets a standard for all of us. His background in social sciences and his initial years in teaching led him to the realization that, until students can read with fluency, and comprehension, they will never . . . Read more about Derek in MyEducationLab.

DEREK BOUCHER
Grades 9–12 social science/reading teacher
Roosevelt High School, California

Education:
BS, biblical/religious studies
BS, social science/teaching
MA, reading/language arts

Teaching Experience:
Grades 9–12 history
(12 yrs.)
Grades 9–12 reading intervention (4 yrs.)

Angelica's tenth grade bilingual Modern World History class is filled with enthusiasm. There are 34 students in the class, all of whom have been in the United States for less than 2 years. Angelica is a young Latina woman whose fluency in both Spanish and English makes her . . . Read more about Angelica in MyEducationLab.

ANGELICA REYNOSA
Grade 10 world history teacher
Roosevelt High School, California

Education:
BS, History and Chicano Studies
MS, Counseling
Teaching Experience:
Grade 10 world history
(3 yrs.)

◼ Concluding Thoughts

Learning to be a teacher . . . teaching so others learn . . . learning to be a better teacher—this life–affirming cycle can be yours. Think of the cycle as a wheel that gathers momentum and takes you on a profound journey. You have begun to grow toward the profession. As a teacher you'll grow within the profession. Read what becoming a teacher has meant to one young man, Jamie Sawatsky, a seventh grade history teacher in Chantilly, Virginia.

> I noticed the change in myself the first time I walked into my classroom. I was no longer Jamie. That was the name of the young man who had delivered pizzas or worked at the office. My newfound teaching life had metamorphosed me into "Mr. Sawatsky." My previous work experiences had taught me a variety of skills, but accepting the title of teacher has cast me into a world where I am charged with the awesome responsibility of sculpting young minds and preparing students for positive participation in their community. When asked why they entered the profession, many teachers respond, "I wanted a chance to make a positive change in the world." In my case, perhaps selfishly, I wanted to be in a profession that would make a positive change in me. With my first year of teaching about to conclude, I can say that I am happy to be a teacher and happy to be "Mr. Sawatsky" (Tell, 2001, p.18).

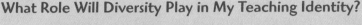

What Role Will Diversity Play in My Teaching Identity?

Student diversity will play a role in your teaching career. Differences among the students you teach will stretch your skills and enrich you professionally and personally. After Concluding Thoughts you will find this segment about how each chapter's content relates to diversity in U.S. schools. Here is the first commentary addressing how diversity will play a role in your teaching identity.

Most teachers are married White women with master's degrees. The second largest group comprises married White women without master's degrees. The next largest group is composed of single White women without master's degrees. Get the picture? We're not a very diverse profession. More men and people of color are needed.

Is it necessary to be the same gender and race as your students? Of course not. But if a student goes through early childhood, elementary, middle, and high school with few or no teachers who are men or minorities, he or she has missed opportunities to expand his or her view of who decides to spend their careers in education. These students have missed role models who may be, at least on the surface, more like so many of them. So if you are a man or a member of a racial minority, or both, thank you for choosing to explore a career in teaching.

One of the roles of teaching discussed in this chapter involves advocating for children and adolescents. This applies to all students, regardless of who they are, what their abilities appear to be, who their parents are, or what language they speak. We ask and answer, "And how are the children? Are they all well?"

■ Chapter in Review

Who teaches in the United States and why?

- Teaching is the largest profession in the United States.
- The majority of teachers are White women, leading to a need for more men and people of color in teaching.
- Almost 90% of teachers believe teaching requires a "true sense of calling."
- The most common reasons for choosing to teach include the desire to work with young people, the value of education to society, interest in a subject, the influence of a teacher or of family, the teaching schedule, job security, and the opportunity for a lifetime of self-growth.

What are the roles of teachers?

- Teachers fill many roles in their classrooms, including facilitators of learning, decision makers, and determiners of classroom climate.
- Teachers should be reflective practitioners and advocates for what's best for students.

How do we prepare to teach?

- States issue a certificate or license to teach in public schools based on their own criteria.
- The traditional path to becoming a teacher is through a university-based teacher preparation program.
- Alternative paths to teacher preparation provide timely, but somewhat controversial, routes to teacher certification.

What is teacher professionalism?

- Teacher professionalism involves a commitment to make students the first priority.
- A profession is an occupation that includes extensive training prior to entering, a code of ethics, and service as the primary product.
- Teaching meets most of the criteria generally agreed upon for a full profession.
- Numerous professional organizations support teachers and teaching.

What are the characteristics of effective teachers?

- Effective teachers may have very different styles of teaching.
- The most important factor in determining teacher effectiveness is the extent of student learning.
- There are established standards for teacher effectiveness through organizations like the Interstate New Teacher Assessment and Support Consortium and the National Board of Professional Teaching Standards.

What's it like to teach at various grade levels?

- The National Association for the Education of Young Children (NAEYC) provides standards for teachers of early childhood students and promotes developmentally appropriate education for young children, birth through age 8.
- Early childhood education can be divided into three levels—preschool, kindergarten, and primary grades.
- Elementary education may encompass a variety of grade configurations, but most elementary schools include kindergarten through grade 5.
- The Association for Childhood Education International (ACEI) provides standards for elementary teachers while advocating for all children.
- Most elementary classrooms are self-contained, although some teachers specialize in subject areas and teach that subject to all students on a grade level.
- The National Middle School Association (NMSA) provides standards for teachers and supports the education of young adolescents, ages 10 through 15.
- Interdisciplinary teams of teachers and specific groups of students are the optimal organizational structures for young adolescents.
- Middle school teachers continually strive to balance academic rigor and developmental appropriateness.
- High schools may be comprehensive in nature as they provide an educational setting for a diverse group of students.
- There are many challenges in determining the best way to provide an education for students ages 14 through 19.

Professional Practice

prac′tice, verb-
1. to do or perform frequently or habitually.
2. to use or exercise for instruction, discipline or dexterity.
3. to use one's knowledge of; to work at, especially as a profession.
4. to put theoretical knowledge to practical use.

prac′tice, noun-
1. a frequent or usual action.
2. the doing of something, often as in the application of knowledge.
3. the exercise of a profession.

At the end of each chapter we are going to practice (verb) for our practice (noun). The word *practice* is frequently used in the world of teaching. We have discussed aspects of our practice in Chapter 1. We will look at the characteristics of best practices of instruction in Chapter 4 and the responsibilities and opportunities of professional teacher practices in Chapter 13.

We will begin by practicing our understanding of what's involved in being teachers in recurring segments entitled Licensure Test Prep. Then we will explore professional standards in Standards Speak.

■ Licensure Test Prep

At the end of each chapter you are asked to respond to multiple-choice and constructed-response items formatted much like licensure exams you will be required to pass before you can begin your teaching career. One of the exams frequently required for either initial licensing or by the end of the first year of teaching is the Praxis™ II Principles of Learning and Teaching (PLT) test. The PLT, like many other exams, is based specifically on the four levels of U.S. education—early childhood, elementary, middle, and high school. This text's emphasis on education at the various levels will help you address the items you will encounter that align with each chapter's content.

The four PLT exams (Early Childhood, K–6, 5–9, 7–12) are 2-hour tests comprising four case histories, each followed by three short-answer (constructed-response) items. These items frequently ask for two responses to a question or a scenario. In addition, the PLT tests include 24 multiple-choice items unrelated to a case history. Some of the multiple-choice items involve brief scenarios, some ask about passages from books about a given topic, and others ask for unrelated information (Educational Testing Service, 2007). If your state requires the Praxis™ Series, you will find basic information, study guides, registration information, and practice items at http://www.ets.org. If your state requires a different exam, ask your instructor about accessing information specific to that exam.

The items in Licensure Test Prep will spark thought and discussion about important issues in education and are valuable regardless of your state's licensing requirements. The rubric for assessing constructed-response items is the same as that presented in the explanation of the Letter to the Editor. See Figure 1.10 on page 20.

Answer multiple-choice questions 1 through 6 and constructed-response item 7.

1. All of the following statements are true about public school teachers in the United States except . . .
   a. 60% are female
   b. almost 60% have master's degrees
   c. 90% are White
   d. about one third have children of their own

2. Which two of the following are the largest teacher organizations in the United States?
   I. NAEYC
   II. AFT
   III. INTASC
   IV. NEA

   a. I and IV
   b. III and IV
   c. II and IV
   d. I and III

3. Renee Ayers has been asked to speak about the many forms of early childhood education at a monthly Rotary Club meeting in Pataskala, Ohio. She should speak about all of the following except . . .
   a. kindergarten
   b. intermediate grades
   c. Regio Emilia
   d. Montessori
   e. primary grades

4. While researching the prevalence of multiage classrooms in U.S. schools, Tim Mendenhall discovers that which of the following configurations occurs most frequently in public elementary schools?
   a. K–5 schools with self-contained K–3 classrooms and specialized teachers for grades 4–5
   b. schools with grades K–2 only
   c. schools with grades 3–5 only
   d. multiage classrooms, grades K–2 and 3–5
   e. self-contained classrooms in grades K–5

5. Deirdre Huger-McGrew plans to attend the annual conference of the National Middle School Association. She will likely hear much about components of middle school strongly endorsed by NMSA, including all of the following except . . .
   a. interdisciplinary teams
   b. academic rigor
   c. content-specific departmentalization
   d. developmental appropriateness
   e. multiple learning and teaching approaches

6. Derek Boucher was chair of the Roosevelt High School committee that recommended a switch from traditional scheduling to block scheduling. Which of the following benefits of block scheduling was likely to have been the most persuasive and compelling for the RHS committee?
   a. Four classes are taken at one time, allowing students to concentrate more on each.
   b. Students may graduate in under 4 years.
   c. Longer blocks of instructional time are provided.
   d. Alternating days for classes give more time for completion of independent assignments.

7. What are two reasons why it is difficult to describe definitive characteristics of an effective teacher? Explain each reason.

■ Standards Speak

We live in the age of standards, or expectations for what we know and are able to do. They do not constitute an education fad or isolated program; standards are foundational to what we do and how we do it. New teacher certification is based in most states on the standards articulated and assessed by the Praxis™ series of exams. Teachers practice their profession according to organizations such as the Interstate New Teacher Assessment and Support Consortium (INTASC) standards and the National Board of Professional Teaching Standards (NBPTS). State departments of education across the United States strive to meet the standards of the National Council for the Accreditation of Teacher Education (NCATE). There are subject area standards and standards that apply to levels of schooling. We will learn about many of the primary standards of INTASC, NBPTS, Praxis™, NCATE, and other professional organizations as they pertain to chapter content through Standards Speak.

In this chapter we looked at many aspects of being a teacher. Let's concentrate on what standards say about reflection and professionalism.

INTASC Standard 9 Professional Commitment and Responsibility

The teacher is a reflective practitioner who continually evaluates the effects of his/her choices and actions on others (students, parents, and other professionals in the learning community) and who actually seeks out opportunities to grow professionally.

NBPTS Core Proposition 4

Teachers think systematically about their practice and learn from experience.

NAEYC Standard 5 Becoming a Professional

Candidates identify and conduct themselves as members of the early childhood profession. They are continuous, collaborative learners who demonstrate knowledge, reflection, and critical perspectives on their work, making informed decisions that integrate knowledge from a variety of sources. They are informed advocates for sound educational practices and policies.

ACEI Standard 5.2 Reflection and Evaluation

Candidates are aware of reflecting on their practice in light of research on teaching and resources available for professional learning; they continually evaluate the effects of their professional decisions and actions on students, parents, and other professionals in the learning community and actively seek out opportunities to grow professionally.

NMSA Standard 7 Middle Level Professional Roles

Middle level teacher candidates understand the complexity of teaching young adolescents, and they engage in practices and behaviors that develop their competence as professionals.

Respond to the following questions in your class notebook and/or discuss your responses with your classmates as directed by your instructor.

1. What sort of scenario can you envision in an early childhood, elementary, middle school, or high school setting that would call on you to exercise professionalism when perhaps others around you are not?

2. What are some ways to keep track of things that happen in your classroom that you believe will require reflection at a time when you can devote at least 10 minutes or so to serious consideration of the issues and incidents?

3. What are some "practices and behaviors" (NMSA, Standard 7) that might help develop your competence as a professional?

■ MyEducationLab

The following interactive features may be found in Chapter 1 of MyEducationLab.

Homework and Exercises

Writing My Own Story
To write your own story by responding to some of the questions in the text accompanied by fingerprint icons, plus others, go to the "Writing My Own Story" section of the Homework and Exercises for Chapter 1 of MyEducationLab.

What's My Disposition?
To reflect on your beliefs and attitudes concerning the teaching profession, go to Chapter 1's "What's My Disposition?" feature of the Homework and Exercises section of MyEducationLab.

Exploring Schools and Classrooms
If your course involves experiences in schools, the questions and prompts in the "Exploring Schools and Classrooms" feature of Chapter 1's Homework and Exercises section of MyEducationLab will guide you as you explore local schools and classrooms.

Virtual Field Experience

To respond to questions and prompts regarding the Choosing Your Teaching Path videos that connect to specific chapter content, go to Chapter 1's Virtual Field Experience section of MyEducationLab. The questions will help you make sense of what you have read in the chapter.

Chapter 2

Schools

Teaching in Focus

Brandi Wade teaches kindergarten at Summit Primary School in Summit Station, Ohio. We first met Brandi in Chapter 1. She has witnessed many changes at her school as families have moved into the once rural area just outside Columbus. Housing developments have sprung up all around the school, and change has been ongoing for several years. The small town of Summit Station is now surrounded by a thriving, suburban-like area, and there are no signs of the rate of growth slowing down. The Licking Heights School District continues to build bigger schools to accommodate the growth.

Summit Primary is the only K–2 school in the district. This is a purposeful configuration. Principal Laura Hill says she likes the format because she has every kindergarten, every first-grade, and every second-grade teacher in the district right in her building. This lends a great deal of consistency to how children are taught and what and when they learn. Even with unprecedented growth, Summit Primary retains its specialty of early childhood education. The grade-level teachers work together as a team to provide instruction that is developmentally appropriate for young children.

Along with the growth has come diversity. Once a school of predominantly White children with a relatively small African American population, all English speaking, Summit Primary now serves children with a variety of heritages who speak one of 16 different languages. This diversity of languages presents a major challenge for the Summit teachers. In Brandi's two kindergarten classes, whose students include twin boys from Somalia, five native languages are represented. A special teacher works with these learners who speak limited or no English to help them acquire the English they need to make learning kindergarten skills an easier and more natural process. Brandi's dedication to all children in her kindergarten classes, regardless of their background, is evident in her interactions and conversations about "her kids."

You watched Brandi's video in the Choosing Your Teaching Path section of MyEducationLab for this text in Chapter 1. Now watch the interview and tour of Summit Primary with principal Laura Hill. Go to Summit Primary, and then click on Laura.

This chapter will explore schools in the United States by addressing these focus questions:

- What is the culture of a school?
- How do the venues of schools differ?
- What is school like at different levels?
- What are the three principle settings of public schools?
- What is an effective school?

Introduction

Schools are centers of our communities, foundations of our citizenry, targets of political and ethical debate, mirrors and shapers of our society, and keepers of the hopes and dreams of parents and children. Without exception the greeting "And how are the children?" should be on the lips and in the hearts of every adult in every U.S. school.

Schools are threads woven through the fabric of American life. Mandatory attendance makes some form of schooling a common factor in our society. As such, we have all experienced schools. But as with all human endeavors, our perspectives differ. We have each lived school in our own unique way. Perspective, however, isn't the only reason we view schools differently. The schools themselves are different. Before we address these differences we will consider that a school, like all established groups and institutions, has a distinct culture or environment that is shaped by people, their shared beliefs, individual and collective actions, and all manner of circumstances.

What Is the Culture of a School?

School culture is the context of learning experiences; it's the prevailing atmosphere of the school. As places where people work together and learn together, schools function according to their cultures. Noted educator Roland Barth (2001) tells us, "A school's culture dictates, in no uncertain terms, 'the way we do things around here.' Ultimately, a school's culture has far more influence on life and learning in the schoolhouse than the state department of education, the superintendent, the school board, or even the principal can ever have" (p. 7).

A school's culture can be a positive force for learning or a negative influence that interferes with learning. It is important to know a school's culture, both the forces that created it and those that perpetuate it. If the culture is positive, recognizing the influential forces and then reinforcing them keeps the culture vibrant and growing. If the culture is negative or apathetic, altering it begins with recognizing the influential forces and finding ways to begin the change process.

From a new teacher's standpoint, a positive school culture may be evident when experienced teachers consistently ask how things are going and offer to help with lessons, materials, managing student behavior, paperwork, and so on. Hearing teachers talking and laughing together, sharing what works in their classrooms, and speaking of students with caring and concerned attitudes demonstrates positive culture. On the other hand, when a school seems to have a territorial atmosphere with cliques of teachers criticizing other teachers and the principal, when offers of assistance are few, when students are spoken of primarily in critical terms, a new teacher will likely sense a negative culture. Because most of the adults in a school are teachers, their influence on school culture is immense.

Teachers and School Culture

Teachers exert a powerful influence on their school's culture. First, teachers' instructional skills and professionalism either improve a school's culture or keep it stagnant or negative. Second, the level of respect teachers engender among their colleagues and in the community either builds a positive culture or serves to drag it down. This level of respect has much to do with the relationships that exist among a school's adults, which, in turn, influence the ways teachers relate to students. All teachers, including

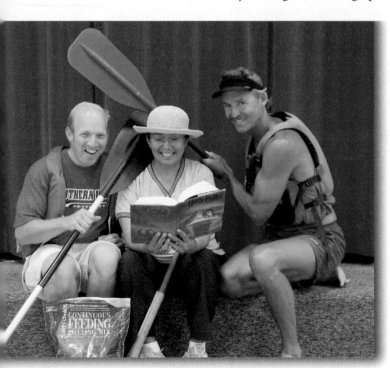

When teachers obviously enjoy each other's company, as with Tim, Brenda, and Chris at Rees Elementary in Utah, the school culture will likely be positive and productive.

those with designated leadership functions as well as those who are new to a school, have considerable influence on school culture. Therefore, teachers must be instrumental in changing their school's culture to move in a positive direction if needed.

Changing School Culture

A school's culture can change. Can it change quickly or easily? Definitely not. Negative to positive culture shifts require strong leadership, ownership of the problems and potential solutions by the adults in the school, and a steady, conscious flow of both actions and attitudes that produce the desired results. On the other hand, changes in a school culture from positive to negative may only require neglect.

All components of American education discussed in this text influence a school's culture. For instance, what is taught in a school can be dynamic and challenging, or mediocre and boring. Not only *what* is taught, but *how* it is taught, influences culture. The level of respect and nurture teachers have toward students influences school culture. As you progress through this book, remember to envision what you read in the context of the complex, living system that is a school. Since students, teachers, parents, community, policies, and politics all potentially influence school culture, we'll explore the many ways schools differ, beginning with types of schools.

■ How Do the Venues of Schools Differ?

U.S. schools vary greatly, from the traditional neighborhood public school to the ultimate private school—the home. This section will look at **school venues,** the variety of ways Americans do school in the more than 120,000 schools in the United States (National Center for Education Statistics [NCES], 2005). Because most of the schools in the United States are public, we will begin by examining them.

Public School Venues

The vast majority of educational settings in the United States are **public schools,** meaning that most of the funding to support them comes through some form of taxation. Public schools are accountable to the community through elected or governmental officials who have policy and oversight responsibilities. We'll examine the governance of schools in Chapter 12.

Public schools come in all shapes and sizes, each with unique characteristics that we will explore throughout this text. Public schools are not only open to every student regardless of socioeconomic status, disability, race, or religion, but in fact must provide a school setting for every child—that's part of being public. Political scientist Benjamin Barber (1997) wrote,

> Public schools are not merely schools *for* the public, but schools of publicness: institutions where we learn what it means to *be* a public and start down the road toward common national and civic identity. They are the forges of our citizenship and the bedrock of our democracy. (p. 22)

Do you have a desire to be part of the "forge" and the "bedrock" of which Barber speaks? What has drawn you to education? Have you considered teaching for a long time, or is it a new idea you are exploring? Remember that when you see a fingerprint in the margin it means that you will be asked to respond to questions based on your experiences and opinions. These questions are included in "Writing My Own Story" in Chapter 2 of the Homework and Exercises section of MyEducationLab at www.myeducationlab.com.

Public schools may be traditional in that they serve most children's needs, or they may be specialized in many ways and for different reasons. They may exist to meet specific student needs, or they may be different because of the community in which they are situated. Before looking at differences among public schools, let's consider the purpose of public schooling in the United States.

Purpose of public schools. For more than two centuries, most people have considered the overarching purpose of American public schools to be the *preservation of our democratic way of life.* That's a powerful concept, one that comes close to being an absolute, or something few, if any, would refute. Since the United States is a constitutional republic, differing views arise about what preservation of the American democratic way of life looks like. Divergent opinions are what democracy allows and, in fact, encourages.

This overarching purpose requires that educators teach principles such as freedom, citizenship and its responsibilities, and respect for law and individual rights. It is also important for students to have opportunities to practice what are considered habits of democracy—tolerance, fair play, hard work—those skills and attitudes that contribute to the preservation of the American way of life and form of government.

Concern has mounted since the attacks of September 11, 2001, for not only the preservation of the American way of life, but also the strengthening and security of the United States and its citizens. The responsibility of fulfilling the primary purpose of public schooling has never been more urgent or necessary. Historian Robert Westbrook (1996) writes,

> The relationship between schooling and democracy is a conceptually tight one. Schools have become one of the principal institutions by which modern states reproduce themselves, and insofar as those states are democratic, they will make use of schools to prepare children for democratic citizenship. (p. 125)

John Goodlad (2004), a respected educator, echoes Westbrook when he writes,

> . . . it would be the height of folly for our schools not to have as their central mission educating the young in the democratic ideals of humankind, the freedoms and responsibilities of a democratic society, and the civil and civic understandings and dispositions necessary to democratic citizenship. (p. 20)

Keep in mind the overarching purpose of public schooling in the United States—the preservation of the American way of life—as we explore options within the U.S. system of public schools, including traditional neighborhood schools, magnet schools, and charter schools.

Traditional public schools. The traditional, or neighborhood school, is still the predominant form of public schooling in the United States. **Traditional public schools** have no admission criteria, other than perhaps residency in a particular attendance zone. Their educational programs are designed to meet the needs of almost all students, with the possible exception of some with severe physical or mental disabilities. Most of us attended a traditional neighborhood public school. Most of the more than 50 million students in grades K–12 in the United States attend public schools.

A public school that provides a comprehensive program of education and includes student and community services, such as after-school and family-education programs, may be considered a **full-service school.** Multiple components are involved in such a school, many of which are made possible through community partnerships with businesses, health-care providers, foundations, and government agencies. These services help students and their families cope with a variety of dilemmas, many of which stem from living in poverty, which often interferes with learning.

The goals of a full-service school may include

- Meeting students' needs, both academic and nonacademic, through extended-day programs, counseling groups, homework assistance, and the like
- Increasing family stability through parent education
- Ceating a safe haven for the community
- Providing role models for all family members
- Responding to physical and psychological needs
- Providing easy access to government services
- Involving community members from all walks of life in public education

Now let's look at three venues of public schools that draw specific groups of students: magnet schools, charter schools, and alternative schools. Each has a structure that uniquely matches the needs of its student population.

Magnet schools. A school with a specific emphasis or theme may be known as a **magnet school.** The curriculum or instructional program of a magnet school is tailored with unique opportunities that attract certain students. A theme may be math, science, or both; performing arts; technology; or high academic expectations and student qualifications. For example, a magnet school with an emphasis on preparation for a career in the trade arts, sometimes called a vocational magnet, would attract students interested in careers in construction, mechanics, cosmetology, culinary arts, and so on.

Some children enter kindergarten with many readiness skills; others do not.

Magnet schools are more expensive to operate than traditional neighborhood schools. Their special programs may require funds for career-related equipment, performance studios, staff with specific expertise, smaller teacher-student ratios, transportation beyond immediate neighborhoods, and other needs. More and more magnet schools are opening and drawing specific groups of students out of the traditional neighborhood schools as parents and students seek more specialized environments. Today approximately 3% of students enrolled in U.S. public schools attend magnet schools. These magnet schools account for about 2% of public schools.

Charter schools. A **charter school** is a public school that is freed in specific ways from the typical regulations required of other public schools. For instance, teachers and administrators in charter schools usually have more control over how they spend their funds and the kinds of classes they offer than their counterparts in traditional public schools. Charter schools are open to all students within a school district and must attract students to stay in operation.

Charter schools are created by people who see a need or an opportunity to fix a problem, such as declining student achievement, or to enhance a particular area, such as student ability in the arts. They may be started from scratch or converted from pre-existing schools. Charter school themes may revolve around a subject area, particular teaching techniques, a social problem, specific grade levels, or anything else the creators imagine and propose.

Charter schools combine freedom and accountability. As such they are examples of the ultimate in **site-based management,** meaning that the governance of a school is in the hands of those closest to it, generally teachers, administrators, and parents. There are more charter schools than magnet schools in the United States, but only about 1.2% of students in the United States are enrolled in charter schools.

Alternative schools. Magnet and charter schools are both alternative forms of school organization. However, in public education, the words *alternative school* take on a unique meaning. If a school is called an **alternative school,** more than likely it is a school designed for students who are not successful in a traditional school setting. Because school districts can't exclude students and attendance is compulsory until age 16, alternative settings have emerged. Alternative schools may be categorized in two ways, remedial and last chance.

Students who need more focused attention to be successful than what the traditional school can provide are in need of remediation, academically, socially, emotionally, or some combination of the three. Once remediation is completed, a student may return to a more traditional setting. Alternative schools with remediation as the primary focus prefer to be viewed as nonpunitive and try to attend to each student's needs as much as possible. Often students who are characterized as being **at risk students**—those in serious danger of not completing school and who may be heading toward nonproductive or counterproductive lifestyles—are strongly urged to attend these alternative schools.

Students who are not successful in a remedial setting may attend public alternative schools that are considered last-chance schools, meaning that the students who attend them have not been successful in terms of academics or behavior in another setting. In most cases the students have gotten into significant trouble in a traditional or remedial school, have been suspended multiple times, have consistently been disruptive in the classroom, or generally have not benefited from other, less intrusive programs. These alternative schools become these students' last chance for success in a public school setting.

In the News

A school that qualifies as both a charter school, because of its vision and unique structure, and an alternative school, because it was developed to meet the needs of students at risk of not succeeding in traditional public schools, is the Seed Public Charter School in Washington, DC. View the In the News video about this school and respond to the prompts. To view this video, go to this text's DVD, click on In the News, and then on this chapter's video, *One Last Chance*.

The wide variety of public schools discussed provides opportunities and choice when parents and students are informed and given ways to explore the options. Table 2.1 summarizes the commonly available public school options.

Did you attend public schools? Were they traditional neighborhood schools, magnet schools, charter schools, or alternative schools? If you attended a variety of public school venues, what differences among them did you experience?

Your Teaching
Fingerprint

As public school enrollment grows, so does private school enrollment. It's important to explore both public and private schools as you consider whether teaching is the career for you. Try to imagine yourself in each setting as you think about your teaching identity.

Private School Venues

The two elements that make schools public—public funding and public accountability—are both absent in **private schools.** About 10% of students in the United States attend private schools (NCES, 2004). Families choose private education for a variety of reasons. Some choose private schools because of the benefits they may provide, such as smaller class size, specific instruction to meet the needs of students with learning disabilities (more on learning disabilities in Chapter 3), or travel and extracurricular opportunities. Still others

In The News

One Last Chance

Ted Koppel and ABC news correspondent Michelle Martin introduce us to a unique charter school. The Seed Public Charter School is the only public urban boarding school in the United States. Located in Washington, DC, Seed provides housing, meals, a safe and clean environment, and an education for seventh- through twelfth-grade students chosen by lottery. Believing that millions of students are being shortchanged, the founders of Seed created an educational structure that allows students, previously thought to be destined to drop out of school because of their environment an opportunity for success.

Watch the video to learn more about Seed and the students and teachers who learn together there. Go to the text's DVD. Click on In the News and then on *One Last Chance.* Then respond to these questions and prompts.

1. Why do the founders of Seed claim that the students they serve need an "entirely new environment" in order to succeed in school?

2. The math teacher says it takes courage for the students to move forward academically. What are two things the Seed students must overcome to be successful in school?

3. What are the purposes of "gates" at Seed? Is the success rate related to them higher or lower than you would have anticipated? Why?

4. What caused Jonathan to say, "You may think because you know my neighborhood that you can judge me for who I may become"?

Table 2.1 Public school venues

Venue	Definition	Admission Criteria	Advantages	Disadvantages
Traditional	Neighborhood school	None	Close to home; sense of ownership	May not have programs of interest or that meet specific student needs
Full service	School that offers student and community services that go beyond academics	None	Draws families in; provides services such as health promotion and community education	None
Magnet	School with specific emphasis or theme	Interest; talent; academic achievement	Specialized curriculum or instruction	May exclude some students; requires more funding
Charter	School freed from some regulatory control of district or state	None; generally first come, first admitted	Site-based decision making; specialized curriculum or instruction	May lack sufficient oversight; danger of "ends justify means" mentality
Alternative	Usually a school for students who are not successful in other public school settings	Behavioral or academic problems	Can provide specialized assistance for students who need it most	May neglect some aspects of school while targeting specific needs; may stereotype or stigmatize students

may choose private education because of family history. Perhaps generations of family members attended a particular private school.

Some families choose private schools because of negative perceptions about local public schools. They may consider public schools inferior or inadequate. Others want to isolate their children from specific ethnicities or races. Still others want their children to have religious instruction or believe that their children's specific mental or physical needs require a private setting. Then there are other families who perceive that a private school may have prestige over the public schools available.

In most instances, public and private schools exist side by side in a community with little rivalry. Yet there may be differences in underlying philosophy that cause friction. Also, unlike their public school counterparts, private schools are not obligated to educate all students, but are able to choose and dismiss students. Thus their classrooms typically have fewer behavior problems, a smaller teacher-student ratio, and stronger parental support. Some private school teachers see this as a trade-off since most of them are paid less than teachers in public schools. Have you considered teaching in a private school for these or other reasons? As you read more about private schools, consider what might motivate you to choose a private rather than a public school for your career.

Your Teaching Fingerprint

Let's explore different venues of private schools, beginning with their affiliations. We'll briefly look at single-gender schools and then at the ultimate private school, the home. This section on private schools concludes with a discussion of for-profit schools.

Affiliations. Most private schools are affiliated with a particular religious sect (denomination). The majority of these are aligned with the Catholic faith. Private schools affiliated with religious organizations are sometimes called **parochial schools.**

Private schools that are not aligned with a religious group exist in many forms and cater to a wide spectrum of needs and wants of students and families. They may resemble charter schools with themes and areas of emphasis, but they are free from all government regulation because they are privately funded.

Single-gender schools. Some private schools are **single gender,** enrolling either all boys or all girls. Because **Title IX of the Education Amendments Act of 1972** prohibits government money from being used for programs that discriminate on the basis of gender, the majority of single-gender schools are private.

A growing body of research supports the opinion that males and females learn differently. In Chapter 3 we will consider these possible gender differences in learning. There are zealots on both sides of this issue and research that supports the academic merits of single-gender schools and classes as well as research that concludes there are no academic benefits.

Homeschooling. Students who receive most of their academic instruction in their homes are considered to be homeschooled. Although it's hard to pinpoint an exact number, we know that there are over 1 million homeschooled students in the United States (NCES, 2004). This figure represents less than 3% of the total U.S. student population. The reasons for parents choosing homeschooling vary, as illustrated in Figure 2.1, but are similar to parental reasons for choosing private over public school venues.

Homeschooling has become a social movement, with parents as political activists, organizers of national networks, and developers of curriculum and materials. As you can imagine, the quality of the education received in the home varies widely. However, on standardized academic achievement tests homeschoolers tend to score 15–30 percentile points higher than students in public schools (Ray, 2006). How students fare socially has not been measured, only openly speculated about. A concern is that children who are homeschooled may miss out on the civic perspective and experiences gained only through going to school with students who are not like themselves in religious beliefs, racial or cultural background, socioeconomic status, or academic aptitude.

Homeschooling has always been part of the human experience. Some notable homeschooled students include Florence Nightingale, Thomas Edison, Margaret Mead, Charles Dickens, Benjamin Franklin, Orville and Wilbur Wright, Woodrow Wilson, and U.S. Supreme Court justice Sandra Day O'Connor.

For-profit schools. Nonreligious private schools are often **for-profit schools.** They may not make a significant profit, but they charge tuition to pay expenses. These schools are managed by someone or some entity that receives a percentage of the money generated. It's capitalism in the schoolhouse.

Figure 2.1   Parental reasons for homeschooling

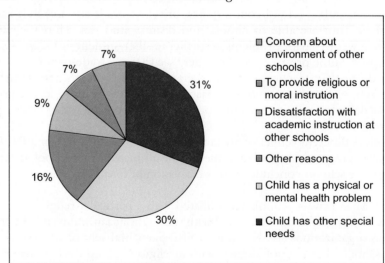

Source: From *National Household Education Survey* (NHES), National Center for Education Statistics, U.S. Department of Education, 2004.

Public schools may also be for-profit, a concept that is controversial. **Education Maintenance Organizations,** or **EMOs** (the educational equivalent of health care's HMOs), have been contracted to take over the management of some public schools. The largest EMO to date manages what are called Edison Schools. Edison Schools, and most other for-profit companies formed to manage schools, have a simple goal—the creation of model schools with research-based instructional programs. A district may contract with a company and pay it whatever the school generates in funds based on number of students. Since income is essentially fixed by the student population, the only way to make a profit is to cut expenses. Bus transportation, areas such as special education and the arts, and numbers of support staff may suffer. For-profit companies may view the concept of education for all as a problem (Kohn, 2002). Additional information on school funding is provided in Chapter 12.

As you can see, there is variety among those schools not directly supported through state funding. Table 2.2 gives an overview of some of the private school venues. Keep in mind that what some may view as advantages may be considered disadvantages by others, and vice versa.

Did you attend private schools? If so, were they religious or nonreligious? If you attended more than one venue of private school, what differences did you experience? Did you attend a combination of public and private schools? If so, what differences did you experience between public and private schools?

Your Teaching Fingerprint

Both public and private schools create choices for families. Let's explore how school choice is manifested in U.S. schools.

Table 2.2   Private school venues

Venue	Definition	Admission Criteria	Advantages	Disadvantages
Religious	School with a religious affiliation	Agreement to either uphold or not interfere with the principles of the affiliation	Allows parents and religious groups to include their traditions and beliefs	Not accountable to any government agency
Nonreligious	School without a religious affiliation	Interest; can afford tuition; students may be rejected for any reason	Specialized curriculum or instruction	Not accountable to any government agency
Single-gender	School for boys only or girls only	Must be gender of school; generally first come, first admitted	May better meet specific learning styles of either boys or girls	Not accountable to any government agency; may not mirror reality of co-ed world
Homeschooling	Students are taught at home or in a home environment	Family member	Provides very specific, one-on-one instruction in a manner desired by parents	Not accountable to any government agency; may isolate student from other cultures and viewpoints; may neglect some aspects of what is commonly agreed upon as necessary curriculum
For-profit	Schools run by individuals or corporations that make and keep monetary gain	Any criteria set by school managers	Can be very specialized	Not accountable to any government agency

School Choice

School choice—letting parents and students decide which schools meet their needs—has a very democratic feel, doesn't it? The reasons for offering choice are as varied as the choice plans available. Increasing parental involvement, providing learning environments more suited to individual students, attempting broader integration, accommodating particular interests and talents, and affording more desirable settings to at-risk or underprivileged students are just a few of the reasons.

Let's consider school choice in the context of competition. Marketplace theory says that competition leads to improvement. But does this apply to schools competing for student enrollment when more students mean more money? If all schools were high performing and differed only in theme or focus, then competition would simply mean appealing to student interests or learning preferences. But when schools gain enrollment while others lose because of real or perceived failure to meet the needs of students, the failing school is left in an even more untenable situation. If we close them down, we may be eliminating the possibility of improving the predominant public school setting—the neighborhood school. On the other hand, no child should be in a school that is not making progress toward improved levels of learning. Answering the question, "And how are the children?" becomes even more complex and important.

For any choice plan, there are two key ingredients for success—information and transportation. Without provisions for both, a choice plan only gives choices to families who seek out information and have the capability to provide transportation out of their neighborhoods.

School choice for students attending public schools is accomplished through three broad approaches, as illustrated in Figure 2.2.

Public-to-public school choice. Allowing for choice among public schools occurs in a variety of ways. The option of attending magnet, charter, and alternative schools versus a traditional neighborhood school within a district is by far the most common manifestation of school choice. Taking this option a step further, **open enrollment** allows students to choose from among all the schools in a school district with a few exceptions, such as magnet schools with specific student qualifications and alternative schools with student enrollment controlled by the district. Open enrollment may extend across district lines as well. As of 2004, 33 states had some form of interdistrict open enrollment, and 15 states required districts to offer open enrollment (Education Commission of the States, 2004). Some large districts, such as Miami-Dade and Milwaukee, have offered some form of open enrollment for decades.

Figure 2.2   School choice options supported by government funding

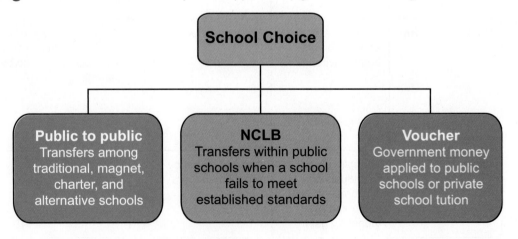

No Child Left Behind. One provision of the No Child Left Behind Act of 2001 (introduced in Chapter 1, page 18) is that parents and students have school choice under certain conditions. The act includes guidelines for grading schools based on their progress toward reaching designated goals dealing with, among other things, student achievement on standardized tests and attendance. Schools are evaluated and given report cards called Adequate Yearly Progress, or simply AYP reports. After two years of failing AYP, students at schools with a high percentage of students in poverty may transfer to a school with a passing AYP report. The school district has the responsibility to provide at least two designated recipient schools that passed AYP for each student and to make transportation available for students who choose to transfer according to this NCLB provision. The transferring student is likely to encounter more positive student role models and teachers with higher morale in the new school than in a school bearing the burden of being labeled a failure.

Middle school students will eagerly participate in class discussion when their interest is piqued by engaging and challenging topics and questions.

Are parents and students likely to take advantage of the choices provided by NCLB? Maybe, maybe not. More will if they are informed of the options in a timely fashion, if they are comfortable that long bus rides won't be necessary, and if the students are not socially committed to staying with their neighborhood friends who opt not to move. These are powerful ifs. Here's another to consider: children are unlikely to instigate the move. If their parents do not explore options, students will likely remain in schools designated as failing under NCLB criteria.

Vouchers. Perhaps the most controversial of current efforts to provide school choice is the **voucher,** a government-issued piece of paper that represents part of the state's financial contribution for the education of a student. Parents choose a school and present the voucher, and the government allocates funding accordingly to the school.

Some vouchers are only for students living in poverty, allowing them to choose a school that perhaps better meets their needs. Other vouchers are awarded to any student within a designated area to use within a school district, or even across district lines. Some vouchers may be used only in public schools, whereas others may be applied to private school tuition or even to schools with a religious affiliation. The viability of voucher plans often sparks debates in state legislatures.

Consider this. Private schools are free to admit or refuse any student. They can decide not to take vouchers from students who don't fit in—for any reason, including gender, race, past or potential achievement, or disability. Likewise, they can recruit and admit the most motivated, highest-achieving students. Public money in the form of vouchers thus has the potential to become a tool of discrimination.

The use of vouchers to attend schools with a religious affiliation is perhaps the most controversial aspect of the program. Many people consider this a violation of the separation of church and state, and this obstacle may lead to the demise of vouchers as school choice alternatives.

To help you understand more about school choice as an issue that will likely affect you as a teacher, this chapter's Letter to the Editor addresses vouchers in Milwaukee, Wisconsin, schools. Milwaukee Public Schools (MPS) serve almost 100,000 students in about 220 schools. About three quarters of the students live in low-income settings. In 2003–2004, 13,000 of Milwaukee's poorest students enrolled in 107 private schools, including schools with religious affiliations. MPS offers a wide variety of school venues to its students, including

- Neighborhood schools (over 160). MPS is making an ongoing, concerted effort to improve neighborhood schools through a program known as the Neighborhood Schools Initiative.
- Open enrollment. Students can attend any public school within MPS and in surrounding districts if space is available.
- Charter schools. These public schools are open to Milwaukee students and sponsored by MPS, the City of Milwaukee, and the University of Wisconsin.
- Chapter 220. This program encourages minority students in MPS to attend suburban public schools and White suburban students to attend MPS.
- Milwaukee Parental Choice Program (MPCP). This is a taxpayer-funded voucher program for low-income students to attend Milwaukee private schools, including religious-affiliated programs (School Choice Wisconsin, 2004).

Advocates and critics of school choice. School choice, regardless of the format, has its advocates and its critics. If we simply pose the question, "Should parents have the right to choose a school that best meets the needs of their children?" most Americans would say yes. Table 2.3 lists several of the pros and cons of school choice, each deserving study to

Letter to the Editor

This letter appeared in the *Milwaukee Journal Sentinel* on July 2, 2004. It concerns the hotly debated practice of using public funds in the form of vouchers to pay private school tuition for low-income students in Milwaukee. The writer is addressing what is perceived as a lack of accountability.

Dear Editor,

I agree, in part, with the editorial of July 2. If school choice is to be funded by the taxpayers of Wisconsin, then there should be some accountability of the schools that receive the funds.

Right now, public schools must participate in the Wisconsin Student Assessment System. Third-, fourth-, eighth- and tenth-grade students are tested using standardized tests. Student testing results are published in the paper. It is only fair that private schools that use public money should also take these tests and have the results published for the taxpayers to read.

If taxpayers are funding schools, then they should see the results of their spending.

Milwaukee citizen

Now it's your turn. Consider the information about Milwaukee public schools in this chapter as you write your own letter to the editor. These questions will help you think through the issues.

1. Do you think public funds generated through taxation should be given to private schools for tuition for students who choose to leave public schools?

2. Does taking public money obligate private schools in any way?
3. Should private schools have to prove that voucher students are achieving? If so, how?
4. Do voucher plans violate the separation of church and state? If so, how do you justify giving public money to private schools that are affiliated with a religion? If not, explain why not.
5. If private schools were to be required to give the same standardized tests given by public schools, would publishing the scores be reasonable? If so, why? If not, why not?
6. If you were a teacher or administrator in a private school, how would you feel about being required by public officials to do anything?

Your letter to the editor should be in response to the *Milwaukee Journal Sentinel* letter—supporting it, adding information, or refuting it. Write your letter in understandable terminology, remembering that readers of newspaper letters to the editor are citizens who may have limited knowledge of school practices and policies. Your letter may be written in your course notebook and shared with classmates as directed by your instructor. Remember to refer to the letter assessment rubric in Figure 1.10, page 20.

Table 2.3   Advocates' and critics' views of school choice

Advocates	Critics
Competition raises the standards, and consequently the performance, of all schools.	Competition destroys cooperation among teachers, schools, communities.
Competition gives parents decision-making power to choose for their children.	Only parents who are vocal advocates for their children will take advantage of options.
Competition forces low-performing schools to go out of business.	Students remaining in low-performing schools suffer.
Choice better accommodates diversity.	Choice leads to the possibility of further segregation.
Choice provides equal opportunities.	Choice exacerbates inequities.

understand its nuances. One thing's for sure. The variety of school settings for career teachers has expanded. It is important to know what choices are available.

As you consider your teaching identity, keep the options in mind, visit various school venues, and explore where you might best fit. Does a particular venue appeal to you? If so, what elements of the particular type of school make it a possible career choice?

Your Teaching
Fingerprint

What Is School Like at Different Levels?

The discussion of the levels of schooling began in Chapter 1, when you met this text's focus teachers (see pages 23–29). Chapter 3 will explore student development and diversity in the four levels. The variations by level in curriculum, instruction, and assessment will be discussed in Chapters 4 and 5, with similarities and differences in the learning environment of each level discussed in Chapter 7. Because this chapter is about schools, the discussion of levels will focus on organization and structure of the four basic levels of school—early childhood, elementary, middle, and high school.

Structure and Organization of Early Childhood Education

Early childhood education is commonly divided into three basic age spans: preschool, kindergarten, and primary grades. Educators seem to agree that early childhood settings should be characterized by warmth, sensitivity, and nurture. Learning through play, with healthy doses of experimentation and discovery, describes a commonly held and balanced early childhood philosophy. Let's briefly explore some of the structural and organizational components of early childhood educational settings.

Preschool. Three fourths of 3- and 4-year-olds in the United States are in some form of child care for at least a portion of each week. These experiences vary enormously from a place to be, where only physical needs are met, to a more structured environment housed in a school setting, known as a **preschool.** In this setting, often designated as a prekindergarten for 4-year-olds, care is enhanced by exposure to basic educational concepts. Preschool education may follow many different models.

The **Montessori** approach to early childhood education, with mixed-age grouping and self-pacing, is growing in popularity and has the reputation of being high quality when faithfully implemented (Morrison, 2003). Teachers in a Montessori setting are primarily guides, with children acting independently to choose learning activities. The **High/Scope**

Summit Primary School, Summit Station, Ohio

approach, widely used in preschool through early elementary settings, is built on consistency and few transitions during the day as children construct meaning for themselves in problem-solving situations within learning centers. The **Reggio Emilia** approach to early childhood education for ages 3 months to 6 years is based on relationships among children, families, and teachers. Close, long-term relationships are built because the teachers in each classroom stay with the same children for up to 3 years (Kostelnik, Soderman, & Whiren, 2004). **Head Start** is the largest provider of government-funded preschool education, employing one of every five preschool teachers in the United States (Barnett, 2003).

More than 40 states invest in preschool initiatives. Hawaii has a statewide public-private partnership called Good Beginnings Alliance. Every county in South Carolina has a public-private partnership board that assesses local needs and develops strategies to address preschool education through that state's First Steps to School Readiness initiative. To promote private sector involvement in preschool education, Kentucky has a program called the Governor's Early Childhood Initiative. Similar programs are available in other states, although some states have yet to attempt to standardize the availability of preschool opportunities.

As you can see, children enter kindergarten with a variety of experiences. The step from kindergarten to first grade is a giant one, so it is crucial that the term *readiness* has become a major part of the vocabulary of early childhood education.

Kindergarten. Once considered an optional bridge between preschool, or no school at all, and the beginning of formal education in first grade, **kindergarten** (meaning "children's garden") has become part of almost every 5-to-6-year-old child's educational experience, some for half a day and others for the entire day. However, kindergarten is mandatory in only 12 states (Morrison, 2003).

What occurs in both whole-day and half-day kindergarten classrooms across the country varies. In some kindergarten classrooms children are involved in literacy-building activities, while in others there's little evidence of any emphasis on literacy (Pianta & LaParo, 2003). Some kindergartens are housed in K–5 or K–6 elementary schools, while others are in primary school settings that may include prekindergarten or kindergarten through grade 2 or 3. Figure 2.3 displays a possible schedule for half-day kindergarten, with teachers following a similar schedule twice a day.

Primary grades. Teachers in primary classrooms, grades 1 through 3, are faced with the challenge of meeting the needs of children with widely varying levels both of readiness for learning and of acquired knowledge and skills. Imagine a first-grade classroom with 5 children who have received very little home encouragement for learning and did not attend kindergarten, 10 children who attended three different kindergartens that varied widely in their approaches, and 4 students who are reading independently. The challenge is to engage them all in learning based on where they are, with a view of unlimited potential.

Figure 2.4 shows a general schedule for a primary classroom. The next section will discuss overlapping grades between early childhood and elementary school and look more closely at differences in first-, second-, and third-grade classrooms.

You have met Brandi and Renee in Chapter 1, both teachers at Summit Primary, Ohio (see page 23). You learned about the structure and organization of Summit Primary in the opening scenario of this chapter as you watched the school tour and interview with principal Laura Hill in the Choosing Your Teaching Path section of MyEducationLab.

Figure 2.3 Sample half-day kindergarten schedule

9:25–9:40	Arrival, morning exercises
9:40–10:40	Learning centers
10:40–10:50	Cleanup
10:50–11:10	Outdoor or gym play/snack
11:10–11:30	Whole-group instruction
11:30–11:45	Small-group time, cooperative activity
11:45–12:00	Art projects
12:00–12:15	Closing exercises/dismissal
Repeat with another group of children 1:20–4:05	

Figure 2.4 Sample primary grade schedule

8:50–9:10	Arrival, daily business, opening activities
9:10–9:30	Whole-group instruction in literacy
9:30–10:30	Small groups rotate through reading and writing centers
10:30–10:45	Recess
10:45–11:45	Math instruction
11:45–12:15	Lunch
12:15–12:30	Read aloud
12:30–1:15	Science (physical education on Tuesday and Thursday)
1:15–1:30	Silent reading
1:30–2:15	Social studies (art on Monday, music on Wednesday)
2:15–2:45	Center time
2:45–3:10	Whole-group review of day, cleanup, dismissal

Now that you know more about early childhood education, can you envision spending your days with the youngest students in American schools? What aspects appeal to you? What aspects do not appeal to you?

Your Teaching Fingerprint

Let's continue our look at school levels by exploring elementary schools.

Structure and Organization of Elementary Education

In Chapter 1 you learned that elementary classrooms may be self-contained, or teachers may share responsibility for a group of children (see page 25). A sample schedule for a second-grade self-contained classroom is provided in Figure 2.5. A sample schedule for a fourth-grade classroom that utilizes a team of three teachers, each teaching a core subject area, is provided in Figure 2.6.

Another possible elementary school configuration with benefits similar to those of multiage grouping is looping. **Looping** occurs when a teacher stays with a particular group

Rees Elementary School, Spanish Fork, Utah

of students for more than 1 year. Among the many positive reasons to loop are the following (Roberts, Kellough, & Moore, 2006):

- A consistent relationship develops between teacher and students and lasts for 2 or 3 years.
- Student learning styles, strengths, weaknesses, interests, behavior patterns, potential, family circumstances, and the like, are well known to the teacher.
- The last few weeks of the school year are often used more productively, and summer reading and project assignments become more meaningful.

In Chapter 1 you met Chris, Brenda, and Tim, teachers at Rees Elementary School, Utah, where both multiage classrooms and grade-specific, self-contained classrooms flourish (see page 24). To learn more about the structure and organization of Rees Elementary, take a school tour and watch an interview with principal Mike Larsen in the Choosing Your Teaching Path section of MyEducationLab. Go to Rees, and then on Mike.

Does staying with the same group of children for more than a year appeal to you? Does teaching all subjects to the same group of children sound like something you would enjoy? Or would you prefer to have an elementary homeroom class to whom you teach one or more subjects with other teachers teaching the remaining areas?

Your Teaching Fingerprint

Now that we have looked at the structure and organization of schools for children, let's examine more closely schools for young adolescents.

Figure 2.5   Sample second-grade schedule (self-contained)

8:50–9:15	Whole-class morning meeting
9:15–9:35	Small-group reading
9:35–9:55	Whole-class instruction in writing/spelling
9:55–10:20	Reading and writing activities
10:20–10:40	Recess and snack
10:40–11:15	Whole-group math instruction/activities
11:15–12:00	Alternating PE (M), art (T), PE (W), music (Th), PE (F)
12:00–12:35	Lunch, recess
12:35–1:15	Alternating social studies and science
1:15–1:45	Alternating computer and library time
1:45–2:00	Read aloud
2:00–2:30	Free-choice centers
2:30–2:50	Reading and writing activities
2:50–3:10	Whole-group class meeting
3:15	Dismissal

Figure 2.6   Sample fourth-grade schedule (three-teacher team)

8:50–9:05	Whole-class meetings in homerooms
9:05–10:10	Block time: Group 1—math Group 2—English language arts Group 3—science/social studies
10:10–10:30	DEAR (Drop Everything And Read) in homeroom
10:30–10:50	Journal writing in homerooms
10:50–11:10	Recess and snack
11:10–12:15	Block time: Group 1—English language arts Group 2—science/social studies Group 3—math
12:15–12:35	Lunch
12:35–1:00	Computer or library time
1:00–2:05	Block time: Group 1—science/social studies Group 2—math Group 3—English language arts
2:05–2:40	PE
2:40–3:00	Alternating art and music
3:00–3:10	Whole-class meetings in homerooms
3:15	Dismissal

Structure and Organization of Middle School Education

Some middle schools are **departmentalized,** with teachers teaching their own subjects and meeting occasionally with other teachers who teach the same subject. With departmentalization, a teacher who, for instance, has Jamal in math does not collaborate with Jamal's social studies or science teacher. The math teacher may not even know who Jamal has for social studies or science.

The preferred organizational structure for middle level education is the student-teacher team, known as an **interdisciplinary team.** A team generally comprises four core subject area teachers and the 80 to 100 or so students they share. If Jamal is on a team, all his teachers know exactly who teaches him each core subject. The team of teachers meets at least three times a week to plan together and discuss student progress and concerns. This kind of teaming is developmentally appropriate for young adolescents.

In some middle schools, students attend six or seven classes a day, each 50–60 minutes long. These classes include the core subjects (English language arts, math, science, social studies) and other subjects that are considered **exploratory** or **related arts.** These may include art, music, physical education, industrial arts, languages, drama, and computer education, among others. Figure 2.7 shows both a traditional, six-period student schedule and a schedule allowing for longer class periods, commonly called a **block schedule.**

Cario Middle School, Mt. Pleasant, South Carolina

Figure 2.7   Sample middle school student schedules

<u>Traditional schedule</u> (5 minutes to change classes)

8:00–8:15	Homeroom
8:15–9:10	Math
9:15–10:10	English language arts
10:15–11:10	Band/art/foreign language/drama (9 weeks each)
11:15–11:45	Lunch
11:50–12:45	Science
12:50–1:45	Computer education/physical education (1 semester each)
1:50–2:45	Social studies
2:50–3:00	Homeroom
3:00	Dismissal

<u>Block schedule</u>

8:00–8:15	Homework
8:20–10:00	English language arts block
10:05–10:55	Related arts rotation
11:00–11:30	Lunch
11:35–1:15	Math block
1:20–2:10	Science and social studies (rotating days)
2:15–3:05	Related arts rotation
3:05	Dismissal

Teaming is successfully implemented at Cario Middle School, where Traci and Deirdre, our two middle school focus teachers, teach. At Cario, each core class is taught for 70 minutes. The students also have one class period for a variety of special classes that are rotated every 9 weeks. They have a 30-minute lunch period and 5 minutes to go from class to class. Cario teachers provide a rich array of clubs and after-school activities from which students may choose.

To learn more about the structure and organization of Cario Middle School, take a school tour and watch an interview with principal Carol Bartlett in the Choosing Your Teaching Path section of MyEducationLab. Go to Cario, and then on Carol.

 Does teaching on an interdisciplinary team appeal to you? Would you enjoy working closely with other teachers to plan for the education of a specific group of young adolescents?

Your Teaching Fingerprint

Structure and Organization of High School Education

High school may be a very recent experience for you, or it may have occurred decades ago. Regardless of the time interval, virtually everyone agrees that high school represents a unique time of life. The 4 years of ninth, tenth, eleventh, and twelfth grade provide vivid memories that many of us choose to relive every 10 years or so as we make our way back to reunions to reminisce, to see what and how our classmates are doing, or perhaps to show off or embellish our own accomplishments. Then there are those of us who would rather forget that time of our lives. Regardless of our feelings or memories from both an academic and a social perspective, high school experiences have a significant and long-lasting impact on our lives.

Some U.S. high schools flourish, with the majority of students learning and thriving, whereas others are considered "broken" according to wide-scale fact-finding reports (Perkins-Gough, 2005). Think about whether high school is the place for you as a teacher as you study Table 2.4, which is an overview of some of the basic types of high schools, the students they serve, and the courses they may offer.

High school teachers typically specialize in one major subject and teach different areas or levels of that subject. All teachers of a subject form a department and meet periodically

Table 2.4 Types of public high schools

Type of High School	Who Attends	Courses Offered
Magnet	Students who are interested in specific subjects or areas of study (sciences, arts, government, etc.)	• for graduation credit • specialized, specific areas of study • college prep and advanced placement
Academic Magnet	Students who qualify through placement tests, past achievement, or teacher recommendation	• for graduation credit • college prep and advanced placement • collegelike courses that require deeper prior knowledge and intellectual ability
Vocational	Students who are interested in trade arts, such as mechanics and cosmetology; students who are not necessarily interested in attending a 4-year college	• for graduation credit • trade-specific • college prep and less academically challenging
Alternative	Students who have not been successful in other types of school settings for behavioral or academic reasons	• for graduation credit • college prep and less academically challenging
Comprehensive	All students except those excluded for reasons stated for alternative schools	• possibly all from above categories

to discuss issues such as course materials, innovations and dilemmas in the subject field, and professional development opportunities. Departmentalization is the primary organizational structure of high schools.

Some high schools adhere to a traditional schedule of six or seven classes a day, each about an hour long. Students attend these classes for two semesters to earn a credit in each. However, alternative schedules are gaining popularity. Blocks of 90–100 minutes allow for more complete cycles of learning, such as completion of labs, reading and reflecting on literature, and proving as well as applying math theories.

Block schedules take one of two forms. Each has benefits. One form is composed of four classes per day, every day, thus allowing four courses to be completed in a semester. One of the major benefits of this type of schedule is that students have only four subjects to study at a time, rather than six or seven. With four courses per semester, students have the opportunity to earn 32 credits in 4 years of high school. The other basic form of block scheduling is the alternating day model. With this schedule, students also receive credit for eight courses a year, but each course meets for 90–100 minutes every other day for two semesters.

Many high school students flourish when attending classes configured using alternative scheduling models.

To learn more about the structure and organization of Roosevelt High School, where Craig, Derek, and Angelica teach, take a school tour and watch an interview with principal Maria Romero in the Choosing Your Teaching Path section of MyEducationLab. Go to Roosevelt, and then on Maria.

Does teaching in a high school appeal to you? If so, what about the structure of a high school makes you want to be part of it? Are your own high school memories fresh enough for you to believe you can be more effective than your teachers were? Is there a teacher who had a profound influence on the direction of your life that you would want to use as a model for your own teaching?

Your Teaching Fingerprint

We will return to discussions of school levels as we address various aspects of the teaching profession. Each time the information will build on previous topics so you will

Roosevelt High School, Fresno, California

have a view of the big picture of what teaching is like in each level. Regardless of the level you decide to teach, your school will be in one of three settings.

What Are the Three Principal Settings of Public Schools?

When it comes to schooling, geography has a major impact. Sometimes a mile or two is significant with regard to educational experiences. The commonly accepted categories of rural, suburban, and urban schools that exist in all 50 states probably conjure up images in your mind, generalized impressions of what each embodies. This section will attempt to refine those images.

Using U.S. Census Bureau guidelines, let's define **rural** as an area with fewer than 2,500 people and a minimum of retail stores and services. Let's define **suburban** as neighborhoods and small-to-medium-size towns that may be located on the fringe of cities or distinct from them. For **urban,** think of cities with large downtowns and dense populations. Now, when you read about the schools typically found in rural, suburban, and urban areas, your mental picture of what the words mean will come into focus.

An in-focus view will reveal some generalities about the context of schooling in each area. The day-to-day realities of children both in and out of school within these three areas may be vastly different in terms of home, family socioeconomic circumstances, and school settings. Many of these differences are economic and reflect the expectations held by parents, community, and educators of what children can do and be. Most teachers can do little to alter the financial realities faced by schools and schoolchildren. However, what teachers can alter are the ways they view students and their potential. It's a matter of values—both teachers' and students'.

As this section explores rural, suburban, and urban schooling, become keenly aware of how things are and what your role might be as an agent of change where inequities exist. Before continuing, think about your own experiences. Did you live in a rural area, a suburb, or an urban setting? If you had the opportunity to live in more than one setting, what do you recall about the differences?

Your Teaching Fingerprint

Rural Schools

About one third of schools across the United States are in rural communities (Carter, 2003). In Montana, over 70% of the state's schools are rural. Twenty percent of Alaska's schools employ three or fewer teachers each (Carter, 2003).

Most rural schools are smaller than urban and suburban schools. However, some draw students from an area that may encompass hundreds of square miles. A single primary school, intermediate school, middle school, and high school, each with more than 800 students, may serve such a large geographic area.

Dennis Griner, a high school teacher in rural Washington, tells us about his experiences in Teachers' Days, Delights, and Dilemmas. If you have never lived in a rural area, you may find his account of life in a small community interesting.

Geographic isolation often means that students may not be frequently exposed to opportunities and experiences found in more populated areas, such as museums and performing arts. Even basic services that people in suburban and urban areas take for granted, such as hospitals and large libraries, may not be readily available.

A high school of 100 to 200 students that is over an hour away from a medium-size town may have difficulty offering ample opportunities for what's commonly viewed as a

Teachers' Days, Delights, and Dilemmas

Dennis Griner
2004 Washington
State Teacher
of the Year

The next time you hear the words "rural education" imagine a place where the school is the heart and soul of community life. Think about a town where the citizens make tremendous sacrifices to provide quality education for the children. On any winter Saturday night, you will find the majority of the townspeople in the high school gym supporting "their" students. After 33 years of teaching in this environment, I can only sing praises of the positive impact this closeness has on young people. The student body and faculty function as extended family. Teachers providing support and encouragement to their students are just as much a part of the experience in a rural school as are the three R's. Students and their families are neighbors and family friends. A walk to the post office could spontaneously become a parent conference on the sidewalk or a discussion with a concerned community member about an issue facing the school. Regardless of the setting (it could just as easily be the grocery store, a school function, or my own backyard) I am still "the teacher." Teachers serve as role models for every young person in town.

As a result of the relationships developed in this environment, teachers can make an even greater difference in the lives of their students. Teachers in rural schools know their students' parents, grandparents, aunts, and uncles, and watch their students mature from pre-schoolers to high school graduates. Attending major events in their students' lives such as weddings, funerals, and celebrations is all a part of rural education.

Rural schools do have challenges as well. Geographic isolation, dropping student enrollment, inequity in funding, and lack of access to technology are but a few. Benefits, however, far outweigh the disadvantages. I can see no higher calling or greater reward for teachers than to invest their careers and their lives in rural education.

well-rounded education. Think about it. In order to offer adequate coursework, a high school must employ certified subject-area teachers. Supporting an algebra II class of 6 costs just about as much as supporting a class of 28. Regardless of class size, the course requires a teacher and a classroom. Small high schools face similar constraints in offering extracurricular opportunities. It may be difficult to offer French club, and debate team, and football and basketball teams, and orchestra, and so on.

Hiring and retaining qualified teachers in small or large rural schools is a significant problem, even though the schools may be community-oriented centers in safe, scenic places. When you graduate with teacher certification, would you consider moving to an isolated rural area where you may be needed, but where there are no shopping malls, no theaters, and few, if any, single people under age 50? The benefits of having ready access to recreation and natural beauty may outweigh any perceived drawbacks. Does this lifestyle appeal to you? If so, why?

Your Teaching Fingerprint

Suburban schools. Suburban schools most often serve students who live in single-family homes with grassy yards in areas dotted with shopping centers, churches, and recreational facilities. Apartment complexes and townhouses are scattered among the well-lit paved streets. Every few miles or so, there's a school.

Many people who live in the suburbs are likely to be somewhere in the middle-class to affluent socioeconomic spectrum. Their communities are basically safe places with adequate public services that provide a minimally comfortable lifestyle. The schools, even in tight state budget situations, generally continue to operate at acceptable levels with tolerable class sizes, textbooks for each child in most subjects, and satisfactory building maintenance. Within suburban schools students generally experience organization and order, extracurricular opportunities, and some degree of community participation and approval.

These factors don't necessarily mean that students are learning at optimal levels, but there are few signs that things are not as they should be.

Many families choose to live in the suburbs and in small-to-medium towns primarily because of what the schools offer their children. Real estate agents have long known that the public school options for specific residential areas have much to do with property appeal. Families desire stability and a satisfactory free education. They buy homes in locations that will fulfill these desires. Do they get what they pay for? Most would probably say yes.

Did you grow up in a suburban area? Do you enjoy the conveniences these areas generally afford? Is this type of location where you want to spend your teaching career? If so, why? If not, why not?

Urban Schools

Most urban school settings are in sharp contrast to those of suburban schools. The facilities tend to be older, part of the fabric of downtowns that may or may not continue to be vibrant community areas. While architecturally appealing, the older buildings are generally more expensive and difficult to maintain and may be in a state of disrepair more often than suburban school buildings.

Urban schools are likely to serve many students who live in low-income settings. Approximately 40% of students in urban areas attend schools where the majority of students are living in poverty. Only about 10% of students in suburban areas attend such schools (Urban Schools, 2000). While funding differences certainly exist between some urban and suburban areas, as poignantly related by Jonathan Kozol in *Savage Inequalities* (1991), some urban schools actually receive more funding per student than do suburban schools. One reason for this is that the federal government has programs that provide extra money for schools with student populations living below certain economic levels. Research supports the assertion that students from low-income families may require more resources to perform at the same levels as students from middle-income families (U.S. General Accounting Office, 2002).

Many urban school settings present some unique challenges. The students in urban schools more often have unstable home lives, and they come to school with greater needs than those that can be met by the curriculum alone. Is this the kind of challenge you might want to tackle? Can you see yourself nurturing

Table 2.5   Comparison of schools in rural, suburban, and urban settings

Setting	Definition of Setting	Percentage of All Public Schools	Advantages	Challenges
Rural	Fewer than 2500 people	31%	Smaller schools; community ownership	Inadequate tax base for funding; difficulty hiring qualified teachers; geographic isolation
Suburban	Neighborhoods and small-medium towns located on the fringes of large cities	44%	Families with higher socioeconomic status; relative ease of hiring qualified teachers	Satisfying various factions in the community; making continuous improvements
Urban	Cities that have large downtowns and a dense population	25%	Possibility of making large gains in student learning	Low socioeconomic status of many families; problems associated with low expectations; low levels of parental/family education

Source: Common Core of Data Surveys, National Elementary and Secondary School Enrollment Model, National Council of Education Statistics, 2003.

A few miles can make a significant difference in the school experiences of students. At Wells High School in San Francisco, students look out the window to see Alamo Hill and the city skyline. Just 30 miles north of the city, students look out the window of Bolinas-Stinson Elementary at sea lions in Bolinas Lagoon.

and guiding students who may depend on you for encouragement to see beyond their current circumstances?

Table 2.5 illustrates some of the general distinctions among rural, suburban, and urban schools. Keep in mind that there are exceptions in every setting and that schools in every setting can make effective teaching and learning connections.

■ What Is an Effective School?

Effective schools meet the learning needs of the students who attend them. How can we recognize one when we see it? What are the characteristics of an effective school? This is exactly where to begin—describing elements of a school that make it effective. As with describing characteristics of effective teachers in Chapter 1 (see pages 17–21), this is also where the discussion gets bogged down—in listing characteristics and trying to find ways to measure whether they exist, and, if they do, to what extent. Theorists and practitioners have attempted to measure schools' effectiveness for decades, and the efforts are not likely to end. Grappling with what elements characterize effective schools keeps the conversation alive. The minute we say, "Okay. This is it. If a school does this list of things in these ways, it is effective," we will box in our thinking and become stagnant. Even so, lists of characteristics lead us to examine school effectiveness and discover weak areas that, if strengthened, increase a school's effectiveness. While they may vary in many ways, we need a picture of what effective schools may look like and what students and teachers do in them.

Characteristics of Effective Schools

Let's look at the recent history of national efforts to make schools more effective. We'll start with the Equal Educational Opportunity Survey in 1966, commonly referred to as the **Coleman Report.** This report concluded that family and community factors, such as poverty and parental levels of education, prevented some children from learning; that no matter what schools did, some children would not be successful in school. Appalled by this assertion, many in the education community adopted the mantra, "All children can learn." President Lyndon B. Johnson responded in the late 1960s with landmark legislation, the **Elementary and Secondary Education Act,** which, among other things, provided extra funding for schools with high numbers of children from low-income homes, called **Title I funding.** In the 1970s President Gerald Ford expanded equal educational opportunity by signing **Public Law 94-142,** making special education services a right, not a privilege. Educators, with governmental assistance, continued to prove that all children can learn.

In the 1970s the **Effective Schools Movement** developed research based on the belief that all children can learn. The purpose of the movement was to find schools deemed effective for all children and to identify common characteristics among these schools. The basic tenets of these identified schools included

- All children can learn.
- Schools control enough of the variables to make it happen.
- Schools should be accountable for measuring achievement to be certain that all children, regardless of gender, race, ethnicity, or socioeconomic status, are learning.
- All schools should have qualified and capable people to ensure that all children learn.

Effective Schools research, led primarily by Ronald Edmonds and Lawrence Lezotte, concluded that there are seven elements relating to effective schools. These elements, or correlates, listed in Figure 2.8, are all associated with improved student learning. Examining schools in light of these elements reveals areas of needed improvement.

Effective schools may be found in rural, suburban, and urban areas. They may be early childhood, elementary, middle, or high schools. They may serve mostly White, middle-to-upper-class students, or they may serve a predominantly minority population from poor homes. School effectiveness exists where students are learning and experiencing positive personal growth, facilitated by teachers who make a difference.

We Make a Difference

We make a difference when we ask ourselves and one another "And how are the children?" According to Kati Haycock, director of The Education Trust, what schools do makes a huge difference in whether students learn. She asserts that what matters most is good teaching (Haycock, 2003). Quality teachers for every student will enhance a school's effectiveness. The education of quality teachers, the hiring and retention of quality teachers, and the continuing professional growth of quality teachers are key elements of effective schools, where a balance exists between students' academic achievement and personal development.

Figure 2.8 The seven correlates of effective schools

1. Clear and focused mission. The school staff shares a commitment to instructional goals, priorities, and accountability and they accept responsibility for students learning their curricular goals.

2. High expectations for success. The school staff believes, and demonstrates that belief, that all students can master essential content and skills.

3. Instructional leadership. The principal is the instructional leader who persistently communicates the school mission to staff, students, and parents.

4. Frequent monitoring of student progress. Student academic progress is measured frequently in a variety of ways. The results are used to improve instruction and student performance.

5. Opportunity to learn and student time on task. Students are engaged in learning essential content and skills for a significant amount of the school day.

6. Safe and orderly environment. Schools are orderly, purposeful, and free from threat of physical harm. The climate is conducive to learning.

7. Positive home-school relations. Parents understand and support the school's mission and have opportunities to play important roles in helping to achieve the school's mission.

Source: From *Correlates of Effective Schools: The First and Second Generation,* by L. W. Lezotte, 1991, Okemos, MI: Effective Schools Products.

Concluding Thoughts

George Albano, 25-year veteran principal of Lincoln Elementary School in Mount Vernon, New York, can answer "And how are the children? Are they all well?" by stating that 99% of his school's fourth graders made it over the New York state achievement bar in English, math, and science even though 60% are African American or Hispanic and more than 50% are eligible for free or reduced-price lunch. He leads an effective school where the achievement gap is nonexistent, and students are in the care of competent teachers who make them feel valued. Mr. Albano puts it this way, "Success comes down to hard work; great and dedicated teachers; an integrated curriculum; lots of art, music, and physical education; the willingness to bend and break rules occasionally; and the complete refusal to let any child fail to learn" (Merrow, 2004, p. 456).

What Role Will Diversity Play in My Teaching Identity

Schools in the United States are becoming more diverse each year. In Chapter 3 we will explore the many ways in which students exhibit diversity. In this chapter we have read that magnet schools, charter schools, and a variety of school-choice options exist in part to ensure greater learning opportunities for students, regardless of who they are, their race, or home setting. The No Child Left Behind legislation (NCLB) provides for students to change schools if they attend one that is not measuring up. In Milwaukee options range from open enrollment to vouchers. Programs such as Head Start and First Steps to School Readiness serve students who, for a variety of reasons, may be disadvantaged.

One of the key provisions of NCLB, enacted in 2002, is that by 2014 the achievement gap between African American and White students will be eliminated. Are we doing enough to close this learning gap that exists among students of different races and socioeconomic status? The answer is a resounding no. In 2005 the gap had actually widened since the initial data were collected in 2002 (Tough, 2006). Does this bode well for the elimination of the gap by 2014?

Your challenge is clear. Be the generation of teachers who figures it out—the teachers who will bring us closer and closer to quality, effective education for all students in the United States.

■ Chapter in Review

What is the culture of a school?

- The culture of a school is the context of the learning experiences as well as adult and student behaviors and attitudes.
- School cultures can be positive forces for learning or negative influences that interfere with learning, and all shades in between.
- Teachers have an enormous impact on a school's culture.

How do the venues of schools differ?

- There is a great variety of schools in the United States, from the traditional neighborhood public school to the ultimate private school, the home.
- Traditional public schools have education programs that suit most students.
- Full-service schools attend to the academic, health, and social service needs of students and families, and, in many cases, of the community.
- A magnet school is a public school with a specific theme or focus.
- A charter school is a public school that operates under a contract negotiated between the initiator of the school and an oversight agency to which the school is accountable. Charter schools are free from many of the regulations that apply to other public schools.
- Alternative schools are schools designed to meet the needs of students who are not successful in traditional schools.
- Private schools may or may not be affiliated with a religious organization.
- Single-gender schools, almost all of which are private, are schools for boys only or for girls only.
- Homeschooling is a growing trend in the United States.
- For-profit schools are run by management companies. The concept is controversial when applied to public schools.
- School choice plans provide students and parents with options in both the public and private sectors.

What is school like at different levels?

- Early childhood education spans birth through age 8, or roughly through third grade.
- Elementary education may include a variety of grade levels, with K–5 or 6 as the most common. Early childhood and elementary overlap on the low end, while elementary and middle overlap on the high end.
- Middle school education usually includes grades 6–8.
- High school education includes grades 9–12.

What are the three principal settings of public schools?

- Urban settings are cities with large downtowns and a dense population. Urban schools are likely to have a high percentage of minority students from low-income homes.
- Suburban settings are distinct locations that include neighborhoods and small-to-medium-size towns that have grown up on the fringe of cities. Suburban schools are likely to have a lower percentage of minorities, with most students coming from middle- or upper-income homes.
- Rural settings are areas with population under 2,500 and few retail stores and services. Rural schools may be all White, all minority, or integrated to some extent, depending on the area.

What is an effective school?

- Effective schools are those that meet the learning needs of the students who attend them.
- Effective schools may have a variety of characteristics, with quality teaching as the most important common element.

Professional Practice

■ Licensure Test Prep

Carefully read, and then reread, the following passage from *A Reason to Teach: Creating Classrooms of Dignity and Hope* by James A. Beane (2005, p. 4). Then respond to multiple-choice items 1–3 and constructed-response item 4.

How many teachers have we all met who say that they really love and care about children and whose classrooms are full of engaging and positive activities? Countless. But too many do not seem to understand that if we really care about young people, we need to do more than just brighten their school days. We need to help young people think more deeply about the issues facing the world. We need to help them put their expanding knowledge to work toward making a better world—help them participate as democratic citizens right now, not later on when they are adults. And if we truly care about young people, we also need to work against the injustice and inequities that too often plague their lives and crush their hopes.

1. With which pair of purposes of schooling do you think James Beane's views most closely align?
   a. sustaining for today and learning academics
   b. preparing for tomorrow and transmitting society
   c. preparing for participation in society and serving individual needs
   d. serving collective needs and reconstructing society

2. Which statement about diversity would James Beane likely consider most important for students to understand?
   a. Diversity among students has always existed, just in different forms.
   b. Diversity is sometimes the reason for students being treated differently and presented with varying opportunities.
   c. Diversity can positively add to a classroom's culture.
   d. Diversity can be a source of conflict, and we should all concentrate on what we have in common in order to promote harmony.

3. In which school venue would James Beane probably prefer his ideals be taught?
   a. In a magnet school because it attracts high-achieving students with special talents who are destined to be leaders who will bring about change
   b. In a charter school because the theme of the school can be determined to include the tenets he proposes
   c. In a full-service public school because it is open to all students and has a component of community involvement
   d. In a homeschooling setting because parents have complete control over what is presented and are likely to be more successful instilling particular values

4. What are two ways in which school choice might more broadly promote James Beane's view of what is important for students to understand? Explain.

Standards Speak

In this chapter we have examined American schools—public, private, rural, suburban, urban. While all the standards related to teaching and learning ultimately affect what happens in schools, read the two that follow and think of how they might apply to you as a new teacher.

NBPTS Middle Childhood/Generalist XI

Accomplished teachers work with colleagues to improve schools and to advance knowledge and practice in their field.

NMSA Standard 2 Middle Level Philosophy and School Organization

Middle level teacher candidates understand the major concepts, principles, theories, and research underlying the philosophical foundations of developmentally responsive middle level programs and schools, and they work successfully within these organizational components.

1. In order to work toward improving schools, it is important to understand what school effectiveness looks like. Choose one of the seven correlates of effective schools listed in Figure 2.8 and explain how you, as a teacher, could promote improvement of this element at a particular level of school.

2. As we have seen in this chapter, each level of school has distinct organizational components. Briefly explain three characteristics that would enable a teacher to work successfully within the middle school organizational component of teaming?

MyEducationLab

The following interactive features may be found in Chapter 2 of MyEducationLab.

Homework and Exercises

Writing My Own Story

To write your own story by responding to some of the questions in the text accompanied by fingerprint icons, plus others, go to the "Writing My Own Story" section of the Homework and Exercises for Chapter 2 of MyEducationLab.

What's My Disposition?

To reflect on your beliefs and attitudes concerning the teaching profession, go to Chapter 2's "What's My Disposition?" feature of the Homework and Exercises section of MyEducationLab.

Exploring Schools and Classrooms

If your course involves experiences in schools, the questions and prompts in the "Exploring Schools and Classrooms" feature of Chapter 2's Homework and Exercises section of MyEducationLab will guide you as you explore local schools and classrooms.

Virtual Field Experience

To respond to questions and prompts regarding the Choosing Your Teaching Path videos that connect to specific chapter content, go to Chapter 2's Virtual Field Experience section of MyEducationLab. The questions will help you make sense of what you have read in the chapter.

Chapter 3

Students

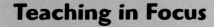

Teaching in Focus

As Craig Cleveland looks around his classroom at Roosevelt High School (RHS) in Fresno, California, while his second-period U.S. History students are making their way to their seats, he sees 32 adolescents—7 sophomores, 21 juniors, and 4 seniors. They are chatting as they make themselves comfortable in the crowded second-floor room. Their primary languages tell much of their ethnic stories—15 speak Spanish, 10 Hmong, 6 English, and 1 Laotian. Thirteen of the 32 speak very little English and write even less.

All 32 students qualify for free or reduced-price meals. Craig knows that students from low-income families struggle more to achieve academically. When measured by standardized tests, over half are considered below basic, or far below basic, in both English language arts and math. In addition, 19 of the 32 have impairments of some kind that are recognized by the school and require special accommodations by teachers.

Craig's challenge today is to pique every student's interest in the question, "Is separate ever really equal?" Watch a segment of Craig's lesson, as well as an interview and room tour in the Choosing Your Teaching Path section of MyEducationLab at www.myeducationlab.com. Go to Roosevelt, and click on Craig.

The students in Craig's class are alike in many ways: they are all adolescents; most are from low-income homes in the same geographic area; and they have all gone through similar developmental stages to become 15-, 16-, 17-, and 18-year-olds. They also have many differences: some are male, and some are female; some were born in the United States, whereas others are recent immigrants; some are Catholic, some Protestant, some Buddhist. When viewed as a group, Craig's students are a wonderful but challenging example of diversity in the American classroom.

In this chapter we will explore the student population in the United States by looking at aspects of similarity as well as aspects of diversity. Here are some questions we'll focus on in Chapter 3:

- How are we similar?
- How are gender differences manifested?
- How does cultural diversity impact us?
- How is language diversity manifested in U.S. schools?
- What impact does diversity in family structure have on students?
- Does diversity of religion influence U.S. schools?
- How does diversity of socioeconomic status affect students?
- How are differences in intellectual ability manifested in schools?
- Who are students with exceptionalities, and how do we serve them?

At the end of this chapter you'll meet 12 students who will be featured throughout this text in pictures, in scenarios, and in the Choosing Your Teaching Path section of MyEducationLab.

Introduction

In the time it takes you to read from the first page of this chapter through page 69, a whole classroom of students will be born. That's right—statistically, every 8 minutes 30 babies are born in the United States. Your entire future kindergarten class, third grade class, middle school social studies class, or high school algebra class may be coming into the world right now.

Statistically, we can predict that of these 30 future American students, 14 will be considered a racial minority, 8 will be born into poverty, and 9 will be born out of wedlock. Of these 30 children, 17 will have parents who divorce before the students graduate from high school, 5 will serve jail sentences, 5 will be victims of violence, 4 will commit a violent crime before the age of 16, and almost half will drop out before finishing high school (National Center for Education Statistics [NCES], 2004; U.S. Census Bureau, 2002). "And how are the children? Are they all well?"

Chances are your classroom won't mirror the statistics you just read. Classrooms vary from little cultural or socioeconomic diversity to a challenging mix of cultural and socioeconomic backgrounds. You may teach in a school with students whose families are financially well off or one with families that move when the rent comes due. You may teach in a stable rural community with conservative values and lifestyles, or you may teach in a transient suburban area that affords a great variety of opportunities and educational options. Mark Twain said that every day children are born who could change the world. We just don't know who they are yet.

The 30 new lives that have begun in this 8-minute time frame may appear to be diverse, but are actually more similar than they are dissimilar. They are individual beings with unique attributes and a variety of needs. But most of all, they are human beings.

How Are We Similar?

We are more alike than we are different, regardless of the degree of influence that genetics and the environment have on us. We all have similar needs, and we also all share developmental stages as we progress from infancy into adulthood. Let's explore these areas of similarity.

Nature and Nurture

There has been much debate on the question of what has the greater influence in determining who we are—nature or nurture. These two concepts are generally presented as oppositional: nature *versus* nurture. Because they both figure prominently into who we are, let's consider them as related, rather than in opposition. **Nature** refers to genetically inherited influences. Not only are certain physical characteristics, such as eye color, skin tone, and adult height, determined by nature, but aspects of our intelligence are established genetically as well. **Nurture** refers to the influences of our environment, which encompasses everything that cannot be accounted for genetically. For instance, the people we meet, the schools we attend, and our economic status are all part of nurture.

Think of the relationship between nature and nurture as one of balance, with the influences of nature on one side and the influences of nurture on the other.

Each child arrives in the world with predispositions, or tendencies, accounted for by nature and over which we have no influence. Teachers do have some control, however, over nurture. That's why we create classroom environments that stimulate growth—physical, intellectual, emotional, social, and moral. This text is designed to help you begin to discover how to do just that. To more fully realize why we need to create this environment, let's examine the importance and relative priority of human needs that we all share.

Figure 3.1   Maslow's hierarchy of needs

As these higher-order needs are met, our motivation to have more increases.

As these more basic needs are met, our motivation to satisfy them decreases.

Source: From *Toward a Psychology of Being,* 3rd ed., by A. H. Maslow, 1999, New York: John Wiley & Sons. Adapted by permission.

Maslow's Hierarchy of Needs

Psychologist Abraham Maslow (1908–1970) developed a theory that links us all together by proposing that human beings experience the same needs. Figure 3.1 shows his classic **hierarchy of needs,** which is widely accepted as an accurate depiction of the order, from bottom to top, in which needs have to be met for healthy and full human development.

Maslow proposed that basic needs for survival and safety must be met first. Once these needs are satisfied, humans are motivated to move up the pyramid toward higher-order needs. Makes sense, doesn't it? If students don't have food and shelter, or if they feel physically threatened, it's unlikely they will be concerned about understanding the Pythagorean theorem. Some circumstances are out of our hands, or perhaps only in our hands for 7 hours a day, 5 days a week, 180 days a year. Providing opportunities and support for needs fulfillment and promoting positive student development during the precious time we have with students will help them ascend Maslow's pyramid and develop in positive ways.

Student Development

Most children progress through predictable, age-related stages of development. The more we know about these developmental stages, the more empathy and support we can offer. We will briefly consider five developmental areas, with accompanying charts to give you an idea of the general chronological progression of development in each area. Keep in mind that our students are individuals who may not experience every characteristic at every level.

Physical development. Patterns of physical development are perhaps the most predictable. Because physical development is easy to measure, we can establish averages from large samples of children and adolescents. Averages are important because they allow us to compare individuals with the norm.

Many older students agree that what they learned during the rapid brain growth period before first grade continues to influence them.

Physical development involves how our bodies appear and how they function. The generalizations found in Table 3.1 are organized according to school levels to help you visualize classrooms and students in early childhood, elementary, middle, and high school settings. Which intrigues you most? Remember that when you see a fingerprint in the margin it means that you will be asked to respond to questions based on your experiences and opinions. These questions are included in "Writing My Own Story" in Chapter 3 of the Homework and Exercises section of MyEducationLab.

Cognitive development. Cognitive (intellectual) development is considered the primary focus of school. Changes in cognition are just as profound, but often much more subtle, than outward physical changes. Yet the brain grows faster than any other part of the body. By age 5, the brain has reached approximately 90% of its full size, while the body is only 30% developed (Feldman, 2006).

Jean Piaget (1896–1980) was one of the most renowned cognitive development theorists. Piaget recognized distinct differences in children's and adolescents' responses to

Table 3.1   Some characteristics of physical development

Early Childhood	• Steady increases in height and weight • Dramatic changes in appearance and abilities • Boundless energy utilizing gross motor skills • Fine motor skills progress, but dexterity is limited • Rapid brain growth • Healthiest time of life
Elementary	• Coordination increases • Use of physical skills becomes controlled • Dexterity improves • Steady growth in height and weight • Significant differences in size among children • Most illnesses are short-term
Middle School	• Onset of puberty leading to reproductive maturity • Sudden growth spurts may change appearance • Specialized gross and fine motor skills develop • Some risk-taking behaviors exhibited
High School	• Sexual/reproductive maturity is reached • Girls complete growth spurt; boys continue to grow • Large appetite accompanies rapid metabolic rate • High level of physical risk-taking activities exhibited

Sources: Bredekamp & Copple, 1997; Feldman, 2006; Gallahue & Ozmun, 1998; McDevitt & Ormrod, 2004.

Figure 3.2 Piaget's model of cognitive development

Sensorimotor intelligence (birth to 2 years of age)

Children primarily learn through their senses as their motor capabilities develop. Children in this stage don't actually "think" conceptually.

Preoperational thought (2–7 years old)

Children begin to use symbols and their grasp of concepts develops rapidly. They begin to think about things and people outside their observable environment. Their viewpoint is generally limited as they have little ability to see things from different perspectives.

Concrete operations (7–11 years of age)

Children begin to think logically. They understand the concept of conservation, that quantities don't change because they are moved. Through manipulation of concrete objects they understand concepts such as number, space, and causality. They begin to see things from varied perspectives and draw conclusions.

Formal operations (11 years of age and on)

Adolescents progress from concrete thinking to the capability of thinking abstractly. They are able to make predictions, experience metacognition (thinking about thinking), and appreciate and use the structure and subtleties of language.

Source: From *Child Development* (pp. 144–152), by T. M. McDevitt and J.E. Ormrod, 2004, Upper Saddle River, NJ: Pearson Education, Inc.

questions that directly correlated to their chronological ages. This was the beginning of his research into the four **stages of cognitive development** encapsulated in Figure 3.2.

Although Piaget's work is still held in very high esteem, researchers have concluded that he based much of his theory on children's deficits rather than on their strengths. Children may be more capable at younger ages than Piaget believed. Teachers benefit from knowing about Piaget's stages, but should never use them to limit how and when the intellectual capabilities of students are stretched.

Rather than looking at deficiencies, noted Russian psychologist Lev Vygotsky (1896–1934) advocated determining children's intellectual abilities and then providing opportunities for intellectual growth. He proposed that a child's cognitive development increases through exposure to new information and that learning takes place within the individual's **zone of proximal development**. This zone is the level at which a child can almost, but not completely, grasp a concept or perform a task successfully. As learning takes place, the zone widens. This theory is akin to **scaffolding**, a concept widely accepted within education that takes its name from the construction term for temporary supports placed around a structure to allow work to be completed. Vygotsky viewed learning scaffolding as the support given to children to help them move through progressive levels of learning.

Additionally, Vygotsky believed that children's learning is shaped by the culture and society around them. The more interactions, the greater the learning as children move forward within their ever-expanding zone of proximal development (Feldman, 2006).

Table 3.2 outlines some of the characteristics of cognitive development. At which level, based on these characteristics, would you most want to work with children or adolescents?

High school students' sense of identity develops during adolescence.

Your Teaching Fingerprint

Emotional development. Human experiences are given meaning through emotions. Both our emotions and our responses to them become more complicated with time.

Table 3.2   Some characteristics of cognitive development

Early Childhood 	• Piaget's preoperational stage • Linguistic ability increases rapidly • Progressively link thinking to language • Understanding of organization and patterns begins • Can learn simple strategies that are modeled • Very intense brain activity • Increased understanding of symbolism • Potential vocabulary of 8,000 to 14,000 words by age 6 • Learn prerequisites for reading
Elementary 	• Piaget's concrete operational stage • Capable of active logical thought • Beginning to be reflective about own thinking (metacognition) • Able to apply learning strategies • Able to view situations from multiple perspectives • Short-term memory capacity increases significantly • Understand number conservation • Potential vocabulary of 13,000 to 20,000 words • Learn to phonetically decode; read aloud
Middle School 	• Beginning of Piaget's formal operational stage • Reasoning ability increasingly more abstract • Increased ability to solve complex problems • Increased ability to use varied learning strategies • Use reading as a means of learning • Often in state of self-absorption • Improved capabilities for metacognition
High School	• Capacity for adultlike thought • Reasoning ability matures with capabilities for abstract reasoning • Realism plays a more active role in decision making • Can discern which learning strategies are effective and when

Sources: Bredekamp & Copple, 1997; Feldman, 2006; Gallahue & Ozmun, 1998; McDevitt & Ormrod, 2004.

Children and adolescents experience a wide array of emotions, including happiness, anxiety, anger, fear, sadness, shame, and pride. For young adolescents, all these emotions and more may be experienced in one class period. Teachers need to be able to identity emotions as well as know how and when to respond to them.

In 1995 Daniel Goleman wrote *Emotional Intelligence*, in which he proposed that a person's **emotional intelligence quotient** (EQ) may be the best indicator of future success in life. EQ involves a set of skills that accompany the expression, evaluation, and regulation of emotions. A high-level EQ indicates an ability to understand others' as well as one's own feelings, respond appropriately to them, and, in general, get along.

Characteristics of emotional development are listed in Table 3.3. These characteristics represent only a portion of what may be observed as children grow emotionally. At what level could you be most helpful to students as they develop emotionally?

Social development. Learning to get along with others is a process that begins when young children sit next to each other in **parallel play,** agreeably sharing the same space but not

Table 3.3 Some characteristics of emotional development

Early Childhood	• Self-concept develops and is influenced by family and society • Most have positive, overconfident self-concepts • Self-conscious emotions such as guilt and pride emerge • Wide variety of emotions develop (happiness, sadness, anger, etc.) • Most emotional ties are with family
Elementary	• Begin to view themselves in terms of psychological traits • Self-concept becomes more complex and differentiated • Coping skills develop (emotional regulation) • Emotional ties beyond family develop
Middle School	• Perceive an "imaginary audience" (belief that own behavior is focus of others' attention) • Belief that what happens is unique to them and shared by no one else • Tend to be emotionally volatile • Experience a drop in self-esteem • Strong emotional ties with friends develop • Frequent mood changes • Begin to establish a sense of identity
High School	• Sense of being invulnerable • May be prone to depression due to biological, environmental, or social causes • Seek autonomy (independence and a sense of control) • Sense of identity develops • Self-consciousness of early adolescence decreases

Sources: Bredekamp & Copple, 1997; Feldman, 2006; Gallahue & Ozmun, 1998; Goleman, 1995; McDevitt & Ormrod, 2004.

communicating. When children begin to share toys and verbally communicate, they are engaged in **associative play.** Progressing to **cooperative play,** children actively coordinate ways to keep the interaction going. When you think about it, these stages of socialization describe how we relate to others regardless of our age. Relating to others and thinking about them (and ourselves) is called **social cognition.** Whether we are simply coexisting (parallel play), communicating when necessary (associative play), or actively engaging with others (cooperative play), we are social creatures.

Relationships matter to us; adolescents are, at times, consumed with them. Relationships are part of America's youth culture, much of which revolves around groups that inevitably form as adolescents search for their identities. It's pretty easy to see which youth subcultures appear to fit most easily into the traditional school setting—generally it's the "cool kids," the "jocks," and the "preppies." Other students may exhibit different developmental patterns and be labeled "nerds," "stoners," "eggheads," "loners," "goths." The names may change, but subgroups live on. As teachers our challenge is to understand and connect with all our students and let them know we care about them,

The social cognition of young children develops into capabilities for cooperative play by the time they enter kindergarten.

Many elementary schools emphasize a character trait a month.

regardless of their social affiliations. Helping students develop positive and productive relationships within society is a major aspect of what teachers do.

As you view Table 3.4, think about the level at which you might be most comfortable dealing with students and their relationships.

Character development. A discussion of character, or moral, development can easily become value laden and situational, that is, dependent on particular religious or ethical beliefs. Even so, there are certain character traits considered positive by almost everyone, including honesty, trustworthiness, fairness, caring, and citizenship (Gathercoal & Crowell, 2000).

Noted developmental psychologist Lawrence Kohlberg contends that people pass through the **stages of moral reasoning** as illustrated in Figure 3.3.

Kohlberg's stages are based primarily on observations of males in Western culture and have been criticized for not being more universal or sensitive to gender differences. Psychologist and colleague of Kohlberg, Carol Gilligan (1982), suggests that differences in the way girls and boys are raised (nurture) can lead to differences in how they view moral dilemmas. According to Gilligan, boys tend to view morality in terms of broad principles of justice, while girls view morality in terms of responsibility to individuals. We'll look more closely at gender differences in the next section.

Table 3.5 lists some of the characteristics of character development. Which level of character development most interests you?

Now that we've established some of the ways we are the same, let's think about ways we may be different. Acknowledging our similarities on one side of the balance scale, and using them to accept and temper our differences on the other side, will help bring who we are, and who our students will be, into perspective. It is important to view diversity as beneficial in both our classrooms and in our society. Finding ways to include all students in the teaching and learning process depends largely on the attitudes and approaches we adopt.

■ How Are Gender Differences Manifested?

"It's a boy!" "It's a girl!" These are the exclamations heard in every delivery room in the United States. The anatomical differences between males and females determine sex; **gender** is the sense of being one sex or the other. Boys and girls, men and women—gender differences are undeniable and are as fundamental as life itself. By age 2, children understand that they are either boys or girls and they label others as well (Campbell, Shirley, & Candy, 2004).

It is common in U.S. households for girls to be encouraged to engage in what are considered gender-appropriate activities, such as playing with dolls and cooking on make-believe stoves, while boys are encouraged to play with cars and throw balls. Household chores are often

Table 3.4   Some characteristics of social development

Early Childhood 	• Relationships with adults centered on direction, care, and protection • Relationships with peers centered on play and entertainment • First friendships are developed • Types of play change from individual to cooperative over time • Empathy emerges • Become aware of other people's feelings
Elementary 	• Increasingly concerned with making and keeping friends • Becoming more assertive • Groups are generally same gender • Status hierarchies develop • Capable of empathy toward people they don't know • Awareness of social conventions and rules • Realize that society has certain rules for behavior
Middle School 	• Conflicts with parents and other adults likely • May suffer identity crisis • Peers become more influential than adults • Popularity, or lack of it, becomes very important • Awareness develops of sexuality and gender-related relationships • Aware that people may have multiple or conflicting intentions
High School	• Identity crisis may lead to social dysfunction • Same-gender groups increasingly give way to mixed-gender groups • Search for autonomy leads to readjustment of relationships • Conformity with others decreases; desire for self-reliance • Gain a more sophisticated understanding of others and their motivations • Often overwhelmed with demands of relationships

Sources: Bredekamp & Copple, 1997; Feldman, 2006; Gallahue & Ozmun, 1998; McDevitt & Ormrod, 2004.

Figure 3.3   Kohlberg's stages of moral reasoning

Stage 1: A rule is a rule, and people obey rules to avoid punishment.

Stage 2: Rules are followed or disobeyed based on rewards.

Stage 3: People obey rules because it's what others expect of them.

Stage 4: Society's rules are what's right, and people conform to expectations.

Stage 5: People follow rules out of obligation to what is agreed-upon behavior in their society. Laws and rules can be changed if society sees a compelling need.

Stage 6: People follow rules that agree with universal ethics. If a law doesn't, they feel free to disobey it.

Source: Adapted from *The Psychology of Moral Development: Essays on Moral Development*, by L. Kohlberg, 1984, San Francisco: Harper & Row.

Table 3.5   Some characteristics of character development

Early Childhood	• Demonstrate heteronomous morality (rules are rigid, unchanging) • Begin to understand intentionality (being bad on purpose) • Aggression declines as language develops • Beginning awareness that actions may cause others harm
Elementary	• Demonstrate incipient cooperation (rules come from shared knowledge) • Increased awareness of others' problems, suffering • Growing recognition that one should try to meet other people's needs as well as one's own • Experience guilt and shame over moral wrongdoing and conflict with self-interest
Middle School	• Strong sense of fairness • Desire to help those less fortunate • Experience roller-coaster emotions
High School	• Understand the need for rules to promote society • Increased concern about fulfilling duty to benefit others • Increased concern about abiding by rules

Sources: Bredekamp & Copple, 1997; Feldman, 2006; Gallahue & Ozmun, 1998; McDevitt & Ormrod, 2004; Powell, 2005; Richardson & Norman, 2000.

assigned by gender, with girls asked to wash dishes and boys asked to cut the grass. Boys and girls sense very quickly that there are expectations based on gender. **Gender stereotyping** occurs when perceived gender differences are assumed for all people, as in assuming that the play and chores described are always appropriate for one gender or the other. **Gender bias** is the favoring of one gender over the other in specific circumstances.

The federal government recognized gender bias in schools in 1972 when Congress passed Title IX of the Education Amendments Act, which states, "No person in the United States shall, on the basis of sex, be excluded from participation in, be denied the benefits of, or be subjected to, discrimination under any education program or activity receiving Federal financial assistance." Title IX has helped correct inequitable treatment of males and females in schools, most notably in athletic programs involving teams.

Social Aspects of Gender

During early childhood, children are friends with whoever is convenient, at day care, in preschool, or in the neighborhood. During the elementary school years children begin choosing friends of the same gender who have similar interests. With the advent of puberty, friends of the opposite gender begin to be included, and this trend continues through high school.

Generalizations about gender differences appropriately begin with phrases such as *tend to*. These two words indicate generalizing, as opposed to stereotyping. Boys tend to base their play on activities, whereas girls tend to base their play on talking. In group play, boys tend to play in more adventurous ways, such as acting out battles and physically challenging each other, whereas girls tend to take on roles that are calm, such as playing house or school. Research shows that boys tend to be more aggressive than girls, at least in physical ways. Boys show what researchers call **instrumental aggression,** or aggression based on attempting to meet a specific goal, such as grabbing a particular toy or establishing dominance in an activity. Girls may be as aggressive, but learn to be so in more subtle ways that may be more emotional than physical. This type of aggression is known as **relational aggression** and may include name-calling, gossiping, or saying mean things just to be hurtful (Underwood, 2003).

Achievement and Gender

In general, researchers have found that boys tend to set higher goals than girls (Bandura, Barbaranelli, Caprara, & Pastorelli, 2001) and attribute their achievement to ability. When they fail, they tend to attribute their failure to lack of effort. On the other hand, when girls meet their goals, they tend to attribute their success to effort. When they fail, they attribute their failure to lack of ability (Vermeer, Boekaerts, & Seeger, 2000). This generalization, illustrated in Table 3.6, is significant for teachers to understand. It indicates that one gender may be conditioned to view failure as the result of a lack of effort, which is easily corrected. The other gender sees failure as the result of a lack of ability, which is not easily corrected.

Until recently it was generally held that boys scored higher than girls in almost every area tested. This academic gender gap has been closing in the last two decades. Although girls as a group may lag behind boys in some areas of science and upper-level math, they are outpacing boys in reading and writing, are more likely to be inducted into the National Honor Society, and are more likely to attend college.

In classrooms many teachers call on boys more often than girls, allow boys to call out answers while scolding girls for doing so, give boys more encouragement to attempt difficult tasks, and generally have higher expectations for boys than for girls. This usually subtle discrimination is almost always unintentional, but nevertheless has an effect on classroom participation (Gober & Mewborn, 2001).

This chapter's In the News video segment addresses the perception that boys are in crisis. Some who study gender differences contend that boys have unique and previously unacknowledged problems dealing with school and achievement. To view this video, go to this text's DVD, click on In the News, then on this chapter's video, *Boys in Crisis.*

In the News

Table 3.6   Boys' and girls' rationale for success and failure

Reasons for	Boys	Girls
Success	High Ability	High Effort
Failure	Low Effort	Low Ability

Source: From "Motivational and Gender Differences: Sixth-Grade Students' Mathematical Problem-Solving Behavior," by H. J. Vermeer, M. Boekaert, and G. Seeger, 2000, *Journal of Educational Psychology, 92,* 308–315.

In The News

Boys in Crisis

This *World News Tonight* report raises the question of whether boys are really in crisis. Headlines are presented that seem to tell us that we need to pay particular attention to the plight of boys. A Harvard researcher says there is something inherently "sad" about boys and tells us that boys are much more likely to attempt suicide than girls and are not as enthusiastic about attending college. After examining test data, however, another researcher says that boys are fine. The Harvard researcher says there's more to the "sadness" of boys, elements that don't show up in test scores. In an interview of recent male high school graduates, we hear one young man say that boys simply don't feel as comfortable seeking help with the various stresses they may face.

Watch the video by going to this text's DVD. Click on In the News and then on *Boys in Crisis.* After watching the video, respond to these questions.

1. What do you think the researcher means when he says there is a "sadness" in boys? Do you agree with his characterization? If so, give an example of why. If not, why not?
2. Do you think that boys are less inclined than girls to seek help with an emotional or social problem? On what do you base your opinion?
3. As a teacher, what could you do to help your male students not be "in crisis," as the headlines presented at the beginning of the video seem to indicate they are?

Sexual Orientation

The sex to which a person is romantically or socially attracted determines a person's **sexual orientation.** Estimates of the percentage of Americans who are gay or lesbian (attracted to the same sex) range from 5% to 10%. It is reasonable to assume that these estimates apply to the American student population as well. Although it has achieved a measure of acceptance, homosexuality remains in many instances the basis of discrimination and focus of hateful attitudes and actions. The two places that we like to think of as safe and supportive—home and school—are often the very places where the most hurtful slurs and overt rejection of gay and lesbian students occur.

The first official guidelines from the U.S. Department of Education relating to students who are homosexual were issued in 1997, when the phrase "gay or lesbian students" was added to the prohibitions against sexual harassment, a topic we'll address in Chapter 10.

Your Teaching Fingerprint Have you ever felt discriminated against because of gender? Are you aware of discrimination in a school setting based on sexual orientation?

Gender Diversity: Implications for Teachers

We don't want to deny that girls and boys are different in some ways, whether the differences stem from nature, from nurture, or from the inevitable combination. However, with awareness we can diminish gender-biased behaviors and attitudes in our schools. The most important contribution we can make toward alleviating gender bias in our classrooms is to treat our students as individuals, realizing that each is unique. In modeling this behavior we will help instill it in our students.

Our goal in creating **gender equity,** the fair and balanced treatment of boys and girls, is to provide learning environments where all students are free from limitations that might accompany gender stereotyping of what they can or should accomplish. Addressing the following questions will help foster gender equity in the classroom:

- Do I use examples of males and females in all roles and occupations?
- Do I encourage girls as well as boys to explore science and math?
- Do I encourage boys as well as girls to read for pleasure and to participate in poetry writing and drama?
- Am I careful to include historical contributions of both males and females?
- Do I have a way of assuring that I call on boys and girls in equal numbers during class discussions?

Now we'll move beyond gender to cultural diversity and its impact on both males and females.

How Does Cultural Diversity Impact Us?

A widely accepted definition of **culture** states that it is a "dynamic system of social values, cognitive codes, behavioral standards, world views, and beliefs used to give order and meaning to our own lives as well as the lives of others" (Delgado-Gaitan & Trueba, 1991). Culture, and the complex combination of elements that compose it, should have a prominent place in any discussion of American education. Geneva Gay (2000) tells us that "culture is at the heart of all we do in the name of education" (p. 8).

Recent research suggests that culture affects perceptions of the characteristics of intelligence. In a study entitled "Who Are the Bright Children? The Cultural Context of Being and Acting Intelligent," Sternberg (2007) tells us that "different cultures have different views of intelligence, so which children are considered intelligent may vary from one culture to another" (p. 148). He contends that teachers' acceptance and understanding of the differences can affect how well students learn. Intriguing idea, isn't it?

Gollnick and Chinn (2006) contend that culture has three primary characteristics. First, culture is *learned*. The language, the ways we behave, the social rules, the expectations, the roles—all these aspects of a culture are learned from family and others who influence our daily lives. The second primary characteristic of culture is that it is sustained and strengthened because it is *shared*. To learn how to "be" in a culture requires mentors, those who share the culture and, in doing so, perpetuate the culture. Third, a culture is *adaptive* to its environment. The culture of a large group of people changes, or adapts, over time in response to many variables.

The characteristics that apply to cultures of groups also apply to cultures of individuals. Each of us has a cultural identity.

Cultural Identity

The interactions of many factors, including language, religion, gender, income level, age, values, beliefs, race, and ethnicity, form a person's **cultural identity.** This identity is adapted throughout a person's life in response to his or her experiences.

The words *race, ethnicity,* and *culture* are often used interchangeably, but they do not have the same meaning. As teachers, we need to understand the meanings of the terms in order to better navigate the complexities of our students' lives. While the color of our skin (race) and the country of our origin (ethnicity) may contribute strongly to our cultural identity, neither encompasses the total concept of culture. Let's consider race and ethnicity separately.

Racial Component of Culture

The word **race,** when applied to a group of people, simply categorizes them according to the physical characteristics they have at birth, such as skin color and facial features. Characterization by race is a social, political, economic, and psychological reality (Mukhopadhyay & Henze, 2003). Some researchers say there are actually as few as three races, whereas others claim that there are more than 300 (Gollnick & Chinn, 2006). Not a very precise way to categorize people, is it?

Guillermo, from Mexico, and Khammany, from Laos, are part of the rich fabric of diversity at Roosevelt High School in Fresno, CA.

The federal government uses race to categorize people in the United States. For census taking, five races are designated: White, Hispanic, Black, Asian/Pacific Islander, and American Indian/Eskimo/Aleut. These categories are indistinct, without consideration of family or country of origin. Beginning in 2000, the census form allowed people to check more than one race. Because race is based solely on physical characteristics, what box would a person check whose mother is Chinese and father is Cuban? Half of Asian immigrants' children marry non-Asians, while 35% of Latino immigrants marry members of other races (Diversity Data, 2000). One of America's best known sports figures, Tiger Woods, can actually check four of the five racial boxes as a "Cablinasian," with Caucasian, Black, Indian, and Asian family ties (Hodgkinson, 2001). Tiger is not alone. According to the 2000 census, about 7 million people indicated that they were multiracial. Table 3.7 shows that in U.S. public schools, 41% of students are non-White. They could mark one or more of the four other races. Note the wide range in percentages by state, with Maine at 4% and the District of Columbia at 96%.

Ethnic Component of Culture

We will use the word **ethnicity** to mean simply an individual's country of origin (Gollnick & Chinn, 2006). Even if families are two, three, or more generations removed from their ancestral country they may still strongly identify with both the country and the people who share their ethnicity. The category of ethnicity often reveals much more about our students than race. Knowing that a student is Hispanic (race) doesn't necessarily tell us much, but knowing that the child is of Cuban, Chilean, or Mexican heritage may be much more revealing and much more personalized (Hodgkinson, 2001).

Your Teaching
Fingerprint

What is your race? What is your ethnicity? How would you define your cultural identity?

Cultural Diversity: Implications for Teachers

The response of many U.S. educators to the fast-paced growth of diversity is **multicultural education,** an approach that celebrates diversity and promotes equal educational opportunities. James Banks (2004), an expert in the field, tells us that multicultural education has several goals, including

- the creation of equal opportunities for students of all cultures
- the development of knowledge, attitudes, and skills needed to function successfully in a diverse society
- the promotion of communication and interaction among groups that work for the common good

Unfortunately, many view multicultural education as simply observing February as Black History Month or including a social studies unit on Native Americans. Chances are these lessons have little impact on the day-to-day lives of students. Sonia Nieto (2003), a leading author on the topic, is concerned about the simplistic ways in which multicultural education is taught in schools. She proposes that multicultural education permeate all areas of schooling. Nieto says that if we ask ourselves the following four questions and then spend our careers as educators answering them, facing the answers, and making continual corrections, we will take multicultural education where it needs to go.

- "Who's taking calculus?" (composition of challenging courses)
- "Which classes meet in the basement?" (distribution of the best resources and facilities)
- "Who's teaching the children?" (distribution of the most effective teachers in our profession)
- "How much are the children worth?" (issue of funding—where the money for education goes and why) (pp. 8–10)

Table 3.7 Percentage of non-White (minority) students in public schools by state

State	Total Students	Minority Students	Percentage of Minority Students	State	Total Students	Minority Students	Percentage of Minority Students
Reporting States	48,540,725	19,926,161	41	Tennessee	936,681	269,541	29
District of Columbia	78,057	74,690	96	Rhode Island	159,375	45,475	29
Hawaii	183,609	146,540	80	Washington	1,021,349	291,137	29
New Mexico	323,066	217,243	67	Michigan	1,757,604	478,955	27
California	6,413,862	4,166,409	65	Massachusetts	980,459	249,148	25
Texas	4,331,751	2,653,701	61	Pennsylvania	1,821,146	431,511	24
Mississippi	493,540	260,269	52	Kansas	470,490	109,208	23
Louisiana	727,709	375,099	52	Missouri	905,941	201,670	22
Arizona	1,012,068	514,413	51	Oregon	551,273	126,668	23
Maryland	869,133	430,663	50	Wisconsin	880,031	186,264	21
Florida	2,587,628	1,260,936	49	Ohio	1,845,428	372,406	20
Georgia	1,552,611	729,218	47	Nebraska	285,542	58,499	20
Nevada	385,401	189,721	49	Minnesota	842,854	166,950	20
New York	2,864,775	1,321,845	46	Indiana	1,011,130	186,754	18
South Carolina	699,198	318,812	46	Utah	495,981	81,922	17
Illinois	2,100,961	895,179	43	Idaho	252,120	40,160	16
New Jersey	1,380,753	581,591	42	Montana	148,356	22,062	15
Delaware	117,668	50,252	43	South Dakota	125,537	18,899	15
North Carolina	1,360,209	567,168	42	Wyoming	87,462	12,277	14
Alaska	133,933	55,052	41	Kentucky	663,885	82,314	12
Alabama	731,220	293,015	40	North Dakota	102,233	12,271	12
Virginia	1,192,092	453,961	38	Iowa	481,226	56,885	12
Oklahoma	626,160	241,311	39	West Virginia	281,215	16,563	6
Colorado	757,693	268,351	35	New Hampshire	207,417	11,938	6
Connecticut	577,203	182,036	32	Vermont	99,103	4,090	4
Arkansas	454,523	136,647	30	Maine	202,084	8,472	4

Source: Public Elementary/Secondary School Universe Survey, 2003–04 and State Nonfiscal Survey of Public Elementary/Secondary Education, 2003–2004, U.S. Department of Education, National Center for Education Statistics, Common Core of Data (CCD), 2006.

Culturally responsive teaching is what teachers do to make multicultural education a reality. Here are five additional questions addressing culturally responsive teaching that will also help move the classroom in the right direction.

- Do I know the culture of each of my students beyond their obvious race and ethnicity?
- In what ways might I help my students see their similarities as clearly as their differences?
- How can I help validate the cultures represented in my classroom?
- How can I promote communication among all students?
- How can I assure equal opportunities for learning for all students?

Now we'll explore four more components of culture—language, family structure, religion, and socioeconomic status.

■ How Is Language Diversity Manifested in U.S. Schools?

We have looked at race and ethnicity as major contributors to our cultural identity. These two factors are largely based on nature and can't be changed. Our language, on the other hand, is rooted in nurture and can be changed. **Language** is our primary means of communication, and through it, we transmit knowledge and pass on our culture.

The United States is a nation of immigrants and their offspring, and its schools reflect this fact. In 2003, assistance was provided through our public schools to over 4 million students who needed help learning to speak and write English (NCES, 2005). Let's discuss some basic information concerning language.

Standard English

A composite of the language spoken by educated, middle-class people in the United States is known as **Standard English** (Wolfram, Adger, & Christian, 1999). There are two forms of Standard English—one that's spoken in our everyday lives, and a more formal version that is written and considered grammatically correct.

Dialects

In the United States there are at least 11 regional **dialects**, or deviations from standard language rules used by identifiable groups of people. You may have been the brunt of jokes when you traveled outside your region, or you may have poked fun at someone in your college dorm who spoke with a regional dialect unlike your own. Black English, sometimes referred to as **Ebonics**, is one of the best-known and most controversial dialects in the United States. In most school settings, Black English, along with Hawaiian Pidgin and Appalachian English, is associated with lower levels of both intelligence and social class (Gollnick & Chin, 2006).

English Language Learners

Students with **limited English proficiency (LEP)** may speak and understand some English, but not enough to be successful in classes taught in English without additional assistance. Non-English speakers and students with LEP are referred to as **English language learners (ELLs)**.

Whether in the mall or filling out a job application, the value of fluency in English is obvious to students who are ELL. Immigrant children often believe that continuing to speak their native language will hurt them in school settings where often language is the most obvious characteristic that sets them apart (Miller & Endo, 2004).

Craig Cleveland's class roll in Table 3.8 mirrors the ethnic mix at Roosevelt High, California. To meet this challenge head on, Craig involves all his students by

- giving them as many curricular and instructional choices as possible
- having them talk to each other about class content in their native languages
- using role-playing (read more about role-playing as an instructional strategy in Chapter 4) to reinforce concepts
- reading picture books that make concepts more transparent
- using written materials in students' native languages when available

You don't have to be in an urban area to have students who are ELL in your classroom. One of our focus schools, Summit Primary, Ohio, has gone from a mostly White, all English-speaking school to one with 16 other languages represented (see Figure 3.4).

Table 3.8   Craig Cleveland's 2nd period class roll

Name	Grade	Primary Language
1. Acevez, Miguel*	12	Spanish
2. Avelar, Margarita	11	Spanish
3. Chavez, Jennah	11	English
4. Conriquez-Reyes, Dan	11	Spanish
5. Douangsavanh, Khammany	12	Laotian
6. Esqueda, Meagan	12	English
7. Garcia, Alberto	11	Spanish
8. Garcia, Diana	11	Spanish
9. Garcia, Guadalupe	11	Spanish
10. Hurtado, Cassandra	11	Spanish
11. Lopez, Crystal	12	Spanish
12. Maldonado, Sarah	11	English
13. Martinez, Andrew Jame	11	Spanish
14. Perez, Yvonne	10	Spanish
15. Rodarte, Silvia	10	Spanish
16. Rodriguez, Antonio	11	Spanish
17. Rodriguez, Daniel	12	Spanish
18. Romero, Norma Angelic*	11	Spanish
19. Sanchez, Javier*	11	Spanish
20. Sepulveda, Elizabeth	11	English
21. Toscano, Guillermo	11	English
22. Valles, Leanna Marie	10	English
23. Vang, Doug*	10	Hmong
24. Vang, Ka Yeng*	11	Hmong
25. Vang, Mong Her*	11	Hmong
26. Vang, Pa*	11	Hmong
27. Vang, Sandda*	11	Hmong
28. Vang, Xoua*	11	Hmong
29. Vang, Zoua*	11	Hmong
30. Yang, Don*	11	Hmong
31. Yang, Gloria*	10	Hmong
32. Yang, Tom*	11	Hmong

*Considered limited English proficient (LEP)

Services Addressing ELL

There are two main approaches to delivering ELL services to students, bilingual education and English as a second language (ESL). Both aim to help English language learners function effectively in all-English settings.

Figure 3.4   Native languages at Summit Primary, Ohio

English	Chinese/Cantonese
Somali	Serbo-Croatian
Russian	Spanish
Macedonian	German
French	Croatian
Creole	Korean
Ohomo	Japanese
Bosnian/Albanian	Tagalog/Filipino
Sierre Leone/Creole	

Bilingual education. One of the primary responses of public education to the needs of English language learners is **bilingual education,** the delivery of instruction in two languages. Perhaps the greatest barrier to bilingual education programs is the lack of teachers who speak both English and another language fluently. In addition to speaking two languages fluently, however, teachers in bilingual programs must also be qualified to teach math, science, social studies, reading, writing, and other subjects.

English as a second language. In **English as a second language (ESL)** programs, students receive individualized assistance once or twice a week for about an hour each session. Unlike bilingual education, ESL services are delivered only in English. With ESL, little or no emphasis is placed on preserving native language or culture, and ESL teachers do not need to speak another language. ESL programs are far less expensive than bilingual programs for school districts to implement if they have limited numbers of students to serve.

Your Teaching Fingerprint

Is English your primary language? If not, what is? Has language ever been a barrier to you? Do you know people who are English language learners?

Language Diversity: Implications for Teachers

Language diversity presents a major challenge for education in the United States. Recent sharp increases in the numbers of both legal and illegal immigrants have resulted in increased numbers of English language learners in U.S. schools, impacting both teaching and learning. We need to focus our attention squarely on meeting this challenge.

Here are some questions to keep in mind as you consider teaching in a language-diverse classroom:

- How can I make my classroom an academically, emotionally, and socially safe place for students who are ELL?
- How can I include the cultures of students who are ELL in my classroom?
- What resources will I need to communicate subject-area concepts to all students?
- How will I communicate with families who are ELL?
- What community services might benefit students who are ELL and their families?

The influx of diverse cultures with varied languages can be a source of richness for the United States, rather than a phenomenon that is feared or avoided. As with other issues, striking a balance between preserving native cultures and assimilating students into the mainstream to enable them to function more successfully in U.S. society is a worthy goal.

Now we turn our attention to the families of our students. We will explore how the differing structures of their relationships affect students.

What Impact Does Diversity in Family Structure Have on Students?

The 1970s *Brady Bunch* television sitcom introduced many Americans to the concept of the blended family. Today, blended families come in a variety of configurations. Many students live with people other than their biological parents. With the divorce rate over 50%, single-parent homes have increased more than 300% since 1980 (U.S. Census Bureau, 2002).

The increasing mobility of American families also adds to the instability of students' home lives. Consider, for example, the increasing influx of both documented (legal) and undocumented (illegal) immigrants and the rapidly growing migrant population. These families may move two to four times a year, with children changing schools, enrolling and withdrawing from the same school multiple times, or simply not going to school (NCES, 2004). Not only is all this mobility potentially harmful for students, but it can also wreak havoc on classroom teaching and learning. We'll take a closer look at immigration in Chapter 10.

Family Diversity: Implications for Teachers

Knowing with whom our students live can give teachers insight into behavior and achievement patterns. Ideally, families are our partners in educating children and adolescents. If this is going to be a reality in classrooms, our tactics for gaining and maintaining family support must be sensitive and flexible. Here are some questions to consider for your classroom:

- How can I restructure volunteer opportunities to include evenings and weekends?
- Are options available for child care that might lead to greater parental participation?
- Can the school provide easily accessible transportation to boost family involvement?
- Can I be more inclusive by practicing simple tactics such as addressing correspondence with "Dear family" rather than "Dear parents"?

Chapter 10 will look more closely at societal issues as they relate to families, and Chapter 13 will discuss teachers' responsibilities toward students' families.

An issue closely related to family is religion, since most children through at least early adolescence follow the religious path of their parents. Let's briefly look at religious diversity in U.S. schools.

Does Diversity of Religion Influence U.S. Schools?

Religion and faith have considerable daily influence on many of our lives. Over 230 million people, or about 4 out of 5 of us, affiliate with a religious group. About 96% of Americans who practice a religion align with Christianity. However, religious diversity exists in urban, suburban, and rural areas in every state, and among Americans who align with a religion, about 1.4% align with Judaism, and about 0.5% align with each of Islam, Hinduism, and Buddhism. Freedom to practice a religion or not is central to our common political, social, and cultural heritage.

Private schools are often established to cater to and promote a particular religion. Public schools are open to all and are obligated to serve all. Although separation of church and state is the official stance, religion has considerable influence on what we do in schools. Most of the issues teachers face in terms of religious diversity can be dealt with positively simply through awareness.

Religious Diversity: Implications for Teachers

Our response to religious diversity must be within legal bounds and delivered with sensitivity. Here are some questions classroom teachers should consider concerning religious diversity:

- How do I make sure tolerance is modeled in my classroom?
- How can I guard against being offensive to students of varying faiths?
- How should holidays be observed?
- How can I best respond to the community in which I live and teach?

The last question will be very important to you. While singing "Jesus Loves Me" at nap time in a southern kindergarten might be not only tolerated, but encouraged, singing the same song in a kindergarten in suburban Denver might be seen as offensive and grounds for dismissal.

Your Teaching Fingerprint What do you remember about family support, or lack of it, in your own K–12 experience? How did your religious affiliation and beliefs impact you and your school experiences?

One area of diversity that supersedes differences of gender, culture, language, family, and religion and has widespread influence on student success in school is socioeconomic status (SES). Let's explore this area now.

■ How Does Diversity of Socioeconomic Status Affect Students?

The gap between the haves and the have-nots is wider in the United States than in most other industrialized nations. We might call this a **privilege gap.** Approximately 11% of the U.S. population lives below the poverty line. A family of four—two parents and two children—that earns less than about $20,000 a year is considered to be in poverty. Although most Americans living in poverty are White, the percentage of the White population in poverty is smaller than that of other races. A family can be above the poverty line but still qualify for free or reduced-price meals. Of all the states, New Hampshire, at 15%, has the lowest percentage of students who qualify for free or reduced-price meals, and Kentucky, at 69%, has the highest percentage (U.S. Census Bureau, 2006).

Challenges of Low SES

The federal government acknowledges that there are unique challenges in teaching low-income students. Title I funding, additional money given to public schools when more than 50% of the students qualify for free or reduced-price meals, is the government's attempt to make school experiences equitable. These funds are intended to help educators better meet the needs of low-income students who often are low-achieving students as well.

The following are some generalizations about the performance of students from low-income settings. As you read them, keep in mind that they are not true of all students from low-income settings, and they may not be true of those in your classroom. Generally, students from low-SES settings.

- may enter first grade having been read to about 25 hours, compared to 1,000 hours in middle-class homes (Neumann, 1999)
- may have been exposed to 30 million fewer words by the age of 4 than children from high-SES settings (Neumann, 2003)
- may be disorganized, lose assignments, not do homework, have many excuses (Payne, 2003)
- may perform poorly on class and standardized tests (Payne, 2003)
- may dislike authority, talk back to adults, not monitor their own behavior, not use middle-class courtesies (Payne, 2003)
- may be physically aggressive (Payne, 2003)
- very often attend schools with inadequate facilities and less-effective teachers (Payne, 2003)

How has your own socioeconomic status affected your school experiences? Were you aware of socioeconomic differences among your classmates? Did this affect how you viewed your own circumstances or the circumstances of other students?

Your Teaching Fingerprint

SES Diversity: Implications for Teachers

Ruby Payne (2003), a recognized expert on the effects of poverty on children, tells us that teachers are in a position to support students and families in poverty by attending to their resource needs, which include

- emotional resources—the stamina to withstand difficult and uncomfortable emotional situations
- mental resources—the ability to learn; to read, write, and compute
- spiritual resources—belief that help is available through a higher power that alleviates hopelessness
- physical resources—having a healthy body
- support systems—knowing who to turn to for everyday and future needs and information

Teachers' Days, Delights, and Dilemmas

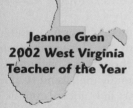

**Jeanne Gren
2002 West Virginia
Teacher of the Year**

When I sat down at my desk, there was a new bouquet of flowers on the corner. Four dandelion stems stood in a little jar of water. No yellow flowers, just one puffy white head of seeds. The other stems were totally barren. Jimmy walked up as soon as I sat down. He was wearing the same torn and dirty t-shirt for the third day in a row. "I just wanted to give you some flowers, Mrs. Gren. These are special for you."

That moment, as much as anything, captures the delights and the dilemmas of teaching children who live in poverty—the hopefulness of a little child wanting to bring flowers to his teacher, tainted by the sad reality of a t-shirt unfit to wear and a few desolate stems. Working in a school with so many students in poverty is more emotional, more devastating, and yet more rewarding, than anything I've ever done. I am, at times, frustrated to tears. Not by the students though. They are mostly bright eyed and eager for every new experience I can offer. I teach in the basement of a 98-year-old building, and, for some of the children in my

class, this is the most beautiful, safest, and cleanest place they have in their lives.

I believe all children can learn. I believe absolutely in maintaining high expectations. But it just takes more time and more effort for some children to get there. Students come to school from the very beginning with incredible differences in experiences, knowledge, and vocabulary. Some of our students come to kindergarten having been read to every night. Their parents talk to them regularly at dinner time. They write notes to their grandparents. These children are already at least 3 or 4 years ahead of their disadvantaged peers, many of whom come from low-income home settings. Some of our students enter kindergarten having never seen a book, never picked up a pencil. They've never eaten dinner without the television blaring. The gap is huge—before we even get started.

I am frustrated beyond measure by the lack of acknowledgment and understanding from some in the public, the media, and policy makers concerning the differences among our children in terms of school readiness and economic background. Difficult conditions, lack of resources, and inconsistent support create almost intolerable working conditions leading to high teacher turnover and many inexperienced teachers where our most expert and highly effective ones should be. Given the startling differences in students' lives, we need to reconsider the push for high-stakes testing with severe consequences that may actually be the greatest threat to leaving our nation's children behind.

I don't want to be in any other school, with any other group of children. They need me—and I want all the dandelion stems Jimmy can gather.

Table 3.9   Facts about Fresno Unified School District and Roosevelt High School, California

	Fresno Unified School District	Roosevelt High School
Enrollment	79,646	2,764
% minority	84	94
% English learners	28	35
% free or reduced meals	82	72

Source: California Department of Education, 2006.

- relationships/role models—having people around who demonstrate appropriate relationships and successful living
- knowledge of hidden rules—knowing how to get along in a particular group (pp. 17–18).

Look for opportunities to observe the privilege gap as you work toward your teaching certification. In this chapter's Teachers' Days, Delights, and Dilemmas we read about a teacher's affection for, and reactions to, a student who lives in poverty.

This chapter's Letter to the Editor is from a California teacher who wants greater acknowledgment of the roadblocks students encounter as a result of low socioeconomic status. To provide context for the letter, here are some facts about education in California.

California K–12 enrollment is over 6 million, roughly the same number of people who live in the entire state of Indiana. This number is predicted to remain around the 6 million mark through 2010, even though the birthrate is decreasing. Why? In simple terms, the number of immigrants is rapidly increasing (California Department of Education, 2006).

The majority of students in California public schools belong to a racial minority. The state's Hispanic school population alone is now larger than its White population. Of California's K–12 students,

- about 25% are English language learners
- more than 20% live in poverty, second only to Texas
- about 3 million, or close to 50%, qualify for free or reduced-price meals (California Department of Education, 2006)

As illustrated in Table 3.9, Roosevelt High School, one of the schools featured on this text's *Choosing Your Teaching Path* video clip, and the Unified Fresno School District face challenges even greater than those indicated in the California state statistics. For years there has been much public attention and debate surrounding the high drop-out rate and sizable achievement gap in the Fresno Unified School District. This debate occurs in many rural, suburban, and urban areas across the United States. Carefully read this chapter's Letter to the Editor and thoughtfully write your own response.

■ How Are Differences in Intellectual Ability Manifested in Schools?

The revered **intelligence quotient (IQ)** affixes a number to intelligence that, in one single freeze-frame, labels us for life. Scores on IQ tests may provide useful information, but they are no longer considered the final answer in determining a child's intellectual

Letter to the Editor

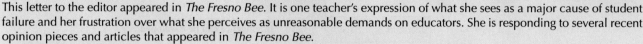

This letter to the editor appeared in *The Fresno Bee*. It is one teacher's expression of what she sees as a major cause of student failure and her frustration over what she perceives as unreasonable demands on educators. She is responding to several recent opinion pieces and articles that appeared in *The Fresno Bee*.

Now it's your turn. You learned about student development and diversity in this chapter. Use what you know to write your own letter to the editor that addresses both the cause of student failure according to Ms. Van Vleet's letter and responsibilities of educators. These questions well help clarify some of the issues.

1. Do you believe teachers and schools should be able to overcome students' personal circumstances and lead them to academic success? If so, how? If not, why not?

LETTER TO THE EDITOR

APRIL 2, 2005

I am a teacher trying to pull, push, drag and even carry 75 seniors to their high school graduation.

It is not for want of trying. The enormous weight of their families' lives keeps them burned out, exhausted and often too sick to keep trying. There is little "American Dream" in their backgrounds, and even less nourishment to strengthen them, fewer homeowners, more transience and interrupted employment.

I used to hear Mayor Alan Autry talk about our schools—but not the jobs that would sustain the families. I've heard the community forums discuss the disarray of our schools—but not address the families these students come from.

I agree it's irresponsible for the teachers union and school district to be at an impasse, but it's immoral for the community to ask even more of its teachers on less pay.

Mary Van Vleet
Clovis

2. When students fail or drop out, do you think it is more the fault of life circumstances (SES, family structure, etc.) or the school's failure to provide adequate support? Explain your view.
3. When students walk through the school doors, do you think teachers should be able to provide an environment for success for all regardless of home dilemmas? If so, how? If not, why not?
4. Do you believe the government should be responsible for getting families out of poverty? If so, how? If not, why not?
5. Do you believe teachers today are faced with responsibilities beyond what should be expected of them? If so, what are some of these responsibilities?

Your letter to the editor should be in response to *The Fresno Bee* letter—supporting it, adding information, or refuting it. Write your letter in understandable terminology, remembering that readers of newspaper letters to the editor are citizens who may have limited knowledge of school practices and policies. Your letter may be written in your course notebook and shared with classmates as directed by your instructor. Remember to refer to the letter assessment rubric in Figure 1.10, page 20.

capacity. We have moved beyond the notion that intelligence is a fixed attribute. Researchers now believe that **intelligence,** a capacity for knowing and learning, can change, as illustrated in Figure 3.5, and is manifested in various ways.

Multiple Intelligences Theory

Harvard psychologist Howard Gardner added an "s" to the word *intelligence* and influenced how we view the concept. In 1983 he theorized that intelligence is multidimensional, that individual brains work in ways that give each of us our own personal intelligences. He called this **multiple intelligences theory (MI).**

Gardner (1999) proposed distinct intelligences that can be activated and connected in very individual ways. Table 3.10 lists eight of the nine intelligences he proposed and shows how each may be manifested in sensitivities, inclinations, and abilities. The ninth intelligence is existential intelligence, described by Gardner in 2005 as the intelligence of big questions. When we consider concepts that are too big or too small to be immediately (or ever) fully grasped, we are thinking in existential ways. For example, considering how big infinity is, imagining how small the increments are when the property of

Figure 3.5 How our views of intelligence have changed

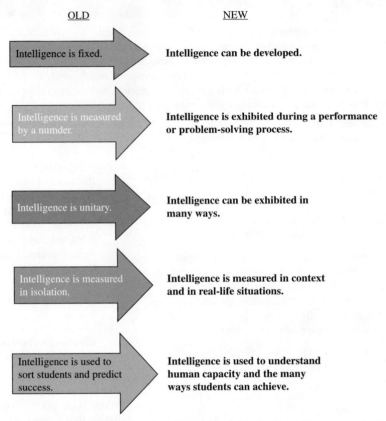

Source: From *So Each May Learn: Integrating Learning Styles and Multiple Intelligences,* by H. F. Silver, R. W. Strong, and M. J. Perini, 2000, Alexandria, VA: Association for Supervision and Curriculum Development.

density is applied, or pondering the meaning of life are intriguing subjects for someone with existential intelligence.

It is important for us as educators to understand the new view of intelligence (Figure 3.5) and to know what to look for in terms of multiple intelligences (Table 3.10) so that we can plan experiences to help students capitalize on their strengths.

Learning Styles

Whereas Gardner's theory of multiple intelligences helps explain different forms of intelligence, theories of **learning styles** give us insight into the variety of ways in which the learning process happens. Perhaps the simplest way to characterize learning styles is through the four commonly accepted **learning modalities,** or preferences: auditory (hearing), visual (seeing), tactile (touch), and kinesthetic (movement). We use all four in the process of learning, but each individual tends to favor one or two over the others. Traditional classrooms rely most heavily on auditory and visual modalities, such as lectures and chalkboard or whiteboard support, especially in the upper grades. Yet active learning techniques, such as the hands-on manipulatives and group work, activate tactile and kinesthetic modalities and may engage students more effectively. Figure 3.6 helps us understand students who learn best through hearing, seeing, touching, or moving.

Several theories deal with learning styles, but the message is the same: we learn in different ways. Incorporating what we know about multiple intelligences and learning styles

Table 3.10 Manifestations of multiple intelligences

Disposition/Intelligence	Sensitivity to	Inclination for	Ability to
Verbal-Linguistic Intelligence	Sounds, meanings, structures and styles of language	Speaking, writing, listening, reading	Speak effectively and/or write effectively
Logical Mathematical Intelligence	Patterns, numbers, and numerical data; causes and effects; objective and quantitative reasoning	Finding patterns, making calculations, formulating hypotheses, using the scientific method	Work effectively with numbers and reason effectively
Spatial Intelligence	Colors, shapes, visual puzzles, symmetry, lines, images	Representing ideas visually, creating mental images, noticing details, drawing and sketching	Create visually and visualize accurately
Bodily-Kinesthetic Intelligence	Touch, movement, physical self, athleticism	Activities requiring strength, speed, flexibility, hand-eye coordination, and balance	Use hands to fix or create and use the body expressively
Musical Intelligence	Tone, beat, tempo, melody, pitch, sound	Listening, singing, playing an instrument	Create music and analyze music
Interpersonal Intelligence	Body language, moods, voice, feelings	Noticing and responding to other people's feelings and personalities	Work with people and help people identify and overcome problems
Intrapersonal Intelligence	One's own strengths, weaknesses, goals, desires	Setting goals, assessing personal abilities and liabilities, monitoring one's own thinking	Mediate, reflect, exhibit self-discipline, maintain composure, and get the most out of oneself
Naturalist Intelligence	Natural objects, plants, animals, naturally occurring issues	Identifying and classifying living things and natural objects	Analyze ecological and natural situations, learn from living things, and work in natural settings

Source: From *So Each May Learn: Integrating Learning Styles and Multiple Intelligences* (Figure 1.3, p. 11), by H. F. Silver, R. W. Strong, and M. J. Perini, 2002, Alexandria, VA: ASCD. Adapted by permission. The Association for Supervision and Curriculum Development is a worldwide community of educators advocating sound policies and sharing best practices to achieve the success of each learner. To learn more, visit ASCD at www.ascd.org.

into our plans for instruction helps us meet the learning needs of more students. Acknowledging that there are many ways to learn leads us to understand that some students have particular difficulties learning, while some learn more quickly and perhaps more deeply than others.

Figure 3.6   Learning styles and learner preferences

Auditory learners tend to . . .
 enjoy reading and being read to
 be able to verbally explain concepts and scenarios
 like music and hum to themselves
 enjoy both talking and listening

Visual learners tend to . . .
 have good spelling, note-taking, and organizational skills
 notice details and prefer neatness
 learn more if illustrations and charts accompany reading
 prefer quiet, serene surroundings

Kinesthetic learners tend to . . .
 be demonstrative, animated, and outgoing
 enjoy physical movement and manipulatives
 be willing to try new things
 be messy in habits and surroundings

Tactile learners tend to . . .
 prefer manipulatives when being introduced to a topic
 literally translate events and phenomena
 tolerate clutter
 be artistic in nature

Source: From *Introduction to Middle School* (p. 62), by S. D. Powell, 2005, Upper Saddle River, NJ: Merrill Prentice Hall. Copyright © 2005 by Merrill/Prentice Hall. Adapted by permission.

Differences in Intellectual Ability: Implications for Teachers

There are differences in intellectual ability; individuals have their own ways of being smart. When we recognize that people also perceive and process knowledge in different amounts and with varying timing, the challenges of teaching become even greater. Here are some questions to keep in mind when considering these challenges:

- Do I view the students in my classroom as a collection of individuals, each with unique ways of being smart?
- Do I continually seek to understand the ways in which my students learn best?
- Do I plan some experiences that address and incorporate each of the multiple intelligences?
- Does my awareness of my students' various learning styles change how I teach?
- Do I consciously seek to identify, and then expand, each student's zone of proximal development?

Now that we know more about how students differ, let's address definitions of, and resources for, students who fall outside the spectrum of what is considered a range of normal development and abilities. These are students with exceptionalities.

Who Are Students with Exceptionalities, and How Do We Serve Them?

Learners with abilities or disabilities that set them apart from other learners are often referred to as **students with exceptionalities.** Heward (2006) tells us that exceptional children

> . . . differ from the norm (either below or above) to such an extent that they require an additional program of special education and related services to fully benefit from education. . . . Thus, exceptional children . . . refers to children with learning and/or

behavior problems, children with physical or sensory impairments, and children who are intellectually gifted or have a special talent. (p. 10)

Some exceptionalities are the result of nature, while others may be the result of injury or illness, aspects of nurture (Heward, 2006).

Two factors are especially important when we consider the education of students with exceptionalities: identification, deciding who has what exceptionality and to what degree, and intervention, determining how best to meet their educational needs.

Students with Disabilities

The categories of exceptionalities considered disabilities, along with the percentage of all disabilities they represent, are shown in Table 3.11. Considering all the categories, about 12% of American students receive **special education services,** services provided by schools to help students function and learn in ways optimal to the individual. This percentage translates into about 6.6 million students. If the current rate of identification continues, the percentage of students receiving special education services in 2010 will be over 14% (Goldstein, 2003).

Many disabilities, especially those that impair daily functioning, such as orthopedic disabilities and hearing, sight, and disease-related impairments, are diagnosed before children enter school. When classroom teachers and parents first recognize learning difficulties, they are encouraged to talk with administrators or school psychologists about their observations. Official identification of students with learning disabilities is typically handled through a team of educators equipped with expertise and diagnostic tools.

A designation of **learning disabled (LD),** which accounts for almost half the students receiving special education services, includes a general category of students with disorders involving problems understanding or using language that results in significant differences between learning potential and achievement (Turnbull, Turnbull, & Wehmeyer, 2007). Misdiagnosis or the absence of diagnosis is problematic; students may not necessarily look as though they have learning disabilities. Many students develop coping strategies

Table 3.11 Categories of disabilities and percentages of students served

Disability	Percentage of Total Students Receiving Special Services
Specific learning disabilities	47.2
Speech or language impairments	18.8
Mental retardation	9.6
Emotional disturbance	8.1
Multiple disabilities	2.2
Hearing impairments	1.2
Orthopedic impairments	1.1
Other health impairments	7.5
Autism	2.3
Visual impairments	.4
Traumatic brain injury	.4
Developmental delay	1.1
Deaf-blindness	.1

Source: From *Individuals with Disabilities Education Act (IDEA) data,* U.S. Department of Education, 2004, Washington, DC: Author.

Students with more obvious disabilities, as opposed to those with learning disabilities and ADHD, which are likely to be diagnosed later, receive special services from kindergarten on.

that mask their learning problems for years, and very possibly for life. Students with LD may

- have difficulties with word recognition and text comprehension
- feel overwhelmed by the idea of getting started
- struggle to organize and use the mechanics of writing
- have difficulty differentiating numbers or copying shapes
- have difficulty identifying, using, and monitoring problem-solving strategies
  (Turnbull et al., 2007)

Intervention for students with LD may include time each day with a special education teacher, often referred to as a **resource teacher,** who will help them develop strategies for school success.

Identification of another disability, **attention deficit/ hyperactivity disorder (AD/HD),** may be as problematic as identification of learning disabilities. Students with AD/HD demonstrate three defining characteristics: inattention, hyperactivity, and impulsivity. AD/HD is defined by the American Psychological Association (APA) (2000) as the frequent existence of these three characteristics in a persistent pattern that is more severe than in others of the same age. The APA estimates that 3%–7% of students in an average class have AD/HD, which falls within the other health impairments category of Table 3.11. The intervention for students with AD/HD may include specific strategies to help modify behavior, or medication. They receive services through special education only if they have impairments other than AD/HD for which they qualify (Turnbull et al., 2007).

Legal Support for Students with Disabilities

Until recently, students with disabilities were often isolated in a room at the end of a hallway—out of sight, out of mind—unless they happened to be seen walking as a group or boarding one of those short buses designed to hold that "special" group of kids. Prior to 1975, most students with disabilities, designated as **special education students,** weren't even in the same facilities as other students; there were no provisions for them to attend public schools. In 1975 the landmark legislation **Public Law 94–142 (PL 94–142)** changed all that.

Today special education is viewed as a service rather than a place to send children (Jackson & Harper, 2002). The **Education for All Handicapped Children Act (PL 94–142)** opened all public schools to students with disabilities and mandated that students with disabilities be given the opportunity to benefit from special education services at no cost to families. The law established six governing principles, listed in Figure 3.7, that apply to the education of students with disabilities.

In 1990 PL 94–142 was amended and renamed the **Individuals with Disabilities Education Act (IDEA).** Students with autism and traumatic brain injury were added to those entitled to services under PL 94–142. A change in attitude and philosophy was also evident in the law when the language changed from "disabled individuals" to "individuals with disabilities." The person comes first, with the disability secondary. In 2004 IDEA was reauthorized as the **Individuals with Disabilities Education Improvement Act.** This latest reauthorization is the most comprehensive yet, including all U.S. laws affecting children with disabilities in one statute (Heward, 2006).

Individualized Educational Programs

Serving students with disabilities (ages 3–21), regardless of the setting or combination of settings, requires an **individualized educational program (IEP)** as prescribed by Principle 3

Figure 3.7 Six principles governing the education of students with disabilities

1. **Zero reject:** A rule against excluding any student.

2. **Nondiscriminatory evaluation:** Requires schools to evaluate students fairly to determine if they have a disability and, if so, what kind and how extensive.

3. **Appropriate education:** Requires schools to provide individualized education programs for each student based on evaluation and augmented by related services and supplementary aids and services.

4. **Least restrictive environment:** Requires schools to educate students with disabilities with students without disabilities to the maximum extent appropriate for the students with disabilities.

5. **Procedural due process:** Provides safeguards for students against schools' actions, including a right to sue in court.

6. **Parental and student participation:** Requires schools to collaborate with parents and adolescent students in designing and carrying out special education programs.

Source: Information from *Exceptional Lives* by R. Turnbull, A. Turnbull, and M. Wehmeyer, (2007), Fifth Edition, Upper Saddle River, NJ: Merrill/Prentice Hall.

Figure 3.8 Components of an IEP

An IEP must include a statement of

1. the student's present level of academic achievement and functional level
2. measurable academic and functional annual goals
3. how the student's progress toward meeting the annual goals will be measured
4. special education and related services to be provided to the student
5. the extent to which the student will not participate with nondisabled students and the regular classroom
6. accommodations necessary to measure the student's achievement on state assessments
7. date of beginning services
8. postsecondary goals and transition services at age 16

Source: Information from *Exceptional Children* (pp. 69–70), by W. L. Heward, 2006, Upper Saddle River, NJ: Merrill/Prentice Hall.

of PL 94–142. An IEP is developed by educators, the family, and others as appropriate and involves a detailed plan to reach specific goals. A student's IEP must be revisited annually and student progress evaluated. While IEP formats may vary, the required elements are listed in Figure 3.8.

An important part of an IEP is the designation of where and with whom students with disabilities will spend their school time. Principle 4 of PL 94–142 explicitly states that students with disabilities will be in the **least restrictive environment (LRE)** possible. The LRE is generally a setting with students who do not have disabilities that also meets the educational needs of the students with disabilities.

Inclusion

Whether you are interested in teaching students with disabilities or not, you may be doing exactly that in a regular inclusive classroom setting if a student's IEP designates it as the LRE. **Inclusion** means that "students attend their home school with their age and grade appropriate peers, participate in extra curricular activities, and receive special

Inclusive classrooms provide opportunities for students with disabilities and students without disabilities to learn and work together.

education and support services, to the maximum extent possible, in the general education classroom" (Rosenberg, O'Shea, & O'Shea, 2006, p. 14).

Many teachers, students, parents, and research studies conclude that the regular classroom is the setting in which many students with disabilities are best educated. However, simply placing students with disabilities in a regular classroom does not mean inclusive practices are in place or that a rigorous learning environment will be maintained. Teachers still must effectively focus on individualized objectives for every student, facilitate interactions and cooperative learning among students at every learning level, and maintain collaborative relationships with students, parents, and special educators. Given this approach, inclusion can be a healthy and positive experience for students without disabilities as well (Heward, 2006). There is a growing trend toward co-teaching involving a regular classroom teacher and a special educator in a single classroom.

Inclusion is not embraced by all. Some parents believe their students with disabilities are better off in smaller, special education classrooms where they are more likely to receive one-on-one attention from teachers specifically trained to work with them. Some regular education teachers are wary of having a student with disabilities placed in their classrooms, an understandable hesitation if they receive little or no training in meeting the emotional, social, and cognitive needs of the students. While the **Council for Exceptional Children** (CEC), the professional organization of special education, endorses inclusion, the official stance is support of a continuum of services with inclusion as a desirable goal, but not the only appropriate option for all students with disabilities.

Assistive Technology

The Technology-Related Assistance to Individuals with Disabilities Act of 1988 authorized funding for **assistive technology** devices and services. These devices and services benefit students with disabilities by helping them communicate, increasing their mobility, and aiding in multiple ways that enhance their capacity to learn. The range of assistive technology includes wheelchairs, voice-activated and touch-screen word processors, sound-augmenting devices, and closed-captioned television (Turnbull et al., 2007). Technology is making it possible for students with disabilities to function and learn at levels unimaginable only a decade ago.

Students Who Are Gifted and Talented

Descriptions of characteristics of students who are **gifted and talented** include phrases such as

- evidence of high performance capabilities
- intellectual, creative, artistic, or leadership ability well beyond average
- excelling in specific academic fields

Identification of students who are gifted and talented can be objective or quite subjective, depending on the criteria accepted by a particular school district. When IQ is used for identification, the threshold number is 125–130, achieved by only about 2%–3% of the general student population. However, evaluating creativity along with IQ testing allows more students to benefit from gifted and talented services.

Services for students who are gifted and talented vary significantly and include pull-out programs, with students working on projects or an accelerated curriculum. In-school options, such as grade skipping, concurrent enrollment in two levels of schooling, curriculum compacting (faster pace), and advanced placement courses (rigorous high school courses with possible college credit for completion), enhance the opportunities of students designated as gifted and talented. There are also specifically designed magnet schools for such students.

When students who are gifted and talented are in regular classrooms, and most are, we can better meet their needs by

- being flexible
- accepting unusual ideas and encouraging alternative solutions to problems
- not being intimidated by the intellectual and creative capabilities of students who have IQs that exceed our own
- differentiating instruction often (more about this in Chapter 4)

Students with Exceptionalities: Implications for Teachers

The most important aspect of teaching students with exceptionalities is to recognize that each student is an individual with learning potential and at least part of his or her mind "amply equipped to thrive" (Levine, 2003, p. 13). Seeing and seeking strengths before, or concurrently with, acknowledging limitations helps us embrace possibilities for each individual, whether in an inclusive classroom or in a special education setting.

Including students with exceptionalities in the classroom is beneficial to all students because instruction is delivered in a variety of ways to engage diverse learners. To do so successfully, teachers need support and time for planning, as well as an appropriate curriculum, materials, and resources. Ongoing professional development is essential.

Here are some questions teachers of inclusive classrooms need to ask:

- Do I take the time to get to know each student as an individual?
- Do I look for the strengths and abilities of all my students?
- Is differentiating instruction a primary goal? (more in Chapter 4)
- Is cooperative learning used frequently in my classroom? (more in Chapter 4)
- Do I continually diagnose the progress of my students and adjust my instruction appropriately? (more in Chapter 5)

During your field experiences, look closely for evidence of inclusion. Ask teachers to help you understand more about students with exceptionalities.

Before meeting our other focus students, let's meet Trista Kutcher. Trista has Down syndrome. This fact makes her exceptional, but so do many other aspects of Trista's life. Trista's family and friends recognize Trista's gifts as well as her clinical disability.

■ Meet the Students

"You just had to be there!" we often exclaim when words just aren't enough. Learning about students and their schools is one of those situations when pictures or video clips can help convey what a thousand words cannot. Is it as good as being there? No, but it helps. In reading this text, you will watch 12 students grow through real-life scenarios and pictures. By watching the video in the Choosing Your Teaching Path section of MyEducationLab, you will meet each student through conversations and parent interviews. We will revisit the students; their teachers, who were introduced in Chapter 1; and their schools, which were introduced in Chapter 2, throughout the text as their stories help to illustrate concepts.

The students are representative in many ways of the students at their schools, but not necessarily of the general student population in the United States. It would be impossible to represent the vast diversity of American students in only 12 profiles. You will

Getting to Know Trista

Trista Kutcher is a very special young lady. Her happy life and remarkable accomplishments are evidence of what dedicated parents and sensitive, knowledgeable education professionals can do to help children, even those with disabilities, realize their potential. Trista has Down syndrome.

Trista's mom, Rebecca, teaches eighth-grade English language arts at Cario Middle School in Mount Pleasant, South Carolina, and Trista's dad, Joe, teaches math at Wando High School where Trista is a freshman. Trista has two younger sisters, Suzanna, age 12, and Samantha, age 4. As a member of the 2003 USA Special Olympics gymnastics team, Trista won five medals at the Dublin, Ireland, games. She is a cheerleader at Wando High and is included in many regular education classes.

After reading Trista's story, watch the interview of Trista and her family and friends in the Choosing Your Teaching Path section of MyEducationLab. Click on Cario Middle School, and then on Trista.

Rebecca has written about many of her experiences as Trista's mom. Here's an abridged version of one of her pieces, entitled "We Danced."

We Danced

Joe and I had the perfect life. . . . We dated in high school and married right out of college. Life was grand! We got pregnant and things were sailing along as we **danced** through life. People would often ask, "What do you want—a boy or a girl?" I never said more than my prayer that the baby would be healthy! Joe's response was that we just wished for "10 fingers and 10 toes." Deep down, however, I really wanted a little girl with blonde hair and blue eyes who would **dance** in a recital, **dance** on the beach, and **dance** into everyone's heart!

The pregnancy was perfect, as was the delivery. Joe and I held Trista Sue and cooed over her late into the night.

A few hours later the music stopped. The doctors told us our little blonde-haired, blue-eyed Trista Sue had Down syndrome. Joe and I no longer felt like **dancing.**

Knowing breastfeeding was important for her in many ways, I wanted to continue her feeding schedule, even though she was still in the hospital. I would wake up during the night at 1:00 and 5:00 and travel to the hospital to nurse her. I would waltz around the room with her in my arms. How wonderful those **dances** were . . . just us, loving each other.

I decided I was going to get Trista involved in activities that every "normal" girl does. At age two I took her to Tapios School of Dance and Gymnastics. I asked the owner if Trista could enroll in her tap and ballet classes. She welcomed her with open arms and taught her to dance with grace and poise.

Around this time Trista's sister, Suzanna, was born. How proud she was to be a big sister! Oh, the mischief they could get into together. Eventually, Trista and Suzanna were in a dance recital together, Trista 6 and Suzanna 3. Suzanna was amazed at the lights and people in the audience. She completely forgot her dance. Big sister to the rescue! Trista decided this was unacceptable and took matters into her own hands. Trista marched across the stage,

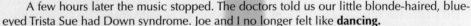

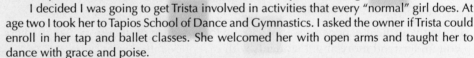

meet Dylan and Sherlonda at Summit Primary, Ohio; Amanda, Hector, and Josie at Rees Elementary, Utah; Patrick and David at Cario Middle School, South Carolina; and Guillermo, Khammany, Hugo, and Mayra at Roosevelt High School, California. In addition to these 11 students you will learn more about Trista, a freshman at Wando High School, South Carolina. These 12 students put faces on our discussions of development and diversity. Take your time as you read about, watch, and listen to these students. Let their stories sink in. Think about

Your Teaching Fingerprint

positioned herself behind Suzanna and proceeded to move her arms and legs for her. The audience rolled with laughter while Trista made Suzanna **dance.**

When Trista started school, we decided she should be included in the regular classroom. Speech was definitely a concern and having her with the other kids would be great modeling. Each of her accomplishments was celebrated by kids in the class and by teachers who were initially worried about how they would teach her.

Through elementary and middle school Trista thrived, making friends and showing all of us what she could do, rather than what she couldn't do. In high school she eats, drinks, and sleeps cheering during the fall and, like her gymnastics, loves it dearly. The other girls could not be more accepting and supportive of her.

> ### Poem written by Trista's sister
>
> Trista-
> Famous, idol,
> Likes to run, jump, and play,
> Annoys me when she says she is right when she is wrong.
> She can do cartwheels—I wish I could.
> She wishes she could play basketball like me.
> I do not like to go to the same parties as she does
> Because then I feel like I have to look after her
> and I cannot have fun.
> It amazes me when she does flips and is not scared.
> It makes me sad when she says hi to someone
> and they do not respond back to her.
> I am proud to tell my friends about all the gold medals she has.
> I like when she smiles and her nose crunches up . . . it is so cute.
> She has Down syndrome.
> She is my sister!
>
> By Suzanna Kutcher
> 12 years old

Along with regular gymnastics competitions, Trista competed in Special Olympics gymnastics. She was the state champion from the age of 8. Being involved provided many opportunities for independence and pride. During the summer of 2002, she received another very important letter. It asked her to be a part of the Special Olympics team USA for the 2003 World Games. As she opened that letter she beamed from ear to ear. This adventure was one of meeting the governor and the mayor, being featured in a commercial, being on the news and in the newspaper regularly, and having an official day in Mt. Pleasant proclaimed by the mayor as Trista Kutcher Day! Everywhere we went people knew her. Suzanna began to make a joke about all of us being her entourage! Never did we think we would be **dancing in her shadow!** She was leading us on the adventure of a lifetime!

The competition in Ireland was tough but she was ready! She won five medals, two of which were gold! As she stood on the podium, she cried and told me later that she was so proud because "She did it"! After the awards ceremony, the audience flooded the gym floor, joined hands, and **danced the Irish jig**. What a celebration!

The **dance** has been wonderful. The music has played non-stop for 15 years! Our dance began with three people on the floor . . . and ended with **a whole community kicking up its heels!**

the ones who speak to you most deeply. Think about the grade levels they represent and imagine in which level you would like tof spend your days. Let them help guide you toward your teaching identity.

After you have read the following brief introductions, go to the Choosing Your Teaching Path section of MyEducationLab to learn more about each focus student. Watch the students and their parents by clicking on each student's school, and then their name.

Dylan Todd
Kindergarten
Summit Primary School
Ohio

Kindergarten   *Dylan with Mom and Dad*

Dylan is the only child of Brandon and Lisa Todd. Their pride is obvious as they talk about what a delightful little boy he is. When Dylan smiles, everyone smiles. When he giggles . . . Read more about Dylan in MyEducationLab.

Who wouldn't think that Dylan is adorable! However, that's not quite enough on which to base a decision to teach in an early childhood setting. Consider the energy level and developmental neediness of the 4–7-year-old. Is this how you want to spend your days?

Your Teaching Fingerprint

Sherlonda Francis
2nd grade
Summit Primary School
Ohio

Kindergarten   *2nd grade*   *Sherlonda with Mom and Dad*

Sherlonda's personality shines. The challenge is to help her develop academically and find success in school so high school graduation will be in her future. Renee Ayers, her teacher, is afraid that if Sherlonda doesn't experience academic success soon, her penchant for socializing may . . . Read more about Sherlonda in MyEducationLab.

Would you like to work with first or second graders, some of whom already read fluently and are successful academically and some of whom struggle to develop basic skills?

Your Teaching Fingerprint

Amanda Wiley
3rd grade
Rees Elementary
Utah

Kindergarten   *1st grade*   *3rd grade*   *Amanda and Mom*

Amanda's mom describes Amanda as "just plain fun." All it takes is 5 minutes of classroom observation to know the description fits. Amanda loves school now, but reading did not come easily for her, and first grade proved to be very challenging. She simply didn't . . . Read more about Amanda in MyEducationLab.

Third grade is when many states begin high-stakes testing of children to show the cumulative results of learning from birth through age 9. It's an exciting time to be with children. Does this age appeal to you?

Your Teaching Fingerprint

Hector Mancia
4th grade
Rees Elementary
Utah

Kindergarten 2nd grade   4th grade   Hector and Mom

Hector's smile would warm the heart of any teacher. As a fourth grader, he is a fluent English speaker, vibrant, curious, and determined to succeed. Hector's family came to Utah from Mexico. One of his biggest challenges is . . . Read more about Hector in MyEducationLab.

Fourth grade is a year when the curriculum becomes more difficult for children. They may struggle academically for the first time. Do you want to teach children who will be in the midst of this phase of changing academic expectations?

Your Teaching Fingerprint

Josie Ford
5th grade
Rees Elementary
Utah

Kindergarten 3rd grade   5th grade   Josie and Mom

Josie is an ideal student. At age 10 she loves school, reads fluently, enjoys math, and is quite proficient on the computer. Josie thrives in a multiage setting with children in grades 3, 4, and 5 spending their days together, sharing both . . . Read more about Josie in MyEducationLab.

Do you remember what it was like to be in fifth grade? Would you enjoy spending your days with kids on the upper end of childhood, poised to enter early adolescence?

Your Teaching Fingerprint

Patrick Sutton
7th grade
Cario Middle School
South Carolina

Kindergarten   2nd grade   5th grade   7th grade

Patrick is a very self-assured 13-year-old seventh grader at Cario Middle School who likes school. He enjoys being with friends the most, and doing homework the least (no surprise here!). He says he likes teachers who challenge him and . . . Read more about Patrick in MyEducationLab.

Seventh grade is a very interesting time for students and teachers (and parents!). Not all seventh graders are as mature as Patrick. Do you remember being in seventh grade? Do you have the temperament, flexibility, and sense of humor to spend your days guiding young adolescents?

Your Teaching Fingerprint

David McBeath
7th grade
Cario Middle School
South Carolina

Kindergarten   *3rd grade*   *5th grade*   *David and Mom*

At 6 feet, 195 pounds, David doesn't appear to be 12 years old.
However, looking at his childlike face and hearing his soft voice, you realize he is a young adolescent whose emotional and social growth have yet to catch up with . . . Read more about David in MyEducationLab.

Would you want to spend your days with students like David who require more encouragement to succeed?

Your Teaching
Fingerprint

Trista Kutcher
9th grade
Wando High School
South Carolina

Preschool   *Kindergarten*   *3rd grade*   *9th grade*

Trista is as friendly as any high school freshman could be. Other Wando students pass her and smile when they say hello. Trista is a cheerleader and athlete, and she has Down syndrome . . . Read more about Trista in MyEducationLab.

Do you have the desire to work closely with students whose daily lives are affected by a disability? Does being a special educator appeal to you?

Your Teaching
Fingerprint

Mayra Reyes
10th grade
Roosevelt High School
California

Kindergarten   *3rd grade*   *6th grade*   *10th grade*

Mayra was born in the United States, yet she speaks fluent Spanish, the language of her family.
Friends are at the center of her life. Mayra would much rather be at school than . . . Read more about Mayra in MyEducationLab.

Do you have a desire to teach adolescents whose lives may be very complex just at a time when life-changing decisions need to be made?

Your Teaching
Fingerprint

Guillermo Toscano
11th grade
Roosevelt High School
California

Kindergarten *3rd grade* *6th grade* *10th grade* *Guillermo and Mom*

Guillermo represents the first generation in his family to finish high school. In conversation, his maturity and thoughtful demeanor are engaging. He says he learns best when . . . Read more about Guillermo in MyEducationLab.

Guillermo has high hopes for his future. As a junior he needs to take his classes seriously as he thinks about going to college. Do you want to guide and inspire students like Guillermo? Is there a particular subject that excites you? Would you like to foster that excitement in high school students?

Your Teaching Fingerprint

Hugo Martinez
11th grade
Roosevelt High School
California

11th grade

Hugo with Mom and Dad

Hugo is a handsome 17-year-old junior at Roosevelt High with a very outgoing personality. Are you wondering why there's only one school picture of him? When Hugo, his mom and dad, and three brothers crossed the Mexican border into California 18 months ago . . . Read more about Hugo in MyEducationLab .

Recent immigrants often bring problems with them, as well as an enthusiasm for the opportunity to go to school. Would you, as a teacher, want to support these students emotionally and cognitively?

Your Teaching Fingerprint

Khammany Douangsavanh
12th grade
Roosevelt High School
California

Kindergartem *2nd grade* *5th grade* *Khammany and Mom*

Khammany is Laotian. She speaks fluent English at school, but only Lao-tian at home. She participates consistently and demonstrates an appreciation for the value of education. As a learner, Khammany says her interest in a subject is . . . Read more about Khammany in MyEducationLab.

Families often put so much hope in the children for whom they want a better life. Would you like to be part of a faculty who teaches many students who are first-generation Americans?

Your Teaching Fingerprint

Concluding Thoughts

In Chapter 1 we began our focus on teaching with the assertion that all children can learn. In Chapter 2 we explored schools and the purposes of education in the United States. Now that we have looked at how students are similar and how they are different, perhaps the concept that all students can learn seems more elusive to you. How, indeed, do we make "all children can learn" a reality given the circumstances that pervade some children's lives?

Understanding the uniqueness of each of us calls for an absolute commitment to individuality. Thomas Jefferson expressed the thought that there is nothing so unequal as the equal treatment of unequals. All children are equal in terms of their right to fulfill their own promise, but certainly children are unequal in the many ways we have discussed in this chapter and more. The spirit of inclusion draws them all in; the unwavering determination to meet their needs requires attention and action based on each individual.

This brings us back to balance—philosophical balance. On the one hand, we have all the similarities shared by our students. On the other, we have their diversity in even more categories than we have discussed. Planning for the teaching and learning process must take both into consideration.

Yes, all children can learn. These complex questions logically follow this statement:

What can they learn?

When can they learn it?

In what ways will they learn it best?

As always, "And how are the children? Are they all well?" should be the center of our focus.

What Role Will Diversity Play in My Teaching Identity?

In this chapter we explored some of the multiple ways we are different, including diversity of gender, culture, language, family structure, socioeconomic status, and intellectual ability. All of these aspects will affect you as a teacher. Regardless of where you fit in this complex maze of diverse characteristics, you will have students who do not fit your profile. This is a fact, and to attempt to change it is both futile and counterproductive. Rather than bemoaning differences, we should embrace them and even celebrate them. Our responsibility is to search for, and then cultivate, student strengths, some of which are the direct result of the diversity that makes each student unique. This responsibility, which is indeed an opportunity, makes teaching an exciting and challenging profession!

Chapter in Review

How are we similar?

- We are all human beings.
- Nature (genetics) influences human traits we are born with.
- Nurture (environment) influences who we are through every aspect of our lives that nature does not determine.
- Human beings share the same basic hierarchy of needs.
- We all experience physical, cognitive, emotional, social, and character development.

How are gender differences manifested?

- Anatomical differences between males and females determine sex, whereas gender is the sense of being male or female.
- Gender determines many of the choices we make and the expectations others have for us.
- Homosexuality is often the basis of discrimination.

How does cultural diversity impact us?

- Race, while a social, political, economical, and psychological reality, is based solely on physical characteristics.
- Racism is a form of prejudice stemming from a belief that one race is superior to another.
- Ethnicity refers to a person's country of origin.
- Culture has many components and is learned, shared, and adaptive.
- Cultural identity relies on many factors, such as race, ethnicity, language, gender, religion, income level, values, and beliefs.
- Multiculturalism involves beliefs concerning the value of looking at the world through the eyes of people who are different from us.
- To be most effective, multicultural education needs to permeate all areas of schooling.

How is language diversity manifested in U.S. schools?

- Language is an aspect of cultural identity that can be changed.
- English language learner services are provided to over 8% of all public school students in the United States.
- Bilingual education, a controversial initiative, involves instruction delivered in two languages.
- English as a second language (ESL) is a pull-out program assisting English language learners in English only.

What impact does diversity in family structure have on students?

- Blended families and family structures other than two biological parents and children are becoming more prevalent.
- The increasing mobility of American families potentially harms students and wreaks havoc on classrooms.

Does diversity of religion influence U.S. schools?

- Religion and faith have considerable influence on lifestyles and choices.
- The religious beliefs of families and communities influence decisions that relate to school issues.

How does diversity of socioeconomic status affect students?

- The gap between the haves and have-nots is wider in the United States than in most other nations.
- SES is the complex interaction of income, occupation, education level, wealth, and power.
- Low-income settings contribute to many at-risk situations and behaviors.

How are differences in intellectual ability manifested in schools?

- There are many different ways to be smart and to exhibit intelligence.
- We all have learning-style preferences.

Who are students with exceptionalities, and how do we serve them?

- Students with exceptionalities include those with disabilities and those considered gifted and talented.
- The concept of least restrictive environment means that students with disabilities are to be placed in the highest-functioning setting possible, usually the regular education classroom.
- Students considered gifted and talented are most likely to be included in the regular education classroom and pulled out for special classes for brief periods of time.

Professional Practice

Licensure Test Prep

Use this scenario to respond to multiple-choice questions 1 and 2 and constructed-response item 3.

> Angelica Reynosa teaches world history at Roosevelt High School in Fresno, California. Hugo Martinez is one of her students. During her 3 years of teaching at Roosevelt she has seen over and over how English language learners struggle not only with adjustments to day-to-day life in the United States, but also with academics. They may have had learning difficulties in their country and language of origin, with little prerequisite knowledge to succeed in their own cultures, much less in American public schools. Angelica, herself bilingual, knows that life and learning were much easier for her because she was born in the United States and grew up speaking both Spanish and English. She wants to more fully understand the obstacles the English language learners in her classes face and how to approach instruction in ways that are meaningful to them.

1. When Angelica begins to look at the data in her school that compares students, she comes to the valid conclusion that
   a. she must adjust her expectations downward in order to have any success with English language learners grasping complex concepts.
   b. English language learners are inherently less capable than English speakers.
   c. many English language learners have had fewer opportunities to be exposed to cultural opportunities that enhance learning that most Americans take for granted.
   d. parents of English language learners do not value education and thus do not pass that value on to their children.

2. One of Angelica's classes is designated as a bilingual class. What is the least advantageous aspect of being in this class for Hugo?
   a. Hugo is with students in world history who are English language learners like himself.
   b. The bilingual classes potentially put students in tracks where they are with English language learners for most of the day.
   c. Instruction is delivered in both English and Spanish.
   d. Parent communication is enhanced because bilingual teachers can speak with adults in Hugo's home in their own language.

3. What two things might Angelica do to help include families of students with limited English proficiency (LEP) in the education of their children? Explain your chosen approaches.

Standards Speak

In Chapter 3, as we looked at student similarities and differences, we addressed a number of standards.

NCATE Standard 4: Diversity

The new professional teachers should be able to apply effective methods of teaching students who are at different developmental stages, have different learning styles, and come from diverse backgrounds.

NBPTS, Proposition 1

Accomplished teachers recognize that in a multicultural nation students bring to schools a plethora of abilities and attitudes and aptitudes that are valued differently by the community, the school, and the family.

INTASC Knowledge, Principle 2

The teacher understands how children learn and develop, and can provide learning opportunities that support their intellectual, social, and personal development.

INTASC Knowledge, Principle 3

The teacher understands how students differ in their approaches to learning and creates instructional opportunities that are adapted to diverse learners. The explanation that follows INTASC Knowledge, Principle 3, addresses differences by name. The list includes

Learning styles
Multiple intelligences
Visual and perceptual difficulties
Physical and mental challenges
Language
Culture
Family

Although you are not yet prepared to deliver instruction or create instructional opportunities, you are now at least aware of some of the ways in which students are the same and some of the ways in which they are different. Awareness is the first step toward any purposeful action.

1. As a kindergarten teacher, how would you find out about the differences among the 16 students in your classroom?
2. As a third grade teacher, how would you find out about the differences among your 22 students?
3. As a seventh grade teacher, how would you find out about the differences among the 100 students on your teaching team?
4. As an eleventh grade teacher, how would you find out about the differences among the 120 high school students you teach?

■ MyEducationLab

The following interactive features may be found in Chapter 3 of MyEducationLab

Homework and Exercises

Writing My Own Story
To write your own story by responding to some of the questions in the text accompanied by fingerprint icons, plus others, go to the "Writing My Own Story" section of the Homework and Exercises for Chapter 3 of MyEducationLab..

What's My Disposition?
To reflect on your beliefs and attitudes concerning the teaching profession, go to Chapter 3's "What's My Disposition?" feature of the Homework and Exercises section of MyEducationLab.

Exploring Schools and Classrooms
If your course involves experiences in schools, the questions and prompts in the "Exploring Schools and Classrooms" feature of Chapter 3's Homework and Exercises section of MyEducationLab will guide you as you explore local schools and classrooms.

Virtual Field Experience

To respond to questions and prompts regarding the Choosing Your Teaching Path videos that connect to specific chapter content, go to Chapter 3's Virtual Field Experience section of MyEducationLab. The questions will help you make sense of what you have read in the chapter.

Part 2

The Work of Teachers

Chapter 4   **Curriculum and Instruction**

Chapter 5   **Assessment and Accountability**

Chapter 6   **Technology in U.S. Schools**

Chapter 7   **Creating and Maintaining a Positive and Productive Learning Environment**

Chapter 4

Curriculum
and Instruction

Teaching in Focus

Chris Roberts is an adventurer. He travels extensively, climbs mountains, and rafts in white water. He could do lots of things with his life—and he does. But his career choice is teaching 9-, 10-, and 11-year-olds at Rees Elementary School, Utah. As you look around his classroom in the Choosing Your Teaching Path section of MyEducationLab, Chris Roberts's personality, interests, and philosophy of life shine through. The cartoons with philosophical messages, the inspirational stories and poems, the giant topographical map of Utah, the newspaper and magazine clippings about people who triumphed over unimaginably difficult circumstances, and the personal family photographs—all of it speaks to who Chris is and what he values.

It takes only a few minutes in Chris's multiage classroom to recognize how his energy and wide range of interests influence how he interacts with students. He teaches all the core elementary subjects, as well as the dance component of the arts emphasis at Rees. When asked what he gets out of teaching, Chris says, "I like to play, I love these kids, and learning is the most exciting thing in the world."

You won't find references to the inspirational and fascinating displays in Chris's classroom in his lesson plans. Nor will you find "Tell the kids about my last dive off the Yucatan" or "Let my students know that life is a wonderful adventure." When Chris infuses his hobbies, interests, travels, and inspirational stories and philosophy into his classroom, he is teaching what we'll define later as the informal curriculum—lessons that aren't in a curriculum guide.

To view Chris's interview, classroom tour, and lesson segment go to the Choosing Your Teaching Path section of MyEducationLab at www.myeducationlab.com. Click on Rees Elementary, and then on Chris.

In this chapter we'll explore what is taught in U.S. schools and the teaching and learning strategies that make content come alive. At the end of the chapter we'll closely examine the teaching strategies used by our 10 focus teachers during their lesson segments in the Choosing Your Teaching Path section of MyEducationLab.

Here are questions we will explore in Chapter 4 as we look at what is taught, and the strategies used to teach it, in U.S. schools:

- **What is the relationship between the learning process and the brain?**
- **What curriculum do we teach in U.S. schools?**
- **How is instruction implemented in U.S. schools?**
- **Are we all teachers of reading and writing?**
- **How do teachers match instruction to school levels?**

Introduction

We move now from the "who" of school—the students and teachers—to the "what" and "how." In this chapter we'll look at the way teachers spend their days with students: what they teach and how they teach it. **Curriculum** is the educational term for what students experience in schools, and **instruction** encompasses the strategies used to convey the curriculum with the desired end result of student learning.

Engaging in **authentic teaching**—teaching what's needed, when it's needed, and doing so appropriately (Lemlech, 2004)—requires a deep understanding of both **content** (what we teach) and a repertoire of instructional strategies that promote learning. Authentic teaching also requires decision making based on understanding students, along with astute observation, critical analysis, and effective management of the learning process. Remember our discussion of the balance between academic rigor and developmental appropriateness on pages 11–12 in Chapter 1? These two vital elements must always be considered in any discussion of curriculum and instruction. Every course you take, every book or article you read, every example of teaching and learning you observe, and every classroom you experience will help you grow professionally into authentic teaching.

Curriculum and instruction are interdependent in the sense that content (curriculum) is meaningless without methods (instruction) to convey it, and those methods are useless without content. Assessment, as a significant piece of the teaching and learning process, is the subject of Chapter 5. These three components—curriculum, instruction, and assessment—are interwoven. Their relationship will become clear after we examine each separately. Think about our 12 focus students, their developmental qualities, and the levels of school they represent as you read about what is taught and how it's taught in U.S. schools. Before continuing this discussion, let's look briefly at how learning and the brain interact.

What Is the Relationship Between the Learning Process and the Brain?

Learning changes us. Better read that again. The implications of this simple statement are profound. **Learning** is a complex and dynamic process involving thinking, perception, experience, and memory. Learning can be so incremental that we hardly notice it occurring, or powerful enough to bring about swift, sweeping change. Learning, in any case, has the power to transform our lives.

We've recognized for a long time that learning changes what we do and how we do it. Those who study how the brain functions are discovering that the process of learning actually results in physical changes in our brains. **Brain-based learning** is looking at learning through study of the brain and then using what is discovered to guide teaching and learning techniques.

The discovery that the brain is physically changed when we learn has resulted in a significantly new way of viewing learning. Educator and biochemist James Zull (2004) likens the brain to modeling clay that is molded and reshaped by the forces of life and learning. Zull cites recent research studies in which scientists have used magnetic resonating imaging (MRI) equipment to literally watch the brain function as people learn new information and skills. The research shows that learning leads to greater capacity for learning. The discovery that as we learn the brain actually grows further confirms what John Dewey (1938) believed about learning as a continual spiral. Learning equips the brain to make new connections, see new problems, or see old problems differently, and then to move on to new learning.

So what motivates learning? Many think that emotions and the brain chemicals they produce actually motivate brain activity (Brembs, Lorenzetti, Reys, Baxter, & Byrnes,

2002). Learning should feel good and be rewarding so that the emotion-generated chemicals and the neuron networks involved in learning work in harmony, enhancing the learning process (Zull, 2004).

The quest to uncover more about how we learn and related brain functioning holds great promise. This research will flourish during your teaching career. As brain-based learning research continues, it will no doubt increasingly influence how we determine curriculum and instructional strategies.

What Curriculum Do We Teach in U.S. Schools?

Curriculum has been defined in many ways. Some view it as solely the content of courses. For our purposes, let's adopt a comprehensive viewpoint that curriculum encompasses all that students experience in school. It's important to understand curriculum from both historical and philosophical perspectives. We'll address these aspects in Chapters 8 and 9.

Four kinds of curricula contribute to the experiences of students in schools. The **formal curriculum** encompasses what is intentionally taught, what are stated as the goals of student learning. The **informal curriculum** is what students learn that isn't written in a lesson plan or necessarily intentionally transmitted to students. The **extracurriculum** includes the organized experiences students have that are beyond the formal curriculum, and the **null curriculum** is what is not taught. These four kinds of curricula are illustrated in Figure 4.1.

We'll spend the most time discussing the formal curriculum, but all four play important roles in shaping the learning process. Keep informal curriculum, extracurriculum, and null curriculum in mind as you read about the formal curriculum and the standards and subject areas that give it shape.

Formal Curriculum

The formal curriculum, sometimes referred to as the explicit curriculum, is what teachers are expected to teach, what students are expected to learn, and what society expects of schools. The formal curriculum is based very explicitly on three foundations: the needs of the subject, the needs of students, and the needs of society (Gunter, Estes, & Mintz, 2007). These three needs were reiterated by John Dewey in two of his most

Figure 4.1 Four kinds of curricula

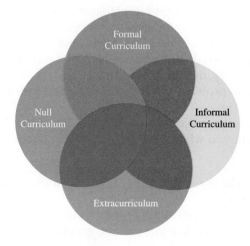

One of the major factors to consider when determining curriculum is the needs of the students.

important books, *School and Society* (1900) and *The Child and the Curriculum* (1902). The titles speak volumes, as does the text, about the interconnectedness of society, students, and the subject matter itself. Dewey (1938) also emphasized that formal curriculum is dynamic, meaning that it is continually changing and evolving.

As we consider the formal curriculum, we acknowledge the guiding contributions of Ralph Tyler (1949), one of Dewey's students (more on both Tyler and Dewey in Chapter 8). Tyler developed what is now called the **Tyler Rationale,** laying out four questions that should be asked throughout the stages of curriculum development:

1. What educational purposes should the school seek to attain?
2. What educational experiences can be provided that are likely to attain these purposes?
3. How can these educational experiences be effectively organized?
4. How can we determine whether these purposes are being attained?

For the twentieth century until about 1990, broad guidelines for what to teach were developed primarily by state planning committees and were based largely on textbook content, federal educational goals, and a "this is the way it's always been" attitude. Individual schools and teachers refined the state or school district guidelines to suit their particular circumstances. However, in 1989 curriculum development moved abruptly into what might be called the *era of standards* when the National Council of Teachers of Mathematics (NCTM) published math standards for grades K–12, the first official set of standards written for a core subject area (NCTM, 2000).

Standards. Very simply put, **standards** define what students should know and be able to do at specific grade levels. Following NCTM's initiative, the professional organizations of the other core subject areas developed standards. Each professional organization is quick to say that its standards are not the curriculum, but should be used for the development of a cohesive curriculum. State departments of education have used the professional organization standards to create standards documents upon which the statewide curriculum is based.

Any discussion of standards encompasses terminology teachers should understand. **Content standards** refer to the specific knowledge students should have and skills they should be able to perform. **Performance standards** or **benchmarks** designate the level of the knowledge or skill that's considered acceptable at a particular grade level. Some standards documents include **process standards** that support content learning by explaining both how the content might best be learned and how to use the content once it is acquired. For example, the five broad areas of NCTM content standards—number and operations, algebra, geometry, measurement, data analysis/probability—are accompanied by five process standards—problem solving, reasoning and proof, communication, connections, and representation.

While grade-level-specific, subject-based standards have brought unprecedented organization to what is taught and when, they are not perfect documents. Their most noted flaws include

- excessive coverage—the sheer volume of standards in any content area may be overwhelmingly impractical
- fragmentation of learning—isolated bits and pieces of knowledge and skills may not be connected and, therefore, lose context and meaning

- details that obscure major ideas—too many details may keep students and teachers from "seeing the forest for the trees"
- broad concepts that are too nebulous—standards written in broad generalities can be open to many interpretations
- a more regimented way of doing school—many experienced teachers find adherence to sets of standards inhibiting when compared to a curriculum that gives more choices.

On the positive side, standards give teachers information about what students should have learned in the past and will learn in the future. Using grade-level-specific standards for planning lessons helps teachers fit their expectations into the bigger picture of student learning over time. Along with standards, another major factor impacts what is taught on a daily basis—the textbook.

Textbooks. One of the most influential determiners of what we teach is the textbook. However, now that adherence to standards in the content areas is mandated by states, textbooks have lost a little of their power to shape curriculum.

Textbooks and their accompanying materials often provide lesson plans, teacher resources, online assistance, workbooks, and tests. We should be aware that textbooks may also pose the following problems:

- Textbook content may not match standards.
- Textbooks may include too many topics, and few in adequate depth.
- There may be readability issues (attempting to be readable for a range of abilities) that may result in dumbing down of content, language, sentence structure, and so on.
- Textbook authors may avoid interesting but controversial topics to please constituent groups.
- Textbooks may lack content or be of poor quality, problems perhaps masked by an attractive presentation.
- Textbooks may exhibit bias related to conservative or liberal ideology, culture, race, gender, and the like, either overtly or by omission.

On the positive side, quality textbooks help organize and sequence course content. Supplementary materials provided with many textbooks provide options for enrichment, remediation, extension, application, and practice of skills. These options allow teachers to more easily tailor content to student needs and readiness.

You probably will not have much choice when it comes to textbooks available for your use. Be conscious of both their value and their limitations, knowing that textbooks have a significant impact on what we teach and what students learn in the subject areas of the formal curriculum.

Subjects of the formal curriculum. Now that we know more about the formal curriculum of schools and the influence of standards and textbooks, we are ready to consider the subjects taught in pre-K–12 classrooms. We generally consider English language arts, math, science, and social studies as the core subject areas. In early childhood and elementary settings classes outside the core curriculum are built into the day. Most middle and high schools require students to take a specific number of courses that are not part of the core. These courses, known as **related arts**, **exploratory**, or **encore courses**, are valuable components of the curriculum that both complement the core and enhance the formal curriculum. Encore subjects include physical education, technology, world languages, music, home arts, theater, and more.

Before reading further, think about your own experiences with English language arts, math, science, social studies, and encore courses. Which appealed to you most? Did its appeal depend on the particular topic, course, or grade level, or perhaps on the teacher's level of enthusiasm and teaching strategies? Remember that when you see a fingerprint in the margin it means that you will be asked to respond to questions

Your Teaching Fingerprint

based on your experiences and opinions. These questions are included in "Writing My Own Story" in Chapter 4 of the Homework and Exercises section of MyEducationLab at www.myeducationlab.com.

English Language Arts. The National Council of Teachers of English (NCTE) and the International Reading Association (IRA) tell us that language development includes reading, writing, speaking, listening, viewing, and study of media. In early childhood, elementary, and middle school, much of the English language arts (ELA) curriculum focuses on skills, including reading, grammar, spelling, mechanics of punctuation and capitalization, editing, and basic research. Reading consists mainly of fiction (short stories and simple books) through fourth grade. In middle school, the focus begins to shift toward a variety of literary forms and writing. High school ELA is primarily literature based.

Communication skills such as oral presentation and persuasive speech have figured more prominently in ELA classes in recent years. The importance of listening is emphasized, as are writing skills.

Mathematics. According to the National Council of Teachers of Mathematics (NCTM, 2000), the need to understand and use math in everyday life has never been greater. From making purchasing decisions to interpreting tables and graphs, math is a vital part of the present, and will be increasingly important in a more complex future. Children in early childhood settings are now exposed to concepts of geometry and data analysis. Elementary and middle school students are asked to write about problem-solving strategies involving scenarios with multiple variables. An increasing number of high school students are taking advantage of advanced placement math courses for college credit.

By viewing math as something students do and connect to real life, NCTM standards ushered in a shift in math education from memorizing procedures to understanding concepts, and from emphasizing isolated mechanical ways of finding solutions to problem solving (NCTM, 2000).

Science. The vision of the National Science Teachers Association (NSTA) is for all students to regularly experience scientific inquiry while bringing together students' many experiences in pre-K–12 science around unifying themes. To do this, teachers emphasize that science is a process involving observation, inference, and experimentation. This is a major shift from content-specific facts to understanding concepts through process and inquiry. Using these skills to explore the content of physical, life, earth, and space sciences will lead students to genuine inquiry. In early childhood and elementary school, NSTA tells us that the meaning and use of unifying concepts and processes such as order, organization, models, change, and function should be emphasized. For instance, young children will learn what it means to measure and how to use measurement tools. In middle and high school, they examine how and why measurement is important in every aspect of science (NSTA, 2005).

Social Studies. The National Council for the Social Studies (NCSS) tells us that the "primary purpose of social studies is to help young people develop the ability to make informed and reasoned decisions for the public good as citizens of a culturally and demographically diverse society in an interdependent world" (NCSS, 2005, p. 1). This is a definite shift from the way social studies was approached for much of the last century. Prior to the influence of NCSS and the curricular changes prompted by standards, social studies was dominated by names and dates to be memorized, with little or no application of concepts to local, national, or international dilemmas.

The NCSS standards are based on 10 themes that are addressed in all school levels but are approached differently based on grade level. For instance, for standard one, culture, students in early childhood and elementary settings may explore food, clothing, and shelter in places that may represent the ethnicities of students in a class. In middle grades a unit on the culture of a country may involve examining the lifestyles of the people and the environment and completing comparative writing exercises. A high school social studies class may address culture through a unit on prayer in schools in which students consider different faiths, examine relevant case studies, argue opposing views, freely voice opinions, and develop supporting rationales (NCSS, 2005).

Technology. The International Society for Technology in Education (ISTE) is a professional organization whose mission is to provide "leadership and service to improve teaching and learning by advancing the effective use of technology in education" (ISTE, 2005). The standards for technology are organized into categories such as basic operations, communication tools, and ethical issues. Almost all schools have computer labs used for classes in information literacy, a broad phrase associated with technology education. In these labs, designated technology teachers teach whole classes of students at a time. We'll explore technology use in schools in Chapter 6.

Foreign Language. The statement of philosophy of the American Council for the Teaching of Foreign Language (ACTFL) tells us that "the United States must educate students who are linguistically and culturally equipped to communicate successfully in a pluralistic American society and abroad" (ACTFL, 2005). To accomplish this mission, high schools and most middle schools offer courses in a variety of world languages, most commonly Spanish and French. Because of the recognition that young children acquire a second language more readily than do young adults, many early childhood and elementary schools offer opportunities to learn a second language.

The Standards for Foreign Language Learning are organized according to five goals that ACTFL calls the "Five C's of Foreign Language Education": communication, cultures, connections, comparisons, and communities (ACTFL, 2005, p. 2).

Physical Education and Health. Leaders of physical education (PE) and health education strongly advocate for more time spent on physical activity and health education. Supporting standards are provided by the National Association for Sport and Physical Education (NASPE) and the American Association for Health Education (AAHE).

In early childhood and elementary schools PE may be unorganized play time, often the responsibility of the classroom teacher, or there may be a designated physical education teacher who conducts whole class sessions two or three times a week. In middle school PE and health are likely to be rotated courses, perhaps covering 9 weeks each year, with health taught by the PE or science teacher. In high school, students are usually required to take only one or two courses in PE and even fewer in health. Given the health risk factors associated with adolescence in society today, implementation of the AAHE standards is especially important for teenagers. In Chapter 10 we'll explore how societal health issues add urgency to the uniform implementation of health and PE standards.

Arts. The National Standards for Arts Education define what students should know and be able to do in the four arts disciplines—music, dance, theater, and the visual arts. Essentially, the standards state that by the end of high school students should be able to communicate at a basic level in the four disciplines and be proficient in at least one art form. The availability of art experiences in music, dance, theater, and visual arts in pre-K–12 schools varies tremendously. In early childhood and elementary schools, the classroom teacher may be responsible for the art curriculum, or the school may have an art specialist. In middle and high school, students usually have a variety of arts classes from which to choose and perhaps a limited number of arts activities.

It is an unfortunate fact that when the budget is tight in many schools and districts, the arts are the first to go. After all, standardized tests don't even mention forms of dance, genres of paintings, composers and their works, or elements of drama. But even while whole programs may be in jeopardy or even canceled, there are ways for classroom teachers to make the arts part of their curriculum. Later in this section we'll look at methods of infusing the arts into other curricular areas.

Career and Tech-Prep Courses. Career and tech-prep cover a broad category of courses usually offered in high school. Some courses are of general interest, such as basic industrial or home arts classes, while some are specific-career-oriented, such as auto mechanics and cosmetology. The federal government supports a program called **School-to-Work**, initiated to bring real-world, work-related skills and understanding to students through courses that introduce them to career possibilities.

Before turning from this overview of formal curricular subject areas to a discussion of the remaining types of curricula that are part of any school's learning process, let's turn briefly to three aspects of the formal curriculum that cross subject area boundaries, illustrated in Figure 4.2: integrated curriculum, multicultural curriculum, and arts-infused curriculum.

Integrated curriculum. When teachers include content and skills from a variety of subjects in lessons, they are utilizing what may be termed an **integrated curriculum.** An integrated curriculum basically involves making connections among subject areas through the use of a unifying topic or theme. Early childhood and elementary teachers do it all the time. They often begin the school day with discussions about the weather of the day (science), time and money (math), and events that may have happened in the past on the specific day (history) and conclude with a story read together by the class (English language arts).

In middle school, teams of teachers may plan whole days, or even weeks, around a theme that brings together research of real-world events and phenomena. Curriculum integration is least common in high school, where teachers are usually organized by departments. This in no way, however, prevents an English (ELA) teacher from teaching about literature through short stories, poems, and novels that reflect a topic covered in the social studies curriculum for the grade level. For instance, if U.S. History is a course taken by most sophomores, the ELA teachers could use period literature that coincides with the progressive history of the United States as taught by the History Department. Likewise, teachers of every subject at every level have opportunities to emphasize multicultural aspects of the curriculum.

Figure 4.2 Crossing subject area boundaries

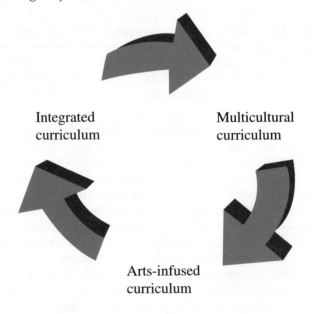

Integrated
curriculum

Multicultural
curriculum

Arts-infused
curriculum

Multicultural curriculum. As diversity in U.S. schools increases, the importance of and demand for a multicultural perspective grows. A **multicultural curriculum** is one that purposefully includes contributions and viewpoints from the perspectives of different cultures, ethnicities, races, genders, and socioeconomic levels. At its best, a multicultural curriculum is accurate, timely, and sensitive, while avoiding tokenism and a sense of forced inclusion (Banks, 2003).

Methods for infusing your classroom with a multicultural curriculum will depend on the grade level and subject area you teach. In early childhood and elementary settings, celebrating historical events and holidays of a variety of cultures helps create awareness of values and traditions within various cultures. In middle and high school settings, making a variety of perspectives part of your classroom discussions and topics, and asking students to research and report on issues of interest to them that include various perspectives, can help forge an understanding of people of different cultures. One of the most effective tools for including a variety of perspectives is through an emphasis on current events in addition to textbook content. For instance, in late 2006 the first elected president of Liberia took office. Ellen Johnson Sirleaf, a 67-year-old Harvard-educated African woman, has the unique perspective of being not only Liberia's first popularly elected president, but also a female president in a male-dominated government and society. Her presidency and her links to the United States can be followed through Internet sources and newspapers, providing students with a wealth of insight that can cross subject area lines.

One way of making learning more relevant and encouraging the celebration of diversity is the infusion of arts into the curriculum.

Arts-infused curriculum. Including arts in the curriculum requires awareness of opportunities, along with purposeful determination to include music, theater, dance, and the visual arts when possible. You don't need to be an artist or musician to display art or play music in the classroom. Encouraging students to create their own works of art to enhance a project takes exactly that—encouragement.

"The arts are the great equalizer in education. Regardless of native language, ability or disability, music, art, and drama are accessible to all" (Gregoire & Lupinetti, 2005). As an equalizer, the arts can provide both expression and success for students of diversity. Cornett (2003) supports eight reasons for integrating the arts into the curriculum. Of these, four can be applied directly to diverse classrooms.

- Arts provide a natural view into the contributions and perspectives of other cultures.
- Arts are primary means of communication.
- Arts provide opportunities for achievement that may not otherwise be available.
- Arts may focus on alternative ways to assess and evaluate.

Two of our focus schools have made major commitments to integrating the arts into their curricula. As discussed in Chapter 1 (see page 28), on the campus of Roosevelt High School (RHS), California, is Roosevelt School of the Arts (RSA), a magnet school with about 500 students. RSA provides access to some of the specialized performance, visual, and media arts classes for nonmagnet students at RHS. In addition, an array of arts is offered in the nonmagnet school through Folkloria, a program designed especially for Hispanic students. Mayra, one of our focus students at RHS, participates in the Folkloria arts opportunities.

Teachers at Rees Elementary, Utah, use state grant funds to provide arts experiences for their students. They bring in talented individuals for days and weeks at a time to be artists-in-residence. In Chapter 1 we met Chris, Brenda, and Tim, each of whom teaches a specialized art form to all three multiage classes of students on a daily basis (see page 24).

While it's hard to imagine objections to infusing arts into the curriculum, there are groups who oppose arts on the grounds that their inclusion detracts from the core subjects. Controversy and curriculum are never far apart.

Controversy and curriculum. The heart of school is what is taught and what is learned. In a society that values opposing views and encourages diversity, the curriculum is sure to be debated. The dynamic nature of debate is healthy, but it can also be frustrating at times for educators.

Religious beliefs, censorship, and philosophical differences all influence what's included in curricula. Societal circumstances and pressures we'll discuss in Chapter 10 may affect curricula as well. One particularly controversial curricular issue in public schools is the ongoing debate over the exclusive teaching of evolution to explain the origin of human beings. Intelligent design, proposed by some who practice Christianity and oppose the teaching of evolution, includes a belief that certain features of the universe and of living things are best explained by an intelligent cause, not by natural selection espoused by evolution. Some people argue for an evolution-only curriculum, while others argue for intelligent design only. Still others propose the teaching of both as theories, incurring the disapproval of many in the scientific community who maintain that evolution is factually based. This chapter's Letter to the Editor centers on this debate.

We've covered a lot of territory since the beginning of this section on formal curriculum. Now let's examine the other three kinds of curriculum in light of what we have learned about the formal curriculum in U.S. schools.

Informal Curriculum

The informal curriculum is what teachers and schools teach and what students learn that is not part of a lesson plan, a curriculum guide, or standards. It encompasses what is

Letter to the Editor

This letter to the editor appeared in the Dallas, Texas, newspaper, the *Dallas Morning News*. It was written by a man weighing in on the debate over what should be taught in science classes about the origin of human beings.

Now it's your turn. As you plan your own letter to the editor, these questions will help you think through the issues involved in the ongoing controversy surrounding some aspects of science education in public schools.

Letter to the Editor
Sept. 11, 2005

Let's teach science, and ID isn't science.

It is painfully obvious that the methods of scientific thought are not being taught in our schools. Recent statements by the ACT academic testing service indicate that only 26 percent of graduating seniors are academically prepared to study science at the college level. Our children are basically illiterate when it comes to science.

The debate about intelligent design and Darwin is not about science but about philosophy. Rigorous scientific thought deals with observable, testable ideas and does not depend on supernatural forces to explain the unknowns. Intelligent design does not constitute science and does not deserve to be part of the science curriculum. Our schools need to return to the task of preparing our children for the future by providing sound intellectual tools of reason and learning.

David Young
DeSoto

1. Do you have any information to refute Mr. Young's statement about students' science illiteracy? If so, what is it?

2. What impact might the inclusion of intelligent design in science have on the science literacy of students? Would the inclusion cause a further decline?

3. Do you agree that the debate is not about science but rather about philosophy? If so, why? If not, why not?

4. Who do you think should make the decision about what is included in public school science about the origin of human beings?

5. What are your personal beliefs and values on this topic? What is your comfort level about making your opinions public?

Your letter to the editor should be in response to the *Dallas Morning News* letter—supporting it, adding information, or refuting it. Write your letter in understandable terminology, remembering that readers of newspaper letters to the editor are citizens who may have limited knowledge of school practices and policies. Your letter may be written in your course notebook and shared with classmates as directed by your instructor. Remember to refer to the letter assessment rubric in Figure 1.10, page 20.

Renee Ayers at Summit Primary develops caring relationships with her students. Here she and Sherlonda share secrets in the positive environment Renee maintains for her students.

learned by students through attitudes, values, and various types of informal teaching situations, such as recess, encounters between students and teacher sponsors in school clubs and organizations, and on field trips when conversations are casual. This informal learning may be positive or negative and is sometimes unintentional.

Regardless of what students learn in terms of content and skills, they learn *us*. They watch us, listen to us, notice their surroundings; they learn more than we imagine. If we are positive, caring, excited about learning, fair, and organized, students learn that

- optimism is more productive than pessimism
- cooperation and empathy matter
- structure and enthusiasm enhance learning
- responsibility is personal and valuable

On the other hand, if we are negative, lack interest in students and subjects, and exhibit a general disdain for our work, students are likely to mirror these qualities. If our classrooms are a mess, if the school building is dilapidated, and if the community is unsupportive, students learn that they may not matter very much.

A middle school science teacher wrestling with the "What should I teach?" question decided to ask her former students what they remembered about her class and what they believed were the most important lessons. She developed a survey and received responses from students she taught in each of her 9 years of teaching. These responses included the following:

"The most important things I learned from you weren't in class, but during the Science Olympiad. . ."

"The [finest] things I learned from you have nothing to do with science."

"The most important thing I learned from you would have to be the ability to be nice to people even if you feel like screaming . . . . The way you acted toward our class and the compassion you showed to our class [taught me this]."

"Self-confidence and how important it is."

"How important science is to society."

"How you encouraged everyone to do their best."

Several students responded that the books she read aloud to them (in science class!) changed their opinions on diversity (Little, 2001, pp. 62–63).

As Catherine Little read the responses she was alarmed at first, thinking that subject matter should have been more prominent. But after reading these comments, is there any doubt students learned science in Ms. Little's class?

John Lounsbury (1991), a noted middle school educator and advocate for young adolescents, would call the responses to Ms. Little's survey the result of **"wayside teaching"** (p. 29). According to Lounsbury, wayside teaching is the teaching we do inside and outside the classroom through our attitudes, values, habits, interest, and classroom climate.

Think about how the informal curriculum affected you. Were there things teachers said to you and attitudes they displayed that spoke volumes to you as a learner? What informal lessons do you remember most from grades pre-K through 12?

Extracurriculum

Activities sponsored by the school but outside the limits of the formal curriculum are considered extracurricular. Although some elementary schools offer extracurricular activities, such as jump rope and craft clubs, most extracurricular opportunities begin in middle school and expand in high school.

Extracurricular activities provide opportunities for active involvement and higher-order and creative thinking for students and for sponsorship and coaching for teachers. Examples include

- Odyssey of the Mind, math and book clubs
- debate, chess, and photography clubs
- band and choral activities
- athletics of all kinds, including cheerleading
- school newspaper, student government, and honor society

Recently there has been renewed interest in the factors that contribute to **school connectedness,** or student bonding and engagement. Lack of school connectedness may lead to disruptive behavior, substance abuse, emotional distress, absenteeism, and dropping out. The importance of doing what it takes to foster connectedness is magnified when we consider that approximately one half of all high school students, whether urban, suburban, or rural, feel "chronically disengaged" from school (Klem & Connell, 2004, p. 262). A major factor that influences school connectedness is participation in extracurricular activities (Blum, 2005). Researchers have found that extracurricular activities "provide all students—including at-risk and gifted students—an academic safety net" (Holloway, 2000, p. 88).

The poster behind Mayra and Roosevelt assistant principal John Lael lists some of the extracurricular possibilities at RHS.

In what extracurricular activities did you participate? What did participation mean to you? In which activities did you want to be involved, but for some reason were not?

Null Curriculum

Now let's turn our attention to what Elliot Eisner (2002) calls the null curriculum. The null curriculum is what *isn't* taught—those concepts and skills thought to be too controversial, too expensive, not important enough, or that simply haven't been considered. Topics considered controversial include almost anything dealing with religion, abortion, homosexuality, and so on. Eisner (2002) tells us that the way certain subjects are taught is simply based on tradition. "We teach what we teach largely out of habit" (p. 103).

The null curriculum may not be as important as the formal curriculum, the informal curriculum, and the extracurriculum, but it is certainly worth thinking about. What's *not* part of the school curriculum may never be considered by students and therefore may have little to do with their futures. Herein lies the danger, discussed earlier, of neglecting a multicultural curriculum. Failing to acknowledge and celebrate differences may contribute to prejudice and exclusionary attitudes in students. Wolk (2007) tells us that the following are often part of the null curriculum and that students and society as a whole would benefit from their inclusion and emphasis: knowledge of self; love of learning; caring and empathy; environmental literacy; social responsibility; global awareness; and money, family, food, and happiness. Did you gain insight in these areas when you were in pre-K–12 school? If so, through what part of the curriculum?

Next we will look at *how* we teach the curriculum— the concepts and strategies of instruction.

Organizations like Junior Reserve Officer Training Corps (JROTC) play a big part in connecting students to schools.

■ How Is Instruction Implemented in U.S. Schools?

Just as curriculum is the "what" of teaching, instruction is the "how." Chapter 3 addressed students' similarities and differences. It's evident that with differing student intelligences, learning styles, and abilities, a variety of instructional strategies is necessary to meet students' needs. Therefore, building a repertoire of instructional strategies is vital. No need to worry—instructional possibilities are practically limitless. Think of knowing and being able to use strategies as filling a figurative instructional toolbox, as illustrated in Figure 4.3.

Having a wide array of instructional strategies in our toolboxes is necessary, but not sufficient. We must also have a thorough grasp of the curriculum and its content, as discussed in the previous sections. **Pedagogy** refers to the combining of curriculum and instruction to foster learning. The role of decision maker, presented as one of the roles of teaching in Chapter 1 (see page 12), is nowhere more crucial than in planning which strategies to use with what curriculum to create an effective pedagogy.

Your Teaching Fingerprint

For clarity, let's summarize what lies ahead as we discuss the importance and use of instructional strategies:

- We'll begin by looking at big ideas of instruction.
- We'll then identify nine categories of instruction that have proven to be effective.
- Finally, we'll examine 12 individual instructional strategies.

Big Ideas of Instruction

Each of the big ideas of instruction shown in Figure 4.4 deserves, and indeed has had, entire books written about it. As you read about them, keep balance in mind. The more big

Figure 4.3　Instructional toolbox

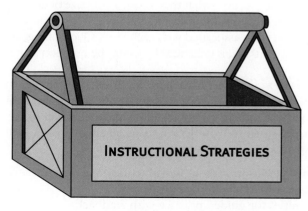

INSTRUCTIONAL STRATEGIES

Figure 4.4 Big ideas of instruction

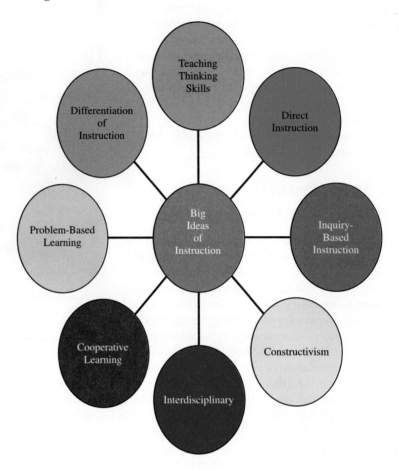

ideas and individual strategies we know how to implement, the better able we are to take a balanced approach in our classrooms to reach students, each with their own unique ways of learning.

Big idea 1: Teaching thinking skills. We think all the time, so what's there to teach? The answer is—*plenty!* Benjamin Bloom first published his taxonomy of thinking in 1956, and it has become a way of organizing and planning for learning experiences for millions of teachers. Simply put, **thinking skills** are those skills that aid in processing information. They grow in complexity and sophistication as we go from level I to level VI of Bloom's taxonomy. All the levels, as illustrated in Table 4.1, are necessary, and none should be neglected. Designing learning experiences that call only for knowledge and comprehension is cheating the minds of students who need to apply and analyze what they know, synthesize or create something new, and evaluate ideas and events. When planning lessons and assessments, teachers should use Bloom's taxonomy and the action verbs associated with each level. Questioning, as an important strategy to promote student thinking, is enhanced by using the question stems in Table 4.1.

Big idea 2: Direct instruction. A widely used big idea of instruction is commonly called **direct instruction.** A lesson that includes a distinct opening, presentation of information, practice, and teacher feedback or review is following the model of direct instruction. In later courses when you learn to write lesson plans, chances are you will use a format that supports direct instruction. The steps include

1. getting students' attention with an introduction
2. presenting new knowledge and/or skills
3. giving opportunities for guided practice with feedback

Table 4.1   Bloom's taxonomy

Level	Explanation	Key Words	Question Stems
I. Knowledge	Recall basic facts/concepts	Name, tell, list, define, match, find	When did _____? Who was _____? Where is _____? Why did _____? Can you list four _____?
II. Comprehension	Demonstrate understanding	Compare, contrast, explain, summarize, classify	How would you compare _____ to _____? What is the main idea of _____? What is meant by _____?
III. Application	Apply knowledge to solve problems	Use, plan, model, solve, build	How would you use _____ to _____? What is the main idea of _____? What is meant by _____?
IV. Analysis	Examine critically to support/make inferences	Categorize, find relationships, conclude	What evidence can you find to conclude that _____? What does _____ have to do with _____?
V. Synthesis	Combine or rearrange to develop alternatives	Adapt, formulate, invent, create, modify, improve	How would you change _____ to form _____? Can you propose a different way to _____? How would you design _____ to _____?
VI. Evaluation	Make judgments, defend, validate	Debate, decide, conclude, prove, recommend	What is your opinion of _____? How valuable is _____ for _____? Why would you recommend _____?

Source: From *Introduction to Middle School* (p. 191), by S. D. Powell, 2005, Upper Saddle River, NJ: Merrill/Prentice Hall. Copyright 2005 by Pearson Education, Inc.

4. assigning opportunities for application (perhaps homework)
5. providing additional feedback/reteaching/review
6. assessing progress

As we look at other big ideas of instruction and at a variety of instructional strategies, think about how each might fit within the direct instruction framework. The word *direct* does not mean that the teacher is always center stage and the students are only receptacles of information. The way new knowledge and skills are presented (step 2) can vary as widely as the range of possible strategies themselves. Engaging introductions, opportunities for practice, ongoing feedback, and assessments of progress are all vital elements of instruction.

Big idea 3: Inquiry-based instruction. When students pursue answers to questions posed by others or developed on their own, they are involved in **inquiry learning.** Observation, questioning, hypothesizing, and predicting are all part of inquiry-based learning, which requires students to move beyond rote memorization to become independent thinkers and problem solvers.

Inquiry-based instruction is not new. All discoveries have come about as the result of questions and answer

The teachers on the opening page of the chapter work together as a team. Here they are taking advantage of young adolescents' imaginations when planning for active student engagement in learning.

seeking. Before students can search for answers or formulate questions on their own, they need knowledge and skills as building blocks. Once these building blocks are in place, then students are ready to inquire and look for answers. Inquiry-based instruction is an effective way of teaching and learning because the ideas we create ourselves are the ones we tend to retain (Renzulli, Gentry, & Reis, 2004).

Big idea 4: Constructivism. **Constructivism** is "an inquiry learning approach that takes advantage of students' own experiences to develop problems that will engage students in active learning" (Lemlech, 2004, p. 56). Piaget and Vygotsky, both discussed in Chapter 3 (see pages 70–71), would be supporters of inquiry-based constructivist teaching. Piaget (1970) advocated discovery learning, with students literally manipulating objects and figuratively manipulating subject matter to discover relationships and construct meaning. Vygotsky's (1978) theory that learning is a social process supports the interactive classroom. Vygotsky's scaffolding and zone of proximal development fit perfectly into the practice of students working their way through concepts with the help of teacher questions and cues.

A constructivist approach to learning considers students' prior learning, involves them in exploration of a concept, and encourages Bloom's higher levels of thinking. Because it's more time-consuming, constructivist teaching and learning should be saved for complex learning, such as proving a scientific or mathematical theory, interpretation of a piece of literature, or analysis of an historical event.

Big idea 5: Interdisciplinary instruction. Any time we make explicit links between subject areas or even between concepts within the same subject, we help students learn more deeply and meaningfully. The term **interdisciplinary** is often used to describe curricular links or connections between subjects.

In early childhood and elementary settings, interdisciplinary instruction is not only possible, but preferable. It often happens naturally because one teacher is responsible for most subjects and a distinct group of students. In middle school, when teachers and students are in teams, interdisciplinary instruction is relatively easy to implement because students are shared and there is time for team planning. As noted in the discussion of integrated curriculum, high school teachers have the most difficulty utilizing all forms of interdisciplinary instruction.

 Your Teaching Fingerprint   What do you recall about your teachers' efforts to connect subject areas when you were in elementary school? How about middle school or high school?

Big idea 6: Cooperative learning. Loosely defined, **cooperative learning** refers to any instance of students working together. It was more strictly defined in the 1980s when Roger and David Johnson designed the following grouping patterns:

- informal groups that meet together for a variety of tasks as needed
- formal groups that complete designated, often long-term, tasks
- base groups whose members support one another with remembering and completing assignments, studying, and sharing resources (Johnson & Johnson, 1999)

Student roles within groups include facilitator, recorder, materials gatherer, timekeeper, and encourager.

Your Teaching Fingerprint   Cooperative learning is a big idea of instruction that can be successfully implemented in early childhood, elementary, middle, and high school settings. It's likely that you have been a member of many cooperative groups during your school experiences. Think about the experiences that were productive and pleasant, as well as those that either failed or were not enjoyable. What made them successful? What contributed to problems with group functioning?

Big idea 7: Problem-based learning. Focusing student attention and effort on a real-life problem that has more than one solution path or product is called **problem-based learning (PBL).** The best PBL experiences involve real-life problems that are relatively complex and require time to solve. The problems should be broad enough to require knowledge and skills in at least three distinct subject areas and should be sufficiently difficult so that students see the need for working together.

Problem-based learning requires intense planning to engage students and facilitate their work through the stages of the cycle. Because individuals and small groups are going in different directions as they gather information and resources, create products, and develop performances, traditional classroom structure rarely exists for the duration of the PBL experience. Teachers need to set high expectations for behavior and use of time as well as practice a personal tolerance for productive chaos.

Big idea 8: Differentiation of instruction. Teachers should vary their instruction based on the needs of students. In 1999 Carol Ann Tomlinson gave this philosophy and practice a name—**differentiation of instruction.** Tomlinson tells us that teachers who differentiate instruction strive to do whatever it takes to diagnose student strengths and weaknesses in terms of readiness, interests, and learning profiles and then differentiate content, process, and product when possible. The *content* is what the students should know, understand, and be able to do. *Process* consists of the ways students make sense of content, typically through activities and practice. A *product* shows what students know and are able to do; it may be, for example, a project, demonstration, test, or display.

Figure 4.5 describes what teachers do in differentiated classrooms. It is clear that differentiated instruction values individuality and requires teachers to use a variety of instructional strategies. Next we will look at categories of instructional strategies that have been shown through research to be effective.

Nine Categories of Effective Instructional Practices

Researchers at Mid-continent Research for Education and Learning (McREL) conducted a **meta-analysis** (a research technique involving the analysis of multiple studies) to determine the most effective instructional strategies that lead to increased learning and retention. From this meta-analysis, concluded in 2001, came the nine categories of effective strategies in Table 4.2. Some of these categories of strategies, such as note taking and homework, are traditional and commonly used, whereas others, such as generating and testing hypotheses, are implemented less frequently. The nine categories of strategies are often intertwined (Marzano, Pickering, & Pollock, 2001). For example, one lesson may involve *identifying similarities and differences* using *nonlinguistic representations* (charts and tables) in a *cooperative group* (several students working together). In order to complete the lesson, students may review their *notes* for *homework*. It's important to know that the McREL researchers have confirmed that all these instructional techniques are effective. As you read about 12 individual strategies, think about how they fit into these nine important categories.

Figure 4.5   Differentiation of instruction

When teachers differentiate instruction they . . .

- begin where students are
- accept and build upon the premise that learners differ
- engage students through different learning modalities
- ensure that a student competes against himself more than he competes against other students
- believe that students should be held to high standards
- ensure that each student realizes that success is likely to follow hard work
- use time flexibly
- are diagnosticians who prescribe the best instruction for their students

Source: From *The Differentiated Classroom: Responding to the Needs of All Learners* by C. A. Tomlinson, 1999, Alexandria, VA: Association for Supervision and Curriculum Development.

Table 4.2 Categories of proven instructional strategies that positively affect student achievement

	Category of Instruction	Impact on Learning
1	Identifying similarities and differences	Identifying concepts/characteristics and then comparing/contrasting them
2	Summarizing and note taking	Study skills of recognizing and recording important knowledge
3	Reinforcing effort and providing recognition	Helping students understand the value of effort and its relationship to success
4	Homework and practice	Opportunities for practicing new and developing skills
5	Nonlinguistic representations	Using visual/graphic organizers to understand relationships
6	Cooperative learning	Grouping that requires each person to contribute to learning and activities
7	Setting objectives and providing feedback	Establishing intended learning, recognizing student progress
8	Generating and testing hypotheses	Understanding a principle, making a conjecture, and applying the knowledge to see if it holds true
9	Cues, questions, and advance organizers	Activating prior knowledge, setting the stage for new knowledge

Source: From *Classroom Instruction That Works* (p. 7), by R. J. Marzano, D. J. Pickering, and J. R. Pollock, 2001, Alexandria, VA: Association for Supervision and Curriculum Development. Adapted with permission.

Instructional Strategies

The big ideas of instruction and the research-based categories of instruction form a framework within which we can place the strategies we use in our classrooms, as illustrated in Figure 4.6. What follows are descriptions of 12 strategies you can begin to put in your instructional toolbox. Right now, they go into your toolbox at the awareness level. As you work with students in field experiences, you will have opportunities to practice them and make them your own.

Lecture. Lecture can be an efficient way to verbally convey knowledge to students using their auditory modality (Chapter 3, see page 92). A well-planned minilecture (10–20 minutes) can be a valuable teaching tool to introduce a topic, describe a situation or problem, or concisely deliver information.

Class discussion. When focused, with lots of participation, a class discussion becomes a conversation that goes beyond teacher questions and student responses. Students should do far more talking than the teacher.

Demonstration. Many concepts are better seen than heard or, better yet, seen *and* heard. Teacher or student demonstration can show steps in a procedure, illustrate what students will later do themselves, and make a concept come alive visually. A demonstration may be

Figure 4.6 Framework for instructional strategies

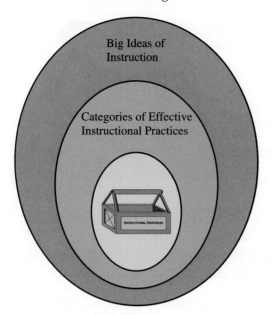

as simple as showing how to solve a math problem by writing on a chalkboard, or as complex as the setup and implementation of a complicated science experiment.

Teacher think-aloud. Making thinking and reasoning audible is a modeling strategy called **teacher think-aloud** that can be used in all subjects and at all grade levels. Teachers talk through how to approach a problem, make sense of new information, use self-restraint in volatile situations, consider options, discard what doesn't work, and begin to refine what makes sense. Students learn through teacher modeling.

Questioning. Effective questioning requires in-depth content knowledge and planning. Asking convergent questions, those that usually have one best answer, allows students to use Bloom's first two levels of thinking—knowledge and comprehension. Divergent questions, those that are more open-ended, allow for many answers and prompt analysis, application, synthesis, and evaluation. Learning to frame questions that are understandable and probing is important for teachers.

Brainstorming. The purpose of brainstorming is to generate as many ideas as possible without judgment on their merit. It's a good way to see what a class knows about a topic (prior knowledge), to find out what students may find most interesting about an upcoming unit, or to start ideas flowing for a writing project. Brainstorming gets students involved and stimulates creative thinking.

Note taking. Simply telling students to take notes may have little value. The supportive skills involving listening, recognizing key words and important points, developing a sense of organization, and efficient methods of summarizing what needs to be written must first be explained and practiced. Note taking skills have lifelong benefits.

Drill and practice. Once students have had at least moderate success with a skill, exercising that skill is appropriate. Drill and practice aid in long-term retention and help students increase accuracy and develop speed.

Graphic organizers. As visual tools, graphic organizers help categorize, sequence, and prioritize concepts and information; show cause-and-effect relationships; and illustrate the similarities and differences of objects and ideas. They may be applied in many ways to

Figure 4.7   Twelve instructional strategies

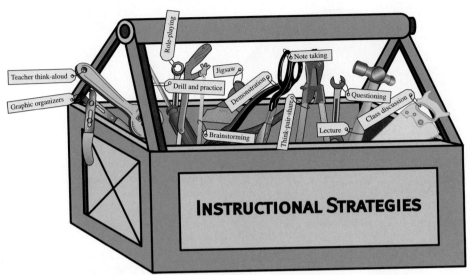

Role play can be an effective method of helping students understand and apply concepts.

promote reasoning and critical thinking. Graphic organizers are also referred to as concept maps, thinking maps, and nonlinguistic representations.

Role-playing. Getting students up and moving as they dramatize a scenario can make a point or prompt students to think in divergent ways. As with class discussion, role-playing becomes more effective with practice.

Think-pair-share. This instructional strategy is both versatile and easy to implement. Once students have been exposed to information, given a prompt, asked a question, or had an experience, the teacher asks them to think about it in a particular way and perhaps record their thoughts on paper. They then share their thoughts with another student. T-P-S involves all students in nonthreatening ways.

Jigsaw. This strategy involves students becoming experts on particular topics within *expert groups* and then teaching those topics to the other students in their *base groups.* Jigsaw is a powerful tool that actively involves students in their own, and one another's, learning.

Now you have 12 strategies to put in your instructional toolbox, as illustrated in Figure 4.7. Which of the strategies do you remember experiencing? Which ones had positive effects on your learning?

In this chapter's Teachers' Days, Delights, and Dilemmas, a teacher tells us about her own learning experience. She talks about finding ways to draw in even the most reluctant students.

■ Are We All Teachers of Reading and Writing?

Reading and writing are vital skills, without which life is difficult and limited in many ways. Regardless of the subject or grade level taught, all teachers need to be teachers of reading and writing.

Reading

An old adage says that children learn to read through third grade and read to learn from then on. National and state education goals reflect the philosophy that every child should

Teachers' Days, Delights, and Dilemmas

Kathy S. Rank
2005 Ohio
Teacher of the Year

Several years ago, some friends and I were out to dinner and we noticed a family conversing at the next table. The family was made up of mom, dad, and two children about the ages of the fourth graders I teach. What caught my attention was the amount of conversation between the children and the parents and, more importantly, the number of questions the children continued to ask and the parents' responses. It suddenly dawned on me that these interactions were most likely missing from some of my students' lives. For the most part, my students do not ask questions or seem to wonder about the world around them. I vowed that when school started in the fall, my new mission would be to get kids to ask questions and to think about what they were doing. As a result, not only did I set up situations to arouse curiosity but I also began to answer questions with other questions, such as, "Gee, I don't know, what do you think?" This questioning strategy went on for several weeks. One day the students were working on a project with partners and I overheard a girl in my room tell another girl that she was going to ask the teacher a question. I had to laugh when I heard this bright young student say, "Don't bother. Mrs. Rank doesn't know anything. Every time I ask her a question, she just says, 'I don't know, what do you think?'"

Kids need someone to listen to them, someone to hear them and validate their thinking. This is critically important, especially in low socioeconomic schools where verbal interactions between children and adults can be minimal. It is difficult for teachers to find enough time in the school day to carry on extended conversations with each student. But communication is essential if students are to learn to wonder and to extend their thinking. It's how we connect with them and encourage connections with the world around them.

Sometimes there are barriers to communicating and connecting with students that seem almost insurmountable. During summer school last year, a young man named Tyrell entered my fifth-grade classroom. He was a walking caricature of a gang member—the pants slung low on the hips, the look, the attitude. He was determined not to learn. Because it was summer school, our director promised us that any student who disrupted class or who didn't want to learn could be sent home. After several disruptions by this student, I moved him to the back of the room so I could continue to teach. I thought that just maybe if I ignored his attempts to be disruptive, he might become interested. I started reading aloud *My Side of the Mountain,* a story of survival and adventure in the Catskill Mountains. Sam, the main character, runs away from home to live in the mountains and reclaim the family land. Tyrell was captivated by this story. As I read, he slowly inched his way to the front of the room. Soon he had moved right up front to join us on the floor. He was also an outdoor kid and knew much about the wilderness and could identify with Sam in the story. From that moment on, I didn't have one more problem with this student. He began to think, ask questions, and learn. How I would have failed him had I sent him home. It is so important to find a way to connect with every student we teach.

Every child can learn—maybe not on the same day or in the same way, but they can learn. This is such an important concept for teachers to keep in mind.

be a reader by third grade. Emphasis is placed on emergent literacy (getting ready to read) and beginning reading (letter/word recognition, story patterns) in pre-K through third grade. Teachers in the early grades expect to be teachers of reading, and often their efforts are supported by reading specialists whose sole responsibility is teaching children to read.

If students don't receive specific literacy instruction beyond third grade, two assumptions in the "read to learn" phase are sure to hinder them. The first assumption is that if a student is a reader in third grade, he or she will continue to be a reader. The second assumption is that if a student reads third-grade material, that student will continue to read grade-appropriate material in subsequent grades. Neither assumption is true.

In middle and high school there is a devastating lack of reading proficiency. "You can't learn much from books you can't read," a young man said to Richard Allington (2002b), noted expert in the field of literacy. That statement became the title of an article Allington wrote to expose the problems of older struggling readers. More than half of the ninth graders in the 35 largest cities in the United States read at the sixth-grade level or below (Vacca, 2002). The average student in a high school classroom is reading below the level of content-area texts (Allington, 2002a), and 25% of adults are functionally illiterate (Moats, 2001).

Reading areas should be inviting for young children.

The prospect of having reading specialists in all middle and high schools is unlikely. Therefore, all of us need to

- first, become convinced that reading is essential in all content areas and at all grade levels
- second, accept the responsibility of promoting literacy throughout grades pre-K–12

Teachers can employ a variety of skill builders to promote student literacy, from decoding letters and words to comprehending the meaning and inference of what is read. Infusing the curriculum with reading and writing is often referred to as reading and writing across the curriculum. Remembering that all teachers are teachers of reading, what can we do to encourage reading regardless of the level or subject we teach? Here are some ideas to keep in mind.

- Give students access to student-friendly, inviting, content-rich reading materials (books, magazines, newspapers, etc.).
- Read aloud to students at all grade levels (and think aloud as you go) to show them how to navigate through difficult text.
- Provide opportunities for silent, oral, and recreational reading.
- Use appropriate before (explain vocabulary, predict), during (graphic organizers, note taking, integrating prior and new knowledge), and after (summarizing, checking for understanding) reading strategies.
- Take a "textbook journey" as a class to help students understand the way the pages are set up, the purposes of the illustrations and data representations, the length and structure of the lessons and sections, the activities and exercises that follow sections, the glossary, and so on.

The more we read, the better readers we become. Students need large amounts of successful reading time—experiences marked by high levels of accuracy, fluency, and comprehension. Stephen Krashen (2002), an expert in reading instruction, agrees. Access to books, recreational reading, and silent reading all lead to improved skills in both decoding and comprehension.

Fluent readers have the skills to be fluent writers. Conversely, students who struggle to read will struggle to write as well.

Writing

Techniques for effective writing in multiple genres have not received as much attention or classroom time as reading instruction. Writing can be integrated into all subjects at all grade levels and may be descriptive, creative, factual/informative, or expository. Teaching students to write involves many components, including sentence formation, punctuation, capitalization, word usage, style, and spelling.

Writing should be incorporated into every subject in meaningful ways. Students may benefit from keeping notebooks or journals in any subject, in which they take notes, record questions about content, reflect on their learning, and so on. Writing essays, biographical sketches, descriptions of events, stories, poetry, and answers to prompts fits naturally into English language arts and social studies classes. Writing narrative explanations of science and math procedures deepens and extends understanding.

Elementary children will gravitate to comfortable settings for silent reading.

Most teachers have very little formal training in techniques for teaching reading and writing. Many, particularly middle and high school teachers, are experts in a content area, and their primary goal is to increase student knowledge and skills in the subject(s) they teach. Encouraging reading and writing increases student literacy and leads to greater student comprehension of specific subject area materials. Formally trained or not, we should all look for opportunities to be teachers of reading and writing.

How Do Teachers Match Instruction to School Levels?

Not every instructional strategy is appropriate for every grade level. Early childhood is not the place for note taking, and high school is not the place for graphing solely with pictures. Some strategies, however, are appropriate for all levels of school. For instance, demonstration, cooperative learning, and think-alouds can be used effectively in early childhood, elementary, middle, and high schools.

Return to the Choosing Your Teaching Path section of MyEducationLab at www.myeducationlab.com and watch the lessons in each of our 10 focus teachers' classrooms. These provide brief glimpses into some of the strategies used at the various levels. Let's discuss them.

Early Childhood Instruction

Active engagement is absolutely necessary in early childhood settings. Early childhood teachers need to be masters of engaging children in meaningful activities and providing an environment for creative and cooperative play. In prekindergarten, children learn prereading strategies and the meaning of numbers, among other basic concepts. In kindergarten through third grade, children learn to read and perform basic problem solving.

In Brandi Wade's kindergarten class at Summit Primary, Ohio, the lesson involves the concepts of less than, greater than, and equal to. The students' prior knowledge includes awareness of the symbolism involved with the concepts and how to count to at least 20 by assigning a number to an object (one-to-one correspondence). Brandi uses what the students already know to engage them in an activity. Here are some strategies in Brandi's lesson:

- demonstration of counting, sorting, writing numbers, choosing correct symbols
- use of manipulatives
- children working at tables where they can observe and help each other (cooperative learning)

In Renee Ayers's second-grade classroom at Summit Primary, Ohio, the students are using and adding to poetry books they have made. They are familiar with the poems (prior knowledge) and use them for reading practice. Here are some strategies involved in Renee's lesson:

- use of materials that have personal meaning to students
- teacher and student read-alouds
- student choice of which poems to read
- independent reading of poems

Can you imagine being the teacher in either Brandi's or Renee's classroom? Do their lessons and styles appeal to you? Do you think your abilities and interests match what you know so far about early childhood education?

Your Teaching Fingerprint

Now let's examine the elementary lessons in the Choosing Your Teaching Path section of MyEducationLab taught by Tim Mendenhall, Chris Roberts, and Brenda Beyal.

Elementary Instruction

For students in elementary settings, reading takes on new purposes beyond learning to decode words. It becomes a tool for acquiring new knowledge in math, social studies, science, and other subjects. Although active engagement remains vital, elementary children

can be expected to read, study, and complete assignments with some measure of independence for brief periods of time. All 12 instructional strategies discussed earlier in this chapter are appropriate in elementary settings.

Tim Mendenhall's multiage (grades 3, 4, 5) classroom at Rees Elementary, Utah, is concentrating on the concepts of estimation, classification, and data representation. Notice that Tim's students use M&M's as a manipulative, much as Brandi's kindergarten students do, but with increased complexity. The students have prior knowledge of estimation techniques and the creation of bar graphs. Here are some of the strategies in Tim's lesson:

- teacher questioning students
- practice estimating and then explaining techniques
- sorting and classifying manipulatives
- working at tables where students can help each other
- conversion of information to data representations

Chris Roberts's multiage class at Rees Elementary, Utah, moved to the gym for their weekly arts lesson in dance. Here are some strategies in Chris's lesson:

- vocabulary presented visually (poster) and audibly, and experienced kinesthetically
- demonstration of dance techniques
- pairs of students working cooperatively
- oral directions for movement

Intermediate students like Hector readily learn about data analysis using M&Ms, much the same way kindergarteners learn about comparing numbers with this simple-to-use manipulative.

In Brenda Beyal's multiage class at Rees Elementary, Utah, the students experience a unique instructional strategy called the creation of tableaus. **Tableaus** involve freeze-frame role playing, with students choosing a book passage, striking a pose that depicts the passage, and holding the pose while a narrator reads the passage. Here are some strategies Brenda uses to support the tableau lesson:

- minilecture on author Eve Bunting
- teacher read-aloud
- graphic organizer to explain tableau
- cooperative group work
- teacher working with groups to give guidance

Can you imagine being the teacher in Tim's, Chris's, or Brenda's classroom? Do their lessons and styles appeal to you? Do you think your abilities and interests match what you know so far about elementary education?

Now let's examine the middle school lessons in the Choosing Your Teaching Path section of MyEducationLab taught by Traci Peters and Deirdre Huger-McGrew.

Middle School Instruction

Young adolescents typically respond positively to active learning opportunities. They are eager to be involved in meaningful experiences that require inquiry and creative problem solving. They also respond to more traditional strategies such as minilectures and note taking if they have been taught to actively listen and record and organize presented material. Variety and frequent shifts in strategies are key to engaging middle school students.

In Traci Peters's seventh-grade math class at Cario Middle School, South Carolina, the students are reviewing topics. They complete a worksheet and are both responding to teacher questions and taking notes. The new learning in this lesson involves students discovering the sum of the measures of the angles of a triangle, then writing generalizations about what they have learned. Here are some strategies Traci uses to support the day's lesson:

- homework to practice and review concepts
- teacher demonstration and questions using overhead projector
- use of manipulatives to discover concept
- working together to check for understanding
- cooperative grouping to write and report generalizations
- teacher working with small groups

In Deirdre Huger-McGrew's class at Cario Middle School, South Carolina, students stay together much of the day as part of C.A.R.E. (Cario Academic Recovery and Enrichment). Deirdre teaches them language arts and social studies, while her teammate, Billy Carol, is responsible for math and science. Here are some strategies Deirdre uses:

- role-playing (pairing students to develop pantomimes)
- group interaction to decide word being portrayed
- activating kinesthetic modality to reinforce vocabulary

Can you imagine being the teacher in Traci's or Deirdre's classroom? Do their lessons and styles appeal to you? Do you think your abilities and interests match what you know so far about middle school education?

Now let's examine the high school lessons in the Choosing Your Teaching Path section of MyEducationLab taught by Derek Boucher, Angelica Reynosa, and Craig Cleveland.

High School Instruction

Students in high school respond to active learning opportunities as do younger students. They work best when the content interests them and when they interact with the subject or topic in ways that require them to be problem solvers.

Derek Boucher's reading class at Roosevelt High School, California, begins with him recommending some books in his classroom library. The students then have time for silent reading before beginning the main focus of the lesson—getting students involved in reading for meaning and then forming their own opinions about a newspaper article. The topic is provocative, and Derek uses small groups for discussion of what the students are learning about persuasive text. Here are some strategies Derek uses:

- appealing to the students' interests
- giving time for independent reading of self-chosen books
- group work to summarize main ideas
- recording on posters used for reporting ideas
- asking students to express opinions

Angelica Reynosa's bilingual World History class at Roosevelt High School, California, demonstrates the power of active engagement in high school. Angelica begins her lesson with a picture on the overhead projector that speaks volumes in any language. Occasionally interspersing English, she asks leading questions to help students interpret what they are seeing. The students then play a rock-scissors-paper game to represent randomness as Angelica gives, and takes away, candy. The students record what they have learned about class struggles in their detailed notebooks, with facts from their textbooks on the right and their personal reflections on the left. Angelica uses many strategies in one lesson, including

- questioning and choral responses
- use of pictures and interpretation
- notebooks for facts and reflections
- game to illustrate concepts
- small group interaction

Using the paper-rock-scissors game to teach about socialism and capitalism intrigues older students.

Craig Cleveland's U.S. History class at Roosevelt High School, California, engages in thought-provoking discussion after he reads a picture book to them about discrimination. The students then read a series of Jim Crow laws, with the purpose of developing role plays in their small groups that illustrate a particular law. The students act out their creations, and then the class discusses what it has seen. This kind of active involvement is excellent for promoting critical and creative thought. Here are some of the strategies Craig uses in his lesson:

- teacher reading aloud to students
- class discussion
- minilecture
- use of quotation to provoke thinking and discussion
- role-playing
- cooperative groups

The 10 lesson snapshots in the Choosing Your Teaching Path section of MyEducationLab last only about 14 minutes altogether. The variety of strategies we see in this brief time is impressive. These experienced teachers are excellent role models and examples of the kinds of people you will want to seek out as mentors.

Concluding Thoughts

John Goodlad, following his landmark study of American high schools, wrote that the typical classroom is a site where "boredom is a disease of epidemic proportion" (1984, p. 9). What a devastating indictment. In the more than two decades since his observations, Goodlad has dedicated his professional life to being part of the solution. It's an effort worthy of our dedication, time, and energy.

Can you picture a classroom full of students deeply immersed in learning? Asking, "And how are the children? Are they all well?" leads us to make authentic teaching our ultimate goal. Now that you know more about curriculum—what it is and where it comes from—you understand the importance of both knowing content and being enthusiastic about it. Now that you know more about instruction—its limitless variety and potential—your ability to envision student engagement has increased.

In closing, read the following quotation from more than half a century ago. It expresses both the purpose of teaching and the criteria for determining effectiveness in the classroom.

Successful teaching is teaching that brings about effective learning. The decisive question is not what methods or procedures are employed, and whether they are old-fashioned or modern, time-tested or experimental, conventional or progressive. All such considerations may be important but none of them is ultimate, for they have to do with the means, not ends. The ultimate criterion for success in teaching is—results! (Mursell, 1946, p. 1)

What Role Will Diversity Play in My Teaching Identity?

Chapter 1 discussed that teachers are facilitators of learning. Now that you know more about what to teach and how to teach it, there's no turning back. A whole career is ahead to build on this basic knowledge. As lifelong learners, teachers continually search for more effective ways to facilitate learning for all students.

A multicultural curriculum, as validation for those students who are diverse in so many ways and as an awareness tool for others, brings the world into your classroom. It broadens your views and your vision—and does the same for your students. Given the array of instructional strategies limited only by creativity and desire, you can engage in multicultural teaching and learning through current events and the arts. You can encourage acceptance and appreciation among all your students in the formal, informal, and extracurriculum. Not to do so is to relegate multiculturalism to the null curriculum. That's unacceptable.

As you learn more about curriculum and continually add to your instructional toolboxes, you also need to prepare to infuse multicultural curriculum into your classroom.

■ Chapter in Review

What is the relationship between the learning process and the brain?

- Learning changes us in small and major ways.
- Learning is complex, personal, and useful.
- The brain physically changes as a result of learning.
- Emotion motivates brain activity.
- The study of brain-based learning holds great promise for future understanding of how best to teach.

What curriculum do we teach in U.S. schools?

- The formal curriculum is what is intentionally taught and stated as student learning goals.
- Standards, defined as what students should know and be able to do, serve as the framework for much of the formal curriculum.
- Textbooks have a great deal of influence on the school and classroom curriculum.
- An integrated curriculum involves linking curricular areas as their contents complement one another.
- A multicultural curriculum purposefully includes contributions and ways of viewing the world from perspectives of different cultures, ethnicities, races, genders, and socioeconomic levels.
- Infusing arts (music, theater, dance, visual arts) into the curriculum provides opportunities for expression that motivate and engage students.
- The informal curriculum is what teachers teach and students learn that is not part of the planned curriculum or standards.
- The extracurriculum comprises activities that are sponsored by the school, but outside the formal curriculum.
- The null curriculum is what isn't taught.

How is instruction implemented in U.S. schools?

- Nine categories of instruction have been proven to increase learning and retention.
- There are big ideas of instruction that serve to ground and provide a framework for strategies.
- Multiple strategies of instruction allow for variety in how the curriculum is taught.

Are we all teachers of reading and writing?

- Reading and writing are essential for success in all subject areas.
- All teachers have the responsibility to promote literacy in their classrooms.

How do teachers match instruction to school levels?

- Some instructional strategies are appropriate for students of all levels.
- Choosing instructional strategies for each of the four levels of school requires thoughtful consideration.

Professional Practice

◾ Licensure Test Prep

What follows is a case study similar to what you will find on the Praxis™ II PLT exam. Read each component and answer multiple-choice questions 1–3 and then constructed-response items 4 and 5. It is wise to read the questions before reading the case so you will be aware of your purpose for reading.

Situation

It is March, and Carrie Fogelman, a first-year teacher in a self-contained 5th grade classroom, is enjoying spring break. One thing's for sure—she has never worked as hard in all her life as she has the past 7 months at JFK Elementary. After spending a few days visiting her parents and brother back in her hometown, Carrie has returned to her apartment and school to prepare her classroom and make plans for the rest of the school year. When she checks her mailbox in the near-empty school building, she finds a note from her principal, Mr. Landford. She also retrieves a notepad with ideas she jotted down before leaving town for break. When she gets to her classroom she sits at her desk and accesses her email. One very welcome message is from Dr. Hagood, one of her favorite professors and her supervisor during her student teaching experience.

Note from Mr. Landford

Dear Carrie,

After spring break, let's find some time to visit. As you know from our talks following my formal observations of your teaching, I have very high regard for the lessons I have seen you teach. Your plans are excellent and your classroom management is above average. I'd just like to visit with you about how the year has gone so far for you and what you have learned about students and teaching since you've been here at JFK.

See you soon!
Mr. Landford

Mr. Landford's notes to himself about what he will discuss with Carrie

- Formal observations positive; very structured lessons
- Informal observations—no complaints, just different from formal visits
- Kids with headphones, others in small groups talking/laughing, appear to be working together
- Email from Mrs. Whitley—very little homework, daughter in group with low achiever and one student who speaks almost no English, book reports?
- Complaint from Mr. Rollins about noise level

Email from Dr. Hagood

Hey, Carrie!

How are you? I was just cleaning out a file drawer and I came across that super unit you and your group did on incorporating environmental concerns into the curriculum. I have a copy of the unit for my files, but I also have all the photos you took of your group working on the project and of the class you conducted to try out some of your ideas on how to motivate kids to care about environmental issues. Would you like to have the pictures?

Have you had a chance to actually do a similar unit in your classroom?

Just let me know where to mail the pics if you want them. Love to hear from you!

Fondly,
Dr. Hagood

Carrie's notepad

- Compare where we are in math with standards and pacing guide
- Go over district reading list to decide what to include by the end of the year
- Ask Ms. Coakley to order more books with CDs for independent reading (Raphael, Enriquez, Marissa)
- Field trip to recycling center—bus? Permission forms? Scavenger hunt?
- Marcus—medication?
- Plan groups for last 9 weeks
- Order *USA Today* for April—whom do I ask?

1. When Mr. Landford formally observes Carrie, he is likely seeing which of the following approaches to instruction?
   a. inquiry-based instruction
   b. constructivist approach to instruction
   c. a prescriptive approach planned by district curriculum specialists
   d. direct instruction

2. Carrie has organized her students into
   a. cooperative groups of students of like ability.
   b. cooperative groups based on matching students who may learn from each other.
   c. cooperative groups that change with each subject.
   d. random groups, allowing students to choose with whom they work.

3. Carrie recognizes that without reading skills, her students will not succeed. She is particularly concerned about the three Hispanic students who were in her class August through November and then moved. They returned in mid-February and say they will be at JFK for the rest of the year. They speak limited English and read even less. An acceptable approach to planning lessons with these students in mind would be to
   a. put them together in a group and spend extra time with them when possible, as well as making sure they receive special services from ESL teachers or others designated to assist LEP students.
   b. concentrate on teaching the students English before attempting to teach them the curriculum.
   c. limit the amount of homework assigned.
   d. use the curriculum of whatever grade level suits the achievement of the students.

4. What are two major ideas of instruction that Carrie appears to incorporate in her classroom that Mr. Landford may not have observed during his formal observations? Explain the evidence that led you to your two choices.

5. Imagine the meeting Carrie will have with Mr. Landford. He is going to ask Carrie about the contents of the email he received, while keeping Mr. Rollins's complaint in mind. He is also going to ask her about instructional strategies and about different techniques she incorporates that he hasn't observed. What are two explanations Carrie might make about her beliefs concerning instruction? Explain each, including evidence for your choices from what you know about Carrie, her beliefs, and her classroom.

■ Standards Speak

This chapter looked at many aspects of curriculum, along with instructional strategies suited to various parts of the curriculum. Many professional organization standards address curriculum and instruction.

NCATE Standard 7 Knowledge, Skills, and Dispositions

The new professional teacher should be able to explain instructional choices based on research-derived knowledge and best practice.

INTASC Standard 1 Knowledge of Subject Matter

The teacher understands the central concepts, tools of inquiry, and structures of the subject being taught and can create learning experiences that make these aspects of subject matter meaningful for students.

INTASC Standard 4 Multiple Instructional Strategies

The teacher uses various instructional strategies to encourage students' development of critical thinking, problem solving, and performance skills.

INTASC Standard 7 Instructional Planning Skills

The teacher plans instruction based upon knowledge of subject matter, students, the community, and curriculum goals.

NMSA Standard 3 Middle Level Curriculum and Assessment

Middle level teacher candidates understand the major concepts, principles, theories, standards, and research related to middle-level curriculum and assessment, and they use this knowledge in their practice.

NMSA Standard 4 Middle Level Teaching Fields

Middle level teacher candidates understand and use the central concepts, tools of inquiry, standards, and structures of content in their chosen teaching fields, and they create meaningful learning experiences that develop all young adolescents' competence in subject matter and skills.

NMSA Standard 5 Middle Level Instruction and Assessment

Middle level teacher candidates understand and use the major concepts, principles, theories, and research related to effective instruction and assessment, and they employ a variety of strategies for a developmentally appropriate climate to meet the varying abilities and learning styles of all young adolescents.

NBPTS Standard 2

Teachers know the subjects they teach and how to teach those subjects to students.

Respond to the following questions in your class notebook and/or discuss your responses with your classmates as directed by your instructor.

1. When choosing instructional strategies, what criteria are most important to consider? Justify your choices.

2. Which comes first, curriculum planning or instructional planning? Why?

3. NMSA Standard 4 includes the phrase "meaningful learning experiences." Choose a grade level and describe how a teacher might recognize a meaningful learning experience for students in that grade.

4. NBTS Standard 2 is simple and straightforward. Choose phrases from other standards that speak to "Teachers know the subjects they teach" and phrases that speak to "how to teach those subjects to students."

 **MyEducationLab**

The following interactive features may be found in Chapter 4 of MyEducationLab.

Homework and Exercises

Writing My Own Story

To write your own story by responding to some of the questions in the text accompanied by fingerprint icons, plus others, go to the "Writing My Own Story" section of the Homework and Exercises for Chapter 4 of MyEducationLab.

What's My Disposition?

To reflect on your beliefs and attitudes concerning the teaching profession, go to Chapter 4's "What's My Disposition?" feature of the Homework and Exercises section of MyEducationLab.

Exploring Schools and Classrooms

If your course involves experiences in schools, the questions and prompts in the "Exploring Schools and Classrooms" feature of Chapter 4's Homework and Exercises section of MyEducationLab will guide you as you explore local schools and classrooms.

Virtual Field Experience

To respond to questions and prompts regarding the Choosing Your Teaching Path videos that connect to specific chapter content, go to Chapter 4's Virtual Field Experience section of MyEducationLab. The questions will help you make sense of what you have read in the chapter.

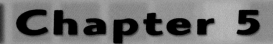

Chapter 5

Assessment
and Accountability

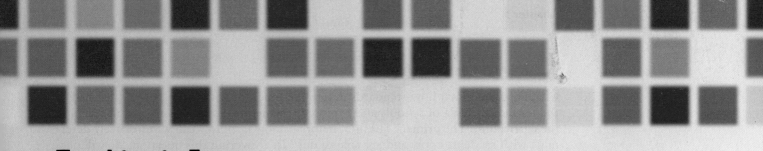

Teaching in Focus

Renee Ayers believes that ongoing assessment is vital to her teaching. The progress her second graders are making at Summit Primary, Ohio, is recorded and analyzed in multiple ways. She even finds ways for her students to view their own progress.

One of Renee's favorite uses of student self-assessment involves writing. She asks her second graders to write the best they can about any topic they choose during the first week of school. She then tucks these little masterpieces away until the last week of second grade, when the students again choose a topic and write about it. Renee surprises her students by giving them their first week's writing to compare. She says it's one of the most joyous celebrations a 7- or 8-year-old can experience. The looks on their faces and their obvious pride in recognizing their progress are priceless!

Renee keeps anecdotal records on her students in two distinct and user-friendly ways. One method involves a clipboard and notecards. She tapes the first card to the board so the bottom of the card and the bottom of the clipboard are even. She writes a student's name on the bottom of the card. Then she tapes another card so that its lower edge lines up just above the name on the first card and writes another student's name on the bottom of that card. She continues this process, taping cards up the board to the clip. She carries this board around as she talks with students about their reading or math or a project they may be working on. In doing so she is practicing teacher observation with the added benefit of recorded notes.

Renee uses another clipboard to hold pages of sticky-back labels. She writes students' names, the date, and her observations about student learning on the labels. Later she simply puts the labels in a notebook on pages designated for each student. This is a quick way to record informal assessments all day and then easily organize them.

Of course Renee also does more formal assessments similar to what most early childhood teachers do. She feels, however, that her informal assessments help her develop the kind of rapport with her students she values and give her clear insights concerning their learning.

Renee models both the attitude and techniques that promote the use of assessment as an integral part of classroom practice. She takes seriously her responsibility to understand her students' strengths and weaknesses, to know their learning profiles, and to monitor their continual progress. Her innovative approach contains ideas you can adapt to your own classrooms. To review Renee's interview, room tour, and lesson go to the Choosing Your Teaching Path section of MyEducationLab at www.myeducationlab.com and click on Summit Primary, and then on Renee.

In this chapter we'll explore assessment—its many forms and multiple purposes. We'll also examine who is responsible for student progress. Here are some of the questions we'll consider in Chapter 5:

- **What is backward design?**
- **What is involved in classroom assessment?**
- **How do teachers evaluate student learning and assign grades?**
- **What are standardized tests, and how are their results used?**
- **Who is accountable for student learning?**
- **What are some of the challenges of accountability?**

◼ Introduction

Chapter 4 described how standards determine much of what is taught and learned in the formal curricula of schools and explored instructional strategies to use in teaching the curriculum. The primary question before us now is: "How can we effectively determine what students know and are able to do?" In answering this question, we will necessarily expand our discussion of curriculum and instruction, since both are interrelated with assessment.

Our discussion will go beyond the common conception that assessment consists mainly of quizzes and paper-and-pencil tests at the end of a chapter. Effective **classroom assessment** is much more, encompassing every deliberate method of gathering information about the quantity and quality of learning. We'll also consider state, national, and international testing, as well as the purposes and categories of all forms of assessment. Envisioning the classroom as the pan and the school as the stove, we should consider assessment one of the three essential ingredients, along with curriculum and instruction (discussed in Chapter 4), required to create a wholesome and academically nutritious "standards stew." All three ingredients must be continually added and constantly stirred throughout the year-long simmering, as illustrated in Figure 5.1.

Assessment results point us naturally toward consideration of who bears the responsibility for student learning—who has **accountability.** The answer is complex and surprisingly controversial. Many would say the student and the teacher, whereas others argue that parents and the community bear much of the responsibility. Still others maintain that state and federal governments bear the ultimate burden of accountability. In this chapter we'll consider the proposition that we are all accountable to ask and answer, "And how are the children? Are they all well?"

Before beginning the discussion of classroom assessment, let's put assessment in perspective in relation to curriculum and instruction by looking at a concept called backward design.

◼ What Is Backward Design?

In 1998 Grant Wiggins and Jay McTighe introduced educators to a concept that links curriculum, instruction, and assessment in meaningful and interconnected ways. **Backward design** is a unique approach to planning for teaching and learning. It starts with deciding on the desired learning results (curriculum), then identifies how to collect

Figure 5.1   Cooking the standards stew

Figure 5.2 Stages of backward design

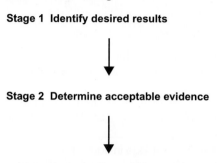

Stage 1 Identify desired results

Stage 2 Determine acceptable evidence

Stage 3 Plan learning experiences and instruction

Source: From *Understanding by Design*, 2nd ed., p. 18, by G. P. Wiggins and J. McTighe, 2005. Alexandria, VA: Association for Supervision and Curriculum Development.

the evidence necessary to know if the results have been achieved (assessment), and finally proceeds to choosing how to help students acquire the desired knowledge and skills (instruction). These three stages, as illustrated in Figure 5.2, constitute backward design. This idea is in contrast to the way many teachers approach planning, which is to think of activities that incorporate standards before considering the desired results of utilizing those activities.

The concept of backward design is not new. Ralph Tyler (1949), the curriculum theorist introduced in Chapter 4, proposed that instructional strategies be planned after considering the changes desired in students. Many teachers call the concept of backward design just plain common sense and say they have used some version of it for years to plan their work. Others find it revolutionary. Let's examine Wiggins and McTighe's conception of what it means to understand and their advice about setting content priorities.

Understanding

In *Understanding by Design,* Wiggins and McTighe (2005) explain that the purpose of the backward design approach is to facilitate true understanding. Their approach echoes Bloom's taxonomy (see Chapter 4, page 124) by emphasizing that to **understand** is to "make sense of what one knows, to be able to know why it's so, and to have the ability to use it in various situations and contexts" (p. 353). Dewey (1933) explained that to understand something is to "see it in relationship to other things: to note how it operates or functions, what consequences follow from it, what causes it" (p. 137).

Wiggins and McTighe (2005) define six facets of understanding, listed in Table 5.1, that deal with what students know and are able to do, putting the focus on student output rather than teacher input.

Content Priorities

Wiggins and McTighe (2005) contend that there is too much for teachers to teach and for students to thoroughly understand in state content standards. The three categories in Figure 5.3 serve to prioritize the content, some of which is worth being familiar with, but doesn't rise to the category of being important to know and do. The most vital knowledge and skills are in the category of big ideas and core tasks. Chapter 4 referred to the big ideas of instruction (see pages 123–127). Wiggins and McTighe similarly define big ideas of content as those that give "meaning and connection to discrete facts and skills" (p. 5). Core tasks are those that are fundamental to the performance of other tasks.

Table 5.1   Six facets of understanding

A Student Who Really Understands . . .	
1. can explain	• provide insightful reasons • avoid or overcome misunderstandings and simplistic views
2. can interpret	• offer powerful interpretations of text, data, situations • offer meaningful accounts of complex situations
3. can apply	• use knowledge in context • extend knowledge in novel, effective ways • self-adjust as needed • see through language/argument that is biased • see and explain the worth of an idea • take a critical stance
4. sees in perspective	• critique and justify a position • place facts and theories in context
5. demonstrates empathy	• feel and appreciate another's point of view • watch and listen sensitively and perceive what others may not • recognize insightful views, even if flawed
6. reveals self-knowledge	• accurately self-assess and self-regulate • accept feedback and criticism without defensiveness • recognize own style and prejudices • regularly reflect on one's learning and experiences

Source: From *Understanding by Design*, 2nd ed., Figure 7.9, pp. 163–164, by G. P. Wiggins and J. McTighe, 2004, Alexandria, VA: ASCD. Used with permission. The Association for Supervision and Curriculum Development is a worldwide community of educators advocating sound policies and sharing best practices to achieve the success of each learner. To learn more, visit ASCD at www.ascd.org.

Figure 5.3   Clarifying content priorities

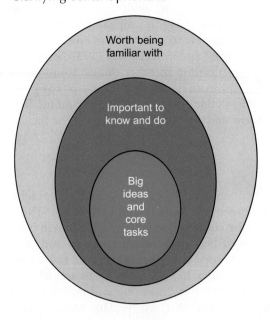

Source: From *Understanding by Design*, 2nd ed., p. 71, Figure 3.3, by G. P. Wiggins and J. McTighe, 2004, Alexandria, VA: ASCD. Adapted by permission. The Association for Supervision and Curriculum Development is a worldwide community of educators advocating sound policies and sharing best practices to achieve the success of each learner. To learn more, visit ASCD at www.ascd.org.

Clarifying content priorities is vital in making decisions regarding the desired results of learning and in planning assessments that provide feedback about student learning. In the classroom, teachers make these decisions and conduct ongoing assessments on a daily basis. Let's discuss the specifics of assessment to discover how they do this.

What Is Involved in Classroom Assessment?

Classroom assessment encompasses all the possible ways teachers determine what students know and can do. It measures what students know and can do against what is in the standards or other learning goals. The assessments developed and used by individual teachers are **criterion referenced.** This means that student scores indicate levels of mastery of a subject and are not dependent on how other students score. In its many forms, classroom assessment serves multiple purposes that are appropriate for the variety of curricula and instructional strategies used in U.S. schools.

Purposes of Classroom Assessment

The mind-set that classroom assessment only serves the purpose of providing grades on a report card is being put to rest in U.S. schools. Determining student achievement is certainly one legitimate reason for classroom assessment, but it is definitely not the only reason.

Just as the National Council of Teachers of Mathematics (NCTM) led the way into the era of standards, this professional organization has also helped broaden our view of the purposes of assessment. Figure 5.4 illustrates NCTM's four purposes of assessment.

Monitoring student progress. Ongoing assessment allows teachers to be continuously aware of where students are in the learning process. It is also important, though, to assess student knowledge and skill levels before beginning a unit of study. This is called **diagnostic assessment** or, more commonly, pretesting. A **unit of study** organizes curriculum, instruction, and assessment around a major theme or distinct body of content. A unit provides planned cohesion. Diagnostic assessment is only possible when desired results have been identified and a plan for collecting evidence has been made, the first two stages of backward design. For instance, a teacher may plan a unit based on the Industrial Revolution. The teacher decides on the major concepts (content) and skills the students should understand and be able to do. The teacher then decides how to determine when

Figure 5.4   NCTM's four purposes of assessment

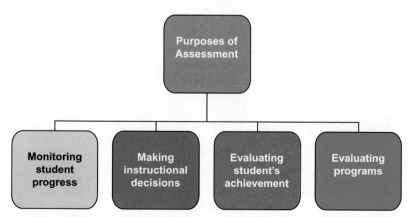

Source: From *Assessment Standards for School Mathematics,* p. 25, by National Council of Teachers of Mathematics, 1995, Reston, VA: Author.

Reading to children and questioning them can be an effective means of formative classroom assessment.

the students have mastered the major concepts, content, and skills. The next step is to formulate an assessment that will diagnose what the students may already know about the topic. This is a diagnostic assessment.

Diagnostic assessment should be followed with a series of assessments in a variety of formats that allow for monitoring student progress. This kind of assessment is called **formative assessment.** Feedback is the key to making formative assessment effective. Feedback needs to be timely and specific enough to make students aware of not only where they are in the learning process, but also what they need to do to move forward. Effective monitoring of student progress provides the information and insight to make instructional decisions that promote student growth. These decisions may involve reteaching or teaching differently to help more students master the unit content and skills.

Making instructional decisions. Assessment can be a waste of time and effort if it does not influence the content, the instructional strategies, and the pacing or sequencing of classroom experiences. A teacher's decisions should be guided not by what materials are available, how last year's class responded, or the fact that a favorite topic already has complete, detailed lesson plans, but rather by the results of ongoing monitoring of student progress through formative assessment.

Evaluating student achievement. Assessment allows teachers to measure if, and how much, students learn. Formative assessments and their results may have a part in the measurement, but **summative assessment** is most often utilized for the purpose of evaluating student achievement. A summative assessment is typically more formal than a formative assessment and involves judging the success of a process or product. Summative assessments most often occur at the end of a unit of study. Paper-and-pencil tests are traditional summative assessments, but they need not be the only format used. Students should be given opportunities to demonstrate what they know and are able to do in a variety of ways, such as completion of a project or performance of an authentic task. When students succeed, teachers can and should recognize accomplishments.

Look closely at Figure 5.5. Notice the flow from diagnostic to formative to summative assessment. The double arrows between formative assessment and instruction indicate that formative assessment helps teachers make decisions about instruction. There is a fluidity between ongoing, formative assessment and what is planned in the classroom. Summative assessment occurs at the end of the formative assessment–instruction ebb and flow.

Evaluating programs. The fourth purpose of assessment may extend beyond the classroom. Instructional materials and formalized programs such as Scholastic 180, the literacy

Figure 5.5   Diagnostic, formative, and summative assessment in the classroom

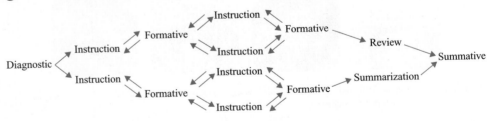

program used by Deirdre at Cario Middle School, South Carolina, are purchased by schools and districts. The components of these programs are monitored for effectiveness, and decisions are made regarding their use based on some form of evaluation.

The purposes of assessment as summarized in Figure 5.4 powerfully influence U.S. schools. Certainly one or two forms of assessment are not adequate to accurately gauge what students know and can do. Fortunately, there is a rich array of assessments for teachers to use in their classrooms.

Forms of Assessment

Students learn differently and should have a variety of opportunities to demonstrate what they know and can do. Although all students in a classroom may be given the same assessment at the same time, varying the assessment format ensures that differing student learning styles and intelligences are accommodated (see Chapter 3, pages 88–92).

Robert Marzano (2000), a researcher with Mid-continent Research for Education and Learning (McREL), tells us there are seven basic forms of classroom assessment that may be used in almost any classroom setting. Table 5.2 lists the seven forms. Read about each

Table 5.2   Seven forms of assessment

Form of Assessment	Characteristics
1. Forced-choice	• multiple choice, matching, true/false, fill-in-the-blank • can be scored objectively • most common form of assessment • choose from among alternatives given
2. Essay	• good for assessing thinking and reasoning skills • opportunity to demonstrate knowledge of relationships • gives information on how students process knowledge • scoring can be subjective
3. Short written responses	• mini-essays • brief explanations of information or processes • scoring more objective than for essays
4. Oral reports	• assess student speaking ability • similar to essay, but more impromptu • require acute listening skills to score
5. Teacher observation	• informal • best for process-oriented and nonachievement factors • good when linked to interview • teacher notes used to record observation results
6. Student self-assessment	• most underused form of assessment • helps develop higher-order metacognitive skills • assessment conference allows student to clarify own level of learning
7. Performance tasks	• require student to construct responses, apply knowledge • require more than recall of information • can assess a variety of forms of knowledge and skills • scoring dependent on task

Source: From *Transforming Classroom Grading*, by R. J. Marzano, 2000, Alexandria, VA: Association for Supervision and Curriculum Development.

and think about if and how it might serve a diagnostic, formative, and/or summative function.

What forms of assessment do you remember from your K–12 experiences? Did you have a preference? If so, what aspects of the different assessments did you prefer? Why? Remember that when you see a fingerprint in the margin it means that you will be asked to respond to questions based on your experiences and opinions. These questions are included in "Writing My Own Story" in Chapter 5 of the Homework and Exercises section of MyEducationLab at www.myeducationlab.com.

Matching Assessment to Curriculum and Instruction

Given all the possible ways to assess what students know and can do, it is important to attempt to create a balanced assessment plan for the classroom. Each method has appropriate uses; each method has limitations. Paying close attention to which assessment is appropriate and when will help ensure assessments are aligned with the curriculum, the instructional strategies, and the needs of the students.

One way to put different assessments together to build an overview of learning is through the use of a portfolio, a popular assessment tool. To create a **portfolio,** students or teachers or both assemble a cohesive package of representative evidence of student learning. A portfolio may serve as

- a compilation of all the work a student does over a period of time. The student may feel a greater sense of accomplishment from reviewing a portfolio than from seeing individual assessments that are quickly discarded.
- a selected collection of work intended to show growth over time
- a display tool for work samples chosen by the teacher, the student, or both to showcase the student's best work

You are likely creating a portfolio, or will be soon, of products related to your education coursework. Your portfolio will show your professional growth. At some point your instructor will evaluate your portfolio and assign a grade that indicates your achievement.

How Do Teachers Evaluate Student Learning and Assign Grades?

Now that we have discussed the purposes and forms of assessment, let's turn our attention to a more detailed discussion about using assessment to evaluate student learning and, ultimately, assign grades. Recall that evaluating student achievement is one of the four purposes of assessment. The result of this purpose is the recognition of achievement or, practically speaking, the assigning of grades.

Evaluation

Evaluation and assessment are often used interchangeably, but they are not the same. Assessment is gathering evidence of student learning (stage two of backward design). **Evaluation** makes judgments about, and assigns values to, the results of assessments. For example, a student writes an essay about the effects of rail travel on the gold rush of the 1800s. The teacher uses the essay as an assessment of what the student has learned in a unit on the events leading to the statehood of California. The assessment provides the evidence to evaluate the quality of student learning.

It is not necessary, nor advisable, to evaluate all evidence of student learning. Referring to our previous example, the teacher may assess the note-taking skills of the student by checking on the completeness of notecards the student filled out during research in the library (first formative assessment). This assessment and teacher feedback help the student make corrections in the research process and move forward with the project. The teacher may simply record a check in the grade book to indicate that student progress was assessed through an examination of notecards. There's no need to make an evaluation at this point. Later the teacher may read through the essay's rough draft and give feedback about it (second formative assessment), yet still not record an evaluation. In this scenario there are two formative assessments without evaluation. When the student turns in the completed essay, the teacher will use a rubric to assess it and then record a summative evaluation.

Rubrics

One of the most productive innovations in assessment is the **rubric,** a tool to help make subjective evaluation more consistent. Rubrics are assessment tools that make explicit what is being assessed, list characteristics of degrees of quality, and provide a rating scale to differentiate among these degrees. Rubrics serve several distinct, yet related, purposes:

- Rubrics provide clear expectations for students about what is expected on a given task or assessment. Therefore, they are instructional tools as well as assessment tools.
- Rubrics allow teachers to consistently differentiate among performance levels.
- Rubrics provide guidelines for student improvement.
- Rubrics make grading more transparent and consistent.

There are two basic types of rubrics. A **holistic rubric** uses one scale for an entire project. In Table 5.3 you can see that a student may receive a score of 0–5 according to the descriptor that most closely matches the work being assessed.

The second type of rubric is the **analytic rubric,** which specifies separate parts of an assessment task, product, or performance and the characteristics of various levels of success for each. An analytic rubric gives much more information than a holistic rubric because the assessment task is broken down into separate components, each judged on its own merit. Table 5.4 is an analytic rubric. This rubric may be used to evaluate a demonstration lesson you might create and deliver in a teacher preparation class.

Along with numbers for scoring, most rubrics include descriptors of what the numbers mean. For instance, on a 0–5 scale, the numbers may mean

5 – Advanced		5 – Highly accomplished
4 – Proficient		4 – Developed
3 – Adequate	or	3 – Developing
2 – Basic		2 – Beginning
1 – Below basic		1 – Preparing to begin
0 – Not attempted		0 – Not attempted

To take advantage of all the benefits of using rubrics to evaluate classroom assessment tasks, products, and performances, teachers should

1. create rubrics for as many tasks as appropriate
2. explicitly teach students how to read and use rubrics
3. distribute rubrics when the task is explained or assigned
4. refer to the rubric when giving directions, answering questions, guiding students, and so on
5. provide anchors (Wiggins & McTighe, 2005), or exemplars, samples of work that fit the various criteria for scoring so that students actually see what a product looks like that earns a particular number
6. inform families about the use and benefits of rubrics so they will understand the evaluation criteria and know how to help guide their students

Many Internet sites provide templates for the creation of rubrics for multiple content areas and performance tasks.

Table 5.3　Sample holistic rubric

Score	Descriptor
5	Student clearly understands the assessment task and the product fulfills all the requirements accurately and completely.
4	Student understands most of the assessment task and the product fulfills the requirements.
3	Student understands just enough of the assessment task to fulfill most of the requirements.
2	Student has little understanding of the assessment task and fulfills a minimum of the requirements.
1	Student does not understand the assessment task and fulfills none of the requirements.
0	Student does not attempt the assessment task.

Table 5.4　Sample analytic rubric

Criterion	4	3	2	1	0
Topic choice	relevant, interesting	appropriate	shallow, lacks interest	very limited	not appropriate
Planned assessment	creative, matches instruction	adequate and appropriate	only addresses part of topic content/skills	does not address topic	not included
Standard(s)/ objective(s)	appropriate, well-written	appropriate	improperly written	not appropriate	not included
Lesson procedures	clear, detailed, could be easily implemented by others	clear and adequately detailed	not detailed enough to be implemented by others	unclear	not included
Handout for class	professional, detailed, few mechanical errors	adequate detail, useful, few mechanical errors	not enough detail, distracting mechanical errors	not useful	not included

Now that you know more about the key elements of evaluating student achievement, let's explore how to put this information to practical use in order to recognize student accomplishments through grades.

Assigning Grades

A **grade** is a judgment of assessment quality (evaluation) with a number attached to it. A student may receive a grade on an individual assignment or assessment based on tools such as rubrics, as well as a grade at the end of what is sometimes called a grading period, for instance, a 9-week or semester time frame. The latter is one number or letter grade that represents the accumulation of many individual grades on individual assessments. This section on assigning grades is an overview of how a grade may be given to represent work and learning over time.

The wisdom of assigning grades has been questioned for decades by many who have viewed grades as harmful to student self-esteem and detrimental to progress (Powell, 2005). Even so, Marzano (2000) states that "Americans have a basic trust in the message that grades convey—so much so that grades have gone without challenge and are, in fact, highly resistant to challenge" (p. 1). Let's explore reasons for grades and some guidelines for grading.

Reasons for grades. Perhaps the most compelling reason for grades is that they are expected by students, families, administrators, and the public in general. In *How to Grade for Learning*, O'Connor (2001) summarizes reasons for grading as follows:

1. Instructional uses: clarify learning goals, pinpoint strengths and weaknesses, motivate
2. Communication uses: inform students and parents about achievement
3. Administrative uses: promotion, graduation, honors, eligibility
4. Guidance uses: help students and parents make educational and vocational plans

Guidelines for grading. O'Connor (2002) gives eight guidelines for grading, most of which involve concepts and principles beyond this text's scope. However, simply reading through the guidelines will help you be aware that guidance is available.

1. Relate grading procedures to learning goals.
2. Relate grades to an individual's achievement on learning goals, not an individual's relative achievement to other students.
3. Grade individual achievement only.
4. Include a sampling of student work, not all work, in a student grade.
5. Update grades to reflect how much learning occurs by the end of the grading period, not a compilation of scores when topics were new.
6. Carefully arrive at a final grade by considering the method of averaging to be used and the significance of zeros.
7. Base all grades on quality assessments.
8. Involve students in the grading process whenever possible and appropriate. (pp. 243–244)

Implementing classroom assessment is primarily the teacher's job. Remember this mantra concerning classroom assessment: "Teach what you test; test what you teach," and return often to the four purposes of assessment discussed earlier in this chapter.

Now let's discuss another kind of assessment, one that teachers don't create, but must be very conscious of when teaching—standardized testing. These tests will be prominent components of your teaching career.

What Are Standardized Tests, and How Are Their Results Used?

In education a **standardized test** is one that is given to multiple groups of students, designed for specific grade levels, and typically repeated annually. These tests are administered and scored under controlled conditions, and their exact content is unknown to everyone except the test makers before they are administered. In this section we'll examine some of the tests, those who are tested, and the purposes and results of standardized tests. We'll conclude this discussion with a look at positive and negative aspects of standardized testing.

Let's begin by examining the difference between standardized tests and standards-based tests. A **standards-based test** is one that is devised according to the content of a specific set of standards. For instance, state standardized tests are also standards based because state content standards are addressed in the writing of the test items. But to say a test is standardized doesn't necessarily mean it's standards based. The content may be derived from textbooks or various curriculum guides, but not necessarily from specific sets of standards.

The first half of this chapter discussed the need for, and value of, multiple assessments to accurately gauge student learning. Keep in mind the previous discussion of classroom assessment as we explore one-shot standardized tests and how their results are used. These are often termed **high-stakes tests**—standardized tests that have far-reaching consequences (sometimes referred to as high-stakes consequences). Read on, armed with the knowledge that a single test administered in one format once a year is very different from ongoing classroom assessment. We will examine international, national, and state-level standardized assessments as well as state-level standards-based assessments.

Standardized Tests in the United States

Standardized tests are given in some form in every public school in the United States. The only international test that compares the United States with other countries is the Trends in International Mathematics and Science Study (TIMSS). The National Assessment of Educational Progress (NAEP) is given to a cross section of students in the United States. Other standardized tests are published by private companies and distributed nationally to states and districts that choose to administer them. In addition, most states administer their own standards-based standardized tests. We will explore each kind of standardized test, beginning with TIMSS.

Trends in International Mathematics and Science Study. As the only international test that compares students worldwide, the **Trends in International Mathematics and Science Study (TIMSS)** has been administered every 4 years since 1995. In 2003, 46 countries administered the TIMSS test to sample populations of fourth and/or eighth graders. Sixteen of these countries tested twelfth graders as well. The TIMSS

- provides achievement data to show trends in performance over time
- fosters public accountability
- allows achievement comparisons among countries

The conditions under which the TIMSS exams are given are not tightly regulated. Some nations do not follow the appropriate guidelines for randomly selecting students. U.S. scores consistently fall in the middle among countries that administer the TIMSS (National Center for Education Statistics [NCES], 2005).

National Assessment of Educational Progress. Often called the nation's report card, the **National Assessment of Educational Progress (NAEP)** is the only standardized test systematically administered to a sampling of students across the United States. The NAEP is administered to fourth, eighth, and twelfth graders in math, reading, writing, science, history, economics, geography, civics, foreign language, and a variety of the arts. The grade levels and subjects are rotated so that not every subject is assessed in every grade each year. The results are not reported by student, school, or district, but only by race, grade level, and state. The NAEP

- allows for the achievement tracking of students at specific grade levels over time, both nationally and by individual states
- provides a basis for state-to-state comparisons
- allows for results tracking for a particular subject area and for comparisons among subject areas

Scores on the NAEP are divided into three categories: basic (partial mastery), proficient (solid performance on grade-level content/skills), and advanced (superior). Many students, unfortunately, do not even achieve at the basic level. With a few exceptions, scores on the NAEP have remained basically the same over the years. One exception occurred in 2005, when fourth- and eighth-grade math scores were the highest since NAEP testing began in 1969. However, in all subject areas except reading, the percentage of twelfth graders at the proficient and advanced levels is consistently lower than the corresponding percentage for fourth and eighth graders. Over the years, scores at all grade levels in social science subjects such as history, civics, and geography have been lower than the scores in other areas. In all subjects, significant gaps remain between the scores of White students and those of African American, Hispanic, and Native American students (NCES, 2006).

General standardized tests. Mandatory testing of students using standardized tests has existed for decades. The most frequently administered general standardized tests include the California Achievement Test (CAT), the Comprehensive Test of Basic Skills (CTBS), the Iowa Test of Basic Skills (ITBS), the Metropolitan Achievement Test (MAT), and the Stanford Achievement Test (SAT) (Popham, 2001). Chances are, you've taken one or more of these tests multiple times.

Many nationally published standardized tests provide detailed score reports for individual students that serve diagnostic purposes when studied by teachers. If given annually, it's possible to track a student's progress in a variety of content and skill areas within a subject.

A major thrust of national standardized tests involves comparing students, both individually and in groups. Comparison is possible because the tests are **norm referenced**, meaning that they are administered to a group of students selected because they represent a cross section of students. The scores of these representative students become the norm against which all other students are compared. Students receive percentile rankings. For instance, if Enrique's reading comprehension performance on the MAT is 78%, this means that 78% of students in his grade-level norm group scored lower than he did, while 22% scored higher.

Two important concepts of standardized assessment are validity and reliability. **Validity** means that an assessment measures what it is intended to measure. Think about how backward design has the potential to increase validity. If desired learning results are known by the test makers, the assessment will likely measure what it's supposed to measure. **Reliability** means that an assessment yields a pattern of results that is repeated and consistent over time. Makers of standardized tests are conscious of the importance of these two concepts. They expend much effort to ensure validity and reliability and to assure the users of the tests that these test components are in place.

State standards-based standardized tests. The newest category of standardized tests in the United States is the standards-based test, with items based on state standards. Almost all 50 states now have their own tests based on specific state standards and usually administered at least to students in third through eighth grade, as required by the No Child Left Behind Act of 2001. As we have discussed, NCLB dramatically changed the public education landscape in the United States in several ways. The act imposes federal requirements on states to develop plans for promoting progress for all students and to be responsible for assessing, evaluating, and recording that progress. NCLB has far-reaching influence; mandatory state testing is only one of the ramifications of the act.

Test results in some states are reported in ways that are useful to teachers as they make instructional decisions, and some are not. For instance, many state tests simply place students in one of four categories, such as below basic, basic, proficient, and advanced. These types of results do not provide information about performance within a particular subject area. In science, for example, the tests do not reveal whether students lack understanding in earth science, biological science, or both. In other words, the results are evaluative and summative, not educative. "Educative feedback is immediate, relevant, and useful, and it promotes student learning" (Reeves, 2004, p. 9). Teachers and other educators have expressed disappointment that many state standards-based tests do not provide educative feedback.

State standards-based assessments are high-stakes tests because there may be drastic consequences associated with inadequate results. For instance, the results are used to make decisions about funding and human resources, which students are promoted or held back, and who graduates and who doesn't (Stiggins, 2001). States threaten (and sometimes follow through) to close schools, dismiss principals and teachers, and then reopen schools with new staffing and perhaps new programs. Schools, districts, and states are judged by test results. Students are allowed to transfer out of schools that have consistently low test

In the News
The Test

High-stakes testing has become a way of life for students in U.S. schools. The state of Florida, during the governorship of Jeb Bush, has taken the consequences of this testing to extremes, as explained in this ABC video. Large numbers of students are being required to repeat grade levels or do not graduate from high school based on the results of a snapshot of their learning taken through the lens of the Florida Comprehensive Assessment Test, the FCAT. We hear proponents of the strict use of test results acknowledge that the test won't fix the ills in the schools, but clarify how bad the problems actually are.

To view this video, go to this text's DVD. Click on In the News, Chapter 5, and then click on *The Test*. Think about our discussion of standardized testing, and then respond to these questions.

1. We hear a parent say of students that the FCAT and subsequent use of the results "takes the wind out of their sails." And then we hear a counselor say that the tests are "deflating." What do they mean by these statements?

2. In the Little Havana section of Miami, 98% of the children are on free or reduced lunch. Most of them live in homes where English is not the primary language spoken. How might these facts skew the percentages of students who are not promoted based on FCAT results?

3. We hear Marie talk about the fact that she works hard in school to earn a 2.8 grade point average and yet cannot graduate because of her FCAT scores. What is your opinion of this situation?

4. Stephanie asks a pertinent question in the video. She wants to know whether the large number of students failing the FCAT might indicate that there is something wrong with the schools and the curriculum, not just a lack of student achievement. How would you answer Stephanie's question?

5. Governor Bush says that there are some positive results of this stricter use of test results and that students who couldn't read before are now doing so. The state is providing multiple opportunities for students to get extra help and retake the tests. What suggestions do you have for how to turn what appears to be primarily a negative issue into one with promise and hope for success?

results into schools that have acceptable results, as explained in Chapter 2 (see page 47). High-stakes, indeed. This chapter's In the News examines the high-stakes consequences in Florida, where large numbers of children and adolescents are repeating grade levels, or not graduating from high school, because of low scores on the Florida Comprehensive Assessment Test (FCAT).

This chapter's Letter to the Editor revolves around the CSAP, the Colorado Student Assessment Program. The principal of a middle school made the decision to have two assemblies before the test was administered, one for eighth graders and one for sixth and seventh graders. Not so unusual, except that all the students in the assemblies were African American. The African American students of Morey Middle School make up about 25% of the total population. An article addressing the assemblies appeared in *The Denver Post* and is shown in Figure 5.6. Read the article carefully before reading the Letter to the Editor. Then respond with your own letter, using the questions to help guide your writing.

Now we'll take a look at some of the good and bad aspects of standardized testing, as well as some absurd situations that have occurred as a result of the current obsession with testing in the United States.

The Good, the Bad, and the Ugly of Standardized Testing

Many educators, parents, concerned citizens, and others loudly criticize standardized testing, particularly state standards-based standardized testing practices. Among the most well known critics are James Popham, Susan Ohanion, Alfie Kohn, Anne Lewis, Richard Stiggins, and David Sadker. Critics of current standardized testing practices are not against assessments that are well-constructed tools for improving instruction. Their criticisms are directed at certain current practices. We hear them say, in essence, "You can't fatten cattle by weighing them," meaning that testing alone won't result in more learning. Alfie Kohn's

Figure 5.6 Article in *The Denver Post*

Pep talk for black students raises eyebrows
By Allison Sherry
Denver Post Staff Writer
March 20, 2007

Before students at Morey Middle School took CSAP tests this year, school administrators pulled all the African-American students into two assemblies and told them that, as a whole, they were not performing as well as their peers at the school. The sixth-, seventh- and eighth-graders were told that the school's principal and assistant principal care about them and that they wanted to hear from them about what they could do to help.

This has sparked controversy at the Denver middle school, where some parents say the achievement gap is so dramatic that drastic conversations such as this must take place. Others, though, decry the assemblies as inappropriate and insensitive because they unfairly single out students by their skin color. "The students were made to feel like they were worse than the white kids," said Stacey DeKraker, whose daughter was at the assembly. "If even one of the students got that message, was it worth it?"

Morey principal Dori Claunch, who has spoken with DeKraker about her concerns, said she decided to call the assembly after winter break because she noticed that black students were lagging behind other ethnic groups at the school.

College fair also broached

Fifty-three percent of African-American sixth-graders at the school are proficient readers. Among white sixth-graders, that number is 89 percent. "The idea of the assembly wasn't just to talk about how African-American kids aren't performing well," Claunch said. "We wanted to talk to our African-American students to let them know we care about them and to let them know they have the best opportunity at Morey." She said she also talked to the eighth-graders about attending a college fair.

Of the roughly 773 students at the school, 24 percent are African-American, and 51 percent are white. Twenty percent of the students are Latino.

"I think it's necessary"

Claunch said several Morey children—in all ethnic groups—are not meeting the school's student-achievement expectations and that the school has interventions for these students. These include "DPS Success," a tutoring program offered before the Colorado Student Assessment Program tests, as well as giving students who are below grade level in reading and math a double dose of those core subjects during the school day.

Claunch, and her assistant principal, Gwen Victor, didn't pull out students from other ethnic groups for an assembly. And that is fine, said Tracey Peters, who has two children at Morey. "I think it's necessary. I'm sorry if our students are being targeted, but when a large group of our students fails to achieve, then drastic measures must be taken," said Peters, who is a member of the school's African-American parent-advisory council. "We can't ignore the problem because it makes us feel uncomfortable."

Must be explained well

Lawrence Borom, head of Denver Public Schools' Black Education Advisory Council, said pulling students out based on race isn't wrong, but it must be explained well. "If you don't let people know what you're doing, if you don't explain it to people, it can be misinterpreted," Borom said. "You have to make sure parents know what's going on, and the message is correct."

DeKraker said she wished she would have known about the assemblies in advance because she would have pulled her daughter out of school that day. "She struggles in school," DeKraker said. "Does she need to be reminded of that in an assembly?"

Source: Reprinted with permission of *The Denver Post.*

(2000) criticism is graphically portrayed when he likens standardized testing to a horror movie monster that swells and mutates and threatens to swallow schools whole (p. 60).

Others, most notably government officials, say that standardized assessment is both valuable and necessary. There's an adage that says, "What we measure, we do." This means

Letter to the Editor

This letter appeared in *The Denver Post* on March 22, 2007. It was written by Dr. Thomas D. Russell, a professor of law at the University of Denver. He is responding to the article reprinted in Figure 5.6, about the assemblies for African American students at Morey Middle School in Denver.

Principal's CSAP pep talk for black students
Re: "Pep talk for black students raises eyebrows," March 20 news story.

However well-intentioned Morey Middle School principal Dori Claunch may have been, her decision to segregate her African-American students in order to deliver a CSAP pep talk may have had an effect exactly opposite to what she intended.

Some years ago, Stanford psychologist Claude Steele discovered that when subjected to racial stereotyping, students perform less well on standardized tests. In one experiment, Professor Steele separated white male Stanford undergraduates into two groups. He told one group that the exam would compare their math skills to Asian students. He said no such thing to the other group. After testing, those white students who had been subjected to the racial stereotype in advance of testing scored lower than the other group. He found the same results with other racial groups including African-Americans.

The performance gap between students of different races, ethnicities or genders is not attributable solely to such stereotyping, of course. Nonetheless, my prediction would be that Ms. Claunch's pep talk had the unintended effect of lowering the CSAP scores of Morey's African-American students.

Thomas D. Russell,
Denver

Now it's your turn. The information about the assemblies and the various perspectives expressed in *The Denver Post* article provide the context for Dr. Russell's letter. Consider this information along with these questions as you formulate your own letter.

1. Dr. Russell talks about research that he feels applies to this incident. Does his conclusion make sense to you? Why or why not?
2. The principal knew the history of the performance of many African American students on the CSAP test. She wanted the students to know that she and the staff cared about them and their success. Do you think this justifies the assemblies? Why or why not?
3. The article does not reveal that both assemblies were actually led by African Americans, one by a teacher and one by the assistant principal. What, if any, influence does this fact have on your opinion of the assemblies? Do you think this knowledge might have influenced the letter writer's stance?

Your letter to the editor should be in response to *The Denver Post* letter—supporting it, adding information, or refuting it. Write your letter in understandable terminology, remembering that readers of newspaper letters to the editor are citizens who may have limited knowledge of school practices and policies. Your letter may be written in your course notebook and shared with classmates as directed by your instructor. Remember to refer to the letter assessment rubric in Figure 1.10, page 20.

that assessment often drives progress. Standardized assessment is intended to do just that on a grand scale.

Figure 5.7 contains statements about the good and the bad of standardized testing. Of course, the statements don't apply to all tests, just as the statements don't paint a complete picture. The issues are much too complex to be adequately examined in a chart. For our purposes, however, Figure 5.7 serves as an overview.

The purpose of considering the good and bad, or the pros and cons, of standardized testing is to develop a sense of balance. Standardized tests serve several positive purposes, as we have seen. Do they serve these purposes adequately? Maybe not. Can we "fatten cattle simply by weighing them"? No. But, used reasonably and as one of several indicators, standardized tests can inform us about instruction that is successful, as well as where improvement is needed. Once again, balance is the best approach.

Your Teaching Fingerprint

Did you approach standardized tests in grades K–12 with confidence? Or did you feel anxious and intimidated on test days? Recalling your own reactions to high-stakes testing will help you approach this fact of life with understanding in your own classroom.

Now that we've looked at the good and the bad, let's briefly touch on some of the ugly aspects of standardized testing. This will give you perspective on the fact that, as with any widespread program, abuses can occur unless management at all levels is both vigilant and consistent. Susan Ohanion, an often-published outspoken critic of standardized

Figure 5.7   Pros and cons of standardized testing

Standardized testing is a **positive** component of public education in the United States because
- many tests align with acknowledged learning goals (standards) and measure progress toward those goals
- administering the same test to large numbers of students allows for comparisons to be made and resources to be allotted where they are most needed
- standardized tests are cost effective because they are administered and scored uniformly
- without testing on a grand scale there is no way to make sure schools and teachers are doing the jobs they are assigned

Standardized testing is a **negative** component of public education in the United States because
- the results are often misused, with consequences that are out of line with the relative importance or meaningfulness of the scores
- the tests are often poorly constructed, with items that are not grade-level or subject-area appropriate
- standardized testing often reduces the curriculum by requiring teachers to concentrate on what is tested and eliminate what is not
- inadequate evidence is available to show a correlation between raising scores on state standardized tests and learning as reflected on the NAEP, ACT, SAT, or other nationally published standardized tests
- test-taking skills have an undetermined effect on raising scores, making increased learning a questionable result of better scores
- low-income, mostly minority, students predictably score below students with higher socioeconomic status, validating the opinion that the tests may actually test what's learned, or not, outside school
- teachers generally support standards, but undue pressure from high-stakes standardized tests can undermine productivity
- standardized tests don't measure important concepts such as cooperation, creativity, and flexibility

testing, refers to the following examples as "weirder and more vicious" than anything she could make up (2003, p. 739). These examples were reported by Ohanion in the June 2003 issue of *Phi Delta Kappan*.

- Tenth graders in one state take a math exam required for high school graduation that consists of items too tough for graduate engineering students.
- In one state, a third grade teacher complained about how difficult certain items were for her students, then discovered the items were subsequently moved to the seventh grade test.
- Parents in one state were told that only 6 out of 90,000 students tested received top marks in writing. Is it possible that the other 89,994 students somehow missed out on writing instruction that would lead them to achieve high scores on an appropriately leveled test?
- In one school, teachers were pulled out of their regular classroom to drill low-scoring students full-time while the other students were left with aides, deprived of their teachers.
- In one state where tests are given in October, teachers stay with their students from the previous year until tests are completed, rather than beginning a new school year in August with a new group of students.
- Some states find ways to actually push students out of school on their 16th birthday if they perform poorly on tests so they won't adversely affect school scores.

Standardized testing is not going away. Recognizing that reality, and making classrooms positive places in spite of testing pressures, is the challenge facing us in this age of

Teachers' Days, Delights, and Dilemmas

Kathy Koeneke Heavers 2005 Colorado Teacher of the Year

Headlines in newspapers across the country call attention to our successes and failures on standardized tests. "School district falls short of No Child Left Behind standards," they announce, and accompanying articles cite the names of schools that did and did not achieve "Adequate Yearly Progress" (AYP). Articles compare results on state-mandated testing and labels are immediately attached in many readers' minds: good school, poor school, mediocre school, achievers, non-achievers . . . Obviously these reports play a big part in the perceptions citizens have about how well our schools are serving children. It is impossible to ignore this major issue.

Standardized assessment has positive purposes. It is important to know on what level students are functioning. Test results allow teachers to individualize instruction according to the specific strengths and weaknesses of each child. ACT and SAT tests allow universities to compare students across the nation and, in theory, assess each student's ability to compete academically on their campuses.

But high-stakes tests also have inherent weaknesses. Most are timed, penalizing students who work at a slower rate. High-stakes testing does nothing to accommodate the students who suffer test anxiety and may freeze under pressure. Minority students, students from migrant families, students of lower socio-economic status, and perhaps students in single-parent households often face more difficult challenges in high-stakes testing. We have yet to come up with a way to create a more equal playing field, even as the tests become the basis by which we judge states, districts, schools, teachers, and students.

A major concern is how we, as teachers, set high standards, improve student achievement, and build public confidence in our public schools. The enormity of this issue has made educators' jobs much more stressful. Recently I received the following email:

"My name is Mary Sullivan and I am getting ready to start my 4th year of teaching middle school math. I'm really struggling with going back this fall to face how my students did on their Colorado Student Assessment Program tests. It has really discouraged me from wanting to continue teaching. I had hoped my summer vacation would change my outlook, but it hasn't. I was wondering if you could give me some words of advice."

I suppose my best response to Mary is that effective teachers acknowledge the challenges and respond by looking for solutions. As frustrating as high-stakes assessment may be, it is here to stay. We must accept the challenge and look together for ways to address the inadequacies and the inequities.

accountability. Classroom teachers can take the reality of standardized testing and use it in beneficial ways by

- modeling mature and reasoned responses to the assessments
- encouraging positive attitudes in colleagues and students
- teaching students that life is full of challenges we may not like or agree with, but that we must meet head on with our best efforts

Read one experienced teacher's philosophy about standardized testing in this chapter's Teachers' Days, Delights, and Dilemmas feature.

Who Is Accountable for Student Learning?

When *A Nation at Risk* was published in 1983, America's public schools were painted as inadequate. Too many students were dropping out or graduating without basic literacy and math skills. People began asking, "Who should be accountable for this sorry state of affairs?" In other words, who should be held responsible for student learning, or the lack of it? Who should ask, "And how are the children? Are they all well?" and accept responsibility for the answer?

Because the United States is a nation that supports individual freedom and responsibility, the "Who's accountable?" question might ultimately be answered, "The students." Of course, students have the choice of listening, participating, behaving, and learning or not.

Given the finest and most equitable opportunities and full support from home, then, yes, students should be held accountable for their own learning. And they are. Teachers grade them, and much of their future success rests on their school accomplishments. But students have very different starting positions when it comes to learning. As explained in Chapter 3, some have built-in family and community support and advantages, but others do not.

Parents and families bear a share of the accountability burden. If students are not supported in terms of adequate shelter and food, encouragement to value education, and physical and emotional surroundings conducive to studying, then families are not doing their part to promote student learning.

The adults who spend the most time with students outside the home are their teachers. Few teachers would ever deny that they are accountable, but most will be quick to add that they are not alone in their accountability. They expect their principals to support their efforts in every way possible, as well as the other adults in the lives of students.

Local school districts and school boards are also accountable for student learning, as they make financial, programmatic, and personnel decisions that affect schools and classrooms.

Communities are accountable for student learning. If financial support of schools (more on this in Chapter 12) and a fundamental respect for education are not present, then communities are failing to accept their portion of accountability. Elected representatives of communities—legislators, members of city councils, mayors, governors—all play roles in accountability because they are responsible for policies that either promote or thwart student learning.

State and federal governments share in accountability for student learning. Chapter 12 will discuss state and federal roles in education. Both levels of government pass laws and deliver mandates that directly affect schools.

So we see that "Who's accountable?" can be answered, "All of us." In other words, "And how are the children? Are they all well?" should be asked and answered over and over by everyone in the United States.

The goal of all who are accountable for student learning should be focused on student success.

What Are Some of the Challenges of Accountability?

State standards-based standardized tests are used on a broad scale to measure student learning. Teacher evaluations often include their students' score reports from year to year. As limited a criterion as this is, it is the measure mandated by No Child Left Behind. In a series of focus groups in 2003, Public Agenda, an education watchdog organization, asked questions about accountability issues. The groups of teachers, parents, students, employers, and professors all overwhelmingly responded that using one test to judge what and how much is learned has questionable merit. They agreed that basing high-stakes consequences on the results of a single test is not appropriate (Johnson & Duffet, 2003). These test results are part of a larger measure of school effectiveness, the Adequate Yearly Progress report.

Adequate Yearly Progress

Schools, principals, and teachers are held accountable for **Adequate Yearly Progress** (AYP). The AYP report consists of elements determined by each individual state, with guidance from No Child Left Behind requirements. AYP data are kept by race, socioeconomic status, and gender. Typical components of the AYP report include graduation rate, attendance, math scores, reading/language arts achievement data, and other indicators of student progress. Failing even one indicator means that a school fails AYP. After failing

Schools are accountable for student success as indicated by AYP scores even if English is not a student's first language.

2 years in a row, schools are placed on an improvement track. The consequences of failing AYP for more than 2 consecutive years range from students being allowed to transfer to a nonfailing school in year 3, to possible state takeover of the school in year 7. All of the consequences are intended to improve student learning. Teachers bear much of the burden of accountability for a school's AYP score.

Teachers and Accountability

The days of assuming a teacher is effective based on pleasant personality or self-declaration of competency are over. It has become absolutely necessary for teachers to follow a curriculum that is standards based. If student scores on state standards-based standardized tests are not acceptable, or at least improving, then teachers do not meet expectations. The standards tell teachers what to teach. Teachers' decisions center on how to make the teaching and learning connection. "In this age of accountability, teacher creativity has less to do with what to teach and more to do with how to teach it" (Jerald, 2003, p. 14).

In addition to following a standards-based curriculum, teachers should adhere to a **pacing guide,** a document that dictates the timing of content coverage. A pacing guide helps guarantee that all grade-level standards are part of the curriculum. Teachers must devise ways to record student progress so that lessons can be planned that take advantage of prior knowledge and move students forward at an appropriate pace.

Assessment Drives Curriculum

From the discussion of backward design in the beginning of this chapter you learned that knowing desired outcomes before designing learning experiences is a meaningful way to approach curriculum and instruction. With test-based accountability and high-stakes consequences, it is inevitable that test content will drive the curriculum. Often what gets tested gets taught, and little else. As long as assessments address a solid curriculum, it may be acceptable for testing to drive the curriculum. However, this approach has some problems. For instance, announcements of which subjects will be tested at which grade levels influence how teachers allocate time, often leading them to exclude valuable curriculum components for the sake of test preparation. In elementary schools in states where only math and language arts are tested, social studies and science are often relegated to 30 minutes or less in the late afternoon. This practice leaves obvious holes in the curriculum to which students are exposed. The consequences of ignoring standards that are not tested show up in later grades when students lack prior knowledge upon which the curriculum may depend. Do you recall the discussion of the null curriculum in Chapter 4 (pages 122–123)? What *isn't* taught can have far-reaching consequences.

Let's briefly consider how teachers and students prepare for high-stakes testing.

Test-Taking Preparation

Test-taking skills are receiving more emphasis in K–12 classrooms. Practicing the format of a standardized test increases students' chances of success. If students are familiar with the way the test looks and the way answer choices are arranged on the answer sheet, the possibility of non-content-related errors is reduced, and the test itself becomes a more accurate assessment of student knowledge and skills. For instance, if students are accustomed to listening to directions and working in silence, test day will not seem quite so extraordinary. If an anticipated test is in multiple-choice format, it's a good idea to occasionally provide classroom assessments in multiple-choice format. If short written response items are anticipated, teaching students to compose succinct, logical answers to prompts should be part of a teacher's instructional strategies. Almost every state provides practice materials that supposedly align with their state tests. Districts and individual schools will often purchase commercially produced materials designed to prepare students for standardized tests and make them available to teachers, or even mandate that they be used.

"Teaching to the test" is a phrase most often viewed negatively. Stop and think for a moment. If the test is a good one that aligns with standards and contains reasonable questions, then teaching to it is a positive thing. "Teaching to the test" means emphasizing particular content and format. There's nothing inherently wrong with this if the practice doesn't limit the curriculum more narrowly than the standards or inhibit the implementation of a variety of engaging instructional practices. However, these are big ifs and may constitute pitfalls in the name of accountability.

Test preparation is an expectation. However, "many teachers . . . experience a disconnect between their vision of a challenging and rewarding career and the day-to-day grind of test preparation" (Renzulli, Gentry, & Reis, 2004). It doesn't have to be this way. Creative teachers are able to weave test-preparation strategies throughout their rich curriculum and instruction in ways that benefit students and expand their learning.

Learning vocabulary is a vital part of success on standardized assessment. A word wall is an effective tool for teaching vocabulary in elementary schools.

Concluding Thoughts

In today's educational and political environment, accountability for student learning falls most heavily on teachers and their schools. Whether student learning occurs, and to what degree, may be gauged by classroom tests. For the sake of coordination of state and national goals, a standardized system is necessary. Given that, a great deal of work is required to create a fair and equitable system that does not stifle imaginative teaching and learning and that yields results teachers can use to make the very best instructional decisions.

Douglas Reeves (2004) tells us that our aim should be to "transform educational accountability policies from destructive and demoralizing accounting drills into meaningful and constructive decision making in the classroom" (p. 1). Both classroom and standardized assessment results should guide the decisions teachers make every day in terms of curriculum and instruction. It is important to see the big picture of teaching and learning that involves the interconnectedness of assessment, curriculum, and instruction.

What Role Will Diversity Play in My Teaching Identity?

Chapter 3 discussed the fact that people learn differently. Chapter 4 explored ways to diversify instruction to meet the needs of learners. This chapter spent considerable time discussing standardized assessment. Generally, a standardized assessment is a paper-and-pencil test in forced-choice format. These high-stakes exams test in only one way. Does that make sense when we know how differently students learn and when teachers are encouraged to differentiate instruction as often as possible?

As we are not likely to see the end of standardized testing, teachers must take advantage of the benefits of this kind of assessment that were stated in the chapter. Teachers must also design classroom assessments to allow students to show what they know and can do in a variety of ways, while continuing to help students master the content, skills, and format they will encounter on standardized exams.

Chapter in Review

What is backward design?

- Planning learning experiences begins with decisions about results and gathering evidence to demonstrate them.
- The concept of understanding is a complex goal of teaching.
- Content priorities include first, vital knowledge and core tasks; then, what is important to know and do; and finally, what is worth being familiar with.

What is involved in classroom assessment?

- The four major purposes of classroom assessment are to monitor student progress, make instructional decisions, evaluate student achievement, and evaluate programs.
- The three major kinds of assessment are diagnostic, formative, and summative.
- The seven basic forms of assessment are forced-choice, essays, short written responses, oral reports, performance tasks, teacher observation, and student self-assessment.
- It is vital to match assessment to curriculum and instruction.

How do teachers evaluate student learning and assign grades?

- To evaluate is to make judgments about quality and quantity.
- Rubrics are instructional and assessment tools that make expectations explicit.
- A grade is an evaluation with a number attached to it.

What are standardized tests, and how are their results used?

- Most standardized tests are high-stakes tests.
- State standardized tests are also standards based.
- The No Child Left Behind Act of 2001 mandates state testing and results monitoring.
- Test content often determines curriculum.

Who is accountable for student learning?

- Teachers, principals, and schools bear much of the burden of accountability.
- Families, the government, and local and state administration are often viewed as less accountable for student learning.

Professional Practice

Licensure Test Prep

Answer multiple-choice questions 1 through 6.

1. Traci Peters will teach a unit on polyhedra in her seventh-grade math classes in March. She believes in thorough planning. In what order should Traci place the following components?
    - I. summative assessment
    - II. reteaching
    - III. formative assessment
    - IV. diagnostic assessment
    - V. standards search

   a. III, II, V, IV, I
   b. V, IV, III, II, I
   c. V, III, IV, II, I
   d. IV, V, III, II, I
   e. V, IV, II, I, III

2. All of the following statements are true about assessment except
   a. students learn differently and should have a variety of opportunities to demonstrate what they know and can do.
   b. it is important to create a balanced assessment plan.
   c. the most frequently used form of summative assessment is the essay.
   d. it is not necessary or advisable to evaluate all of the evidence of student learning.

3. The only standardized national test regularly administered across the country in K–12 schools is the
   a. NAEP.
   b. TIMSS.
   c. ITBS.
   d. NCLB.
   e. SAT.

4. Which of the following statements is/are true?
   I. A norm-referenced test yields test scores that tell teachers which topics in a unit they have recently taught have been mastered by their students.
   II. If a test has reliability, it compares student score data accurately.
   III. If a test has validity, it measures what it is intended to measure.
   IV. Most standardized tests yield valuable diagnostic information.
   V. Analytic rubrics provide more detailed information than do holistic rubrics.

   a. III only
   b. I, III, and V
   c. IV and V
   d. III and V
   e. II only

5. A portfolio is a valuable assessment tool that may serve as
   a. a compilation of all the work a student does over a period of time.
   b. a selected collection of work intended to show growth over time.
   c. a display tool for work samples chosen by the teacher, the student, or both to showcase the student's best work.
   d. b and c only
   e. a, b, and c

6. At a professional development session in Spanish Fork, Utah, Tim Mendenhall learned about rubrics and how they can be used to assess student work with many benefits for both teachers and students. All of the following statements are true about the use of rubrics except
   a. rubrics make objective grading more subjective.
   b. rubrics are actually instructional tools as well as assessment tools.
   c. rubrics allow teachers to consistently differentiate among performance levels.
   d. rubrics make grading more transparent and consistent.
   e. rubrics provide clear expectations for students.

■ Standards Speak

In this chapter we examined assessment and accountability. All major teaching and learning professional organizations address assessment in their standards. Read the following standards and then respond to the questions.

INTASC Standard 8 Assessment of Student Learning

The teacher understands and uses formal and informal assessment strategies to evaluate and ensure the continuous intellectual, social, and physical development of the learner.

NBPTS Core Proposition 3

Accomplished teachers . . . employ multiple methods for measuring student growth and understanding and can clearly explain student performance to parents.

NMSA Standard 3 Middle Level Curriculum and Assessment

Middle level teacher candidates understand the major concepts, principles, theories, standards, and research related to middle level curriculum and assessment, and they use this knowledge in their practice.

NMSA Standard 5 Middle Level Instruction and Assessment

Middle level teacher candidates understand and use the major concepts, principles, theories, and research related to effective instruction and assessment, and they employ a variety of strategies for a developmentally appropriate climate to meet the varying abilities and learning styles of all young adolescents.

NCATE Standard 1 Knowledge, Skills, and Dispositions

Teacher candidates accurately assess and analyze student learning, make appropriate adjustments to instruction, monitor student learning, and have a positive effect on learning for all students.

Respond to the following questions in your class notebook and/or discuss your responses with your classmates as directed by your instructor.

1. Why is it important to use a variety of assessments in your classroom?
2. How can you make assessment an important part of your instructional plan?
3. How might you enhance communication between your classroom and families concerning the learning progress of your students?
4. How can you communicate the importance of standardized tests for your students to their families?

■ MyEducationLab

The following interactive features may be found in Chapter 5 of MyEducationLab.

Homework and Exercises

Writing My Own Story
To write your own story by responding to some of the questions in the text accompanied by fingerprint icons, plus others, go to the "Writing My Own Story" section of the Homework and Exercises for Chapter 5 of MyEducationLab.

What's My Disposition?

To reflect on your beliefs and attitudes concerning the teaching profession, go to Chapter 5's "What's My Disposition?" feature of the Homework and Exercises section of MyEducationLab.

Exploring Schools and Classrooms

If your course involves experiences in schools, the questions and prompts in the "Exploring Schools and Classrooms" feature of Chapter 5's Homework and Exercises section of MyEducationLab will guide you as you explore local schools and classrooms.

Virtual Field Experience

To respond to questions and prompts regarding the Choosing Your Teaching Path videos that connect to specific chapter content, go to Chapter 5's Virtual Field Experience section of MyEducationLab. The questions will help you make sense of what you have read in the chapter.

Chapter 6

Technology
in U.S. Schools

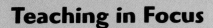

Teaching in Focus

Deirdre Huger-McGrew has always enjoyed technology. In fact, she has been a full-time technology teacher and has kept up with what's cutting edge for both personal interest and professional use. As the English language arts and social studies teacher for Cario's C.A.R.E. program, discussed in Chapter 1 (see page 26), Deirdre believes that computer skills are essential for students and uses computer technology as an integral part of instruction. In the video for this text, you saw Deirdre's classroom and the way computers are arranged for student use. To take another look at Deirdre's classroom and review her interview, go to the Choosing Your Teaching Path section of MyEducationLab, click on Cario Middle School, and then on Deirdre.

The Scholastic READ 180 program Deirdre chose for her students, all of whom are below grade level in reading skills, is one of only a few programs designed to teach older students to read with fluency and comprehension. Reading intervention is accomplished through individualized instruction based on both ability level and specific need. READ 180 follows an extremely comprehensive cycle of instruction that includes

1. *a brief anchor video that provides background information to help the student understand what will be read*
2. *text about the video written at the student's predetermined reading level*
3. *prompts that allow the student to access help in decoding words, phrases, or the whole passage*
4. *comprehension questions*
5. *a summary of how many words and phrases are correctly read and how many questions are correctly answered*
6. *opportunities to reread the passage with varying levels of support to build speed and accuracy (Hasselbring & Bausch, 2006)*

The students in Deirdre's class have access to a library of books specifically related to the topics presented in the computerized videos and reading passages, as well as audiotapes of most of the books, allowing them to follow along as they listen. In the video for this text, you also met David, one of Deirdre's students. In the interview with David's mom you heard about how she encourages David to listen to tapes to increase his reading proficiency. So the instructional strategies used in Deirdre's classroom are reinforced at home. To review David's story, go to the Choosing Your Teaching Path section of MyEducationLab, click on Cario Middle School, and then on David.

This chapter will look at the technology that impacts curriculum, instruction, and assessment in U.S. schools. The focus questions for this chapter will facilitate understanding of whether, and in what ways, technology is changing the way we learn.

- What guides the use of technology in U.S. schools?
- What technological tools are available to enhance curriculum, instruction, and assessment?
- Does technology make a difference in student learning?
- How do teachers use technology in their classrooms?
- What issues surround and affect the use of technology in schools?
- What does the future hold for technology in schools?

Introduction

Technology is changing our world: how we communicate, how we work, how we play, how we care for our health—the list goes on. But is technology changing the way we learn? Helping you form your own opinion on the issues related to this question will be the primary focus of this chapter. Although the word *technology* conjures up images of devices with digital components, it's actually a much broader term encompassing any device that assists people in doing what they do. Applying this broad definition of technology to schools, **educational technology** includes any device that assists teachers in teaching and students in learning.

Older or more commonplace educational technology—low-tech—and newer or more innovative technology—high-tech—are both commonly used in school settings. The boundary between what is low-tech and what is high-tech is continually shifting as a result of both societal changes and human inventiveness.

Long ago in the United States, the one-room schoolhouse accommodated children and adolescents of all ages. Individual slates, paper with coal, chalk, or pencils, and eventually the textbook constituted the technology of the day. As schools became larger, and students were divided according to age or ability, teachers needed tools for group instruction. The classroom chalkboard was introduced. The overhead projector was considered innovative in the 1950s, and televisions became available in limited school settings in the 1960s. In the late 1970s calculators and computers arrived in schools, but it was the 1990s that ushered in computers as everyday components of pre-K–12 classrooms. Today teachers regularly use televisions or monitors with VCRs and DVD players, computer software, Internet research tools, digital and video cameras, and more.

In this chapter the emphasis will be on what's available in terms of educational technology. When the word *technology* is used, assume we are discussing higher, rather than lower, technology. Your challenge as a teacher is to possess the knowledge and skills required to utilize available educational technology and to have the tenacity and interest to watch for and learn about what's on the educational technology horizon. "No longer an 'extra,' technology promotes collaboration, cooperation, communication, critical thinking, personal expression, and differentiation. It is a tool for increasing student achievement and motivating students to learn" (George, 2004, p. 2).

As technology advances, today's students are increasingly referred to as the "MEdia Generation," digital learners in "techno-drenched atmospheres" that are "gizmo-intensive" (McHugh, 2005, p. 33). "No generation has ever had to wait so little to get so much information" (Renard, 2005, p. 44). Relying exclusively on paper, pencil, textbook, and a chalkboard as tools of instruction will likely result in lost opportunities. Today's teachers can use technology to effectively and efficiently make teaching and learning connections with students. As educators we have the responsibility to guide students in ways that will help them excel in our technology-rich society.

What Guides the Use of Technology in U.S. Schools?

As with other aspects of teaching, direction for technology use is found through standards. Let's consider subject area organization standards, grade level organization standards, and the standards of the organization that specifically addresses technology in education, the International Society for Technology in Education (ISTE).

Subject Area Organization Standards

The most recent versions of teacher preparation standards in the four core subject areas—English language arts, math, science, social studies—include general expectations for incorporating technology into the classroom. The National Council of Teachers of English (NCTE), the National Council of Teachers of Mathematics (NCTM), the National

Science Teachers Association (NSTA), and the National Council for the Social Studies (NCSS) all include technology-related standards for teacher preparation. Figure 6.1 provides portions of the technology-related standards of these organizations. Professional organizations for other subject areas also include technology-related teacher competency standards.

Grade Level Organization Standards

Grade level professional organizations address the need for technology competence for teachers. The National Association for the Education of Young Children (NAEYC) standards specify that early childhood teachers should "demonstrate sound knowledge and skills in using technology as a teaching and learning tool" (NAEYC, 2001, p. 18). The Association for Childhood Education International (ACEI) standards recommend that teachers of elementary students plan to use a variety of instructional approaches, including the effective use of technology (ACEI, 2005). The National Middle School Association (NMSA) states that teachers will "incorporate technology in planning, integrating, implementing, and assessing curriculum and student learning." NMSA also says that teachers will "maintain currency with a range of technologies, and seek resources to enhance their professional competence" (NMSA, 2002, p. 10). At the high school level the situation is somewhat different because no one professional organization represents the entire level. High school teachers are primarily guided by the subject area professional organizations.

Figure 6.1   Technology-related standards of professional subject area organizations

National Council of Teachers of English

Standard 8: Students use a variety of technological and information resources (e.g., libraries, databases, computer networks, video) to gather and synthesize information and to create and communicate knowledge.

National Council of Teachers of Mathematics

Technology Principle: Mathematics instructional programs should use technology to help all students understand mathematics and should prepare them to use mathematics in an increasingly technological world.

National Science Teachers Association

The science and technology standards establish connections between the natural and designed worlds and provide students with opportunities to develop decision-making abilities. They are not standards for technology education; rather, these standards emphasize abilities associated with the process of design and fundamental understandings about the enterprise of science and its various linkages with technology.

National Council for the Social Studies

Science, Technology, and Society Standard—Modern life as we know it would be impossible without technology and the science that supports it. But technology brings with it many questions: Is new technology always better than old? What can we learn from the past about how new technologies result in broader social change, some of which is unanticipated? How can we cope with the ever-increasing pace of change? How can we manage technology so that the greatest number of people benefit from it? How can we preserve our fundamental values and beliefs in the midst of technological change? This theme draws upon the natural and physical sciences, social sciences, and the humanities, and appears in a variety of social studies courses, including history, geography, economics, civics, and government.

Source: From NCTE, 1996; NCTM, 2000; NSTA, 2005; NCSS, 2005.

Figure 6.2 ISTE National Educational Technology Standards for Teachers

Teachers should

- demonstrate understanding of technology operations and concepts
- plan and design effective learning experiences supported by technology
- implement plans for using technology to increase student learning
- use technology when implementing a variety of effective assessment strategies
- use technology to enhance their productivity and professionalism
- understand the social, ethical, legal, and human issues surrounding the use of technology

Source: From *Educational Technology Standards and Performance Indicators for All Teachers,* by ISTE, 2005. Retrieved April 14, 2007, from http://cnets.iste.org/teachers/t_stands.html

International Society for Technology in Education

The International Society for Technology in Education (ISTE) provides detailed descriptions of the knowledge and skills that should be part of U.S. education for pre-K–12 teachers and students. These standards are organized into the National Educational Technology Standards for Teachers (NETS for Teachers) and for Students (NETS for Students). An overview of the NETS for Teachers is given in Figure 6.2. NETS for Students, provided in Figure 6.3 is the framework for ISTE's Profiles for Technology Literate Students, organized by school level. We'll explore these profiles later in the chapter.

ISTE standards set the expectation that teachers will demonstrate introductory knowledge, skills, and understanding related to technology. ISTE asserts that teachers should use what they know and can do to help students meet their standards.

What Technological Tools Are Available to Enhance Curriculum, Instruction, and Assessment?

This section will briefly describe some of the educational technology tools that may be available to classroom teachers. This discussion is meant to heighten your awareness, not to teach you how to use the technology. Knowing what's available will help you frame a philosophy about technology use as you develop ideas on how technological tools might enhance your future classroom.

When asked if technology has affected the way they teach, 86% of a large sample of teachers responded "a great deal" or "to some extent" (Prensky, 2006). In looking at technology available in schools, there are two broad categories to consider: teaching tools and tools for teachers. Teaching tools are low- and high-tech resources that enhance curriculum, instruction, and assessment when used by teachers to teach and students to learn. We will look briefly at both low-tech and high-tech teaching tools. Tools for teachers are those technologies that expedite or enhance the work of teachers and, consequently, curriculum, instruction, and assessment in the classroom. Many technologies accommodate both categories. Later in the chapter we will explore how our 10 focus teachers utilize various technology tools.

Low-Tech Teaching Tools

Let's discuss some of the low-tech teaching tools that are available in most schools and classrooms in the United States. Although low-tech tools may seem simplistic, using them effectively and efficiently requires planning and practice. We'll look at chalkboards and white boards, television, subject area aids, and a variety of other low-tech classroom teaching tools.

Figure 6.3 The ISTE® National Educational Technology Standards and Performance Indicators for Students

1. Creativity and Innovation

Students demonstrate creative thinking, construct knowledge, and develop innovative products and processes using technology. Students:

    a. apply existing knowledge to generate new ideas, products, or processes.
    b. create original works as a means of personal or group expression.
    c. use models and simulations to explore complex systems and issues.
    d. identify trends and forecast possibilities.

2. Communication and Collaboration

Students use digital media and environments to communicate and work collaboratively, including at a distance, to support individual learning and contribute to the learning of others. Students:

    a. interact, collaborate, and publish with peers, experts or others employing a variety of digital environments and media.
    b. communicate information and ideas effectively to multiple audiences using a variety of media and formats.
    c. develop cultural understanding and global awareness by engaging with learners of other cultures.
    d. contribute to project teams to produce original works or solve problems.

3. Research and Information Fluency

Students apply digital tools to gather, evaluate, and use information. Students:

    a. plan strategies to guide inquiry.
    b. locate, organize, analyze, evaluate, synthesize, and ethically use information from a variety of sources and media.
    c. evaluate and select information sources and digital tools based on the appropriateness to specific tasks.
    d. process data and report results.

4. Critical Thinking, Problem-Solving & Decision-Making

Students use critical thinking skills to plan and conduct research, manage projects, solve problems and make informed decisions using appropriate digital tools and resources. Students:

    a. identify and define authentic problems and significant questions for investigation.
    b. plan and manage activities to develop a solution or complete a project.
    c. collect and analyze data to identify solutions and/or make informed decisions.
    d. use multiple processes and diverse perspectives to explore alternative solutions.

5. Digital Citizenship

Students understand human, cultural, and societal issues related to technology and practice legal and ethical behavior. Students:

    a. advocate and practice safe, legal, and responsible use of information and technology.
    b. exhibit a positive attitude toward using technology that supports collaboration, learning, and productivity.
    c. demonstrate personal responsibility for lifelong learning.
    d. exhibit leadership for digital citizenship.

6. Technology Operations and Concepts

Students demonstrate a sound understanding of technology concepts, systems and operations. Students:

    a. understand and use technology systems.
    b. select and use applications effectively and productively.
    c. troubleshoot systems and applications.
    d. transfer current knowledge to learning of new technologies.

Source: Reprinted with permission from *National Educational Technology Standards for Students, Second Edition,* © 2007, ISTE® (International Society for Technology in Education), www.iste.org. All rights reserved.

White boards are low-tech tools used in most classrooms at all levels.

Chalkboards and white boards. Many concepts can be visually demonstrated by students and teachers using boards and chalk or markers. However, writing on boards can be a difficult skill for teachers to master, as it involves deciding what and when to write, using legible script, and managing to write and pay attention to students at the same time.

Many teachers use classroom sets of small white boards on which students write individual responses to questions. These individual boards give everyone the opportunity to record and display responses, and help teachers informally assess knowledge and skills.

Television. It's hard for most of us to imagine life without television as a source of both entertainment and information. Most classrooms in U.S. schools are equipped with televisions that may be used to view educational programming and videos that correlate with topics in the curriculum.

A controversial use of classroom televisions surfaced in 1990, when Christopher Whittle, noted entrepreneur and founder/CEO of Edison Schools (see Chapter 2, page 45), introduced Channel One, a 10-minute daily news broadcast with 2 minutes of commercials. When schools agree to air Channel One daily, they are given thousands of dollars worth of equipment, all regularly serviced for free. Channel One's many critics say it represents the worst of commercialism. After all, the students in schools that broadcast Channel One form a captive audience, and some say that the 10 minutes of news has not proven to be academically beneficial to students. Did you experience Channel One? If so, what do you remember about it? Is the content of Channel One, or a similar newscast for adolescents, something you might want to use to prompt discussion in a middle or high school classroom?

Your Teaching Fingerprint

Remember that when you see a fingerprint in the margin it means that you will be asked to respond to questions based on your experiences and opinions. These questions are included in "Writing My Own Story" in Chapter 6 of the Homework and Exercises section of MyEducationLab at www.myeducationlab.com.

Math and science manipulatives. The philosophical shifts from teacher demonstration to student inquiry in teaching math and science, and from paper-and-pencil computation and problem solving to the manipulation of concrete objects, have permeated all grade levels. Referred to as hands-on learning, this use of everyday objects, attribute blocks, algebra tiles, simple-to-complex lab materials, and similar items for teaching and learning requires students to *do* math and science, not just read about the concepts.

Social studies teaching aids. Whereas reading about history, geography, civics, and economics provides necessary background and factual information, stimulating student curiosity and deepening their understanding is accomplished through the appropriate use of other teaching tools readily available in today's classrooms. Maps, globes, timelines, and videos all bring social studies alive for students in ways that reading chapters in textbooks can't.

Other classroom tools. A wide variety of low-tech teaching tools can be used to enhance any subject area as well as to more efficiently accomplish routine tasks. Bulletin board space should routinely be changed to display current administrative information, student work, and subject-related information, as well as inspirational and motivational posters. Organizational and storage bins make materials available to students and can facilitate handing in and returning assignments. When desks or tables are used for cooperative work, many teachers provide containers of everyday supplies, such as colored pencils, scissors, glue, and rulers, for each table.

The overhead projector is one of the most common teaching tools and can be found in most U.S. classrooms. Using it efficiently can enhance any subject by allowing teachers to demonstrate a procedure, such as a math algorithm, or guide students in note taking while still facing the class.

Low-tech teaching tools may seem old school, but they play a significant role in facilitating the teaching and learning connection in the classroom. Setting up your classroom so that these materials and resources are readily accessible will provide more on-task time for teaching and learning. Efficient use of low-tech tools also leaves more time for incorporation of high-tech teaching tools.

High-Tech Teaching Tools

Teaching tools are generally considered high-tech if they involve computers or computer-based technology. However, a designation of high-tech may be short-lived. What's considered high-tech today may soon be considered low-tech as this rich field evolves. Let's look at computers, software, and Internet use.

Computers. Life in the United States is influenced in almost every arena by computers, and schools are no exception. Think about the many ways in which computers impact your life, both in and out of school. Since the 1970s computers have been changing what we do, as well as how we do it, in classrooms across the country. Today most K–12 classrooms have at least one computer for student use, and many have multiple desktop or laptop computers. Most K–12 schools have computer labs that can accommodate an entire class at once, providing each student access to his or her own computer. Teachers use computers in a variety of ways to facilitate instruction and usually have access to multiple types of software.

Software. Computer programs that are written to perform specific applications are referred to as **software.** Application software and instructional software are both used in schools.

Application software falls into three basic categories: word processing, spreadsheet, and database programs, all of which are used in schools. Word processing is the most commonly used software tool, and it supports many types of instruction. The use of spreadsheets and databases to search for and organize information can provide curricular enhancements in most subjects and grade levels.

PowerPoint is perhaps the most popular presentation program in the classroom, used by teachers to deliver instruction and by students to demonstrate skills and display the product of a project. Multimedia presentations can be created using PowerPoint.

Streaming video allows students to view video that is either stored on a site or live as it downloads on the computer. Many teachers project streaming video in their classrooms to illustrate their lessons.

Instructional software is designed specifically for student use to learn about concepts or practice skills related to a subject area. M. D. Roblyer (2006) categorizes instructional software in five groups: drill and practice, tutorial, simulation, instructional game, and problem solving, as illustatated in Figure 6.4. Scholastic READ 180, used at Cario Middle School, South Carolina, is an example of tutorial software.

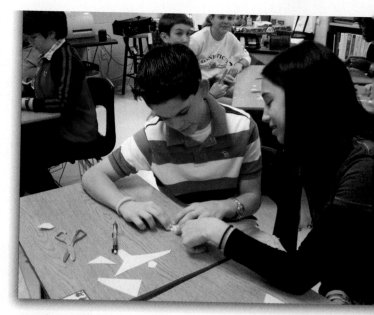

Simple manipulatives, such as these used in Traci Peter's class at Cario Middle School, help students understand math concepts.

Overhead projectors are staples in most classrooms in the United States. They are simple to use and give teachers flexibility for presentation of material, whether new information or review.

Figure 6.4 Categories of instructional software

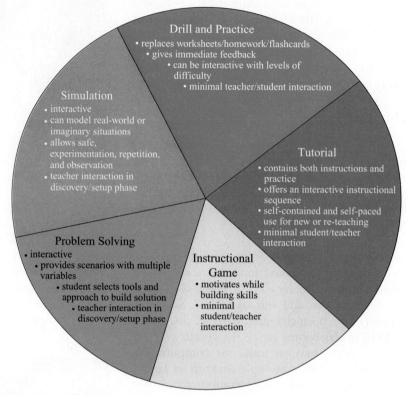

Source: From *Integrating Educational Technology into Teaching*, p. 63, by M. D. Roblyer, 2006, Upper Saddle River, NJ: Merrill/Prentice Hall.

Handheld computers may be used to share information, commonly referred to as beaming.

Your Teaching Fingerprint

Handheld Computers. The portability of these pocket-sized computers gives teachers and students flexibility to move around while using them and to move class sets of computers from place to place. Basic software tools can be used with handheld computers that have small folding keyboards. Handheld computers also provide a convenient way for students and teachers to share information and products simply by pointing one computer at another, commonly referred to as beaming.

Classroom Networks. Networks connect computers so that users can share and exchange resources and information, and entail the active participation of students. Networked classrooms are therefore learner oriented.

The Internet. The most widely used network is the **Internet.** The most common Internet service that links sites is the World Wide Web (WWW) or, as Tom March (2006) refers to it, the new "Whatever, Whenever, Wherever." Through the World Wide Web people around the world can search for information, share resources, and communicate. This powerful computer tool is used by students in almost every school setting as they access information using search engines such as Google, Yahoo, and Dogpile. Table 6.1 illustrates the growth in the percentage of public schools with Internet access. When did you first use the Internet? How do you use it today for school, work, or personal purposes? How has the Internet impacted your educational experiences?

Table 6.1   Percentage of public schools with Internet access, 1994–2003

School Characteristics	Year					
	1994	1996	1998	2000	2002	2003
All public schools	35	65	89	98	99	100
Instructional Level						
Elementary	30	61	88	97	99	100
Secondary	49	77	94	100	100	100
School Size						
Less than 300	30	57	87	96	96	100
300–999	35	66	89	98	100	100
1,000 or more	58	80	95	99	100	100
Locale						
City	40	64	92	96	99	100
Urban fringe	38	75	85	98	100	100
Town	29	61	90	98	98	100
Rural	35	60	92	99	98	100
Percent Minority Enrollment						
Less than 6%	38	65	91	98	97	100
6–20%	38	72	93	100	100	100
21–49%	38	65	91	98	100	99
50% or more	27	56	82	96	99	100
Percent of Students Eligible for Free or Reduced-Price School Lunch						
Less than 35%	39	72	92	99	98	100
35–49%	35	59	93	99	100	100
50–74%	32	53	88	97	100	100
75% or more	18	53	79	94	99	100

Source: Compiled from "Survey on Advanced Telecommunications in U.S. Public Schools, K–12," FRSS 51, 1994; "Survey on Advanced Telecommunications in U.S. Public Schools, K–12," FRSS 57, 1995; "Advanced Telecommunications in U.S. Public Schools, Fall 1996," FRSS 61, 1996; "Internet Access in U.S. Public Schools, Fall 1997," FRSS 64, 1997; "Internet Access in U.S. Public Schools, Fall 1998," FRSS 69, 1998; "Internet Access in U.S. Public Schools, Fall 1999," FRSS 75, 1999; "Internet Access in U.S. Public Schools, Fall 2000," FRSS 79, 2000; "Internet Access in U.S. Public Schools, Fall 2001," FRSS 82, 2001; "Internet Access in U.S. Public Schools, Fall 2002," FRSS 83, 2002; and "Internet Access in U.S. Public Schools, Fall 2003," FRSS 86, 2003; National Center for Education Statistics, Fast Response Survey System, Retrieved November 2, 2006, from http://nces.ed.gov/surveys/frss/publications/2005015/

An increasingly common use of the Internet is the development of **WebQuests**, inquiry projects in which most or all of the information is obtained through the Internet. Instructions for a WebQuest typically call for it to include information that introduces a topic, a description of the task to be completed, suggested sources to be explored, guidance about the project product, and directions for a closing. Through WebQuests teachers can guide students as they research topics electronically (Renard, 2005).

Computer resources can also be used to link multiple media sources in the same presentation. **Multimedia** is just what it sounds like—more than one medium used to communicate information. For instance, a student presentation on African wildlife might include text, audio, video, graphics, and animation. When all of these elements are digital, the term for multimedia becomes **digital media**. **Hypermedia** is an advanced form of multimedia with all the sources of media hyperlinked to other documents. Resources available to be linked as hypermedia include audio from CDs, video resources from digitized and prerecorded videos, photos that are scanned or taken with digital cameras, graphic images from clip art or software, and text from word-processed files (Shelley, Cashman, Gunter, & Gunter, 2006). Teachers use multimedia and hypermedia for a variety of purposes, including presentations to accompany demonstrations, the creation of virtual tours, and documentation of field trips (O'Bannon & Puckett, 2007).

As teaching tools, computers, software, and the Internet can be integral parts of today's classrooms. They can also support teachers in many aspects of their work.

Educational Technology Tools for Teachers

Computers have streamlined the work of teachers by becoming tools that increase productivity in lesson planning, record keeping, communicating with students, parents, and colleagues, and professional development. Let's examine each of these areas.

Lesson planning. The Internet abounds with resources for teachers to use as they prepare lessons. Some of the most widely used and comprehensive teacher websites are listed in Figure 6.5. Although the Internet can be valuable for lesson planning, teachers need to be aware that just because a plan appears complete, there's no guarantee that the lessons meet necessary curriculum standards or provide for the needs of diverse learners (discussed throughout Chapter 3). However, the websites of national professional organizations are reliable Internet sources for standards-based lesson ideas. These organizations were discussed in Chapter 4 (see pages 116–117).

Figure 6.5 Internet sources to assist with lesson planning

- Education World
  http://www.education-world.com/
  Includes many subjects, professional development
  technology integration, multiple resources

- Eisenhower National Clearinghouse
  www.enc.org
  Multiple math and science resources for all
  grade levels

- Lesson Planet
  http://www.lessonplanet.com
  Resources, tools, lessons in many subjects

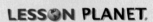

- Ed Helper
  http://www.edhelper.com
  All grades, seasonal lessons, includes special education

- Teachers.net Lesson Bank
  http://teachers.net/lessons/
  Allows you to search, submit, or request lessons;
  covers multiple subject areas and grade levels

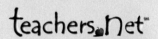

- A to Z Teacher Stuff
  http://atozteacherstuff.com/
  Lesson plans, thematic units, teacher tips,
  discussion forums for teachers, downloadable
  teaching materials

- The Educator's Reference Desk
  http://www.eduref.org/
  Resource guides; lesson plans in all subject areas,
  including foreign language and vocational

Note: Education World logo © EducationWorld.com, reprinted with permission.

Record keeping. Software specifically designed for recording grades and attendance is often referred to as an electronic grade book. Two examples of electronic grade books are Easy Grade Pro at http://easygradepro.com and Gradekeeper at http://www.gradekeeper.com.

Communication. The Internet enhances our capacity for rapid, effective communication. Now rather than having to physically go to another school or even pick up a telephone, teachers can almost instantly learn from each other by conversing through email and chat rooms. They can also communicate with students, assess assignments, give feedback, and even hold informal conversations with parents. Some teachers have their own websites to help inform their students and families. At the school and district levels, websites provide information for both families and the community.

Professional development. Teachers can use the Internet to remain current in their fields. Many organizations provide online staff development sessions, and teachers can access professional journals and book excerpts online.

Given the array of technological tools designed to aid in instruction, as well as those designed to increase teacher productivity, we assume that technology makes a difference in terms of student learning. Does it? This issue is more complex than you may think.

■ Does Technology Make a Difference in Student Learning?

As explained in Chapter 5 (see page 154), scores on the National Assessment of Educational Progress (NAEP) have remained virtually unchanged for U.S. students over the years, with no appreciable increase since the advent of higher technology, namely, computers, in the schools. There is little widespread concrete evidence that student learning increases as use of technology grows.

Technology has tremendous potential to impact student learning, but simply having students use technology does not mean their learning increases. Increased learning hinges on how technology is integrated into classroom curricula and instruction. Let's take a look at attempts to verify technology's impact on student learning.

Research on the Impact of Technology

The scant scientifically based research on the impact of technology on learning has shown little generalizable increase in student learning (Cradler, 2003). Yet schools and all levels of government continue to pour millions of dollars into technology, specifically computers, for pre-K–12 students. In 1997 there were approximately 21 students for every computer in public schools in the United States. In 2002, schools averaged 4 students per computer. In the 5 years between 1997 and 2002, large sums of money were spent on computers and accompanying software. *Education Week's* "Technology Counts" report indicates that the 4-to-1 ratio still applied in 2006 (Swanson, 2006). What do we have to show for this investment in computer technology? Certainly not revolutionary changes in student learning, at least not by current assessment measures (Morrison & Lowther, 2005).

The most comprehensive and ongoing compilation of research studies on the impact of technology is conducted by the **Center for Applied Research in Educational Technology (CARET),** a project of the International Society for Technology in Education and funded through the Bill and Melinda Gates Foundation. CARET's continuing study has identified conditions for effectively integrating technology into curricula and instruction. Figure 6.6 encapsulates some of these study results.

Reasons for Using Technology

CARET has also provided reasons for using technology in schools: growth in problem-solving skills, increased motivation for learning, preparation for the workforce, and meeting the needs of specific groups of students, namely, students with disabilities. All these

Figure 6.6 Integrating technology into curriculum and instruction

Technology is effectively integrated into curriculum and instruction when

- applications align with state curriculum standards
- students have opportunities to collaborate
- students become proficient with the technology before applying it to lessons and assignments
- teachers have support and mentoring from colleagues in the implementation of innovative efforts
- teachers are given time to design, experiment with, and receive feedback regarding lessons involving technology
- it is systematically incorporated into classroom lesson plans

Source: From *Questions and Answers,* by the Center for Applied Research in Educational Technology (CARET). Retrieved July 3, 2007, from http://caret.iste.org/index.cfm?fuseaction=topics

represent student learning that may result from the appropriate application of technology. We'll briefly examine each.

Growth in problem-solving skills. Using technology tools in problem solving results in a more student centered classroom. When a whole school uses technology in inquiry and problem solving, positive changes occur (Morrison & Lowther, 2005).

Simulation software provides models of situations that require students to solve problems by working through dilemmas that have changing variables. Many websites also allow for student interaction. A prime example is the National Council of Teachers of Mathematics site called Illuminations (http://illuminations.nctm.org/).

Entire classes can use computers to inquire or problem solve as they share information and skills in a networked classroom (discussed earlier). Some math and science teachers have reported significant improvement for middle school students on standardized tests, which they attribute to classroom networking (Roschelle, Penuel, & Abrahamson, 2004). Although not yet reflected in NAEP test results, this is one encouraging sign of improvement in student learning, using traditional assessment as evidence.

Increased motivation for learning. When students find lesson-appropriate websites and are able to navigate to the information needed, they find the process motivating and memorable. "Commanding information is an empowering experience that builds upon itself, leading to more interactive learning" (Tienken, 2003, p. 9).

Almost everyone in the United States has either played a video or computer game or witnessed games being played. The motivation for playing the game is the game itself. Electronic games are certainly not the answer to problems in education, but the motivation they engender serves as a lesson in the power of games (Jenkins, 2005).

Preparation for the workforce. Computers are used in the workplace primarily because they're functional, not because they are motivating or fun. The widespread use of computers is a result of enhanced efficiency and flexibility. Experts tell us that by 2010 virtually all occupations will involve the daily use of computers (Shelley et al., 2006). Obviously, aspects of student learning defined by computer knowledge and skills play a role in preparing students for the workplace.

In talking about features of the 21st-century landscape, Prensky (2006) tells us that the best thing we can do for students' technology literacy is prepare them to use the technology that currently exists and to be able to recognize the appropriateness of emerging technology that enhances the workplace. Many states and districts have implemented initiatives to do just that—prepare students to contribute to the future through technological knowledge and skills. Let's consider Maine's initiative.

Maine Learning Technology Initiative. In January 2005 the state of Maine brought together key leaders to participate in a summit meeting called Education, Technology, and the Future of Maine. Representatives from the Maine Departments of Education, Labor, and Economic and Community Development met with noted experts to discuss essential elements necessary to propel Maine's economy forward. The group made it clear that education and Maine's economy are inextricably linked. A conclusion published at www.Maine.gov states, "Education at all levels must be prepared to respond creatively to the increasing realities of the 21st-century workplace."

This historically significant Maine summit supported the Maine Learning Technology Initiative (MLTI) of 2002, dubbed the largest educational technology project in the history of the world by former Maine governor Angus King. The project, funded through corporate contributions and state money, proposed to provide a laptop for every seventh and eighth grader in the state to eliminate the "digital divide," or the differences in accessibility of technology among various groups. The Maine Department of Education envisions Maine students among the most technologically literate in the world. In 2005 the University of Southern Maine issued a report showing that the majority of students and teachers believed the laptops had improved the quality of teaching and learning. Most teachers reported increased student engagement, and most students were looking forward to seventh grade when they could use laptops all day long, as illustrated in this chapter's Letter to the Editor. One teacher summed up the impact of MLTI by saying,

> Demonstrating knowledge now goes beyond filling in circles on a multiple choice test; instead students use remote controls to guide their classmates through multimedia demonstrations of learning. The issue of gender and economic equity has faded; the efficiency of teaching and learning has improved; and going to school is much more fun for both teachers and students. (MLTI, 2005, p. 19)

Letter to the Editor

This letter to the editor appeared in the Portland, Maine, newspaper, the *Portland Press Herald*. It was written by a sixth grade student to express his support for the Maine Learning Technology Initiative (MLTI).

Student's Enthusiasm Tied to Computers

JANUARY 13, 2006

I am a sixth-grade student hoping to use a laptop next year. I believe that Maine schools should continue the laptop program because our school's computer lab is a bit small, even for one class of sixth-graders.

Researching is more efficient on a laptop because everyone can be working at once instead of waiting for a book from the library or a computer in the lab.

Many teachers have a Web site where you can see your grades, get class work and get assignments for extra-credit work.

Using the computer also can help teach responsibility and value because a computer is a valuable object and needs to be handled with care and respect. It also needs to be returned in good condition.

I don't like to write and sometimes am not too excited about the subjects we are studying in school. Using a computer makes it easier for me to get my information across, and I am much more enthusiastic about going to school. In subjects that are interesting to me, I can do research and learn more than I usually would.

Jack Baker
Freeport Middle School

Now it's your turn. Your letter to the editor should express your views of the benefits and limitations of providing laptop computers for all students. These questions will help you frame your thinking.

1. MLTI currently provides one-to-one computer access only for seventh and eighth graders. Are 2 years enough for Maine students to become computer literate? Why or why not?

2. Would computer access for 2 years serve to convince students that technology use makes them more productive and able to solve problems more effectively and efficiently? Why or why not?

3. If taxpayers fund about half of the initiative, what indicators of success should they expect to see?

4. Think about a grade level or subject you may want to teach. How do you envision utilizing one-to-one computer access?

Your letter to the editor should be in response to the *Portland Press Herald* letter—supporting it, adding information, or refuting it. Write your letter in understandable terminology, remembering that readers of newspaper letters to the editor are citizens who may have limited knowledge of school practices and policies. Your letter may be written in your course notebook and shared with classmates as directed by your instructor. Remember to refer to the letter assessment rubric in Figure 1.10, page 20.

Table 6.2   Matching technology resources to the needs of at-risk students

Learning Difficulties	Strategies
Difficulty remembering things to do, sequence of tasks	• Provide a reminder service: http://www.iping.com. • Use a specialized prompting device: Job Coach at http://www.attainmentcompany.com.
Inability to read and comprehend at grade level	• Provide digital text in a text-to-speech program: ReadPlease at http://www.readplease.com. • Provide instructional materials with multiple levels: http://www.windows.ucar.edu.
Difficulties in written expression	• Use a predictive word processor; e.g., *Co:Writer* (http://www.donjohnston.com) or *WordQ* (http://www.wordq.com). • Offer support for dictation: http://www.idictate.com.
Difficulties in math computations and concepts	• Use online calculators: WebMath at http://www.webmath.com. • Use teaching tools such as Virtual Math Manipulatives at http://matti.usu.edu/nlvm/nav/vlibrary.html.

Source: From *Integrating Educational Technology into Teaching,* p. 420, by M. D. Roblyer, 2006, Upper Saddle River, NJ: Merrill/Prentice Hall. Reprinted with permission.

Meeting the needs of students with disabilities. Almost half of students with disabilities are classified as learning disabled. According to Hasselbring and Bausch (2006), "Assistive technologies can act as a lifeline to students with learning disabilities" (p. 72). Table 6.2 suggests strategies for helping students with learning difficulties so that they have the same opportunities for success in the classroom that are available to students without disabilities.

Increasing the use of technology by children and adults with disabilities is the mission of the Alliance for Technology Access (ATA). This network of assistive technology resources is working "toward a world in which all people with limitations have ongoing and effective use of critical technology tools that are adaptable, accessible, affordable, and available, along with the training and support necessary to integrate these tools into their lives" (ATA, 2006, p. 1).

As we conclude our look at whether technology makes a difference in student learning, consider what Brenda Dyck (2004) has to say.

> Those waiting for technology to deliver increased test scores and automatically engage learners can expect to be disappointed. But, technology can be a catalyst for creating a new model of school. Learning about how these new tools work is the easy part. More challenging and pivotal will be how effectively we alter our conception of the learning, and finally, school itself. (p. 23)

Assistive technology such as cochlear implants and teacher microphones help students with disabilities function and flourish in the classroom.

Altering our conception will require careful examination of the factors involved in the application of the technology available to classroom teachers.

How Do Teachers Use Technology in Their Classrooms?

Let's examine some of the variables that influence the educational quality of classroom computer use. These variables include the role of teachers, the utilization of instructional models, the presence of essential conditions for success, technology-integration strategies, and developmental appropriateness.

Variable: Role of Teachers

The teacher is a facilitator in a classroom where technology has an integral place in teaching and learning. Facilitation is a facet of a broader view of what it means to teach. When a teacher facilitates effective use of technology, meaningful learning can be fostered, an open and supportive environment can be established, and the needs of diverse learners can be met (Morrison & Lowther, 2002).

Variable: Instructional Delivery and Problem-Solving Models

There are three basic approaches to computer use in schools involving the categories of instructional software described in Figure 6.4. **Computer-assisted instruction (CAI)** uses instructional software that is self-contained and self-paced. CAI allows individual students, including students with special needs, English language learners, and those in advanced placement courses, among others, to work on skills they need in ways that don't depend on other students or require a great deal of teacher time. CAI most commonly uses drill-and-practice software.

Tutorial and problem-solving software, as well as any computer program that diagnoses student progress and adjusts accordingly, offer **computer-managed instruction (CMI)**. Students advance in self-paced ways and learn new concepts and skills with CMI.

Interactive simulation software may be used in inquiry-based lessons where students control much of the input, and teachers guide the discovery process. This approach, referred to as **computer-enhanced instruction (CEI),** is less structured than CAI and CMI. Table 6.3 summarizes some of the characteristics of each of these three approaches to computer instruction. The challenge for teachers is to find ways to meaningfully incorporate the approaches into classroom instruction.

Table 6.3   Computer use to assist, manage, and enhance learning

	CAI Computer-Assisted Instruction	CMI Computer-Managed Instruction	CEI Computer-Enhanced Instruction
Purpose	drill-and-practice tutorials	diagnose, move students forward, monitor progress	assists with inquiry learning
Teacher's role	make sure program is at appropriate level	monitor student use to assure progress	facilitates student use of computer
Teacher-student interaction	may be minimal during use	may be minimal during use	may be substantial and high quality during inquiry process
Advantages for students	self-pacing, low risk	self-pacing, continual new challenges built on previous experiences	unlimited resources for self-paced research

Variable: Essential Conditions

As stated previously, simply having computers in a classroom or a computer lab doesn't guarantee their effective use. When the International Society for Technology in Education introduced its National Education Technology Standards for teachers, summarized in Figure 6.2, and for students, in Figure 6.3, teachers began to identify barriers to the productive use of computer technology. Using their feedback, ISTE developed the essential conditions, listed in Figure 6.7, that teacher preparation programs and schools must meet to realize the potential benefits of computer technology.

Variable: Integration of Technology

When essential conditions are in place, teachers must understand how to use technology in meaningful ways for both delivery and problem solving within the curriculum. Using technology in this way is sometimes referred to as **integration literacy** (Shelley et al., 2006). Technology, as a support for both curriculum and instruction, should not drive either, but rather should make both more meaningful. Some basic steps to technology integration for teachers who practice integration literacy are to

- identify the goals to be accomplished within the curriculum
- identify an appropriate technology tool that will help accomplish these goals
- develop innovative ways to teach a diverse population of learners
- carefully and continually plan to facilitate learning (Shelley et al., 2006, pp. 342–343)

The five phases of the planning checklist shown in Figure 6.8 provide a comprehensive list of the issues involved in guiding the integration of technology, regardless of grade level.

Variable: Technology Use by Grade Level

Just as curriculum, instruction, and assessment vary by grade level, so does technology implementation. Yet implementation varies not only by level, but also by teacher. Technology that works as a learning tool for one third grade teacher might not work for another. One tenth grade U.S. history teacher might assign a project that requires Internet research, whereas another may rarely even refer to the Internet, much less encourage its use.

We'll explore technology use in the four levels of school by examining ISTE guidelines of what students should be able to do at specific grade levels. You'll notice that the ISTE Profiles for Technology Literate Students include some very ambitious thresholds of proficiency. Some of the tools necessary for students to learn about and practice skills are not readily available in many school settings. Even where tools are accessible, they may be used infrequently in instruction for a variety of reasons, some of which will be discussed

Figure 6.7   Essential conditions for powerful use of technology

- A shared vision for technology integration
- Access to hardware, software, and other resources
- Educators skilled in technology use
- Professional development to support technology use in teaching and learning
- Content standards and curriculum resources
- Appropriate teaching and assessment approaches
- Community and policy support
- Technical assistance

Source: Information from *National Educational Technology Standards for Teachers: Preparing Tomorrow's Teachers to Use Technology Project,* by the International Society for Technology in Education, 2004. Retrieved July 3, 2007, from http://cnets.iste.org/teachers/t_esscond.html#chart

Figure 6.8 Technology integration planning checklist

Phase 1: Determine Relative Advantage—Why Use Technology?
_____ Do I have topics, curriculum objectives, or insights I have difficulty teaching?
_____ Are any of the above a good match for a technology-based solution?
_____ What is the relative advantage of the technology-based solution?
_____ Is relative advantage sufficient to justify the effort and expense of using these solutions?

Phase 2: Decide on Objectives and Assessments— How Will I Know Students Have Learned?
_____ What outcomes do I expect of students after instruction to show me they have learned?
_____ What is the best way for me to assess students' learning (e.g., written tests, products)?
_____ Do the assessment instruments (e.g., tests, rubrics) exist or do I have to develop them?

Phase 3: Design Integration Strategies—What Teaching Strategies Will Work Best?
_____ Will the instruction be single subject or interdisciplinary?
_____ Will students work as individuals, pairs, small or large groups, whole class, a combination?
_____ Should activities be directed, constructivist, or a combination of these?
_____ What strategies should I use to encourage female and minority student involvement?
_____ What sequence of activities should I teach?
_____ Will students have enough time to learn the technologies before I begin grading?
_____ Do I have demonstrations of equipment and the software skills students will need?

Phase 4: Prepare the Instructional Environment—Are Essential Conditions in Place to Support Technology Integration?
_____ How many computers and copies of software do I need to carry out the activities?

_____ How many computers and copies of software are available?
_____ Over what time period and for how long will technology resources be needed?
_____ Do I need to schedule time in a lab or media center?
_____ Do I need to schedule projection devices or large-screen monitors for demos?
_____ What other equipment, software, media, and resources will I need?
_____ Are the uses I am planning legal according to copyright laws?
_____ Have I provided for students' privacy and safety?
_____ Have I made all necessary access provisions for students with physical disabilities?
_____ Am I familiar with troubleshooting procedures specific to the hardware or software?
_____ Have I built in time to test-run an equipment setup before students arrive?
_____ Have I built in time to back up important files? Have I trained students to back up theirs?
_____ Do I have a backup plan if I cannot use the resources as I had planned?

Phase 5: Evaluate and Revise Integration Strategies— What Worked Well? What Should Be Improved?
_____ Were objectives achieved? What evidence do I have to indicate success?
_____ Have I solicited feedback from students about how to improve activities?
_____ Do data and comments indicate changes are needed to improve outcomes?
_____ Are there other ways to arrange technology resources or activities to improve results?

Source: From _Integrating Educational Technology into Teaching,_ p. 63, by M. D. Roblyer, 2006, Upper Saddle River, NJ: Merrill/Prentice Hall. Reprinted with permission.

later in the chapter. In addition to examining the ISTE profiles, we'll look at how the 10 teachers featured in the Choosing Your Teaching Path section of MyEducationLab utilize both low-tech and high-tech tools in their classrooms. Their implementation of technology provides examples and is not necessarily representative of the overall integration of technology in U.S. schools.

Early Childhood. Creative early childhood teachers can incorporate technology in their classrooms while designing experiences that are developmentally appropriate for young children, as illustrated in Brandi's and Renee's classrooms at Summit Primary, Ohio. Prior to the end of second grade, students should be given the opportunity to show competence in using and communicating about developmentally appropriate technology. Figure 6.9 lists the 10 recommended competencies of technology literate students, grades pre-K–2, as prescribed by ISTE.

Figure 6.9   ISTE profiles for technology literate students, grades pre-K–2

Performance Indicators:
All students should have opportunities to demonstrate the following performances.

Prior to completion of Grade 2 students will:

1. Use input devices (e.g., mouse, keyboard, remote control) and output devices (e.g., monitor, printer) to successfully operate computers, VCRs, audiotapes, and other technologies.
2. Use a variety of media and technology resources for directed and independent learning activities.
3. Communicate about technology using developmentally appropriate and accurate terminology.
4. Use developmentally appropriate multimedia resources (e.g., interactive books, educational software, elementary multimedia encyclopedias) to support learning.
5. Work cooperatively and collaboratively with peers, family members, and others when using technology in the classroom.
6. Demonstrate positive social and ethical behaviors when using technology.
7. Practice responsible use of technology systems and software.
8. Create developmentally appropriate multimedia products with support from teachers, family members, or student partners.
9. Use technology resources (e.g., puzzles, logical thinking programs, writing tools, digital cameras, drawing tools) for problem solving, communication, and illustration of thoughts, ideas, and stories.
10. Gather information and communicate with others using telecommunications, with support from teachers, family members, or student partners.

Source: Reprinted with permission from *National Educational Technology Standards for Students: Connecting Curriculum and Technology,* © 2000, ISTE® (International Society for Technology in Education), iste@iste.org, www.iste.org. All rights reserved.

Brandi Wade. Kindergarten teacher Brandi Wade employs a variety of low-tech tools in her classroom, including the overhead projector. She introduces manipulatives, such as pattern blocks, on the overhead before setting up a learning center where children use them individually or in small groups. Brandi uses tape and CD players in centers where children listen to recorded books and follow along on the hard copy. She conducts singing and puppet plays with recorded music and introduces different cultures through music as well. Additionally, Brandi uses cartoon-format videos, primarily for science and historical topics, such as *Hiawatha* and *Mouse on the Mayflower.* She often plays the video of a book the class has read together and asks students to compare and contrast the book version with the video version.

Brandi has two computers in her kindergarten classroom. She encourages children to type words and original sentences and watch them appear on the monitor. For students who do not have home computers, this is especially intriguing. As a class, the kindergartners, with Brandi's assistance, research topics such as the size of the world's largest pumpkin and the average number of pets in a home.

Renee Ayers. Second grade teacher Renee Ayers routinely uses low-tech tools, such as large and individual white boards, egg timers, CD and tape players, and an overhead projector.

Renee also uses high-tech tools, such as a digital camera, in a variety of ways as part of instruction. One of her students' favorite projects involves taking autumn and spring walks they call their "Ohio wildflower hikes." Each student takes a picture of a flower or berry and uses the Internet to identify the plant. Renee then creates a PowerPoint presentation, interspersing pictures of the children. After the spring walk the students compare autumn flowers and berries to spring growth as part of a unit focusing on plants, seasons, and change.

Renee has two computers in her classroom for student use: one for word processing original compositions and one for reinforcing specific math skills.

Renee and her second graders have an email pen-pal class about 300 miles away. Using a computer projector, the students can participate in composing questions and responses. They excitedly wait for the other class to answer their emails.

Do the uses of technology in early childhood settings and the developmentally appropriate ISTE guidelines intrigue you? Can you picture yourself in a pre-K–2 classroom with students who are beginning to use technology?

Your Teaching Fingerprint

Some teachers, like Roxie Ahlbrecht, a second grade teacher at Robert Frost Elementary School in Sioux Falls, South Dakota, seek out innovative ways to incorporate technology both to deliver instruction and to introduce exciting ways to approach problem solving. Read more about Roxie and her classroom in Teachers' Days, Delights, and Dilemmas.

Elementary. ISTE-recommended competencies for technology literate students in grades 3–5 add to the early childhood guidelines primarily in the areas of using telecommunications

Teachers' Days, Delights, and Dilemmas

**Roxie Ahlbrecht
2004 South Dakota
Teacher of the Year**

I have been walking into a classroom daily for the last 48 years. My classroom today has a few similarities to the one I attended as a first grader. The students enter each morning with news to share and stories to tell. We start each day with the Pledge of Allegiance, and students are just as eager to help each other as my fellow first graders were in our one-room country schoolhouse almost five decades ago.

It is there that the similarities begin to dissipate. In my second grade classroom, the pledge is followed by a daily email message from our principal. This message is projected on our SmartBoard, a large screen connected to a computer that teachers and students can write and draw on. It includes the announcements for the day, schedule changes, and behavior and academic expectations. I use it as part of our shared reading each morning. I have the ability to highlight phrases or sentences to focus students' attention. Through this process, I am able to introduce reading strategies, vocabulary, and reading fluency to my whole class. When students come to words they do not know, I encourage them to decode them. This whole group activity at the beginning of the day is rich with teachable moments and opportunities for extensions.

Technology in my classroom continues to grow. We now do at least three online, collaborative projects each year. While technology can be an equalizing factor, it also allows for enrichment opportunities. Currently, I use Kidspiration, PowerPoint, KidPix, or Microsoft Word to challenge my students. Using these technology tools, my students are much more inclined to put forth greater effort because they know their work will be shared with our class on the SmartBoard and with classes around the world through online collaboration. There is nothing like looking at a child's eyes when they first see their work on the Internet or SmartBoard. Their excitement and motivation are palpable!

I love using the SmartBoard in our writing lessons. It allows us to save unfinished lessons to work on later, or to call back up when the topic or skill resurfaces. Part of the fun of using the SmartBoard is writing on it. When the opportunity arises, students want to be prepared to take a turn. I believe their attention increases with SmartBoard interactive lessons. My students write text more descriptively, using far more detail. We even correspond with mentor authors who are a mouse click away and are always happy to provide a model for my students as they experiment with different writing styles.

Technology is growing and changing rapidly. Teaching resources no longer fit in the right-hand drawer of our desks. If we are going to educate and prepare our students to succeed in a changing world, we need to work with the technology available to us today efficiently and effectively. Our students are going to grow up in a world where the career possibilities are endless and the skills they will need are beyond our imaginations. Yes, things have changed over the last five decades or so. But what hasn't changed is students' love of learning when teachers employ strategies that engage their eager minds.

to communicate with others and accessing information in order to problem solve and become self-directed learners. By the end of fifth grade, students should be able to evaluate information sources, an ability that developmentally sets elementary students apart from early childhood students. The list of recommended competencies for elementary students is provided in Figure 6.10.

The teachers and students at Rees Elementary, Utah, have access to a fully equipped computer lab. Principal Mike Larsen gives us a glimpse of the lab in the Choosing Your Teaching Path section of MyEducationLab. Click on Rees Elementary, then on principal Mike Larsen to watch the building tour again. Notice how technology has been incorporated throughout the building.

Chris Roberts. Multiage teachers Chris Roberts, Tim Mendenhall, and Brenda Beyal all use overhead projectors, white boards, and videos in their classrooms as instructional delivery tools. Using the three computers in their classroom, Chris Roberts's students experience drill-and-practice, tutorial, and simulation software. Chris also regularly incorporates music into his classroom activities using a CD player and drums. Chris often uses maps and globes to give his students a sense of "how big and wonderful the earth is."

Tim Mendenhall. Tim's computers are configured in what he calls his mini-lab. He requires students to do Internet research, practice their math lessons, and take computerized tests. On the low-tech side, Tim uses flip charts more often than any other instructional delivery aid.

Figure 6.10   ISTE profiles for technology literate students, grades 3–5

Performance Indicators:
All students should have opportunities to demonstrate the following performances.

Prior to completion of Grade 5 students will:
1. Use keyboards and other common input and output devices (including adaptive devices when necessary) efficiently and effectively.
2. Discuss common uses of technology in daily life and the advantages and disadvantages those uses provide.
3. Discuss basic issues related to responsible use of technology and information and describe personal consequences of inappropriate use.
4. Use general purpose productivity tools and peripherals to support personal productivity, remediate skill deficits, and facilitate learning throughout the curriculum.
5. Use technology tools (e.g., multimedia authoring, presentation, Web tools, digital cameras, scanners) for individual and collaborative writing, communication, and publishing activities to create knowledge products for audiences inside and outside the classroom.
6. Use telecommunications efficiently and effectively to access remote information, communicate with others in support of direct and independent learning, and pursue personal interests.
7. Use telecommunications and online resources (e.g., e-mail, online discussions, Web environments) to participate in collaborative problem-solving activities for the purpose of developing solutions or products for audiences inside and outside the classroom.
8. Use technology resources (e.g., calculators, data collection probes, videos, educational software) for problem solving, self-directed learning, and extended learning activities.
9. Determine when technology is useful and select the appropriate tool(s) and technology resources to address a variety of tasks and problems.
10. Evaluate the accuracy, relevance, appropriateness, comprehensiveness, and bias of electronic information sources.

Brenda Beyal. Brenda Beyal uses primary sources in her classroom whenever possible, along with other resources her students access through the Internet. She engages students in instruction with authentic objects. Her favorite items relate to her Native American heritage. These low-tech items enrich her lessons in all subject areas. Brenda's students are encouraged to use audiotapes occasionally as they follow along in books. Hearing good readers read with inflection and attention to punctuation helps students become better readers.

Does the use of technology at the elementary level interest you? Can you see yourself with students in grades 3–5 exploring topics and problem solving according to ISTE guidelines for this developmental level?

Your Teaching Fingerprint

Middle School. ISTE-recommended competencies for students as they complete eighth grade emphasize student familiarity with computer software and hardware to the degree of being able to recognize and diagnose problems. They are also expected to be knowledgeable about evolving technology and its subsequent effects on society. In addition, middle school students are expected to make decisions about the appropriateness of technology tools for various purposes, a developmentally advanced competency beyond the capabilities of most elementary students. The list of 10 ISTE competencies for middle school students is shown in Figure 6.11.

Traci Peters. Seventh grade math teacher Traci Peters at Cario Middle School, South Carolina, has six computers in her classroom, including a laptop. She creates PowerPoint presentations to accompany her lessons and projects them on a large television monitor. The other five computers have drill-and-practice and tutorial software

Figure 6.11   ISTE profiles for technology literate students, grades 6–8

Performance Indicators:
All students should have opportunities to demonstrate the following performances.

Prior to completion of Grade 8 students will:
 1. Apply strategies for identifying and solving routine hardware and software problems that occur during everyday use.
 2. Demonstrate knowledge of current changes in information technologies and the effect those changes have on the workplace and society.
 3. Exhibit legal and ethical behaviors when using information and technology, and discuss consequences of misuse.
 4. Use content-specific tools, software, and simulations (e.g., environmental probes, graphing calculators, exploratory environments, Web tools) to support learning and research.
 5. Apply productivity/multimedia tools and peripherals to support personal productivity, group collaboration, and learning throughout the curriculum.
 6. Design, develop, publish, and present products (e.g., Web pages, videotapes) using technology resources that demonstrate and communicate curriculum concepts to audiences inside and outside the classroom.
 7. Collaborate with peers, experts, and others using telecommunications and collaborative tools to investigate curriculum-related problems, issues, and information, and to develop solutions or products for audiences inside and outside the classroom.
 8. Select and use appropriate tools and technology resources to accomplish a variety of tasks and solve problems.
 9. Demonstrate an understanding of concepts underlying hardware, software, and connectivity, and of practical applications to learning and problem solving.
10. Research and evaluate the accuracy, relevance, appropriateness, comprehensiveness, and bias of electronic information sources concerning real-world problems.

Source: Reprinted with permission from *National Educational Technology Standards for Students: Connecting Curriculum and Technology,* © 2000, ISTE® (International Society for Technology in Education), iste@iste.org, www.iste.org. All rights reserved.

for student use. Traci's students also often use Cario's computer lab. When not engaged in other projects, they complete practice standardized tests online to help prepare them for South Carolina's annual standards-based test, the Palmetto Achievement Challenge Test (PACT).

Traci uses an overhead projector daily for sample problems, homework assignments, and practice exercises, along with diagrams she either draws or photocopies onto transparency sheets. Traci also uses a variety of manipulatives to teach the concepts of seventh grade math. Toward the end of seventh grade, students study equations and functions. Traci teaches them how to use the graphing components of the TI-83 calculators Cario Middle School provides for student use.

Deirdre Huger-McGrew. We got a glimpse of Deirdre Huger-McGrew's use of technology in the opening scenario of this chapter. In addition to READ 180, Deirdre has her own website and a class page used for sharing information with her students. She posts discussion questions through email to get her students to talk about books they're reading. These emails give students writing practice, opportunities to send and receive attachments, and occasions to learn netiquette (the correct way to email).

Middle school students use technology in more sophisticated ways than elementary students. Would you like to be part of this developmentally maturing process? If so, why is the middle school level intriguing to you?

High School. The recommended competencies for high school students include more analysis and evaluation than those for middle school students. ISTE guidelines for technology literate twelfth graders emphasize responsibility for understanding the impact of use, and reliance on, technology in the workplace and society. The high school competencies are listed in Figure 6.12.

As we saw in Chapter 3, many students at Roosevelt High School (RHS), California, are English language learners (ELLs). The RHS library is equipped with computers that allow students to learn English using visual communication on the screen and audio communication through headsets. As the students use programs such as Accelerated Reader (AR), they learn basic computer skills. AR allows students to read at their diagnosed appropriate levels and then answer questions that measure comprehension. In afterschool programs, students in the bilingual classes have opportunities to use the computers in the library and receive individual help from teachers and other school personnel. In the Choosing Your Teaching Path section of MyEducationLab, you got a glimpse of the computers earlier as you toured Roosevelt High with the assistant principal. To review the tour, click on Roosevelt High School, then on principal Maria Romero.

Angelica Reynosa. In Angelica Reynosa's segment of this text's video, she uses the overhead projector as one means of adding visual stimulation to her lessons at RHS. In the lesson video segment showing her World History course, Angelica uses a powerful drawing depicting class struggle. She also frequently uses videos to help her bilingual students grasp concepts and understand background information.

Derek Boucher. Derek Boucher uses videos in his history and reading classes. He introduces books on topics students have seen in videos, leading students to be more motivated to read. Derek also uses the overhead projector and white board during group lessons. When Derek assigns writing projects, he requires that at least a portion of the research be conducted using the Internet.

Craig Cleveland. Craig Cleveland uses videos and the overhead projector for delivery of instruction and for student inquiry. He often requires his students to conduct Internet research. As Craig's video segment shows, he uses music to enhance his teaching. Craig's low-tech approaches using the guitar and piano bring his lessons to life and capture attention that may otherwise not be tapped. To review high school lessons at RHS using low-tech

Figure 6.12   ISTE profiles for technology literate students, grades 9–12

Performance Indicators:
All students should have opportunities to demonstrate the following performances.

Prior to completion of Grade 12 students will:

1. Identify capabilities and limitations of contemporary and emerging technology resources and assess the potential of these systems and services to address personal, lifelong learning, and workplace needs.
2. Make informed choices among technology systems, resources, and services.
3. Analyze advantages and disadvantages of widespread use and reliance on technology in the workplace and in society as a whole.
4. Demonstrate and advocate for legal and ethical behaviors among peers, family, and community regarding the use of technology and information.
5. Use technology tools and resources for managing and communicating personal/professional information (e.g., finances, schedules, addresses, purchases, correspondence).
6. Evaluate technology-based options, including distance and distributed education, for lifelong learning.
7. Routinely and efficiently use online information resources to meet needs for collaboration, research, publication, communication, and productivity.
8. Select and apply technology tools for research, information analysis, problem solving, and decision making in content learning.
9. Investigate and apply expert systems, intelligent agents, and simulations in real-world situations.
10. Collaborate with peers, experts, and others to contribute to a content-related knowledge base by using technology to compile, synthesize, produce, and disseminate information, models, and other creative works.

Source: Reprinted with permission from *National Educational Technology Standards for Students: Connecting Curriculum and Technology,* © 2000, ISTE® (International Society for Technology in Education), iste@iste.org, www.iste.org. All rights reserved.

and high-tech tools, go to the Choosing Your Teaching Path section of MyEducationLab, click on Roosevelt, and then on the teacher's name.

In high school settings technology use can be integrated as part of the everyday process of learning in many progressive ways. Would you like to learn about and implement technology to assist students in grades 9–12? Does their maturing development that allows them to evaluate the potential of technology in the workplace appeal to you as a future facilitator of learning?

Your Teaching Fingerprint

Now that we have reviewed the current technology standards at each school level and have seen a variety of technology applications in the classrooms of our focus teachers, let's consider the issues involved in the use of technology in schools.

What Issues Surround and Affect the Use of Technology in Schools?

As you might imagine after reading about technology in schools, there are many issues involved in the integration of technology into classrooms. We will explore some of these issues, examine their impact on schools, and look for possible ways to enhance the positive and minimize the negative.

Equity

Socioeconomic status and minority designation have widely been considered the biggest roadblocks to educational access (Corporation for Public Broadcasting, 2003). This results in what is often called the **digital divide**. Some people fear that technology may further divide society along socioeconomic and ethnic lines, thus widening the existing gap between the haves and have nots. Table 6.2 revealed that Internet access in schools appears to be equal regardless of minority status, socioeconomic status, and level, size, and location of schools. Given these statistics, how can a digital divide exist?

The divide is twofold. First of all, even with equal access, technology is often used differently among schools and among specific student populations. The quantity of computer use in schools is not as important as the quality or type of computer use (Wenglinsky, 2005). Students in Title I schools that have a majority of students from lower socioeconomic settings may have daily access to computers, but they are more likely to use them for remedial work, such as drill and practice. In schools that are not designated as Title I, students are more likely to use computers for higher-order learning activities, such as problem solving (Roblyer, 2006).

The second aspect of the digital divide involves home access to computer technology. A recent study shows that about 77% of students ages 7–17 from higher-income homes (earning more than $75,000 annually) use a home computer regularly. For low-income homes (earning less than $15,000 annually), the percentage drops dramatically, to 29%. White and Asian American students are twice as likely as Latino, African American, or Native American students to use word processing or desktop publishing applications in home settings (Azzam, 2006).

What can we do? In a report entitled *Measuring Digital Opportunity for America's Children: Where We Stand and Where We Go from Here* (Lazarus, Wainer, & Lipper, 2005), the Children's Partnership presents five recommendations for advancing Information and Communications Technology (ICT) as part of a "digital opportunity action agenda" (p. 9):

1. . . . identify and capitalize on the ICT advances of proven value
2. . . . invest in powerful but not-yet-developed ways in which ICT can help meet national goals for children
3. . . . create benchmarks necessary to hold ourselves accountable for providing digital opportunities to all children
4. . . . ensure that every child has access to ICT tools where it matters—at home, at school, and in the community. Parents and young people must be well informed about the opportunities and risks found through the Internet.
5. . . . develop a long-range research agenda that can inform our decisions and actions in deploying technology effectively for children and young adults over the next decade

Safety and Privacy

We continually hear about safety and privacy issues involving technology. From identity theft to online pornography, predators are striking often and in ingenious ways. In 2000 Congress passed the Children's Internet Protection Act (CIPA) to help protect children from these predators by requiring that all public libraries install filtering software to block websites that contain obscene images or content. Many parents and K–12 schools have similar blocks to filter content and protect student identities.

What can we do? While the federal government, school district policies, and filtering software all help protect students' privacy and ensure their safety, teachers can play an even greater role than agencies or devices. Close monitoring of Internet use and lessons on smart usage of technology can positively influence students as they become more skilled in the use of technological tools.

Safekids.com offers *Kids' Rules for Online Safety,* recommending 10 ways to keep students safe while using the Internet. Posting and reiterating these rules in the classroom may save the identity, even the life, of a child. Teachers can have a major impact on the preservation of privacy and safety of students by emphasizing these rules, shown in Figure 6.13.

Figure 6.13   Kids' rules for online safety

1. I will not give out personal information such as my address, telephone number, parents' work address/telephone number, or the name and location of my school without my parents' permission.
2. I will tell my parents right away if I come across any information that makes me feel uncomfortable.
3. I will never agree to get together with someone I "meet" online without first checking with my parents. If my parents agree to the meeting, I will be sure that it is in a public place and bring my mother or father along.
4. I will never send a person my picture or anything else without first checking with my parents.
5. I will not respond to any messages that are mean or in any way make me feel uncomfortable. It is not my fault if I get a message like that. If I do I will tell my parents right away so that they can contact the service provider.
6. I will talk with my parents so that we can set up rules for going online. We will decide on the time of day that I can be online, the length of time I can be online, and appropriate areas for me to visit. I will not access other areas or break these rules without their permission.
7. I will not give out my Internet password to anyone (even my best friends) other than my parents.
8. I will check with my parents before downloading or installing software or doing anything that could possibly hurt our computer or jeopardize my family's privacy.
9. I will be a good online citizen and not do anything that hurts other people or is against the law.
10. I will help my parents understand how to have fun and learn things online and teach them things about the Internet, computers and other technology.

Source: Rules 1 through 6 are adapted from the brochure *Child Safety on the Information Highway* by SafeKids.Com founder Larry Magid. (© 2004 National Center for Missing and Exploited Children). Rules 7 through 10 are copyrighted by Larry Magid (© 2005). Retrieved December 28, 2006, from http://www.safekids.com/kidsrules.htm

Standards and Accountability

The pressure to meet designated state and national standards may lead teachers and administrators to question the wisdom of using the time and resources necessary to plan and implement the sometimes complex process of technology integration. Under these circumstances, drill-and-practice and tutorial software may be considered the best, and sometimes the only, way to use technology in the classroom.

What can we do? Many approaches are available to teachers to promote the use of technology for both presentation and problem solving, even in this era of standards and high-stakes testing, including the following:

- Teachers should thoroughly understand their subject and grade-specific standards in order to recognize opportunities to utilize technology in their classrooms.
- Teachers should take the initiative to seek out new ways of using technology to accomplish curricular goals.
- Because No Child Left Behind (NCLB) requires government-funded programs (public schools) to demonstrate scientifically based research results, teachers should look for and be involved in research attempts to determine the usefulness of technology in increasing student learning.

Funding

Educators and legislators are increasingly questioning the funding expended on technology given accountability demands and NCLB-imposed requirements. Ringstaff and Kelley (2002) examined research findings to calculate the learning return on investment in technology. They concluded that justifying technology expenses is becoming more difficult because of the lack of research evidence of its effectiveness in teaching and learning.

In the 1990s money seemed plentiful to support technology use in schools. It was almost a bandwagon environment as money was earmarked to purchase initial equipment and services, many times without considering what's known in business as the total cost of ownership. Frequently schools lack the money in their budgets to pay for total cost of ownership items such as maintenance, long-term network access and security, licenses, and eventual hardware replacement. In this situation technology amounts to what Warhaftig (2005) refers to as a "costly gift" (p. 61).

Federal and state governments, businesses, and organizations continue to invest billions of dollars in hardware and software for schools. These dollars have stretched a little further, however, since 1996, when Congress passed the Telecommunications Reform Act that allows technology for schools to be purchased at discounted prices or at an education rate (E-Rate).

What can we do? Obviously teachers won't have the capacity to purchase expensive technology tools or financially support their use. However, individual teachers or groups of teachers can apply for **grants** to pay for initial technology or continuing technology support. Grants are funds provided by a source to pay for equipment or services requested by teachers and others.

Equally as important as acquiring funding for technology is documenting the use of technology and its positive effects on student learning in the classroom. This kind of documentation can serve to support the continued use of funds to both purchase and maintain appropriate levels of technology in schools.

Online Plagiarism

Because online access to information and full documents has grown exponentially, the possibility of plagiarism has also increased. Not only are there more sources to be copied, but the sheer number makes detection more difficult. Plagiarism involving students using what they find on the Internet as their own is sometimes called **cybercheating**.

Teachers also need to be concerned about violating copyright laws that either prohibit the copying of material or limit the amount that may be copied. Copyright issues can be complex and involve not only the document but also the intended use. What constitutes fair use of a particular document may not be considered fair use for a different document.

What can we do? Teachers concerned about students' work being authentic need to watch for signs such as vocabulary that is advanced for the students' grade level or citations that are perfectly referenced in a format to which students have not been exposed. Online services such as www.turnitin.com and www.plagiarism.org can help teachers detect cybercheating.

School districts generally provide guidelines for teachers that explain how copyright laws apply to materials teachers may use. Teachers should carefully read and follow district guidelines and ask should they have questions.

Professional Development for Teachers

Many teachers do not feel prepared to integrate technology into their classrooms in ways that lead to optimal student use. Often the professional development available for teachers centers on lower-order questions regarding the "what" of technology tool use rather than the "higher-order how and why questions that prompt real understanding of the true potential of computers in instruction" (Burns, 2006, p. 52). Teachers require ongoing and higher-order professional development to effectively integrate technology into curriculum, instruction, and assessment.

What can we do? Teachers should seek out professional development in their school or district settings, through coursework, or in sessions at conferences that focus on higher-order applications of technology. All teachers, regardless of their expertise, must continue to broaden their technological horizons because the world of technology is continually changing, growing, and evolving.

What Does the Future Hold for Technology in Schools?

Today's technology is yesterday's science fiction; today's science fiction is tomorrow's technology. Given this somewhat simplistic adage, remaining in step with the innovation and refinement of technology is a Herculean task. Most teachers can't do it alone. With the demands of keeping up with content and standards, planning lessons, attending to paperwork and certification issues, and so on, teachers' professional lives are full. However, the fullness of teachers' days will neither stop the technological revolution from occurring, nor exclude pre-K–12 schools from incorporating technology into curriculum, instruction, and assessment.

What's on the educational technology horizon? Let's look at just a few of the technological innovations that may be familiar to some of you (and may have been part of your pre-K–12 experiences) and totally new to others.

Innovation: Computers for All

In 2003 Norris, Sullivan, Poirot, and Soloway reported on the results of a survey administered to over 4,000 K–12 classroom teachers in large and small districts across the United States. The teachers overwhelmingly stated that technology does not have an impact on teaching and learning because it isn't being used. The reason technology is not being used is a real lack of access to it. The study revealed that although virtually every school has Internet access and every classroom has at least one computer, that's not nearly enough to have an impact. A strong case is made for classroom computer access in a one-to-one computer-student ratio—a "computers for all" policy. The Norris et al. study concluded that "the strongest predictor of teachers' technology use were measures of technology access" (p. 16). The long-held belief that technology use or nonuse rests almost solely with a teacher's attitude toward it was debunked in this study. The authors emphatically conclude, "If students don't have access to classroom computers, then classroom computers can't possibly have a measurable impact on students' learning!" (p. 25).

Innovation: Wireless Technology

Wireless technology is not new. Over 100 years ago Marconi sent the first wireless messages using radio waves. Over a century of research and many inventions later, we see wireless technology impacting schools in a variety of forms, including handheld technology and mobile laptop labs. Access to the Web and other innovations through wireless technology is dominating much of the first part of the 21st century, to the point of being commonly labeled a wireless revolution.

Innovation: Software Programs

Continual innovations in software capabilities lead us to believe there is no limit to what we can do by integrating human ingenuity and technological advances. Some of the software programs currently in use as resources for students with disabilities include text-to-speech, speech-to-text, and handwriting-recognition-to-text features. Not only do these programs serve as assistive technology, but their capacity to personalize and individualize content and move the learner along a logical path toward higher-order thinking and learning is remarkable.

Innovation: Digital Portfolios

Multimedia collections of students' work that are stored and reviewed in digital format are known as **digital portfolios**. Digital portfolios may showcase products, prove mastery of standards, and communicate to parents and others what students are learning.

Niguidula (2005) has identified a set of essential questions schools need to address when considering moving to digital portfolios.

1. Vision: What skills and content should students master and demonstrate in their portfolios?
2. Purpose: Why do we collect student work?
3. Audience: Who are the audiences for portfolios?
4. Assessment: How do the entries in portfolios reflect the school's assessment vision, and how can we assess the quality of those entries?
5. Technology: What hardware, software, networking, and technical support will our school need to implement a digital portfolio assessment system?
6. Logistics: How will students enter work into digital portfolios?
7. Culture: Is discussing student work already a part of our school culture? (Niguidula, 2005, pp. 44–47)

Establishing and maintaining digital portfolios is a major commitment of time and resources. These and other questions should be carefully considered before beginning.

Innovation: Authentic Audiences

Collaborating on projects and then sharing them through Web publishing takes the Internet beyond the role of mere information dispenser and includes students in an interactive role as publishers of information. Digital tools such as blogs, wikis, and podcasts allow students to work with people outside their schools and share results with a wide authentic audience in what is referred to as the Read/Write Web (Richardson, 2006).

Millions of bloggers, or those who contribute to Weblogs, or **blogs**, share content and perspectives. Many of these are high school students. For example, at Hunterton High School in Flemington, New Jersey, students communicate with authors of literature they are studying through blogs. They also communicate with students in Krakow, Poland, as part of a Holocaust unit (Richardson, 2006).

A **wiki** is a website serving as an information source that anyone can edit at any time. An online encyclopedia with more than 500,000 entries can be accessed at Wikipedia.org. Entries are changed by contributors who add information as desired. Because anyone can alter the content, the accuracy of information found on a wiki may be questionable.

A **podcast** is like a radio program distributed on the Web. Examples of podcasts include museum tours, weekly classroom reports, oral histories, and interviews. The audiences for podcasts may be small, but Richardson (2006) equates creating a podcast to publishing a project as opposed to simply turning it in to the teacher.

Innovation: No More Books

Moving to a "no more books" environment requires a large monetary investment and teachers with the skills and desire to be part of the project. An example of a bookless school is Empire High School, just outside of Tucson, Arizona, the state's first completely wireless, all-laptop school. The 350 students have access to texts, classics, articles, and e-media through Apple iBooks. States such as Illinois, Maine, New Hampshire, and Virginia have cited dramatic improvements in student engagement, absenteeism, and discipline since supplying laptops for all students in entire classrooms, schools, and even counties (Colin, 2005).

Innovation: Distance Learning and Virtual Schools

Web-based courses are becoming increasingly more prevalent in pre-K–12 settings. **Distance learning** involves the acquisition of knowledge and skills through instruction delivered by technology. Learning is not place based. Many online and offline skills and tools are needed to make distance learning effective. Course management systems such as WebCT and Blackboard help teachers design and deliver courses. Well-designed distance learning courses include four essential characteristics:

- effective course structure
- engaging, collaborative activities

- an interactive learning community
- effective assessment strategies (Roblyer, 2006, pp. 242–243)

Distance learning provides opportunities for students to participate in coursework that may not otherwise be available. Students in rural areas or in very small schools can take courses along with students attending large schools with wide arrays of curricular offerings. All students who enroll in distance learning courses may benefit from access to experts, communication resources that support collaboration, ideas from multiple sources, online course materials, and tutorials.

Virtual schools are schools that deliver instruction only through distance learning. In 2002 a nonprofit foundation called Virtual High School, Inc. (VHS), supported a consortium of more than 200 virtual high schools in 28 states and 8 countries (*Technology Counts*, 2002).

The basic question remains, "Can an online school replace face-to-face experiences?" Of course virtual schools can't replicate a traditional school, but they have other advantages we are only beginning to tap. Innovations make virtual schools more and more attractive as the debate over their value continues.

Have you participated in online courses or experienced online components in your pre-K–12 or college classes? What aspects did you most enjoy or benefit from? What aspects of online study did you not like? Why?

Your Teaching Fingerprint

Concluding Thoughts

The headline of the September 25, 2000, issue of *U.S. News and World Report* read "Why Computers Fail as Teachers." The reason is simple—computers aren't teachers. There are good teachers who use computers daily for instructional delivery. There are good teachers who rarely or never purposefully incorporate computer technology into classroom learning experiences. Likewise, there are poor teachers who use technology daily and poor teachers who are true technophobes. An influx of technology can make a good school even better. An influx of technology will not, however, make a bad school good.

In the 1980s and '90s some people feared that computers would replace teachers. Supporters of technology in the classroom hoped not for the replacement of teachers, but rather for comprehensive and widespread integration of technology requiring teachers to play significant roles as facilitators of higher-order thinking. Neither has happened. Norris et al. (2003) reported, "By and large classrooms and schools go about their daily business ignorant of the profound changes caused by computing technologies in many other areas of everyday life" (p. 15). Larry Cuban (2001), noted expert on education and change, contends that technology was "oversold" in terms of its impact on teaching and learning. Thoughtful educators are now examining what Burns (2005) calls the "gap between intention and implementation."

Teachers will use technology when they see compelling reasons to do so. These reasons must include a curriculum that is a rich mix of what Prensky (2006) calls traditional, predigital "legacy" knowledge and 21st-century digital-based learning. Instructional uses of technology will flourish when computers are as available in the classroom as pencils and books. When assessment is not only administered by computers, but also requires that problem-solving skills be demonstrated with solutions that can only be obtained through the use of technology, then teachers will embrace the potential. Integrating current and emerging technology will no doubt enhance the teaching and learning connection. In *The Information Commons Handbook*, Don Beagle (2006) relates the recent past to the future when he says,

> Throughout much of the last century, people shared a collective understanding of the way information was organized and accessed. Change seemed continuous but controlled. The computer age initiated by the electronic revolution of the 1980s and 1990s transformed this relatively stable process of development, splintering it through the refractive lenses of new paradigms and possibilities. As it did so, it redefined how, where, and why people used information. These radical changes brought about a new vision of knowledge and forever transformed the ways we learn. (p. xv)

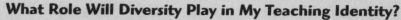

What Role Will Diversity Play in My Teaching Identity?

The digital divide is real. There may be little we can do about student access to technology in their homes. However, what we *can* affect is how technology is utilized in our classrooms and schools. In schools where the majority of students are from low-income settings, computers are likely to be used for remediation, rather than for enrichment. While instructional software is appropriate in all schools at times for drill-and-practice and tutorial purposes, computers can do much more to promote higher-order thinking and problem solving.

Knowing that some students have little or no opportunity to use computers outside school should prompt us to design assignments that will involve all students in the possibilities that high-tech brings to our lives.

Because of this transformation, the future of technology in pre-K–12 schools is both exciting and mind-boggling. Prensky (2006) asks us to consider that "Schools are stuck in the 20th century. Students have rushed into the 21st." He asks, "How can schools catch up and provide students with a relevant education?" (p. 8). Prensky further tells us that our students are no longer younger versions of ourselves, but rather "digital natives" who fluently speak the language of technology. He advises educators to "Listen to the natives" (p. 9). As "digital immigrants," many teachers retain a predigital "accent." Students can lead the way into the future because they are growing up in a technological world. We would be wise to listen to and learn from these digital natives.

Chapter in Review

What guides the use of technology in U.S. schools?

- Standards of subject area organizations and grade level organizations all include guidance concerning technology.
- The International Society for Technology in Education has set expectations for teachers and students regarding technology use in schools.

What technological tools are available to enhance curriculum, instruction, and assessment?

- Teachers have two broad categories of technology to consider: teaching tools and tools for teachers.
- Low-tech tools require thought, planning, and practice to be used effectively and efficiently.
- Television is a technology staple in most classrooms.
- High-tech tools, such as computers, educational software, and the Internet, have the potential to affect teaching and learning.
- Tools for teachers include tools for lesson planning, record keeping, communication, and professional development.

Does technology make a difference in student learning?

- Insufficient research has been conducted on the impact of technology.
- There is little evidence, as measured by traditional assessment, that the use of technology positively impacts student learning.
- Effective use of technology can lead to growth in problem-solving skills, increased motivation, better preparation for the workforce, and improved ways of meeting the needs of students with disabilities.

How do teachers use technology in their classrooms?

- Facilitating technology use in the classroom requires teachers to rethink their roles.
- There are essential conditions that support the use of technology for both delivery of instruction and problem solving.
- Integrating technology in the classroom leads to meaningful usage that enhances teaching and learning.
- Technology use varies by grade level.

What issues surround and affect the use of technology in schools?

- A digital divide exists in schools based on socioeconomic status and ethnicity. The divide is twofold: how technology is actually used in the schools, and home access.
- School personnel must be continually vigilant to keep students safe and protect their privacy when they are using technology.
- Securing continued funding, preventing security risks and online plagiarism, and keeping teachers up-to-date in terms of professional development are challenging issues for technology use in schools.

What does the future hold for technology in schools?

- Research tells us that only when all students have one-to-one access in schools will computers have a measurable impact on student learning.
- Software programs of the future will allow for the amazing interaction of digital text, voice, and handwriting.
- The use of digital portfolios and authentic audiences for collaboration and products will be meaningful implementations of technology.
- Future delivery systems, including those that do away with traditional hard-copy books, will impact how teachers teach and students learn.
- Distance learning and virtual schools will affect increasing numbers of students in the future.

Professional Practice

■ Licensure Test Prep

1. The ISTE Profiles for Technology Literate Students include progressively more complex standards for each level of school from early childhood to high school. Following are additions that are made to each level's particular standards. Place the additions in order as they build from early childhood to elementary, then from elementary to middle school, and from middle school to high school.

   I. responsibility for understanding the impact of use, and reliance on, technology in the workplace and society
   II. using telecommunications to communicate with others, and accessing information in order to problem solve and become self-directed learners
   III. making decisions about the appropriateness of technology tools for various purposes

   a. I, II, III
   b. II, I, III
   c. II, III, I
   d. III, II, I

2. All of the following statements apply to the digital divide except
   a. schools with large populations of students from low-income homes are less likely to have Internet access than schools with fewer students with low socioeconomic status.
   b. socioeconomic status is a factor in the creation of the digital divide.
   c. technology is often used differently among schools and among different school populations.
   d. minority designation is considered a contributing factor to the digital divide.

3. In the 1990s, when funding appeared to be plentiful for technology in schools, the primary factor not considered by those who sought funding and those who granted it was
   a. technology is steadily, although gradually, losing its importance in K–12 education.
   b. the total cost of ownership is proving to be an unplanned burden for schools.
   c. one-time grant funding never fosters sustainable programs.
   d. the cost of new hardware exceeds the budget of most districts.

4. All of the following statements are true except
   a. almost all occupations involve some sort of technology.
   b. instructional games are considered instructional software.
   c. multimedia collections of students' work that are stored and reviewed in digital format are known as digital portfolios.
   d. there is substantial evidence that the use of technology in the classroom improves learning.

5. Craig Cleveland at Roosevelt High School in Fresno, California, is an effective teacher and communicator. However, Craig does not make use of high-tech tools very often. He regularly uses an overhead projector and a television with DVD/VCR capabilities. What are two high-tech tools Craig might use in his history classes to enhance his instruction? Explain your choices and briefly describe how Craig might use each.

6. Brenda Beyal at Rees Elementary, Utah, promotes collaboration among her students and plans experiences that actively involve them in their own learning. Explain two ways Brenda might meet ISTE Profiles for Technology Literate Students, Grades 3–5, number 5, in her class. Describe the tools she might use and how she could incorporate them.

   ISTE Profiles for Technology Literate Students, Grades 3–5. Use technology tools (e.g., multimedia authoring, presentation, Web tools, digital cameras, scanners) for individual and collaborative writing, communication, and publishing activities to create knowledge products for audiences inside and outside the classroom. (from Figure 6.9)

Standards Speak

This chapter's section entitled What guides the use of technology in U.S. schools? briefly looked at subject area and grade level standards. The following are other standards that address the use of technology in schools.

INTASC Knowledge Principle 4

The teacher knows how to enhance learning through the use of a wide variety of materials as well as human and technological resources (e.g., computers, audiovisual technologies, videotapes and discs, local experts, primary documents and artifacts, texts, reference books, literature, and other print resources).

NCATE Standard I: Candidate Knowledge, Skills, and Dispositions

The professional teacher . . . should be able to integrate technology into instruction effectively.

NBPTS Proposition 3

Teachers know about the breadth of options available to them, such as . . . working with computers.

Respond to the following questions in your class notebook and/or discuss your responses with your classmates as directed by your instructor.

1. Until the mid 1990s there was little or no mention of technology in standards. Why are guidelines now necessary for technology use in schools?

2. Both INTASC and NBPTS standards speak of variety and options. Why is it important for teachers to know about and use many different resources and tools in the classroom?

■ MyEducationLab

The following interactive features may be found in Chapter 6 of MyEducationLab.

Homework and Exercises

Writing My Own Story

To write your own story by responding to some of the questions in the text accompanied by fingerprint icons, plus others, go to the "Writing My Own Story" section of the Homework and Exercises for Chapter 6 of MyEducationLab.

What's My Disposition?

To reflect on your beliefs and attitudes concerning the teaching profession, go to Chapter 6's "What's My Disposition?" feature of the Homework and Exercises section of MyEducationLab.

Exploring Schools and Classrooms

If your course involves experiences in schools, the questions and prompts in the "Exploring Schools and Classrooms" feature of Chapter 6's Homework and Exercises section of MyEducationLab will guide you as you explore local schools and classrooms.

Virtual Field Experience

To respond to questions and prompts regarding the Choosing Your Teaching Path videos that connect to specific chapter content, go to Chapter 6's Virtual Field Experience section of MyEducationLab. The questions will help you make sense of what you have read in the chapter.

Chapter 7

Creating and Maintaining a Positive and Productive Learning Environment

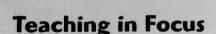

Teaching in Focus

When Jeff walked into Tim Mendenhall's multiage classroom at Rees Elementary School, Utah, in late September, he had one of those "I don't want to be here" looks. His entrance was more of a shuffle than a walk, and his demeanor was obvious to other students as well as to Mr. Mendenhall. Jeff had just moved to Spanish Fork from Los Angeles. He was 12 and entering fifth grade for the second time. Tim sensed that Jeff would prove to be quite a challenge. When it was time for the third, fourth, and fifth graders in Tim's multiage class to go out for recess, Tim asked Jeff to spend the time with him so they could get to know each other. Jeff's first words were, "Why do I have to be in here with all these babies?"

Fortunately for Jeff he had come to a school and a homeroom with structure, and a teacher with a classroom management philosophy that responds to students as individuals. Tim applies a theory that might be called game therapy. He believes in playing with kids—on the field and in the classroom. He tells us, "If you earn the kids' respect by being respectful, consistent, and fun, there are few problems. If you make learning enjoyable and meaningful, then students stay on task and want to be with you. Wanting to learn, wanting to be with you, and wanting to do whatever you have planned is motivation enough to behave."

Tim had his work cut out for him. Jeff had no intention of joining in. The first week or so he sat silently and sullenly. He resisted any kind of group work and refused to take part in classroom and outside games until Tim tossed a basketball his way. He threw it back. Tim shot at the basket and missed. Jeff picked up the ball, tossed it up, made the basket, and grinned. That's all Tim needed to plan his strategy. Back in the classroom he placed a three-ring binder filled with basketball player cards on Jeff's table.

Jeff had the potential to be very disruptive to the classroom community Tim had so carefully built. By being sensitive and purposeful, Tim was able to avoid power struggles and give Jeff a behavioral comfort level. Although behavior didn't become a problem, Jeff continues to struggle academically. That's the challenge Tim faces daily. At the same time, Tim has cleared a major hurdle because he has won Jeff's respect and Jeff wants to be with him.

Later in the chapter we'll examine guidelines Tim has developed that help him maintain a positive and productive learning environment. To review Tim's portion of the video, go to the Choosing Your Teaching Path section of MyEducationLab at www.myeducationlab.com, click on Rees Elementary, and then on Tim Mendenhall.

Here are the focus questions this chapter will explore.

- **How do teachers create a positive learning environment?**
- **What routines contribute to maintaining a productive classroom environment?**
- **How do teachers establish expectations, incentives, and consequences?**
- **How can I develop a classroom management plan?**

■ Introduction

Creating and maintaining a positive and productive learning environment is complex and compelling—complex because there are multiple variables to consider, and compelling because without a positive and productive learning environment, teaching has little effect. New and experienced teachers alike are often puzzled by the whole process. They often think of the learning environment in narrow terms of student cooperation and student misbehavior. But the learning environment is so much more. When teachers expand their view to include the elements discussed in this chapter, it becomes clear that creating and maintaining a positive and productive learning environment is indeed a puzzle, one with many interlocking pieces that depend on one another to form a complete, stable picture. Some of the most important pieces of the puzzle are shown in Figure 7.1.

It's not too soon to begin thinking about the learning environment you want to create in your future classroom as you continue your journey toward becoming a teacher. Some of the content of this chapter may seem too detailed for where you are on your journey, but there is a purpose in reading about it now. When you are in classrooms observing the work of teachers, having read about the topics in the chapter will prompt you to notice elements of the learning environment that might otherwise escape your attention. You will no doubt take a course devoted to the study of and planning for the learning environment. Consider this chapter an introduction for such a course, piquing your interest to discover more about the classroom learning environment as you continue your courses and fieldwork.

This chapter will examine the physical surroundings and the student-teacher sense of community that are both so vital to the learning environment. It will explore student routines that lead to greater productivity. Classroom management, a major part of maintaining a positive and productive learning environment, will be addressed in the context of three primary components: expectations, incentives, and consequences. Information about both routines and classroom management is augmented by examples from our 10 focus classrooms at the four levels of school. The chapter concludes with information about developing a classroom management plan that supports a positive and productive learning environment.

Figure 7.1   A positive and productive learning environment

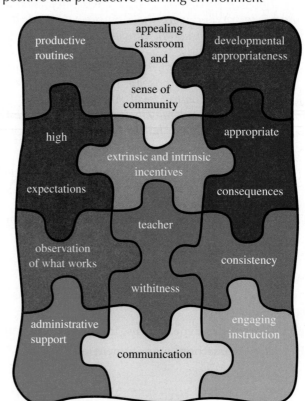

How Do Teachers Create a Positive Learning Environment?

A positive learning environment doesn't just happen. It takes planning, continuing effort, and a watchful eye. The physical layout of the classroom, its appearance, and the degree of usefulness and efficiency achieved within it all work in unison to set the stage for a teacher to build community with and among students. In this section we consider community—what it is and how to establish this important aspect of teaching and learning. We then examine the classroom management philosophy of Jacob Kounin to prepare for a discussion of classroom routines, expectations, incentives, and consequences. Let's begin with the most obvious and least complex element of the learning environment, the physical space.

Physical Space

A welcoming, well-organized, student-friendly environment goes a long way toward helping accomplish both learning and affective goals. The layout of desks and equipment, what's on the walls, the organization—everything about a classroom matters. This kind of classroom doesn't happen by accident. John Dewey's wisdom concerning the physical surroundings of learning included his statement that "any environment is a chance environment so far as its educative influence is concerned unless it has been deliberately regulated with reference to its educative effect" (1944, p. 19). The job of a teacher includes deliberately staging the classroom itself to be an "educative influence." Think about the classrooms in your pre-K–12 experiences. Were they conducive to learning, or distracting? Why? How do you envision your future classroom's appearance? Remember that when you see a fingerprint in the margin it means that you will be asked to respond to questions based on your experiences and opinions. These questions are included in "Writing My Own Story" in Chapter 7 of the Homework and Exercises section of MyEducationLab at www.myeducationlab.com.

Your Teaching Fingerprint

Teachers seldom have much to say about which classroom they are assigned to or the general condition of the school building. You may have gone to school in well-kept, relatively modern buildings; in older, stately surroundings; or in a dilapidated structure beset with never-ending maintenance problems. Your teachers may have had clean, comfortable spaces to decorate, or they may have fought off bugs and fungus in a dingy, poorly lit room plagued with a leaky roof. Teachers are responsible for making the most of room assignments. Even under dismal circumstances, designing a classroom can be both challenging and fun. Do it for your students, and do it for yourself. The classroom truly is "home away from home."

Deirdre's classroom at Cario Middle School takes on a home-like appearance with the addition of furniture other than desks.

Home away from home. As a teacher you will spend 8 to 9 hours a day for almost 200 days every year in your classroom. Early childhood and elementary students will spend almost all of their days in the classroom with you, whereas middle and high school students will generally spend about one sixth of their school time in any one classroom. The classroom atmosphere is important for all students, but is particularly influential for students who may, through circumstances beyond their control, find that school and their classrooms are the cleanest, most welcoming environments in their lives.

If space allows, adding a comfortable couch, chairs, lamps, rugs, plants, curtains, and other homey items does wonders for inviting students in to learn. Deirdre Huger-McGrew (Cario Middle School, SC) created a reading center in her classroom with a couch, chairs, tables, and lamps, as shown in the video in the Choosing Your Teaching Path section of MyEducationLab. Click on Cario Middle, then on Deirdre.

Early childhood and elementary classrooms should be cheerful and organized for learning. This one includes clusters of desks and supplies for group word, a cubby and coat hook for each student, plants to care for, a word wall, and more.

Seating arrangement. The arrangement of desks and tables in a classroom depends on a number of variables, including the level of the school, the subject(s) taught, and available floor space and furniture. Traditional rows of desks are fine for whole group instruction, whereas clusters of desks or students sitting together at tables work well for group work. Ideally, the arrangement will be flexible so seating can accommodate various instructional strategies.

Proximity. Whatever the seating arrangement, one vital element to keep in mind is **proximity**—the accessibility of teacher to students. The teacher needs to be able to approach each student quickly and easily, without having to negotiate narrow pathways that could lead to stumbling or a complex maze that makes it difficult to work one-on-one with students. Students also need to have visual access to boards and screens.

Organizational schemes. Equipping classrooms with necessary supplies as well as bins, shelves, and cabinets is important. In early childhood and elementary classrooms teachers must deal with a variety of supplies, including all kinds of paper, crayons, scissors, markers, and stickers, as well as learning toys. To review the kinds of items you may find in the early grades, watch Brandi Wade's classroom tour in the Choosing Your Teaching Path section of MyEducationLab. Click on Summit Primary, and then on Brandi Wade. To review a high school classroom library, click on Roosevelt High School, then on Derek Boucher. Organizing classroom items in easily accessible bins, shelves, and cabinets makes classroom activities much more efficient.

Wall space and interest centers. Creative teachers often find ways to entice students to come into the classroom and browse. The walls and tables in a classroom offer tremendous opportunities to create spaces students will want to explore just to see what's up. Think back to the classroom video segments in the Choosing Your Teaching Path section of MyEducationLab. Brenda Beyal (Rees Elementary, UT) uses her classroom to display artifacts from her Native American culture, and Angelica Reynosa (Roosevelt High School, CA) displays Hispanic cultural items. Tim Mendenhall (Rees Elementary, UT) has a science corner complete with Rosie, the pet tarantula, as well as a reading area with couches. Fellow team member Chris Roberts displays objects from his worldwide travels, along with inspirational pieces that are meaningful to him. Additionally, Traci Peters (Cario Middle School, SC) has a bulletin board displaying family photos and her own personal memorabilia from seventh grade. To take another look at these classrooms, go to the Choosing Your Teaching Path section of MyEducationLab. Click on your school of interest, and then on the teacher's name.

Your Teaching Fingerprint

Do you remember classrooms that seemed to invite you in? What do you remember about them?

A simple yet potentially powerful use of wall space is the organized display of student work. Although preprinted posters are appropriate on classroom walls, they should not be used to the exclusion of attractively posted and regularly updated student work. Displaying student work fosters student ownership of the classroom. Some teachers only display traditionally exemplary work, such as tests that received A's or perfectly colored maps. This practice stops short of being optimally effective if half or more of the students never see their work displayed because their achievement on traditional assignments never rises to the top of the class. Ingenious teachers who know students well incorporate creative assignments that give average, and even below average, achievers opportunities to excel. Recall from this text's video that Chris Roberts displayed student artwork that he actually purchased from his kids. This gives him an opportunity to choose pieces created by students who may not otherwise be recognized for their work. To see Chris's art, go to the Choosing Your Teaching Path section of MyEducationLab, click on Rees Elementary, and then on Chris Roberts.

It is well worth the time to thoughtfully arrange physical classroom space, which in many ways shapes the interactions of the people who inhabit the classroom and contribute to the classroom community.

Building Community

A **classroom community** is not just a place, but it is also a way of actively learning together. Dewey (1944) expands on this thought by telling us that people in a community are "like-minded," that they have common beliefs, understandings, and aims (p. 4).

Lemlech (2004) contends that in order to build a classroom community where like-mindedness of learning is experienced, it is necessary to incorporate the building blocks illustrated in Figure 7.2.

The caring classroom. To accomplish Lemlech's classroom vision, a teacher must care—about curriculum, instruction, assessment, society, the past, the present, the future, and, most of all, about students. Nel Noddings, noted educator and author, believes strongly that care is the vital foundation for building community. She tells us, "Caring is the very bedrock of all successful education" (1992, p. 27). As Angela Lumpkin writes, "When students know that their teachers genuinely care, they respond by exerting greater effort to reach their potential" (2007, p. 158).

A caring classroom centers on relationships—between the teacher and the students and among the students themselves. Taking a personal interest in students is the first step in developing caring relationships. Linda Darling-Hammond (1997) states, "Environments that attend to students as individuals also help heighten the probability that school relationships will be characterized by respect and caring rather than by demeaning interactions, threats, and sanctions" (p. 137).

Figure 7.2 Building blocks of classroom community

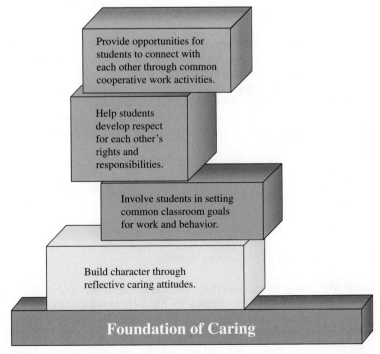

Source: From *Teaching in Elementary and Secondary Classrooms* (p. 5), by J. K. Lemlech, 2004, Upper Saddle River, NJ: Merrill/Prentice Hall.

So how do we get to know individual students? Early childhood and elementary classrooms of 15–30 students allow teachers to know their students and their families well. The numbers are manageable, and teachers have most of the day, every day, to develop relationships. Middle and high school teachers are challenged by both numbers and time, since they may have 60–120 students a year in their classes for only a small portion of each school day. Marzano (2003b) suggests a number of ways teachers can get to know students, shown in Figure 7.3. The positive actions he suggests constitute wayside teaching, a concept discussed in Chapter 4 (see page 121).

Classroom climate. Once community is built in the classroom, maintaining that sense of what Dewey calls like-mindedness can be thought of as maintaining **classroom climate**, the everyday environment of teacher and students working together. You were introduced to the concept of classroom climate in Chapter 1.

One of the most powerful statements concerning classroom climate was penned by Haim Ginott, an admired teacher and Holocaust survivor. You've seen this quotation before, in Figure 1.5. Read and reread Ginott's words now, in Figure 7.4, and consider the awesome responsibility teachers bear.

Kounin's Philosophy

For decades Jacob Kounin (1970) observed and analyzed videotapes of teachers he eventually categorized as either effective or ineffective classroom managers. He then described what effective managers do. Many teachers and theorists have expanded on Kounin's work over the years as they have described how teacher behavior influences student behavior.

To create and maintain a positive and productive learning environment, Kounin tells us teachers must practice **withitness.** This term refers to a teacher's awareness of what's going on in the whole classroom, which enables the teacher to step in when needed to keep the environment positive. Teacher withitness often surprises students, as they perceive the teacher must have eyes in the back of his or her head. Withitness allows teachers to do what Kounin calls **overlapping,** which means multitasking, or taking care of several things at once. A teacher who has withitness and the ability to overlap can help a small group with an assignment, see a student pestering another student, give a "cut it out" look

Figure 7.3   Ways to develop student-teacher relationships

- Talking informally with students before, during, and after class about their interests
- Greeting students outside of school, such as at extracurricular events or at stores
- Singling out a few students each day in the lunchroom, and talking to them
- Being aware of and commenting on important events in students' lives, such as participation in sports, drama, or other extracurricular activities
- Complimenting students on important achievements in and outside of school
- Including students in the process of planning classroom activities, soliciting their ideas and considering their interests
- Meeting students at the door as they come into class and saying hello, making sure to use each student's name

Source: From *What Works in Schools: Translating Research Into Action* (pp. 100–101), by R. J. Marzano, 2003, Alexandria, VA: Association for Supervision and Curriculum Development.

Figure 7.4   Teacher's role in classroom climate

"I've come to the frightening conclusion that I am the decisive element in the classroom. It's my personal approach that creates the climate. It's my daily mood that makes the weather. As a teacher, I possess a tremendous power to make a child's life miserable or joyous. I can be a tool of torture or an instrument of inspiration. I can humiliate or humor, hurt or heal. In all situations, it is my response that decides whether a crisis will be escalated or de-escalated, a child humanized or de-humanized." (Ginott, 1993, p. 15)

while answering a question, and checking the clock to see how much time remains in the class period.

In addition, Kounin says effective classroom managers understand the **ripple effect,** an effect that occurs when one action directly affects another. He tells us that the "cut it out look" given to one student may help deter another student from the same off-task behavior. This is a positive ripple effect. Similarly, but with negative results, if the teacher interrupts the whole class, loudly saying, "Jeremy, stop that right now. You do nothing but continually disturb," other students may perceive that the teacher overreacted and begin to display the same pestering behaviors (Lemlech, 2004).

Jacob Kounin's research has yielded the common-sense view that teachers who know what's going on, who can switch from one activity to another smoothly, and who can maintain positive momentum will be successful in maintaining a positive classroom environment. As you continue reading this chapter about classroom routines, expectations, incentives, and consequences, keep withitness, overlapping, and the ripple effect in mind.

What Routines Contribute to Maintaining a Productive Classroom Environment?

A **routine,** sometimes referred to as a procedure, is an expected action that occurs in a given circumstance to accomplish a task efficiently. When routines are in place in the classroom, teachers have more time to teach, and students have more time to learn.

Practicing Routines

The whole point of a routine is to save time and increase efficiency. It is important to practice routines in the first weeks of school. In this way, the routines become habits. Three important reasons for routines that help preserve time on task are getting student attention, responding to interruptions, and transitioning from one activity to another.

productive routines

Student attention. When students are engaged in class activities, and the teacher wants to make an announcement, give directions, or remind students of the time, an attention getter is necessary. Turning the classroom lights off and on is a universal method, as is simply speaking loudly enough to be heard. An excellent method for getting attention that doesn't require electricity or vocal chords merely involves the teacher raising a hand and students doing likewise. Students know to stop talking as their hands go up. Once there is silence, the teacher talks while students listen. If rehearsed repeatedly during the first weeks of school, this method (and a variety of others you'll observe in field experiences) will become automatic. Having one method, practicing it, and consistently using it will return big dividends.

Responding to interruptions. Class interruptions constitute a real frustration for teachers. The most frequent culprit is often the public address (PA) system. The routine of students instantly "freezing" will allow the announcement to be heard and any necessary action to be taken quickly.

In all levels students have legitimate reasons for leaving a particular class to go to another. Perhaps it's a resource class, a special counseling group, a remedial reading class, or a gifted and talented program. The students involved need to practice the routine of watching the clock and leaving when it is time or watching the doorway for someone who may arrive to escort them. These comings and goings should not be allowed to interrupt the whole class. Students occasionally need to go to the restroom or get a drink of water during class time. Teachers should establish routines for these occasions as well.

When a visitor (an administrator, teacher, student, or parent) enters the classroom, the routine of students noticing and working more quietly will allow the teacher to respond without interference. This routine will not come naturally for students; it must be practiced.

Routines are needed to make transitions orderly.

Transitions. When students change activities or locations they are in **transition,** the time when most classroom disruptions happen (Boynton & Boynton, 2005). In early childhood and elementary schools children may transition between learning activities three or four times before going to recess or a special area class such as music or physical education. Then it's back to the classroom until lunch, perhaps followed by another recess, then back to class. Teachers typically have routines for all these transitions.

In middle and high schools the transitions between classes provide opportunities for misbehavior. Students may be in crowded, rushed circumstances, where social dilemmas can easily surface. A routine for teachers that can decrease the likelihood of misbehavior involves merely standing outside classroom doors during class transition time. Within the classroom, teachers need routines that are understood and practiced to facilitate teaching and learning.

Routines in the Four Levels of School

The nature and number of classroom routines vary greatly depending on the school level. Early childhood and elementary classrooms have many more elements to which routines apply than do middle school classrooms, and high school classrooms have even fewer. But there are some elements at all four levels that call for routines. For instance, attendance must be taken one or more times daily. Distribution of materials and entering and leaving the classroom also occur daily. Let's take a look at some of the routines of our focus teachers.

Early Childhood. Brandi Wade and Renee Ayers, teachers at Summit Primary, Ohio, both attest to the powerful influence of routines in the early childhood classroom. In fact, Brandi states emphatically, "I can't stress enough the importance of establishing routines in the classroom." The kindergarten and second grade routines Brandi and Renee implement in their classrooms center on the activities of

- paying attention
- gathering supplies
- moving about the room
- working in groups
- playing with, and putting away, games and toys
- reacting to interruptions
- going to the restroom
- lining up and moving through the building
- sharpening pencils
- keeping desks in order
- filing and retrieving folders

Brandi and Renee provide a personal routine for each student in the form of classroom jobs that help develop responsibility. These routines/jobs make life in the classroom run more smoothly and increase instructional time. Some of the jobs include board eraser, floor patrol (uses small broom and dust pan), computer helper (turns off computers at the end of the day), and gardener (waters plants).

Each morning Renee follows a routine that organizes her students. She uses a pocket chart (plastic hanging chart with clear pockets) to display her daily classroom schedule in terms second graders can read. She can change the activities as needed so the students know ahead of time what to expect. A sample of the contents of Renee's pocket chart is shown in Figure 7.5.

Children enjoy having jobs in the classroom. Assigning jobs builds a sense of responsibility and pride in completing tasks.

Figure 7.5   Second grade pocket chart schedule

9:30 Welcome/Morning Work
Calendar/Morning Message
Self-Selected Reading
Working with Words
Restroom Break/Snack
Writing
10:55 Music
12:35 Lunch
1:05 Recess
Guided Reading
Restroom Break
Math
Science/Social Studies
4:00 Dismissal

Source: From Renee Ayer's classroom at Summit Primary School, Ohio

Elementary. Many elementary teachers deal with classroom elements that require routines similar to those found in early childhood classrooms. Students in grades 3 through 5, however, are developmentally able to adhere to more complicated routines. Chris Roberts, Tim Mendenhall, and Brenda Beyal work as a team at Rees Elementary, Utah. They have established similar routines because they share students throughout the day, as discussed in their teacher profiles in Chapter 1 (see page 24). Chris, Tim, and Brenda expect their students to come and go between classrooms and throughout the school responsibly. Within each classroom the routines vary, but basically, they deal with

- gathering materials
- turning in homework assignments
- borrowing library books
- dismissal procedures for walkers, bus riders, and car riders

Middle School. Because Deirdre Huger-McGrew at Cario Middle School, South Carolina, has one relatively small group of students half a day and another small group for the other half (see Chapter 1, page 27), she finds it relatively easy to get the students to follow routines that make the classroom run smoothly. These routines revolve around

- computer use
- gathering and returning materials
- restroom and water breaks

Traci Peters, seventh grade math teacher at Cario, believes in the value of structure. The routines she establishes include

- passing in and handing back papers
- borrowing supplies from the bins in the room
- obtaining restroom passes, used only during the first and last 5 minutes of class

High School. Students in high school can be expected to understand routines. There are generally fewer to deal with, but they are no less important than in the earlier grades. Craig Cleveland, Derek Boucher, and Angelica Reynosa, teachers at Roosevelt High School, California, have routines addressing

- entering and leaving class
- paying attention
- working in groups
- checking out and returning materials
- responding to class interruptions, such as announcements, hand-delivered messages, and visitors.

Establishing developmentally appropriate routines, teaching the routines, and then practicing them goes a long way toward increasing the effectiveness and efficiency of the classroom. Also necessary for classroom effectiveness and efficiency are developmentally appropriate expectations, incentives, and consequences.

■ How Do Teachers Establish Expectations, Incentives, and Consequences?

When you read the title of this chapter you may have thought it was just a fancy way to refer to a chapter on **classroom management,** the establishment and enforcement of rules and disciplinary actions. After reading to this point, you can see that creating and maintaining a positive, productive learning environment encompasses much more than the traditional notion of classroom management.

There is no single recipe for effective classroom management that works all the time in every classroom. Classroom management is something you will think about, read about, and observe throughout your teacher preparation program. Teachers have always struggled with this part of their work. Figure 7.6 contains a picture of a piece of paper found in a 1934 book entitled *Mental Hygiene of the School Child* by P. M. Symonds. It appears to be a list of attributes the writer thought were important to instill in students. There is wisdom in many of the 34 items. Take a few minutes to read them before continuing this section that will give you a sense of some of the challenges involved in classroom management, as well as possible solutions involving expectations, incentives, and consequences.

Expectations, a word with positive connotations, will be used in place of *rules,* a word with negative connotations. **Incentives** will be used in place of the overused and value-laden word *rewards.* **Consequences** imply more natural ramifications for wrongdoing than does the word *punishment,* which can be arbitrary.

engaging
instruction

Before discussing expectations, incentives, and consequences, let's consider the concepts of prevention and intervention. When it comes to student misbehavior, teachers have only two options: they can prevent it, or they will need to intervene. Obviously, prevention is more desirable.

The best way to prevent behavior problems in the classroom is through engaging instruction. Read how engaging instruction figures prominently in one experienced teacher's plan for her classroom learning environment in Teachers' Days, Delights, and Dilemmas.

The three concepts of expectations, incentives, and consequences are interdependent. As with several concepts discussed so far, though, they will be treated separately here for the sake of organization and clarity.

Figure 7.6 Notes from 1934

Good Habits of Mental Hygiene.

1. The child should learn good personal and social habits.
2. A child should learn that he can get attention by doing worth-while things.
3. A child should learn to have the glow of satisfaction in doing things well.
4. A child should learn to try things alone without fear.
5. A child should learn to be glad to try new things.
6. A child should learn to meet situations without excitement, fear, shrinking, or worry, BUT with interest, zest, and confidence.
7. A child should learn to accept some things on authority without demanding the reasons.
8. A child should expect to see the reason for most things that he does.
9. A child should learn to be sensitive to the good, the true, and the beautiful.
10. A child should learn to act because of the value of an activity in itself.
11. A child should learn to be willing to reject habitual standards in favor of more intelligent standards.
12. A child should learn to see himself objectively and to accept facts about himself at face value.

13. A child should learn to face facts, accept facts, and act on facts.
14. A child should learn to admit his mistakes, errors, and faults.
15. A child should learn to place blame where it belongs.
16. A child should learn to accept criticism without due emotion.
17. Children should learn to be helpful to others.
18. Children should learn to attempt tasks without delaying.
19. A child should acquire a sense of humor.
20. a child should learn to work and play with others.
21. A child should learn to work and play alone.
22. The child should learn to be cheerful and enthusiastic when doing monotonous tasks.
23. A child should be taught always to try to improve, BUT without impatience.
24. A child should learn to be satisfied with a creditable degree of perfection

Expectations

Teacher expectations impact students in significant ways and affect students' academic performance and behavior. Teacher expectations may become self-fulfilling prophesies for some students. Therefore, it is vital to set and communicate high expectations.

Whether to include students in the process of establishing expectations is a personal decision. Proponents of what is sometimes called a **democratic classroom**, one that promotes choice, community, authentic learning, and relevant, creative curriculum (Wolk, 2003), encourage student participation in the establishment of behavioral expectations. You'll learn more about how Chris Roberts at Rees Elementary, Utah, practices this approach later in the chapter.

Behavioral expectations. Establishing behavioral expectations is generally a teacher task. However, other influences affect this task, including expectations previously established by the school district and those held by the grade level or the whole school staff. Under no circumstances should an individual teacher set expectations lower than grade-level, team, or whole-school expectations. However, teachers can certainly add to, or make more stringent, their own classroom expectations. For instance, if school expectations include a "no

high

expectations

214   Chapter 7

Teachers' Days, Delights, and Dilemmas

Kathleen H. Thomas
2004 Delaware
Teacher of the Year

Setting the tone for instruction starts on the first day of school when you begin to create a climate in your classroom. In order to establish a business-like learning community in my high school classroom, our rules are posted as "Five P's to Practice Professionalism": Be Prompt, Prepared, Polite, Productive, and Positive. These rules can be adapted to any grade level. Establishing your rules and classroom management system may be the easy part; enforcing your expectations takes time, modeling, and constant positive enforcement. As you implement your plan, be firm, fair, and consistent. Compliment your students on a regular basis when they demonstrate the behavior that you are seeking. If something is not working, re-evaluate the plan, then re-address the issue honestly with your students. Effective teachers are constantly adjusting and modifying their classroom instruction as well as their classroom management techniques.

I am very vocal about my expectations for my students' achievement and behavior. I teach and model routines and procedures and give positive feedback constantly, even for little things like students getting into their cooperative teams quickly and quietly. I establish rapport with my students, but am not too familiar. I am honest, upbeat, caring, and professional. My students know that I care about them and that I believe they are capable of reaching very high standards both in terms of academics and their behavior. I purposely model and explain character traits that are important to their success in school and in life. I constantly make the real-world connections between what we are doing and how our lessons will help them in the future.

One of the keys to classroom management is lesson design. Actively involving students in engaging instruction is a teacher's best classroom management tool. Proactive teachers plan their lessons carefully, have extra activities on hand, and are flexible enough to re-adjust as needed. I often use cooperative learning to allow my students opportunities to work together and to allow me the chance to use direct instruction with each team as I constantly monitor their progress and check for understanding. They are intellectually engaged for a majority of each class period. I constantly stress that what we are doing is important. We complete a lot of performance assessment activities using a combination of wireless laptops and art supplies. Chaos is not an issue because of the classroom routines that have been taught and established. I teach each and every routine, even something as "simple" as putting supplies away. Again, I give my students positive attention at every opportunity. Remember, in any classroom, the "power of positive" is one of the best tools to use for student management.

gum" rule, then a teacher cannot allow gum chewing in the classroom. On the other hand, if there is no schoolwide rule against gum chewing, a teacher may nonetheless establish the expectation that students will not chew gum in his or her particular classroom.

Teachers must establish what DeVries and Zan (2003) call **norms**, expectations that are foundational, including physical norms for preserving the health and safety of students, moral norms pertaining to respect for others, and societal norms for politeness and individual responsibility.

How do teachers set behavioral expectations? The answer, in large measure, depends on the developmental stage(s) of the students. With young children, most expectations have to be made very explicit, for example, "Don't bother classmates," "Share materials willingly," "Don't tease." For older children and adolescents, many expectations can be summed up with statements such as "Treat one another respectfully."

Examples of behavior, some mild, some moderate, and some severe, that fall short of expectations include

- talking or moving around the classroom at inappropriate times
- disturbing others (of course, there are thousands of ways students might do this!)
- tardiness and excessive absences
- off-task behaviors (missing materials, working on an assignment that is not the current task, daydreaming, sleeping)
- unauthorized leaving of the classroom
- cheating, lying

- using obscene or vulgar language
- defacing property
- verbal or physical noncompliance (refusing to do what is asked)
- theft and vandalism
- fighting or inflicting violence
- being under the influence of illegal substances

Sample expectations. Some teachers choose to keep their lists of expectations short and general, as illustrated in Figure 7.7. Notice that none of the sample lists of expectations mentions cheating, lying, vulgar language, vandalism, theft, substance abuse, or violence. As stated earlier, most teachers lump all of these negative actions under the word *respect*, assuming that if students show respect, they won't engage in any of these behaviors.

What classroom expectations, or rules, do you remember in your pre-K–12 experiences? Were they clear and rational, or were they ambiguous and nonsensical? On what do you base your opinion? What would you set as the most important expectation for your future classroom?

Why would students choose to live up to classroom expectations? Many do so because they are accustomed to living up to expectations at home or in other settings. Some students require specific incentives to comply with expectations. Most students fall somewhere in between.

What Mr. White expects of you:

I expect you to....

1. Take responsibility for your work and grade.
2. Respect your teachers, peers, and surroundings.
3. Follow ALL directions.
4. Raise hand before speaking.
5. Come in quietly and ready to learn.

What you can expect from Mr. White:

(Positive Consequence)

You can expect....
1.) a smile.
2.) verbal praise.
3.) a positive call home.
4.) tangible rewards (candy, pencils, etc).

OR

(Negative Consequence)

You can expect....
1.) a warning.
2.) a minor referral for lunch or after school detention
3.) a negative call home.
4.) a major referral.

Setting expectations and consequences, and then making them public and explicit, helps bring order and civility to the classroom.

Your Teaching Fingerprint

Incentives

An incentive is a reason for doing something. For instance, a first grade student may stay in line while walking to music class (expectation) because the teacher told the class

Figure 7.7   Sample lists of classroom expectations

1. Pay attention.
2. Listen when others talk.
3. Treat each other with courtesy.

---

1. Work all class period.
2. Complete all assignments.
3. Stay in the area you are assigned.
4. Show respect at all times.

---

1. Respect each other and the teacher at all times.
2. Talk quietly so as not to disturb others.
3. Ask for help by raising your hand.
4. Follow all classroom procedures.

---

1. Arrive on time for class every day.
2. Have all materials needed to participate fully.
3. Maintain a respectful attitude.

---

1. Respect yourself.
2. Respect others.
3. Respect property.

extrinsic and intrinsic incentives

if everyone stayed in line, the music teacher would be pleased (incentive). Keep in mind that incentives that motivate one individual may have little effect on another. If the first grade student didn't like music or the music teacher, pleasing that teacher would not serve as an incentive. Teachers are responsible for understanding their students well enough to provide the bases for incentives that will motivate students in terms of behavior, academics, personal growth, and so on.

There are two basic kinds of incentives—extrinsic and intrinsic. **Extrinsic incentives** are those that are imposed, or that originate outside the individual. **Intrinsic incentives** are those that come from within and result from students' natural drives.

Extrinsic incentives. Most theorists (and indeed probably most of your professors) downplay the value of extrinsic incentives in the classroom. And they are right. Extrinsic incentives are less desirable than intrinsic incentives. Extrinsic incentives are dependent on people other than the student. For instance, if a fourth grade teacher offers a popcorn party on Friday if the class has fewer than five names recorded for misbehavior during the week, then students depend on one another to behave and on the teacher to keep his or her word. They apply peer pressure, again external, in order to achieve the Friday incentive. Do you think the students will be just as motivated to behave acceptably the next week without the promise of a popcorn party? Probably not. When extrinsic incentives are taken away, positive results are less likely to be reinforced. When teachers employ extrinsic motivation, they are taking on the full responsibility for motivating their students (Erwin, 2003). Even so, extrinsic incentives are common in all levels of school.

In early childhood and elementary classrooms extrinsic incentives may include

- extended time for recess
- a movie at the end of the day
- special food treats
- free time for students to explore classroom centers on their own
- music to accompany an activity
- more time to engage in a favorite activity
- stickers, certificates

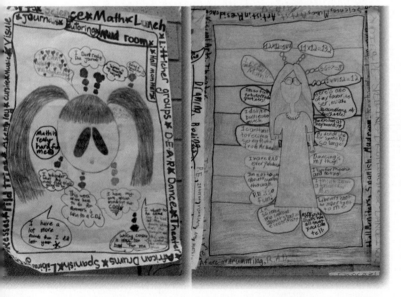

Finding ways for students to express who they are can help teachers get to know them better. This is an important key to creating and maintaining a positive and productive learning environment.

At some point in your field experiences you will likely encounter extrinsic incentives in the form of a **token economy,** a system of distributing symbolic rewards (tokens) for appropriate behavior and withholding or taking away rewards for inappropriate behavior. At a designated time, students can exchange their tokens for something they value. Principal Susan McCloud at T.C. Cherry Elementary School in Bowling Green, Kentucky, reports that the culture of Cherry changed remarkably when her teachers began concentrating on positive behavior and incentives rather than negative behaviors and punishment. One major aspect of the change was the establishment of a token economy, in which students accumulated Cherry Pit Points that they could later "spend" at the Cherry Pit Store. Principal McCloud says this token system gives the students a sense of power and control when they think, "'Hey, I can behave and if I do, I get things that I want'" (2005, p. 49).

In middle school, extrinsic incentives tend to be similar to those in early childhood and elementary schools. As you learned in Chapter 3 (see pages 73), a primary overarching influence for young adolescents revolves around friends. Many middle level teachers capitalize on this developmental trait by promising socializing time at the end of a class period or at the end of a week in exchange for appropriate behavior. High school teachers take advantage of adolescent tendencies in the same way. In middle and high school, extrinsic incentives tend to be less tangible and more social in nature, such as the use of praise as a motivator.

Part of maintaining a productive environment involves learning to follow directions.

Praise. Praise may be a powerful extrinsic motivator for some students. It is extrinsic because it is dependent on someone else, the praiser. It is important for teachers to keep certain guidelines in mind to optimize the value of praise. Specific praise is more effective than general praise. For instance, saying to a student, "Your participation in today's activity helped your whole group stay on task. Thanks, Marcus," is more valuable than simply saying, "Nice work" as Marcus's group leaves the classroom. Using the student's name is also important. Whether to praise in private or in public depends in large measure on the developmental level of the students. Most early childhood and elementary students enjoy being praised in front of their classmates. Young adolescents and high school students are often embarrassed by public praise. A compliment in private is generally more motivational and increases the likelihood of the desired behavior being repeated.

Logic of Extrinsic Incentives. In a perfect world extrinsic incentives would not be necessary. We would all behave appropriately because it's the right thing to do. We would all work hard to reach our potential and to benefit others. Real teachers in real school settings understand the theories that reject extrinsic incentives; they also understand that much of society runs as smoothly as it does because of extrinsic motivation. Ask how many people who work in service industries (fast-food restaurants, dry cleaners, etc.) actually get out of bed and go to work because they are internally motivated to do their jobs. How they do their jobs—their attitude, attention to quality, drive to be successful—may indeed be intrinsically motivated. But chances are, most go to work to earn money.

Ideally, students complete assignments and behave appropriately because they want to (intrinsic motivation). But there are tasks (drill and practice, assignments with no readily apparent value) and behaviors (walking in a straight line, being quiet when a visitor enters) that simply may not be internally motivating for some students in some settings. When it comes to extrinsic and intrinsic incentives, most teachers use a mixture to meet the real needs of their real classrooms.

Intrinsic incentives. For lasting results, intrinsic incentives, such as the satisfaction of completing an assignment that is challenging or behaving appropriately in an assembly, have the most value. Helping students understand why a particular behavior is desirable builds an internal "want to" that is motivating. When an individual behaves appropriately because of intrinsic motivation, chances are the desired behavior not only lasts, but spreads to other aspects of life with positive results.

The best classroom management involves **student self-monitoring.** This is the ultimate in intrinsic incentives because when students assume control of their own behavior, they develop a sense of ownership. Sounds good, doesn't it? We all want this for our students and our classrooms. However, helping students move toward this ideal when they may be used to being told what to do, when to do it, and how to do it, with the promise of rewards for compliance, is a difficult task. Teaching for obedience is much easier than teaching for responsibility. Methods of accomplishing student self-monitoring are beyond the scope of this text, but this discussion may plant the seed that will give you the intrinsic motivation to think about, read about, and plan for a classroom full of self-monitoring students.

Meeting student needs. Akin to intrinsic motivation is the concept that when student needs are met, misbehavior is less of an issue. When student needs are met, students behave appropriately because (1) they want to, and (2) there's little need to do otherwise. Glasser's *Choice Theory* (1998) says that there are five basic needs that constitute the source of all intrinsic motivation: survival, love and belonging, power, freedom, and fun. Glasser contends that giving students what they need will get teachers what they want: student responsibility and more appropriate behavior. Erwin (2003) tells us that when teachers understand these needs it is possible to "transform your classroom into a place where students . . . behave in respectful, responsible ways" (p. 21). Figure 7.8 includes ways in which teachers can address Glasser's five basic needs.

As with other aspects of teaching, teachers must remember that their classrooms are likely to include diverse groups of students. What is valued and what is motivating may be quite varied. Knowing students well—their cultures, their home settings, their disabilities, and more—is vital in understanding how to help them behave in respectful and responsible ways. We'll look more closely at this issue later in the chapter.

Now let's turn our attention to consequences, or what takes place when students do not respond favorably to incentives.

Consequences

Proactive prevention strategies, coupled with a system of incentives that helps students self-monitor their behavior, is the best approach to classroom management. But when expectations are not met, and prevention isn't enough, teachers must intervene. Intervention usually involves consequences. There are two guidelines teachers should follow to help ensure that consequences are reasonable, fairly applied, and not overly reactive, punitive, or exclusionary. First, consequences should match the inappropriate behavior. Second, consequences should focus on the behavior, not on the person, preserving both the student's dignity and the teacher-student relationship. Let's examine these two guidelines.

Figure 7.8 Addressing Glasser's five basic needs

Survival
- Provide opportunities to get food, water, fresh air
- Maintain behavior guidelines that promote safety and respect
- Develop routines that add a sense of order and security

Love and Belonging
- Learn names and personal information quickly
- Greet students as they enter the classroom
- Let students know you personally
- Teach cooperation
- Engage students in ways that show them they are valued

Power
- Give students a voice in the classroom
- Be conscious of a variety of learning styles
- Teach personal responsibility
- Allow for second and third chances to demonstrate learning

Freedom
- Give choices
- Use a variety of instructional strategies

Fun
- Use games in instruction
- Engage students in brain teaser activities

Source: From "Giving Students What They Need," by J. C. Erwin, 2003, *Educational Leadership, 61*(1), 21–23.

Matching consequences to misbehavior. Consequences should match misbehavior both in appropriateness and in severity. Although it would be impossible to design a distinct consequence for every type of misbehavior, teachers should attempt to match consequences whenever possible. For instance, if a student writes on desks or lockers, an appropriate consequence would involve cleaning during a school-required detention. If a student wastes class time, spending free time making up class work would be appropriate. If teasing and hurt feelings are involved, perhaps an apology and reading a short story about how hurtful teasing can be may be effective. Most schools have a standard list of consequences ranging from mild to severe. As with expectations, these consequences need to be applied in the classroom. Teachers can go beyond schoolwide agreed-upon consequences by developing and implementing consequences tailored to the misbehavior of their own students.

What do you remember about consequences in your pre-K–12 experiences? Which appeared to be effective and why? What kinds of consequences make sense to you?

Let's examine some commonly used consequences that range from unobtrusive to involving law enforcement.

Unobtrusive Interventions. The variability of both students and misbehavior dictates a wide range of consequences, beginning with consequences that do not disrupt instruction. There are nonverbal and verbal ways to address relatively minor behavior problems such as student inattention; minor off-task behaviors like daydreaming, doing something other than what is expected, and not using proper materials; leaving a designated area; pestering another student; and many others.

Nonverbal interventions include moving closer (proximity) to the offending student, giving a disapproving look, stopping mid-sentence for a moment to gain student attention, making an established gesture, and so on. To be effective, nonverbal interventions take thought and proactive behavior on the part of the teacher. The best way to learn about nonverbal interventions is to watch experienced teachers make them work.

Verbal interventions can resolve minor problems if delivered quickly, calmly, and in ways that match the offense. From saying, "Everyone needs to listen," to using the offending student's name in a classroom scenario, to a class discussion about why a particular behavior is inappropriate, teachers' words can make a difference. Whatever is said should purposefully lead students back to focus on instruction or learning activities.

Simply asking a student to move to another part of the classroom temporarily, or permanently, may solve some minor misbehavior problems. Withdrawing privileges is another tactic some teachers use successfully.

Teacher-Prescribed Consequences. Teachers must move beyond unobtrusive nonverbal and verbal intervention when misbehavior warrants. The timing of this escalation depends on a number of variables, including school level, student needs, and assessment of possible damage or danger involved with the behavior, among others.

Time-out is a consequence often used in early childhood and elementary classrooms. Students are isolated, usually within the classroom, and not allowed to participate in whatever is going on. Time-out works well as a consequence if not overused and if classroom instruction and activities are engaging, making isolation undesirable.

Detention is a consequence often used at all grade levels. It is most effective when it involves isolation and requires the student to give up time he or she would rather spend elsewhere. Some teachers, teams of teachers, and whole schools find that lunch detention works well. Students assigned to lunch detention are separated from others and required to eat lunch alone in silence. After-school detention is typically used for completion of assignments or for school-related chores such as cleaning or helping in some way. Weekend detention, sometimes called Saturday school, is generally reserved for more serious, or repeated offenses.

Boynton and Boynton (2005) describe the concept of sending a student out of the classroom with the purpose of reflection and planning for better choices as **processing.** Students may be sent to another classroom, the hallway, the library, or a designated room, sometimes called a behavior improvement room (BIR). An important part of processing is what Marzano (2003a) refers to as "written self-analysis" (p. 84). He recommends that students analyze what part they played in the misbehavior, how others contributed, how it should be resolved, and what might prevent it from happening again. Processing is appropriate for minor misbehavior that occurs repeatedly or student disruptions that aren't resolved through unobtrusive nonverbal or verbal interventions.

Serious Consequences. Some misbehavior calls for consequences beyond what an individual teacher may assign. Misbehavior involving physical violence, loud or threatening verbal abuse, vandalism, theft, and possession of illegal substances or weapons dictates the involvement of building-level administrators who may elect to involve law enforcement. Such serious misbehavior often results in suspension, either in school or out of school, or expulsion. Classroom teachers should not attempt to handle such misbehavior alone.

Corporal, or physical, **punishment** is still practiced in some states today. Interestingly, the perceived need for such punishment dates back to the very beginning of the United States. Figure 7.9 provides a portion of a teacher's journal dated 1776 that describes a "bad boy" and the philosophy of the day about "curing" the student. Most teachers will recognize at least some of the traits described by Master Lovell in at least a few of the students they have known. Reading about history, here and throughout Chapter 8, provides a perspective that shows the struggles teachers face in today's classrooms are not necessarily new.

School districts that practice corporal punishment must follow guidelines governing its use that have resulted from court cases. These guidelines include giving specific warnings that a behavior may result in physical punishment, having more than one adult present, and ensuring that the punishment is reasonable and humane (Dunklee & Shoop, 2002). Although corporal punishment has vocal critics and its practice has fallen out of favor with most districts and educators, some people still believe it is warranted. This belief is voiced in this chapter's Letter to the Editor.

Focus on the behavior, not the person. Teachers should avoid equating a behavior with the character of the person exhibiting it. Children and adolescents are developing and growing. Their misbehavior often results from fleeting moods, spontaneous impulses, and poor decision making linked to immaturity.

Constructive Correcting. Assigning consequences in ways that serve as student learning experiences is both productive and constructive, productive in that students sense that they are viewed as individuals, and constructive in that students may use the experience to build their understanding of why certain behaviors are unacceptable. Correcting students in constructive ways can turn something negative into a growth experience. For instance, a

Figure 7.9 Master Lovell's journal

A Bad Boy is undutiful to his father and mother, disobedient and stubborn to his master, and ill-natured to all his playmates. He hates his books and takes no pleasure in improving himself. . . .

He is always in mischief, and when he has done a wrong, will tell twenty lies to clear himself. He hates to have anyone give him good advice, and when they are out of sight, will laugh at them. He swears and wrangles and quarrels with his companions, and is always in some dispute or other. . . .

He is frequently out of humour, and sullen and obstinate, so that he will neither do what he is asked, nor answer any question put to him.

In short, he neglects everything that he should learn, and minds nothing but play and mischief. He grows up a confirmed blockhead, incapable of anything but wickedness and folly. . . . [T]o make a bad boy into a good one, he should be thrashed daily for some reason or other, and locked securely in a closet. There he can meditate upon his sins and thus avoid his fate.

Source: From Going to School in 1776, by J. L. Loeper, 1973, New York: Macmillan.

Letter to the Editor

This message was posted June 11, 2005, as part of the *Community Voice* of the *Tennessean,* Nashville's newspaper. Thisonline extension provides opportunities for Nashville area residents to voice their opinions, similar to traditional letters to the editor. The letter was written by a local teacher.

JUNE 11, 2005

As a Metro public school teacher, I deplore the elimination of corporal punishment in the elementary schools. The past three years have resulted in an increase in bullying, intimidation, and threats not only to other children but to staff itself. My school (K–4) has had teachers assaulted by 5 year olds this year! The fear of not having good ADA—average daily attendance— has paralyzed administration into ignoring repeat offenses until they often turn into zero tolerance issues. If teachers aren't given tools to keep order in class, this already bad situation will worsen. . . . We have a new generation of parents who have no respect for schools, teachers, the law or anybody. And their children are entering school now! Sugarcoat it all you want; I see it every day. Teachers spend more time keeping order than actually teaching. Visit your child's school and get involved! Demand discipline and good order! It's worse now than you think.

Now it's your turn. This chapter has given you information about possible consequences for misbehavior as well as insight into the controversial nature of corporal punishment. These questions will help you formulate your own letter.

1. Do you think there are ever instances that justify corporal punishment? If not, why not? If so, what might those instances be?
2. If you support the writer, what justification do you propose? If you do not support the writer, what would you say to an experienced teacher who believes in administering corporal punishment?
3. If you do not agree with corporal punishment, what alternative can you suggest? If you do agree with corporal punishment, how would you explain the need for it in a public forum?

Your letter to the editor should be in response to the *Community Voice* of the *Tennessean* letter—supporting it, adding information, or refuting it. Write your letter in understandable terminology, remembering that readers of newspaper letters to the editor are citizens who may have limited knowledge of school practices and policies. Your letter may be written in your course notebook and shared with classmates as directed by your instructor. Remember to refer to the letter assessment rubric in Figure 1.10, page 20.

consequence for using the word *retard* in a joking manner may be viewing a video about children with Down syndrome that explains their mental retardation and the coping strategies they are taught. The disrespect shown by using *retard* as a slang word will hopefully be corrected with increased understanding.

Boynton and Boynton (2005) tell us that the goal of correcting students should be to have them reflect on their actions, be sorry for their misbehavior, and determine to make better choices next time. How teachers correct students makes a difference. If done constructively, the chances of a student walking away hating the teacher and planning to misbehave again, but not get caught, are diminished. Steps to use when correcting a student and assigning a consequence are listed in Figure 7.10.

Starting Fresh. When focus is placed on the misbehavior, not on the student, it is possible for the student to see beyond the incident and consequence to the possibility of a fresh start. Chris Stevenson (2002), noted expert on middle level education, advises us to have an attitude that says to students, "Redemption is always close, not closed" (p. 219). In other words, when a student misbehaves and a consequence is assigned, the student deserves to be given a fresh start.

Family Communication. When communicating with the family of a student who misbehaves, it is vital to focus on the misbehavior, not the person. In essence, if a student is maligned rather than the misbehavior, then the family is maligned, with a negative effect on the family-school relationship. A wise teacher emphasizes the positive and the potential before discussing the misbehavior.

Figure 7.10   Steps to use when correcting students

1. Review what happened.
2. Identify and accept student's feelings.
3. Review alternative actions.
4. Explain the building policy as it applies to the situation.
5. Let the student know that all students are treated the same.
6. Invoke an immediate and meaningful consequence.
7. Let the student know you are disappointed that you have to invoke a consequence to his or her action.
8. Communicate an expectation that the student will do better in the future.

Source: From *The Educator's Guide to Preventing and Solving Discipline Problems* (p. 13), by M. Boynton and C. Boynton, 2005, Alexandria, VA: Association for Supervision and Curriculum Development.

If a teacher has already had a positive family communication, such as a complimentary note sent home or a pleasant meeting at Back-to-School Night, then a phone call about a behavior problem may work wonders. For some students, just the threat of a call is enough. For other students, a call home is meaningless. For instance, parents may not be available for a call; they may have received many such calls, perhaps for over 10 years already, and may not care; or the phone may be disconnected.

Parent or family conferences can be effective if they are handled professionally and result in an agreed-upon, enforceable plan to correct the problem. We'll look more closely at guidelines for parent-student-teacher conferences in Chapter 13. Were you ever involved in a teacher-initiated family conference because of behavior issues? If so, how did you feel about it? Did your behavior improve? If so, in what ways? Do you have friends or siblings who were involved in such a conference? Do you remember their reactions?

It's important to keep in mind that incentives and consequences should be balanced. Clear consequences for what is unacceptable must strike a healthy balance with incentives for what is acceptable (Marzano, 2003b).

Now that we have considered ways to create a positive learning environment, how routines contribute to a productive learning environment, and some of the basics of expectations, incentives, and consequences, we are ready to explore developing a classroom management plan.

How Can I Develop a Classroom Management Plan?

Considering elements that contribute to a successful classroom management plan will create an awareness of what to look for in field experiences throughout your teacher preparation program as you observe teachers dealing daily with learning environment issues.

This section will look briefly at what selected theorists and researchers have to say about classroom management; the necessity of considering students' special needs, societal context, and developmental stages; and some general guidelines for planning and implementing classroom management.

Prominent Theories of Classroom Management

If you presented a classroom management scenario to a room full of teachers and asked them how they would respond, you'd no doubt hear as many solutions as there were teachers. A foolproof recipe for classroom management doesn't exist. Many new teachers are dismayed to hear this, because a recipe or formula would make life much easier. But take heart! Teachers can take advantage of what experienced theorists have to say, as well as research-based strategies, to garner ideas to consider in developing personalized classroom management plans.

Table 7.1 Overview of selected theories of classroom management

Theorist	Model	Basic Beliefs
Skinner	Behavior Modification	Teachers use positive and negative reinforcements or rewards and punishments to modify or shape students' behavior.
Glasser	Choice Therapy and Quality Schools	Schools help satisfy students' psychological needs and add quality to their lives. Teachers teach, manage, provide caring environments, and conduct class meetings in a way that adds quality to students' lives.
Gordon	Teacher Effectiveness Training	Teachers teach self-discipline, demonstrate active listening, send "I-messages" rather than "you-messages," and teach a six-step conflict resolution program.
Canter	Assertive Discipline	Teachers and students have rights in the classroom. Teachers insist upon responsible behavior and use a hierarchical list of consequences to manage behavior.
Kounin	Instructional Management	Teachers use effective instructional behaviors (teaching techniques, movement management, and group focus) to influence student behaviors.
Curwin and Mendler	Discipline with Dignity	Teachers protect the dignity of students. Teachers are fair and consider individual situations (as opposed to rigid rules), list rules that make sense to students, and model appropriate behaviors.
Gathercoal	Judicious Discipline	Teachers provide behavioral guidelines for property loss and damage, threats to health and safety, and serious disruptions of the educational process. They also demonstrate professional ethics and build a democratic classroom.

Source: From *Classroom Management: Models, Applications, and Cases* (pp. 12–14), by M. L. Manning and K. T. Bucher, 2003, Upper Saddle River, NJ: Merrill Prentice Hall.

Table 7.1 contains an overview of what some well-known theorists have to say. Teachers can pick and choose various elements based on their personal styles and the students in their classrooms.

Consider the Students

We have already discussed the importance of considering all aspects of students' lives when planning for curriculum, instruction, and assessment. This outlook is equally important in planning for the learning environment. The many ways in which students are diverse must be considered, especially when it comes to incentives and consequences. A classroom management plan must take into account students' special needs, the societal context, and their developmental stages.

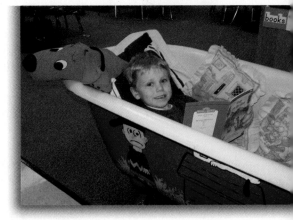

A classroom management plan should take into consideration the attributes of the students it will affect.

Special needs. Chapter 3 (see pages 92–97) discussed students with special needs, designated as requiring unique services in order to optimize their learning potential. These unique services often bring with them specific guidelines for classroom management. The best way to find out what the guidelines are for a student with special needs in your classroom is to talk with the person in your school who has oversight responsibility for the student's education, usually one of the special educators in your building. You will be referred to the student's Individualized Education Program (IEP) (see Chapter 3, pages 94–95), which will contain information about any variances from what are considered normal, reasonable incentive-and-consequence systems that are necessitated by the student's disability.

Recall the discussion of the Individuals with Disabilities Education Act (IDEA) in Chapter 3 (see page 94). This legislation includes provisions for the development of a management plan through a team of educators utilizing a process known as **functional behavioral assessment (FBA).** FBA looks for events and actions that may lead to misbehavior and devises strategies to help students abide by classroom expectations (Gable, Hendrickson, Tonelson, & Van Acker, 2000).

Societal context. Students don't leave their home lives on the schoolhouse steps at 8.00 A.M., to be picked up again at 3:30 P.M. when they leave the classroom. The societal context in which they are growing up colors their attitudes, aptitudes, and reactions. You name it, they bring it with them into the classroom. The answer to the familiar questions, "And how are the children? Are they all well?" should guide the development and implementation of a classroom management plan.

What motivates one child to follow routines and expectations may be meaningless to another. Student perceptions, regardless of whether the source may be culturally or socioeconomically based, influence their reactions to expectations, incentives, and consequences. Some of the everyday areas about which perceptions may differ are listed in Figure 7.11.

To understand this issue of differing perspectives, read about students different from yourself and what experienced educators and sociologists have to say about sensitivity and insightful management options. Some of the best sources of information, Ruby Payne, Lisa Delpit, Alfie Kohn, Jonathan Kozol, S. A. Perez, and others, remind us that diversity exists within specific groups, as well as among groups.

developmental appropriateness

Chapter 10 will look at a variety of social issues that affect students in the United States. Many of these issues may impact the day-to-day functioning of classrooms as teachers strive to match their classroom management systems to students' developmental levels.

Developmental appropriateness. Understanding human development is absolutely essential when writing and implementing a classroom management plan. Let's take a look at how some of our 10 focus teachers maintain learning environments through classroom management plans that match their personal styles and respond to the developmental stages of their students.

Early Childhood. Brandi Wade at Summit Primary, Ohio, works to create a safe, loving, consistent environment for kindergartners. She attempts to match misbehavior with logical consequences. For instance, if during group time on the classroom carpet a child is disruptive, the child must go back to his or her desk, continuing to listen, but not sitting with the rest of the children.

Brandi uses a system that is theme related, and her expectations for behavior increase as the year progresses. For instance, her expectation in September may be for students not to argue as form lines to leave the room. If students "earn" 15 apples in their class apple basket for meeting this expectation, they may enjoy an apple-tasting party. To review Brandi's segment of the video, go to the Choosing Your Teaching Path section of MyEducationLab. Click on Summit Primary, and then on Brandi Wade.

Figure 7.11   Differing student perceptions

Students might have differing perceptions about
• making eye contact • standing close to others • competing with others • receiving attention, positive or negative, in front of peers • behaving appropriately or inappropriately

Source: From *Classroom Management: Models, Applications, and Cases* (p. 9), by M. L. Manning and K. T. Bucher, 2003, Upper Saddle River, NJ: Merrill/Prentice Hall.

Do the behavior and classroom management dilemmas of early childhood sound like something you might find intriguing? Do you already have ideas about the learning environment you want to implement with young children?

Elementary. Chris Roberts, multiage teacher at Rees Elementary School, Utah, has a classroom management–learning environment philosophy best related in his own words.

> Maintaining a positive environment really boils down to a quote I follow by Ron Miller, "Our work is not about curriculum or a teaching method. It is about nurturing the human spirit with love." I do my best to have unconditional love for my students. I think my students feel that and do their best to work hard and learn all they can. We don't have "rules," but we do have "agreements." I believe that language change is important. Kids are smothered in rules. We meet together a lot in the beginning of the year and do experiential activities to build teamwork. We talk about how we want our village to be. We write down our discussions and sign an agreement that we will do our best to show respect for ourselves, others, and property. We continually assess how we are doing all year long. I write a lot of letters to my students telling them I appreciate the positive things they are doing. (From email communication with Chris Roberts, November 11, 2005)

In the opening scenario of this chapter you read about Tim Mendenhall and a new student who came into his classroom with a history of misbehavior and poor academic performance. Tim applied his classroom management plan to help Jeff acclimate to Rees Elementary and make behavioral progress, a necessary step toward academic success. The general guidelines of Tim's management plan are presented in Figure 7.12.

To review Chris's and Tim's portions of the video, go to the Choosing Your Teaching Path section of MyEducationLab. Click on Rees Elementary, and then on Chris and Tim.

Elementary children are learning about themselves and their relationships with others. Do Chris's and Tim's approaches appeal to you? Can you envision yourself managing an elementary classroom?

Middle School. We saw in the opening scenario of Chapter 1 (see page 3) that Traci Peters at Cario Middle School, South Carolina, invests a lot of time in getting to know her students and attending school events to support their participation. Building relationships is foundational to Traci's classroom management plan.

Traci and her students abide by the five basic behavior guidelines agreed upon by the entire staff of Cario Middle School and listed in Figure 7.13. The Charleston County School District requires teachers to give conduct grades for each student in every 9-week grading period. Employing a system commonly found in many schools, Traci gives demerits for misbehavior. She has a system for converting demerits into letter grades. She also uses a "three strikes, you're out" policy. After three demerits in her classroom in a quarter, a student must talk with a building-level administrator. Traci says, "Basically, I give kids a chance to be kids, but at the same time I expect them to respect me and those around them." She tells us that parent communication is a major help in managing a middle school classroom.

Young adolescents, perhaps more than any other age group, experience wide fluctuations in levels of maturity. Making sure "Redemption is always close, not closed," as Stevenson admonishes, may be difficult. Does managing a classroom of these changeable, and wonderful, students appeal to you?

High School. Many people think classroom management does not present a significant challenge in high school classrooms. This may be true in some high schools, but not in all. However, a high school administrative team and staff with expectations for respect and consistent consequences can generally run a positive and productive campus.

Students who are disruptive in high school are often sent out of the classroom, instructed to see an administrator, and may be given **suspension,** or sent off school grounds,

Figure 7.12 Tim Mendenhall's guidelines for classroom management

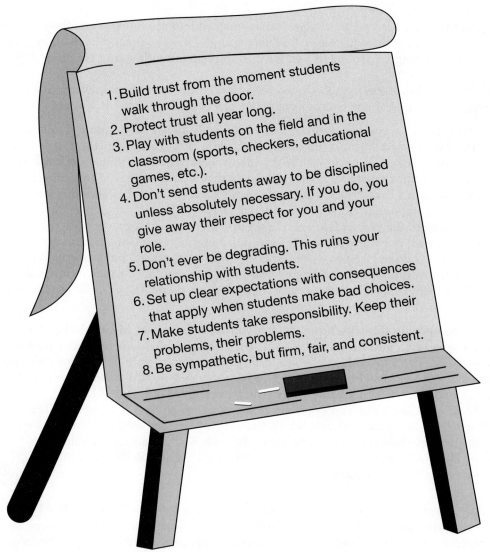

1. Build trust from the moment students walk through the door.
2. Protect trust all year long.
3. Play with students on the field and in the classroom (sports, checkers, educational games, etc.).
4. Don't send students away to be disciplined unless absolutely necessary. If you do, you give away their respect for you and your role.
5. Don't ever be degrading. This ruins your relationship with students.
6. Set up clear expectations with consequences that apply when students make bad choices.
7. Make students take responsibility. Keep their problems, their problems.
8. Be sympathetic, but firm, fair, and consistent.

Source: From email communication with Tim Mendenhall, November 12, 2005.

Figure 7.13 Cario Middle School student expectations

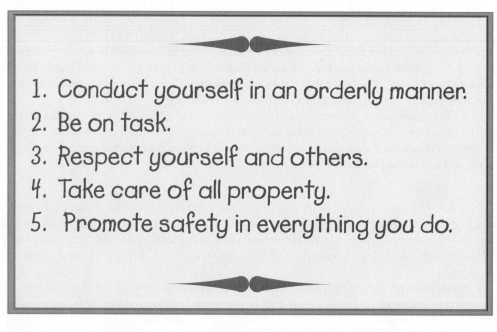

1. Conduct yourself in an orderly manner.
2. Be on task.
3. Respect yourself and others.
4. Take care of all property.
5. Promote safety in everything you do.

for a specified length of time. This severe consequence should be reserved for extreme cases. Most high school students understand behavioral expectations and the rationale behind them. If adolescents ages 15 through 19 are disruptive in the classroom, they know exactly what they're doing and in some cases, do it because they know they can get away with it or perhaps because they want to be suspended.

Roosevelt High School, California, publishes school rules as well as its Student Code of Conduct in a student handbook. The school rules on which Roosevelt teachers build their classroom expectations are shown in Figure 7.14. The Code of Conduct covers expectations for a safe environment, closed-campus rules and exceptions, the necessity of ID tags, absences, the use of electronics, and a sexual harassment policy. In addition, the Fresno Unified School District maintains a zero-tolerance policy for possession of firearms, weapons of any kind, explosives, controlled substances, and attempted or actual harm to another person. Immediate suspension occurs for violations, many times resulting in **expulsion,** or permanent removal from school.

Our three focus teachers at Roosevelt High, Craig Cleveland, Derek Boucher, and Angelica Reynosa, seldom have misbehavior in their classrooms that a certain look or a private word won't remedy. They are instead often faced with the dilemma of students not engaging in learning. So rather than overt misbehavior, a lack of desire or enthusiasm for the whole educative process often challenges them. This can be an even more perplexing problem than dealing with students who are disruptive.

If all adults consistently monitor students and hold them to expectations similar to those of Figure 7.14, behavior problems in the classroom can be minimized. Problems that occur outside the classroom, perhaps in the school courtyard, on the sidewalks, or in the hallways, can also be minimized when the entire school staff makes it their business to be present and visible during transitions.

Do you have the desire to establish caring relationships with maturing adolescents who wish to be treated as adults, but who may not have the self-control or self-motivation to match? Could you be fair, firm, and consistent in order to help them grow into their potential? What characteristics do you have that indicate your abilities?

Your Teaching Fingerprint

Figure 7.14   Roosevelt High School behavior guidelines

Roosevelt High School students are required to conduct themselves in an appropriate, acceptable manner at all times when present in school, in classrooms and hallways, on school grounds, and at school sponsored events.

Students are to:

1. Treat others with consideration and dignity.
2. Respect the property of others.
3. Be punctual and prepared for class.
4. Follow the direction of all staff.

General Guidelines

We have discussed some of the most important elements of developing and implementing a classroom management plan. Figure 7.15 presents Boynton and Boynton's (2005) concise version of the crucial components of an effective system.

Certain guidelines are nonnegotiable when establishing a classroom management plan. Although it is impossible to address all of them within the scope of this book, here are several important ones:

- **Always stay within school and district policies and guidelines.**
- **Use positive, rather than negative, statements when establishing expectations.** Students need to know what they *should* do, not just what they *shouldn't* do. For instance, the expectation "We will show respect for others when working together or apart" is more likely to gain compliance than "We will not be disrespectful of others when working together or apart." Plant positive thoughts in students' minds to promote productive habits of appropriate behavior.
- **Consistently apply expectations and consequences.** Some teachers set an expectation and have different consequences based on the number of times a student's behavior is outside the expectation. This sort of consequence layering in no way undermines the consistency of consequences.
- **Explore conflict resolution and peer mediation.** This approach involves students trained as go-betweens to help other students work through their differences and agree to disagree amicably. Look for such programs as you observe and interact in schools.
- **Communicate and document.** Once established, a teacher's classroom management plan should be explicitly taught to students, the building administrators should receive a written plan, and parents and families should be informed of it. An aspect of communication often neglected by teachers is documentation, or record keeping. When a consequence is applied, document it.
- **Ask for help.** There are some behavior issues that classroom teachers should not handle alone. Physical violence, overt bullying, and verbal abuse of students or adults cannot be tolerated in a classroom setting. Episodes of this nature must be dealt with immediately by building administrators who, in turn, may involve law enforcement. A supportive and decisive administrator can be one of the most valuable assets to teachers and the classroom management process.

Don't Be Part of the Problem

Think back to your days in prekindergarten through twelfth grade. Can you remember a classroom behavior problem actually getting worse because of something a teacher did or didn't do? Were you ever in a class when student misbehavior escalated so that it was almost out of control even as the teacher yelled for attention? How about out-of-control behavior in the presence of a teacher who repeatedly used "shhhh" to ask for silence? Neither approach works.

Figure 7.15 Components of an effective classroom management system

Five components that, when implemented correctly, are crucial for establishing an effective classroom discipline system include

1. Positive teacher–student relationships
2. Strong content instruction
3. Clearly defined parameters of acceptable student behaviors
4. Use of effective monitoring skills
5. Appropriate consequences

Source: The Educator's Guide to Preventing and Solving Discipline Problems (p. v), by M. Boynton and C. Boynton, 2005, Alexandria, VA: Association for Supervision and Curriculum Development.

Purposefully embarrassing students should never be a teacher tactic. The result may be serious psychological damage to the student. Another likely result is the student's loss of respect for the teacher who has displayed his or her own version of misbehavior.

Avoid making threats without following through. This practice can have disastrous results in a classroom. A teacher repeatedly saying, "If you don't stop that I'll . . ." may cause the immediate misbehavior to escalate, and guarantees future problems because students won't believe that the teacher will follow through.

Teachers should never allow a classroom confrontation to escalate into a power struggle. When a student loses control of his or her temper and directs remarks at a teacher, and the teacher reacts in kind, the opportunity to be a mature, reasonable role model is lost. No one wins. Giving a student time to calm down and gracefully save face will provide a chance for student and teacher to talk about the situation. In some exaggerated cases, avoiding a power struggle prevents physical violence and gives time for administrators to get involved in a resolution.

Concluding Thoughts

Students don't just learn academic subjects in our classrooms. They learn how to exist in society. They learn limits of what they can and can't do in terms of behavior. A positive and productive learning environment is safe—physically, emotionally, and academically. When students feel safe they are more likely to participate, learn, and grow.

Creating and maintaining a positive and productive learning environment is hard work. Teachers can learn how to cultivate appropriate relationships with students, how to establish routines that foster productivity, and how to thoughtfully develop classroom management plans that are effective. With diligence and consistent monitoring, a positive and productive learning environment can be maintained.

Well-managed classrooms are marked by civility. Some students come to school without a clear idea of what civility looks like because they don't live in the midst of it. Teachers must model civility, orchestrate an environment that fosters it, and then expect nothing less of students.

Chapter in Review

How do teachers create a positive learning environment?

- The physical layout, appearance, usefulness, and overall appeal of the classroom either enhance the learning environment or detract from it.

What Role Will Diversity Play in My Teaching Identity?

A positive and productive learning environment can only be maintained if expectations, incentives, and consequences are thoughtfully established with students' similarities and differences in view. You can accomplish this through

- knowing your students well—their home settings, their cultures, their abilities and disabilities
- creating a physical space that is inviting and safe (remember that your classroom may be the most appealing place in a child's life)
- using wall space to display posters and information from a variety of perspectives, thereby validating those perspectives in the eyes of some students
- establishing a foundation for caring by helping students get to know each other and finding ways to encourage them to respect the viewpoints and rights of classmates

Teachers must continually look at students through eyes that see possibility, not past performance, and set high expectations for all of them. Basing expectations on race or socioeconomic status is wrong and harmful. Keep in mind the power of a teacher as described in Figure 7.4. The teacher is, as Ginott says, the "decisive element in the classroom" that creates the climate.

- A caring classroom climate helps teachers and students build a sense of community.
- Teacher awareness, ability to multitask, and recognition that one action directly affects another are valuable assets in creating a positive learning environment.

What routines contribute to maintaining a productive classroom environment?

- The types of routines needed vary by school level, but their importance at all levels cannot be overemphasized.
- Students need to practice routines so that they become productive habits.

How do teachers establish expectations, incentives, and consequences?

- Successful classroom management is a prerequisite for successful teaching and learning.
- The best prevention of behavioral problems is engaging instruction.
- Many issues and situations require teachers to establish behavioral expectations, incentives for achieving these expectations, and consequences for not fulfilling them.

How can I develop a classroom management plan?

- Prominent theories and classroom observations provide background and strategies for new teachers to use to formulate management plans.
- Teachers should consider student needs and development when formulating a plan.
- Classroom management plans are most effective when expectations are stated positively, when expectations, incentives, and consequences are applied consistently, and when teachers model appropriate behavior.

Professional Practice

Licensure Test Prep

Here is a description of first-year English teacher Jim Clausen. After reading about Jim, answer multiple-choice questions 1–5 and constructed-response item 6.

About Jim

Jim Clausen just submitted first semester grades for his 86 students. His high school is on the block system that allows students to take four classes per semester, with each meeting daily for 90 minutes. Jim has three classes of freshman English and a 90-minute planning period every day. This is pretty much an ideal schedule, or so his department chair, Mrs. Landry, told him when he landed the job at South High (SHS), a school of about 2,000 students. He had attended SHS and decided to move back home after college and live with his parents just until he could get a handle on paying off his college loans and save enough to afford an apartment of his own. That part of his life was working out fine. His parents seemed to enjoy having him around, and they understood his need to come and go as he pleased, as he had in college.

What wasn't going so well was the mismatch between what he envisioned his teaching day would be and what it actually turned out to be. He was anxious for holiday break, not just for time off, but for a chance to really think about his situation. Jim loves books. He has been an avid reader since he picked up his first R. L. Stine scary book in fourth grade. His imagination had soared, and he began reading all the mystery books in the library. Then came *Harry Potter* and *Lord of the Rings*. Jim's taste matured, and he grew to appreciate a variety of genres. His sophomore year in college he decided to become a high school English teacher and set his sights on one day teaching literature at a university. Jim pictured the fun and fulfillment of teaching upper-level high school students who would fall in love with literature just as he had. He made that clear when he applied for a job at SHS. The principal, Mr. Everett, remembered Jim and was delighted to have him become part of his faculty. However, the only position available was teaching freshman English.

Jim's first semester

How could kids have changed so drastically in only a few years? Jim didn't remember himself and his friends acting this way. It's not that his students weren't enthusiastic, just not about anything academic. Jim had played football and was a pretty popular guy, so it's not as if he wanted his students to be nerds or spend all their time reading and studying, but he expected them to do their reading assignments, pay attention in class, and study for tests. A few did, but not the rest. They came to class without their materials, talked or slept while he attempted to conduct class discussions, and did miserably on exams. What was wrong with these kids?

The grades Jim turned in were dismal. There were only 7 A's and 29 B's. The rest were C's and D's, with 22 F's. The F's meant that the students would have to repeat freshman English.

1. Jim knew from his education classes that spending time reflecting on situations was a good way to come up with a plan. He was disappointed at the end of most days that he had not been able to spend much time thinking about the big picture of his teaching, even though he had 90 minutes a day. Which of the following is *not* a plausible reason Jim had postponed thinking his situation through until the end of the semester?
   a. As a first-year teacher he needed every available minute to prepare for his classes.
   b. He kept thinking it would all get better.
   c. He was caught up in the autumn school spirit surrounding football season.
   d. The things he tried all came up short, and he knew he needed more time to regroup and think it all through.

2. The 22 students who failed Jim's class would
   a. benefit from block scheduling in that they would have room in their schedules to repeat freshman English and still get in the credits necessary to graduate.
   b. likely repeat freshman English the summer before their sophomore year because block scheduling restricts the number of classes that may be taken in a year.
   c. be held back as freshmen the following year.
   d. more than likely be in Jim's freshman English class again in the spring because of the size of South High.

3. Because so many of Jim's students either talked or slept during his lesson, all of the following were probably true except
   a. Jim had not yet acquired the ability to demonstrate what Kounin calls withitness.
   b. Jim went beyond the required readings of the district.
   c. Jim had not yet mastered the skill of overlapping.
   d. Jim was a recipient of the effects of negative rippling.

4. When Mrs. Landry saw Jim's grades, she should have
   a. attributed them to Jim's high expectations for student learning.
   b. assumed he would relax a bit in the second semester and his students would do much better.
   c. decided Jim should be moved to a senior classroom assignment where his high expectations would most likely be met.
   d. planned to observe and work more closely with Jim to try to help him do a better job of teaching the freshmen.

5. Place the following strategies in order from most helpful to least helpful in terms of their potential to make the most difference in Jim's success in the second semester.

I. Mr. Everett could tell Jim he will find a place for Jim to teach upperclassmen next year.

II. Mrs. Landry could share with Jim some ways to teach that are conducive to 90-minute periods.

III. Jim could join the National Council of Teachers of English and order books published by them.

IV. Jim could be given time to observe other English teachers both in and outside his building to learn new teaching techniques.

a. I, II, III, IV
b. II, III, I, IV
c. II, IV, III, I
d. IV, II, III, I

6. Describe two strategies Jim could use in the second semester to engage his freshman class in their own learning.

Standards Speak

This chapter explored the creation and maintenance of the learning environment and components of a successful classroom management system. Although these topics permeate almost all aspects of teaching, relatively few standards address the learning environment.

INTASC Knowledge Principle 5

The teacher uses an understanding of individual and group motivation and behavior to create a learning environment that encourages positive social interaction, active engagement in learning, and self-motivation.

NBPTS Standard 3

Teachers are responsible for managing and monitoring student learning.

NMSA Standard 1, Performance 3

Middle level teacher candidates create positive, productive learning environments where developmental differences are respected and supported, and individual potential is encouraged.

Respond to the following questions in your class notebook and/or discuss your responses with your classmates as directed by your instructor.

1. The INTASC standard refers to encouraging positive social interaction. If you walked into a classroom at a specific grade level, what behaviors might you see that would indicate the existence of positive social interaction?

2. The NBPTS standard says that teachers are responsible for monitoring and managing student learning. What does this statement have to do with student behavior?

3. The NMSA standard talks about respecting and supporting developmental differences. How can a classroom management plan be consistent (as the chapter emphasizes) and developmentally responsive to differences at the same time?

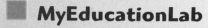 ## MyEducationLab

The following interactive features may be found in Chapter 7 of MyEducationLab.

Homework and Exercises

Writing My Own Story

To write your own story by responding to some of the questions in the text accompanied by fingerprint icons, plus others, go to the "Writing My Own Story" section of the Homework and Exercises for Chapter 7 of MyEducationLab.

What's My Disposition?

To reflect on your beliefs and attitudes concerning the teaching profession, go to Chapter 7's "What's My Disposition?" feature of the Homework and Exercises section of MyEducationLab.

Exploring Schools and Classrooms

If your course involves experiences in schools, the questions and prompts in the "Exploring Schools and Classrooms" feature of Chapter 7's Homework and Exercises section of MyEducationLab will guide you as you explore local schools and classrooms.

Virtual Field Experience

To respond to questions and prompts regarding the Choosing Your Teaching Path videos that connect to specific chapter content, go to Chapter 7's Virtual Field Experience section of MyEducationLab. The questions will help you make sense of what you have read in the chapter.

Part 3

Foundations of Education in the United States

STARTOWN SCHOOL
Founded 1904. First graded school in what is now City of Newton. From 1914 to 1931 was site of Startown Farm Life School, an innovative state-supported high school integrating agriculture and home economics in curriculum. Continues as an elementary school.

Chapter 8 **History of Education in the United States**

Chapter 9 **Philosophical Foundations of Education in the United States**

Chapter 10 **The Societal Context of Schooling in the United States**

Chapter 11 **Ethical and Legal Issues in U.S. Schools**

Chapter 12 **Governing and Financing Public Schools in the United States**

Chapter 8

History of Education in the United States

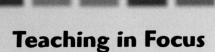

Teaching in Focus

Angelica Reynosa, world history teacher at Roosevelt High School, California, knows that her task of helping sophomores understand historic events and their impact on today's world is a complex one. Most of the 31 students in the class you observed in the video for this text, located in the Choosing Your Teaching Path section of MyEducationLab at www.myeducationlab.com, are new to the United States. Some of them may have picked up English through classes at Roosevelt or simply from living in Fresno. Many live in homes where only Spanish is spoken. These students haven't grown up steeped in the U.S. social studies curriculum, and reciting the Pledge of Allegiance each morning since they were 5. As a second-generation American herself, Angelica understands at least some of her students' challenges.

Angelica has always loved to study history. She views the subject she teaches as a living, breathing entity that's filled with problem-solving scenarios and intrigue. Her teaching philosophy dictates that she engage her students, not merely give reading assignments. The objective of the lesson you observed is: "Students will participate in an activity that will help them grasp the reasons for the rise of Marxist Theory. They will experience the 'haves' and 'have-nots' of the capitalist system and critically evaluate the benefits and drawbacks of capitalism and socialism." That's an ambitious objective, and one that takes lots of thought and planning. To review Angelica's lesson segment on the video, go to the Choosing Your Teaching Path section of MyEducationLab. Click on Roosevelt, and then on Angelica.

Many of Angelica's students fall into the have-nots, similar to the people Angelica describes in her lesson. They may be in the United States illegally, crowded into the homes of extended family while their parents look for work or hold low-paying jobs. There's so much Angelica wants them to understand about the world. She wants them to see the big picture included in the world history curriculum and help them grasp the significance of how various forms of government enhance or inhibit people's lives. She wants them to understand how knowledge of history is meaningful for their futures and how it can give them perspective about their roots and cultural struggles.

Similarly, knowing the major events and turning points in the history of education will give you some perspective as you explore education in the United States. The major questions guiding this chapter include:

- What were the major influences, issues, ideologies, and individuals in 17th-century American education?
- What were the major influences, issues, ideologies, and individuals in 18th-century American education?
- What were the major influences, issues, ideologies, and individuals in 19th-century American education?
- What were the major influences, issues, ideologies, and individuals in 20th-century American education?
- How can I be aware of education history in the making?

■ Introduction

Americans often take for granted many of the underlying concepts of public education in the United States. Among these are free public schools; compulsory education; classrooms that welcome students regardless of race, culture, socioeconomic status, abilities or disabilities; and separation of church and state. In the relatively short history of the United States, spanning less than 4 centuries, education has evolved into a system that mirrors the democratic principles on which the country was founded.

Americans typically value education, both as a means to an end and as a worthwhile endeavor in itself. Most have faith that education will lead to a better life, and the more education, the better. However, different views arise when it comes to the how, where, and when of providing educational opportunities for the children in the United States. As you grapple with the questions and possibilities surrounding U.S. education, it's helpful to realize that not much is actually new. Most of the basic arguments and concepts behind each dilemma, and each suggested solution, have surfaced in just slightly different forms throughout U.S. history. You've probably heard it said that people who don't understand history are doomed to repeat it. Let's put a more positive and useful spin on the adage. Learning from the history of education—and the lessons are many—may keep us from repeating past mistakes. Recognizing yesterday's valiant and often brilliant examples of doing what's best for students will guide our present efforts.

History is not dull or dry. Real people in real places used problem-solving techniques to address and solve real issues as they arose and made history in the process. Remember this as we take a very abbreviated journey to examine some of the major personalities and events that shaped both the history of the United States and the history of U.S. education. To help put events and people into a meaningful context, timelines are provided that highlight events in U.S. history on one side and events and people in U.S. education on the other. We will consider the history of American education—the influences, issues, ideologies, and individuals—one century at a time. Each century's timeline is color coded.

One of the best ways to consider the history of American education is through the lives of the people who created that history. In the perspective gained by time, history makers have emerged. Those described here are representative of the hundreds of thousands who have made positive contributions to the education of youth in the U.S. Notice that each history maker profiled in this chapter is enclosed within a colored border that reflects the century in which the person made the most significant contributions to education.

Now let's begin our journey through the centuries, as we explore the history of American education.

■ What Were the Major Influences, Issues, Ideologies, and Individuals in 17th-Century American Education?

The founding of Jamestown, Virginia, in 1607 by roughly 100 men is used to mark the formal beginning of America's colonization. Previous voyages to the New World were mostly prompted by the hope of finding riches. The English Puritan religious sect who settled in Plymouth, Massachusetts, 23 years later included men, women, and children. Families came to begin new lives in a place where they hoped to be free to worship their God in their chosen ways. Culturally, the first colonists had their roots in England; religiously, the first colonists opposed the Church of England because it lacked tolerance for any doctrine other than its own. The Church of England in the 17th century was an extension of the English government. To escape being forced to abide by the Church of England's doctrine, the Puritans, who held that the Bible in its literal (or pure) form is the source of all wisdom, sought to establish English-style colonies with their own

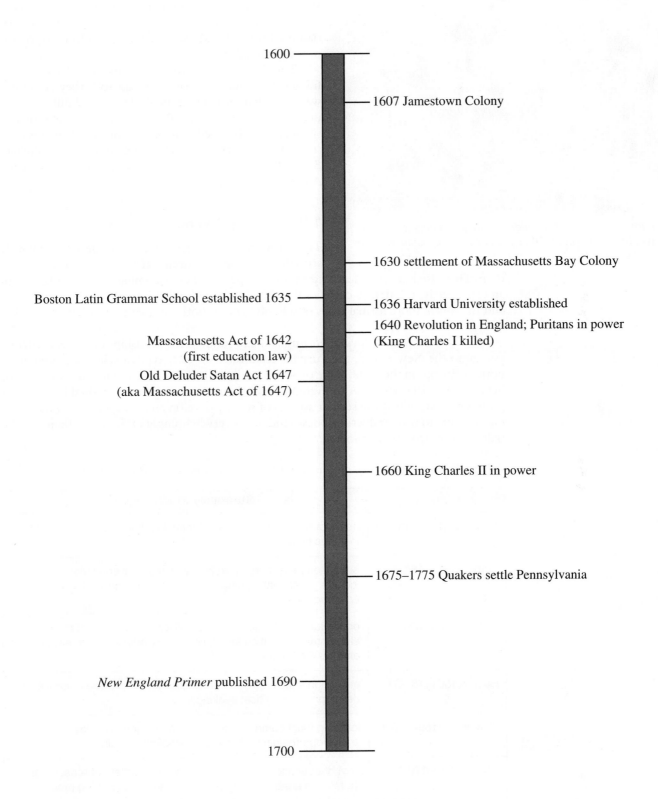

1600

1607 Jamestown Colony

1630 settlement of Massachusetts Bay Colony

Boston Latin Grammar School established 1635

1636 Harvard University established

1640 Revolution in England; Puritans in power
(King Charles I killed)

Massachusetts Act of 1642
(first education law)

Old Deluder Satan Act 1647
(aka Massachusetts Act of 1647)

1660 King Charles II in power

1675–1775 Quakers settle Pennsylvania

New England Primer published 1690

1700

Puritans believed that children were just little adults who would remain sinful if they did not ward off Satan through Bible study.

biblical interpretations to guide them. They were not, however, particularly more tolerant than the Church of England they had escaped. For instance, because Roger Williams, one of the prominent Puritans of the 17th century, espoused separation of church and state, he was banished from the Massachusetts Bay Colony to what is now Rhode Island.

The Puritans believed that people were basically sinful and that children would remain so if they could not ward off Satan by reading the Bible and faithfully upholding its principles. To the Puritans, children were merely small adults who needed to learn scripture. Play was considered a waste of time, and discipline was stern (Pulliam & Van Patten, 2007). This attitude carried over into early American schools.

17th-Century American Schools

The early colonists recognized the need to provide schooling for their children—at least for their male children. They also knew that learning a trade was perhaps best accomplished by working with an expert artisan. Later, as colonies flourished in New England, the middle Atlantic area, and the south, more formal types of schools grew in both number and variety.

Early colonial schools. Having left England and suffered the hardships of the transatlantic voyage to the New World, the Puritans established an early type of schooling influenced both by European theorists, some of whom are listed in Table 8.1, and by Puritan religious beliefs and social customs. Although the first colonial schools were established for religious purposes, they helped the secular aspects of society develop and prosper as well by teaching students to read and write. These students, overwhelmingly White boys, then had the skills to participate in commerce.

Table 8.1   Influence of major theorists on early American education

Theorist	Summary of Influence
Erasmus (1466–1536)	need for systematic training of teachers; liberal arts education includes classics
Luther (1483–1546)	education necessary for religious instruction; education should include vocational training; need for free and compulsory education
Calvin (1509–1564)	education serves religious and political establishments; elementary education for all; secondary education for leaders; emphasis on literacy
Bacon (1561–1626)	education should advance scientific inquiry; provide rationale for development of critical thinking skills
Comenius (1592–1670)	learning must come through the senses; general body of knowledge (paideia) should be possessed by all
Locke (1632–1704)	goal of education is to promote the development of reason and morality to enable men to participate in the governing process

Source: From *Foundations of American Education*, by L. D. Webb, A. Metha, and K. F. Jordan, 2007, Upper Saddle River, NJ: Merrill/Prentice Hall.

At first, the earliest Puritan settlers educated their children within their own homes, but **dame schools** soon became common. Dames were respected women who, usually without formal schooling, had learned to read and write, and who turned their homes into schools where parents paid to have their children educated. Some children went from a dame school, which was essentially the first American elementary school, or from no schooling at all, to an apprenticeship that required them (virtually all boys) to move into the home of a master. The master taught them a trade and often also taught them basic literacy skills. Girls usually stayed home and learned homemaking skills from their mothers.

As education moved from individual homes into schools throughout colonial America, notable differences in education emerged among colonies in different geographical areas. Figure 8.1 is a map of colonial America showing the three basic geographical areas we will discuss next.

Schools in the New England colonies. In 1630 the Massachusetts Bay Colony was established, followed by Rhode Island, Connecticut, and New Hampshire. These four colonies made up early New England. Their inhabitants tended to be very much alike, sharing the Puritan faith and English roots. They tended to settle in towns that made formal education a relatively easy endeavor. Dame schools were commonplace for New England children, who learned basic reading, writing, and arithmetic skills, all within a religious context. Girls in New England were allowed to attend the dame schools, although their curriculum was different and focused primarily on homemaking. The elementary education of a dame school was generally the extent of what girls received in terms of formal schooling for much of the colonial period.

In 1635 the first **Latin grammar school** was established in Boston for boys whose families could afford education beyond the dame school. The word *grammar* is associated with elementary school today, but was a term for secondary schools in the 17th century. Students learned higher levels of reading, writing, and arithmetic, along with classical literature. The Latin grammar schools were considered the forerunners of modern high schools and specifically prepared boys to attend Harvard University, established in 1636 (Tehie, 2007).

Figure 8.1   The 13 original colonies

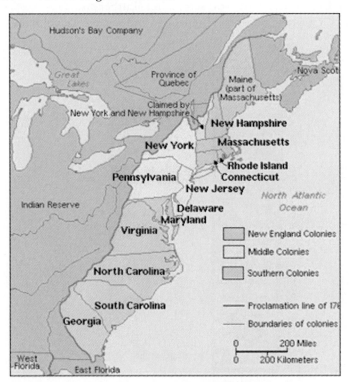

Only the wealthiest New Englanders went beyond dame schools. Schooling opportunities and apprenticeships for White boys from poorer families were either less desirable or nonexistent. Girls, African Americans, and Native Americans had even fewer opportunities for educational advancement.

Some Puritan leaders recognized the benefits of educating all children, at least all White children. The **Massachusetts Act of 1642** was the first **compulsory education law** in the New World. Although the law required all White children to attend school, it did not specify how or where children would get an education. Nor did the law provide funding, making it the first **unfunded mandate**—a legally enforceable law without provision for monetary support. Five years later, the Massachusetts Act of 1647, also known as the **Old Deluder Satan Act** because education was considered the best way to fight the devil, established that every town of 50 or more households must provide a school. Again, no funding was attached, and either parents or the whole community contributed to supporting a school and teacher. These two acts, along with Puritan determination, led to the New England colonies having about the same literacy rate as England by 1700 (Cohen, 1974).

The *New England Primer* was first published in 1690 for children in upper elementary and secondary levels. The book was a perfect example of the interrelatedness of education and religion in colonial New England. Published for over 150 years with few substantial changes over its lifetime, the *New England Primer* included a spelling guide based on the alphabet denoted in brief rhymes and pictures. The *New England Primer* also included the Lord's Prayer, the Apostles' Creed, the Ten Commandments, a list of the books of the Bible, and the numbers 1–100. At the end of the primer was the Puritan catechism. Figure 8.2 contains a sample from the *New England Primer*.

Schools in the middle colonies. New York, New Jersey, Pennsylvania, and Delaware made up the middle colonies. Their population was much less homogeneous than that of New England. Settlers came from Sweden, the Netherlands, Germany, France, and other parts of Europe, along with people of the Quaker faith who primarily settled in Pennsylvania.

Whereas schools in the New England colonies were very much alike in the 17th century, no one kind of school could satisfy the diversity of the middle colonists. Each religious sect established its own brand of schooling: Lutherans, Presbyterians, Jews, Mennonites, Catholics, Quakers, Baptists, Huguenots, and so on. The colonies attempted

Figure 8.2
New England Primer

to license schools, but did not provide financing. The middle colony schools were mostly private, or parochial, a term typically associated with religion (see Chapter 2, page 43). These parochial schools often taught a greater variety of subjects than the New England schools and included topics such as business, bookkeeping, and navigation.

Schools in the southern colonies. Like the middle colonies, the southern colonies were settled by diverse groups, but the settlers were even more widespread geographically. During the period from the late 1640s until about 1660, between the reigns of King Charles I and King Charles II, England experienced a revolution. During this time Puritans took over in England, and many supporters of Charles I moved to the southern colonies, adding further to the diversity.

In the southern colonies of Virginia, Maryland, Georgia, and the Carolinas, more so than in New England or the middle colonies, opportunities for education were based almost exclusively on social class. Children of plantation owners and wealthy merchants either attended private schools or were taught at home by tutors. These privileged students went from elementary to secondary schools either in the south or in Europe. Children who lived on small farms or children of laborers experienced whatever education was available through charity schools run by people who believed education should be more widely available, apprentice programs, or church schools. The children of slaves received no formal education in the southern colonies during the 17th century. In general, colonists were not concerned about making education available to all children. Most people in colonial America, including the first teachers, never considered the question, "And how are the children? Are they all well?"

Teachers in Colonial America

During the 17th century there was no formal system of teacher preparation. The closest parallel would have been apprentices assigned to Quaker teachers, who themselves lacked formal training in the education of both children and teachers. In dame schools the teachers were widows or housewives who could read and write to some unspecified degree of proficiency. Men who taught in the first elementary schools often did so for very short periods of time before beginning official training for the ministry or law.

Many teachers were indentured servants who taught in exchange for passage to the New World. Often people were teachers because they were not successful in other occupations; some were even of questionable character or conduct (Pulliam & Van Patten, 2007).

Teachers in the secondary schools (Latin grammar schools) enjoyed more status than those in elementary level schools. They often had more education themselves, and many had college training (Ornstein & Levine, 2006).

Many teachers in both the 17th and 18th centuries participated in the curious custom of boarding 'round. To save lodging money, towns required teachers to live with the families of their students for one week at a time. This practice did nothing for the dignity of the teacher or the profession. Pay was low, about what farmhands made, and without permanent homes, teachers often thought of themselves as expendable part-time employees (Good, 1964). Figure 8.3 contains a description of the life circumstances of an itinerant teacher and an excerpt from the journal of a female teacher who lived with her students' families.

Now that we have explored 17th-century American education, let's look at the progress made in the 18th century.

■ What Were the Major Influences, Issues, Ideologies, and Individuals in 18th-Century American Education?

The relatively benign colonial period in American history continued until about 1750. This period ended as a result of the spillover of European nationalistic conflicts onto colonial soil and subsequent attempts by Britain, in particular, to recover war costs through colonial

Figure 8.3   Teachers in the American past

About Silas Crocker:
Mr. Crocker is an itinerant schoolteacher, going from village to village in search of employment. During the summer months he earns a living plowing, mowing, and carting manure. In the winter, he teaches school. Having the reputation as the greatest "arithmeticker" in the county, he is a respected schoolmaster. Most of the schoolrooms in the area are familiar with this tall, gaunt master.

From Mistress Robbins's Journal:
My name is Elizabeth Robbins, and I am in my seventeenth year. I have been engaged to teach at Litchfield. A committee of the subscribers examined me and asked that I read passages from the Old Testament. They seemed pleased when I did not stumble over the big words. . . . I was hired for a period of five months, at four dollars a month.

I find a wretched schoolhouse, in the road, as it were, with a tiny fireplace. At first, it was easy, as the older scholars stayed away. When the school is full, however, it is very difficult to teach. The older boys make threats against me. They are generally lawless, and in the habit of using profane language. I have to resort to using severe corporal punishment to maintain order.

Source: From *Going to School in 1776*, by J. L. Loeper, 1973, New York: Macmillan.

taxation. Having emerged as the dominant colonial power in North America, England embarked on a system of taxation without representation in its colonies. This system swayed nationalistic feelings from loyalty to England to allegiance to the colonies themselves.

Representatives to the First Continental Congress (1774) in Philadelphia met to discuss how to claim their rights as British citizens in America. The Declaration of Independence soon followed, as did the writing of the Constitution, and then the Bill of Rights. The United States of America rapidly took shape (Boyer & Stuckey, 2005).

The timeline for the first and second halves of the 18th century appears quite out of balance in terms of noteworthy events, both for American history and for American educational history. The first half of the century was one of geographic growth on American soil and the maturation of economic and political ideas. Future leaders, such as Benjamin Franklin (1706–1790) and Thomas Jefferson (1743–1826), were born and grew up not only to pave the way for the new nation, but also to influence the direction in which 18th-century education was heading.

Benjamin Franklin (1706–1790)

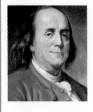 A pudgy, bookish man with long curly hair and little square glasses, flying a kite in the middle of a thunderstorm, is the image most have of Ben Franklin. Inventor and philosopher extraordinaire, Franklin contributed to American education in many valuable ways. In the mid-18th century he espoused educating America's youth in the practical and useful arts and trades. In addition to the traditional study of reading and math, he was the first to propose the study of history that included not just past politics and wars, but also customs and commerce. He founded the Library Company of Philadelphia in 1731 to promote reading by subscription to help tradesmen and farmers become as intelligent as gentlemen of other countries. In his *Proposals Relating to the Youth of Pennsylvania* (1749), Franklin said that wise men view the education of youth as "the surest foundation of . . . happiness. . . ." (Franklin, 1931, p. 151).

(Franklin, 1931; Good, 1964)

18th-Century American Schools

In 1751 Benjamin Franklin established the Franklin Academy, a school that was oriented toward real-world, useful learning. The academy was built on the principles Franklin espoused in 1749 in his work, *Proposals Relating to the Youth of Pennsylvania*, which, among other things, encouraged the use of English rather than Latin for literacy instruction. The Franklin Academy offered mathematics, astronomy, navigation, accounting, bookkeeping, French, and Spanish. One significant contribution of the Franklin Academy was its provision for students to choose some courses, the forerunner of today's electives.

Private **academies** sprang up across America. These schools were designed to teach content intended to prepare students to participate in business and trade. They

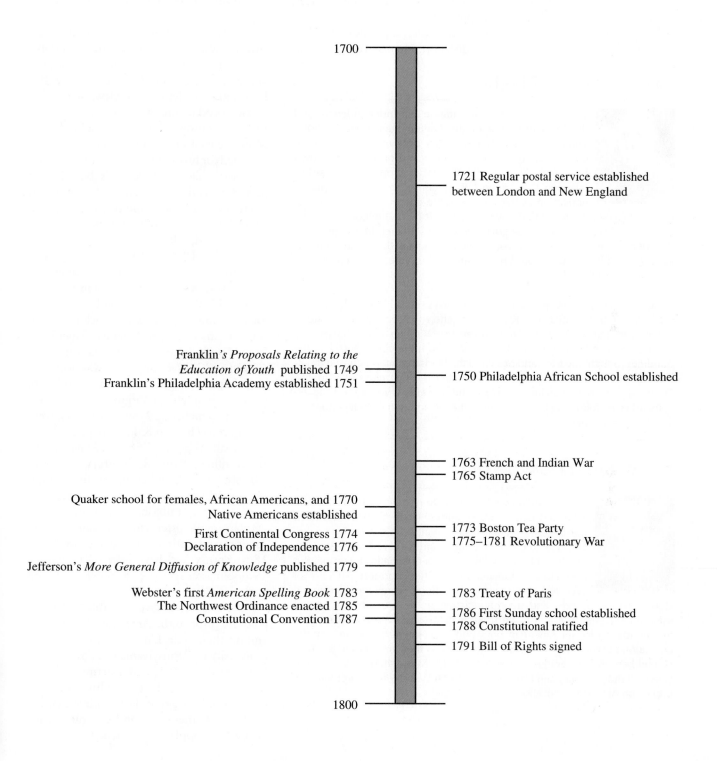

1700

1721 Regular postal service established
between London and New England

Franklin's *Proposals Relating to the
Education of Youth* published 1749
Franklin's Philadelphia Academy established 1751

1750 Philadelphia African School established

1763 French and Indian War
1765 Stamp Act

Quaker school for females, African Americans, and 1770
Native Americans established

1773 Boston Tea Party
1775–1781 Revolutionary War

First Continental Congress 1774
Declaration of Independence 1776

Jefferson's *More General Diffusion of Knowledge* published 1779

Webster's first *American Spelling Book* 1783
The Northwest Ordinance enacted 1785
Constitutional Convention 1787

1783 Treaty of Paris

1786 First Sunday school established
1788 Constitutional ratified

1791 Bill of Rights signed

1800

met not only intellectual needs, but also economic needs. In addition to these academies, **town schools** were established for whole communities. Although some schools still limited curriculum to reading, writing, and the classics, specialized schools in the form of academies became popular.

Thomas Jefferson had political, practical, and intellectual motives for his interest in and attention to education. He believed that education was essential to the maintenance of a viable republic (recall the discussion of the purpose of public education in Chapter 2, page 40). Education, in Jefferson's view, would increase production and preserve health. In 1779 he proposed the Virginia Bill for the More General Diffusion of Knowledge that provided for broader availability of education for more children. Jefferson's bill did not pass the Virginia legislature, but it raised awareness of the need and potential value of education among both lawmakers and the public (Good, 1964).

Thomas Jefferson (1743–1826)

As author of the Declaration of Independence and the third president of the United States (1801–1809), Thomas Jefferson believed that only through education could people preserve freedom and promote their own happiness. Historian S. Alexander Rippa (1997) said of Jefferson that "none has so consistently viewed public education as the indispensable cornerstone of freedom" (p. 55). Jefferson believed that government must be by the consent of the governed, and he wanted those governed to read. In fact, he suggested to President John Adams that anyone who was given the opportunity to learn to read but didn't, should not be allowed to vote. President Adams disagreed with this idea.

Disappointed by the Virginia House of Burgess's refusal to pass his Bill for the More General Diffusion of Knowledge, Jefferson spent the years following his presidency establishing the University of Virginia (UVA). It was truly his university in the beginning. He designed both the curriculum and the buildings, bought the trees and designed the landscaping, purchased the library books, chose the faculty, and admitted the first class of students. Thomas Jefferson died on July 4, 1826—one year after UVA opened and exactly 50 years following the adoption of the Declaration of Independence.

(Good, 1964; Rippa, 1997)

In the 18th century many Quakers came to America. They believed that education should be all-inclusive, and in Philadelphia in 1770 Quakers established a school for elementary students that included girls, African Americans, and Native Americans. In the South, however, formal education for African and Native Americans was nonexistent, despite a high literacy rate for White men and women. In Virginia, for example, 9 out of 10 men, and 2 out of 3 women were able to read (Button & Provenzo, 1989).

Noah Webster (1758–1843) had a profound influence on 18th-century American schools, particularly because of his writing. His most important work was the *American Spelling Book*, published in 1783. Some scholars say Webster had more influence on American education than anyone else in the 18th century and have referred to him as "Schoolmaster of the Republic" (Webb et al., 2007).

Noah Webster (1758–1843)

More than any other education statesman of the late 18th and early 19th centuries, Noah Webster reshaped the English language and literature into America's own. He was intensely patriotic and believed that America needed not only political independence from Europe, but also cultural independence. The enormous success of Webster's *American Spelling Book*, which included moral stories, lists of words, and a pronunciation guide, put an end to the importing of English books to be used as textbooks. Webster believed in free education for all American boys and girls. Interestingly, he saw the education of women as an absolute necessity as they are the first teachers of children. A Yale graduate, member of the Massachusetts legislature, lawyer, writer, scholar, and businessman, Noah Webster had a tremendous impact on American education.

(Good, 1964; Gutek, 2005; Webb et al., 2007)

Several colleges were established in the colonies prior to the American Revolution, among them Yale University in 1701, the University of Pennsylvania in 1753, Brown University in 1764, and Dartmouth College in 1769. At first, theology was the most popular degree; later, other majors, such as law, medicine, and commerce, increased in popularity (Cohen, 1974).

Education as a Priority

Education received a boost in priority with the passage of the **Northwest Land Ordinance of 1787,** which divided federally owned wilderness land into townships and required the building of schools. Article Three of the Ordinance proclaimed "Religion, morality, and knowledge being necessary to good government and the happiness of mankind, schools and the means of education shall be forever encouraged."

Education is not directly mentioned in the U.S. Constitution ratified in 1788. However, the Tenth Amendment in the Bill of Rights states, "The powers not delegated to the United States by the Constitution, nor prohibited by it to the states, are reserved to the States respectively, or to the people." Thus, from the inception of the United States to the present, except for the occasional federal mandate, states have grappled independently with educational issues.

As the new nation of the United States of America approached the 19th century, a surge of energy was directed toward education. Leaders and policies emerged that would place American education squarely in the foreground of thought and action.

What Were the Major Influences, Issues, Ideologies, and Individuals in 19th-Century American Education?

By 1800 American geography lessons included maps showing 17 states. By the end of the century the Union comprised a total of 45 states. During this unprecedented period of rapid geographical growth the United States also established a functioning and flourishing economy, endured a protracted test of the strength of its union (the Civil War), and matured into a stable, respected political entity.

With the election of President Andrew Jackson in 1828, the birth of the Democratic Party brought changes to American politics, turning a nation governed largely by an aristocratic society to one based in greater measure on government of, by, and for the people. Westward expansion propelled by the continuing desire for individual independence and opportunity took the growing nation all the way to the Pacific Ocean.

Cultural and economic differences between an increasingly industrialized North and an agrarian South grew and festered in the 19th century. The rift erupted into the Civil War in 1861 as Southern states seceded from the Union and formed the Confederacy.

Although the most commonly perceived reason for the Civil War is slavery, other actual issues surrounding the onset of hostilities revolved around states' rights and economics. Over 600,000 Americans on both sides lost their lives before the North and South were reunited in 1865.

On the post–Civil War education front one fact was crystal clear—both the classical educational system popular in the northeast and the one-room schoolhouse approach adopted during western frontier days were increasingly incapable of meeting the needs of the country.

Of all the issues facing the American population as the 19th century drew to a close, the most significant were associated with the Industrial Revolution. Poverty-level wages, a workforce that would soon include too many children, unchecked immigration, and abysmal working conditions all reflected poorly on the country's ability to cope with the abuses actually brought about by its wonderful spirit of inventiveness. Each of these issues would have to be faced and solved, and the educational system revamped to meet the needs of the more commerce- and industry-based society that was on the horizon.

Horace Mann and the common school movement made it possible for some Black children to be educated in public schools.

19th-Century American Schools

The 19th-century in the United States was characterized by a wide variety of schools. There were town schools, primarily in the northern states; charity schools, run by churches and philanthropic groups; and widely varying dame schools serving as small venues for

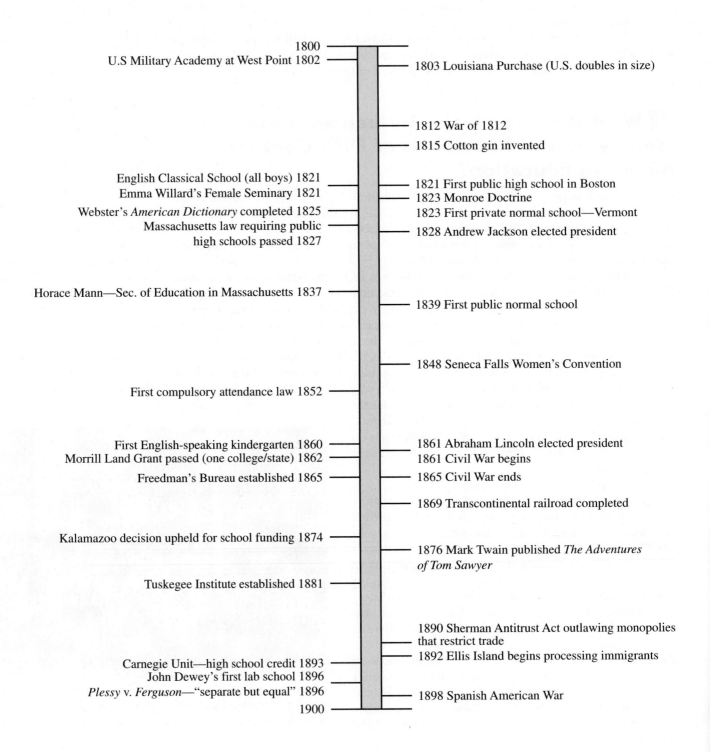

1800

U.S Military Academy at West Point 1802

1803 Louisiana Purchase (U.S. doubles in size)

1812 War of 1812

1815 Cotton gin invented

English Classical School (all boys) 1821
Emma Willard's Female Seminary 1821
Webster's *American Dictionary* completed 1825
Massachusetts law requiring public
high schools passed 1827

1821 First public high school in Boston
1823 Monroe Doctrine
1823 First private normal school—Vermont
1828 Andrew Jackson elected president

Horace Mann—Sec. of Education in Massachusetts 1837

1839 First public normal school

1848 Seneca Falls Women's Convention

First compulsory attendance law 1852

First English-speaking kindergarten 1860
Morrill Land Grant passed (one college/state) 1862
Freedman's Bureau established 1865

1861 Abraham Lincoln elected president
1861 Civil War begins
1865 Civil War ends

1869 Transcontinental railroad completed

Kalamazoo decision upheld for school funding 1874

1876 Mark Twain published *The Adventures
of Tom Sawyer*

Tuskegee Institute established 1881

1890 Sherman Antitrust Act outlawing monopolies
that restrict trade

Carnegie Unit—high school credit 1893
John Dewey's first lab school 1896
Plessy v. *Ferguson*—"separate but equal" 1896

1892 Ellis Island begins processing immigrants

1898 Spanish American War

1900

local education. Religious schools grew as families banded together with others of the same denomination and country of origin. Academies of all descriptions, some prestigious and some humble, flourished in the first half of the 19th century. In the South most educational opportunities still belonged to the wealthy; in the West most frontier children did not attend school. The obvious lack of consistency and opportunity did not mirror the ideals of America's founders, who saw education as a means to accomplish the goal stated in the Preamble to the U.S. Constitution to "promote the general Welfare. . . ."

Let's look at some of the categories of schools in 19th-century America.

Common schools. The system of free public schools that exists today had its beginnings in the common schools movement, first established about 1830. **Common schools** were community-supported elementary schools for all children established in response to a variety of economic, social, and political factors. Because free public education was a new concept, the common schools were debated, with many citizens seeing their value and others remaining skeptical, as illustrated in Table 8.2. Horace Mann was the champion of common schools. In fact, he was widely regarded as a champion of children in general and of the basic American ideal of opportunity for all.

In common schools, and most other schools of the 19th century, the works of William Holmes McGuffey had the most significant impact on what children learned. McGuffey's

Horace Mann (1796–1859)

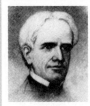

Widely known as the Father of American Education, Horace Mann had a profound influence not only on early American schools, but also on modern schools. He believed that regular attendance in schools with quality teachers would serve to equalize opportunities for poor, African American, and disabled children. He vigorously advocated for common schools.

As attorney and state legislator turned education advocate, Mann established the first normal school to prepare teachers in 1839 in Lexington, Massachusetts. Mann was not afraid of controversy as he pushed for separation of church and schools, not a popular stance in 19th-century America. Even as an avowed religious man, he was often criticized from church pulpits. As the first secretary of education for the Massachusetts Board of Education, which he helped establish in 1837, and throughout his life, Horace Mann spoke eloquently and worked tirelessly as a champion of schools and students.

Not only was Horace Mann an advocate for free quality education, but he also worked for the abolition of slavery and the limiting of alcohol as a social problem and was a vocal supporter of women's rights.

(Chartock, 2004; Mann, 1891)

Table 8.2   Merits of and objections to the common school from various viewpoints

Group	Merits
From the viewpoint of . . .	**common schools provided . . .**
the working class	avenues for social and economic mobility
some in business and industry	an increase in the supply of literate and trained workers
social groups	means of controlling crime and social unrest
people of the frontier	symbols of civilization and ways to keep literacy and citizenship alive in the wilderness
Group	**Objections**
From the viewpoint of . . .	**common schools were objectionable because . . .**
private school proponents	free schools meant fewer private school students
some in business and industry	they decreased the workforce of children who opted for school instead of jobs
some political leaders	of their apprehensions that an overeducated citizenry might question authority

W. H. McGuffey (1800–1873)

Far from the overly pious and drab books that painted a dreary picture of the worth of children and first appeared in American schools, W. H. McGuffey's six-volume set of *McGuffey's Readers* included stories and poetry that appealed to the interests of students. The volumes were geared to specific levels and paved the way to the separation of elementary school into grade levels. The volumes sold over 1 million copies between 1836 and 1906 and helped students learn to read and study while instilling in them virtues such as patriotism, morality, and a work ethic. McGuffey, as a minister, professor, and college president, indelibly left his mark on American education.

(McNergney & McNergney, 2007; Webb et al., 2007)

books differed from the unimaginative literature of previous centuries. The McGuffey readers included stories that promoted truth, honesty, and hard work.

As common schools increased in number, their inconsistencies became more and more apparent. Some were housed in acceptable buildings with adequate supplies and appropriate heating and lighting. Other common schools were housed in dilapidated, poorly heated and lit, filthy surroundings.

Secondary schools. When the English Classical School opened for young men in Boston in 1821, intended to replace the Latin grammar school, it marked the beginning of the public high school. In 1824 the school's name was changed to the Boston English High School. In 1838 a coeducational high school opened in Philadelphia. This school offered three tracks: a classical (Latin) curriculum (4 years), a modern language curriculum (4 years), and an English curriculum (2 years) (Webb et al., 2007).

Before the Civil War, high schools were almost exclusively found in the North, and always in cities. Because children could learn to read in common schools, and reading was considered sufficient education by many citizens, high schools were slow to grow in number.

In the aftermath of the Civil War, with Reconstruction and rapidly growing industrialization, economic growth spurred the establishment of more schools—not just common schools, but also secondary schools. High schools began to flourish about 1850, and by 1870 had replaced academies as the dominant secondary school. In 1874 a case in the Michigan Supreme Court called the **Kalamazoo case** established that the legislature could tax for support of both common and secondary schools, propelling public high schools into school systems in every state (Ornstein & Levine, 2006).

Friedrich Froebel (1782–1852)

When the first English-speaking kindergarten in the United States opened in Boston in 1860, it was the direct result of the work of Friedrich Froebel, widely viewed as the father of the kindergarten or "children's garden." Froebel thought of young children as flowers that would blossom into healthy adults if given the opportunity to be creative in an active curriculum. His emphasis on self-development and self-expression is the theoretical basis for early childhood education.

(Johnson, Musial, Hall, Golnick, & Dupuis, 2005)

Kindergarten. Early childhood education in the United States developed after elementary (common schools) and high schools (secondary schools). In Europe, Swiss educator Johann Pestalozzi (1746–1827) developed the theory of child-centered education and the concept of individual differences among children. German educator Friedrich Froebel (1782–1852) agreed with Pestalozzi, but took child-centered education further. Froebel was a proponent of an activity-based curriculum in an early childhood setting, where children are encouraged to be creative and expressive. This setting was called a kindergarten, or "children's garden" (recall our discussion of early childhood education in Chapter 2, pages 49–51). The first English-speaking kindergarten in the United States was established in 1860 in Boston. By 1873 kindergartens had become part of many public school systems (Chartock, 2004).

With the establishment of kindergarten, common school, and high school, the need for specially prepared teachers grew.

Teacher Preparation

Prior to Horace Mann's proposal that teachers receive special training, few completed any form of secondary education. Other than an occasional young man who was studying for the ministry and gave a brief term to a school, teachers were inadequately and inconsistently prepared. Notable exceptions were the teachers prepared at the Troy Female Seminary, the first institution of higher learning for women in the United States, established in Troy, New York, in 1821 by Emma Willard (1787–1870).

The first **normal school**, a publicly funded institution dedicated exclusively to preparing teachers, was established 18 years later, in 1839 in Lexington, Massachusetts. Catherine Beecher (1800–1878), along with Horace Mann, was instrumental in making teacher preparation a priority in normal schools (Holmes & Weiss, 1995).

As these first specially prepared teachers entered their classrooms, they seldom encountered children with disabilities, children of color, or children of poor immigrants. This situation would change with time.

19th-Century Education for Children with Disabilities and Minorities

The 19th century was marked by meager, yet important, advances in education for children with disabilities, children of color, and children of poor immigrants. Let's look briefly at each of these groups.

Emma Willard (1787–1870)

While boarding schools were teaching girls how to be polite, proper wives who could serve tea and make gentile conversation, Emma Willard was formulating plans for a school to teach girls and women useful, solid skills in homemaking as well as content and pedagogy to enable them to be teachers or to enter other professions. In 1821 she established the Troy Female Seminary, the first institution of higher learning for females. Before the first normal school was established in 1839 by Horace Mann and others, the Troy Seminary had prepared over 200 teachers. Emma Willard is also credited with the establishment of home economics as a legitimate subject area. Willard wrote textbooks, traveled extensively, and was a lifelong activist for women's rights.

(Chartock, 2004; Good, 1964; Webb et al., 2007)

Catherine Beecher (1800–1878)

Although Catherine Beecher's sister, Harriet Beecher Stowe, author of *Uncle Tom's Cabin*, may have more name recognition, Catherine had a great impact on the establishment of teacher training schools, or normal schools. In 1832 she established the Western Institute for Women, partially because she saw a need for better-educated teachers. The institute was not publicly funded and did not prepare teachers exclusively, but spawned other institutions of higher learning for women. In 1839 Beecher, along with Horace Mann and others, started the first publicly supported normal school for teacher preparation.

(Holmes & Weiss, 1995)

Children with disabilities. A few innovative schools were established in the 19th century for students with certain disabilities. In 1817 Thomas Gallaudet established the first school for the deaf in Hartford, Connecticut. In the mid-19th century physician Samuel Howe was influential in the establishment of the first school for blind children, the Perkins School for the Blind in Watertown, Massachusetts (Cubberly, 1934). Social mores of the day demanded that any educational opportunities for children with disabilities be separate from those for children without disabilities.

As you learned in Chapter 3 (see pages 92–96), children with disabilities remained apart from other children in public schools until 1975, when the Individuals with Disabilities Education Act (IDEA) changed the way schools and teachers approached the education of these special children.

Children of color. Children of color in 19th-century America were primarily Native American, Mexican American (in the South and Southwest), or African American. Let's consider each separately.

Native American Children. In 1824 the U.S. government established the Bureau of Indian Affairs and began placing whole tribes of Native Americans on reservations. Most of what little formal schooling Native American children received was provided by missionaries, whose efforts were fueled by a desire to convert the children to Christianity. The missionary schools were not consistently organized or maintained (Chartock, 2004).

A further goal of most efforts to educate Native American children in the 19th century was assimilation, that is, making the children more like White children or, in the terms of the time, "civilizing" them. It wasn't until the 1970s that the U.S. policy

Prudence Crandall (1803–1889)

Way ahead of her time, and incredibly courageous, Prudence Crandall believed strongly in the rights of African American students to an education. Her Quaker roots and her own education under a noted abolitionist, Moses Brown, helped shape her steadfast belief in equal opportunity. In 1830 Crandall founded a school for neighborhood girls in Canterbury, Connecticut. When she admitted an African American girl, Sarah Harris, Crandall and her school became the target for vandalism and ostracism. White parents withdrew their daughters. When Crandall established a school populated entirely by African American girls, it was destroyed by outraged Whites. Sarah Harris went on to teach many years in Louisiana, thus carrying on Prudence Crandall's legacy.

(Lincoln & Meltzer, 1968)

The doctrine of separate but equal was evident in schooling in the United States until well past the middle of the 20th century.

All-Black schools and all-White schools were the norm through the 19th and much of the 20th centuries.

changed from one of assimilation to fostering self-determination, encouraging Native Americans to take charge of their own education, whether on reservations or in other public schools. Today, even though the percentage of Native Americans under age 20 is greater than the corresponding percentage in the general White population, a smaller percentage of Native Americans participate in formal education (Ornstein & Levine, 2006).

Mexican American Children. At the end of the Mexican-American War in 1848, Mexico gave the United States vast territories comprising what are now Arizona, California, Colorado, Nevada, New Mexico, and Utah. Like Native Americans, Mexican Americans were targets of efforts at assimilation. For much of the 19th century most Mexican American children had few, if any, educational options. When they did attend school, teachers generally tried to Americanize them. Jumping forward into the 20th century, the passage of the Bilingual Education Act (1968) established bilingual programs that validated the children's native language. The dramatic increases in numbers of Mexican and Mexican American children in the schools as a result of both legal and illegal immigration has created an ongoing challenge for educators. We'll look more closely at this issue in Chapter 10.

African American Children. Although the education of Native American and Mexican American children was far from ideal and was inconsistently implemented, at least it didn't face legal objection by state or federal governments. The education of African American children in the 19th century did. For example, when Prudence Crandall admitted an African American student, Sarah Harris, to the school she founded in Connecticut in 1830, the school was forced to close. Crandall reopened the school for girls and enrolled 15 African American students from other states. The Connecticut legislature subsequently passed the **Black Law,** a law that specifically forbade a school intended to educate African Americans from other states without the permission of local authorities.

Prior to the Civil War, **Black Codes** were enacted, predominantly in the South, prohibiting the education of slaves. Some White people feared that educating slaves would give the slaves a sense of self-importance and that they might begin to think they were created equal and had certain inalienable rights as stated in the Declaration of Independence. In 1850, with increasing numbers of free African Americans in the North desiring education, the Massachusetts Supreme Court upheld the decision in *Roberts* v. *City of Boston* that separate-but-equal schools did not violate the rights of African American children. This ruling solidified the practice of separate but equal. At the end of the 19th century, the practice was reinforced by the ruling in a similar case, *Plessy* v. *Ferguson* (more on court cases in Chapter 11).

Following the Civil War, hundreds of teachers sponsored by church groups moved from the North to the South to educate freed African Americans. The Freedman's Bureau was established and opened 3,000 schools in the South to educate African American children. By 1869 about 114,000 African American students were being educated in these schools. Along with common school subjects, these new schools added industrial training in an effort to prepare African American students for employment (Gutek, 2005). Hampton Institute, founded in 1868, was an institution of higher education that emphasized industrial skills and teacher preparation.

The most famous graduate of the Hampton Institute was Booker T. Washington. Following graduation he became Hampton's first African American teacher. Washington was a major supporter of vocational education for African Americans. He viewed learning practical skills as a way of advancing socially and economically in the United States. In 1881 Washington founded the Tuskegee Institute in rural Alabama. By 1890 Tuskegee had 88 faculty members and over 1,200 students, making it one of the larger colleges in the South (McNergney & McNergney, 2007).

Children of poor immigrants. The United States is a nation of immigrants. The country's motto, *E Pluribus Unum,* means "from many, one." The issue of how to educate the many and have a strong one is not new. From 1870 to 1900 the United States experienced an influx of almost 2 million immigrants, many from Asia and eastern Europe, and many whose primary language was not English (Boyer & Stuckey, 2005). The immigrants needed schools to teach not only practical skills, but also language and American values and ideals.

Many immigrants were very poor, but their skills were needed in the rapid industrialization of the United States. As the economy grew, so did the tax base for supporting free elementary schools and high schools. The number of free public schools increased dramatically as the country attempted to cope with its industrial growth and with the many coming to its shores to become one nation (Gutek, 2005; Takaki, 1993).

Most poor immigrants had no means of providing for their families when they first arrived in the United States, generally in the already heavily populated cities of New York and Chicago. **Settlement houses** were established by reformers to address the problems of urban poverty. These were community service centers that provided educational opportunities, skills training, and cultural events. Jane Addams (1860–1935), raised in a wealthy Quaker home, established the most famous of the settlement houses, Hull House, in Chicago in 1889.

Now let's take a look at the growth of higher education in 19th-century America.

Higher Education

In 1862 President Lincoln signed a congressional bill called the **Morrill Act.** Through this act the government granted states 30,000 acres of land for every senator and

Booker T. Washington (1856–1915)

As a steadfast believer that education was the way to advance socially and economically, Booker T. Washington spent his life working for educational opportunities for African American students. From graduating from, and then teaching at, the Hampton Institute to the founding of the Tuskegee Institute in Alabama in 1881, Washington promoted his message that African Americans needed vocational skills to get and keep good jobs. Washington led the Tuskegee Institute until his death in 1915.

(Chartock, 2004; McNergney & McNergney, 2007)

Jane Addams (1860–1935)

Raised in a wealthy home with an abolitionist Quaker father, Jane Addams set her sights on becoming a doctor. However, because of back problems, she quit her studies and determined to dedicate her life to helping the urban poor. She founded Hull House in an old, run-down Chicago mansion. Located in the middle of an immigrant neighborhood, Hull House provided education for both children and adults. Addams recruited college-educated young women to work at Hull House. Many later used what they learned there to propel them to make major contributions to social reform. For years Hull House served as a model for other successful settlement houses, which numbered almost 100 by 1900.

Addams tirelessly promoted women's suffrage (right to vote) and was president of the Women's International League for Peace and Freedom from 1919 until her death in 1935. In 1931 she received the Nobel Peace Prize.

(Boyer & Stuckey, 2005)

representative it had in Congress in 1860. The income the states could generate from this land was to be used to support at least one college. The Second Morrill Act of 1890 further stipulated that no grants would be given to states where college admission was denied because of race unless the state provided a separate-but-equal institution. As a result of the Morrill legislation, 65 land-grant colleges were established, including the Universities of Maine (1865), Illinois (1867), and California (1868); Purdue University (1869); and Texas A&M (1871) (Rippa, 1997).

As colleges flourished, more progressive ways of educating children and adolescents also began to grow. The discussion of 20th-century education begins with progressive education, first introduced at the close of the 19th century.

■ What Were the Major Influences, Issues, Ideologies, and Individuals in 20th-Century American Education and Beyond?

The 20th century was a time of extremes in the United States. The country survived two world wars, numerous regional conflicts in Korea, Vietnam, and elsewhere, and a protracted period of dire economic stress. It also thrived in years of unprecedented economic prosperity. The populace of the United States grew increasingly aware of its own diversity. Periods of rampant racial tension necessitated healing and both legal and educational responses on a national level.

In schools, the beginning of the century ushered more of the components of John Dewey's progressive education into classrooms.

Progressive Education

In 1896 John Dewey established the first laboratory school at the University of Chicago to test the principles of **progressive education.** The progressive method was very different from the traditional 19th-century approach to education. What started with students learning in cooperative groups and letting their interests guide what they learned about traditional subjects grew into a major movement with far-reaching implications. The influence of John Dewey was tremendous as the United States moved from the 19th to the 20th century.

The progressive movement gained momentum during the first quarter of the 20th century and flourished until the end of World War II. The influences of progressivism are still evident in the 21st century. The basic principles of progressive education are summarized in Figure 8.4. These principles show the sharp contrast between the philosophy of progressivism and the established ways of doing school discussed earlier. John Dewey's primary focus was the implementation of schooling as a means of social reform and the improvement of life for Americans.

Figure 8.4 Basic principles of progressive education

1. Education is life, not just preparation for life.
2. Learning should be directly related to the interests of the child.
3. Learning through problem solving should be emphasized more than rote memorization of subject matter.
4. The role of the teacher is to facilitate learning more so than to direct it.
5. Cooperation among students should be emphasized more than competition.
6. Democracy should be practiced to encourage the free interplay of ideas that leads to growth.

Source: From *Introduction to the Philosophy of Education* by G. F. Kneller, 1971, New York: Wiley.

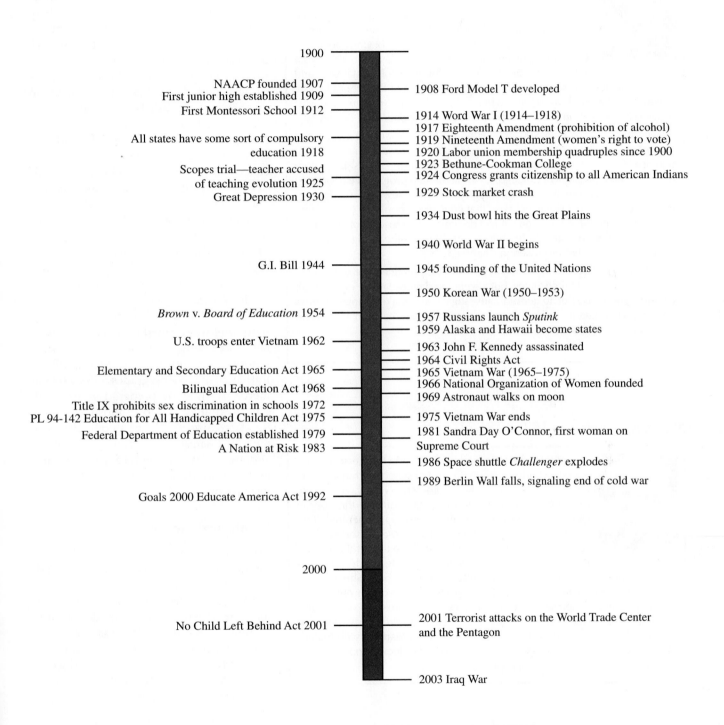

1900

NAACP founded 1907
First junior high established 1909
First Montessori School 1912

All states have some sort of compulsory
education 1918
Scopes trial—teacher accused
of teaching evolution 1925
Great Depression 1930

G.I. Bill 1944

Brown v. Board of Education 1954

U.S. troops enter Vietnam 1962

Elementary and Secondary Education Act 1965

Bilingual Education Act 1968

Title IX prohibits sex discrimination in schools 1972
PL 94-142 Education for All Handicapped Children Act 1975
Federal Department of Education established 1979
A Nation at Risk 1983

Goals 2000 Educate America Act 1992

2000

No Child Left Behind Act 2001

1908 Ford Model T developed

1914 Word War I (1914–1918)
1917 Eighteenth Amendment (prohibition of alcohol)
1919 Nineteenth Amendment (women's right to vote)
1920 Labor union membership quadruples since 1900
1923 Bethune-Cookman College
1924 Congress grants citizenship to all American Indians
1929 Stock market crash

1934 Dust bowl hits the Great Plains

1940 World War II begins

1945 founding of the United Nations

1950 Korean War (1950–1953)

1957 Russians launch Sputink
1959 Alaska and Hawaii become states
1963 John F. Kennedy assassinated
1964 Civil Rights Act
1965 Vietnam War (1965–1975)
1966 National Organization of Women founded
1969 Astronaut walks on moon

1975 Vietnam War ends
1981 Sandra Day O'Connor, first woman on
Supreme Court
1986 Space shuttle Challenger explodes

1989 Berlin Wall falls, signaling end of cold war

2001 Terrorist attacks on the World Trade Center
and the Pentagon

2003 Iraq War

255

John Dewey (1859–1952)

Think about all the things that happened in the United States during John Dewey's life, from the Civil War to the Korean War. He lived and wrote a very long time. In terms of education, many consider Dewey the most influential American of the 20th century. He was a professor of philosophy and pedagogy at the University of Chicago and at Columbia University. In Chicago, Dewey's son attended a school run by an ardent follower of Pestalozzi and Froebel. Dewey was so impressed with the approach of the school that he began researching, thinking, and writing about it. What we know today as progressive education was given an intellectual foundation by Dewey.

Dewey wrote more than 500 articles and 40 books, among which *The School and Society* (1900) and *The Child and the Curriculum* (1902) had perhaps the greatest impact on American education. In his laboratory school at the University of Chicago, he implemented progressive education and introduced projects such as carpentry, weaving, sewing, and cooking into the curriculum. Dewey believed that education should be experiential and child centered, rather than subject driven. He proposed that education is best served when the whole child is considered—including all the aspects of development discussed in Chapter 3.

John Dewey believed that democracy should be practiced not only in the governance of the United States, but also in the day-to-day life of a school. Children should be free to question, investigate, and make changes in their environments. Learning the principles of democracy early in life would serve them well later as adults.

(Dewey, 1956; Rippa, 1997)

Maria Montessori (1870–1952)

A compassionate medical doctor, Maria Montessori established a children's house, a kind of school within a house, for poor children in early 20th-century Italy. As people recognized transformation in these children they began studying Montessori's methodology and opening other children's houses, later referred to as Montessori schools. As Maria Montessori herself said, "The task of the child is to construct a man [or woman] oriented to his environment, adapted to his time, place, and culture" (1967, p. xiv). She believed that children are capable of integrating aspects of the world around them through the use of their senses. Children ages 3–6 are the ideal participants in the Montessori method. Montessori insisted that children's environments be carefully constructed to allow them to sense their learning with materials, such as letters made of sandpaper and colored objects to count.

(Chartock, 2004; Good, 1964; Montessori, 1967)

Junior High and Middle School

The need for a bridge between elementary and high school became apparent as the high school developed into a 4-year institution and the courses taught there became more standardized in content. Educators began to delineate the kinds of preparation necessary for high school success. High school teachers and administrators asked for basic preparation in algebra and English before high school. Writers such as G. Stanley Hall began recognizing a period of life called adolescence and acknowledging that adolescence was different from childhood. This new viewpoint led to a change in the configuration of schools; elementary schools shifted from eight grades to five or six, and the remaining two or three grades became the province of junior high schools. Later in the century, junior high most frequently encompassed grades 7 through 9.

In the 1960s another concept of schooling was formed to meet the unique needs of young adolescents—the middle school (Alexander & McEwin, 1989). Rather than viewing grades 5–8 or 6–8 as merely a time of preparation for high school, middle school philosophy called for recognition of the unique developmental qualities of young adolescents and use of developmental appropriateness in the school, in both curriculum and instruction.

Montessori Method

Although Maria Montessori (1870–1952) was developing a philosophy of early childhood education in Italy and other parts of Europe in the beginning of the 20th century, the Montessori method, described in Chapter 2 (see page 49), was not widely implemented in the United States until the 1950s. Today many Montessori principles can be found in early childhood settings across the United States.

Important African American Leaders

Two particularly influential people in 20th-century education were African Americans W. E. B. DuBois and Mary McLeod Bethune. DuBois believed that African Americans should pursue higher education in order to become leaders in politics and education. He sharply disagreed with Booker T. Washington's philosophy that African Americans would best serve themselves and their race by pursuing vocational arts and skills to prepare them to compete in the workplace with White people.

Mary McLeod Bethune was influential in both education and government policy. Her long career as a teacher, as well as college instructor and founder, took her from her home in South Carolina to college experiences in Chicago, to Florida, where she founded Bethune-Cookman College, and all the way to Washington, D.C., where she served as an advisor to President Franklin D. Roosevelt in the 1930s (Chartock, 2004).

This chapter's Teachers' Days, Delights, and Dilemmas is written by Burt Saxon, a teacher whose career has, in large measure, been focused on the African American community in New Haven, Connecticut. Both W. E. B. DuBois and Mary McLeod Bethune would be pleased to see the accomplishments of Burt's students.

The Last Five Decades

In this section we will examine schools decade by decade, beginning in the 1950s.

1950s. The *Leave It to Beaver*, white-bread world of Ward and June Cleaver and their two sons was experienced by many families in the United States and was typical of the social paradigm during the period of unprecedented economic growth and prosperity following World War II. In 1957, however, the "all's right with the world" syndrome was shaken by the Soviet launch of *Sputnik*, the first satellite to venture into space. The **National Defense Education Act of 1958** called for strengthening of science, math, and foreign language programs. Teachers were given training in the use of new methods and materials in hopes of bringing American student learning up to, and beyond, the levels of learning in other countries.

W. E. B. DuBois (1868–1963)

As a champion for equality of Africans and African Americans, W. E. B. DuBois spent his life as a scholar, a writer, and a reformer. In 1895 he was the first African American to earn a doctorate from Harvard. From 1895 through the 1950s he was a college professor and a civil rights activist. He organized worldwide conferences of Black leaders. DuBois considered Africa the homeland of all Black people and wrote about the dual citizenry of Black people who had left Africa in his 1903 book, *The Souls of Black Folks.* In 1907 he cofounded the National Association for the Advancement of Colored People (NAACP). Disillusioned by lack of progress for people of African descent in the United States, DuBois embraced socialism. At age 93, he joined the Communist Party and moved to Ghana, where he died at age 95.

(Boyer & Stuckey, 2005)

Mary McLeod Bethune (1875–1955)

Born in South Carolina of former slave parents, Mary McLeod Bethune was educated in a Presbyterian mission school and attended Moody Bible Institute in Chicago. The school in her hometown of Mayesville was for Whites only. Although Bethune originally wanted to be a missionary to Africa and was often quoted as saying the drums of Africa still beat in her heart, she dedicated her life to educating African American students. She established a school in Florida that became a normal school to train female African American teachers. Later the school evolved into Bethune-Cookman College, a 4-year coeducational college with mostly African American students.

In the midst of her work with education, Bethune became good friends with Eleanor Roosevelt, who drew her into government service, specifically, the National Youth Administration (NYA), a branch of the Works Progress Administration (WPA) created by President Franklin D. Roosevelt. In 1935 Bethune founded the National Council of Negro Women, an umbrella group for all organizations working on behalf of African American women.

(Boyer & Stuckey, 2005)

Another major factor in the American schools of the 1950s was the increasing pressure to desegregate. After all the years of separate-but-equal schools, the Supreme Court upheld the complaints of the National Association for the Advancement of Colored People (NAACP) made on behalf of a Kansas family in the now famous ***Brown v. Board of Education*** ruling of 1954. Chief Justice Earl Warren declared that segregating children based solely on race was wrong and illegal. Some schools integrated peacefully, while others did not.

While the launching of *Sputnik* triggered immediate changes in American education, and desegregation came to the forefront as an ongoing issue with significant moral implications, another, quieter, yet very important change was also taking place in the 1950s. Educators began to examine curriculum more carefully as a result of the thinking of Ralph Tyler (1902–1994), an educator discussed in both Chapter 4 (page 114) and Chapter 5 (page 145). Tyler proposed that data concerning the needs of the learner, the needs of society, and the needs of the subject area should all be considered in the process of developing curricula. Tyler believed that learning should have both specific objectives and appropriate assessments, two concepts deeply engrained in teacher preparation.

Teachers' Days, Delights, and Dilemmas

Burt Saxon
2005 Connecticut
Teacher
of the Year

My students are descendants of a long line of freedom fighters. Their ancestors include Frederick Douglass, Sojourner Truth, and Harriett Tubman. Their family trees include Dr. King and Cesar Chavez—and Thomas Jefferson too.

Teaching at Hillhouse High School in New Haven, Connecticut, has been the greatest opportunity of my life—far greater even than the opportunity of teaching at Yale University. Emma Ruff, New Haven's first African American teacher and Connecticut's first female high school principal, gave me the opportunity to teach the so-called talented tenth of New Haven's African American community. That is New Haven at its best. That is America at its best.

Emma Ruff gave me the chance to teach not only the descendants of freedom fighters and creative geniuses, but also the descendants of those who worked the fields, built the factories, took care of the children, the sick, and the aged, and toiled for low pay. Their children and grandchildren deserve better and I, like all my colleagues here, have tried to help them acquire the skills to take advantage of their increasing opportunities in the United States.

Even with my students' rich heritage and exceptional gifts, U.S. history can be tough to teach. Surveys of students across the country suggest it is one of the least popular subjects. To teach it well, you need to keep trying to get your students' attention each and every day. Today with 5 minutes left in the period, I asked my U.S. history students what had been their favorite topic so far this year. Robnisha said, "Nothing. No offense, but I just want to get a good grade so I can get into college." Most of the class agreed. I asked if they thought they would be more interested in the civil rights movement, and Patricia said, "It's the same thing every year." I told them we were not going to learn about Dr. King this year, but about people like Bob Moses. Then they asked me who Bob Moses was, and I told them that people in the civil rights movement considered him a saint. I told them he has spent the rest of his life trying to improve mathematics instruction for African American students. Their eyes brightened a bit, but they looked like they thought I was making all this up. I told them I had mentioned Bob Moses to Dr. James Comer a few months ago, and he had smiled and said he had just seen Bob Moses a few weeks before. Their interest was piqued because they realized Bob Moses was a real, flesh-and-blood man. They even asked how many other civil rights leaders were still alive and what they were doing now.

This was my opportunity to make U.S. history come alive with accounts of people both in our past, and in our present, that make a difference in our daily lives. History is indeed relevant to my students and to all students in the United States.

1950

1960

1970

1980

1990

High school students from 5 decades voted by their classmates to be Most Likely to Succeed.

Another influential person in American education, Benjamin Bloom (1913–1999), headed a group that composed what has become known as Bloom's taxonomy of learning objectives (discussed in Chapter 4, pages 124–125). The taxonomy was introduced in 1956 and continues to influence how educators think about and write learning objectives today.

1960s. The 1960s were characterized by a more outspoken U.S. citizenry. The election of a young, vibrant president, John F. Kennedy, gave rise to a sense of idealism among younger voters. After the assassination of President Kennedy in 1963, Lyndon Johnson attempted to continue in this vein with what he called the War on Poverty and the creation of the Great Society. Both the Kennedy and Johnson administrations allocated large amounts of money to break the cycle of poverty in the United States (Boyer & Stuckey, 2005). For example, the **Vocational Education Act of 1963** quadrupled the amount of money allocated for vocational education.

The following year, the **Civil Rights Act of 1964** stipulated that if schools discriminated based on race, color, or national origin, they would not be eligible for federal funding. Similarly, in a series of court battles, the Supreme Court continued to strike down school segregation.

In 1965 Congress passed the **Elementary and Secondary Education Act (ESEA),** which provided extra money for school districts with low-income families. Project Head Start was also established to boost the early learning of children ages 3 to 6 from low-income homes. In 1968 the **Bilingual Education Act** (Title VII of the ESEA of 1965) provided funds to assist non-English-speaking students (mostly Hispanic) who were dropping out of high school at a rate of about 70%.

1970s. During the first half of the decade, the country's attention was focused on the Vietnam conflict and the administration of President Richard Nixon. Public trust in establishment institutions was repeatedly shaken, resulting in a general lack of confidence in schools and teachers.

The number of students in public schools decreased during the 1970s, while private schools and homeschooling grew. Public school students' test scores dropped. Many perceived the need to implement a back-to-basics curriculum, and demands for accountability increased.

At the same time, some good things happened in 1970s education. Title IX of the Education Amendment Acts, which prohibited sexual discrimination in any education program receiving federal funding, took effect in 1975. In Chapter 3 you read about PL 94–142, the Education for All Handicapped Children Act, which passed in 1975. This important legislation granted children with disabilities the right to an education that meets their needs

Ralph Tyler (1902–1994)

Upon his death, a news release from the Stanford University News Service called Ralph Tyler "the grand old man of educational research." Ralph Tyler's contributions to education were many, with his impact on curriculum development perhaps the most meaningful. Of the 16 books and over 700 journal articles he wrote, the one with perhaps the most impact was among his first, *Basic Principles of Curriculum and Instruction*, published in 1949.

Tyler's commonsense approach to curriculum development involved

- determining the goals of the school
- selecting learning experiences useful in attaining the goals
- organizing instruction around the experiences
- and then deciding how best to evaluate the learning

Tyler conducted a groundbreaking longitudinal analysis of 30 schools and the careers of their students called the Eight-Year Study (1933–1941). This study focused on the opportunities students had who stayed in school rather than joining the workforce during the depression.

Tyler is also responsible for initiating the National Assessment of Educational Progress (NAEP) test in the 1960s, still the only test that evaluates the U.S. school system rather than the success of the students in it. Ralph Tyler was often heard to make two statements: "I never wanted to be anything but a teacher," and "I never met a child who couldn't learn."

(McNeil, 1995; Stanford News Service, 1994; Tyler, 1949)

Benjamin Bloom (1913–1999)

Following the 1948 convention of the American Psychological Association, Benjamin Bloom chaired a team that examined the cognitive, affective, and psychomotor domains of educational activity. From their work came what today is known as Bloom's taxonomy, a way of classifying levels of intellectual behavior important in learning. These six increasingly complex levels are

- Knowledge
- Comprehension
- Analysis
- Application
- Synthesis
- Evaluation

As part of his work at the University of Chicago, Bloom observed that about 95% of all classroom questions were at the knowledge (recall) level. The taxonomy provides a way to structure both activities and questions that run the gamut of intellectual processing.

Bloom also did extensive work in the area of assessment. He was influenced by Ralph Tyler and recognized that comparing students wasn't as important in terms of assessment as helping students master the learning.

Benjamin Bloom's work has been both condensed and expanded over the years by scholars and practitioners. His contributions to education are meaningful and enduring.

(Bloom, 1956; Eisner, 2000)

In spite of the 1964 Civil Rights Act, some schools remain segregated.

in the least restrictive environment (Chapter 3, page 94). Additionally, in 1979 President Carter elevated the federal office of education to a department, making its secretary a member of his cabinet.

1980s. During the 8 years of Ronald Reagan's presidency (1981–1989) federal funding for elementary and secondary education declined by 17%. Even so, the quality of education received renewed attention for two basic reasons. The first reason was concern over economic competition with Japan. Many Americans believed that the United States had begun to compare unfavorably with Japan, in part because of inferior schools.

The second reason for the renewed attention to education was the release in 1983 of a report commissioned by President Reagan called ***A Nation at Risk: The Imperative for Educational Reform***. The language of the report was strong, referring to public education in the United States as a "rising tide of mediocrity." In response, various proposals for reform and improvement surfaced. The *Paideia Proposal* (1982) by Mortimer Adler called for a core curriculum based on Great Books. The 1989 Carnegie Council on Adolescent Development report, *Turning Points: Preparing American Youth for the 21st Century,* validated the middle level philosophy of the National Middle School Association, which called for small learning communities, the elimination of tracking, and careful guidance.

Restructuring became a buzzword in education. Some of the efforts included year-round schools, longer school days, longer school years, and more funding for technology.

1990s. The 1990s might be labeled as the era of standards, as discussed in Chapter 4 (see pages 114–115). Along with the standards came tests designed to determine whether students had met the standards. The emphasis shifted from the input of education (what teachers do, funding, support) to the output of education (student learning). President Bill Clinton brought increased attention to education as he promised to be an effective "education president." He formalized Goals 2000, listed in Figure 8.5.

Teachers began taking on leadership roles in schools and in school districts. There was more collaboration among parents, the community, students, administrators, and teachers. Record enrollments resulted in a teacher shortage. President Clinton, in addition to providing federal support for the recruitment of 100,000 new teachers, joined policy makers in asking states to raise teacher standards (Webb et al., 2007).

And beyond. The defining legislation of the first decade of the 21st century is the No Child Left Behind Act of 2001 (NCLB). The act is the reauthorization of the Elementary and

Figure 8.5 Goals 2000

By the year 2000

- all children will start school ready to learn
- the high school graduation rate will increase to at least 90%
- all students in grades 4, 8, and 12 will demonstrate competency in English, math, science, foreign language, civics and government, arts, history, and geography
- all teachers will have access to programs for improvement of professional skills
- U.S. students will be first in the world in math and science achievement
- every adult American will be literate and prepared to compete in a global economy
- every school will be free of drugs, violence, and the unauthorized use of firearms and alcohol, and will offer a disciplined environment conducive to learning
- every school will promote partnerships to increase parental involvement

Secondary Education Act (1965) and calls for accountability of schools and school districts to states, and of states to the federal government. No Child Left Behind was formulated as a response to evidence that students were being promoted without mastering concepts and were graduating without basic literacy skills. NCLB has been discussed numerous times in previous chapters and will surface again in future chapters.

A major challenge of NCLB is that individual states determine the standards used for curricula and instruction as well as the tests to measure what students know. Wide disparities exist in both standards and tests among states. This situation is becoming increasingly obvious as state test results are compared to results of the National Assessment of Educational Progress (NAEP) discussed in Chapter 5 (see page 154).

How Can I Be Aware of Education History in the Making?

Time gives us perspective. We can look at the history of American education and determine which of the various influences, issues, ideologies, and individuals have most affected the course of schools, teachers, and students. What is less than obvious is which of these influences, issues, ideologies, and individuals are making a difference or initiating significant change now. Fifty or 100 years from now, it may be evident.

Education issues come and go, often in predictable cycles. The notable individuals involved in education at any given point are numerous. Sifting through them to determine who has significant and long-term influence generally only happens with time. The danger of listing contemporary movers and shakers in any field is the inevitable omission of names. Given that risk, Table 8.3 is an attempt to provide a partial list of individuals and their contributions that are currently influencing American education. You will no doubt hear and read about these individuals as you pursue a degree in teaching. Table 8.3 also contains empty rows to allow you, your instructor, and your classmates to add names and contributions.

Reading professional journals, continuing to take courses, attending conferences, having conversations with colleagues—all of these activities will help you stay abreast of the individuals in the forefront of our work as teachers. History is in the making all around us. In classrooms across the United States excellent teachers are the real heroes of education. Figure 8.6 provides you with the opportunity to write about a teacher who has influenced you. If you decide to be a teacher, then the history of American education has been changed, and the person you write about in Figure 8.6 helped make it happen.

What Role Will Diversity Play in My Teaching Identity?

For most of the first century after the Europeans arrived on the east coast of North America, the only students thought worthy of education were White male children. Diversity of race, gender, and socioeconomic status was nonexistent in formal education settings. The Quakers were the first to include females and children of color in schools in 1770. In the 1830s common schools were opened to all children, but their inconsistencies did little to improve education for minorities. The first schools specifically created to meet the needs of some children with disabilities were established around 1850 and served a very limited number of students. African American students began attending schools established for them in the 1870s. In 1896 the *Plessy* v. *Ferguson* case resulted in the separate-but-equal stance that lasted until *Brown* v. *Board of Education* in 1954, when the Supreme Court declared that separate is inherently unequal.

The history of segregation is relevant today. We struggle even now in the 21st century with inequities. Many children of color and children from low-income homes still attend substandard schools with a disproportionate number of underqualified teachers. Segregation, though no longer ordered by the courts, occurs in every state. This form of discrimination will be part of your reality in the classroom, and your responsibility to remedy as a teacher in American schools.

Table 8.3 History in the making

Individual	Theory, Field of Research, Written Works
Mortimer Adler	Paideia Proposal; core curriculum based on Great Books
James Banks	multicultural education
David Berliner	educational researcher; teacher effectiveness
Marva Collins	tireless advocate for all children; founder of Westside Preparatory School
James Comer	Comer Model; emphasis on social context of teaching and learning
Larry Cuban	expert on change in education
Linda Darling-Hammond	*The Right to Learn*; teacher quality and preparation
Marian Wright Edelman	Children's Defense Fund; advocate for all children
Elliot Eisner	arts education; curriculum reform
Jaime Escalante	outstanding high school math teacher in urban Los Angeles
Paulo Freire	*Pedagogy of the Oppressed*; education gives power to the poor
Howard Gardner	multiple intelligences theory
William Glasser	choice theory of human behavior
John Goodlad	*A Place Called School*; democracy and education; teacher education
Maxine Greene	existentialism; *Landscapes of Learning*
E. D. Hirsch	*Cultural Literacy: What Every American Needs to Know*
Ivan Illich	social reconstructionism; *Deschooling America*
Herbert Kohl	*36 Children*; the value of teachers and teaching differentiated instruction
Jacob Kounin	classroom management
Jonathan Kozol	*Savage Inequalities: Children in America's Schools*; study of urban children
Sonia Nieto	multicultural and bilingual education
Nel Noddings	caring in the classroom; teacher reflection
Robert Slavin	Success for All program; early intervention
Theodore Sizer	Coalition of Essential Schools; necessity of community in school environment; *Horace's Compromise*
Kay Toliver	outstanding teacher in urban New York City
Carol Ann Tomlinson	differentiated instruction
Grant Wiggins/Jay McTighe	*Understanding by Design*; development of curriculum, instruction, and assessment

Figure 8.6 History in the making

```
          Educators Positively Affecting American Education
    _____
    _____
    _____
    _____
    _____
    _____
    _____
    _____
    _____
```

Concluding Thoughts

This brief look at the history of education in the United States has been written from a majority culture viewpoint (White, middle class) primarily using sources having the same lens. Encapsulating 400 years into one brief chapter involves choices that have inherent limitations. Be aware of this when you consider any aspect of history. Understand that there's always more to the story.

American education has been more reactionary than trailblazing, more foundational than earthshaking. In an ideal world educators would be ahead of dilemmas, and the teaching and learning in U.S. schools would lead the way toward solutions to the country's problems. And indeed this is true, but in a subtle way. The adage "Teachers make all other professions possible" elevates teachers to indispensable heroes, although they are largely unheralded as such.

The history of education in the United States parallels the history of the country. Although once relatively simple and perceived as manageable, education in the United States is now incredibly complex and often unwieldy, with issues to match. In spite of the lessons to be learned from studying the history of American education, there remain unacceptable conditions for learning in some schools, unequal opportunities for children based on such factors as socioeconomic status and race, and international test results that show mediocre performances by U.S. students. Together we will face many challenges as we strive to effectively build on the past in order to do a better job of educating in, and for, the future, asking, "And how are the children? Are they all well?"

Chapter in Review

What were the major influences, issues, ideologies, and individuals in 17th-century American education?

- Many of the original colonists came to America seeking religious freedom and established schools to bolster their beliefs.
- Colonial schools primarily served White males.
- Education differed greatly among the New England, middle, and southern colonies.

What were the major influences, issues, ideologies, and individuals in 18th-century American education?

- Private academies served as secondary schools that went beyond what was taught in dame schools and town schools.
- Influential leaders, such as Benjamin Franklin, Thomas Jefferson, and Noah Webster, contributed to the expansion of educational opportunities.
- Education became a state responsibility by virtue of not being addressed in the Constitution.

What were the major influences, issues, ideologies, and individuals in 19th-century American education?

- Common schools were the first public, free American elementary schools.
- Following the Civil War, the first high schools began to flourish to meet the new economic demands of an increasingly industrialized United States.
- Kindergarten, with an activity-based curriculum, became common by the end of the 19th century.
- Teacher preparation institutions called normal schools were created to respond to the need for more teachers with increased and consistent preparation.
- Few educational opportunities existed for children with disabilities, children of color, or children of poor immigrant parents.
- Land-grant colleges were established as a result of the Morrill Acts.

What were the major influences, issues, ideologies, and individuals in 20th-century American education?

- John Dewey and the philosophy of progressive education fostered more active student participation in a school system based on democratic principles.
- Junior highs, and then middle schools, bridged the gap between elementary and high schools.
- Interest in science and math education increased following the launch of *Sputnik*.
- During the 1970s the Education for All Handicapped Children Act and Title IX increased educational opportunities for all children.
- *A Nation at Risk* served as a wake-up call for education in the United States.
- Curriculum standards emerged in the 1990s as the defining criteria for the quality of teaching and learning.
- The No Child Left Behind Act of 2001 represents the most significant federal impact on education in decades.

How can I be aware of education history in the making?

- Teachers should assume the responsibility of staying current with major shifts in educational concepts and trends. Time provides perspective. As history unfolds, those most influential will emerge in prominence.

Professional Practice

▇ Licensure Test Prep

Answer multiple-choice items 1–11 and constructed-response item 12.

1. The Puritans who settled on America's east coast believed all of the following except
   a. children were just little adults who needed to learn scripture.
   b. play was considered a waste of time.
   c. tolerance of differences is an absolute.
   d. English-style colonies were desirable.

2. A Latin grammar school in the 17th century
   a. was primarily for boys from wealthy families.
   b. was the first elementary school.
   c. promoted the education of all children.
   d. was the only option available to girls.

3. Teachers in colonial schools
   a. were trained in teacher education colleges.
   b. were often indentured servants.
   c. were men who specifically chose teaching as a career.
   d. were often revered for their success in other fields.

4. The establishment of academies in the 18th century was attributed to
   a. Thomas Jefferson.
   b. Benjamin Franklin.
   c. John Dewey.
   d. Noah Webster.

5. Which statement is true of 19th century schools?
   a. In the South, education was primarily focused on the wealthiest.
   b. Children in the western frontier learned in mobile schools that traveled with them.
   c. Religious schools were declining.
   d. Consistency of educational opportunity was the hallmark of the century.

6. The system of free public education as we know it today had its beginning in the
   a. normal school.
   b. kindergarten.
   c. academy.
   d. common school.

7. Specific preparation of teachers has occurred in
   I. Quaker apprenticeships.
   II. normal schools.
   III. Latin grammar schools.

   a. I and II only
   b. II and III only
   c. I and III only
   d. All of the above

8. All of the following are true of Booker T. Washington except
   a. he founded the Tuskegee Institute
   b. he supported vocational education for African Americans
   c. he never actually graduated from college
   d. he viewed education as a way to advance socially and economically

9. Which act was directly related to the establishment of higher education?
   a. The Morrill Act
   b. The Progressive Education Act
   c. The Old Deluder Satan Act
   d. The Northwest Land Ordinance of 1787

10. Progressive education, still influential today, includes which of the following principles?
    I. Competition among students increases learning.
    II. The role of the teacher is to facilitate.
    III. Education is life, not just preparation for it.
    IV. Learning is best accomplished through problem solving.

a. I and II only
b. I, II, and III only
c. II, III, and IV only
d. All of the above

11. Which statement is true?
    a. Ralph Tyler's major sphere of influence was in the area of curriculum.
    b. Benjamin Bloom was a colleague of Booker T. Washington.
    c. Mary McLeod Bethune was among the originators of the normal school.
    d. Maria Montessori developed the first kindergarten.

12. Business and industry had mixed reactions to the establishment of common schools. What is one reason business and industry favored the establishment of common schools? What is one reason business and industry objected to the establishment of common schools?

■ Standards Speak

This chapter explored the history of education in the United States. Although not speaking directly to this topic, some standards imply the importance of understanding this vital aspect of preparing to teach.

NBPTS Standard 5

Teachers are members of learning communities.

INTASC Standard 9 Professional Commitment and Responsibilities

The teacher is a reflective practitioner who continually evaluates the effects of his/her actions on others and who actively seeks out opportunities to grow professionally.

Respond to the following questions in your class notebook and/or discuss your responses with your classmates as directed by your instructor.

1. As part of a learning community, what role do you think the history of that community might play?

2. As reflective practitioners teachers have a bounty of resources and information from which to draw. How might the history of education or of an individual school be made part of the reflective process?

■ MyEducationLab

The following interactive features may be found in Chapter 8 of MyEducationLab.

Homework and Exercises

Writing My Own Story

To write your own story by responding to some of the questions in the text accompanied by fingerprint icons, plus others, go to the "Writing My Own Story" section of the Homework and Exercises for Chapter 8 of MyEducationLab.

What's My Disposition?

To reflect on your beliefs and attitudes concerning the teaching profession, go to Chapter 8's "What's My Disposition?" feature of the Homework and Exercises section of MyEducationLab.

Exploring Schools and Classrooms

If your course involves experiences in schools, the questions and prompts in the "Exploring Schools and Classrooms" feature of Chapter 8's Homework and Exercises section of MyEducationLab will guide you as you explore local schools and classrooms.

Virtual Field Experience

To respond to questions and prompts regarding the Choosing Your Teaching Path videos that connect to specific chapter content, go to Chapter 8's Virtual Field Experience section of MyEducationLab. The questions will help you make sense of what you have read in the chapter.

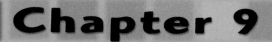

Chapter 9

Philosophical Foundations of Education in the United States

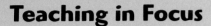

Teaching in Focus

Brenda Beyal's passionate approach to teaching is evident in every aspect of her work—curriculum choices, teaching methods, relationships with students, interactions with colleagues, and the learning environment she has created in her classroom. In her interview on this text's video, Brenda tells us she considers her choice to teach a "calling." She had planned to be an engineer until she took a course that addressed the needs of children with disabilities. That's when she knew teaching would be her life's work. She has taught for over 20 years, most of them spent in a multiage classroom at Rees Elementary, Utah. To review Brenda's video segment, go to the Choosing Your Teaching Path section of MyEducationLab at www.myeducationlab.com, click on Rees Elementary, then on Brenda.

Brenda's classroom is very student-friendly, with tables and a couch rather than desks in rows; a large classroom library with books for all reading levels on a wide range of topics; multiple cabinets of art supplies; display boards of student work; and an area filled with Native American art, posters, and artifacts that have personal meaning to Brenda because of her Native American heritage.

Brenda was one of the originators of the multiage concept (see Chapter 1, pages 24–25) at Rees Elementary. She wanted to have longer-term relationships with individual students. She saw the benefits of children at different stages of maturation being together for several years. She also liked the idea of collaborating with other teachers in creative ways. With colleagues Chris and Tim, Brenda maintains an arts-infused curriculum by teaching all three classes of multiage students an art form. Brenda's specialty is visual arts, evident by the amount of artwork in her classroom.

Each day is filled with opportunities, according to Brenda, who finds purpose and beauty all around her as she fulfills her calling. Toward the end of the chapter we'll translate what we know about Brenda into a philosophy of education.

Some people spend their entire careers studying philosophy. This chapter provides only a very brief survey of some of the components of philosophy that apply to education. The major questions addressed in Chapter 9 include

- What is a philosophy of education?
- What are four branches of philosophy?
- How do five prominent philosophies of education affect teaching and learning?
- How do I begin to develop my personal philosophy of education?

■ Introduction

The word *philosophy* may bring to mind an image of Socrates, with white-robed students sitting placidly at his feet, or perhaps of some lonely guy in a windowless office thinking deep thoughts but having little or no social life. The purpose of this chapter is to expand your view. We study philosophy to learn about ourselves and our world. Every time we make a decision, form an opinion, or take an action, we are expressing a philosophy.

Let's begin by defining philosophy, discussing what it means to have a philosophy of education, and the importance of a philosophy to teachers. There are branches of philosophy just as there are branches of medicine (cardiology, oncology, dermatology) and branches of law (civil, criminal, tax), each having its own definition. This chapter will explore four branches of philosophy and the basic questions that frame each. There are also schools, or categorizations, of philosophy, each giving direction to part of the wide gamut of possible philosophical thought. From these schools of philosophical thought, five philosophies of education have emerged. The chapter will examine how each philosophy affects what teachers do in the classroom. The chapter concludes with guidelines to help you purposefully develop your own philosophy of education.

The contents of this chapter on the philosophical foundations of education should not be dismissed as irrelevant theory. On the contrary, the concepts should be seriously considered and internalized. This won't happen with a quick read-through and a glance at the figures. The chapter is relatively brief, allowing time to read it twice or even three times, purposefully reflecting on the content to make it personally meaningful.

■ What Is a Philosophy of Education?

Let's begin by taking a look at the word *philosophy.* The Greek *philo* means "love," and *sophos* means "wisdom." **Philosophy,** then, means "love of wisdom." Philosophy is a means of answering fundamental questions. It is not just a boring, stuffy subject, but rather a vibrant way of discovering and expressing ways of being and acting.

If you've ever considered questions such as "Who am I?" or "What's my purpose in life?" you have engaged in philosophical thought. Every attitude and action is determined by some deeper basic beliefs, conscious or unconscious. To bring a philosophy to the surface of your consciousness requires consideration of your values and views about life. It necessitates reflection on circumstances, reactions, assumptions, intentions, and so on.

Most people don't have a formally defined philosophy. If asked, they would likely shrug and say, "I've never thought about it," or, "I don't have time for that kind of useless stuff." But if you could study a person's attitudes and actions over a relatively brief period of time, you could probably make some statements about the person's basic philosophy. This is particularly true for teachers and the work they do. A teacher's **philosophy of education,** whether written or not, is the teacher's love of wisdom regarding teaching that expresses itself in attitudes and actions every day in the classroom.

Why Is a Philosophy of Education Important?

A teacher's philosophy of education affects every decision the teacher makes in the classroom. Allan C. Ornstein (2003) expresses the far-reaching impact of a philosophy of education when he writes:

> Philosophy enters into every important decision about curriculum, teaching, instruction, and testing. When an educational official or policy maker calls for stiffer standards, or emphasis on a particular course of study or content area, this represents a philosophy. The methods and materials a teacher chooses to use in a classroom reflect a professional judgment, which reflects philosophy. When a teacher decides to increase the homework load or assign a particular author, he or she is acting on the basis of philosophy. In short, choices reflect philosophy—and whether we recognize our own

philosophy in education, it is out there and it influences our behavior and attitudes in classrooms and schools. Philosophy then operates overtly and covertly, whether we know that it is operating or not. (p. 17)

Getting Started on Your Philosophy of Education

All prospective teachers will likely be asked to write a philosophy of education. This means you will look closely at established philosophical viewpoints; you will analyze what these viewpoints mean to teachers and their work; then you will either state with which philosophy you agree or with which combination you most closely align. Let's examine this assignment. Your experiences with education are likely limited to your own K–12 schooling and a year or two of college, and, perhaps, your life experiences that may include children of your own. You have never been a teacher, nor have you spent much time talking with teachers about their own philosophical views. The conclusions you draw about your own philosophy of education based on limited reading and limited experience will no doubt be a work in progress. But it's a start, and an important one.

An educational philosophy should not be a static document that you write because you have to and then never look at again. People change and grow, often in response to personal experiences. Your philosophy will change and grow. Read about Karen Heath's experience of writing an initial philosophy of education as a college assignment and her subsequent experiences leading her to rewrite her philosophy in this chapter's Teachers' Days, Delights, and Dilemmas.

To get started on your own philosophy of education, read about four established branches of philosophy and how they may look in the classroom.

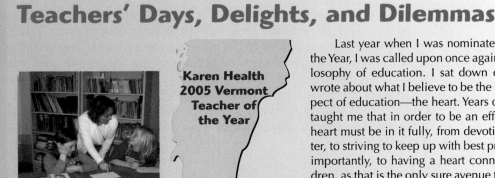

Teachers' Days, Delights, and Dilemmas

Karen Health 2005 Vermont Teacher of the Year

One of the ubiquitous rites of passage for preservice teachers is the completion of a philosophy of education. When I was a senior in college 22 years ago, having just completed my student teaching, one of the final requirements before being certified was to complete such a document. I was still a student, and much of what I thought about and wrote was largely theoretical. I wrote about the need for children's differences to be recognized, the importance of process in education, and freedom within a structured environment. "A Personal Philosophy of Education," as it was titled, went subsequently into a box in an attic while I ventured across the country and, a few years later, settled into a home in Vermont where the box was moved to a new attic, gathering dust with other college relics.

Last year when I was nominated to be Teacher of the Year, I was called upon once again to produce a philosophy of education. I sat down one weekend and wrote about what I believe to be the most important aspect of education—the heart. Years of experience have taught me that in order to be an effective teacher, my heart must be in it fully, from devotion to subject matter, to striving to keep up with best practices, and, most importantly, to having a heart connection to the children, as that is the only sure avenue to effective student learning.

It took a bit of digging, but I found the old college box, and at the very bottom of it lay my original philosophy of education. I took it like a treasure into the afternoon sun in our yard and carefully read not just a philosophy, but also the mind-set of an idealistic 21-year-old. Surprisingly, I still agreed with everything I had written, but there was a distinct lack of mention of anything having to do with relationships. I guess that is the aspect of teaching that I have truly learned over time.

Though my first written document sat untouched for 23 years and my newest one was just composed, I have always carried with me a philosophy of education. It brings stability to my work as initiatives and programs come and go. From a fairly benign population of children in a wealthy college town to an inner city Boston high school, my philosophy is the backbone of what I do as a teacher. It directs what and how I teach and, most importantly, how I interact with my students. It is the core of who I am as a teacher.

What Are Four Branches of Philosophy?

Because the study of philosophy is based on questions and the pursuit of answers, four commonly held basic branches of philosophy are best explored through the questions addressed in each. Metaphysics, epistemology, axiology, and logic each has its own unique category of questions that will aid in understanding its primary content and purposes. As you read this section, think about how the philosophical questions may apply in early childhood, elementary, middle, and high school classrooms.

Metaphysics

Metaphysics addresses the search for reality and purpose (Jacobsen, 2003). The word *metaphysics* means "beyond the material or the physical." Those who study metaphysics look for answers that go beyond scientific experiments. To understand more about metaphysics, first read the questions associated with this branch of philosophy, then read about how metaphysics may be manifested in the classroom.

- What is reality?
- What is a human being in the grand scheme of things?
- Do cause-and-effect relationships exist?
- Does reality change, making the search for truth meaningless?
- What is the meaning of life?
- Are people born either good or evil?
- Does life have a purpose?
- Are people free to make decisions, or is everything predetermined?

Metaphysics in the classroom. Curriculum is based on what we know about reality. Those who make decisions about what to teach are expressing a view of reality. When teachers attempt to inspire students to look to the future and find reasons for studying and learning, they are expressing metaphysics-related beliefs that life has purpose and that people can make decisions that affect the future. For instance, in a middle school career exploration class, a teacher may ask students to think about what they consider important in life. The teacher may then ask how aspects of a career in business management, for example, might help the students and others affected by a particular business to concentrate on what is considered important.

Epistemology

Epistemology addresses the dilemma of determining truth and ways of acquiring knowledge. The skeptic says it's impossible to know what the truth is, whereas the agnostic says there is no truth and, therefore, no need to look for it. Some people who are skeptics or agnostics in one area of their lives may believe that truth exists and can be determined in other areas. Consider the questions posed in the study of epistemology and then read how epistemology may look in a classroom.

- What is truth?
- Does truth depend on circumstances or on the person seeking it?
- How do we acquire knowledge?
- What are the limits of knowledge?
- Is knowledge changing or fixed?

Epistemology in the classroom. Curriculum standards are stated as truths. When teachers consider that there are absolute truths in the curriculum that students need to know, they are dealing with epistemological questions.

There are commonly held beliefs about where knowledge comes from and how it is acquired. Teachers tend to organize instruction or to use some instructional strategies more than others depending on their own views. For instance, believing that students learn best when they discover knowledge themselves will lead a teacher to practice constructivist strategies (see Chapter 4, page 126).

Once teachers have determined what is true about their content area (or have accepted the curriculum standards as truths), they are ready to consider how they want students to know or discover these truths. Consider the following sources of knowing, based loosely on Eisner (1985):

1. We know based on *authority*. This belief puts the teacher, the textbook, and other sources of information squarely in the middle of instruction.
2. We know based on *experience*. This belief leads to active learning involving the students' senses and the gathering of data.
3. We know based on *reasoning and logic*. This belief says that we think through situations and problems and draw conclusions.
4. We know based on *intuition*. This belief bases truth on a feeling about the answers.
5. We know based on *divine revelation*. This belief is in the power of the supernatural to reveal knowledge or truth.

The first three ways of knowing are the ones most often employed in the classroom. Knowing based on authority leads to reading assignments, lectures, review of the appropriate literature, and many traditional ways of teaching. Knowing based on experiences would lead to the use of manipulatives in math, survey research in social studies, and experiments in science. Knowing based on reasoning is what most teachers promote in the classroom. Learning to use higher-order thinking skills and moving through Bloom's taxonomy (see Chapter 4, page 124) are part of knowing based on reasoning.

Axiology

Axiology addresses values, both in ethics and aesthetics. **Ethics** is the determination of what's right and what's wrong. **Aesthetics** is the determination of what is beautiful and artistic. Both ethics and aesthetics require judgments. Consider the questions posed in the study of axiology and then read about how axiology may look in the classroom.

- What is valuable?
- What values should a person possess?
- What is right, and what is wrong?
- What is just, and what is unjust?
- How should life be lived?
- How should we judge the quality of what we see, hear, and touch?
- What is the quality of an artistic expression?
- What is beauty?

Integrating the arts into curriculum develops students' aesthetic senses and capitalizes on their interests and talents.

Axiology in the classroom. Teachers deal daily in their classrooms with questions of axiology. Ethics deals with how students treat one another, how they respect property, and how they make decisions about right and wrong in the classroom community. When a school adopts a character education program to help students establish attitudes about respect, it is acknowledging that ethics matters.

Deciding what is aesthetically pleasing also involves axiology. Part of what teachers do is help students recognize and appreciate beauty in any form. For instance, a math teacher who encourages students to explore geometry in nature and to discover the artistry of the geometric structures is prompting them to expand their definition of what is beautiful.

School itself expresses a value. Requiring children to attend school suggests the belief that it is right to give students the opportunity to learn (Nelson, Carlson, & Palonsky, 2000). Also, teachers are expected to possess certain values and to behave in ethical ways. Chapters 11 and 13 will explore some of the ethical responsibilities of teachers.

Figure 9.1   Deductive and inductive reasoning

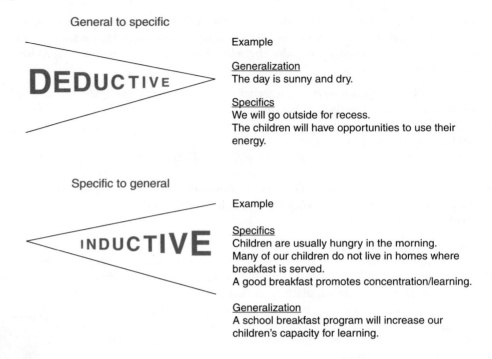

General to specific

DEDUCTIVE

Example

Generalization
The day is sunny and dry.

Specifics
We will go outside for recess.
The children will have opportunities to use their
energy.

Specific to general

INDUCTIVE

Example

Specifics
Children are usually hungry in the morning.
Many of our children do not live in homes where
breakfast is served.
A good breakfast promotes concentration/learning.

Generalization
A school breakfast program will increase our
children's capacity for learning.

Logic

Logic is reasoning that avoids vagueness and contradictions. Simply put, people use logic when they think to understand a situation, solve a problem, or draw a conclusion. Two basic kinds of reasoning, or logic, are commonly addressed in school. **Deductive reasoning** is a process that begins with a general statement, from which more specific statements are assumed to be true. **Inductive reasoning** works the other way: given some specific statements, a general conclusion may be assumed. Figure 9.1 illustrates these two types of logic. Consider the questions posed in the study of logic and then read how logic may look in the classroom.

- What makes sense?
- Is an idea or conclusion valid?
- How can we get from point A to point B in a way that makes sense?
- Is there a foundation for a particular argument?

Logic in the classroom. Teaching thinking skills—teaching the use of logic—is a major emphasis in many subject areas. An essay question that asks students to judge the outcome of a government program as good or bad (axiology) is asking them to use inductive reasoning, to look at individual results and draw a conclusion. A test that asks students to explain how to apply a theorem using particular variables is prompting them to use deductive reasoning. A teacher who intervenes in a student squabble and says, "Now stop and think about this," is asking students to think clearly, using logic and reasoning.

Review the four branches of philosophy and their defining questions in Table 9.1. The basic questions can be applied to the five schools of philosophical thought expressed as philosophies of education in the following section.

■ How Do Five Prominent Philosophies of Education Affect Teaching and Learning?

Just as knowing about individual branches of philosophy helps lay the groundwork for understanding what philosophy encompasses, exploring five prominent philosophies that have direct implications for education will provide a framework for writing one of your

Table 9.1 Four branches of philosophy

Branch of Philosophy	Defining Questions
Metaphysics	What is reality? Does life have a purpose?
Epistemology	What is truth? How do we acquire knowledge?
Axiology	What is right, and what is wrong? What is beauty?
Logic	What makes sense? Is there a foundation for a particular argument?

own. The five philosophies featured in this section are not the only ones that directly impact the work of teachers. A few others will be discussed briefly at the end of this section.

Chapter 4 explored teacher-centered and student-centered curricula and instruction (see pages 123–127). The five philosophies discussed here fall fairly neatly into these two categories: essentialism and perennialism are teacher-centered approaches, whereas progressivism, social reconstructionism, and existentialism are more student centered, as illustrated in Figure 9.2. Keep this in mind as you read about the five philosophies. Also remember to think about early childhood, elementary, middle, and high school classrooms as you consider each philosophy of education.

The discussions that follow mention prominent proponents of each philosophy. You will recognize many of them from Chapter 8.

The discussion of each philosophy is accompanied by a diagram of a tree. The analogy of a philosophy of education to a tree is appropriate in many ways. The tree trunk represents teaching. The root system is a particular philosophy, or a combination of philosophies, of education providing the strength and foundation of the tree: the philosophy literally grounds the tree. The branches of the tree represent the work of teachers. Each trunk-attached branch supports smaller branches with plentiful leaves that represent student learning.

Now we'll explore each of the five philosophies.

Essentialism

Essentialism is a philosophy of education based on the belief that there is a core curriculum that everyone in the United States should learn. This core can shift in response to societal changes, but should always be basic, organized, and rigorous. When you hear someone praise the concept of back to basics, chances are that person is an essentialist.

Figure 9.2 Teacher- and student-centered approaches

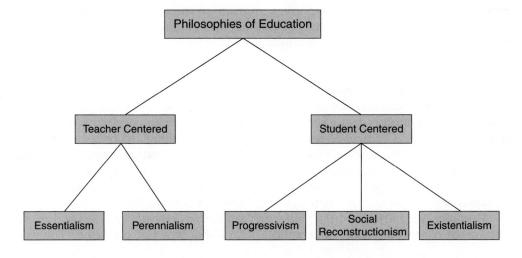

Essentialism has ancient roots, but in the 20th century it grew as a backlash to progressivism, discussed in Chapter 8 (see page 254), and later in this section. Whereas progressivism puts student interests at the center of curriculum and instruction, essentialism puts little stock in what students want in terms of what and how they learn. Essentialism gained impetus from the launching of *Sputnik* by the Soviet Union in 1957 and again from the publication of *A Nation at Risk* in 1983 (both discussed in Chapter 8, pages 257 and 260). Supporters of the essentialist philosophy are vocal about their view that schools have dumbed down the curriculum with nonessential courses, resulting in lower test scores (Ravitch, 2000). Essentialists favor high expectations for students, along with testing to measure mastery of standards.

An essentialist philosophy of education puts the teacher front and center as an intellectual and moral role model. Direct instruction is encouraged, but other instructional methods are used if they prove effective. Students are expected to listen and learn as they follow the rules of the classroom.

One prominent proponent of essentialism is E. D. Hirsch (1928–), author of *Cultural Literacy: What Every American Needs to Know* (1987). Hirsch lists events, people, facts, discoveries, inventions, art, literature, and more that he believes all Americans should know about to be culturally literate. Another proponent of essentialism is Theodore Sizer (1932–), founder of the Coalition of Essential Schools, a group of 200 schools that pledge to promote the essentialist goals of a rigorous curriculum based on standards. Sizer (1985) insists that students clearly exhibit mastery of content as well as evidence of developing thinking skills.

Your Teaching Fingerprint

Take a few minutes to study the essentialism tree in Figure 9.3. Visualizing how teachers might translate the elements of essentialism into their classrooms will help you understand this philosophy of education. Can you identify with some of the elements of essentialism? If so, which ones? Do some of the aspects of essentialism in the classroom appeal to you as a prospective teacher? Are there some aspects that do not appeal to you? Remember that when you see a fingerprint in the margin it means that you will be asked to respond to questions and prompts based on your experiences and opinions. These questions are included in "Writing My Own Story" in Chapter 9 of the Homework and Exercises section of MyEducationLab at www.myeducationlab.com.

Perennialism

Perennialism is a philosophy of education based on a core curriculum and in that regard is similar to essentialism. The difference lies in what constitutes the core. The word *perennial* means "everlasting" and is often used when talking about flowers. A flower that is a perennial blooms in season, is dormant for a time, and then blooms again, year after year. A flower that is not a perennial is an annual. An annual must be replanted each year. Perennialism, as a philosophy of education, says that there is a curriculum with themes and questions that endure, that are everlasting. In contrast, the curriculum of essentialism is considered basic and core, but its components may change as society changes and, as such, the essentialist curriculum is more comparable to an annual.

Perennialists believe that even as life changes and times change, the real substance and truths of life remain the same. The wisdom students need may be obtained through the study of **Great Books,** the writings of those considered to be the great thinkers through the history of Western civilization, such as Homer, Shakespeare, Melville, Einstein, and many others. Perennialists do not endorse choices in the curriculum or elective courses, and they ascribe to a rigid curriculum for elementary, middle, and high schools.

Teachers who practice perennialism as a philosophy of education desire to be in control of the classroom. They dispense knowledge and lead discussions of classics that require rigorous, logical thought by students. Differences in students are rarely considered, as all are expected to learn from the classics (Webb, Metha, & Jordan, 2007).

Mortimer Adler (1902–2001), author of the *Paideia Proposal* (1982), is perhaps the best-known recent proponent of perennialism as a philosophy of education. The word

Figure 9.3   Essentialism tree

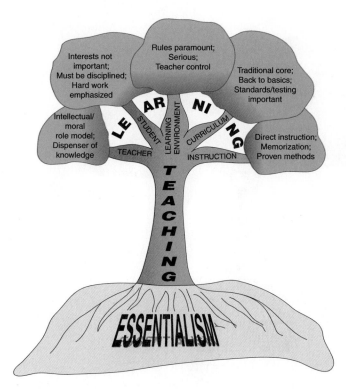

paideia refers to a state of human excellence. Adler said that schools should use intense study of the classics to strive for excellence in students (Pulliam & Van Patten, 2007). Adler founded the Great Books of the Western World program at the University of Chicago in 1930 (Adler, 1982).

Take a few minutes to study the perennialism tree in Figure 9.4. Visualizing how teachers might translate the elements of perennialism into their classrooms will help you understand this philosophy of education. Can you identify with some of the elements of perennialism? If so, which ones? Do some of the aspects of perennialism in the classroom appeal to you as a prospective teacher? Are there some aspects that do not appeal to you?

Your Teaching Fingerprint

Progressivism

Progressivism is a student-centered philosophy of education that focuses on a curriculum that is of interest to students. Progressivism was introduced in Chapter 8 on the history of education in the United States (see page 254). To progressivists, education is more than preparation for the future—it is life itself. The progressive philosophy of education endorses experiential learning full of opportunities for student discovery and problem solving.

Constructivism and pragmatism are philosophies of education that fall within the broader philosophy of progressivism. Constructivism, a way of approaching instruction discussed in Chapter 4 (see page 126), builds on progressivism, as students are challenged to construct, or discover, knowledge about their environments. Process is valued in progressivism, often more than product. The theory is that students who learn through the processes of construction, discovery, and problem solving will be better able to adapt to a changing world. Another philosophy, **pragmatism,** says that student-centered perspectives integrated with firsthand experiences are most effective (Chartock, 2004).

Teachers who ascribe to progressivism act primarily as facilitators of learning, serving as resources and guides to students who explore, gather evidence, and draw conclusions.

Figure 9.4 Perennialism tree

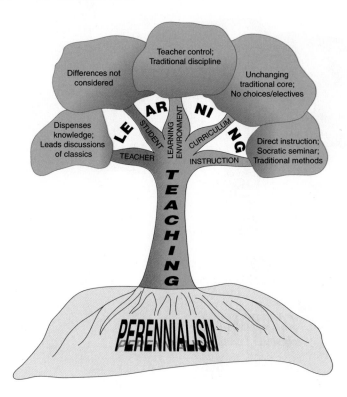

Derek at Roosevelt High School adheres to the progressive philosophy of education as he facilitates gathering of information and drawing conclusions to help his students become critical thinkers.

Real-world problem solving is intended to promote individual student development (Gutek, 2005).

As discussed in Chapter 8 (see pages 854–856), John Dewey (1859–1952) was the most prominent of all the proponents of progressivism, beginning in the late 19th century and continuing well into the 20th century. Dewey supported a balance between valuing established content with structured learning activities and planning experiences that interest, motivate, and actively involve students. Although progressivism fell out of favor in a call for more rigor in the late 1950s, many tenets of the philosophy continue to be part of today's most widely utilized instructional strategies.

Take a few minutes to study the progressivism tree in Figure 9.5. Visualizing how teachers might translate the elements of progressivism into their classrooms will help you understand this philosophy of education.

Can you identify with some of the elements of progressivism? If so, which ones? Do some of the aspects of progressivism in the classroom appeal to you as a prospective teacher? Are there some aspects that do not appeal to you?

Your Teaching Fingerprint

Social Reconstructionism

More than any other philosophy of education, **social reconstructionism** looks to education to change society, rather than just teach about it. Social reconstructionism as a philosophy of education calls on schools to educate students in ways that will help society move beyond all forms of discrimination to the benefit of everyone worldwide. This philosophy addresses such topics as racial equality, women's rights, sexism, environmental pollution, poverty, substance abuse, homophobia, and AIDS. Proponents of other educational philosophies often avoid such topics, thus relegating the topics to the null curriculum (see Chapter 4, page 122).

Figure 9.5 Progressivism tree

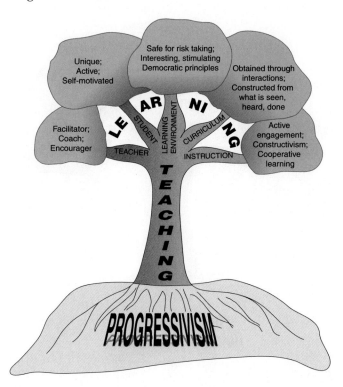

According to some educators, Theodore Brameld (1904–1987) founded the philosophy of social reconstructionism following World War II. Brameld based the philosophy on two premises: (1) people now have the capacity to destroy civilization, and (2) people have the potential to create a civilization marked by health and humanity (Brameld, 1956). The basic tenets of social reconstructionism, however, go back to the early Greeks and, more recently, to Karl Marx, who called for a social revolution that would bring about equity among all people (Jacobsen, 2003).

Teachers who ascribe to social reconstructionism promote active student involvement in societal problems. They plan experiences for students to explore issues and possible solutions, but avoid moralizing. They promote democracy and freedom to make choices, while helping students discover the consequences of particular lines of reasoning and action. All of this occurs within an educational context that focuses on reading comprehension, research techniques, analysis and evaluation skills, and writing as a form of persuasive communication.

Major proponents of social reconstructionism as a philosophy of education include George Counts (1907–1974), Paulo Friere (1922–1987), and Ivan Illich (1926–2002). In his book *Dare the School Build a New Social Order?* (1932), George Counts wrote about his view that schools should equip students to deal with world problems. Paulo Friere, in *Pedagogy of the Oppressed* (1970), wrote about his personal experiences in working with poor, illiterate peasants, which led him to the philosophy that education is the key to empowering the poor to control and improve their lives. In his book *Deschooling Society* (1971), Ivan Illich promoted a radical view. He wrote that schools as we know them should be eliminated because they do nothing to decrease poverty. He contended that schools actually prevent what he saw as real education, a process he viewed as happening in more informal ways. While "deschooling" American society will likely not happen, the social reconstructionist views of Illich have prompted important questions (Chartock, 2004).

Take a few minutes to study the social reconstructionism tree in Figure 9.6. Visualizing how teachers might translate the elements of social reconstructionism into their classrooms will help you understand this philosophy of education. Can you identify

Your Teaching Fingerprint

Figure 9.6   Social reconstructionism tree

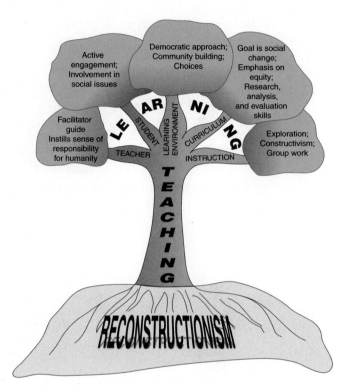

with some of the elements of social reconstructionism? If so, which ones? Do some of the aspects of social reconstructionism in the classroom appeal to you as a prospective teacher? Are there some aspects that do not appeal to you?

Existentialism

The primary emphasis of **existentialism** is on the individual. As a philosophy of education, existentialism contends that teachers teach the whole person, not just math, reading, science, or any other particular subject. Each student searches for personal meaning and personal understanding. If learning about a subject increases a student's sense of self, then it's worthwhile. Practices such as standardization, tracking, and testing do not fit into an existentialist viewpoint. Because meaning is personal, each student has the freedom to make, and responsibility for, his or her own choices and actions. Existentialism rejects traditional education. Few schools practice existentialism as an educational philosophy, and most that do are private. However, there are teachers in both public and private classrooms who practice some elements of existentialism.

The existentialist teacher honors each individual student by arranging for learning experiences from which each student may choose. The classroom atmosphere must be stimulating and full of choices. The student's job is to make choices and then take responsibility for those choices. Teachers and students have a great deal of individual contact, participating in learning that is self-paced and self-directed (Greene, 1978). A teacher who follows existentialism as a philosophy of education teaches best by being a role model and demonstrates the importance of a discipline by pursuing academic goals related to the subject area.

A. S. Neill (1883–1973) was one of the most influential proponents of existentialism. He founded the Summerhill School in England following World War I. Learning by discovery was the primary feature of Summerhill. The student as an individual was emphasized and exploration for the sake of learning had few restrictions (Neill, 1960).

Maxine Greene (1917–) is the most well known proponent of existentialism. She refers to a heightened level of personal awareness as "wide-awakeness." Greene refutes critics of existentialism who say that the philosophy in practice allows children to run free and out of control. She maintains that freedom has rules that allow others to be free as well (Greene, 1995).

Take a few minutes to study the existentialism tree in Figure 9.7. Visualizing how teachers might translate the elements of existentialism into their classrooms will help you understand this philosophy of education. Can you identify with some of the elements of existentialism? If so, which ones? Do some of the aspects of existentialism in the classroom appeal to you as a prospective teacher? Are there some aspects that do not appeal to you?

Your Teaching
Fingerprint

Other "isms"

There are other isms that may impact educational philosophy. Let's look briefly at some of them.

Idealism is a philosophy based on the belief that ideas are the only reliable form of reality. Idealists believe that because the physical world changes continually, ideas are what should be taught. Taking the opposite stance, **realism** is based on the belief that some facts are absolutes whether recognized by all or not. Realists contend that the only way to know these absolutes is to study the material world.

Romanticism, or naturalism, as a philosophy of education contends that the needs of the individual are more important than the needs of society. Many early childhood and elementary educators incorporate into their classrooms the tenets of romanticism that say young children are born good, pure, and full of curiosity and that their individual interests should be validated with opportunities to explore and manipulate elements of their environment.

Postmodernism grew out of a sense that those in power control those who don't have power. Postmodernists

Elements of romanticism may be found in early childhood settings as young children are encouraged to explore and discover concepts through play.

Figure 9.7 Existentialism tree

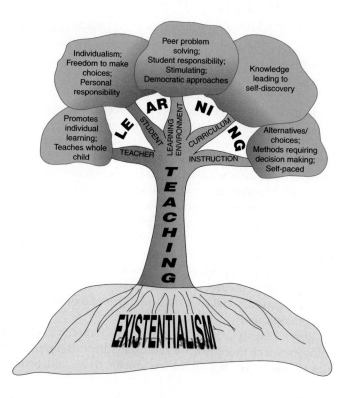

believe this control is manifested through major institutions such as schools. As discussed in Chapter 8 (see pages 258–260), the decades of the 1960s and 1970s were times of unprecedented outcry for justice and equality through the civil rights movement, the feminist movement, and a renewed concern for the poor. Postmodernist philosophy grew as a response to these cultural stirrings. The postmodern curriculum includes perspectives on history and literature by a variety of authors representing different lifestyles. Proponents of postmodernism contend that they are attempting to strike a balance of power among all people and that intellectual growth from multiple perspectives is one avenue for doing so. Critics of postmodernism contend that the philosophy seeks to promote political purposes rather than intellectual purposes (Ozmon & Craver, 2008).

You will likely encounter other isms as you participate in future teacher preparation courses. The ones you have read about so far provide many choices for you to consider as you begin the process of writing your own philosophy of education.

■ How Do I Begin to Develop My Personal Philosophy of Education?

Throughout this text the concept of balance has been emphasized. When it comes to developing a philosophy of education, balance is important. If, as you read about the prominent philosophies of education, you found yourself aligning with parts of one and parts of another and thinking, "How will I weigh all this and decide?" you are certainly not alone. Very few educators can place themselves squarely in one camp or another. Picking and choosing from among the components of several philosophies is referred to as taking an eclectic approach. This entails balance. Chartock (2004) tells us that it is natural for teachers to lean toward one philosophy or approach more than another, but that prescribing to only one philosophy will not serve the needs of all children. She continues by stating, "For every belief there is an equal and opposite belief and data to support both. That's why the field of education is never dull" (p. 136). Never dull, indeed.

Revisiting the Trees

Let's return for a moment to the analogy of philosophy as a tree. Many aspects of a tree's growth are directly analogous to teaching and learning. Do you recall seeing a cross section of a tree trunk? Elementary students learn that you can count the rings to determine the age of a tree because each year of growth not only takes a tree skyward, but also wraps another layer around it. So it is with teaching experience. Each year, previous experiences aren't shed, but are wrapped in new experiences.

Trees have two kinds of roots: anchor roots, which grow deeper with time and hold the tree upright against most winds, and feeder roots, which shoot out in all directions and draw in nourishment. Have you ever noticed a makeshift fence or stakes with colored tape around the base of a tree when construction is nearby? The purpose of this barrier is to let workers know that digging closer would likely damage the tree. Although a tree can survive the loss of some feeder roots, the diameter of the feeder root system is generally the same as that of the canopy of the tree's branches and leaves. Cutting away feeder roots will diminish the canopy in like proportion. Looking back at the five tree diagrams it's important to know that the size and stability of the philosophical root system determine the effectiveness of the learning canopy.

Reread the opening scenario of this chapter about Brenda Beyal. The philosophy tree in Figure 9.8 represents Brenda's philosophy and was developed based on her interview, room tour, and lesson on this text's

Brenda, one of the focus teachers at Rees Elementary, demonstrates her skills during a field trip with her students.

Figure 9.8 Brenda's philosophy tree

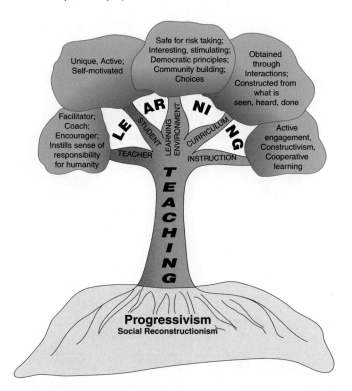

Aspects related to branches of philosophy that are addressed in Brenda s class include:

Epistemology—ways of knowing
Brenda's calling as knowing based on divine revelation

Axiology—What is just and unjust?
Smoky Night theme

Axiology—How should we judge the quality of what we see, hear, and touch?
Arts-infused curriculum

video in the Choosing Your Teaching Path section of MyEducationLab. Revisit Brenda by clicking on Rees, and then on Brenda Beyal. As you examine the tree, think about evidence, given what you know about Brenda, to support the elements on the tree.

Your Turn

Now it's your turn to grow a philosophy tree. The root system will consist of an anchor philosophy, the philosophy with which you most closely align. There's no need to as- cribe to every tenet of this anchor philosophy, but it should express most of your cur- rent beliefs about teaching and learning. Other philosophies may be part of the feeder root system. The branches and leaves of the tree's canopy will be a mix of what you be- lieve about the roles of teacher, students, the learning environment, the curriculum, and instruction. Keep in mind that the deeper and wider the philosophy root system, the stronger and more stable the trunk will grow and the richer and more extensive the canopy will be.

Figure 9.9 is a tree waiting for you to make it your own. Your philosophy tree can be a valuable component of the teaching portfolio you will no doubt develop as part of your teacher preparation.

Figure 9.9   My philosophy tree

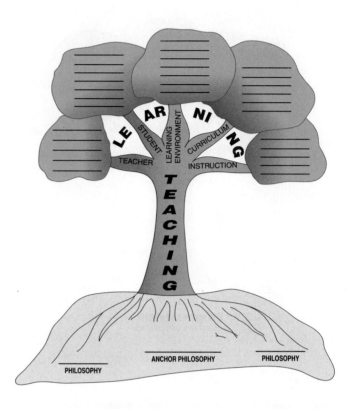

You may take one of several valuable approaches to growing your philosophy tree. One approach is to answer the questions, within the context of teaching and learning, associated with each branch of philosophy. In other words, when considering epistemology, the question "What is truth?" may become "Is this part of my curriculum verifiable?" When considering axiology, the question "What is valuable?" may become "Is this worth spending time on in my classroom?" Your answers to such questions will help you examine your philosophical views. There are many questions that may be asked, with each philosophy of education contributing unique responses. Table 9.2 relates the branches of philosophy to philosophies of education and provides sample questions and relevant responses aligned with the various philosophies of education.

Another approach to growing your philosophy tree is to spend some time thinking about your favorite teachers in early childhood, elementary, middle, and high school. Why did you admire them? What made them special? Your answers need to go beyond "She was so nice" or "He just stands out in my mind." To help you think through the reasons particular teachers had positive effects on you, put their names on the chart in Table 9.3. Then think about how they appeared to view their roles as teachers, how they related to students, how they created and maintained the learning environment, and their approaches to curriculum and instruction. Table 9.3 will help organize your recollections.

A sincere, honest start to the development of a philosophy of education will help grow you into the teaching profession. Having opportunities to talk about your philosophy and listen to your classmates, your instructor, and teachers in the field will make you more comfortable articulating your stance. The more you think, talk, and listen, the more confident you will become that you are grounded in your reasons for how you approach your role, your students, the learning environment, the curriculum, and instruction.

Table 9.2   Sample questions and philosophical responses

Question (Branch)	Essentialism	Perennialism	Progressivism	Reconstructionism	Existentialism
What is real? (metaphysics)	elements of core curriculum; may change	elements of core curriculum; unchanging	what can be verified through the senses	what can be verified through research and analysis	based entirely on the individual's perspective and experience
How do we acquire knowledge? (epistemology)	from a combination of the classics and science	from the never-changing classics	from individual experiences and discovery	from individual and group searches for meaning and justice	through individual quests; making choices
What is valuable? (axiology)	core of knowledge that responds to some societal shifts	changeless core of knowledge	determined by individual interacting with own culture	whatever makes society more just and equitable	whatever leads to greater self-knowledge
What makes sense? (logic)	classics provide generalizations; specifics are deduced; observation and analysis of specifics may lead to generalization	deductive reasoning from truths of classics	discovered through problem solving	weighed against potential benefit or harm to society	whatever enhances individual freedom and increases personal responsibility

Table 9.3   My favorite teachers' philosophical bents

Teacher's Name	Teacher's Role	Interactions with Students	Learning Environment	Curriculum	Instruction	Aligned with Which Philosophy?

Concluding Thoughts

This chapter may appear to be a rather simplistic approach to understanding what it means to have a philosophy of education. Chances are this is not something you've ever seriously considered. Now you have some background about major branches of philosophy, as well as philosophies of education. You have been prompted to think about, and tentatively declare, which philosophy represents your primary beliefs about teaching and learning. You also know that an eclectic approach is not only natural, but will actually benefit the diverse groups of students you will no doubt encounter.

Thoughtful teachers who are not necessarily swayed by gimmicks and fads, who have basic beliefs about teaching and learning that guide their practice, and who can articulate the bases for decisions are teachers who will positively affect student learning throughout their careers. This applies to early childhood, elementary, middle, and high school teachers equally. A carefully considered philosophy of education provides the framework for professionals in the classroom.

What Role Will Diversity Play in My Teaching Identity?

As you write your philosophy of education, a prominent topic you will need to address is your view of the role of diversity in your teaching identity. Some of the questions to think about include:

- Is it my job to consider student diversity when I plan for instruction?
- Do I have a desire to understand the many ways students may vary?
- Do I value particular kinds of diversity among students?
- Are there certain ways that students may vary that I want to eliminate? If so, what are they?
- Am I determined to make my classroom a safe haven for students who have very diverse opportunities outside school?
- Do I believe all students can learn? What qualifiers, if any, do I believe are acceptable to attach to an "All students can learn" statement?

Teacher-centered philosophies tend to be less tolerant of, and consequently less involved with, considerations of diversity. More student-centered philosophies entail recognition of, and planning for, diversity in the classroom. As you think about your teaching identity and begin to grow your anchor roots, how you approach student diversity will be a dominant factor.

Chapter in Review

What is a philosophy of education?

- We all have philosophies that guide our decisions, attitudes, and actions.
- A teacher's philosophy of education affects every decision about teaching.

What are four branches of philosophy?

- Metaphysics addresses the search for reality and purpose.
- Epistemology addresses the dilemma of determining truth and ways of acquiring knowledge.
- Axiology addresses values, in both ethics and aesthetics.
- Logic is reasoning that avoids vagueness and contradiction.

How do five prominent philosophies of education affect teaching and learning?

- Essentialism is a philosophy of education based on the belief that there is a core curriculum that is responsive to the times and that every American should know.
- Perennialism is a philosophy of education based on the belief that there is a changeless core curriculum that every American should know.
- Progressivism is a philosophy of education that focuses on a curriculum that is of interest to students and experiential learning.
- Social reconstructionism is a philosophy of education that endorses a curriculum that benefits society by promoting equity.
- Existentialism is a philosophy of education that focuses on the individual's search for meaning.

How do I begin to develop my personal philosophy of education?

- Incorporating components of more than one philosophy of education into your personal philosophy is an eclectic approach.
- Growing an effective philosophy tree requires a strong root system with philosophical grounding to enhance both teaching and learning.

Professional Practice

■ Licensure Test Prep

Carefully read, and then reread, the following passage from *A Letter to Teachers: Reflections on Schooling and the Art of Teaching* by Vito Perrone (1991, p. 33). Then respond to multiple-choice item 1 and constructed-response item 2.

> To engage students constructively, the school day needs more continuities, not more fragmentation. Work that can truly be valued takes time, sometimes hours and days. It is hardly reasonable to expect a child to complete a fine piece of artwork in ten- or twenty-minute intervals, twice a week, or produce a well-organized, thoughtful description, a poetic or narrative story within ten minutes. Teachers know this but claim that in this current basic skills, testing, "academic" environment, they don't have the time any more for work of that quality.
>
> Moreover, and possibly more important, life in classrooms is shaped by the expectations that are held for children. No matter how good a school might appear physically or how many books and computers exist, if teachers don't believe firmly that *all* children have important interests, intentions, and strengths that need to be seen as starting points for ongoing learning, they are failing children, their families, and their communities. . . .

1. To which prominent philosophy of education do you think Vito Perrone most closely aligns?
   a. existentialism
   b. essentialism
   c. social reconstructionism
   d. progressivism
   e. perennialism

2. Philosophy is a means of answering fundamental questions. What are two fundamental questions Vito Perrone answers about his philosophy of education in this brief narrative? Explain your choices.

Items 3 and 4 are not directly related to the Perrone quotation.

3. Each branch of philosophy has unique questions associated with it. All of the following branches have appropriate questions after them except
   a. Metaphysics—What is just and what is unjust?
   b. Epistemology—What is truth?
   c. Axiology—What is beauty?
   d. Logic—Is an idea valid?

4. Which philosophy of education is considered teacher centered?
   a. progressivism
   b. existentialism
   c. perennialism
   d. social reconstructionism

Standards Speak

In this chapter you discovered that almost every question, every scenario, and every decision may be categorized according to the branches of philosophy or the prominent philosophies of education. Teaching standards are no exception.

INTASC Knowledge Principle 1

The teacher understands major concepts, assumptions, debates, processes of inquiry, and ways of knowing that are central to the discipline(s) s/he teaches.

NBPTS

Accomplished teachers are models of educated persons . . . and the capacities that are prerequisites for intellectual growth: the ability to reason and take multiple perspectives, to be creative and take risks, and to adapt to an experimental and problem solving orientation.

Respond to the following questions in your class notebook and/or discuss your responses with your classmates as directed by your instructor.

1. Consider the INTASC standard. Determine which branch of philosophy you think the standard addresses most readily and explain why.
2. The NBPTS standard has implications for both branches of philosophy and philosophies of education. Write a narrative that explains the connections.

MyEducationLab

The following interactive features may be found in Chapter 9 of MyEducationLab.

Homework and Exercises

Writing My Own Story

To write your own story by responding to some of the questions in the text accompanied by fingerprint icons, plus others, go to the "Writing My Own Story" section of the Homework and Exercises for Chapter 9 of MyEducationLab.

What's My Disposition?

To reflect on your beliefs and attitudes concerning the teaching profession, go to Chapter 9's "What's My Disposition?" feature of the Homework and Exercises section of MyEducationLab.

Exploring Schools and Classrooms

If your course involves experiences in schools, the questions and prompts in the "Exploring Schools and Classrooms" feature of Chapter 9's Homework and Exercises section of MyEducationLab will guide you as you explore local schools and classrooms.

Virtual Field Experience

To respond to questions and prompts regarding the *Choosing Your Teaching Path* videos that connect to specific chapter content, go to Chapter 9's Virtual Field Experience section of MyEducationLab. The questions will help you make sense of what you have read in the chapter.

Chapter 10

The Societal Context of Schooling in the United States

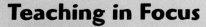

Teaching in Focus

After reading the title of this chapter, and perhaps glancing at the topics, you may be asking why this opening scenario would be about Brandi Wade, a kindergarten teacher. The answer is actually simple—social issues do not suddenly appear in the lives of adolescents. The social context of students' lives surrounds them from birth. By the time they get to kindergarten, many influences have already shaped them.

Brandi is very aware of the fact that her students enter kindergarten with individual histories as well as present circumstances. They do not come to her, as educators once proposed, as blank slates. Many already have strikes against them not of their own making, such as poverty or a family that doesn't value education. Brandi understands the saying, "There's nothing so unequal as the equal treatment of unequals." Think about that for a minute.

Her 12 years in the classroom have allowed Brandi to see her first group graduate from high school, or not. She has watched her students progress through primary, elementary, middle, and high school. She has seen some cope and thrive, and others become involved in destructive lifestyles. One thing she knows for sure is that success is more likely for some than for others. Thus she continually adjusts and differentiates.

In early December Brandi decided that she needed to change some of her routines and instructional strategies. She had lived with her kindergartners 5 days a week for more than 3 months, and she knew some of them were not yet thriving. Her experience had taught her that treating these 5- and 6-year-olds equally was not going to meet their needs.

Brandi's decision to make some general changes in her classroom, including a new seating arrangement, a new rule-and-consequence system, a heavier reliance on one-on-one instructional strategies, and a buddy plan, came as a result of her consideration of the students in her class.

Brandi's realistic view that some of her students will struggle more than others lowers neither her hopes nor her expectations for all her students. Regardless of the strikes against them, Brandi maintains that her children can and will learn. She knows that the challenges for children may come in many forms. Students raised in poverty face particular challenges. Children who are minorities face other challenges. Children who live in relative wealth, but with few restraints or little structure, will be challenged in other ways. All of Brandi's students will need academic and interpersonal skills, along with self-confidence and the ability to make reasoned decisions. All are, or will be, at risk in some way.

This chapter will examine elements that make up the complex societal context in which schooling occurs. The discussion of these elements will include the following questions:

- **How do family, community, and society impact students in the United States?**
- **How do socioeconomic status and race affect students in the United States?**
- **How do health issues affect students in the United States?**
- **What effects do bullying, theft, and violence have on students and schools in the United States?**
- **How do truancy and dropping out affect youth in the United States?**

Before beginning the discussion, let's look again at the faces of some of our focus students as kindergartners. These are children who will encounter dilemmas and choices as they grow, just like the students in your future classroom if you decide to accept the challenges of teaching. Remember their faces, as they represent children in the United States whose lives are affected both positively and negatively by societal influences.

■ Introduction

The question asked repeatedly in this text is "And how are the children?" In no other chapter is this question more appropriate than in this one. This chapter will explore some of the societal issues that impact students and schools in the United States. These issues do not affect all students or all schools, but they do reach into all areas—urban, suburban, and rural. They affect White, African American, Hispanic, Asian, and Native American children and adolescents in both affluent settings and impoverished neighborhoods. And they affect both U.S. citizens and noncitizens because some students in U.S. schools are not U.S. citizens, as you will see in the discussion of immigration.

James Garbarino (1999), a professor at Cornell University specializing in human development and family studies, tells us that children are growing up in a socially toxic environment. By this he means that just as our physical environment contains toxins, so has the social context of children's lives become poisoned in a number of ways. Garbarino is quick to point out that toxins in our social world have always existed, but now we are more informed and more aware of them. Students may face toxins such as dysfunctional families, poverty, discrimination, the availability of substances to abuse, violence—all factors largely outside the school's sphere of direct influence.

Some students go through childhood and adolescence relatively unscathed, while others are repeatedly victims or perpetrators. Which students are at risk, or less likely to succeed within our schools? Chapter 3 looked at many ways in which students are different—gender, culture, ethnicity, race, language, family, religion, socioeconomic status, intellectual ability, and exceptionalities. These sources of diversity may also be the roots of social issues that become toxins in the lives of children and adolescents. All students are at risk at some point, in some way, and to some degree. However, those students who are at risk much of the time, and in many ways, are perhaps most in need of attention.

This chapter includes a variety of charts, tables, and graphs, statistical and visual representations to help you grasp the impact of societal context on students. Examine each one with care to more fully understand the lives of the students you will teach. Think about the level at which you might best help children and adolescents emerge healthy and successful from their prekindergarten through high school experiences.

We will examine how family, community, and society in general impact students, both positively and negatively. Then we'll dive into issues that are not positive: poverty, racial discrimination, substance abuse, risky sexual activity, obesity, suicide, bullying, harassment, violence, truancy, and dropping out. These are not pleasant topics, but they need to be discussed because schools have a large role to play in the lives of students. The influence of teachers, even in the face of tremendous societal dilemmas, can provide refuge for students who need role models and guidance. Teachers are powerful when they take seriously their responsibilities and opportunities to care for and nurture the students in their classrooms. Each section in this chapter concludes with a segment entitled What Can Schools and Teachers Do? These segments provide ways for schools and teachers to help support students as they avoid or address the negative effects of their own personal societal contexts.

■ How Do Family, Community, and Society Impact Students in the United States?

The most basic societal unit of humankind is the family. Families exist within communities, and communities make up the larger building blocks of any society. This relationship, as illustrated in Figure 10.1, creates a pattern of influence that is undeniable. An individual is

Figure 10.1   Individual, family, community, society

Some children grow up in homes that shelter them from many of the less desirable societal influences.

Teachers are obligated by law to report suspected child abuse. Some symptoms are more noticeable than others.

influenced by the family, the family is influenced by the community, and the community is influenced by society. When children are very young, the family has the most direct influence. As they grow, the community plays a bigger role in children's lives. The influence of society grows immensely stronger with age.

For some children, family life is idyllic and supportive; for others it is not. Some children's families live in communities that are peaceful and caring; others live in the midst of destruction and violence. Although they all live within the same society, some children in the United States are shielded from negative influences by family and community and others are not.

Family

Chapter 3 (see page 85) explored the family as a source of diversity. Regardless of what a family may look like or the societal pressures the family may experience, members of families can support student success or thwart it.

Many children and adolescents are victims of child abuse and neglect, which places them squarely in the at-risk category. In general, **child abuse** is any act that results in death, serious harm, or exploitation; **child neglect** is a form of abuse resulting from the failure to act in the best interest of the child. Child abuse is reported on average every 10 seconds in the United States, and three children die each day as a result of abuse (Tenneyson Center for Children, 2006).

Information from the National Child Abuse and Neglect Data System (NCANDS) indicates that approximately 899,000 children were victims of child abuse or neglect in 2005. The maltreatment rate was 12.1 per 1,000 children (U.S. Department of Health and Human Services [DHHS], 2005). Although these numbers are disturbing, they represent only the tip of the iceberg. A study conducted in Colorado and North Carolina reported that as many as 60% of deaths by abuse are not reported as such. In order for a case of abuse or neglect to be included in government statistics, it must be reported, meet the established definition, and be investigated. Some forms of neglect and sexual and emotional abuse have few recognizable symptoms to a casual observer. The maltreatment can remain undiscovered for an entire childhood. The 899,000 recorded cases could actually represent millions of victimized children and adolescents. It is also appalling to realize that over 80% of the 1,490 reported fatalities due to child abuse in 2004 were predominantly those most vulnerable, children under the age of 7 (Child Welfare Information Gateway, 2006a).

It is difficult to determine the scope of the toll that child abuse takes on children and adolescents in the United States. For many, it's hard to imagine the reasons or the results of such cruelty. Even harder to imagine is that much of the neglect and abuse is at the hands of family and caregivers, those who should be the most trusted by the children. For some students, teachers and school personnel are actually their most trusted adults.

Your Teaching Fingerprint

How familiar are you with child and adolescent abuse and neglect? Do you have personal experiences? Do you know people who were victims of abuse? Remember that when you see a fingerprint in the margin it means that you will be asked to respond to questions and prompts based on your experiences and opinions. These questions are included in "Writing My Own Story" in Chapter 10 of the Homework and Exercises section of MyEducationLab at www.myeducationlab.com.

What can schools and teachers do? School personnel are among those considered mandatory reporters of suspected abuse. Also included are social workers, health-care workers, mental health professionals, child-care providers, medical examiners or coroners, and law enforcement officers. As you will learn in Chapter 11, teachers should report suspicions to administrators or guidance counselors. As citizens, teachers may also report suspicions of abuse to any Child Protection Services agency or to Childhelp at 800-4-A-CHILD (800-422-4453).

As a teacher, you may be the adult who comes between a child and a lifetime of suffering or, worse, death. Knowing the signs of neglect and abuse is an important first step. Figure 10.2 shows a list of signs provided by Child Welfare Information Gateway (2006b).

Figure 10.2   Recognizing child abuse

The following signs may signal the presence of child abuse or neglect.

In general, the child:

> Shows sudden changes in behavior or school performance.
> Has not received help for physical or medical problems brought to the parents' attention.
> Has learning problems (or difficulty concentrating) that cannot be attributed to specific physical or psychological causes.
> Is always watchful, as though preparing for something bad to happen.
> Lacks adult supervision.
> Is overly compliant, passive, or withdrawn.
> Comes to school or other activities early, stays late, and does not want to go home.

In general, the parent:

> Shows little concern for the child.
> Denies the existence of—or blames the child for—the child's problems in school or at home.
> Asks teachers or other caretakers to use harsh physical discipline if the child misbehaves.
> Sees the child as entirely bad, worthless, or burdensome.
> Demands a level of physical or academic performance the child cannot achieve.
> Looks primarily to the child for care, attention, and satisfaction of emotional needs.

In general, the parent and child:

> Rarely touch or look at each other.
> Consider their relationship entirely negative.
> State that they do not like each other.

Here are the signs of child physical, sexual, and emotional abuse, as well as the signs of neglect.

Signs of Physical Abuse

Consider the possibility of physical abuse when the **child:**

> Has unexplained burns, bites, bruises, broken bones, or black eyes.
> Has fading bruises or other marks noticeable after an absence from school.
> Seems frightened of the parents and protests or cries when it is time to go home.
> Shrinks at the approach of adults.
> Reports injury by a parent or another adult caregiver.

Consider the possibility of physical abuse when the **parent or other adult caregiver:**

> Offers conflicting, unconvincing, or no explanation for the child's injury.
> Describes the child as "evil," or in some other very negative way.
> Uses harsh physical discipline with the child.
> Has a history of abuse as a child.

(continued)

Figure 10.2 *continued*

Signs of Sexual Abuse

Consider the possibility of sexual abuse when the **child:**

> Has difficulty walking or sitting.
> Suddenly refuses to change for gym or to participate in physical activities.
> Reports nightmares or bed wetting.
> Experiences a sudden change in appetite.
> Demonstrates bizarre, sophisticated, or unusual sexual knowledge or behavior.
> Becomes pregnant or contracts a venereal disease, particularly if under age 14.
> Runs away.
> Reports sexual abuse by a parent or another adult caregiver.

Consider the possibility of sexual abuse when the **parent or other adult caregiver:**

> Is unduly protective of the child or severely limits the child's contact with other children, especially of the opposite sex.
> Is secretive and isolated.
> Is jealous or controlling with family members.

Signs of Emotional Abuse

Consider the possibility of emotional abuse when the **child:**

> Shows extremes in behavior, such as overly compliant or demanding behavior, extreme passivity, or aggression.
> Is either inappropriately adult (parenting other children, for example) or inappropriately infantile (frequent rocking or head-banging, for example).
> Is delayed in physical or emotional development.
> Has attempted suicide.
> Reports a lack of attachment to the parent.

Consider the possibility of emotional abuse when the **parent or other adult caregiver:**

> Constantly blames, belittles, or berates the child.
> Is unconcerned about the child and refuses to consider offers of help for the child's problems.
> Overtly rejects the child.

Signs of Neglect

Consider the possibility of neglect when the **child:**

> Is frequently absent from school.
> Begs or steals food or money.
> Lacks needed medical or dental care, immunizations, or glasses.
> Is consistently dirty and has severe body odor.
> Lacks sufficient clothing for the weather.
> Abuses alcohol or other drugs.
> States that there is no one at home to provide care.

Consider the possibility of neglect when the **parent or other adult caregiver:**

> Appears to be indifferent to the child.
> Seems apathetic or depressed.
> Behaves irrationally or in a bizarre manner.
> Is abusing alcohol or other drugs.

Source: From *Recognizing Child Abuse and Neglect: Signs and Symptoms,* by Child Welfare Information Gateway, 2006. Retrieved April 22, 2007, from http://www.childwelfare.gov/pubs/factsheets/signs.cfm

Community

Previous chapters have discussed the concept of community as it refers to relationships in a classroom. In this section, **community** will refer to the neighborhood, town, city, or county in which a student lives. The members of a community are those who live within a specific geographic vicinity, those with whom students may come in contact through everyday activities or when seeking services, such as shopping and doctor's care. The community of a student who lives in a large metropolitan area may comprise just a portion of the city. The community of a student who lives in a suburb or a large town may comprise just that suburb or town. The community of a student who lives in a rural area may extend into a nearby town or city.

Far too many students in the United States grow up in deplorable conditions in communities that prove to be toxic to their present and future well-being.

Most towns, cities, and counties provide services such as medical facilities, utilities (electric, gas, water), welfare and Medicaid, some form of counseling or assistance, law enforcement, recreation opportunities, and schools. The available services vary. Some students and their families live in communities that support healthy lifestyles. In these communities traditional measures of success—economic stability, nonviolent approaches to problem solving, education—are valued and promoted.

Some students and their families have access to government services, particularly in urban communities, that they would not ordinarily have access to on their own, such as medical care, child-care facilities, and tutoring, to name a few. Students in many rural areas must travel to take advantage of services generally provided at the county level.

Unfortunately, some students live in communities that are not only nonsupportive, but may actually be harmful to them. Some neighborhoods and communities are filled with violence and drugs, where children and adolescents are exposed to unhealthy lifestyles. Think about the community in which you spent a portion of your childhood. Was it a supportive community with people and services that contributed to your overall well-being? Or did you encounter situations that made it more difficult to grow and learn?

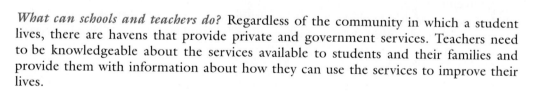

Your Teaching Fingerprint

What can schools and teachers do? Regardless of the community in which a student lives, there are havens that provide private and government services. Teachers need to be knowledgeable about the services available to students and their families and provide them with information about how they can use the services to improve their lives.

Society

This chapter is all about both the support and the problems present in American society. For many children, societal problems will be mitigated by positive forces, such as supportive families, higher socioeconomic status, or membership in the majority race. Other children will suffer proportionately more from negative societal influences. Regardless of sheltering forces, or lack of them, all children and adolescents are at risk of harm because of the complex societal context in which we live. However, many of the negative societal influences discussed in this chapter are more prevalent in families and communities in poverty, and their children often also face race-related roadblocks to success.

▪ How Do Socioeconomic Status and Race Affect Students in the United States?

Societal issues related to socioeconomic status (SES) and race affect school-age children and adolescents. This section will look at the problems that arise as a result of poverty and racism.

Low Socioeconomic Status (SES)

The privilege gap (see Chapter 3, page 86) between the haves and the have-nots is a societal dilemma that can't be quickly fixed, despite increased federal funding, primarily through Title I discussed in Chapter 2 (page 60), for schools with large populations of students living in low socioeconomic conditions. Some educators spend their entire careers seeking solutions to equity issues.

Chapter 3 (see pages 86–87) presented some generalizations about students who live in low-SES settings. These generalizations are summarized in Figure 10.3. Remember, though, that while generalizations may be useful for understanding children and planning learning experiences, it is important not to lump all low-income students together as a group and design programs based on one element of their lives—their socioeconomic status (Landsman, 2006). This kind of categorizing flies in the face of all we know about student learning differences and the value of getting to know students individually. Only by getting to know their students can teachers set appropriate goals and expectations for each.

Your Teaching Fingerprint

With what socioeconomic status (SES) group(s) are you most familiar? How did your own SES affect your school days? Most of us have little experience with what it's like to be truly poor. Although poverty was never part of Kayla Brown's personal life, she suddenly recognized it in the lives of her students. In the In the News video *A Teacher's Mission*, you can see her proactive response to the shocking realization that some of her students simply didn't have enough to eat.

What can schools and teachers do? Landsman (2006) advises us to have "a practical awareness of the students' physical needs coupled with a passion for teaching" (p. 28). She gives examples of teachers who fit this description:

- Doug is a middle school science teacher who keeps granola bars in his desk drawer for students who are so hungry that they fall asleep in his class. He also goes to the cafeteria for free breakfast with students who are hungry but may be embarrassed to go in alone.
- George is a high school teacher who collaborates with social workers to get clothes for students who need them and allows homeless students to leave school materials with him.

Figure 10.3   Generalizations about children in low-income settings

Over 10% of school-age children and adolescents live below the poverty line and may have experienced, or may exhibit, the following:

- enter first grade having been read to about 25 hours, compared to 1,000 hours in middle-class homes
- have been exposed to 30 million fewer words by age 4 than children of high SES
- are disorganized, lose assignments, do not do homework, have many excuses
- perform poorly on class and standardized tests
- dislike authority, do not monitor behavior, do not use middle-class courtesies
- are physically aggressive

Sources: Neuman, 2003; Payne, 2003.

In The News

A Teacher's Mission

Elementary teacher Kayla Brown thought hunger was something she saw in third world countries on TV until she found herself staring it in the face as one of her students picked up his lunch plate and licked it voraciously. She discovered that his lack of energy and enthusiasm could be traced to one factor—he was hungry. Kayla's life changed that day.

This *ABC News* video features Backpack Buddies, a program developed by Kayla Brown and volunteers from her church to help families that struggle because of low-paying jobs and lack of opportunity often associated with limited education and from a myriad of misfortunes that beset many people in the United States. Food is donated, organized, and distributed in backpacks so that children who eat breakfast and lunch free at school 5 days a week will also have food for dinner and snacks.

To view this video on your text's DVD, go to In the News, Chapter 10, and then click on *A Teacher's Mission*. Think back to Maslow's hierarchy of needs (Chapter 3, see page 69) and the discussions of poverty in this text as you consider these questions.

1. Teachers are responsible for students during the school day. Children from low-income homes can eat breakfast and lunch for free during the school week. Given these facts, what would drive a teacher to do what Kayla Brown did?

2. Kayla's school has seen a recent rise in standardized test scores. The counselor and others credit Backpack Buddies for the increase. On what might they base their claim?

3. The concept of a full-service school was discussed in Chapter 2 (see page 40). Should schools attempt to address social problems? Or should other government agencies only work directly with social issues such as poverty and hunger?

• Mary is principal of a middle school where local businesses contribute classroom supplies instead of asking students and parents to provide them. For Christmas 2005 the staff gave bags to homeless students filled with practical items and gift certificates to grocery stores. They report that the toughest students soften and begin to trust the adults at school.

In these examples the teachers' classrooms are open before and after school and at lunch for informal talks.

Figure 10.4 contains a lengthy list of strategies for teaching students who live in low socioeconomic conditions. "Teachers need to see assets and possibility where conventional eyes often see a dead end" (Landsman, 2006, p. 32).

Racism

Even though race has been discredited as a legitimate, precise way to categorize people, still, "race and racism profoundly structure who we are, how we are treated, how we treat others, and our access to resources and rights" (Mukhopadhyay & Henze, 2003, p. 669). **Racism** is a form of prejudice stemming from a belief that one race is superior to another that may be perpetuated by individuals or even government policies (Gollnick & Chinn, 2006). Recall the information presented in Table 3.7 (see page 81), which provides numbers and percentages, by state, of K–12 public school students who are non-White: non-White students account for about 40% of the almost 50 million students in U.S. public schools.

The number of teachers belonging to racial minorities is definitely not keeping up with the rapid growth in the population of minority students. Although this situation exists in virtually every state, Portland, Oregon, has recognized the mismatch and is attempting to do something about it. Figure 10.5 contains excerpts from an article that appeared in Portland's newspaper, *The Tribune*, in 2005. Read this article and

Figure 10.4 Strategies for teaching economically struggling students

- Assume that all students can learn complex and creative material.
- Create a classroom that gives students as much control as possible while maintaining safety and structure. Let students' interests drive the curriculum.
- Do not assume common behaviors or states of mind for all low-income students or parents.
- Focus on the assets that students bring to the classroom: resiliency, perseverance, flexibility, compassion, and hope.
- Understand that you cannot change the world, but that you can work within your classroom and community to effect change. Advocate for small class sizes.
- Build a network of colleagues who are finding ways to challenge low-income students. Meet in the media center on Fridays to talk about "what went right this week."
- Maintain your "other life" so that you can go into the classroom ready to meet kids wholeheartedly and without resentment.
- Find ways to provide the necessities, such as winter coats, art materials, and a place to wash clothes. Look in the community for resources—for example, a place for students to do homework.
- Find respectful ways to survey students about their home situations. Make yourself available for students to talk with you. Refer them for help when they share serious problems or speak of a lack of basic needs at home.
- Ask students to do jobs for you to help them feel important and in control of something in their lives.
- Do not single out kids or indicate in front of others that you know they are homeless or poor.
- "Cut deals" with students, helping them find realistic ways to meet work requirements.
- Convince students that "I believe you can learn and I will listen to you and give you meaningful work to do."

Source: From "Bearers of Hope," by J. Landsman, 2006, *Educational Leadership, 63*(5), pp. 26–32.

consider the dilemma. Then read this chapter's Letter to the Editor and compose your own response.

Discrimination

It's illegal to discriminate by race in American public schools. So that should be the end of the discussion, right? You will never find a public school policy that says, "If you are a racial minority, you must attend schools with peeling paint and inadequate, poorly maintained bathrooms," or, "If you are a child of color you may not experience advanced classes or be in gifted programs." It would be against the law.

However, official policies of nondiscrimination often are not manifested in the day-to-day realities of children and adolescents in American public schools. Even in classrooms where a rich social diversity exists, subtle forms of racism may be at play. The most subtle may be silence, with no ill intent on the part of the teacher. Polite and Saenger (2003) tell us that "the most pernicious and pervasive silence in . . . school classrooms is the silence surrounding the subject of race" (p. 275). Children are aware of physical differences of race at a very early age. Avoiding the subject doesn't make children's questions go away; they simply go unasked and unanswered. If children are not given opportunities to explore their own identities, as well as those of others around them, they will move from elementary to middle to high school carrying increasingly "complex feelings about race and racial issues, including pride, ignorance, anger, shame, ambivalence, and alienation" (Lewis-Charp, 2003).

Another subtle form of discrimination in schools is what has become known as the soft bigotry of low expectations. Whether these expectations are the result of an assumption about abilities and intelligence, of previous experiences with students of various races, or of some other factor, low expectations for some students amount to racism.

Figure 10.5   Portland, Oregon, minority report

Minority report

By TODD MURPHY   Issue date: Fri, Jun 17, 2005
The Tribune

It's a gap that makes the much-discussed "achievement gap"—the educational achievement gap between white kids and kids of color—look like a crack in the sidewalk.

The wider educational gap is between the overwhelming number of white teachers in Portland schools and the relatively paltry number of teachers of color.

Consider these numbers:

- While 40 percent of Portland Public Schools students during the 2003–04 school year were minorities, only 12 percent of the PPS teachers during that year were. (2003–04 is the most recent year for which the Oregon Department of Education has tabulated details on Oregon teachers.)
- At the 27 Portland district schools where the majority of students were minorities, on average only about 2 in 10 teachers were minorities.
- The number of black teachers in the district actually decreased about 12 percent between the fall of 2000 and the fall of 2003—from 172 to 151.
- While the percentage of Hispanic students in the Portland district increased from about 9 percent to almost 12 percent between the fall of 2000 and the fall of 2003, the percentage of Hispanic teachers increased about one-half percent—from 2.6 percent to 3.1 percent.

Paltry numbers of minority teachers are not unique to Portland. The issue has been a national education concern for years. So why does the number of minority teachers matter?

Because, educators and advocates for minority students say, minority students—many of whom struggle in school—need to see that people who look like they do can be successful.

"No matter how well-intentioned a teacher may be in relating to the cultural orientation of the students, there still is a significant value in the student being able to have a direct correlation with someone who is his or her own ethnicity. And being able to parallel the success of that individual with their own opportunities," said Charles Hopson, principal of Portland's Franklin High School. "It's just a process of affirmation."

All of that can and does influence the achievement gap in learning between poor and minority students and white students from middle- and upper-class families, educators say.

"Culture is the fundamental aspect of the student you encounter coming into your school, (and) you have to value and affirm students culturally if you're going to close the achievement gap," said Hopson, who is black.

Portland Superintendent Vicki Phillips said that . . . her administration is "committed to having a diverse work force at every level of the system. . . . And we're going to have to be aggressive about it. Creative and committed."

Landsman (2006) says, "I believe that a true test of any country's morality is whether it gives all children a fair and equal chance to achieve their potential as human beings" (p. 29).

Reflect on your racial identity. How has this identity affected you as a student? How does your own racial identity impact your beliefs about, and attitudes toward, those with racial identities other than your own?

Your Teaching Fingerprint

Immigration and Classroom Success

Immigrant children and adolescents in our classrooms help all students understand that people view the world differently. They contribute to our classrooms by increasing our knowledge and appreciation of diversity and by providing our classrooms with richer learning experiences. By 2010, children of immigrants will constitute at least 25% of K–12 students nationwide (Urban Institute, 2005).

Teachers often need to make an extra effort to understand how immigrant children may respond to many aspects of school in the United States. Without sensitivity to

Letter to the Editor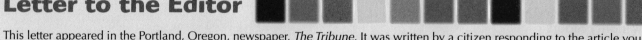

This letter appeared in the Portland, Oregon, newspaper, *The Tribune*. It was written by a citizen responding to the article you just read in Figure 10.5.

LETTER TO THE EDITOR

JUNE 25, 2005

I wholeheartedly agree that Portland needs many more minority teachers in our schools ("Minority report," June 17). However, my reasons are very different from the several education experts quoted in the article.

I feel that it is every bit as important for white students to be exposed to teachers from other races, religions and cultures. My parents taught my siblings and me that racism was the result of ignorance and intellectual laziness. They insisted that we all expose ourselves to as many cultures, religions and languages as possible.

I partially disagree with Franklin High School Principal Charles Hopson, who said that "you have to value and affirm students culturally if you're going to close the achievement gap." If racism and discrimination are the reason for the achievement gap between minorities and whites, why do Japanese-Americans, Korean-Americans, Jews, Chinese-Americans and Cuban-Americans scholastically outscore and, later in life, out-earn most white and black Americans? . . .

We do need many more teachers of different cultures and ethnicities. But I don't believe that more minority teachers will *solve* the achievement gap. Public schools can be a good place to start, but the parents of underachieving students need to do their part as well by showing their kids by example. Read to them when they are little. Pay attention, and help them with their homework. Insist on studies before recreation. And please, please teach them that it's so much cooler to be a geek than a "playa."

Jo G. Haemer
North Portland

Now it's your turn. Write a letter as a future teacher expressing your views about the perceived need for more teachers who are racial minorities. These questions will help you frame your thinking, but should not limit or determine what you write.

1. How important do you think it is for racial minority students to be in classrooms with racial minority teachers? Why?
2. What is the impact of White students having only White teachers throughout their prekindergarten through high school years?
3. What is the impact of minority students having only White teachers throughout their prekindergarten through high school years?
4. Is it possible for a teacher who is not of the same race as a student to understand that student's life experiences thoroughly enough to relate subject matter and life skills effectively to the student? Why or why not?
5. What might be done to increase the number of non-White teachers in our public schools?

Your letter to the editor should be in response to the *Tribune* letter—supporting it, adding information, or refuting it. Write your letter in understandable terminology, remembering that readers of newspaper letters to the editor are citizens who may have limited knowledge of school practices and policies. Your letter may be written in your course notebook and shared with classmates as directed by your instructor. Remember to refer to the letter assessment rubric in Figure 1.10, page 20.

differences, racism may become part of their classroom experiences. Ariza (2002) gives us some examples of differences that may be manifested in a classroom with children who are immigrants or the children of immigrants.

- Manes is a student from Haiti whose parents have gone to great lengths and considerable risk to ensure an education for their children. In Haiti, teachers rarely send communications home with students. Weeks after sending home notes that required parental attention and signatures, a frustrated teacher assumes Manes's parents don't care. However, they simply didn't know to look in Manes's book bag for notes and papers requiring their attention.
- Hong, a student from Southeast Asia, has had a cold and sore throat. A common ethnic remedy in her country of origin is to rub a coin up and down on an area that is causing illness in order to draw out the pain. When Hong arrives at school with what appear to be bruises on her neck, the teacher suspects child abuse.
- Mohammad, a son of recent immigrants from the Middle East, is Muslim. Normally an active, cheerful child, he became withdrawn and wanted to change his name

following the 9/11 tragedy in 2001 so that no one would associate him with his religion or with terrorists.

- Maria, a 7-year-old whose family is from Columbia, routinely carries a baby bottle filled with milk in her lunch box. Her classmates teased her, and her teacher asked if she had mistakenly put her baby brother's bottle in her lunch. She was humiliated. The teacher later discovered that it is both proper and commonplace in some areas of Columbia for primary children to drink from bottles.

Immigration and the laws addressing it continue to be a major source of contention and animosity in the United States. Regardless of the political infighting and social stigmas, the immigrant children and adolescents in our classrooms are just that—children and adolescents. They deserve the same care and consideration teachers give to all students. Read about one teacher's experiences with immigration in this chapter's Teachers' Days, Delights, and Dilemmas.

What can schools and teachers do? The authors of *Black Men Emerging* (1999), Joseph White and James Cones, tell us that there are three basic steps to confronting racism.

1. **Explore the issue of racism intellectually.** Read about racism and minority groups and discuss what you read with other teachers. Attend sessions at conferences that explore issues of racism and how to combat it in the classroom.
2. **Engage in dialogue about racism.** Start conversations with families, students, and the community about racial issues. Be open to frank talk and serious exchange of ideas.
3. **Immerse yourself in other cultures.** If you are White, attend a Black church service or a Kwanza celebration where you can join in and begin to understand traditions and perceptions. If you are Jewish, attend a Christian service. If you are non-Hispanic, join in Cinco de Mayo festivities. There are simple suggestions that will help begin an understanding that the United States is made up of rich diversity.

Teachers' Days, Delights, and Dilemmas

Deb Perryman Illinois Teacher of the Year 2004

I teach the very fine students of Elgin High School in Illinois. EHS is an urban school serving 2,200 students speaking 56 languages. Official records show that 50% of our kids are living at or below the poverty level. However, we know that the percentage is much higher due to our large immigrant population. These families do not yet qualify for government assistance.

I remember the stories my grandparents told me of the hard times they had coming to the United States from Ireland. They faced name-calling and worked dangerous jobs for low wages. I am thankful for all of the risks they took because I have so many opportunities. I remember my great grandpa yelling at the top of his lungs during dinner. He wasn't mad, but nearly deaf after many years working as a boilermaker. That is the first time I can remember thinking to myself, "I will

never treat another person the way my grandparents have been treated."

The immigration process is very complicated. As of May 2005 Illinois has a law (HB 60) that is providing possibilities for thousands of students. It buys time for those students seeking citizenship to actually complete the process, while continuing their education. It gives me hope and, best of all, gives hope to students who are children of immigrants.

I have a set of twins I am working with now. When they entered the United States from Mexico 10 years ago, their parents went to the Immigration and Naturalization Service and began their road to citizenship. They have diligently tried to meet every stipulation and deadline, only to find themselves basically still on square one because of bureaucracy involved, along with our overloaded, and understaffed, naturalization system. Now the boys are ready for college, and the family is threatened with deportation.

I will continue to champion the cause of protecting immigrant children from arbitrary harm. I will ask the hard questions. When will we accept the next wave of immigrants without prejudice? When will we realize that every generation before us has come to the land of opportunity to get or create jobs and live productively?

In our classrooms we need to be sensitive to each and every student, listen to interactions and guard against racial slurs of any kind, hold high expectations for all students, and continually seek to understand and appreciate differences that may accompany race.

How Do Health Issues Affect Students in the United States?

Some health issues pose immediate and obvious dangers to children and adolescents. Underage alcohol consumption and abuse of both legal and illegal drugs alter mental states and lead to overt behavioral changes. Other health issues are just as insidious, but their effects are incremental; their negative consequences occur gradually and are generally not accompanied by alarm. For instance, tobacco use and obesity among children and adolescents rarely push adult panic buttons, but can lead to deadly consequences.

Rates of substance abuse—specifically of alcohol, legal and illegal drugs, and tobacco—are not rising. Early sexual experiences are declining, along with the teen pregnancy rate. However, some health professionals say that the overall health of children and adolescents is worsening because of dramatic increases in obesity rates. This section will look at all of these health issues plus the ultimate health issue, death by suicide.

Substance Abuse

We don't have to look very hard for information about the negative effects of substance abuse, specifically alcohol, tobacco, and drugs. **Substance abuse** is a pattern of alcohol or drug use that can lead to detrimental and habitual consumption, impaired functioning at school and work, and legal difficulties (Schlozman, 2002). The guarded good news is that substance abuse does not appear to be escalating, as indicated by the results of one study presented in Figure 10.6. Another study, by the U.S. Substance Abuse and Mental Health Services Administration, confirms the decrease in substance abuse between 2002 and 2004 (Leinwand, 2006). Data from 2005 indicate that since the beginning of the 21st century, abuse has increased for only three categories of substances: sedatives, OxyContin, and inhalants. The bad news continues to be that substance abuse is extremely dangerous and can be deadly. Even if the statistics show leveling or a decline, one child or adolescent harmed by substance abuse is one too many.

Despite lower rates of consumption, alcohol usage remains widespread, with about 75% of high school seniors and 40% of eighth graders consuming more than just a trial taste of alcohol (U.S. Department of Health and Human Services, 2005). Even though

Figure 10.6 Percentage of high school seniors reporting substance use at least once during the past 30 days

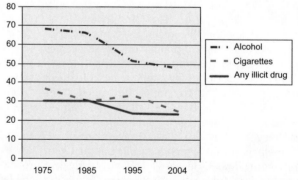

Source: From *Youth Indicators 2005: Trends in the Well-Being of American Youth,* by M. A. Fox, B. A. Connolly, and T. D. Snyder, 2005, Washington, DC: National Center for Education Statistics. Retrieved April 23, 2007, from http://nces.ed.gov/pubs2005/2005050.pdf

teenage alcohol consumption in 2005 was substantially less than in the 1980s, binge drinking, defined as five drinks in a row at least once in 2 weeks, appears to be on the rise.

The heartbreaking stories of automobile accidents involving intoxicated or high adolescents at the wheel spur groups like Mothers Against Drunk Driving (MADD) and Students Against Drunk Driving (SADD) to continue their awareness campaigns. According to MADD (2004), of the 6,409 15–20-year-olds killed in 2003 in automobile accidents, 36% (or 2,283) died due to underage drinking. In 2000, about 60% of 15–20-year-old fatalities on prom or graduation weekend were caused by underage drinkers. The public service messages on television and medical segments in the media raise awareness of the dangers of misusing illegal and legal substances, including tobacco. Smokeless tobacco use appears to be increasing, although fewer teenagers smoke cigarettes than in the 1990s.

It is a heart-breaking fact that thousands of adolescents die each year as a result of underage drinking and driving.

The highly publicized "Just Say No" campaign and the program many of you experienced in elementary school, Drug Abuse Resistance Education (DARE), have been criticized for lack of effectiveness. But all these efforts together, plus factors that haven't been studied or named, have indeed made a difference, although not enough of a difference.

When do children and adolescents begin drinking alcohol and using drugs? Most statistics begin with eighth graders, although a limited amount of research has focused on 12-year-olds. Overall, approximately 21% of eighth graders, 38% of tenth graders, and 50% of twelfth graders have used illegal drugs, with an even higher percentage trying alcohol. However, elementary teachers and principals know that experimentation with alcohol, drugs, and tobacco begins even earlier. In fact, younger students report use of inhalants, one of the substances growing in use, at a higher level than high school students (U.S. Department of Health and Human Services, 2005).

Children and adolescents often have an unfounded sense of immortality. Do you remember thinking, "Well, sure. Some people are hurt by this, but it won't happen to me"? The students in your future classrooms will likely often have this attitude. They grossly underestimate the serious consequences of abusing alcohol, drugs, and tobacco. The risk of addiction is high.

What can schools and teachers do? In 1995 the Supreme Court ruled that schools can arrange to randomly test student athletes for drugs. In 2002 another ruling included those who voluntarily participate in activities such as cheerleading, band, debate, and so on. In 2006 the government reported that about 600 of the approximately 15,000 school districts in the United States had implemented random drug testing. Some people believe that just the threat of testing is a deterrent (Sullivan, 2006).

Teachers need to be informed about the warning signs—often sudden, negative changes in behavior and academic performance—of alcohol and drug abuse. They need to be articulate when it comes to describing the consequences of substance abuse of all kinds. They must take the problem seriously. Here are some suggestions for positively influencing students:

1. Develop strong relationships with students and understand their perceptions concerning substance abuse, some of which are listed in Table 10.1.
2. Become a trusted mentor for individual students at risk for using alcohol, drugs, and tobacco.
3. Promote honest discussions about real-world issues including substance abuse.
4. Use active instructional techniques such as role-playing to teach refusal skills.
5. Make information available about community services related to prevention and intervention of substance abuse.

Table 10.1   Harmfulness of drugs as perceived by 8th, 10th, and 12th graders (2005)

How Much Do You Think People Risk Harming Themselves (Physically or in Other Ways), if They	Percentage Saying "Great Risk"		
	8th	10th	12th
Try marijuana once or twice	31.4	22.3	16.1
Smoke marijuana regularly	73.9	65.5	25.8
Try inhalants once or twice	37.5	45.7	
Try inhalants regularly	64.1	71.2	
Try crack once or twice	49.6	57.0	48.4
Try crack occasionally	69.4	76.9	63.8
Try one or two drinks of an alcoholic beverage (beer, wine, liquor)	13.9	11.5	8.5
Take one or two drinks nearly every day	31.4	32.6	23.7
Have five or more drinks once or twice each weekend	57.2	53.3	45.0
Smoke one or more packs of cigarettes per day	61.5	68.1	76.5
Use smokeless tobacco regularly	40.8	46.1	43.6

Source: From *Monitoring the Future: National Results on Adolescent Drug Use,* by L. D. Johnston, P. M. O'Malley, J. G. Bachman, and J. E. Schulenberg, 2005, Bethesda, MD: U.S. Department of Health and Human Services. Retrieved April 15, 2006, from http://monitoring_the_future.org/pubs/monographs/overview2005.pdf

Sexuality-Related Concerns

Fewer never-married 15-to-19-year-olds are having sexual experiences now than did in the 1990s. From 49% of girls and 55% of boys in 1995, the percentage in 2002 was down to 46% for both girls and boys. By racial subgroups within the ninth-through-twelfth-grade population, 42% of Whites, 51% of Hispanics, and 67% of African Americans have had sexual intercourse. Condom use has increased slightly for sexually active adolescents, but there remains significant cause for concern regarding the spread of sexually transmitted diseases (STDs) and of the HIV virus that leads to AIDS (Education Vital Signs, 2006a). In one widespread survey, about 90% of high school students reported that they had been taught about HIV/AIDS in schools (NCES, 2005). Did you receive sexuality-related information in middle or high school? Was it presented in concise, helpful ways? Do you agree with including sexuality-related information in the curriculum? Why or why not?

Your Teaching Fingerprint

Teen birth rate. As illustrated in Figure 10.7, except for the first half of the 1990s, the teen birth rate has continually declined since 1960 when teen births hit an all-time high of 89.5 per 1,000 girls ages 15 to 19. A decrease in sexual intercourse among adolescents has contributed to the decline, but it is also speculated that a more informed student population and greater availability of both contraceptives and abortion options has helped keep the teen birth rate on the decline. Even with the incidences of teen births decreasing, the United States still has the highest teenage birth rate among developed countries. About 1 million teenage girls get pregnant annually, resulting in over 400,000 babies. More than four out of five teen mothers are unmarried, putting them and their babies at greater risk of living in poverty (Infoplease, 2004).

Homosexuality. Chapter 3 addressed homosexuality from the perspective of diversity (see page 78). Sexual orientation is an issue that evokes strong sentiments that spill over onto school grounds. "Tragically, public schools have become front lines in the culture war over homosexuality—and the biggest losers are the kids caught in the crossfire of incendiary rhetoric and bitter lawsuits" (Haynes, 2006, p. 3). In an effort to find a process that will allow educators and students alike to civilly discuss issues of sexual orientation, a document

Figure 10.7 Teen birth rate

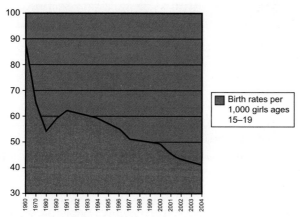

Source: From "Births to Teenagers in the United States, 1940–2000, by S. J. Ventura, T. J. Matthews, and B. E. Hamilton, 2001, *National Vital Statistics Report,* 49(10). Retrieved May 12, 2007, from www.cdc.gov.mill1.sjlibrary.org/nchs/data/nvsr/nvsr49/nvsr49_10.pdf; *New Report Shows Teen Births Drop to Lowest Level Ever,* by the National Center for Health Statistics, 2006. Retrieved May 12, 2007, from www.cdc.gov.nchs/pressroom/06facts/births05.htm; and *Teen Birthrates Continue to Decline,* by Infoplease, 2004. Retrieved April 7, 2006, from http:///www.infoplease.com/ipa/A0193727.html

entitled "Public Schools and Sexual Orientation: A First Amendment Framework for Finding Common Ground" was endorsed in 2006 by organizations including the American Association of School Administrators and the Association for Supervision and Curriculum Development (First Amendment Center, 2006). Will documents such as this end teasing and harassment aimed at adolescents who are, or are perceived to be, homosexual? Perhaps eventually official documents may have some effect, but probably not a lot, nor will the effects come quickly enough to spare many hurt feelings and prevent acts of violence toward individuals.

What can schools and teachers do? Schools should provide health education courses for at least middle and high school students that include open and honest information concerning matters of sexuality, with a forum for asking and answering questions. Teachers should show informed sensitivity to students grappling with sexuality-related issues. As with substance abuse, refusal skills are important, and they are more likely to be demonstrated by students who perceive a sense of control over their lives. The physical and emotional dangers of early sexual activity, STDs and HIV/AIDS, and teen pregnancy can be communicated in nongraphic and noncontroversial ways, often couched in terms of self-respect.

Some schools have established sex education programs and clinics that provide access to birth control information and devices. Such programs are controversial. Many districts support special schools for pregnant students and new mothers. These schools help young women stay in school and graduate.

In the classroom, treating all students with respect is vital. Not allowing students to use derogatory language about sexual orientation will help keep a respectful atmosphere. Among upper elementary and middle school students, saying "That's so gay" is a sign of disapproval. They often use the phrase lightly, while its implications can deeply hurt students who perceive themselves to be homosexual. Simply saying, "We don't use that phrase in this classroom or this school" and then sticking to it is an example of creating a more respectful atmosphere.

Childhood Obesity

Americans rank obesity as a health problem second only to cancer. The number of children who are obese has tripled since 1975 (Haskins, Paxson, & Donahue, 2006). The commonly

Table 10.2   Computing body mass index (BMI)

BMI	Status
Below 18.5	Underweight
18.5–24.9	Normal
25.0–29.9	Overweight
30.0–39.9	Obese
40 and above	Morbidly obese

Note: weight in pounds/(height in inches)^2 × 703 = BMI

Source: From *Understanding Human Development* (p. 248), by G. J. Craig and W. L. Dunn, 2007. Upper Saddle River, NJ: Prentice Hall.

held definition of **obesity** involves the body mass index (BMI), a measure of how much a person weighs relative to height, as illustrated in Table 10.2 (Paxson, Donahue, Orleans, & Grisso, 2006). Use the BMI formula to determine your own weight status. Are you surprised by what you discover about yourself? Do you think it's wise to make children and adolescents face the reality of where they are on the scale? Why or why not? What difference might this knowledge make to them?

Your Teaching Fingerprint

What's considered normal weight for children and adolescents varies with their age. But take a look at a line of children walking down an elementary hallway or adolescents gathered around the school commons and it is evident which students are grossly overweight or on their way to becoming so.

Researchers are studying the causes and consequences of childhood obesity. Figure 10.8 lists seven factors that contribute to what the authors of the study cited call an "epidemic of childhood obesity" (Paxson et al., 2006).

The consequences of childhood obesity include serious health issues such as type 2 diabetes, heart disease, sleep disorders, asthma, joint dysfunction, and mental health problems. What used to be considered adult health problems are now serious health problems for adolescents and even children. As a result of weight issues, today's children may live shorter and less healthy lives than their parents (Paxson et al., 2006).

Serious social and psychological problems are also consequences of childhood and adolescent obesity. Being teased, loneliness, low self-esteem, and other consequences result from being a severely overweight child or teenager (DeAngelis, 2004).

While researchers are not saying that obesity causes lower academic performance, the link between obesity and lower achievement may reveal serious academic consequences. Seriously overweight children are twice as likely to be in special education and remedial classes from an early age. A recent study of approximately 11,000 kindergartners found that overweight children had significantly lower reading and math scores when compared to children in the normal weight range. These academic difficulties continued through first grade (Story, Kaphingst, & French, 2006).

What can schools and teachers do? In 2004 Congress passed the Child Nutrition Reauthorization Act, mandating that all schools participating in the federal school meal program develop comprehensive wellness policies focusing on the following:

Physical activity, healthy food choices, and lessons relating to the dangers of obesity may help curb the alarming trend of childhood obesity.

Figure 10.8 Factors contributing to childhood obesity

1. Increases in television and computer game use that have led to a new generation of "couch potatoes"
2. The explosive proliferation of fast-food restaurants, many of which market their products to children through media campaigns that tout tie-ins to children's movies and TV shows
3. Increases in sugary and fat-laden foods displayed at children's eye level in supermarkets and advertised on TV
4. Schools that offer children junk food and soda while scaling back physical education classes and recess
5. Working parents who are unable to find the time or energy to cook nutritious meals or supervise outdoor playtime
6. The exodus of grocery stores from urban centers, sharply reducing access to affordable fresh fruits and vegetables
7. Suburban sprawl and urban crime, both of which keep children away from outdoor activities

Source: From "Introducing the Issue," by C. Paxson, E. Donahue, T. Orleans, and J. A. Grisso, 2006, *The Future of Children, 16*(1), 3–15.

1. What children and adolescents eat in school
   - provide more nutritious school breakfasts and lunches
   - limit à la carte items to healthier foods
   - reduce or eliminate vending machines or stock only nutritious foods
2. How physically active students are in school
   - provide daily physical education (PE) in elementary and middle school
   - increase high school PE requirements and provide more extracurricular physical activity options
3. Providing in-school health and nutrition education

Teachers can encourage all of the elements of a wellness policy by serving as role models for healthy living. Eating nutritious, balanced meals and snacks in school and showing evidence of an active lifestyle that includes exercise will go a long way toward influencing students. Teachers can help prevent childhood and adolescent obesity by being vocal advocates for students' health.

Suicide

The ultimate health issue and absolute tragedy for young adolescents (10–14) and adolescents (15–19) is suicide. Although teen suicide has decreased by 25% since 1990, it remains the third leading cause of death among teens, trailing only accidents and homicide. In 2003, 244 young adolescents ages 10 to 14, and 1,487 adolescents ages 15 to 19, died as a result of suicide. For every suicide it is estimated that there are 100 to 200 attempts. Girls are much more likely to attempt suicide than boys, but boys complete the act of suicide four times as often as girls (American Association of Suicidology, 2003).

Depression is a mental illness characterized by a deep sense of sadness and a loss of interest or pleasure in activities. Students who are depressed are 14 times more likely to make a first suicide attempt. In fact, over half of all adolescents who suffer from depression will eventually attempt suicide (American Psychiatric Association, 2005a). Depression is one of the factors contributing to suicide attempts, as shown in Figure 10.9. One or more of the factors listed are usually present when an adolescent attempts suicide, but it is possible that none of them are evident. The American Psychiatric Association (2005b) tells us that "Teenagers who are planning to commit suicide might 'clean house' by giving away favorite possessions, . . . they may also become suddenly cheerful because they think that by deciding to end their lives they have found the solution" (p. 2).

What can schools and teachers do? The American Psychiatric Association (2005b) advises that simply taking time to talk with troubled adolescents about their emotions and

Figure 10.9   Strongest factors for attempted suicide in youth

- Depressed mood
- Substance abuse
- Frequent episodes of running away
- Family violence or disruptions
- Periods of incarceration
- Withdrawal from friends and/or family
- Difficulties dealing with sexual orientation
- No longer interested in or enjoying activities that once were pleasurable
- Unplanned pregnancy
- Impulsive, aggressive behavior or frequent expressions of rage
- Feelings of loneliness, hopelessness, and rejection
- Experiences of loss, humiliation, trauma

Source: From *Let's Talk Facts About Teen Suicide,* by the American Psychiatric Association, 2005. Retrieved April 6, 2006, from www.healthyminds.org/multimedia/teensuicide.pdf

problems can prevent what they call the "senseless tragedy of teen suicide" (p. 2). Here are some guidelines for dealing with adolescents at risk for suicide attempts.

- Understand and recognize factors that may indicate suicidal tendencies such as those in Figure 10.9.
- If you suspect suicidal tendencies, always notify others such as a mental health professional or a school counselor who may, in turn, contact family members.
- Be willing to listen, rather than lecture.
- Find ways to involve students in service learning that takes them "outside" themselves.
- Reassure adolescents that depression and suicidal tendencies are treatable.

Your Teaching Fingerprint   Do you have experience with substance abuse, risky sexual behavior, or obesity? Have any of the issues discussed in this section touched you personally? Do you know people who risk their health for short-term gratification?

Now we'll move from health issues to a discussion of how children and adolescents harm each other through acts of aggression.

What Effects Do Bullying, Theft, and Violence Have on Students and Schools in the United States?

Even one student bullied or victimized is unacceptable. Recent data indicate that school-age students are victims of all kinds of minor crimes about as often at school as away from school. However, with serious violent crimes, such as rape and murder, the difference between in-school and away-from-school victimization is dramatic: a student is 70 times more likely to be murdered and 240 times more likely to commit suicide away from school than on school grounds. Although widespread publicity of individual violent acts would lead us to believe otherwise, crime in schools has steadily decreased since the early 1990s (NCES, 2005). To continue this positive trend and protect students to a greater degree, teachers must be knowledgeable about possible threats and prepared to take steps to eliminate all crimes against students.

Let's look next at bullying, often ignored, but both harmful and often the precursor to more serious offenses. We'll then turn to victimization of students through theft and violent acts.

Bullying

In the aftermath of the 1999 Columbine High School tragedy, people across the United States asked, "How could something like this happen?" Psychologists, counselors, principals, teachers, parents, as well as the print and electronic media began to speculate about what might have led Dylan Klebold and Eric Harris to kill their schoolmates and a teacher and then turn the guns on themselves. From conversations with people who knew Dylan and Eric, the conclusion was drawn that they were adolescents who felt alienated from other students and from school. A report from the Safe Schools Initiative (2000), jointly undertaken by the U.S. Department of Education and the Secret Service, states that of the 37 incidents of school violence leading to fatalities that were studied, three quarters involved perpetrators who felt similarly alienated, persecuted, or bullied.

The In the News video *Lessons Learned* provides information about one school's response to the possibility of campus violence. Watch teacher and student reactions to increased security.

Although the extreme violence of Columbine cannot be entirely explained by examining student relationships, interest in interactions among students has grown. Bullying, often considered just "what kids do," has become a topic of concern. **Bullying,** or relationally aggressive behavior, is "a type of emotional violence where individuals use relationships to harm others. Examples include exclusion from a group and rumor spreading" (Ophelia Project, 2006, p. 3). In addition, bullying may involve physical aggression, such as shoving, tripping, and taking personal items. "Bullying is a weapon of people driven by the need for power. Bullying can be a single interaction—verbal, physical, or emotional—but it is always crafted to cause fear and to exert power" (White-Hood, 2006, p. 30). Bullying may be linked to current and future psychological and behavioral difficulties, including depression, dropping out of school, substance abuse, risky sexual behavior, abnormal eating habits, delinquency, and suicide.

According to the 2005 School Crime and Safety report, almost twice as many middle school students as elementary or high school students experience bullying. Interestingly,

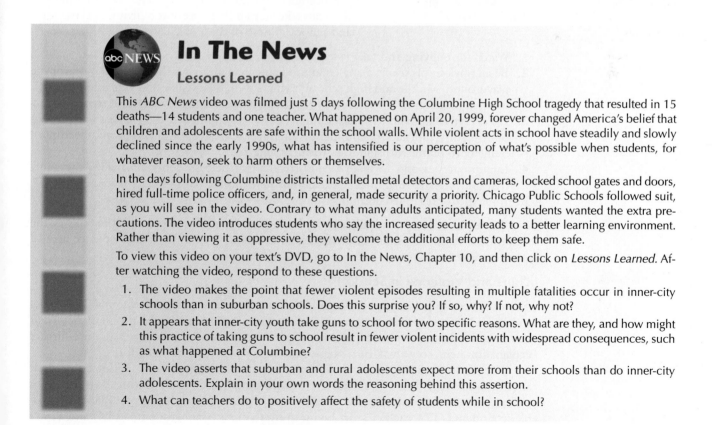

In The News
Lessons Learned

This *ABC News* video was filmed just 5 days following the Columbine High School tragedy that resulted in 15 deaths—14 students and one teacher. What happened on April 20, 1999, forever changed America's belief that children and adolescents are safe within the school walls. While violent acts in school have steadily and slowly declined since the early 1990s, what has intensified is our perception of what's possible when students, for whatever reason, seek to harm others or themselves.

In the days following Columbine districts installed metal detectors and cameras, locked school gates and doors, hired full-time police officers, and, in general, made security a priority. Chicago Public Schools followed suit, as you will see in the video. Contrary to what many adults anticipated, many students wanted the extra precautions. The video introduces students who say the increased security leads to a better learning environment. Rather than viewing it as oppressive, they welcome the additional efforts to keep them safe.

To view this video on your text's DVD, go to In the News, Chapter 10, and then click on *Lessons Learned*. After watching the video, respond to these questions.

1. The video makes the point that fewer violent episodes resulting in multiple fatalities occur in inner-city schools than in suburban schools. Does this surprise you? If so, why? If not, why not?

2. It appears that inner-city youth take guns to school for two specific reasons. What are they, and how might this practice of taking guns to school result in fewer violent incidents with widespread consequences, such as what happened at Columbine?

3. The video asserts that suburban and rural adolescents expect more from their schools than do inner-city adolescents. Explain in your own words the reasoning behind this assertion.

4. What can teachers do to positively affect the safety of students while in school?

rural students are more likely to be bullied than suburban or urban students (U.S. Department of Justice, 2005).

Almost everyone has been teased or called names at some point, and most people have teased others or been guilty of name-calling. When teasing becomes malicious and repetitive, when its intent is to embarrass, hurt, or isolate, it crosses the line into bullying. When rumors are intentionally spread to destroy the reputation of another, gossip becomes bullying. Most teachers can identify students who bully as well as those who seem to be magnets for taunts and subtle forms of emotional aggression. Do you recall being bullied? Did you know students who were relentlessly bullied in school? Did you know students who bullied others? How did you feel toward those who bullied others? How about toward those who were bullied?

Your Teaching Fingerprint

Bullying in middle school is a growing threat to the physical and psychological well-being of young adolescents.

What can schools and teachers do? In 2004 Congress amended the Safe and Drug Free Schools Act to include bullying and harassment. This addition requires all schools that receive federal funding to actively prevent bullying and to respond to all instances of it. School districts are developing policies and mandating antibullying programs. Books such as *Odd Girl Out: The Hidden Culture of Aggression in Girls* (Simmons, 2002) and *Best Friends, Worst Enemies: Understanding the Social Lives of Children* (Thompson & Grace, 2001) shed new light on the ramifications of relational aggression, for both the aggressor and the victim. Books like these and established antibullying programs indicate that many times bullies were themselves bullied at some point or perhaps abused in some way by family members. Most scenarios are complex. Even when teachers don't understand all the circumstances and are not trained to work through the psychological maze of causes for episodes of bullying, they can take steps to help prevent bullying in classrooms and schools. Some of these steps are:

1. Watch for bullying and take it seriously.
2. Be an obvious presence. Early childhood and elementary teachers should monitor the playground. Middle and high school teachers should be visible and vigilant in the hallways, at lunchtime, at bus drop-off areas, at extracurricular events, and so on.
3. Do everything possible to help students develop genuine self-esteem that will prevent bullying driven by lack of confidence. An intact self-esteem will also prompt victims of bullying to better withstand the torment and to seek assistance.
4. Incorporate lessons, formally or informally, that help students internalize the belief that bullying and relational aggression in all forms are harmful and absolutely wrong.
5. Implement prescribed antibullying programs with sincerity and purpose.

Research indicates that bullying may be the last significant step before the bully or the victim turns to more violent and dangerous behavior, such as theft and violence against other students.

Theft and Violence in Schools

The occurrence of theft and violence in schools has decreased since the mid 1990s, yet widespread crimes against students by other students continues to be problematic. Theft accounts for the major portion of crimes reported in schools and doesn't require further explanation here, so we will turn our attention to violence in its many forms.

The most common forms of violence are physical fights, with about equal fault among fighters, and simple assault involving a perpetrator and a victim. Both forms of violence involve boys about twice as often as girls. A larger percentage of Black and Hispanic students (17% each) report being in fights than Asian students (13%) and White students (10%). In 2003, 15% of urban students reported fighting on school grounds, compared with 10% of rural students (NCES, 2005).

According to the U.S. Department of Justice (2005), theft, violence, and serious violent crimes occur more frequently in urban areas than in suburban or rural areas. Serious violent crimes include rape, sexual assault, robbery, and aggravated assault. In 2003, students ages 12–18 reported being victims of serious violence while at school at a rate of 6 per 1,000. Gangs are often associated with violent activities, although the number of students belonging to gangs is small. Urban students report about twice as much gang presence as suburban students, and three times as much as rural students. Hispanic and Black students report greater levels of gang presence than other racial groups (U.S. Department of Justice, 2003).

Have you experienced theft or violence as a student? Have you seen any of these activities take place in school? Did the perpetrators suffer consequences? What was your reaction to these crimes?

What can schools and teachers do? To help ensure the safety of students from early childhood through high school settings, schools have formulated a variety of plans and policies, ranging from programs that foster respect among students to overt ways of increasing security, such as installing surveillance cameras and metal detectors, requiring ID badges, locking school entrances during school hours, and using drug-detection dogs in random sweeps. Some school districts have adopted **zero tolerance** policies, meaning that there are nonnegotiable consequences for certain infractions. For instance, the consequence for fighting may be automatic suspension for 3 days. Possession of a weapon may result in automatic expulsion.

Individual teachers may be able to have the greatest effect on school safety and security by being aware and watchful. Most instances of discipline problems will be similar to those discussed in Chapter 7. Although they may occur, violent episodes are relatively infrequent considering the approximately 27 million students in school each day. When students take weapons to school or there is a student fatality on school grounds, it is reported in the news. Rather than being frightened day in and day out, think through how you would respond to a variety of scenarios, primarily, how you would get help from nearby teachers, administrators, counselors, school security officers, and the like.

Bullying and violence don't have a single source or cause. They originate from complex situations that didn't begin in an instant and won't be fixed quickly or with one solution. A multifaceted approach is needed that emphasizes civility, tolerance, and respect for dignity and life. Teachers must live these values and take every opportunity to pass them on to students, whether in early childhood, elementary, middle, or high school settings.

The next section will explore the problems that truancy can cause, the horrific dropout rate, and the consequences of not completing high school.

How Do Truancy and Dropping Out Affect Youth in the United States?

Dropping out of school has been called "the silent epidemic" by researchers at the Bill and Melinda Gates Foundation—"silent" because it has been covered up and ignored for decades, and "epidemic" because the problem has reached near panic proportions (Bridgeland, Dilulio, & Morison, 2006). One of the most accurate predictors of dropping out is truancy.

Many schools have resource officers whose presence on campus helps prevent acts of violence.

Truancy

Nonattendance of compulsory education, not including excused absences generally granted for health reasons, is called **truancy** (Focus Adolescent Services, 2006), often referred to as cutting class or skipping school. According to a 2005 poll of 467 ethnically and racially diverse students who dropped out of public high school in urban, suburban, and rural areas, 43% said they missed too many days of school and could not catch up. Not

only does truancy indicate who is most at risk of dropping out, but it also correlates strongly with juvenile delinquency, according to the Los Angeles Office of Education. In Van Nuys, California, a 3-week sweep of the city for truant middle and high school students correlated with a 60% drop in shoplifting arrests. School officials concluded that when they're not in school, there's a likelihood that truant-prone students are committing crimes (Focus Adolescent Services, 2006).

On any given day, about 5% of students are absent from U.S. schools. At some schools, however, the rate may be closer to 20% (MacDonald, 2004). Truancy is a problem not only for individual students and their future success, but also for families and communities. Absenteeism for any reason causes students to fall behind. With too many absences, students may feel lost in class, resulting in low self-esteem and a sense of resignation. Families suffer the consequences of truancy as they watch someone they love drift toward academic failure. Communities suffer, not just because of crime, but because of the possible loss of productive, self-sufficient citizens.

Truancy is an indicator that students are at risk of dropping out. The appalling fact is that over one third of students in the United States drop out of middle and high school.

According to a study by the Center for Social Organization of Schools at Johns Hopkins University, when truant students were asked why they skipped school, about half said they just didn't want to go to school; about a fourth said they felt pushed out or bullied; and the remaining fourth reported external problems, many of them family related. The researchers found this information encouraging because they contend that 75% of the truancies, or all except those attributed to external problems, can be altered by school actions that give students reason to be in school as well as safe environments free of bullying (MacDonald, 2004).

Beyond the moral obligation to get truant students back in school, there are increasing monetary reasons for schools to establish antitruancy programs. States have policies that financially reward schools for attendance rates and improvement. No Child Left Behind requires 95% of students to be present on testing days.

What can schools and teachers do? Schools need to maintain accurate attendance records and communicate all absences to families. Although it sounds obvious, many schools do not pay attention to absences and do not call students' homes to ask about students who don't show up. Often parents and guardians don't know there's an attendance problem until it appears insurmountable.

Because student engagement is key to boosting attendance, some schools are establishing after-school programs that motivate students with a wide range of activities. The Los Angeles School District, reeling from the loss of millions of dollars of federal funding because of poor attendance, has a new program called Count Me In, giving tangible incentives, such as tickets to professional sports events, to students who improve attendance (MacDonald, 2004).

Teachers must develop relationships with students that let them know they matter. Engaging, relevant instruction and a "we miss you when you're gone" attitude go a long way toward doing away with the "I just didn't want to go" syndrome expressed by so many truant students. Catching the problem in the truant stage will help prevent the travesty of dropping out.

Dropping Out

For decades states reported grossly inflated high school completion numbers, with most percentages above 80% and many above 90%. Although the desire to portray success is understandable, honestly acknowledging how many students graduate from high school is the first step to fixing the problem of high dropout rates. And there definitely is a problem. In 2005 the Education Trust, the Bill and Melinda Gates Foundation, the Urban Institute, and other education groups independently confirmed that the high school completion rate in the United States hovers around 65%, compared with 77% in 1969 and 70% in 2000. The problem has steadily worsened (Educational Testing Service, 2005).

The U.S. Department of Education defines **high school completion,** or graduation, as the "percentage of students, measured from the beginning of high school, who graduate from a high school with a regular diploma in the standard number of years" (Hall, 2005, p. 4). Prior to 2005 students who left school but indicated that they would seek a GED certificate or who simply never returned to school after numerous absences were not considered dropouts. States are now pressured to track entering ninth graders as they progress toward graduation to portray more accurate numbers. Graduation rates by state, from New Jersey with the highest to South Carolina with the lowest, are listed in Table 10.3.

Table 10.3 Graduation rates by state

State	Graduation Rate, %	State	Graduation Rate, %
New Jersey	86	Ohio	71
Idaho	80	West Virginia	71
North Dakota	80	Arkansas	71
South Dakota	79	Oklahoma	70
Minnesota	79	California	69
Wisconsin	78	Colorado	69
Iowa	78	Arizona	67
Utah	78	Hawaii	66
Vermont	78	District of Columbia	65
Connecticut	77	Louisiana	65
Nebraska	77	Texas	65
Montana	77	Kentucky	65
Pennsylvania	76	North Carolina	64
Illinois	75	Delaware	64
Maryland	75	Alaska	64
Kansas	74	Washington	63
Michigan	74	Alabama	61
New Hampshire	74	New Mexico	61
Virginia	74	New York	61
Oregon	74	Mississippi	58
Rhode Island	74	Tennessee	58
Missouri	73	Georgia	56
Indiana	72	Nevada	55
Maine	72	Florida	53
Wyoming	72	South Carolina	51
Massachusetts	71		

Source: From *Getting Honest about Grad Rates: How States Play the Numbers and Students Lose,* by D. Hall, 2005, The Education Trust. Retrieved January 2, 2007, from http://www2.edtrust.org/NR/rdonlyres/C5A6974D-6C04-4FB1-A9FC-05938CB0744D/0/Getting_Honest.pdf

Fewer than one third of students in U.S. schools are African American, Hispanic, or Native American, yet more than half of high school dropouts belong to one of these groups (Swanson, 2004). Figure 10.10 illustrates graduation rates by race. In addition, students from low socioeconomic settings are about 6 times more likely to drop out than students from high socioeconomic settings (Kaufman, Alt, & Chapman, 2001).

Why do students drop out of school? The reasons are complex and often overlapping. Figure 10.11 lists the top eight reasons given by dropouts in a survey conducted by Bridgeland, Dilulio, and Morison in 2005. You can mix and match the reasons to form plausible scenarios. For instance, boredom in a particular class may lead a group of students to identify with one another and to ditch school occasionally; skipped classes may then lead to academic problems, more absences, and finally dropping out. Dropping out often results from a slow process of disengagement, with costly ramifications that may last a lifetime. Some of the negative consequences include the following:

- Nearly half of dropouts ages 16–24 are unemployed (Thornburgh, 2006).
- High school dropouts earn $9200 less per year than high school graduates (Paulson, 2006).
- Dropouts constitute a disproportionate percentage of all prisoners and of prisoners on death row; 67% of the latter did not complete high school (Thornburgh, 2006).

Dropping out of high school today is to a student's social health what smoking is to his or her physical health—an indicator of a host of poor outcomes to follow, from low

Figure 10.10   Graduation rate by race

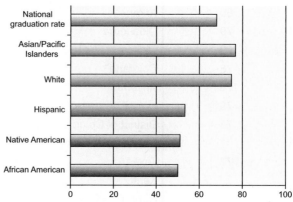

Source: From *The Real Truth About Low Graduation Rates,* by C. B. Swanson, 2004, Washington, DC: Urban Institute. Retrieved April 26, 2006, from http:///www.urban.org/UploadedPDF/411050_realtruth.pdf

Figure 10.11   Top reasons dropouts identify as major factors for leaving school

High school dropouts say they

- were not motivated or inspired to work hard (69%)
- found classes to be uninteresting (47%)
- were failing in school (35%)
- started high school poorly prepared (35%)
- would have been required to repeat a grade to graduate (32%)
- had to get a job and make money (32%)
- became a parent (26%)
- had to care for a family member (22%)

Source: From *The Silent Epidemic: Perspectives of High School Dropouts* by J. M. Bridgeland, J. J. Dilulio, and K. B. Morison, 2006. Retrieved April 8, 2006, from http://www.civicenterprises.net/pdfs/thesilentepidemic3-06.pdf

lifetime earnings to high incarceration rates to a high likelihood that the dropout's children will also drop out of high school and start the cycle anew (Thornburgh, 2006).

What can schools and teachers do? There are no simple solutions to the problem of students dropping out of school. But much of the dilemma is solvable with purposeful effort that focuses on the whole child. Addressing an isolated problem area will likely not be enough, but addressing several areas of concern may produce the desired result of keeping students in school.

In most instances, the students who drop out are capable of succeeding academically: 90% are passing when they drop out, and 70% are confident they could complete the program of study (Education Vital Statistics [EVS], 2006b). Educators don't need to dumb down the curriculum. Efforts to retain students should center on some or all of the following suggestions:

1. Know the warning signs. For instance, sixth graders who don't attend school regularly, receive poor marks for behavior, or fail math or English for any reason have only a 10% chance of graduating (EVS, 2006b). So this group of sixth graders can be targeted for intervention.
2. Establish ninth grade academies. Many schools have found success in separating ninth graders and providing them with extra counseling and support.
3. Consistently provide engaging curricula and instruction.
4. Maintain a safe environment and a welcoming climate.
5. Ensure an adult advocate for every student at every grade level. This person may be a classroom teacher, counselor, mentor, or administrator who has a specific responsibility to stay connected to the student.
6. Improve home and school communication.
7. Provide flexible, and alternative where needed, school configurations.

Concluding Thoughts

There's a saying, "We cannot control the wind, but we can adjust our sails." The social issues that negatively affect students are complex and multidimensional. They don't begin with us, and most won't be completely resolved through us. However, with that reality in view, we can begin to focus on positive steps to prevent or halt risky behaviors and their impact on children and adolescents. Controlling the wind may not be within our reach as teachers, but adjusting our own and our students' sails is indeed possible.

What Role Will Diversity Play in My Teaching Identity?

Diversity in the classroom has multiple sources: the privilege gap, disparities in opportunities for students of different races and cultures, students who are victims or perpetrators, differences in sexual orientation, students who are likely to abuse substances, and those who have better-honed refusal skills. All students may be at risk of being alienated in some way and at risk of dropping out. As a teacher, you will be inserted into the volatile mix of students as a role model and representation of hope for the children and adolescents in your classroom. As part of your teaching identity you may encounter very few of the negative societal influences described in this chapter. Many of you, however, will deal daily with these kinds of dilemmas. We all need to see students through eyes that see assets and possibilities. We need to see individual realities and do what we can to provide a safe haven where encouragement prompts growth. Challenging? Of course. Rewarding? Sometimes. Is it work you can love? Yes.

■ Chapter in Review

How do family, community, and society impact students in the United States?

- Families, communities, and society in general can support student success or thwart it.
- Children and adolescents who are victims of child abuse or neglect are at risk physically, emotionally, socially, and academically.
- Communities can provide vital services for students and their families.

How do socioeconomic status and race affect students in the United States?

- The privilege gap between the haves and have-nots is a societal dilemma with far-reaching ramifications for children and adolescents.
- Racism is a form of prejudice stemming from the belief that one race is superior to another.
- Racism may take the form of inaction through silence or of low expectations for certain students.
- Immigrants and their children require special attention to ensure success in school.

How do health issues affect students in the United States?

- The rates of most forms of substance abuse have recently decreased, yet even one child or adolescent harmed by it is too many.
- Children and adolescents often have an unfounded sense of immortality, which makes them feel they will not be harmed if they use substances such as inhalants, alcohol, legal and illegal drugs, and tobacco.
- Risky sexuality-related behavior can result in emotional distress, sexually transmitted diseases, and unplanned pregnancy.
- Teasing and harassment about homosexuality can be the root of distress for students in and out of school.
- Childhood obesity is near epidemic proportions and has long-term negative effects on students.
- Suicide is the third leading cause of adolescent deaths, with contributing factors that may be recognizable, leading to intervention.

What effects do bullying, theft, and violence have on schools and students in the United States?

- Bullying can be verbal, physical, or emotional and is intended to exert power and cause harm.
- Violent acts in school include simple assault (usually fighting), sexual assault, and aggravated assault (definite perpetrator and victim) and occur most frequently in urban areas and among high school students.

How do truancy and dropping out affect youth in the United States?

- Truancy is a reliable predictor of dropping out.
- The dropout rate in the United States is over 30%, with long-term negative effects for students, families, communities, and the country.
- Reasons for dropping out are many and complex, with financial, self-esteem, and crime-related consequences.

Professional Practice

■ Licensure Test Prep

Answer multiple choice questions 1–3 and constructed-response items 4 and 5.

1. All of the following are appropriate responses by teachers to suspected child abuse except
   a. report suspicions to the principal.
   b. be understanding if academics are affected.
   c. immediately contact the parents in an effort to stop the abuse rapidly.
   d. determine to better understand how to recognize abuse.

2. Which health issue for American public school students is steadily worsening in the 21st century?
   a. tobacco use
   b. obesity
   c. alcohol consumption
   d. teen pregnancy

3. Which statement relating to children and low-income settings is not true?
   a. About 25% of school-age children live in poverty.
   b. Children in low-income settings may have been exposed to 30 million fewer words by age 4 than children in high-income settings.
   c. Childern from low-income settings are likely to be physically aggressive.
   d. Children in middle-class homes may have been read to about 1,000 hours before beginning school compared to 25 hours for children in low-income homes.

Following are two segments from *Multicultural Education in a Pluralistic Society* by Gollnick and Chin (2006). Respond to the question related to each segment.

> Because students in settings with limited diversity do not have the opportunities to interact with persons from other cultural backgrounds, they should learn to value diversity, rather than fear it. They should come to know that others have different perspectives on the world and events that are based in different experiences. (p. 360)

4. Explain two ways a teacher might bring the world into the classroom for a population of middle-income White students and expand their views about diversity.

> The current traditional curriculum is based on the histories, experiences, and perspectives of the dominant group. The result is the marginalization of the experiences of other groups . . . . Diversity existed in the United States when Europeans arrived and became greater with each passing century. To teach as if only one group is worthy of inclusion in the curriculum is not to tell the truth. It suggests that only one group is important and that if you belong to another group, you are inferior to the one that is being taught. How would you feel if you never saw yourself, your family, or your community in the curriculum? (p. 361)

5. It is important to be aware of what Gollnick and Chin are talking about as you decide what and how to teach. In a classroom of mostly minority students from low-socioeconomic-status homes, how would you make sure students are not marginalized as described in this quotation? Explain your answer.

■ Standards Speak

This chapter explored societal issues that adversely affect American students. Let's look at how various professional standards address teacher responsibilities regarding these issues.

NBPTS Standard

[Accomplished teachers] strive to acquire a deep understanding of their students and the communities from which they come that shape students' outlooks, values and orientations toward schooling.

NCATE

Teacher candidates consider school, family, and community contexts in connecting concepts to students' prior experience and applying the ideas to real-world problems.

INTASC Knowledge, Principle 10

The teacher understands how factors in the students' environment outside of school (e.g., family circumstances, community environments, health and economic conditions) may influence students' life and learning.

Respond to the following questions in your class notebook and/or discuss your responses with your classmates as directed by your instructor.

1. How should knowledge of family and community impact teacher expectations of students?

2. How can teachers use real-world concepts to make the curriculum and the skill of problem solving relevant to students?

■ MyEducationLab

The following interactive features may be found in Chapter 10 of MyEducationLab.

Homework and Exercises

Writing My Own Story
To write your own story by responding to some of the questions in the text accompanied by fingerprint icons, plus others, go to the "Writing My Own Story" section of the Homework and Exercises for Chapter 10 of MyEducationLab.

What's My Disposition?
To reflect on your beliefs and attitudes concerning the teaching profession, go to Chapter 10's "What's My Disposition?" feature of the Homework and Exercises section of MyEducationLab.

Exploring Schools and Classrooms
If your course involves experiences in schools, the questions and prompts in the "Exploring Schools and Classrooms" feature of Chapter 10's Homework and Exercises section of MyEducationLab will guide you as you explore local schools and classrooms.

Virtual Field Experience

To respond to questions and prompts regarding the Choosing Your Teaching Path videos that connect to specific chapter content, go to Chapter 10's Virtual Field Experience section of MyEducationLab. The questions will help you make sense of what you have read in the chapter.

Chapter 11

Ethical and Legal Issues in U.S. Schools

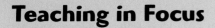

Teaching in Focus

Derek Boucher teaches Modern World History and U.S. History at Roosevelt High School in Fresno, California. He is also the reading intervention teacher for sophomores and juniors, many of whom are English language learners. It is in this capacity that Derek feels a keen sense of responsibility toward building his students' literacy skills. He tirelessly searches for ways to engage his students in reading.

Derek believes that to transform students into readers, it is important to make reading both satisfying and focused on meaning. The nature of the content is what pulls students into the process. Consequently, Derek continually builds his classroom library. He selects books and magazines that will capture student imagination. In the Choosing Your Teaching Path section of MyEducationLab at www.myeducationlab.com, Derek talks about his classroom library and some of the selections he has made. He engages students in literature by selecting topics and sources that capture student interest, yet contain embedded skills instruction. In his lesson Derek uses a newspaper article that gives examples of sexual stereotyping to draw students in. To revisit Derek's classroom, go to the Choosing Your Teaching Path section of MyEducationLab, click on Roosevelt High School, and then on Derek.

Derek's passion for teaching compels him to grow professionally. He tells us, "Professional literature has changed my life as a teacher. That's why I'm an avid reader of books and journals that push me to think more deeply and conceptually about teaching and pedagogy." Derek regularly expresses his views on curricula and reading instruction by writing letters to the editor and opinion pieces for newspapers and magazines. He extends his influence in this way because he sees it as the right thing to do.

This chapter will explore the ethical values that lead to the level of commitment Derek demonstrates. It will examine how teacher and student rights and responsibilities are granted and enforced by law, as well as the nature of the relationship between ethics and laws. The questions we'll consider include:

- What does it mean to be an ethical teacher?
- How do laws affect schools, teachers, and students?
- What are the legal rights of teachers?
- What are the legal responsibilities of teachers?
- What are the legal rights of students?
- How does the law impact the relationship between school and religion?

■ Introduction

The United States has laws for a reason—they make it possible for people to live together as a nation. They prompt civility in neighborhoods, towns, cities, states, and across the country. Consider the chaos and disorder that would happen if there were no traffic laws or laws against robbery, for example.

The U.S. Constitution sets the standard for how the United States functions as a republic. Based on constitutional principles, a hierarchy of federal, state, and local laws has been developed. Public schools are subject to these laws, some of which affect schools' day-to-day operations more directly than others. This chapter will explore how public schools function within the context of these laws and the legal system. It will discuss teachers' legal rights and responsibilities, students' legal rights, and how laws impact the relationship of schools and religion.

It is important to read about actual people and events that have helped shape the fabric of laws that affect education. In doing so you'll gain perspective and more fully understand how laws affect the daily work of teachers. The cases in this chapter are not fictional. They are true. Read carefully and think about the implications for your future career in an early childhood, elementary, middle, or high school classroom.

Before discussing laws, we'll consider what it means to be an ethical teacher. Although not concrete or legislated, a person's or group's ethics guide teacher relationships and decision making. By virtue of being the adult in a classroom of students, a teacher has power. And with that power comes responsibility. Laws don't cover many of the most important aspects of teaching. A teacher's personal belief system about right and wrong and what constitutes obligation, along with ethical codes provided by professional organizations, guide teaching practices in areas where no laws have been established.

■ What Does It Mean to Be an Ethical Teacher?

Laws tell us what we can and can't do. Ethics tell us what we should and shouldn't do. Ethics are standards of conduct based on moral judgments. Because ethics are grounded in personal belief systems, what is ethical in one person's view might not be ethical from another's perspective. Although most of the time what is lawful is also ethical, and what is ethical is also lawful, this is not always the case. For instance, abortion is legal in the United States, but it is considered unethical by many U.S. citizens. For some people with strong antiabortion beliefs, acting on personal ethics may mean becoming involved in unlawful forms of protest against a legal activity.

Let's bring these concepts into the reality of the classroom by examining what it means to be an ethical teacher. Although the following section on ethics is short, it carries a lot of meaning for the attitudes and actions of teachers.

Ethics for Teachers

An ethical teacher is guided by a set of beliefs that lead to attitudes and actions focused on what's best for students. Being ethical means taking the high road and behaving professionally in the midst of big issues as well as in everyday decision making in the classroom.

Howe (1996) tells us there are six characteristics that form a conceptual basis for making ethical decisions. The first characteristic, appreciation for moral deliberation, means understanding that situations are complex and care must be taken to ensure that the rights of all involved are protected. The second characteristic, empathy, refers to the ability to mentally put oneself in the place of others in order to appreciate a variety of perspectives. Knowledge, the third characteristic, is necessary to have a clear view of the dilemma at hand. Dealing with knowledge requires reasoning, the fourth characteristic, and courage, the fifth characteristic, is needed to act on that reasoning. Finally, the sixth characteristic, interpersonal skills, allows teachers to effectively communicate with others about their ethical deliberations. These six characteristics are described in Figure 11.1.

In addition to cultivating Howe's desirable characteristics, teachers can turn to ethical guidelines provided by professional organizations for help.

Figure 11.1 Six desirable characteristics for teachers as they make ethical judgments

1. Appreciation for moral deliberation: ability to see complex moral dimensions of a problem and realization that care is needed to protect the rights of all parties
2. Empathy: ability to "get inside the skin of another"
3. Knowledge: facts to enable us to put issues in context
4. Reasoning: reflecting systematically on an issue and moving step-by-step to a conclusion
5. Courage: the willpower to act in what we perceive to be the right way, rather than just the comfortable way
6. Interpersonal skills: communicating about issues sensitively and tactfully

Source: From "A Conceptual Basis for Ethics in Teacher Education," by Kenneth R. Howe, May/June 1996, *Journal of Teacher Education, 37*, p. 6.

Professional Ethics

Most professions have codes of ethics. The largest teacher organization, the National Education Association (NEA), has a code of ethics (see Figure 11.2). The NEA Code of Ethics is divided into two sections, teacher commitment to students and teacher commitment to the profession. Take a few minutes to read the code. Notice that the majority of points begin with the words *shall not*.

It is important for teachers to understand what they "shall not" do, as these kinds of guidelines can be helpful in keeping out of ethical trouble. However, there are many "shalls" involved in practicing ethical teaching also. If these positive elements are internalized, practicing ethical teaching becomes habitual. Ethical teachers *shall*

- put students' best interests ahead of other considerations
- involve families often and positively
- support colleagues and work collaboratively
- create and maintain a productive learning environment
- diversify instruction to address student differences

The law does not dictate any of these actions; ethical attitudes and beliefs call for them. Similarly, Derek's attitudes and actions—both in and outside the classroom—with regard to the teaching profession, described earlier in the chapter, stem from his ethics.

In this chapter's Teachers' Days, Delights, and Dilemmas, you will read one teacher's account of the days following Hurricane Katrina, a major storm that devastated much of the Gulf Coast in 2005. Again, there is no law governing how educators respond to such tragedies, but the ethics of caring for others in time of dire need directs both attitudes and actions.

Now that you have considered what it means to be an ethical teacher and some of the ways ethics can guide teachers, it's time to look at more concrete guidelines that determine actions in many circumstances. Next, we'll examine laws and how they affect schools, teachers, and students.

How Do Laws Affect Schools, Teachers, and Students?

The U.S. government, its legal system, and the laws that affect schools, teachers, and students are based on a balance of rights and responsibilities. The government and legal system achieve a viable balance of power through the interaction of the three branches of government: executive, legislative, and judicial. Since the founding of the United States of America, four basic sources of law have directly impacted the everyday work of all teachers: the U.S. Constitution, federal laws, state and local laws and policies, and case law. This section will examine each separately.

Figure 11.2 National Education Association Code of Ethics

Preamble

The educator, believing in the worth and dignity of each human being, recognizes the supreme importance of the pursuit of truth, devotion to excellence, and the nurture of the democratic principles. Essential to these goals is the protection of freedom to learn and to teach and the guarantee of equal educational opportunity for all. The educator accepts the responsibility to adhere to the highest ethical standards.

The educator recognizes the magnitude of the responsibility inherent in the teaching process. The desire for the respect and confidence of one's colleagues, of students, of parents, and of the members of the community provides the incentive to attain and maintain the highest possible degree of ethical conduct. The Code of Ethics of the Education Profession indicates the aspiration of all educators and provides standards by which to judge conduct.

The remedies specified by the NEA and/or its affiliates for the violation of any provision of this Code shall be exclusive and no such provision shall be enforceable in any form other than the one specifically designated by the NEA or its affiliates.

PRINCIPLE I

Commitment to the Student

The educator strives to help each student realize his or her potential as a worthy and effective member of society. The educator therefore works to stimulate the spirit of inquiry, the acquisition of knowledge and understanding, and the thoughtful formulation of worthy goals.

In fulfillment of the obligation to the student, the educator—

1. Shall not unreasonably restrain the student from independent action in the pursuit of learning.
2. Shall not unreasonably deny the student's access to varying points of view.
3. Shall not deliberately suppress or distort subject matter relevant to the student's progress.
4. Shall make reasonable effort to protect the student from conditions harmful to learning or to health and safety.
5. Shall not intentionally expose the student to embarrassment or disparagement.
6. Shall not on the basis of race, color, creed, sex, national origin, marital status, political or religious beliefs, family, social or cultural background, or sexual orientation, unfairly—
    a. Exclude any student from participation in any program
    b. Deny benefits to any student
    c. Grant any advantage to any student
7. Shall not use professional relationships with students for private advantage.
8. Shall not disclose information about students obtained in the course of professional service unless disclosure serves a compelling professional purpose or is required by law.

PRINCIPLE II

Commitment to the Profession

The education profession is vested by the public with a trust and responsibility requiring the highest ideals of professional service.

In the belief that the quality of the services of the education profession directly influences the nation and its citizens, the educator shall exert every effort to raise professional standards, to promote a climate that encourages the exercise of professional judgment, to achieve conditions that attract persons worthy of the trust to careers in education, and to assist in preventing the practice of the profession by unqualified persons.

In fulfillment of the obligation to the profession, the educator—

1. Shall not in an application for a professional position deliberately make a false statement or fail to disclose a material fact related to competency and qualifications.
2. Shall not misrepresent his/her professional qualifications.
3. Shall not assist any entry into the profession of a person known to be unqualified in respect to character, education, or other relevant attribute.
4. Shall not knowingly make a false statement concerning the qualifications of a candidate for a professional position.
5. Shall not assist a noneducator in the unauthorized practice of teaching.
6. Shall not disclose information about colleagues obtained in the course of professional service unless disclosure serves a compelling professional purpose or is required by law.
7. Shall not knowingly make false or malicious statements about a colleague.
8. Shall not accept any gratuity, gift, or favor that might impair or appear to influence professional decisions or action.

Source: Retrieved May 22, 2006, from http://www.nea.org/aboutnea/code.html?mode=print

Teachers' Days, Delights, and Dilemmas

Tessie Adams
Domangue
2005 Louisiana
Teacher of the
Year

In 2005 a natural disaster forever changed Louisiana. Hurricane Katrina brought unprecedented damage and chaos not only to our state, but to the entire system of public education. Following the initial shock of human and property loss, the thoughts and efforts of families and educators turned to the children most affected— those who lost their homes or schools, or both. They needed shelter for their physical needs, and a sense of normalcy for their mental well-being.

Hundreds of thousands of students needed to go to school. Districts across the state and the nation opened their doors. Children were given free lunch status. Communities accepted families and donated food, clothing, and basic living supplies. They opened their homes and their hearts. Foundations were quickly established to receive donations and get what people needed to at least temporarily function. I made pleas on local television for donation of uniforms so that children placed in schools would more readily blend in. I established a foundation called REAL—Reviving Education and Learning—to assist teachers in replenishing their classrooms with supplies. School districts and teachers worked together to help ensure as many students as possible got back into school where they could feel safe and have a sense that eventually all would be well.

Some families have left our state permanently and many more have left the coastal area most devastated by Hurricane Katrina. The Louisiana Department of Education is working tirelessly to get schools up and running. This is extremely difficult for many reasons, one of which is the lack of ability to predict the number of families that will actually return to hard-hit areas and the number that will never return. It will take years for a complete cleanup and stabilization.

My elementary school was not badly damaged by the hurricane. Our classrooms were affected, however, by the influx of students displaced by Katrina. In the beginning we experienced an acute shortage of supplies. However, the generosity of the people of America came through, and students received books, paper, pencils, and so on, so that teaching and learning could more easily resume.

Much of the shock has worn off as families have accepted their circumstances. The anger and sorrow, in many cases, have been replaced by hope and resilience. Nowhere in our teaching contracts will you find a job description that includes "You will open your classroom and your heart to an influx of children who desperately need a school home filled with compassion and a sense of normalcy." And yet that's exactly what happened all across Louisiana—not because teachers were following some dictate, but because it was and is the right thing to do.

U.S. Constitution

The Constitution does not specifically mention education. However, certain amendments directly impact teachers and schools.

First Amendment. The First Amendment to the Constitution, shown in Figure 11.3, guarantees, among other things, freedom of speech and religion and prohibits government (i.e., public school) advancement of religion. The relationship between law and religion will be discussed later in this chapter.

Freedom of speech, as guaranteed in the First Amendment, applies to schools. As you read this chapter you'll recognize how often the First Amendment is cited as a guide in decision making on educational issues. The Association for Supervision and Curriculum Development (ASCD) established The First Amendment Center to help educators better understand how to apply the tenets of this amendment in schools. The website,

Figure 11.3 First Amendment

Congress shall make no law respecting an establishment of religion, or prohibiting the free exercise thereof; or abridging the freedom of speech, or the press; or the right of the people peaceably to assemble, and to petition the government for a redress of grievances.

www.firstamendmentschools.org, is designed to provide resources to assist schools in implementing the guiding principles of the First Amendment.

Abiding by the First Amendment has never been more challenging. American society is becoming more diverse and complex every day. Perhaps the most effective way to protect the liberties Americans enjoy is to ensure that students in the United States understand that both freedom and restraint are needed if First Amendment guarantees are to apply equally to all. Educators should purposefully uphold the principles of freedom and democracy in order to "protect religious-liberty rights, encourage freedom of expression, promote academic freedom, ensure a free student press, and support broad-based involvement in school governance. Acting responsibly, students, teachers, administrators, staff, parents, and community members can do much to uphold the rights of every citizen" (Haynes, Chaltain, Ferguson, Hudson, & Thomas, 2003, p. 20).

Fourth Amendment. The Fourth Amendment protects citizens from unreasonable search and seizure and, in doing so, protects the basic privacy and security of all people in the United States. This amendment has a lot to do with students' rights to privacy. For instance, do students have the right to keep whatever they want in a locker assigned to them? Under what circumstances can adults in the school examine the locker contents? This topic is discussed later in the chapter.

Fourteenth Amendment. The Fourteenth Amendment protects the rights of due process and guarantees equal protection to all citizens. For teachers, this amendment pertains to job security and the right to be heard if charges are made against them. Later, the chapter will examine how this amendment affects both teachers and students.

The general guidelines of the U.S. Constitution, specifically the First, Fourth, and Fourteenth Amendments, provide the framework for the federal laws that affect schools, teachers, and students.

Federal Laws

The federal statutes written and passed by Congress (the legislative branch of the U.S. government) have a major impact on the daily work of teachers and the operation of schools. For example:

- The Civil Rights Act of 1964 officially ended more than 50 years of overt racial segregation in public schools by declaring: "No person in the United States shall on the grounds of race, color, or national origin, be excluded from participation in or be denied the benefits of, or be subjected to discrimination under any program or activity receiving federal financial assistance." Unfortunately, however, segregation still exists in public schools in many areas.
- Federal Title IX legislation (1972) opened many doors, specifically to girls, by prohibiting discrimination based on gender.
- The Individuals with Disabilities Education Act (1975, 1990, 2004) guarantees the rights of students with disabilities to a free education in the least restrictive environment. To refresh your memory on IDEA and other laws affecting students with disabilities, reread pages 94–95 in Chapter 3.

Another federal law you've read about many times throughout this text is the No Child Left Behind Act of 2001. The impact of this federal law has changed the way schools do business and will no doubt continue to do so for years to come. For instance, states must now establish specific curricular standards, as discussed in Chapter 4 (see pages 114–115). Also, students must be tested annually to determine if the state's standards are being met by an increasing percentage of students, as you learned in Chapter 5 (see pages 155–156). The consequences for not consistently improving may range from a loss of funding to the closing of schools.

NCLB legislation represents significant federal involvement in state and local schools. Any legislation that wields this kind of power will most certainly be controversial. To look

In The News
No Child Left Behind

Sweeping legislation always has ardent supporters, and just as ardent detractors. No Child Left Behind was controversial at its inception and remains so today. In this ABC News video, journalist Dan Harris discusses a bipartisan report issued in 2005 that said the NCLB law is flawed in fundamental ways. The focus of the report is a boy in Texas who did not go to school on the days the state standardized tests were administered that would have categorized him as proficient or not. The child was acting on his father's belief that "They go to school to prepare for the test, not for life."

To view this ABC News video, go to this text's DVD. Click on In the News, Chapter 11, and then *No Child Left Behind*.

This chapter explores school governance, and Chapter 5 looked at assessment in its many forms. No Child Left Behind has been discussed on numerous occasions. Think about this video, as well as what you have read and discussed in your class, when you respond to the following questions.

1. According to the video, some states are contemplating challenging their obligation to comply with NCLB. This would likely mean a loss of federal funding tied to the legislation. Given what you know about how schools are financed, and assuming the federal government would continue Title I funding, what financial impact might opting out of NCLB have on schools?
2. What does the state senator from New York mean when he says that NCLB is a one-size-fits-all law?
3. From what you know about No Child Left Behind, do you think it has the potential to make a real and lasting difference in American public schools? If yes, why? If no, why?

more closely at what some believe to be the flaws of NCLB, watch and then reflect on this chapter's In the News video.

State and Local Laws and Policies

The U.S. Constitution stipulates that anything not specifically addressed by it becomes a state issue. Consequently, state and local laws and policies affecting education vary from state to state, and from district to district within each state. Some of the issues addressed by state and local laws and policies include curriculum standards (Chapter 4) and assessment mandates (Chapter 5) as well as funding and governance, which will be explored in Chapter 12. The guidelines for teacher certification are left up to states, with some federal stipulations, as discussed in Chapter 1 (see page 12).

Next let's examine how decisions concerning specific circumstances and dilemmas influence what happens in schools.

Case Law

Many legal decisions concerning education are based on precedence—what has been done in the past and what the judicial system has decided with regards to specific rights and responsibilities. The cases brought before the courts are deliberated and settled based on what the U.S. Constitution says, what federal law dictates, and what state and local governing bodies have established. All of these aspects are considered, hopefully with heaping doses of common sense, as decisions are made by the courts.

Case law is based on the doctrine of *stare decisis,* a Latin phrase meaning "let the decision stand." This means that once a decision is made in a court of law, that decision sets a precedent for future cases of a similar nature until challenged or overturned. There is a large body of federal case law on which state and local cases rely for precedence. A decision made by the U.S. Supreme Court establishes case law until either the Supreme Court changes the ruling or an amendment to the Constitution alters the decision. Unfortunately, many school and local government officials have not abided by this principle. Since the Supreme Court doesn't have an enforcement arm, continued court action is sometimes necessary to bring school districts into compliance. For instance, the famous *Brown* v. *Board of Education* (1954) court decision ruled that separate schools are not equal and opened

Figure 11.4   Relationship of laws and ethics

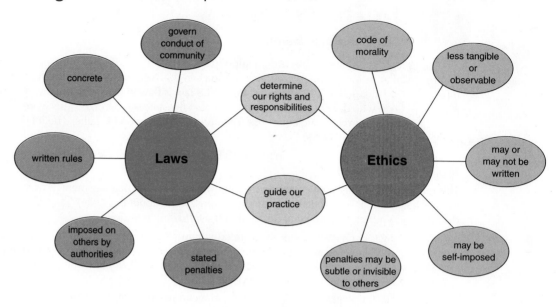

many schoolhouse doors for African Americans. Occasionally during the last 50 years, however, decisions have been made that do not comply with the *Brown* results, and more court action has been needed (LaMorte, 2005).

Now that you have read about laws derived from the Constitution, federal legislation and courts, state and local entities, and the role of case law, you are ready to look at the rights and responsibilities of teachers and students. First, however, take a few minutes to examine Figure 11.4. Consider the relationship between laws and ethics. Laws and ethics both determine rights and responsibilities that guide teachers' practice. Laws are concrete, whereas ethics may vary by person and circumstance. Laws are written with stated penalties for breaking them. The penalties or consequences of violating ethics may be subtle or invisible to others. Figure 11.4 shows how laws and ethics differ in a number of ways, yet still share some qualities.

Throughout this chapter discussions of the legal rights and responsibilities of teachers, the rights of students, and the relationship between schools and religion will cite sample case law. Read these cases carefully. As you do, consider whether teaching, given the variety of legal and ethical guidelines inherent in the profession, is the career for you. Also, ask yourself, "How will these laws and ethical dilemmas have an impact on the grade level I may want to teach? In what settings might this law be most likely to affect what I do?" Remember that when you see a fingerprint in the margin it means that you will be asked to respond to questions and prompts based on your experiences and opinions. These questions are included in "Writing My Own Story" in Chapter 11 of the Homework and Exercises section of MyEducationLab at www.myeducationlab.com.

Your Teaching
Fingerprint

What Are the Legal Rights of Teachers?

Teachers in the United States are entitled to the same rights as other Americans, but some rights are occasionally tempered by the opinions of either the community or the court when there is concern that teachers' individual rights may impact classroom effectiveness. In addition, there are legal rights that apply specifically to the teaching profession. Most teachers will never find themselves in positions where their legal rights are threatened in any way. The day-to-day realities of teaching rarely involve legal challenges.

This section will examine rights associated with teacher employment, freedom of expression, and academic freedom, as well as the rights of teachers in their personal lives.

Employment Legalities

Being employed by a school district entails understanding your rights and responsibilities. You will sign a contract, possibly have tenure in your future, and have procedures for filing grievances if things go wrong or if dismissal is threatened. Let's look at contracts, tenure, and procedures for if things go wrong.

Teaching contracts. In Chapter 1 (see pages 12–14) you learned that there are both traditional and alternative pathways to teacher licensure and certification and that states issue a teaching license or certificate when they determine that a candidate is qualified. A license or certificate is a prerequisite to signing a contract for a teaching position in public schools.

A **contract** is an agreement between parties that states the rights and responsibilities of each. When teachers begin jobs in schools they sign initial contracts. When teachers continue in the same job from year to year, they sign contracts annually. Teachers sign contracts with boards of education, the governing bodies of school districts. Chapter 12 will examine school governance. Teaching contracts typically include a formal offer of employment, the salary, and a description of the position. Signing a teaching contract means that you will abide by district policies. It is very important to carefully read and understand the policies and the contract. Both are extensive and may be written in complex language. Don't hesitate to ask for an explanation.

Contracts are binding on both parties. If you sign a contract and then back out or take a different job, or if the district backs out, you or the district can be sued for damages involving **breach of contract.**

Tenure. Continuing contract status is known as **tenure.** A teacher with tenure is entitled to a contract each year unless the district has reason not to renew it or the teacher decides to go elsewhere. In most states tenure doesn't guarantee a particular position in a particular school, but it does guarantee employment in the district.

Some object to the concept of tenure because it requires more steps to fire, or dismiss, a teacher who has it. However, even teachers with tenure cannot keep their jobs if it is shown that they are incompetent, display immoral behaviors, are insubordinate, or are involved in any of a wide array of behaviors considered unprofessional conduct. These are broad terms that are open to interpretation by districts and courts.

Dismissal. Teachers have been dismissed for many reasons, some of which sound outrageous to us today. Historically, teachers have been dismissed for not attending a particular church, for wearing pants in public (a female teacher), for marrying or becoming pregnant during the school year, and even for moving to a neighboring town. More recently the courts have ruled for dismissal due to, among others, the following reasons:

- insubordination
- neglect of duty
- conduct unbecoming a teacher
- incompetence
- physical or mental health problems
- engaging in illegal activities
- causing or encouraging disruptions

The general direction of court cases that consider dismissal tends more toward personal liberty today than in the past.

The two overriding questions asked when considering dismissal are: "Is the educational process significantly disrupted by the action?" and "Is the teacher's credibility significantly harmed among students, colleagues, families, and the community?" Some teacher offenses are considered by the courts to be remediable, meaning that given assistance and time, a teacher may be able to correct the problem and be effective in the classroom. For instance, if a district begins dismissal procedures because a tenured teacher's classroom management skills are considered very poor, the court will likely say the teacher has a right to try to remediate those

TEACHER'S CONTRACT

SUBD. 10, SECTION 47, TITLE 7, CONSOLIDATED SCHOOL LAW, SUBD. 11,
SECTION 15, TITLE 8 AND SECTION 17, TITLE 15

I _Josie M. Long_ of _Tully_ county of _Onondaga_ a duly qualified teacher, hereby contract with the board of trustees of district no. _10_ town of _Homer_ county of _Cortland_ to teach the public school of said district for the term of _34_ consecutive weeks, except as hereafter provided, commencing _Sept. 8_ 1908 at a weekly compensation of _9_ dollars and _25_ cents payable at the end of each thirty days during the term of such employment.

And the board of trustees of said district hereby contract to employ said teacher for said period at the said rate of compensation, payable at the times herein stated.

Said board of trustees reserve the right to provide for a vacation or vacations of not more than _6_ weeks in the aggregate, during said term, which vacation shall not count as a part of the term of service above referred to.

Dated _Aug. 13_ 1908

Josie M. Long } Teacher

J. P. Carty } Trustees

This contract shall be executed in duplicate and one copy thereof given to the teacher and one retained by the board.

Compared to modern teacher contracts, early 20th century contracts were basic and simple.

skills. On the other hand, some actions are considered irremediable in that they are so unprofessional that a district is not obligated to provide assistance. Conviction in a criminal case or having sexual relationships with a student are examples of actions for which districts may begin immediate procedures toward dismissal.

Most districts require teachers to serve successfully for about 3 years before offering them a continuing contract, or tenure. During these first 3 years or so teachers can be dismissed for suspected incompetence or because of a general **reduction in force** of the district teacher population. Such a reduction may result from lower student numbers, budget cuts, or program cancellation. Reduction in force (rif) may also apply to tenured teachers. However, the general rule of "riffing" is that the last hired are the first to go.

Due process. When a tenured teacher is threatened with dismissal, the steps the district must take to pursue the charges against the teacher are called **due process.** Due process is an important principle that requires guidelines to be followed to ensure that individuals are protected from arbitrary or capricious treatment by those in authority. Both the Fifth and the Fourteenth Amendments to the Constitution state that no person will be deprived of life, liberty, or property, without due process of law. The procedures of due process vary by state, but generally a teacher must be

1. notified of the proposed changes
2. given reasonable time to examine evidence
3. told who will be called upon as witnesses
4. given the right to legal representation
5. provided with a hearing before an impartial jury, panel, and/or judge
6. given the opportunity to call witnesses and cross-examine the district's witnesses

7. afforded a decision based on evidence
8. provided a transcript of the proceedings
9. given the right to appeal

Even though due process has been in force for many years and will likely continue to be part of the profession, outcomes of hearings based on due process may vary by location and according to the times (LaMorte, 2005). For instance, until the 1970s, if an unmarried teacher lived with someone of the opposite sex, the teacher could go through due process procedures and be dismissed. Today, it would be very rare for a teacher's living arrangements to serve as grounds for dismissal.

Teachers affiliated with unions may go on strike when collective bargaining does not result in satisfactory changes.

Unions and collective bargaining. While not exclusively related to getting and keeping a job, collective bargaining is a right practiced in most states by teacher unions. States often allow unions to negotiate with school boards concerning elements of teacher contracts and working conditions. The two major teacher organizations that act as unions, the National Education Association (NEA) and the American Federation of Teachers (AFT), were discussed in Chapter 1 (see page 15). States have their own affiliates of NEA or AFT to represent teachers in more local ways. Individual teachers and groups of teachers can file **grievances**, or formal complaints against a district. NEA and AFT, or their state affiliates, often represent teachers who file grievances. NEA and AFT, as unions, can also call for teacher strikes when collective bargaining does not result in changes that satisfy the large groups of teachers who affiliate with the unions.

How do you feel about teachers going on strike and removing themselves from the classroom for a period of time during which collective bargaining takes place? Should teachers be allowed to strike because of grievances about their work environment (salary, hours, class size, etc.) if it means closing schools during the process? Why or why not? Does the level of school make a difference to you when considering this question? For instance, would 4- or 5-year-olds be more adversely affected by a teacher strike than adolescents?

Your Teaching Fingerprint

One of the most treasured freedoms enjoyed by teachers in their work environment is the right to conduct classes with a measure of freedom of expression. Let's explore this important aspect of teaching as it relates to law.

Freedom of Expression

There are many ways to express opinions and beliefs, including symbolic, written, and verbal expression. Symbolic expression generally involves making a statement by what is worn—a style of clothing, a political button, particular colors, an armband, a ribbon. Some symbolic statements are socially acceptable, even desirable. For instance, ribbons showing support for breast cancer research or bracelets commemorating important days in history are considered appropriate. However, wearing an armband to protest an ongoing war or a shirt with inflammatory or offensive words or pictures may be legal outside school, but ruled unacceptable in school and can serve as possible grounds for dismissal. For teachers, freedom of symbolic expression has limits, especially if it disrupts the school or classroom.

As with symbolic expression, written and spoken expression must not interrupt the education process. Teachers have the right to express themselves through letters to the editor, written articles, conversations, speeches, debates, and so on. Since the often-quoted case of *Pickering* v. *Board of Education,* 1968, the courts have generally ruled on the side of teachers' rights to freedom of spoken and written expression, even when that expression involves harsh criticism of a school, district, or personnel connected to education. In *Pickering,* an Illinois teacher wrote a sarcastic letter to the editor criticizing the school superintendent and school board for funding practices. The board fired Pickering, and the state supreme court upheld the dismissal. Pickering appealed to the U.S. Supreme Court. Justice Thurgood Marshall stated that the problem was one of balance between personal rights of the teacher and the district's right to promote efficient public service through its employees. The court ruled in favor of Pickering and his right to openly debate questions without fear of retaliatory dismissal.

However, if the expression is intended to incite unprofessional behavior, the courts may rule against the teacher. John Stroman was fired for encouraging teachers to call in sick as a form of protest against some administrative decisions. In *Stroman* v. *Colleton County School District,* 1992, the Supreme Court ruled in favor of the school district on grounds that encouraging others to lie is unprofessional.

One form of freedom of expression that specifically applies to the teaching profession is academic freedom. This freedom is cherished by teachers, but is restricted by public school curricula.

Academic Freedom

Academic freedom is a form of expression that allows teachers to use their judgment in making decisions about what to discuss, what to assign as readings, what teaching strategies to use, and so on. Like the other freedoms, academic freedom has limits that courts have upheld in many cases.

One recurring issue involves the courts' attempts to balance the right of academic freedom with a district's desire for students to learn a specific curriculum. Districts and states set the curriculum teachers must teach. When teachers exercise academic freedom and go beyond or eliminate parts of this curriculum, problems occur because either (a) including the additional topics does not leave time for the prescribed curriculum, or (b) the nonprescribed topics are controversial and may be deemed inappropriate.

In this era of standards and high-stakes testing, not teaching the prescribed curriculum is likely to become evident over time. The line between what is appropriate in the classroom, and what is not is the most common cause of disagreements between districts and teachers with regard to academic freedom. Some of the topics deemed inappropriate in the public school classroom when they are not part of the curriculum include sexuality-related issues, gun control, abortion, some political issues, and any topic involving offensive language. For instance, in *Keefe* v. *Geanakos,* 1969, a Massachusetts high school English teacher assigned an article from the *Atlantic Monthly* that contained offensive language. He was fired because he would not agree never to give the assignment again. A court decision reinstated Keefe and stated that because some of the school's library books contained the same words and students would likely not be shocked by them, parental complaints about the words did not dictate what was proper in the classroom.

Some teaching methods may be deemed inappropriate if a teacher cannot substantiate the approach using professional opinions and research. In *Murray* v. *Pittsburgh Board of Education, 1996,* a teacher used a motivational technique with at-risk high school students called "Learnball," which involved dividing the class into teams. The teams elected leaders and determined class rules. Competition between teams involved rewards, such as listening to the radio and shooting baskets with foam balls. The school board ordered the teacher not to use the method. Murray sued the board but lost. The courts determined that the school board had the right to set policy against particular teaching methodologies.

Summaries of the four cases in this section concerning freedom of expression, plus two others of interest, are given in Figure 11.5. Perhaps even more controversial than academic freedom are the issues involved in teachers' personal lives.

Figure 11.5 Case law: Freedom of expression

> ***Pickering* v. *Board of Education* (1968)**
> Teacher kept job after publicly criticizing school board
>
> ***Keefe* v. *Geanakos* (1969)**
> Teacher kept job after assigning controversial readings
>
> ***Kingsville Independent School District* v. *Cooper* (1980)**
> **Teacher uses role-play to teach about racial relations**
>
> A teacher was dismissed when she refused to stop using role-play simulations to teach about post–Civil War American history. Parents complained that the activity caused racially charged sentiments in their children. The court of appeals reinstated the teacher with back pay. The court determined that the district violated the teachers First Amendment rights.
>
> ***Krizek* v. *Cicero-Stickney Township High School* (1989)**
> **Teacher showing R-rated movie**
>
> A teacher was dismissed for showing an R-rated movie to her class as a modern-day parallel to *Our Town* by Thornton Wilder. She apparently told her students they would be excused if their parents objected, but she did not communicate directly with the parents. The court upheld Ms. Krizek's dismissal, saying the movie was a planned event and not an inadvertent mistake and that her methodology was problematic.
>
> ***Stroman* v. *Colleton County School District* (1992)**
> Teacher fired for encouraging others to lie
>
> ***Murray* v. *Pittsburgh Board of Education* (1996)**
> Teacher may not use instructional strategy considered unorthodox by school board

Sources: From *The Principal's Quick-Reference Guide to School Law: Reducing Liability, Litigation, and Other Potential Legal Tangles,* by D. R. Dunklee and R. J. Shoop, 2002, Thousand Oaks, CA: Corwin Press; *School Law: Cases and Concepts* (8th ed.), by M. W. LaMorte, 2005, Boston: Allyn and Bacon; *Teachers and the Law* (6th ed.), by L. Fischer, D. Schimmel, and L. R. Stellman, 2003, Boston: Allyn & Bacon.

Figure 11.6 Excerpt from 1920s teacher contract

> I promise to abstain from all dancing, immodest dressing, and any other conduct unbecoming a teacher and a lady. I promise not to go out with any young men except in so far as it may be necessary to stimulate Sunday School work.
>
> I promise not to fall in love, to become engaged, or secretly marry.
>
> I promise to sleep at least eight hours at night [and] to eat carefully . . . in order that I may be better able to render efficient service to my pupils.

Source: From *Teachers and the Law,* by L. Fischer, D. Schimmel, and L. R. Stellman (p. 265), 2003, Boston: Allyn & Bacon.

Teachers' Personal Lives

A teacher has a right to a personal life. However, the position of teacher carries with it some restrictions that other professions may not. The notion that teachers are role models entails some limits that have been upheld in court when teachers have been dismissed because of aspects of their personal lives. To lend some perspective to this discussion, take a look at an excerpt from an actual teacher contract from the 1920s, shown in Figure 11.6. As late as the 1960s teachers were quickly and without challenge fired for adultery, drunkenness, homosexual conduct, illegal drug use, cohabitation with the opposite sex, or becoming pregnant while single.

Personal conduct and job performance. The notion that teachers can be automatically fired for what is considered by the community as immoral behavior was rejected by the California Supreme Court in *Morrison* v. *State Board of Education,* 1969. The court found that grounds for dismissal must include evidence that the personal conduct of a teacher adversely affects job performance. The Morrison case involved a teacher who had a brief homosexual relationship with another teacher. When the superintendent found out, Morrison's teaching license was revoked on the grounds that his immoral conduct was contrary to the moral standards of the people of California. The court ruled in favor of Morrison and said the term *immoral* was interpreted too broadly. No evidence was found to connect Morrison's personal life and his professional work.

In *Morrison,* the California Supreme Court said it was dangerous to allow the terms *immoral* and *unprofessional* to be interpreted too broadly. "To many people, 'immoral conduct' includes laziness, gluttony, selfishness, and cowardice. To others, 'unprofessional conduct' for teachers includes signing controversial petitions, opposing majority opinions, and drinking alcoholic beverages" (Fischer, Schimmel, & Stellman, 2003, p. 266). The court ruled that a teacher should not be fired because someone disapproves of the teacher's personal life unless it directly relates to his or her professional work. Part of the ruling stated, " 'Today's morals may be tomorrow's ancient and absurd customs' " (Fischer et al., 2003, p. 265). Generally the courts have ruled that teachers have the right to privacy in regard to procreation, marriage, child rearing, and other activities in the home (Underwood & Webb, 2006).

Since 1969 other cases have been brought by teachers who felt they were wrongly dismissed. The courts continue to look for evidence that particular conduct adversely affects job performance. In *Eckmann* v. *Board of Education,* 1986, an Illinois teacher was fired when she became pregnant while unmarried and decided to raise the child as a single parent. The judge found in favor of the teacher and said that she had a due process right to conceive and raise her child, even out of wedlock, and without school board intrusion (Fischer et al, 2003). Eckmann kept her job. In contrast, in what may seem like a frivolous situation, in *Tardif* v. *Quinn,* 1976, a high school teacher was not rehired because she refused to stop wearing short skirts. The court recognized the teacher's constitutional right to choose her grooming, but ruled that the right did not extend to wearing whatever she pleased during the school workday. The teacher did not get her job back.

As with personal conduct, if a district wants to fire a teacher for health reasons (e.g., obesity, disabilities, AIDS), it must show a direct link between the health problem and impaired classroom function. And there is a considerable gray area when it comes to

- conviction for committing a misdemeanor or felony
- possession or use of illegal drugs
- overuse of alcohol

Figure 11.7 summarizes the cases in this section along with several others that concern teachers' personal lives. There is one area of misconduct that receives very little tolerance: misconduct with students.

Misconduct with students. The most clear-cut decisions involving the firing of teachers on moral grounds involve misconduct with students. When a teacher's personal life or habits intersect a student's in illegal or morally questionable ways, then it is relatively easy for a school district to dismiss a teacher for

- sexual relations with students
- profane, abusive language directed at students
- allowing students to drink alcohol
- encouraging students to be dishonest

Your Teaching Fingerprint

Do you think the role of teacher carries with it personal restraints? Would you be willing to alter your lifestyle somewhat to conform with what a particular community considers moral and professional behavior? At what level of school do you think it is most important for teachers to serve as representatives of community values?

Now that you have seen how the law interacts with, and in some cases determines, the rights of teachers, let's examine the legal responsibilities of teachers.

Figure 11.7   Case law: Teachers' personal lives

***Morrison* v. *State Board of Education* (1969)**
Teacher keeps position because behavior does not directly affect job performance

***Tardif* v. *Quinn* (1976)**
Teacher challenges dress code but does not keep job

***Thompson* v. *Southwest District* (1980)**
Teacher unmarried cohabitation
A female teacher was fired because she lived with her boyfriend. While she didn't particularly keep the arrangement a secret, when the school board suspended her for immorality, they publicized it. The court ruled that it was unfair to make the issue public in an attempt to gain support. In addition, the court found that living with her boyfriend did not diminish the teacher's classroom effectiveness. The board lost, and the teacher kept her job.

***Eckmann* v. *Board of Education* (1986)**
Single teacher raising child keeps job

***Ware* v. *Morgan County School District* (1988)**
Teacher using obscene language toward students
A Colorado high school music teacher took a misbehaving student outside and used obscene language to tell him he was a disgrace to the band. The teacher was fired, and the court sided with the school district.

***Elvin* v. *City of Waterville* (1990)**
Teacher having sexual relations with minor
A divorced fourth grade female teacher was fired for having sexual relations with her 15-year-old male neighbor. Although the boy had never been her student, the court agreed with the school district's decision to fire the teacher, saying she had proven herself unfit to teach. The judge added that public awareness of her conduct undermined her ability to deal with

Sources: From *The Principal's Quick-Reference Guide to School Law: Reducing Liability, Litigation, and Other Potential Legal Tangles,* by D. R. Dunklee and R. J. Shoop, 2002, Thousand Oaks, CA: Corwin Press; *School Law: Cases and Concepts* (8th ed.), by M. W. LaMorte, 2005, Boston: Allyn and Bacon; *Teachers and the Law* (6th ed.), by L. Fischer, D. Schimmel, and L. R. Stellman, 2003, Boston: Allyn & Bacon.

What Are the Legal Responsibilities of Teachers?

Teachers have many responsibilities. Some are dictated by laws, while others are dictated by state, district, or school policies. Some responsibilities are governed by ethical and professional guidelines, many of which you'll read about in Chapter 13. This section will look at legal responsibilities of teachers, including avoidance of liability, copyright issues, and the reporting of child abuse.

Liability

To be **liable** means to be responsible for. We generally hear the term in a negative sense, for instance, "He was found liable for the accident" or "That will raise my liability insurance premium." In a positive sense, though, liability is what teaching is all about—accepting responsibility for students while they are under our supervision. This is why we study child development, subject matter, instructional and assessment strategies, guidelines for health and safety, school law, and so on. However, being held liable when something goes wrong is far from positive. Depending on the severity of the issue, liability for a situation can end a career.

Teachers serve *in loco parentis*—in place of parents. They are bound by law to care for and protect children in the school setting as a parent would and are held to a standard of reasonableness. Teachers, schools, and districts are frequently sued over issues related to liability. For a school employee to be considered liable for something, the following four components must be proven to be present:

1. The person has a legal duty to protect students.
2. The person fails to act within reason and provide the appropriate standard of care.

Teachers serve in loco parentis, *or in place of parents. They are bound by law to care for and protect children in the school setting as a parent would.*

3. There is a causal connection between the person's conduct and the result of the injury.
4. Actual damage occurs to the injured person. (La Morte, 2005)

Let's examine a case with these four components in mind. In the case of *Mancha* v. *Field Museum of Natural History,* 1971, students aged 12–15 had gone on a field trip with teachers to the Chicago Natural History Museum. The students were allowed to tour the exhibits on their own. One student was beaten up by teenagers from another school. In this case, the teachers had a legal duty to protect students (1), and there was actual damage (4). The court had to decide if the teachers failed to act within reason and provide an appropriate standard of care (2) and if there was a causal connection between the teachers' conduct and the result of the injury (3). The teachers were not held liable for the student's injuries because the court determined there was minimal risk at the museum, and the teachers could not reasonably have been expected to directly supervise them.

In a similar case the same year, an eighth grader sustained a severe eye injury when a student threw rocks during a baseball game. The teacher involved in *Sheehan* v. *St. Peter's Catholic School,* 1971, had accompanied the students outside but then returned to the building. The courts determined that the teacher left the area and therefore was not properly supervising the students. She was found liable for leaving students alone in a potentially dangerous setting.

Additional cases involving teacher liability are summarized in Figure 11.8. Have you considered the many ways things may go wrong for teachers and students? Were you ever involved in a situation where a teacher's liability was questioned? If so, what were the circumstances? Think about scenarios at the various levels of school. At which level do you think your liability would be greatest? Why?

Your Teaching Fingerprint

Figure 11.8 Case law: Teacher liability

***Kaufman* v. *City of New York* (1961)**
Teacher supervising basketball
A boy was seriously injured when he bumped heads with another boy during a basketball game. The court ruled that any amount of supervision could not have prevented the accident and that the school and teacher were not liable.

***Morris* v. *Douglas County School District* (1965)**
Teacher's lack of caution on field trip
A first grade teacher took her students on a field trip to the Oregon coast. A large wave washed a log onto a student who was wading in the water causing serious injury. The court found that the teacher was liable because this kind of injury is not uncommon, and the teacher was responsible for the safety of the young children in her care.

***Mancha* v. *Field Museum of Natural History* (1971)**
Teacher allowing students to self-guide during field trip is not held liable for injury

***Sheehan* v. *St. Peter's Catholic School* (1971)**
Teacher is found liable for student injury

***Station* v. *Travelers Insurance Co.* (1974)**
Teacher leaving students during class is held liable for student injury

---

Sources: From *School Law: Cases and Concepts* (8th ed.), by M. W. LaMorte, 2005, Boston: Allyn and Bacon; *Teachers and the Law* (6th ed.), by L. Fischer, D. Schimmel, and L. R. Stellman, 2003, Boston: Allyn & Bacon.

Accidents happen—in the classroom, the hallway, the cafeteria, the science lab, the gym, on school grounds, on field trips, and so on. Using good judgment in the *in loco parentis* role will be enough for most teachers. But occasionally students are injured, and teacher liability may be questioned. Liability insurance is a good idea. Teacher organizations offer reasonably priced policies that are recommended even for student teachers. These organizations often also provide legal assistance to members who find themselves involved in a school-related lawsuit. A common school-related legal issue involves copyright laws.

Copyright Laws

Copyright laws are intended to protect the rights of creators of intellectual property and to prevent others from copying or distributing it without permission. Intellectual property includes written material, original audio and visual work, and computer programs. Copyright laws also provide guidelines for authorized use of someone else's intellectual property.

There are three conditions under which copyrighted materials may be used: the user has permission from the copyright owner, the work is in the public domain, or the use is considered "fair use." A work is in the **public domain** if it is more than 75 years old or is published by a government agency. **Fair use,** or the "face-to-face teaching exemption, allows the nonprofit reproduction and use of certain materials for classroom use without permission of the copyright owner" (Underwood & Webb, 2006, p. 87). Generally, fair use stipulates that the material copied must be for educational purposes and that the amount copied must fall within certain guidelines, some of which are listed in Figure 11.9. Teachers may not, however, make copies of consumable products such as textbooks, workbooks, and standardized test materials. If copies could be freely made of these kinds of materials, then their creators and publishers would lose money because the need for them would diminish.

Because teachers often want students to create work using certain computer software, it is important to know that computer software is copyrighted and that fair use guidelines do not apply. Some software publishers allow one backup copy to be made, but more than

Figure 11.9 Guidelines for classroom copying

1. A single copy may be made of any of the following for your own scholarly research or use in teaching:
   - a chapter from a book
   - an article from a periodical or newspaper
   - a short story, short essay, or short poem
   - a chart, graph, diagram, drawing, cartoon, or picture from a book, periodical, or newspaper

2. Multiple copies (no more than one per student) may be made for classroom use if each copy gives credit to the copyright holder and passes three tests.
   - The brevity test includes guidelines such as poems of fewer than 200 words and prose of fewer than 2,500 words.
   - The spontaneity test generally says that you are inspired to copy and use material for the sake of teaching effectiveness and there was not time to ask and receive permission.
   - The cumulative effect test generally restricts the length of time copied material is used and how many instances of copying take place in a period of time.

3. Teachers cannot copy individual works and put them together to serve as an anthology.

4. Students cannot be charged for the photocopying of copyrighted works.

Source: From *School Law for Teachers: Concepts and Applications,* by J. Underwood and L. D. Webb, 2006, Upper Saddle River, NJ: Merrill/Prentice Hall.

this is illegal. Additionally, commercially produced videos may not be copied. Copies made of television programs can be kept for 45 days and then must be erased or destroyed.

With the Internet serving as a major research tool in classrooms today, teachers must be aware that what is on the Internet is not in the public domain. Because the Internet is international, laws governing its use are somewhat unclear. Following fair use guidelines is a safe way to use Web resources.

Whether using written works, audiovisual materials, computer software, or information from the Internet, teachers must take copyright laws seriously. School districts have policies based on fair use guidelines. A school's media specialist is often a helpful, knowledgeable source of information about what is lawful and what is not. Teachers should ask if there is any question about how they plan to use any form of intellectual property.

While copyright laws are important, a much graver responsibility is inherent in being a teacher—recognizing and reporting child abuse.

Reporting Suspected Child Abuse

A teacher who has a reasonable suspicion of child abuse or neglect has a legal obligation to report it to a school counselor or administrator, who in turn will report it to a social services agency or the police. Teachers don't have to be certain that they are correct. They are granted immunity and may not be sued for reporting their suspicions (Fischer et al., 2003).

Figure 10.2 (see page 293) presented signs of abuse or neglect. It is a good idea for teachers to keep such a list at their desks for easy reference. Teachers should never become too busy to be observant. Physical abuse may be visually evident and difficult to miss. However, sexual abuse may be more subtle in terms of symptoms, and emotional or mental abuse may be even more difficult to detect. Reviewing the signs periodically, watching for behavioral or emotional changes, and reporting suspicions of abuse or neglect to administrators or school counselors will help protect students. This is a teacher's legal and ethical responsibility and simply the right thing to do.

Teacher responsibilities obviously include protecting their students however and whenever they can. Teacher responsibilities also include safeguarding students' rights, some of which are discussed in the next section.

■ What Are the Legal Rights of Students?

You may notice that there isn't a section of this chapter devoted to students' legal responsibilities. If there were, the section would be short. Students have the responsibility to go to school as long as it is compulsory (usually to age 16, but to age 18 in some locations). That's about it in terms of legal responsibilities. Although we hope students take responsibility for their learning and behavior, unless their behavior crosses the boundary and becomes illegal or extremely disruptive, there are no other laws binding them.

Students do have rights, however. They do not leave their constitutional rights at the schoolhouse door. This section will consider two basic areas of student freedom. One area is freedom of expression involving what students can do with regard to symbolic freedom, freedom of speech, and freedom of the press. The other basic area is freedom from particular actions and situations. This area may be thought of as legal protection for students. This section will specifically address search and seizure, sexual harassment, particular disciplinary actions, the right of nonparticipation, privacy protection, and the right to nondiscrimination.

Freedom of Expression

Before 1969 students were not recognized as having First Amendment rights to freedom of expression. The U.S. Supreme Court's decision in *Tinker* v. *Des Moines Independent Community School District,* 1969, provided a clear message that a student is entitled to freedom of expression (LaMorte, 2005). The case involved three students who wore armbands to protest the Vietnam War. They were suspended and subsequently sued the district. In this monumentally important case the U.S. Supreme Court ruled that teachers and students do not "shed their rights to freedom of speech or expression at the schoolhouse gate." The *Tinker* case has been cited repeatedly since 1969.

However, court challenges since *Tinker* have served to balance the rights of students to express themselves and the necessity of limiting personal freedom to ensure the safety and well-being of others. For students, understanding the need for this balance is a lesson in the principles of democracy.

Freedom of symbolic expression. The *Tinker* decision so influenced how students are viewed in relation to freedom of expression that it is known as the *Tinker Doctrine.* This doctrine extends to symbolic freedom. As with other rights, students are allowed to express their views symbolically through what they wear as long as it doesn't disrupt the educational process.

Dress Codes. Since the 1960s numerous lawsuits have been initiated over the restrictions imposed by dress codes, but the U.S. Supreme Court has not ruled on the issue. In 1972 Justice Black wrote that the U.S. Constitution doesn't require the courts to bear the burden of supervising clothing or hairstyles.

However, schools are concerned about immodest dress and unusual hairstyles because they could disrupt the educational atmosphere of the classroom as well as lead to more serious issues. For instance, violence generated by gangs and groups such as the "trenchcoat mafia" (the students associated with the 1999 Columbine school shootings) has prompted educators to identify and attempt to ban insignia clothing and hats associated with specific groups. LaMorte (2005) lists the following as school concerns:

- "T-shirts depicting violence, drugs (e.g., marijuana leaves), racial epithets . . . ;
- ripped, baggy, or saggy pants or jeans;
- . . . colored bandanas;
- baseball or other hats;
- words shaved into scalps,
- brightly colored hair . . . ;
- exposed underwear;
- . . . tattoos, . . . pierced noses . . . ;
- and decorative dental caps" (p. 172)

These forms of symbolic expression are not protected by the First Amendment because they may contribute to school unrest. Most dress codes outlaw some or all of the items in LaMorte's list. However, because some of the items are associated with particular cultures, it is difficult for schools to designate them without appearing to be biased. Rules designating shirt length, requiring belts, and prohibiting exposed midriffs are more generic but still hard to enforce.

Uniforms. Dress codes are often ambiguous, leaving much room for interpretation. They can infringe on learning time if teachers are expected to watch for and report violations. Thus some schools and entire districts choose to impose a uniform policy, giving students several modest, relatively plain choices of clothing. Currently, more than half the states have schools with uniform policies. Some large cities, such as Long Beach, California; Chicago; and San Antonio, Texas, require at least elementary students to wear uniforms. In 2002 Memphis, Tennessee, became the nation's first large public school district to adopt a uniform policy in all of its 175 schools.

Public schools that impose uniform policies must provide an opt-out clause for parents who don't want their children to participate. For instance, some parents may not

While some schools ban earrings other than in ear lobes, others allow multiple piercings as long as they do not disrupt the education process.

want their children to wear a uniform because it conflicts with the clothing traditions of their religion. Other parents may request to be exempt simply because their children don't want to wear the uniform and are persistently making that clear. Private schools do not receive government support and, unlike public schools, may impose a uniform policy on all students without allowing them to opt out.

Did your schools have dress codes or uniforms? What do you remember about them? Did you feel that your freedom of expression was restricted by what the schools said you could and couldn't wear? As a future teacher, do you like the idea of dress codes or uniforms? Why or why not? Are they more important at particular levels of school?

Freedom of speech. The freedom of speech implied in *Tinker* was challenged in 1986 when a student made a speech containing sexual innuendo in a high school assembly. He was reprimanded and subsequently sued the school, claiming that his freedom of speech was denied. The case, *Bethel School District No. 403* v. *Fraser,* 1986, went to the U.S. Supreme Court, where the adolescent lost. The court ruled that a school does not have to accept indecent or offensive speech.

While students enjoy free speech, it does have limits. An individual student's freedom of speech, as well as freedom of the press, must be balanced against the school's ability to maintain a safe and civil atmosphere, where all students are shown respect.

Students often enjoy expressing personal taste in their choices of clothing and shoes.

Freedom of the press. School publications have long been fertile ground for disputes about students' rights to express themselves. In attempts to make school newspapers relevant and truly student owned, students tend to write about what's on the minds of classmates, no matter how controversial. However, it is clear from court decisions such as *Hazelwood School District* v. *Kuhlmeier,* 1988, that teachers and administrators may exercise editorial control over school publications. In this case, two articles written by students for a Missouri high school newspaper were deleted by the principal. The main topics of the articles were teen pregnancy and divorce, and they contained references to sexuality the principal thought inappropriate for younger students. In addition, even though their names were changed, the principal was concerned that students written about in the articles were identifiable. The Supreme Court ruled in favor of the district, stating that educators may exercise substantial control over school-sponsored publications and events.

Did you ever sense that your freedom of speech or press was restricted in some way? Were you on a newspaper staff? Did anyone censure or limit in any way how students could express themselves in the paper? If so, how? What was your reaction?

For all three forms of expression—symbolic, speech, and written—students' rights must be balanced with what is in the best interest of the school population. The adults in charge—school board members, district personnel, administrators, and teachers—must be vigilant and protect student rights while also protecting those who may be adversely affected by the exercise of those rights. Further protection for students comes in the explicit policies regarding the areas described in the next section.

The Right to Be Protected

Freedom of expression refers to what students may do. The right to be protected is freedom from actions that may be imposed on students. Some topics related to student rights to protection are addressed next.

Search and seizure. The Fourth Amendment provides for citizens to be secure from unreasonable search and seizure. This right applies to students in schools as well, to a point. The courts have attempted to balance the student's right to privacy and the school's need to know. The key term is *reasonableness*. In *New Jersey* v. *T.L.O.*, 1985, two high school girls were accused of smoking in the bathroom. One admitted it, and one (T.L.O.) denied it. In the principal's office T.L.O. was asked to empty her purse. In it were cigarettes, cigarette-rolling paper, marijuana, a pipe, a roll of money, and a list titled "People who owe me money." The student was turned over to juvenile court. She sued the school for invasion of privacy. The U.S. Supreme Court ruled against her and maintained that the search and seizure were reasonable.

In most cases the courts have ruled against schools that arbitrarily and routinely search lockers, use drug-sniffing dogs, and search through students' clothes. Privacy is upheld as a right unless a search is deemed reasonable. But school lockers are part of school property. If there are reasonable suspicions of contraband in lockers, they may be searched.

Drug testing as a form of search of students remains controversial among the general public. However, since about 2000 most court decisions have ruled that drug testing is permissible for all students who participate in extracurricular activities, making no distinction between basketball and debate teams.

If there is reasonable suspicion for a search, the search itself must be reasonably conducted. Age and gender need to be considered. Walking through a metal detector or putting a book bag through a detector is noninvasive and considered reasonable if there have been problems with weapons at the school. Searching lockers, either by hand or using dogs, is more invasive, but reasonable if there is suspicion. Asking students to empty their pockets and take off coats may be called for and is reasonable. However, strip searches are very invasive and should only be done if there is probable cause (more stringent than reasonable suspicion) and by proper authorities, not by teachers. The courts have been split on the legality of strip searches. In elementary school strip searches are typically supported by the courts, whereas in middle and high school they are sometimes not supported by court decisions. This kind of intrusive search should not be done by teachers alone under any circumstances.

School lockers are part of school property. If there are reasonable suspicions of contraband in lockers, they may be searched.

Did you ever experience any form of search as a student in K–12 schools? What experiences do you recall of teachers or administrators acting on their suspicions of contraband? Have you or has anyone you know been subjected to a locker or clothing search? If so, what were the circumstances and how did you or the other person respond? Do you think teachers and administrators should be able to conduct random searches?

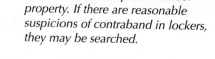

One area of student rights in which teachers definitely should be involved is detecting and preventing sexual harassment.

Sexual harassment. According to the American Association of University Women (AAUW) (2001), **sexual harassment** is behavior with sexual implications that is neither wanted nor welcome. It interferes with a person's life. Sexual harassment may include obvious looks with lewd intent, taunts with sexual innuendo, touching, kissing, groping, and any actions or behaviors that have sexual connotations. The AAUW conducted a survey in 1993, and again in 2001, of eighth through eleventh grade students to gauge the extent of sexual harassment in schools. The survey revealed that 80% in both grade levels experienced sexual harassment. The results served as a wake-up call for schools as sexual harassment came into the public eye. However, a positive change is that in 2001, 69% of respondents, as opposed to only a small percentage in 1990, reported knowing about school policies against sexual harassment and the consequences for harassing. Awareness has increased, but the problem persists.

This chapter's Letter to the Editor highlights an incident of sexual harassment that occurred in 2006 in Mt. Lebanon, Pennsylvania. Excerpts from two articles published in the *Pittsburgh Post-Gazette,* shown in Figure 11.10, set the stage for the letter. While one or more high school students described in the articles may have been dismissed by some with the attitude of "Oh, well, boys will be boys," the young women, their families, and the community

Figure 11.10 Articles dealing with sexual harassment

Explicit ranking of high school girls sparks outrage in Mt. Lebanon

"Top 25" list details students' looks, bodies

Wednesday, April 26, 2006

By Mary Niederberger and Nikki Schwab, *Pittsburgh Post-Gazette*

The Mt. Lebanon School District and Mt. Lebanon police are investigating the distribution of an anonymous document that features sexually explicit descriptions of 25 girls at the high school.

The document, titled "Top 25 in 2006," ranks the girls in order from one to 25. It includes their names, grade levels and photos.

Each girl is assigned a letter grade for her breasts, buttocks and face, followed by a brief description of each girl in crude and vulgar terms.

There are references to girls performing oral sex and comments about their height and weight. . . .

"I think that it's outrageous, the equivalent of a written rape on our daughter," said the father of one girl, who didn't want his name published to protect his daughter's identity.

He and another parent said they are frustrated that the district hasn't disciplined the students who created the publication. . . .

The second father said he has done some investigating and talked to students, including his children, who told him that ballots to choose the "Top 25" were circulated at high school basketball games and that students had been seen reading the list in the school cafeteria.

He said he embarked on his investigation after [the] Mt. Lebanon High School principal . . . told him that the list was not a district matter because none of the activities involved with it took place on school grounds. . . .

Mt. Lebanon Police Chief Thomas A. Ogden Jr. said the "Top 25" list is "in very poor taste," but that his department could not substantiate that any crime had been committed. . . .

[School officials] said the district is examining to see whether the publication violates the district's sexual harassment policy. . . .

Mt. Lebanon suspends student for role in list

"Too little, too late," one girl's father says

Friday, May 5, 2006

A Mt. Lebanon High School student has been suspended for his involvement with a vulgar "Top 25" list of female students.

School officials wouldn't comment on any action taken, beyond a letter issued yesterday by Superintendent George D. Wilson, which states:

"Those proven to be responsible will receive consequences that include disciplinary action, a requirement for atonement and character education. However, since this is a student disciplinary matter, I am prohibited from releasing any confidential information."

The letter was mailed to high school parents and posted on the district's Web site. . . .

Although the disciplinary action wasn't announced, the district must follow procedures set in state law when a student is removed from school.

If a suspension is longer than three school days, the student and parents must be offered an informal hearing within five days of the suspension. Formal hearings are required for expulsions, which by definition are longer than 10 school days.

The fathers of two of the girls whose names were on the list were angry when they read Dr. Wilson's letter.

"Way too little, way too late," said one of the fathers, who repeatedly has criticized the superintendent for not taking immediate action on the list when it was presented to him in early April. . . .

In his letter, Dr. Wilson said he was "appalled" by the actions of any student who participated "in any way." . . .

The superintendent's letter said the district will reinforce with all students "the importance of treating each other with respect and dignity. . . . Schools cannot control popular culture, but, together with the home, we exert a strong influence on how our students conduct themselves."

The district has a policy prohibiting sexual harassment.

were clearly harmed and outraged by the sexual harassment perpetrated by some students. Read the articles and the Letter to the Editor, then respond with a letter of your own.

When students report incidents that appear to be sexual harassment, teachers must take their complaints seriously. The ruling in *Davis* v. *Monroe County Board of Education,* 1999, determined that educators can be held liable if they do not respond to complaints of sexual harassment. A fifth grade girl in Georgia was groped and verbally sexually harassed by a classmate. She and her parents repeatedly reported it to the school, but it continued. The family filed a lawsuit, and 6 years later the U.S. Supreme Court ruled in a 5-to-4 decision that the school failed to act appropriately to protect the girl.

Teachers must also be conscious of their own behavior with students to prevent it from being misconstrued as harassment. In the 2001 AAUW survey, 7% of the respondents said that teachers sexually harassed them. Teachers must be constantly aware of how their actions may be perceived by students.

Have you ever experienced what you considered sexual harassment? What were the circumstances? Was it addressed by anyone, or did it go unnoticed by everyone but you? How did it make you feel? Have you ever been guilty of sexually harassing someone else?

Your Teaching Fingerprint

When sexual harassment is detected, the school is likely to take disciplinary action. The range of possibilities, governed by both common sense and lawful procedures, is broad.

Letter to the Editor

This letter to the editor appeared in the Pittsburgh, Pennsylvania, newspaper, the *Post-Gazette*. It was written in response to the situation at Mt. Lebanon High School described in Figure 11.10.

Now it's your turn. In this chapter you learned how prevalent sexual harassment is among students. These questions will help guide your consideration of how best to express your own response to the situation described in the *Pittsburgh Post-Gazette* article and in Ms. Shapiro's letter.

Women objectified

MAY 6, 2006

It is a sad comment on the state of our society that young men from a highly rated school district find nothing wrong in objectifying young women, humiliating them and possibly betraying their trust.

Does it really matter whether the list was compiled on school property? Obviously the school district and the parents of these young men fell down on the job when it came to instilling respect and good values in these young men.

And one has to wonder if the list had been a ranking of male students, teachers, administrators and/or police officers based on parts of their anatomies, whether the uproar and response would have been swifter, with more concern for the victims.

Celia Shapiro

1. Would it be possible to determine if the list was made on school grounds? Even if the list was not written on campus, is it the school's responsibility to investigate and discipline students?
2. Whose responsibility is it, as the writer puts it, to instill respect and values? Who should be held responsible for the actions of the perpetrators? Why?
3. Do you agree that a similar incident with male victims might have received swifter action? Why or why not?
4. The articles refer to due process rights in disciplinary actions. Do you have a sense that these rights will be granted? Why or why not?
5. Are the parents overreacting? Explain your reasoning.
6. The superintendent says there will be a "requirement for atonement." What do you envision this might be?

Your letter to the editor should be in response to the *Pittsburgh Post-Gazette* letter—supporting it, adding information, or refuting it. Write your letter in understandable terminology, remembering that readers of newspaper letters to the editor are citizens who may have limited knowledge of school practices and policies. Your letter may be written in your course notebook and shared with classmates as directed by your instructor. Remember to refer to the letter assessment rubric in Figure 1.10, page 20.

Disciplinary action. The need for disciplinary action is a fact of life in schools. The U.S. court system has been clear that schools have the right to administer a variety of punishments based on policy. Relatively minor rule infractions call for relatively minor consequences or punishment that may be administered at the classroom or school level. However, corporal punishment, or physical punishment, is controversial and subject to guidelines. Exclusionary discipline, or discipline that takes students out of school, such as suspension and expulsion, carries with it the need for student due process, or steps that protect student rights (Pauken, 2006).

Corporal Punishment. Chapter 7 briefly talked about corporal punishment in the discussion of classroom management (see page 220). Fewer than half of states allow corporal punishment, which may take the form of paddling or spanking. Even so, in many states that allow corporal punishment, efforts are under way to outlaw it. Individual districts may choose not to allow corporal punishment even if allowed by the state. People who are in favor of corporal punishment say it's necessary and educationally sound, while those who oppose it call it archaic, cruel, inhumane, and unjustifiable (LaMorte, 2005).

In *Ingraham* v. *Wright,* 1977, the Supreme Court found that corporal punishment does not violate the tenets of the Constitution. In this case two boys were paddled, causing bruises that kept them out of school for a few days. The court commented that schools can be held liable for injuries, but that students are not entitled to due process before district- or state-sanctioned corporal punishment is administered. The most common restrictions in states that permit corporal punishment are that only an administrator can spank or paddle a student and there must be an adult witness. Teachers can lose their jobs if they violate state laws or local policies related to corporal punishment, as upheld by courts in Texas, Michigan, Pennsylvania, and other states (Fischer et al., 2003).

Exclusionary Punishment. Excluding students from school through suspension or expulsion has been ruled a denial of property rights to an education. Suspension is time out of school that may range from 1 day to less than a semester, but is usually 10 days or less. **Expulsion** is more permanent and is generally for a semester or for an indefinite period.

Exclusionary punishment carries possible long-term consequences that may exceed the seriousness of the original offense. Any time away from school can be harmful to students in many ways, as discussed in the truancy section of Chapter 10 (see page 312). For instance, if a brief suspension causes a student to miss an exam, grades will suffer. Being out of school more than 10 days makes it almost impossible for a student to catch up. An expulsion almost always means a grade must be repeated. For some students a lengthy suspension or expulsion may make admission to college difficult or impossible. Students' future success depends in large measure on school success.

Students are entitled to due process when exclusionary punishment is imposed or when the rule infraction and resulting punishment will become part of a student's permanent record. In the case of *Goss* v. *Lopez,* 1975, several Ohio high school students were suspended for up to 10 days without receiving a hearing. The students maintained complete innocence and were never informed of what they were accused of doing. When a federal district court agreed with the boys in their suit against the school, administrators appealed to the U.S. Supreme Court, where the decision went in favor of the students again. The justices wrote that students have a property right in school and that they may not be withdrawn without due process that includes

- written notification of time and place of hearing, along with a description of the procedures to be followed
- list of evidence to be presented and names of witnesses
- description of the substance of witnesses' testimonies
- taped or written record of the proceedings and findings
- notification of the right to appeal (Fischer et al., 2003)

Have you ever received corporal punishment in a school setting? If so, how did it make you feel? Have you ever been suspended or expelled? If so, did the exclusionary punishment take care of whatever behavior it was intended to curb? How do you feel about these extreme punishments? Are they ever justified? If not, why not? If so, under what circumstances?

Just as due process protects students, so does their right not to participate in particular aspects of school.

Student right of nonparticipation. Students have a right to refuse to do several things in schools. Here are some that have been upheld in the courts.

- Students may refuse to recite the Pledge of Allegiance.
- Students may refuse to dance, even when it is part of the physical education curriculum.
- Students may have other literature substituted for the planned curriculum if they object for religious or other reasons.
- Students may opt out of certain courses (usually dealing with sex education) if they and their parents object to content.
- Parents may refuse to follow guidelines that require students to be immunized.

This list will no doubt grow as parents and students have their voices heard in the courts. Administrators and teachers need to be aware of students' rights to nonparticipation, or at least question the legitimacy of insisting on compliance with school policies and traditions. Likewise, educators need to be aware of privacy rights of students and families.

Student records: access and privacy. The **Family Educational Rights and Privacy Act (FERPA) of 1974,** commonly called the **Buckley Amendment,** allows parents and guardians access to their students' academic records and requires written parental permission for the records to be shared with anyone else. When students turn 18, they have control over who sees their records.

The Buckley Amendment establishes the minimum standards of privacy of records, with some states and districts going beyond to allow students access to their own records. Some items, however, are not subject to student or parent viewing. For instance, teachers' grade books, notes kept by teachers for their own use, and the private notes kept by school law enforcement teams typically remain inaccessible to others.

The extent to which student records must be kept private was tested when an Oklahoma parent challenged the long-standing practice of students grading each others' work in *Owasso Independent School District* v. *Falso,* 2002. The parent sued an Owasso school saying peer grading was embarrassing and often inaccurate. Because of conflicting court actions the case ended up in the U.S. Supreme Court, which ruled unanimously that day-to-day grading is not covered by FERPA. The Buckley Amendment, as with other laws, applies to all students without discrimination.

Right to nondiscrimination. Students (and teachers) may not legally be discriminated against by public schools. Discrimination cases that have been tested in U.S. courts have resulted in the following principles:

- Students of any race, religion, or disability may attend U.S. public schools.
- Students who are married, are parents, or are divorced may attend the same public schools as those who are not.
- Students with HIV/AIDS pose no significant risk to others and may attend public schools.

Not only are all students guaranteed the right to attend public schools, but the right has also been extended to extracurricular activities.

Figure 11.11 summarizes the cases in this section plus others that deal with students' rights. As an aspect of students' rights to nondiscrimination, religion is an emotionally charged topic, and the law is involved in setting boundaries between religion and school.

Figure 11.11   Case law: Student rights

***Tinker* v. *Des Moines Independent Community School District* (1969)**
The rights of students to wear armbands to protest the Vietnam War was upheld.

***Goss* v. *Lopez* (1975)**
Students suspended without due process; court ruled that school attendance is a property right.

***Ingraham* v. *Wright* (1977)**
Corporal punishment may be administered without due process.

***New Jersey* v. *T.L.O.* (1985)**
Student's purse searched after she was caught smoking; court ruled search was reasonable.

***Bethel School District No. 403* v. *Fraser* (1986)**
Student reprimanded for lewd language; court ruled school has the right to censure to avoid disruption.

***Hazelwood School District* v. *Kuhlmeier* (1988)**
Schools have the right to censure controversial articles in school publications.

***Isaacs* v. *Board of Education of Howard County* (1999)**
Student protesting "no hats" rule
A high school girl in Maryland was not allowed in school because she wore a head wrap to celebrate her cultural heritage and was in violation of the "no hats" rule. A judge ruled in favor of the school and commended the reasons they had for the rule, including

1. hats increase horseplay and conflicts
2. hats block teachers' and students' views in classrooms
3. hats allow students to hide drugs and other contraband
4. hats foster a less respectful learning climate

The judge concluded that it was unrealistic to expect schools to make hat-by-hat decisions.

***Davis* v. *Monroe County Board of Education* (1999)**
Student was sexually harassed; court ruled the school failed to act to protect her.

Sources: From *The Principal's Quick-Reference Guide to School Law: Reducing Liability, Litigation, and Other Potential Legal Tangles,* by D. R. Dunklee and R. J. Shoop, 2002, Thousand Oaks, CA: Corwin Press; *School Law: Cases and Concepts* (8th ed.), by M. W. LaMorte, 2005, Boston; Allyn & Bacon; *Teachers and the Law* (6th ed.), by L. Fischer, D. Schimmel, and L. R. Stellman, 2003, Boston: Allyn & Bacon.

How Does the Law Impact the Relationship Between School and Religion?

The First Amendment makes it clear that the founders of the United States did not want government to have any say in how or whether citizens worship. Since public schools are government entities, they may neither establish religion nor interfere with the free exercise of it. As clearly stated as it is in the Constitution, the issue is anything but clear-cut in practice.

In 1998 President Clinton asked Secretary of Education Richard Riley to prepare guidelines based on law and court decisions to help educators determine the rights of students and staff regarding religion and public schools. These guidelines, adapted to question format in Figure 11.12, remain applicable in the beginning decade of the 21st century.

There are few topics as charged with emotion and passion, and hence with such potential to polarize people, as religion. The next sections of this chapter will explore several of the issues presented in Figure 11.12.

Religion and Compulsory Education

Compulsory education laws require students to attend school through a certain age. *Pierce* v. *Society of Sisters,* 1925, established that compulsory education laws could be met through

Figure 11.12 Guidelines for religious expression in public schools from the U.S. Department of Education

Can students pray in school?

Yes. Student may pray individually or in a group as long as they are nondisruptive. For instance, students may pray before meals or tests to the same extent they may engage in comparable nondisruptive activities.

Can students read religious materials and discuss religion among themselves?

Yes. Students may read and talk about religion to the same extent as they may read and talk about anything else in school.

Can students meet to express their religious beliefs during the school day and on school grounds?

Yes. Students may meet for nondisruptive purposes during their lunch periods or other noninstructional time during the school day, as well as before and after the school day. This includes religion-related meetings.

Is it legal to have organized prayer at sporting events or other school functions?

No. Under current Supreme Court decisions, school officials may not mandate or organize prayer at any school-sponsored event or graduation.

Can teachers participate in religious meetings while at school?

No. Teachers and school administrators, when acting in those capacities, are representatives of the state and are prohibited from soliciting or encouraging religious activity and from participating in such activity with students.

Can teachers teach about religions in school?

Yes. Teachers may teach *about* religion, including the Bible or other scripture: the history of religion, comparative religion, the Bible (or other scripture)-as-literature, and the role of religion in the history of the United States and other countries. They may also prompt students to consider religious influences on art, music, literature, and social studies.

Can teachers display religious-related holiday items or encourage the celebration of religious holidays in school?

No. Although public schools may teach *about* religious holidays, including their religious aspects, and may celebrate the secular aspects of holidays, schools may not observe holidays as religious events or encourage students to do so.

Is it acceptable for students to express religious beliefs in school assignments?

Yes. Students may express their beliefs about religion in the form of homework, artwork, and other written and oral assignments free of discrimination based on the religious content of their work. The assignments should be graded according to the standards the lesson is intended to address.

If a lesson may be considered offensive by a student and/or the student's family, can the student opt not to participate?

Yes. Schools can excuse individual students from lessons that are objectionable to the student or the students' parents on religious or other conscientious grounds.

Can students opt out of a particular dress code or uniform for religious reasons?

Legally, the answer is no. However, schools have discretion to interpret this in ways that make sense in their communities.

Can students wear religious messages or symbols on their clothes?

Yes. The restrictions are the same as for any other comparable messages. Schools cannot single out religion-related messages and symbols to prohibit.

Source: Secretary's Statement on Religious Expression, by Richard W. Riley, 1998. Retrieved November 12, 2006, from www.ed.gov/inits/religionandschools. Adapted.

attendance at private or parochial schools (discussed in Chapter 2, pages 42–43). In the 1970s, Amish families asked to be exempt from compulsory education beyond eighth grade on the grounds that attendance in upper grades would have a negative effect on their traditions and way of life. The Supreme Court ruled in their favor in *Wisconsin v. Yoder,* 1972. This ruling is known as the "Amish exception." If non-Amish parents wish to isolate their children from public or private school beyond a particular grade (under age 16), they must show that school will somehow destroy their religion. Chapter 2 (see page 44) described homeschooling, a legal option with very few requirements or restraints. Because families aren't required to supply a reason for homeschooling, it is unknown how many families use their right to home-school their children as a way to avoid compulsory education laws. Another law that may be skirted through silence is the ruling against prayer in school.

Students may pray together on school grounds as long as it is not disruptive to the education process.

Prayer in School

Students may pray silently or quietly in small groups in school. But that's it. Legally there may be no school-sponsored public prayer, even nondenominational prayer (Underwood & Webb, 2006). This prohibition includes prayer at graduation ceremonies, football games, assemblies, and so on. In the case of *Santa Fe Independent School District* v. *Doe,* 2000, a Texas school district allowed students to vote on whether to have prayer and who would deliver it before football games. Groups of Mormon and Catholic students, alumni, and parents filed a suit claiming the district was violating the First Amendment. The U.S. Supreme Court ruled against the district, contending that the school would be endorsing a specific religion depending on who delivered the prayer.

Some communities choose to violate the First Amendment principle of separation of church and state by endorsing prayer in school-related settings. If challenged, they would likely lose in court. Some school boards even begin their meetings with prayer, often careful not to use language that would offend Christians or Jews. However, these prayers may offend Muslims, Buddhists, and other religious groups, as well as atheists. Regardless of who is present, prayer is not legal in public education meetings. However, prayer is allowed on school grounds when the facility is used by a religious group during nonschool hours.

Religious Organizations Meeting on School Grounds

If a school building is used before or after hours for organizations of any kind, it may also be used for organizations that are religious in nature. In *Good News Club* v. *Milford Central School,* 2001, the Supreme Court ruled that a private Christian organization for children ages 6 to 12 in New York could use a public school for weekly after-school meetings. Although some lower courts have ruled that teachers may be involved in student religious organizations on their own time, generally school employees may not sponsor the groups (Fischer et al., 2003). Nor may teachers sponsor or celebrate religious aspects of holidays in their classrooms.

Religious Holidays

Observing specific religious holidays in class is not allowed. This is a visible and controversial aspect of mixing school and religion. The longest traditional school breaks or vacations (other than summer) occur during Christian celebrations—December break at Christmas and spring break at Easter. The most controversial break is what was formerly called Christmas break and is now generally referred to as the winter holiday. The traditional holiday student presentation used to be called the Christmas Program; now the choral/band event may be the Holiday Program or the Winter Program. Students may sing Christmas songs with religious messages, such as "Silent Night," but these songs may not dominate the program.

Holiday displays that depict Christian or Christmas symbols may be used if they are balanced with other cultural symbols such as a Jewish menorah. They must be temporary and help show diversity (Underwood & Webb, 2006). Parents and students may request to be exempt from activities focused on holidays.

Holidays occur sporadically, but the public school curriculum is ongoing. Teachers face decisions about what to teach all day, every day.

Religion and Curriculum

Must schools do away with all reference to religion in order to separate church and state? The answer is no. It is permissible to teach about religion, but not with the purpose of convincing students that a particular belief should be followed. Use of the Bible, Talmud, Koran, and other religious books for teaching literature and history is permissible, as long as one is not endorsed over another.

Perhaps the greatest point of tension concerning religion and curriculum is the theory of evolution. In the so-called Scopes Monkey Trial, 1925, a high school teacher was convicted of violating a Tennessee regulation against teaching anything that contradicted the biblical Genesis account of the creation of humans. Although the conviction was overturned on a technicality, controversy over the teaching of evolution in schools has continued. In 1982 Louisiana passed the Balanced Treatment Act, which required the teaching of both creationism and evolution. The U.S. Supreme Court ruled the act illegal because it endorsed creationism, a Christian view, to the exclusion of other views. Some school districts, and even whole states, have attempted to give equal time to what some Christians believe about creation as embodied in the literal translation of the Bible, and evolution. Some districts have attempted to outlaw the teaching of evolution or to require a disclaimer stating that it is only a theory, and one of many that tries to explain the origin of humans. As you saw in Chapter 4 in the study of curriculum, this controversy is not likely to go away anytime soon.

Figure 11.13 summarizes the cases in this section plus two others that affect how religion and schools coexist. Did you or your family ever have religion-based views that

Figure 11.13 Case law: Religion in schools

***Wisconsin v. Yoder* (1972)**
Amish allowed to end formal education at eighth grade

***Stone v. Graham* (1980)**
Parents protest posting of Ten Commandments
A Kentucky statute required the posting of the Ten Commandments on the wall of every public school classroom. The plaques were purchased with private funds and had a notation describing them as secular. The posting was declared unconstitutional on the grounds that merely stating that the Ten Commandments (rooted in Judeo-Christian beliefs) were secular did not make them so.

***Herdahl v. Pontotoc County School District* (1996)**
Parent protested prayer in public school
A Mississippi mother sued a K–12 school for having prayers following morning announcements on the intercom. The court ruled that the practice violated separation of church and state because students are a captive audience. This case is an example of violations of already established law that continue to go through the judicial system.

***Santa Fe Independent School District v. Doe* (2000)**
Public prayer at school events violates the First Amendment because the school would be endorsing a specific religion, depending on who delivered the invocation.

***Good News Club v. Milford Central School* (2001)**
Student Christian group allowed to use school facilities

Source: From Education: The Practice and Profession of Teaching, *by R. F. McNergney and J. M. McNergney, 2007, Boston: Allyn & Bacon;* Teachers and the Law, *by L. Fischer, D. Schimmel, and L. R. Stellman, 2003, Boston: Allyn & Bacon.*

conflicted with events at your school? Were your views conservative (opposition to dancing, nonacceptance of evolution theory, nonparticipation when certain movies were shown, etc.)? Or were there restrictions imposed that you believed unnecessary?

For some people there is a direct connection between religious beliefs and ethics. For others, ethics deal solely with what is humane and civil in the relationships of people and events. The judicial system interprets the laws that govern what people can and can't do in schools; ethical guidelines speak to what people should and shouldn't do.

Concluding Thoughts

This chapter may seem overwhelming to you. In Chapter 10 you read about the negative influences of society on students, and in this chapter you've learned about legal responsibilities to which teachers must adhere, along with the rights legally afforded to teachers. It's a lot to comprehend.

Controversial issues, such as sex and AIDS education, Internet usage, school choice, high-stakes testing, school uniforms, protection for homosexual students, and funding for public education, continue to emerge and will no doubt prompt legal questions. The courts will interpret the Constitution or rely on case law to settle disputes. Teachers need to stay current on how laws affect what takes place in classrooms and schools.

When you choose to teach you make a commitment to a service profession. You take on the serious responsibility to not only abide by laws, but to continually promote what is ethical for students and for yourself in the big issues as well as in the seemingly minor issues that test you every day. You commit to thoughtful and deliberate decision making, the courage to do what's right for students, and the good sense to ask for advice and guidance when needed.

What Role Will Diversity Play in My Teaching Identity?

It is the teacher's responsibility to recognize all kinds of diversity among students and to make sure they are treated fairly and afforded the same rights. Your teaching identity may place you in schools where diversity doesn't appear to be much of a factor in the education of students, or it may place you in schools where the amount and kinds of diversity among students will require you to be vigilant and serve as a monitor of how laws and rules are enforced.

Serving *in loco parentis* goes beyond nondiscrimination. It's more than making sure laws and rules are followed that prevent blatant mistreatment of students because they are different in some way. Acting in place of parents while students are in their care requires teachers to be proactively responsive to each and every child in ways that take their differences into account. Because of diversity, students may require different kinds of protection and motivation. This is where teacher ethics come into play.

Chapter in Review

What does it mean to be an ethical teacher?

- Laws tell us what we can and can't do. Ethics tell us what we should and shouldn't do.
- To be an ethical teacher means to be guided by a set of beliefs that lead to attitudes and actions focused on what's best for students.

- Six characteristics that help teachers make ethical decisions include appreciation for moral deliberation, empathy, knowledge, reasoning, courage, and interpersonal skills.
- The National Education Association provides a professional code of ethics for educators.

How do laws affect schools, teachers, and students?

- The laws that affect schools, teachers, and students are based on a balance of rights and responsibilities.
- Four basic sources of law directly impact the work of teachers: the U.S. Constitution, federal laws, state and local laws and policies, and case law.

What are the legal rights of teachers?

- The legalities of employment include contracts, tenure, and dismissal.
- Due process involves a set of guidelines that must be followed to ensure that individuals are protected from arbitrary or capricious treatment by those in authority.
- Teachers enjoy the same rights as other citizens, including freedom of expression, whether symbolic, written, or spoken, but with restraints based on the responsibilities of teaching.
- Academic freedom is a form of expression that allows teachers to use their judgment concerning what and how to teach.
- Teachers have some restrictions on their personal lives that other people do not have because of the nature of the profession.

What are the legal responsibilities of teachers?

- Teachers serve *in loco parentis* and are responsible to care for and protect the students they supervise.
- Among other things, teachers have the legal responsibility to avoid liability, abide by copyright laws, and report suspected child abuse.

What are the legal rights of students?

- Court decisions attempt to balance the rights of students to express themselves and the necessity of limiting personal freedom to ensure the safety and well-being of others.
- Students have freedom of symbolic expression, speech, and the press.
- Student privacy is protected from unreasonable search and seizure.
- Students have the right not to be sexually harassed.
- Students have due process rights when facing serious disciplinary action.
- Students and parents have rights concerning privacy and access to records.
- Students may not legally be discriminated against by public schools.

How does the law impact the relationship between school and religion?

- The First Amendment says that government (public schools) can neither establish religion nor interfere with the free exercise of it.
- Public prayer is illegal in public school. Religious organizations may meet and pray in school facilities outside regular school hours.
- It is permissible to teach about religion, but not with the purpose of persuading students to believe in a particular religion.

Professional Practice

Licensure Test Prep

Answer multiple-choice items 1–6.

1. The NEA Code of Ethics
   a. is divided into three sections: teacher commitment to students, teacher commitment to the profession, and parent commitment to the education of children.
   b. inspires teachers by addressing the positive side of ethical behavior.
   c. primarily lists what teachers should not do.
   d. is a code used by school districts on teacher contracts.

2. Which statement is true?
   a. What is lawful is generally legal.
   b. What is ethical is always legal.
   c. What is legal is always ethical.
   d. There is little relationship between what is lawful and what is ethical.

3. Laws that stem from real situations result in
   a. constitutional law.
   b. state law.
   c. federal law.
   d. case law.

4. Recent court decisions to dismiss teachers include all of the following behaviors except
   a. neglect of duty.
   b. pregnancy outside marriage.
   c. causing or encouraging civil disruptions.
   d. physical or mental problems.

5. Jennifer Blandon teaches fifth grade at Morrow Elementary School. Her class has just finished reading *Holes*. Although the movie made from the book is available on DVD, Jennifer wants her students to take a field trip to the theater that is showing the movie as a matinee. She also thinks the event will serve as a reward for the hard work the class has done on their projects related to the book. When permission slips go home to parents, two students return the forms with notes from parents saying that their children are not allowed to go to theaters for religious reasons. Jennifer didn't realize that some people do not go to theaters. She needs to quickly make a decision about how to proceed. Which option most effectively meets the needs of all the students?
   a. Rent the DVD and ask the media specialist to show it for the two students who stay behind.
   b. Develop an enjoyable project related to *Holes* for the two students to work on while the class is on the field trip.
   c. Call the parents to tell them about the trip and try to persuade them to allow their students to attend.
   d. Cancel the field trip and show the whole class the *Holes* DVD.

6. Sadie Nix is passionate about a lot of things. She is vocal about issues and supports causes with enthusiasm. Which of the following symbolic expressions might get Sadie into trouble with her administrators?
   a. ribbon to support AIDS research
   b. support ribbons for military troops
   c. political buttons in support of school board candidates
   d. black armband worn to protest an unpopular war

Standards Speak

INTASC Knowledge, Principle 10

The teacher understands and implements laws related to student rights and teacher responsibilities (e.g., for equal education, appropriate education for handicapped students, confidentiality, privacy, appropriate treatment of students, reporting in situations related to possible child abuse).

NBPTS

Teachers employ technical knowledge and skill, yet must be ever mindful of teaching's ethical dimensions.

Respond to the following questions in your class notebook and/or discuss your responses with your classmates as directed by your instructor.

1. The INTASC standard says that a teacher "understands and implements laws. . . ." Is it a teacher's responsibility to explore laws as they relate to teaching?

2. If an ethical dilemma arises, what should a relatively new teacher do? Should the teacher seek advice? Under what circumstances might a teacher make decisions based on personal ethics without consulting another teacher or administrator?

MyEducationLab

The following interactive features may be found in Chapter 11 of MyEducationLab.

Homework and Exercises

Writing My Own Story

To write your own story by responding to some of the questions in the text accompanied by fingerprint icons, plus others, go to the "Writing My Own Story" section of the Homework and Exercises for Chapter 11 of MyEducationLab.

What's My Disposition?

To reflect on your beliefs and attitudes concerning the teaching profession, go to Chapter 11 "What's My Disposition?" feature of the Homework and Exercises section of MyEducationLab. the Homework and Exercises folder of MyEducationLab for this text.

Exploring Schools and Classrooms

If your course involves experiences in schools, the questions and prompts in the "Exploring Schools and Classrooms" feature of Chapter 11's Homework and Exercises section of MyEducationLab will guide you as you explore local schools and classrooms.

Virtual Field Experience

To respond to questions and prompts regarding the Choosing Your Teaching Path videos that connect to specific chapter content, go to Chapter 11's Virtual Field Experience section of MyEducationLab. The questions will help you make sense of what you have read in the chapter.

Chapter 12

Governing and Financing Public Schools in the United States

Teaching in Focus

Chris Roberts and Brenda Beyal teach in multiage classrooms of third, fourth, and fifth graders at Rees Elementary, Utah, along with colleague Tim Mendenhall, as explained in Chapter 1 (see pages 24–25). You have gotten to know all three through this text's video. You may review the classrooms and interviews of each teacher on this unique team by going to the Choosing Your Teaching Path section of MyEducationLab at www.myeducationlab.com. Click on Rees Elementary, and then on the teacher's name.

Multiage classrooms are not the norm. Teachers or administrators must have an interest in initiating the concept. Chris, as a former special education teacher, is very aware that students of different ages can actually learn at the same level and rate. Brenda, a teacher who routinely finds ways to individualize instruction, knows that the learning capabilities of students the same age can vary widely. Experience taught them both that 8–12-year-olds may be able to grasp some concepts at the same time from basically the same experiences, whereas other concepts may come easily or prove more difficult for individual students regardless of age. This knowledge prompted Chris and Brenda to join together to establish multiage classes.

Chris and Brenda, as accomplished and respected teachers, had workable plans to go with their idea. After hours of talking and planning, and with the support of their principal at Rees Elementary, the idea of multiage education was approved by district authorities.

Chris and Brenda knew a little about what was involved in establishing multiage classes, but they learned so much more from working through the approval process, beginning with the principal, then the district director of elementary education, and, finally, the school board and superintendent. Although school board approval was almost automatic once the district director of elementary education endorsed the plan, Chris and Brenda still needed to present their ideas in a formal meeting of the board and superintendent.

Most teachers get to know the system of public school governance and where funding comes from only when the need arises or when a particular issue demands their attention. Developing an overview now will help you put what you read in the newspaper or see on TV—about school board proceedings, hiring of administrators, legislative decisions, test score reports, and so on—in context.

This chapter will review all levels of public school governance, as well as how public schools are financed. As we explore the complex array of individuals and groups that have governing and financial authority over public schools in the United States, we'll consider the following questions:

- How does the federal government influence public education in the United States?
- What is the state's role in public education?
- How do school districts function?
- What is the management structure of individual schools?
- What other entities impact the governance of public schools in the United States?
- How are public schools financed?
- How are funds for education spent?

■ Introduction

Exploring how schools are governed and financed may seem boring, or overwhelming, or both. Some teachers appear to have no desire to know about either topic. It's true that a teacher's primary responsibility is the classroom and the students that go in and out 180 days a year. But not to know or care about the larger system within which individual schools function is not to fully participate in the teaching profession.

A complex system of people and policies makes it possible for teachers to teach and students to learn. How are the geographic boundaries drawn that determine who attends your school? If the principal is your boss, who is the principal's boss, and what's the chain of command? Who decides whether your school building gets a new wing and how it is financed? Who decides what standardized tests your students take? Why do you have so many forms to fill out? These questions, and a myriad more, are all related to the governance and financing of public schools in the United States.

Teachers can't make programmatic changes themselves. For instance, when Chris and Brenda decided they wanted to have multiage classes, they needed permission to change the organizational structure at their school. In some districts principals are allowed to make such decisions. In others, each school has a committee of parents, community members, teachers, and administrators that makes programmatic decisions. In yet other districts, district school boards must approve requests for programmatic changes. Making decisions such as these is a basic function within a structure of school governance.

This chapter will discuss the layers of school governance illustrated in Figure 12.1. While local governance most directly affects what happens in schools, the discussion here will begin with the more remote, yet important influences at the federal and state levels. School governance begins with the Constitution, which, by not addressing education, leaves this particular responsibility to individual states. As you probably already realize, however, during the last century the federal government has gradually assumed some programmatic and financial responsibilities. Consequently, both federal and state governments share influence as they delegate responsibility to the individual school districts within which schools function. As the chapter explores each layer of governance, details will be added to charts similar to the one in Figure 12.1. Also, other people and groups that impact school governance will be discussed briefly. Once the governance stage is set, we'll examine where money comes from and how it is distributed throughout the public education system.

Figure 12.1 Overview of American public school governance

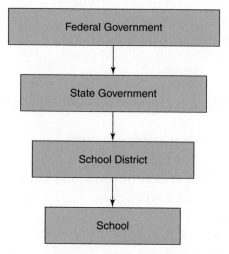

■ How Does the Federal Government Influence Public Education in the United States?

Throughout the last century the federal government played an increasingly significant role in the functioning of schools through the institutions and agencies shown in Figure 12.2, among others. Let's take a look at each.

Presidential Influence

Almost every presidential candidate in the 20th century included education in the campaign platform; most had boldly articulated plans and promises. President Ronald Reagan (1980–1988) was the first president to experience the U.S. Department of Education (established in 1857) as a cabinet-level agency during his entire presidency. President Bill Clinton (1992–2000) was proactive in efforts to ensure equitable educational opportunities, and he worked vigorously toward achieving the objectives of *Goals 2000,* an ambitious list of goals for students in U.S. public schools that have not yet been met. President George W. Bush's legacy (2000–2008) regarding education centers on the No Child Left Behind Act of 2001, which has been discussed throughout this text. The U.S. Congress and federal courts, as well as the U.S. Department of Education, play important roles in the governance of public schools in the United States.

Congress and the Courts

The U.S. Congress has passed many influential laws regarding education, and the federal court system has made numerous rulings impacting education, as we saw in Chapter 11. For example, in 1944 the Serviceman's Readjustment Act, also known as the GI Bill, was signed into law by President Franklin Roosevelt to provide veterans with college tuition, room, and board. The GI Bill continues to provide higher-education opportunities for

Figure 12.2 Federal government role in American public school governance

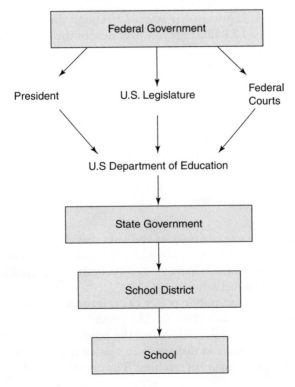

American veterans. The Bilingual Education Act of 1968 made provisions for English language instruction. The Education for All Handicapped Children Act of 1975 was the first to guarantee a free public education for students with disabilities, as discussed in Chapter 3 (see page 94). The most recent major federal legislation regarding public education, the No Child Left Behind Act of 2001, has had the most impact on K–12 students of any federal legislation to date.

U.S. Department of Education

The U.S. Department of Education has had some influential secretaries over the years. The term *secretary* as used here indicates the head of a presidential cabinet-level department. The secretary of education is chosen and appointed by the president, hence the position is political. The incumbents' favor with citizens and educators rises and falls with the popularity of the president and the party in power. The secretary of education influences policies established by the U.S. Department of Education, which has a sizable budget and exercises its power through these policies and programs. The federal government sponsors programs that impact schools and students. For instance, Head Start and the National School Lunch Program both benefit children in low-socioeconomic settings.

Funding provided to schools by the federal government (more on this later in the chapter) is distributed in the form of assistance to implement approved programs and to conduct educational research. The funds are also used as leverage to help ensure that state departments of education comply with specific mandates, such as guidelines and policies related to attempts to equalize educational opportunities for all children, and widespread testing programs. In many cases states may choose whether to comply with U.S. Department of Education policies. However, the federal government withholds funds from states and their schools when states choose not to comply.

Think about how students would benefit if every person at the federal level who plays a role in public education continually asked and answered the question, "And how are the children?"

What Is the State's Role in Public Education?

Each state has its own unique governance system, although the various systems share many common elements. Figure 12.3 illustrates an overview of the basic structure that exists in most states.

State Government

State constitutions call for states to utilize a balance of power with three major branches of government, similar to what exists at the federal level. Governors have executive authority, legislatures have lawmaking authority, and state courts uphold and interpret laws as well as establish constitutional guidelines. Governors, as leaders of state governments, have tremendous influence on public schools. A governor's attitude toward education is quite public and has far-reaching influence.

Governors. Governors impact state policies and laws that directly affect schools. In many states the governor appoints the state's chief education officer, as well as members of the state board of education. Governors make budget recommendations and can veto bills that might benefit or adversely affect schools.

One of the most respected public policy organizations in Washington, D.C., is the **National Governors Association (NGA).** The NGA Center for Best Practices is an on-line clearinghouse that provides governors and the public with information about public education, including such topics as disparities in academic achievement, turning around low-performing schools, and quality of teaching. The organization describes policy options

Figure 12.3   State government role in American public school governance

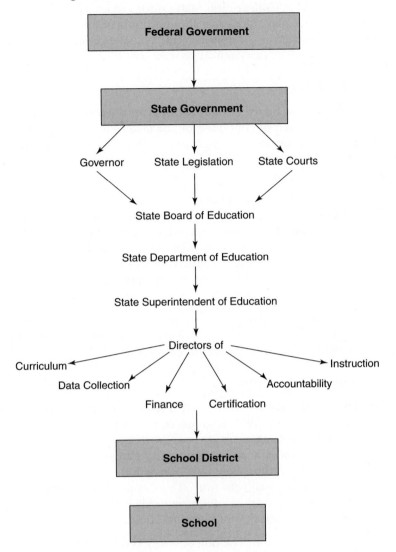

for states, identifies how states cope with dilemmas pertaining to education, helps governors establish and maintain quality education in their states, and counsels them on how to work effectively with state legislatures (National Governors Association [NGA], 2006).

State legislatures. Members of state legislatures have significant influence on public education. State legislators impact schools as they determine

- state laws that affect every aspect of public education
- how state chief officers of education and state school board members are selected
- responsibilities of state-level school officials
- how taxes are used to support schools
- the general direction of the curriculum
- the length of the school day and year
- aspects of teacher employment, including issues involving tenure, retirement, and collective bargaining

There are no requirements in terms of educational background or experience for members of state legislatures. Teachers and school administrators sometime question the wisdom of decisions made in the legislature. Having conversations, inviting legislators to visit schools, and writing letters are vehicles for influencing legislative viewpoints. It is, however, more difficult to influence decisions made in state courts.

State courts. When state laws require interpretation, or when there is a question of conflict with the state or the U.S. Constitution, state courts can impact public education. State courts hear arguments and make decisions about school compliance with state laws that are often written in broad terms. In doing so, the courts examine policies developed by the state board of education to carry out these state laws.

State Board of Education

Almost every state has a **state board of education,** generally comprising seven to nine volunteers who are either elected or appointed by the governor. State legislatures give state boards oversight authority; in other words, state boards act in regulatory and advisory capacities. State boards of education make major decisions concerning the operation of public schools as they

- set goals and approve standards and assessments for schools
- establish the standards by which schools are accredited (allowed to function)
- advise the governor and the legislature on educational issues
- make many of the decisions about how state funds are used
- represent and report to the public on education issues
- serve as the governing body of the state department of education (National Association of State Boards of Education, 2005)

While the state board of education is primarily a policy-making body with broad responsibilities, the many detailed responsibilities that deal with education on a statewide basis are overseen by the state's department of education.

State Department of Education

A **state department of education** (also known as state office of education or department of public instruction) operates under the guidance of the governor, legislature, and state board of education. These state agencies are large, with a complex array of responsibilities and employees. While governors, state legislators, and state board members may not have expertise in education, most of those who hold nonclerical positions within a state department of education are professional educators. There is one notable exception. The chief state officer, or state superintendent of education, is likely to be either publicly elected or a political appointee and may not be a professional educator.

State superintendent of education. The one person given the responsibility of managing the state department of education may be called **state superintendent,** chief state education officer, or commissioner of education. This person may either be elected by the voters or appointed by the governor or state school board (Council of Chief State School Officers, 2006). The state superintendent position is both public and political. The superintendent is in charge of the bureaucracy that is usually centralized in the state's capital city. Additionally, the superintendent travels throughout the state as the acknowledged authority on how schools operate and are assessed for effectiveness. The superintendent oversees all the responsibilities of the state department of education.

State department of education responsibilities. The state superintendent of education generally has a large staff of individuals with varied expertise. The people who work as department directors are in charge of divisions within the state department that address, among other things,

- teacher certification (or licensure)
- curriculum standards and accountability
- instruction (usually a director for each content area)
- special education
- school levels (high, middle, elementary, early childhood)
- technology

- charter schools
- teacher professional development
- state budget funds
- communication and public relations
- collection and reporting of school data

The No Child Left Behind (NCLB) legislation requires states to ensure that all students, regardless of their differences, score at the proficient level on state standardized assessments by 2014, or the states will lose federal funding. This mandate has increased the involvement and power of statewide beauracracies. It is not uncommon for a state department of education to take over the operation of a school, or even of an entire school district, that is deemed unsatisfactory according to NCLB. As state departments of education wield this power, they should consistently ask and answer the question, "And how are the children?"

Directors at the state level are in charge of teacher certification, curriculum standards and accountability, content area instruction, levels of schools, educational technology, teacher professional development, and more.

How Do School Districts Function?

A **school district** is an organizational structure of local schools defined by geographic boundaries. Figure 12.4 provides an overview of the basic structure that exists in most school districts.

Typically a school district will include at least one **feeder system** of schools—early childhood/elementary schools that feed into middle schools that feed into a particular high school. There are about 15,000 school districts in the United States. In the early-to-mid-20th century there were almost 10 times as many. The decrease occurred as officials realized it was more efficient to combine small districts and share services and administration. Interestingly, the entire state of Hawaii is one school district, whereas the state of Texas has more than 1,000 separate districts (National Center for Education Statistics [NCES], 2002).

School districts vary greatly in size, from one building that houses all grade levels of students, as in Gilpin County School District in Colorado with about 300 students, to New York City public schools, with over 1 million students. Small and large districts have distinct advantages as well as limitations. Small and medium-size districts have the advantage of accessibility. Teachers feel as though they can be heard in policy matters and parents often sense a distinct connection to the schools and faculty. In very large districts teachers may sense that they are far removed from where policy decisions are made. Large districts generally have the advantage of having numerous services available and specialists to oversee the many aspects of life in schools and classrooms. In small and medium-size districts, individuals tend to have an array of duties, and fewer curricular and service options are offered. Regardless of size or complexity, each district has a school board and a superintendent who function as leaders of central administration.

Were your K–12 experiences in a small, medium, or large district? How do you think the size of your district affected the operation of your schools? Were you aware of any advantages or limitations because of the size of your district? Did you attend school from kindergarten through twelfth grade in one feeder system, or did you move frequently? Remember that when you see a fingerprint in the margin it means that you will be asked to respond to questions and prompts based on your experiences and opinions. These questions are included

Your Teaching Fingerprint

Figure 12.4   School-district role in American public school governance

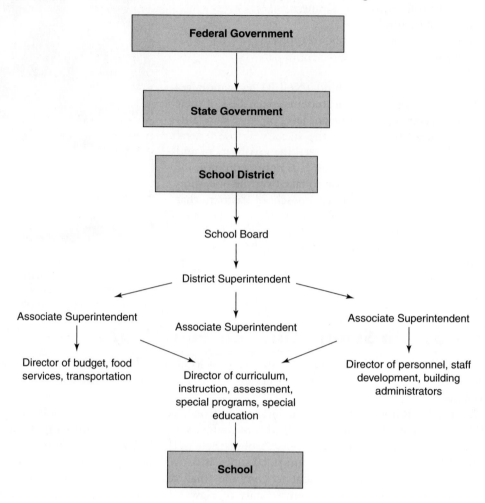

in "Writing My Own Story" in Chapter 12 of the Homework and Exercises section of MyEducationLab at www.myeducationlab.com.

District School Boards

District school boards are unique American institutions composed of elected citizens who volunteer their time. Most members are noneducators, and only a third of them receive any kind of compensation. This form of governance originated in the locally controlled schools of the colonies and in the common schools movement you learned about in Chapter 8 (see pages 249–250) (Hess, 2002). District school board members are responsible for setting policies that affect the operation of schools.

Board elections. It is costly to campaign for a school board seat, especially in medium to large districts (20,000 students plus). There are two basic kinds of school board elections: both at-large and single-member elections allow citizens to vote for representative members. In at-large elections, voters may vote for any candidate regardless of the area in the district the candidate represents. So if there are five distinct areas in a school district, each will have specific candidates who live in the areas, but *every* voter in the *entire* district may vote for their choices regardless of where they live.

In single-member elections, only those who live in a specific area can vote for the representatives in their area. The single-member process has the potential to elect more representative school board members because neighborhoods with large minority populations are more likely to have candidates and voters who share ethnicity and socioeconomic status. The school board profile in Figure 12.5 reveals that the majority of school board members are White males over the age of 40 with incomes exceeding $50,000. District school board members are not representative of the families of many students in the United States.

Board duties. In a 2002 poll sponsored by the National School Boards Association, the five biggest concerns and responsibilities of school board members from small, medium, and large districts were funding, student achievement, teacher quality, improving technology, and special education (Hess, 2002). Dealing with these concerns and fulfilling other duties require numerous meetings and research. Among other responsibilities, school board members

- decide how much money will be spent on teacher salaries, facilities improvement, instructional materials, and so on
- hire and fire personnel, both professional and classified (clerical, custodial, etc.)
- approve and evaluate programs that may affect some or all schools, teachers, and students within the district
- make curricular decisions within state guidelines
- determine organizational policy

School boards and the public. Have you observed the functioning of a district school board, either firsthand or through television news or newspapers? What impressions did you have? You have likely witnessed the controversial nature of being a school board member. School board members are easy targets for both verbal and written chastisement of the

Figure 12.5 Profile of school board members

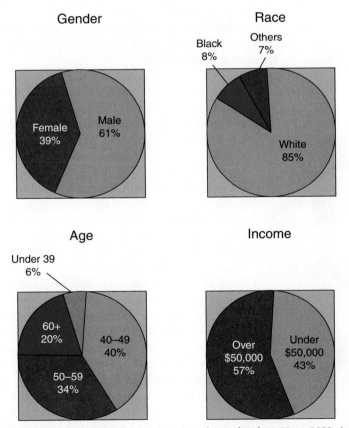

Source: From *School Boards at the Dawn of the 21st Century,* by Frederick M. Hess, 2002, Arlington, VA: National School Boards Association. Available at http://www.nsba.org/site/docs/1200/1143.pdf

community. It's a rare moment indeed when school board members are not perceived by some segment of the population as incompetent, downright stupid, or even evil. As trustees of public schools, their often unappreciated position requires them to make hard decisions. When one group feels slighted or excluded, the board hears its complaints and makes decisions. When it makes fiscal (monetary) sense to close a school, parts of the community storm the board with emotionally charged, often valid, objections. The board listens and makes decisions. When community groups work diligently to help improve education for all students and present research and suggestions, the board listens and makes decisions. When teachers take positions on issues such as board choices to transfer administrators, or program alterations, they make their case to the school board. The board listens and makes decisions.

Your Teaching Fingerprint

With all this responsibility, and frequent community wrath, why would any citizen want to be a school board member? Many do it as a service to the community. They have a genuine interest in doing what they can to benefit local schools. Others see the position as a source of power and visibility, and perhaps a stepping stone to other elected positions. Regardless of their motivations, school board members dedicate long hours to the governance of public schools, including the hiring of a chief executive officer.

District Superintendent and Staff

A **superintendent** functions as the school district's chief executive officer. The superintendent is hired by the board and serves at their pleasure, which means the board can also dismiss the superintendent. The superintendent is expected to both advise the board and carry out board policies. As largely noneducators, board members usually choose an educator as superintendent to keep schools running smoothly and successfully on a day-to-day basis. It can be an awkward arrangement when school board members go beyond policy making into what is considered the authority of the superintendent, for instance, when board members get involved in day-to-day operations. This practice is sometimes referred to as **micromanagement.**

In small districts, superintendents may handle all the responsibilities listed in Figure 12.4. The larger the district, the more necessary it is for the superintendent to delegate duties. Associate or assistant superintendents handle specific duties, as illustrated in Figure 12.4, and may have staff members who supervise subject area directors. Medium and large districts may also have associate superintendents in charge of each level of school—early childhood, elementary, middle, and high. They work with district curriculum and instruction directors to coordinate efforts. Larger districts also have associate superintendents in charge of areas such as personnel, facilities, and finance. All these district administrators should consistently ask and answer, "And how are the children? Are they all well?"

Community members not involved in education, as well as many parents of school-age children, sometimes complain that there are too many administrators and non–classroom teachers doing supervisory work rather than directly teaching children. Before making this judgment, citizens need to recognize the complexity and enormity of doing school right. From the U.S. Constitution and the federal and state governments to the school districts, many people and organizations work hard to support teachers and students in their classrooms.

Teachers, families, and community members voice their questions and opinions at public school board meetings.

What Is the Management Structure of Individual Schools?

Now we will consider individual schools—the places where teachers and students interact. Within the school building, the management structure often depends on both the size and the level of the school. Figure 12.6 lists some of the people who may contribute to the management structure. The one constant person in almost all school-building-level management structures is the principal.

Principals

The **principal** oversees every aspect of school life and answers to the district for all that occurs at the school. The principal's role involves administrative tasks such as facility maintenance, attendance, discipline, parent and community relationships and communication, transportation, and all manner of paperwork. Principals are also instructional leaders with knowledge of, and experience with, the teaching and learning process. Instructional leaders have the ability to make positive suggestions and model practices that enhance student learning (Sergiovani, 2001). A principal who is an instructional leader focuses teachers on improved learning for all students. Many principals who are confident in their administrative and instructional leadership skills believe in the benefits of sharing leadership with teachers and members of the community, as noted in the following discussion.

Site-based management. In *Leadership Capacity for Lasting School Improvement* by Linda Lambert (2003), we are told that the most effective principals build leadership capacity in teachers and others who are sincerely interested in student learning. **Site-based management** is a form of local school governance that puts much of the decision-making power regarding curriculum, textbooks, student behavior, staff development, budget, and hiring in the hands of teachers and family or community members. Principals who want to share leadership and management of schools employ some or all of the actions listed in Figure 12.7. Serving on a site-based management team gives teachers deeper insight into the role of the principal.

Figure 12.6 Local public school governance

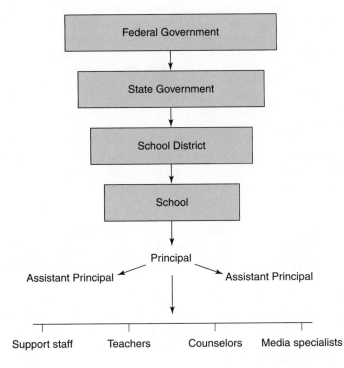

Figure 12.7 Building leadership capacity

Principals who build leadership capacity in teachers and others

- develop a shared vision based on community values
- organize, focus, and sustain the conversations about teaching and learning
- insist that students' learning is at the center of the conversation
- protect and interpret community values, assuring a focus on and congruence with teaching and learning approaches
- work through the evaluation and district personnel systems to dismiss ineffective teachers
- work with all participants to implement community decisions
- develop reciprocal relationships with the larger system, such as by securing support and resources

Source: From *Leadership Capacity for Lasting School Improvement,* by L. Lambert, 2003, Alexandria, VA: Association for Supervision and Curriculum Development.

Teachers' Days, Delights, and Dilemmas

Dana Boyd
2007 Texas
Teacher
of the Year

As a teacher I recognize that the learning that takes place in my classroom is in large measure dependent on what I view as the big picture of public education. I have a professional responsibility to be involved. From grade-level committees, to involvement in our Campus Educational Improvement Committee, to participation in the Texas State Teachers Association, I am determined to have my voice heard in matters that affect teaching and learning.

There are issues that I know I can affect. My school is given a budget to spend in ways that are tailored to our student population. Teachers have a voice in how a portion of the money is spent. Our principal works closely with each grade level as teachers make decisions about curriculum and instruction. Serving on textbook adoption committees gives us a voice in the materials available in our classrooms. Even with the

mandates of No Child Left Behind, teachers are free to make decisions about how to present content related to our state standards.

Then there are issues that seem somewhat beyond my personal ability to affect. Most of the teachers I know feel that children are overtested. It's not that we are against accountability. Of course we believe we have a responsibility to teach so that children learn. But while those outside the public schools tend only to applaud grand leaps in test scores, classroom teachers see even small steps of growth in individual children as reason for celebration.

Another issue that bothers me is that children in districts with many low-income families generally find themselves in underfunded schools. I know this is true for most of the nation. Of course this isn't right, but it's such a big and often complicated issue that I often feel powerless to make a difference.

The Texas State Teachers Association has over 2.8 million members. This organization advocates for improvement in education for all children even as it works to improve salaries, rights, and benefits for all educational employees. While one voice may be overwhelmed, it's hard to ignore millions!

I love what I do in the classroom. Teaching is a wonderful profession. And as a professional, my involvement at all levels is important.

In this chapter's Teachers' Days, Delights, and Dilemmas, the 2007 Texas Teacher of the Year tells about her involvement not only in a site-based decision-making committee, but also in a variety of other areas beyond her individual classroom responsibilities.

Your Teaching
Fingerprint

Understanding the role of principal. What do you remember about your schools' principals? Were they accessible, or did they seem aloof? Did you view them as disciplinarians to be feared, or as friendly adults who were helpful to teachers, parents, and students?

Figure 12.8 Focus principals

Laura Hill
Summit Primary
School, Ohio

Mike Larsen
Rees Elementary
School, Utah

Carol Bartlett
Cario Middle School,
South Carolina

Maria Romero
Roosevelt
High School,
California

Your memories of the principals you have experienced may factor into how you view your first principal when you become a teacher. As a beginning teacher, your principal will have a major impact on you. He or she will select you and ask that the school board hire you, will determine the grade level or subject you will teach, will likely assign a teacher mentor for you, will evaluate your teaching performance, and will make the decision whether to offer you a contract for the following year. Principals have multiple responsibilities and answer to various constituencies, including superintendents, community members, families, and teachers. They are often privy to information that impacts their decisions, some of which they cannot share with their staffs. Too many teachers tend to pass judgment on a principal's decisions and sometimes hold grudges. As a new teacher you need to realize that you won't always understand why or how decisions are made. Your best path is to be supportive of your principal and helpful to the programs and people aligned with your school's mission. Never be quick to side with fractious or very verbal teachers who are quick to criticize and who may attempt to undermine the school administration.

On this text's video, you met four principals: Laura Hill at Summit Primary School (Ohio), Mike Larsen at Rees Elementary (Utah), Carol Bartlett at Cario Middle School (South Carolina), and Maria Romero at Roosevelt High School (California). Their pictures are in Figure 12.8. Review their approaches to leadership that shine through their descriptions of their schools, students, and teachers by going to the Choosing Your Teaching Path section of MyEducationLab. Click on the school name, and then on the principal's name. Do these four principals appear to be the kinds of leaders you could respect? Would you want to teach in their schools?

Figure 12.9 illustrates gender and racial characteristics of school district superintendents and principals at the secondary (high school/middle school) and elementary levels. You will notice that the overwhelming majority of these school leaders are White, and, with the exception of elementary leaders, are also male. Regardless of their gender or race, most principals in all but small schools (fewer than 400 or so students) generally receive help in fulfilling their administrative and instructional leadership roles from assistant principals.

Your Teaching
Fingerprint

Assistant Principals

The position of assistant principal entails a variety of duties. If there is only one in a school, then the responsibilities may be general and similar to the principal's, or as specific as the principal chooses to make them. When there are multiple assistants, they generally have designated areas of responsibility. For instance, a medium-size elementary school (400–700 students) may have a principal and one assistant who may do various aspects of the principal's job, depending on day-to-day needs. A large middle school (more than 1,000 students) may have a principal and three assistants, each responsible for a grade level. A principal of a large high school (more than 1,500 students) may have more than three assistants, who specialize in student discipline, athletics and extracurricular activities, transportation and materials, and so on. Teachers will often work with assistant principals.

Figure 12.9 Profile of school administrators

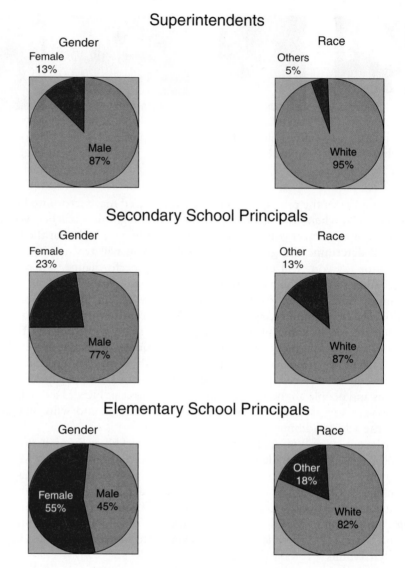

Source: From *Characteristics of School Principals,* by the National Center for Education Statistics, 2001. Retrieved July 8, 2006, from http://www.nces.ed.gov. Also from *The Study of the American Superintendency,* by T. E. Glass, L. Bjork, and C. C. Brunner, 2000, Arlington, VA: American Association of School Administrators.

A teacher in a large school may be more connected with the assistant principal(s) than with the principal. Teachers who assume extra responsibilities will likely become part of the school management team, along with the principal and the assistant(s).

Teacher Leaders

A growing number of teachers with specialized training are relieved of some or all of their classroom teaching duties in order to lead a grade level or be an in-school subject area expert. For instance, a school may have an instructional coach, a teacher who works with individual teachers as they improve or add to their toolboxes of instructional strategies (see Chapter 4, page 130). Another school may have a math specialist who teaches math to all fourth and fifth graders, regardless of their homeroom. These teacher leaders become part of the school management team along with the principal and assistant principal(s). Chapter 13 will explore ways that teachers can serve in specific leadership capacities, as well as how all teachers can be leaders.

Assistant principals may be perceived as stern in their role of student disciplinarian, and yet be approachable as supporters of teachers.

Many individuals and organizations impact public schools in the United States. We have looked at those who hold positions inside and outside the school building. Now we'll look at other influences.

■ What Other Entities Impact the Governance of Public Schools in the United States?

The actual governance of public schools is in the hands of the individuals and groups discussed so far in this chapter. Their decisions about policies and laws, however, are influenced by many constituencies. Among them are parents, businesses, universities, and special interest groups.

Parents

Parents, including step-parents, foster parents, and guardians, have the potential to be among the most influential players in the education of children. Parents, by virtue of their position, are influential in the lives of their own children and, if they are informed and involved in schools, can make a positive difference in the lives of many children in their local schools. One question is, "How can they do this?" But perhaps even more important to ask is, "Why don't they do it more often?" Chapter 13 will examine this issue.

One way for parents to be involved in the life of the school is through the Parent Teacher Association (PTA), a national organization with millions of members at thousands of schools across the country. School PTAs have varying degrees of impact. Some groups boast large numbers of members whose only involvement is the payment of small annual dues ($2–$10). Other groups have very active members who volunteer to help out at school in a variety of ways. Although individual PTAs contribute to school life, rarely do they impact decision making bodies.

Parents also have opportunities to serve on committees that address school issues. In some school districts, parents are encouraged to be part of site-based management groups sometimes called School Improvement Councils (SIC) and Local School Councils (LSC). Being part of an SIC or LSC is a serious responsibility that far too few family members are willing to accept. Parents are usually busy providing for their families and often feel that their time is too limited to commit to membership of an SIC. Some parents may be intimidated by the process or may feel they are not qualified to represent their and other families.

Parents can volunteer to help in schools and classrooms and impact the quality of students' school-related experiences. In what school activities do you recall parent volunteers participating? Were your parents members of a PTA or other organized school group? What do you remember about their involvement?

Your Teaching Fingerprint

Now let's consider how partnering with businesses can support and improve education in public schools.

Businesses

Businesses have a vested interest in education. Having competent employees is a major key to business success, and these employees are likely to be products of public education. Large businesses and their chief executive officers are increasingly becoming involved in education summits, or organized meetings with specific purposes, to advocate for school improvement. This is a positive step since business leaders can potentially support schools and students in meaningful ways.

Business leaders can be influential in supporting educational initiatives. Some businesses offer scholarships to promising students. Other businesses, those that are locally owned as well as national franchises, form partnerships with schools to sponsor events, such as science fairs, and to contribute resources to enhance school activities. Additionally, some large businesses give employees paid time to volunteer in schools and will match funds their employees donate to schools. The potential impact of school-business partnerships is great, as is that of school partnerships with universities.

Universities

Schools of education and teacher educators have important influence on schools because the majority of classroom teachers are prepared on university campuses. Future teachers learn about the concepts in this text and more as they go through teacher preparation programs. The more teachers know, the better prepared they are to take active roles in influencing policies and working toward school improvement.

Teacher educators have the knowledge, and hopefully the will, to exert influence by expressing their views to school administrators, school board members, and legislators. They can serve on School Improvement Councils, curriculum revision and textbook adoption committees and, in general, be active in local, state, and national education associations. University faculty also impact schools through research focused on classroom programs and practices and by facilitating staff development. These activities can form the foundation for recommendations on policy changes and promoting effective practices.

Special Interest Groups

When a group of people join together with a common mission and work to have an impact they are often called a **special interest group.** An example would be a group composed of parents of children who have special needs. For instance, in many areas informal groups of parents of children with autism or Down syndrome band together to help assure more effective services for their children.

Sometimes community members join forces to form local watchdog groups, meaning they keep an eye on school district accountability by examining policies and practices. One such group is the Charleston Education Network (CEN). This group of citizens meets regularly to review happenings in, and policies of, the Charleston County School District in South Carolina, where one of this text's four focus schools, Cario Middle, is located. Members of CEN often fund or conduct research on issues, articulate findings and viewpoints, and lobby school board members and state legislators to bring about change. Groups like CEN offer effective services by asking hard questions and being persistent in their search for answers.

On the national level, groups like the Public Education Network (PEN) tirelessly advocate for children. In addition to activities similar to those of CEN, PEN gathers articles and research results on education issues and distributes them through its website to help individuals and organizations stay informed. You can subscribe for free to *PEN Weekly NewsBlast* at http://news.publiceducation.org and receive valuable updates on many education issues.

Now that we have examined governance structures of public schools and those who influence these structures, we will explore how schools are financed and how the money is spent.

How Are Public Schools Financed?

Free public education—think about it. What a remarkable and noble concept. But is it really free? Hardly. It's true that students don't pay tuition. Their parents do, however, often pay fees for specific items, such as science equipment, gym clothes, band instruments, and workbooks, as well as vague charges for grade level fees. Parents are also asked to supply certain materials each school year. But these expenses barely make a dent in what it costs for a K–12 education. So where does all the money come from? Mainly from local, state, and federal taxes. Regardless of how much families pay into the system through taxes, all children are entitled to attend public schools.

As you previously learned, each individual state has the responsibility of governing its public schools. This applies to financing as well. Consequently, rather than one centralized system for financing public education in the United States, there are 50. Let's look at where the money comes from.

Sources of Education Funding

Although a variety of groups and individuals contribute money to public education, most of the funding comes from federal, state, and local governments in the proportions shown in Figure 12.10. It's interesting to note how these three major sources of funding have shifted over the years from local funding as the primary source in the early part of the 20th century, to local and state sources currently sharing funding responsibilities at approximately the same levels. Figure 12.11 illustrates these historical shifts in the proportion of funding from each major source. As the number of K–12 students and the cost of educating them have grown, most states have increased both the amount and the percentage of their contributions. Although Figure 12.11 would seem to indicate a decrease in local funding, that is not the case; rather, the states' average proportion of total funding has simply increased. The call for equitable funding, regardless of race, socioeconomic status, or geographic location, has led states to increase their portion of funding responsibility (Biddle & Berliner, 2002). States have also come to recognize that the quality of public education has lifestyle and economic implications. As indicated in Figure 12.11, the federal government's contribution to public schools is relatively small, with an increase occurring about the time of the release of the 1983 report, *A Nation at Risk* (discussed in Chapter 8, see page 260), and remaining fairly stable since then. Let's examine each source of funding in more detail.

Federal funding. The federal government budget is supported through income taxes, investments, and various charges for services and goods. Federal government contributions to public education account for only about 2% of the U.S. government budget (U.S. Department of Education, 2006).

Figure 12.10 Percentage of revenues received from federal, state, and local sources for public elementary and secondary schools

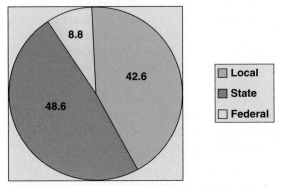

8.8

42.6

48.6

Local
State
Federal

Source: From *Rankings and Estimates: Estimates of School Statistics, 2005* (p. 94), by National Education Association, 2005, Washington, DC: National Education Association.

Figure 12.11   Revenues for public elementary and secondary schools, by source of funds, 1920–2004

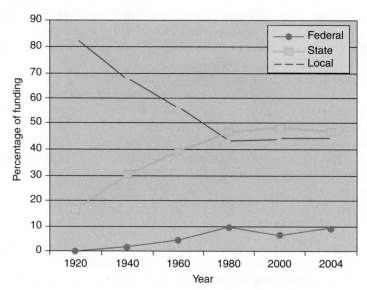

Source: From *Overview of Public Elementary and Secondary Students, Staff, Schools, School Districts, Revenues, and Expenditures: School Year 2004–2005 and Fiscal Year 2004,* by National Center for Education Statistics, Common Core of Data, 2005. Retrieved January 7, 2007, from http://www.nces.ed.gov; *Statistics of State School Systems: Revenues and Expenditures for Public Elementary and Secondary Education,* by National Center for Education Statistics, 2001. Retrieved August 2, 2006, from http://www.nces.ed.gov

The federal government supplies 5% to 10% of the total education budget. Although this doesn't sound like a lot, federal contributions have a major impact on public schools because the money is allocated as **categorical grants,** or funds earmarked for specific purposes. Head Start, Title I, the Bilingual Education Act, and the Education for All Handicapped Children Act (all discussed previously and included in the glossary) are examples of categorical grants. As a group, these and other grants are referred to as **entitlements,** meaning that certain segments of the population have specific needs, and the federal government deems these individuals as entitled to extra assistance.

The Republican administration of Ronald Reagan attempted to diminish the influence of the federal government on schools while still funding their efforts. In the 1980s some federal funding changed from categorical grants to **block grants,** which provide funding with few restrictions for its use. This type of funding allows states and school districts the freedom to use the money in ways that meet their specific needs.

The No Child Left Behind Act of 2001, as a reauthorization of the 1965 Elementary and Secondary Education Act, involves federal funds tied to school improvement as prescribed by the act's specific guidelines. Schools must meet the mandates of NCLB in order to receive the funds. In most cases, states attempt to protect federal funding by complying with the mandates so as to supplement support of schools. Unfortunately, the cost to schools to meet the government mandates sometimes far exceeds the money tied to successful compliance.

State funding. About half of the funding for public education comes from state sources. This is an average, with the percentage of funding varying from state to state. State money for schools is basically raised through taxes, such as:

• state income taxes based on personal earnings
• state corporate taxes based on company earnings
• state sales tax added as a percentage of the cost of goods and services

- excise tax or tax on luxury items such as boats and travel trailers
- "sin" taxes on items some consider vices, such as alcohol and cigarettes

As of 2006, 42 states also had lottery games with portions of the funds specifically earmarked for education (North American Association of State and Provincial Lotteries [NAASPL], 2006). Although lottery-based funding may sound appealing and, indeed, has been used productively in most instances, there are inherent problems. First, gambling through state-run lotteries appears to attract a disproportionate number of low-income individuals who often have little schooling. Many people disagree with the concept of a lottery system for this reason (Brimley & Garfield, 2004). Second, although lottery funding is initially viewed as extra, or found money to supplement other, more stable sources, over time having this easy source of funds often leads to reducing the amount of more stable funding. In other words, a state's attitude may be "We have all this lottery money so we don't need to give schools as much from the state budget." This is risky business, from both state and local standpoints, considering the uncertainty of a lottery's ability to consistently provide money for schools.

Local funding. The source of local funding for schools is primarily **property taxes.** Values of property are determined, and a small percentage of the assessed amount (usually less than 1%) is collected annually and used for local services. Most goes to schools (Brimley & Garfield, 2004). On the surface, using property taxes to finance education seems reasonable. After all, everyone benefits from an educated citizenry. However, as illustrated in Figure 12.12, many people believe an alternative method of funding public education should be imposed. In 1978 California was the first state to put a limit on how high property taxes could go. California's Proposition 13 was a model for other states. Now almost all states impose what is called a **tax cap** on local property taxes, or an upper limit to taxation.

Figure 12.12 Sample community responses to property taxes and their use to fund schools

We moved into this home in 1968. We made the last of our monthly mortgage payments the same year we both retired. Our pensions were supposed to give us enough income to stay right here for as long as our health allows. But year after year the value of the house goes up, with all the new stores and shopping centers popping up in the area. Our property taxes have doubled. If they go much higher, we may have to move. We raised our kids, and now they're raising their own. I'm all for good schools, but not if we lose our home.

I have a good job that allows my wife, who used to be a third grade teacher, to homeschool our two kids. We live in an upscale neighborhood and are very happy with our lives. But what we're not happy about is the way our property taxes are skyrocketing. I believe in public education, but we can afford to homeschool while the kids are young, and then they'll go to our church's private 6–12 school.  Why should I have to pay exorbitant property taxes for schools I'll never use?

I don't have kids and never plan to. I like my life as it is, with good friends and a job that calls for me to travel to interesting places. I bought a great downtown loft apartment with payments I can afford. However, now that this area of downtown is being revitalized, the value of my place is on the rise, along with escalating property taxes. I understand that most of this money goes for public schools. Well, the school a few blocks away sure doesn't look like much of my money, or anyone else's, is being spent there. If that school represents how this school district is spending my money, I'll vote for any decrease of the spending cap.

Impact of Reliance on Property Taxes. Let's consider what reliance on property taxes for almost half of public school funding might mean for different communities. A district composed of middle-to-upper-socioeconomic-status suburban neighborhoods with prospering retail stores and a couple of thriving industries will likely generate a healthy amount of money with a relatively low percentage of the assessed property value. In this case people who own homes and businesses pay what might be considered reasonable taxes on their property and appear to have adequate funding for schools. Now, think about a district in a very rural area, with a lot of land, but few homes, with families who drive out of the area for jobs or who work in the few businesses located in the district. In this case, home and business owners may have to pay a much larger percentage of the assessed value of their property to support schools. There may simply not be enough property value to generate adequate funding. Finally, consider a densely populated urban area, with many people who are renters in high-rise buildings, and often living on government subsidies such as welfare. An area such as this may have large numbers of children and few home owners. In some urban areas, business and industry provide an adequate tax base, but in others the base is very low, resulting in inadequate school funding.

Relying on property taxes to provide a substantial portion of support for public education can create a gap that further exacerbates the socioeconomic problems discussed in Chapters 3 (see pages 86–88) and 10 (see pages 296–297). And, as you have seen, where there are socioeconomic gaps, there are almost certainly achievement gaps. In states with tax caps, it may not be possible for communities to raise the percentage of the tax on assessed property value, even when the majority of people believe it should be done in order to support their schools. They are stuck with the limit, despite unfair and nonproductive funding. If you hear or see an expression such as "Drop the cap, end the gap," you'll now better understand the meaning of this slogan. Read more about the funding gap in Figure 12.13. With all the problems inherent in using property taxes as the primary source of local funding, alternatives are often sought.

Figure 12.13 The funding gap

"Closing the achievement gap is a familiar theme these days. But lurking behind the achievement gap is another contentious issue: funding. Excellence in education doesn't come without a price tag." This statement by Amy Azzam, associate editor of *Educational Leadership,* begins her 2005 special report, *The Funding Gap 2004,* a study conducted by the Education Trust.

The study used the financial data from the U.S. Census from each of the more than 14,000 school districts. The focus of the study was on funding disparities by state between high-poverty and low-poverty districts, as well as between high-minority and low-minority districts. The results revealed that more than half the states provided less money to high-poverty districts than to low-poverty districts. This translates into less money for high-minority areas since there tends to be a higher concentration of minorities in high-poverty areas.

The disparities become even more glaring when we consider the fact that it costs more for high-poverty districts to meet the same standards as low-poverty districts, by some estimates as much as 40% more. Education Trust found that with this cost adjustment, 36 states provided an average of $1,348 per student less for high-poverty versus low-poverty districts. Some states had disparities as high as $2,500 per student.

Given the study results, Education Trust recommends that states

- reduce reliance on local property taxes
- spend extra money to help low-income children
- do away with funding gaps among individual schools within districts

Azzam closes her report by stating, "Closing the achievement gap starts with closing the funding gap. Only by providing the necessary resources can states help ensure quality education for all students."

Source: From "The Funding Gap," by A. M. Azzam, 2005, *Educational Leadership, 62*(5), p. 93. Association for Supervision and Curriculum Development.

Local Funding Alternatives. Some communities are attempting to support public education through an increase in sales tax. For instance, when sales tax is raised from 6% to 7%, an extra penny is collected for every dollar spent on taxable goods. This translates into a sizable amount of money. For a district, such an increase could mean less dependency on property taxes as the source of local funding.

Another way school districts acquire funds is to borrow money through what is called a **bond referendum,** an amount of money stipulated for specific projects. When using a bond referendum, the school board asks voters in their district to approve the borrowing of the money (the bond) that will be repaid over a period of time. Bond referendums can be for hundreds of millions of dollars. In some states, boards are not required to ask voters for permission to borrow money for schools. The request may need only city or county council approval. Such is the case for a 2006 bond requested by the district school board in Charlotte, North Carolina.

Funding in Charlotte. Peter Gorman, newly appointed superintendent of the Charlotte-Mecklenburg Schools (CMS), recognized very quickly the need for new schools and the renovation of older facilities. The CMS school board voted 7–1 to support Dr. Gorman's plan.

The Charlotte newspaper, *The Charlotte Observer,* editorialized its support of the $171 million bond as expressed on July 18, 2006. Then, in a surprising decision, the county council voted against the plan. At that point Superintendent Gorman and the school board began looking for other ways to finance badly needed school improvements. Figure 12.14 contains portions of the *Charlotte Observer* editorials, one before the county council's negative vote, and one after it. The Letter to the Editor from a CMS student is in response to the situation in Charlotte.

Lease-Purchase Option. A recent option for schools to acquire new facilities has been approved in some states. The option involves authorizing private companies to build schools with the agreement that they will be leased back by the school district. After a designated period of time, the district buys the buildings from the private development company or may move out and find a new location. Supporters of this lease-purchase plan say it enables schools to be built more quickly and less expensively, and building does not require voter approval.

Private donations. In addition to federal, state, and local funding, many districts and individual schools receive private gifts of either money or goods. These gifts rarely account for more than 3% of the total amount of school funding (Brimley & Garfield, 2004). Individuals and foundations may contribute to a particular program or project and have a significant impact on that particular segment of school life. However, states, districts, and schools should be cautious about considering private gifts when planning budgets. These sources are often one-time donations or may prove to be unstable.

This chapter's In the News feature is a story of how private funds and public schools can work together to achieve success—at least cautious success at this point in the tale. Learn about the Village Academy in Delray Beach, Florida, by going to this text's *In the News* DVD. Click on Chapter 12, then on *The Power of the Neighborhood School.* The account pulls together many of the concepts discussed so far in this book. You will hear about the achievement gap, segregation and integration, community involvement in schools, class size, high expectations, and more.

In the News

Now that we have considered the various sources of public school funding, let's look at how the money is spent to educate students in public schools.

How Are Funds for Education Spent?

Earlier this text discussed property taxes and how the ability to generate money varies greatly from state to state and district to district. The amount each state spends on public education varies greatly as well. Rather than totals per state, the number that is most meaningful is the amount of money spent per pupil.

Figure 12.14   Charlotte-Mecklenburg Schools

The Charlotte Observer
Editorial, July 18, 2006 (before county council vote)

Unite for schools
Commissioners should strongly support building plan

New Charlotte-Mecklenburg Schools Superintendent Peter Gorman threw down a gauntlet to this community in a commentary on Sunday's Viewpoint page. The Mecklenburg Board of County Commissioners should take heed as they vote tonight on a citizen panel's recommendation to build and renovate public schools.

Superintendent Gorman said "anything less than the best education for every child is a moral and ethical failure—and we can't afford to pay the social costs it brings. . . . Education is the most important indirect form of economic development. Schools are our most important social investment, and we need to treat them with the respect and care they deserve."

That's true, but in recent years, this community has allowed our schools and our students to become pawns in political games that have had a lot to do with adults' political agendas and little to do with educating children.

Political disagreement is inherent in a diverse community, but at times it has led us to abandon common sense. The defeat of public school bonds last fall is a good example. Surveys indicate most Mecklenburg voters agreed that the school needs on the Nov. 7 referendum were legitimate. Yet many opposed the bonds—or didn't vote—because they didn't like or trust the school system and its too-often bickering board members.

Dr. Gorman knows that image and those attitudes are barriers to meeting school needs. He has aggressively set about changing both. But he also says clearly that the public and public officials have to do their parts as well.

One place to begin is by ending the divisive politicking over school building needs and getting on with fixing inadequate schools and building new ones to accommodate soaring enrollment growth. . . .

The Charlotte Observer
Editorial, July 19, 2006 (after county council vote)

"No" to school funds
Mecklenburg commissioners reject sensible compromise

Hardly anyone doesn't think fast-growing Mecklenburg County needs to build and renovate schools. But in 2005 county commissioners split over a $427 million bond proposal for that purpose, and voters defeated it. Then last night the commissioners rejected a reasonable proposal for moving forward. It was a stunning victory of politics over progress.

After the 2005 bond defeat, County Manager Harry Jones urged commissioners to create a citizens' School Building Solutions Committee to recommend ways to move ahead. Jim Martin, a Republican former governor, agreed to chair it.

The committee recommended $171 million to fund some projects now, using money that doesn't require voter approval, and a bond referendum of up to $400 million next year. The school board voted 7–1 to support the proposal. But county commissioners would not compromise. . . .

The county will fall even further behind in meeting school needs because five commissioners said if we won't do it my way we won't do anything now. Here are their names: . . .

Tell them what you think. . . .

Source: Reprinted with permission from *The Charlotte Observer.* Copyright owned by *The Charlotte Observer.*

Expenditure per Pupil

The average amount of money spent from federal, state, and local sources on an individual student is called the **expenditure per pupil.** A comparison of expenditures per pupil by state is found in Figure 12.15. Keep in mind when you look at this figure that the cost of living, and consequently the cost of education, as well as student needs vary from state to state and region to region. Does almost three times the learning occur in

Letter to the Editor

This Letter to the Editor appeared July 20, 2006, in *The Charlotte Observer*. It was written by a rising high school senior who suggests school decisions should be made by students.

Let Students Decide Since it Affects Us Most

I am reminded why I am so eager to leave this circus of a school system. Some commissioners shunned the construction plan because their voters would not have supported it. Here's an idea: Let students vote since we're the people who have to suffer on inadequate campuses with barely enough books and materials for classes. Do not let your selfish goals (to be elected and re-elected) ruin our educations.

Derek Gomes
Charlotte

1. Derek calls Charlotte-Mecklenburg Schools a "circus of a school system." Based on what you have read, is his anger rightly placed or misplaced? Support your position.
2. Derek states that some commissioners voted against the plan because the voters in their constituent areas would not have supported it. Is it ever all right for a representative to go against the perceived will of those he or she represents? Why or why not? Is it "selfish" to act in a way the voters might want in order to be re-elected? Why or why not?
3. How do you feel about students having a voice in issues such as facility maintenance and construction? At what age would they have the maturity necessary to understand financing and the obligations and ramifications of committing to financial debt? Support your views.

Now it's your turn. This chapter presented information about how schools are governed and financed. You know that situations are often much more complicated than it would appear to those who read about the issues in the newspaper without firsthand knowledge of the intricacies involved. These questions will help you write your own letter to the editor.

Your letter to the editor should be in response to *The Charlotte Observer* letter—supporting it, adding information, or refuting it. Write your letter in understandable terminology, remembering that readers of newspaper letters to the editor are citizens who may have limited knowledge of school practices and policies. Your letter may be written in your course notebook and shared with classmates as directed by your instructor. Remember to refer to the letter assessment rubric in Figure 1.10, page 20.

In The News

The Power of the Neighborhood School

The first new school to be built in Delray Beach, Florida, in 30 years is Village Academy. In the 2000 ABC video you see Village Academy as a K–2 school. By 2007 it was a school for K–8, with plans to add a grade a year through twelfth grade. Before 2000 many of Delray's children (mostly poor, mostly minority) took long bus rides to get to schools attended primarily by White children from mostly middle- to upper-class families. Village Academy changed not only the length of the bus ride, but also the attitudes of an entire community.

To view this video, go to this text's DVD, Chapter 12, and then on *The Power of the Neighborhood School*. After watching the video, respond to these questions.

1. Given what you learned about the drop-out epidemic in the United States (Chapter 10, pages 313–315), what are some plausible reasons for the high drop-out rate of minority students bused to other areas from Delray Beach?
2. In the video you hear the Village Academy founder say that he has replaced diversity as a goal with the development of the power of community. What does he mean by this?
3. Given what you learned in Chapter 2, what elements of the Village Academy qualify it as a full-service school?
4. In the video you hear that the school has many extras provided through private funding from a philanthropist. Why is this private–public school partnership having the positive results you see at Village Academy?

Washington, D.C., where expenditures per pupil are over $13,000, as in Utah, where per pupil spending is about $5,000? The answer, of course, is no. Look back at Figure 12.13, which points out that children of poverty require 40% more spending. Spending more to educate students who need extra services to succeed in school is being responsive to differences that often relate to race, socioeconomic status, or disability. There

Figure 12.15   Average expenditures per pupil by state, 2003

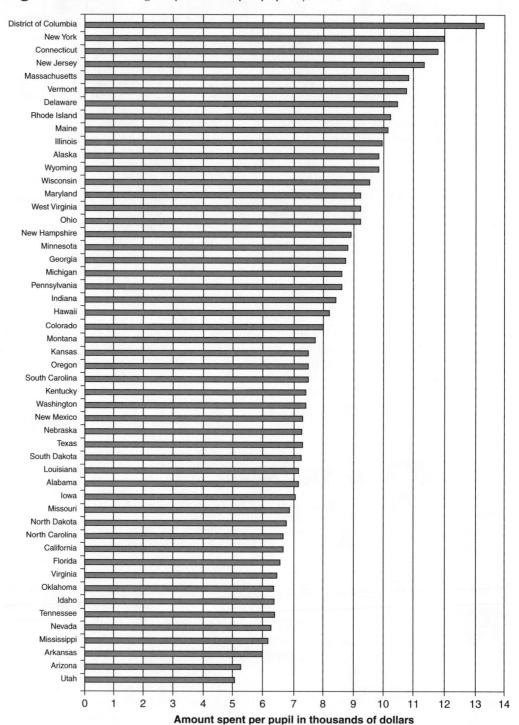

Amount spent per pupil in thousands of dollars

Source: From *Educational Vital Signs,* National School Boards Association, 2005.

are so many variables to consider, including the percentage of teachers who are experts in their teaching fields, state-of-the-art or dilapidated facilities, large or small class size, and more. They all cost money.

You can see from Figure 12.16 that the national average expenditure per pupil has continually increased since 1995 and is projected to remain on this steadily rising course at least through 2014. Everything required to fund education becomes more expensive, as with any large enterprise. When gas prices rise, so does the cost of transportation. When

Figure 12.16 Expenditures per pupil

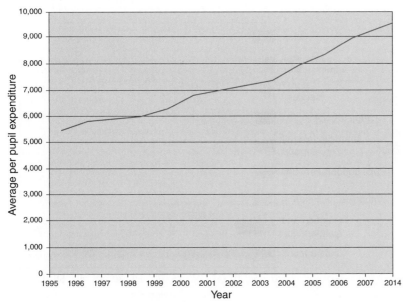

Source: From *Projections of Education Statistics to 2014* (Table 33), by National Center for Education Statistics, 2005, Washington, DC: U.S. Department of Education. Available at http://nces.ed.gov/pubs2005/2005074.pdf

construction costs rise, so does the cost of building new schools. The more diversified student populations become, the more expensive it is to hire personnel to meet their needs. It is understandable that public education is criticized for increased spending when there appears to be little progress in terms of test scores. It is a complicated issue as schools continue to struggle with the connection between spending and levels of learning.

What is your view of the connection between spending on education and student achievement? On what do you base your opinions? Let's continue to look at other ways in which education funds are spent.

Allocation of Education Funding

With any large endeavor there are administrative and other costs that affect, either directly or indirectly, the cause or people served. So it is with education. It would be wonderful if 90% of an education budget could go directly into the classroom to pay teachers, buy books and supplies, and provide the latest technology. But as you saw earlier in this chapter, support for the work of individual teachers in their classrooms requires (at least as the education system is currently configured) people in district and state positions. Some of the current programs with the greatest impact require national level support as well.

Figure 12.17 outlines education's major spending categories. Although several of the spending categories are vague, considering that there are more than 14,000 school districts, labeling only about 10% of the spending as "Other" and "Other support services" isn't bad. Let's look at the rest of the categories.

- *General administration* includes district-level administrators.
- *Pupil transportation* mainly involves school buses. The buses must be purchased, maintained, and filled with gas, and drivers must be paid.
- *Instructional staff support* includes curriculum and instruction specialists, teacher training, and teacher assistants.
- *Pupil support services* include school psychologists, nurses, behavior specialists, home liaisons, and others who work with students with needs, special and otherwise (not including special education teachers).
- *School administration* refers to principals and assistant principals and funds needed to support their positions. Notice that about twice as much is spent at the school level versus the district level.

Figure 12.17 Distribution of public elementary and secondary school system spending, 2003–2004

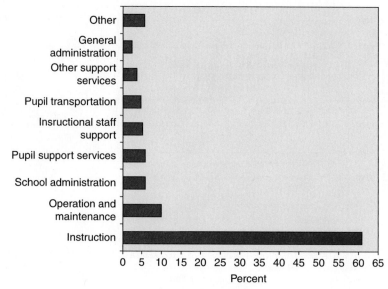

Source: From *Public Education Finances 2004,* by U.S. Census Bureau, 2006. Retrieved January 7, 2007, from http://ftp2.census.gov/govs/school/04f33pub.pdf

- *Operation and maintenance* includes anything related to facilities—building repair, custodial staff, lights, water, heat, air-conditioning, grounds, and so on.

In 2004 over 60% of school spending went directly toward instruction. The bulk of this money is spent on teacher salaries. The rest buys books, classroom supplies, technology, and so on. Committing 70% or 80% of funds to instruction would be great, but in order to do that, less money would have to be spent in other categories. Allocation of funds poses a dilemma with which state and district school boards wrestle continually.

Concluding Thoughts

This chapter is an overview of school governance and finance. As such, it does not describe the political, economic, and social climates that determine the particular form governance and financing take. You have probably considered alternative ways to govern schools and finance them as you have read. There are many possibilities, all with benefits and drawbacks.

The only way teachers can hope to understand and possibly influence the more political aspects of education in the United States—basically what happens outside the individual classroom—is, first of all, to be informed. It's actually very interesting to learn about the support systems that help us do what we do in the classroom. You can be engaged by keeping up with education-related current events at all levels and informed by reading education journals and books. The second step to affecting the bigger picture of education is to have the will to be involved, to step outside the classroom doors and advocate for children in the larger arena of the community, the district, the state, and the nation. Chapter 13 explores the responsibilities and opportunities teachers have to affect how education is done in the United States.

As you continue your teacher preparation program, be aware that classroom teachers do not operate as islands unto themselves. The governance and finance systems and related areas continually function to support, or in some cases inhibit, teaching and learning.

What Role Will Diversity Play in My Teaching Identity?

Were you struck by the lack of diversity among those in public school governance? From school boards to superintendents to principals, the majority are White. This composition does not mirror student populations. You learned in Chapter 3 that about 40% of students in public schools belong to racial minorities. Does this out-of-balance situation mean that there will be a lack of sensitivity to, and validation of, many of our students? As teachers we need to be watchful to make sure the answer to this question is consistently no.

What is inevitable is the lack of role models in the ranks of school leadership. This makes it even more imperative for teachers to teach in a multiculturally enhanced environment where the leadership achievements of individuals representing a variety of races are highlighted.

Chapter in Review

How does the federal government influence public education in the United States?

- The president, the U.S. Congress, and the federal court system endorse specific programs and make and enforce laws that impact schools.
- The U.S. Department of Education initiates programs and mandates the compliance of states using federal money as leverage.

What is the state's role in public education?

- Each state has its own unique governance system.
- State governors, legislatures, and court systems all impact the functioning of education within the state.
- A state board of education is a volunteer policy-making body that has oversight responsibilities.
- A state department of education functions under the leadership of a state superintendent and many administrators who work to support schools and teachers.

How do school districts function?

- A school district is made up of schools defined by geographic boundaries.
- District school boards set policies that affect the operation of schools.
- A district superintendent is the chief executive officer of a school district and may have a staff with specified duties.

What is the management structure of individual schools?

- The principal oversees every aspect of a school and answers to the district for all that occurs.
- Assistant principals and teacher leaders play important roles in school management.

What other entities impact the governance of public schools in the United States?

- Parents and families have the potential to positively impact student success in school.
- Businesses have a vested interest in effective schools that prepare their employees and consumers. Business-school partnerships benefit both.
- Universities and teacher education faculty prepare teachers and impact education.
- Special interest groups are composed of concerned citizens who work for the benefit of specific causes within schools.

How are public schools financed?

- On average, state and local funding share about 92% of the funding burden equally, with federal funds accounting for most of the rest.
- Federal funds are either earmarked for specific purposes in the form of categorical grants or given for states to use at their discretion in the form of block grants.
- State funds are generated primarily through sales taxes and income taxes.
- Most local funds usually come from property taxes, a controversial source.
- Private donations provide boosts to specific programs and efforts but account for a very small percentage of total school funding.

How are funds for education spent?

- The amount spent on each student, the expenditure per pupil, varies greatly from state to state.
- Over half of the money spent on public education goes for expenses related to classroom instruction. The rest is spent on support services, including administration, facilities, and transportation.

Professional Practice

■ Licensure Test Prep

Answer multiple-choice questions 1–8.

1. What governmental body has the major responsibility for public schools in the United States?
   a. the U.S. legislature
   b. the Supreme Court
   c. each county's commissioners
   d. individual states

2. Which governmental body or individual sets goals and approves standards for schools, establishes requirements for school accreditation, and advises the governor on education issues?
   a. the state school board
   b. the state superintendent of education
   c. the secretary of the federal department of education
   d. local school boards

3. An organizational structure of local schools defined by geographic boundaries is a
   a. school liaison committee.
   b. school district.
   c. site-based management team.
   d. legislative region.

4. Local school boards may do all of the following except
   a. be elected by the people of the district.
   b. decide how much money will be spent on teacher salaries.
   c. decide to administer state exams or not.
   d. hire and fire personnel.

5. Jared is a new teacher at Hawkins Middle School. When he interviewed for his position he met with the principal for about an hour. Then he spent an afternoon with a team of teachers he would join after he was hired. When he arrived at school one November morning, he was told that the principal had asked the four seventh grade team leaders to meet with her that afternoon about the possibility of moving teachers around to form new teams. Jared is very uncomfortable with the possibility of upsetting the teams because first, he likes working with his teammates and second, he doesn't think it's good for young adolescents to have their teams change during the year. Which of the following courses of action would best demonstrate Jared's professionalism?
   a. Asking the school secretary to quietly slip a note to the principal asking for a few minutes to talk about the issue
   b. Joining other teachers while students are in related arts classes to formulate a plan to counteract what they believe the principal plans to do
   c. Continuing his regular duties and avoiding talking about the issue if possible
   d. Gathering journal articles about the value of team consistency and giving them to the principal

6. All of the following may be considered special interest groups in their influence on public education except
   a. middle school teacher teams.
   b. parents bound together by the fact that their children have special needs.
   c. citizens who meet to discuss issues.
   d. the Public Education Network.

7. Which statement about the financing of public education is true?
   a. The federal government does not allocate funds for any particular group because it abides by equality of funding guidelines.
   b. The state and federal governments share about equally in financial support of public schools.
   c. Taxation is the major source of money for public education.
   d. State education lotteries fund almost a quarter of district needs.

8. The average amount of money spent on students is called
   a. block grant funding.
   b. expenditure per pupil.
   c. individualized accounting.
   d. legal apportionment.

■ Standards Speak

Teachers' relationships with the system of education, including district, state, and national influences, are defined broadly by the admonition to be professional. However, a few of our organizations specifically address this aspect of being a teacher through their standards for teacher preparation and growth.

INTASC Principle 10, Knowledge

The teacher understands schools as organizations within the larger community context and understands the operations of the relevant aspects of the system(s) within which s/he works.

NBPTS

Accomplished teachers can evaluate school progress and the allocation of school resources in light of their understanding of state and local educational objectives.

NAEYC, Standard 5, Becoming a Professional

Candidates can identify and conduct themselves as members of the early childhood profession. . . . They are informed advocates for sound educational practices and policies.

Respond to the following questions in your class notebook and/or discuss your responses with your classmates as directed by your instructor.

1. Why do you think it's important for teachers to understand the larger governance context within which individual schools function? In what situation(s) might this understanding be useful?

2. The NBPTS standard talks about "state and local educational objectives." How do these broader educational objectives affect what you do as a classroom teacher?

3. How can a classroom teacher inform parents and families about the influence of district and state policies on the day-to-day operation of the local school?

4. The NAEYC standard words "informed advocates" are powerful. All teachers are likely to be advocates of children by virtue of their chosen profession. But what is the difference between being an advocate and being an informed advocate?

■ MyEducationLab

The following interactive features may be found in Chapter 12 of MyEducationLab.

Homework and Exercises

Writing My Own Story
To write your own story by responding to some of the questions in the text accompanied by fingerprint icons, plus others, go to the "Writing My Own Story" section of the Homework and Exercises for Chapter 12 of MyEducationLab.

What's My Disposition?
To reflect on your beliefs and attitudes concerning the teaching profession, go to Chapter 12's "What's My Disposition?" feature of the Homework and Exercises section of MyEducationLab.

Exploring Schools and Classrooms
If your course involves experiences in schools, the questions and prompts in the "Exploring Schools and Classrooms" feature of Chapter 12's Homework and Exercises section of MyEducationLab will guide you as you explore local schools and classrooms.

Virtual Field Experience

To respond to questions and prompts regarding the Choosing Your Teaching Path videos that connect to specific chapter content, go to Chapter 12's Virtual Field Experience section of MyEducationLab. The questions will help you make sense of what you have read in the chapter.

Part 4

Growing Toward
the Teaching Profession

Chapter 13 **Teacher Responsibilities and Opportunities**

Chapter 14 **Charting My Teaching Course**

Chapter 13

Teacher Responsibilities and Opportunities

Teaching in Focus

You have become acquainted with our 10 focus teachers through this text's video in the Choosing Your Teaching Path section of MyEducationLab, and through the scenarios and pictures throughout the text. In this chapter about responsibilities and opportunities, these same individuals share their unique experiences as classroom teachers in segments entitled In Their Own Words. As you read what they have to say, consider their perspectives as early childhood, elementary, middle, and high school teachers. Think about the level or levels that appeal to you. Think also about how these teachers' perspectives either align with your initial impressions as you begin teacher preparation or challenge the way you believe teachers might feel or act.

This chapter considers to whom and to what teachers bear responsibility, as well as the opportunities that may occur in facing the challenges of those responsibilities. The following questions will guide the discussion.

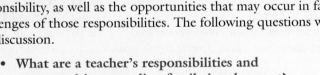

- What are a teacher's responsibilities and opportunities regarding family involvement?
- What are a teacher's responsibilities and opportunities regarding the community?
- What are a teacher's responsibilities and opportunities regarding colleagues?
- What are a teacher's responsibilities and opportunities regarding systemic involvement?
- What are a teacher's responsibilities and opportunities regarding the teaching profession?
- What are a teacher's responsibilities and opportunities regarding self-growth?
- What are a teacher's responsibilities and opportunities regarding students?

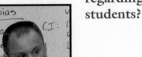

Introduction

Responsibility and opportunity have a symbiotic relationship. You may recall from biology that when organisms are symbiotic, they have a close relationship that is advantageous to both. Responsibilities and opportunities are so close that they flow into one another. When responsibilities are fulfilled, opportunities are created; when opportunities are recognized, their benefits incur responsibilities.

Throughout the chapter an hourglass is used to model the close and mutually advantageous relationship between responsibility and opportunity. Like sand flowing from one chamber into the other, when responsibility is on top and is being fulfilled, it flows into opportunity. Conversely, when we seize the day and make the most of opportunities, we are turning the hourglass over and watching the sands of our efforts create new responsibilities, as illustrated in Figure 13.1.

Teaching is a profession with serious responsibilities. As teachers, we affect the life and future of every student we encounter. We have the most positive impact when our responsibilities range beyond the classroom walls. What we do both inside and outside the classroom matters.

With every responsibility comes opportunity. We have opportunities to do things right, to go above and beyond the minimum. Teaching presents opportunities for growth—our own and of those we touch. Students, families, community members, colleagues—all are within our power to influence as we ask and answer, "And how are the children?"

What Are a Teacher's Responsibilities and Opportunities Regarding Family Involvement?

"The way schools care about children is reflected in the way schools care about the children's families" (Epstein et al., 2002, p. 7). Chapter 3 (see page 85) looked at the diverse configurations of families in the 21st century, from two biological parents and siblings, to group foster homes with numerous children. Regardless of how a family might look, the gap between families and school can be bridged when families see teachers and schools as their partners, working diligently for the welfare of the children (Lightfoot, 1978).

Central to most families is someone who fills the parental role. Chapter 3 (see page 85) talked about accommodating diverse living situations by addressing written communication

Figure 13.1   The relationship between responsibility and opportunity

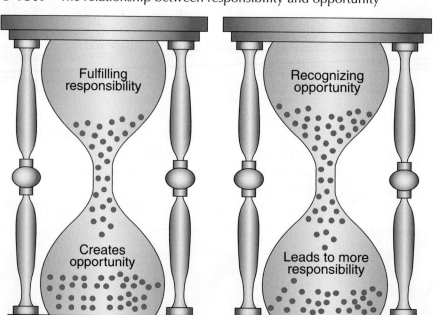

to "Family" rather than using the more limiting language of "Parents." However, this section will use the word *parent* because most of your communication with students' homes will be with the adult(s) filling the parental role.

Most new teachers find that they are not prepared to address home issues. To help you begin considering your responsibilities and opportunities regarding parental involvement in schools, this section is more detailed than those that follow. It will address why parental involvement is important, how to promote it, and barriers to making parental involvement a reality.

Why Parental Involvement Is Important

Parents are a child's first teachers. During those critically important years between birth and age 4, parents (and their choice of child-care providers) have the greatest impact on children. For the rest of childhood and adolescence, parental modeling and attitudes influence students' success in school. Involving parents in the life of the school benefits the educational process in many ways.

Marzano (2003) tells us that parental involvement increases academic achievement and attendance rates and leads to more positive attitudes and behavior of students in the classroom. That's a formula for success! Whereas all students benefit from parental involvement, low-income and culturally diverse students are particularly more likely to succeed when family members communicate with, and are active in, the life of the school (Epstein et al., 2002). Let's explore ways to develop meaningful partnerships between schools and families.

How to Involve Parents

Parental involvement can take many forms, from consistently encouraging students to complete homework, to attending parent-teacher conferences, to volunteering regularly in the school or classroom, or even to serving on a district school board. Parental involvement extends primarily to parents' own children, whereas other kinds of involvement affect a whole class or grade level. Still other types of involvement affect students in an entire school and beyond.

James Comer (2005), a professor at Yale University School of Medicine's Child Study Center since 1968, endorses the development of "a yearlong, school-wide schedule of activities designed to support instruction and to create positive relationships in the school" (p. 40). This schedule may include

- parent volunteer opportunities
- parent-student-teacher events, such as family math night and career exploration workshops
- student performances, such as chorus and band concerts, sports events, and club activities

Through participation, parents show support for both students and teachers. In turn, they gain a sense of connection with the education of their children. Many teachers welcome parents into their classrooms to help with classroom activities, prepare materials, and work one-on-one with students who may need extra help.

Parental involvement can positively affect not only their own children, but also whole classes and schools.

Joyce Epstein and others (2002) developed a framework for involving parents that includes six types of involvement. You'll notice as you examine Table 13.1 that the framework is quite comprehensive. Epstein and her colleagues contend that helping families grow together and become strong in their relationships among themselves results in higher-achieving students. With regard to the first type of involvement, parenting, Epstein suggests that schools offer workshops, videotapes, discussion or support groups, and home visits to help parents develop their parenting skills. By improving skills, and the confidence this generates, the other five types of involvement are more likely to follow.

Involving parents in their child's schooling is a teacher's responsibility. Therefore, teachers must communicate and conference. Let's examine each.

Table 13.1 Epstein's framework of six types of involvement

Type 1	Parenting	Help all families establish home environments to support children as students.
Type 2	Communicating	Design effective forms of school-to-home and home-to-school communication about school programs and their children's progress.
Type 3	Volunteering	Recruit and organize parent help and support.
Type 4	Learning at home	Provide information and ideas to families about how to help students at home with homework and other curriculum-related activities, decisions, and planning.
Type 5	Decision making	Include parents in school decisions, developing parent leaders and representatives.
Type 6	Collaboration with the community	Identify and integrate resources and services from the community to strengthen school programs, family practices, and student learning and development.

Source: From *School, Family, and Community Partnerships: Your Handbook for Action* (2nd ed.), by J. L. Epstein, M. G. Sanders, B. S. Simon, K. C. Salinas, N. R. Jansorn, and F. L. VanVoorhis, 2002. Thousand Oaks, CA: Corwin Press.

Parent communication. Teachers are responsible for communicating with parents. Events such as Back-to-School Night, Open House, and parent conferences (discussed in detail in the next section) all provide opportunities for teachers to talk about their curriculum, classrooms, and students. New teachers should ask experienced teachers about the format and general procedures for these events.

In addition to schoolwide and regularly scheduled forms of communication, there are many other ways teachers can invite parents to participate in their students' education. Here are some communication tools you may use:

1. Welcome letter. Sending a letter to families/parents at the beginning of the school year is a good way for you to introduce yourself, inform parents about policies and procedures that are specific to your class, tell parents about volunteer opportunities, and let parents know how and when to reach you. A sample letter is shown in Figure 13.2.
2. Classroom newsletter. Weekly or monthly newsletters sent home with students can keep parents informed and give them ideas for how to encourage students to complete school assignments and homework. If you tell parents to expect a newsletter at certain times, make sure to follow through. Equally important, make sure the written communication you send home is error free. Have a colleague proofread what you have written. Be aware that some principals require all newsletters be cleared through their office.
3. Homework hotline. Many schools have a telephone system that allows parents to hear messages and homework assignments. The success of such a system depends on the regularity with which teachers update information.
4. Phone calls. Not all phone calls home have to signal trouble at school. Using the telephone to communicate good news is powerful. Imagine a parent saying "Hello" and then hearing, "Good afternoon, Mrs. Lawson. This is Annie Morgan, Brandon's math teacher. I just wanted to tell you that Brandon took the lead today in his group's problem-solving activity. I was so proud of how he worked with the other students to come up with a unique solution!" Now imagine the grin that spreads across Mrs. Lawson's face, especially when Brandon is often the object of not-so-great school communication. The teacher has taken a very positive step toward having

Figure 13.2 Sample welcome letter

Dear Parents/Family,

It is my pleasure to welcome you and your student to my chemistry class this semester. This is my first year teaching at South High, and I'm excited about teaching my favorite subject! I have an undergraduate degree in chemistry with a minor in secondary education. A major goal for me is to make the content of chemistry come alive for your student!

As you probably know, South High will be on what is known as the block scheduling model this year. What this means for your student is that chemistry, and most of the other subjects, will be one semester long. Our class will meet every day for 90 minutes. This will work very well for the content of this course because the students and I will be able to complete lab experiences all in one class period rather than having to start and stop midstream with the traditional 50-minute class. If you would like more information on our new schedule, please go to our school website and click on "Changes at South High."

Here are a few things to keep in mind as you talk with your student about chemistry class:

- Safety is emphasized in every aspect of our class. Your student is asked to follow specific safety-related guidelines while handling all lab substances and equipment.
- I will post class materials (text, lab manual, notebooks, etc.) needed for each day's class for a week at a time outside my classroom door. Students are expected to come to class prepared.
- It is very important for students to keep up with reading assignments in order to be ready for class and labs. Please encourage your student to stay on track by reading all assigned material.

I hope you will share your student's school experiences this year by having regular discussions with him/her about life at South High. We sincerely invite you to attend school events, parent-student-teacher conferences, and other opportunities to be part of the education of your student. Please contact me if you would like to visit my classroom. You are very welcome to do so!

Please feel free to contact me about any aspect of our chemistry class. Your comments and questions help us do a better job of teaching and make learning more productive for your child. This is going to be a terrific school year!

Sincerely,

Name
Phone#
Email address

Mrs. Lawson as an ally should she need assistance in the future to help correct an undesirable trait Brandon might demonstrate. She has also encouraged Brandon to continue his positive behavior.

However, some phone calls home are not positive. You need to call home if you see a negative change in a student's achievement or attitude, if a student's behavior is unacceptable, if homework or assignments are not completed, and so on. These calls need to be handled professionally. If possible, it's best to have negative discussions in person so there can be face-to-face dialogue. The initial call may be an invitation for such a meeting. Always prepare for phone calls, positive or negative, before dialing. Tips on how to do this are in Figure 13.3.

5. **Electronic communication.** Parent and teacher communication via email has become the norm in some areas. It can be done day or night, without disturbing the receiving party. When using email, don't be sloppy. Use a salutation as well as uppercase and lowercase letters. Do not use faddish abbreviations. The guidelines for both written and telephone communication apply to email communication as well.

Figure 13.3 Tips for calling parents

Here are some tips for making the most of phone calls to parents:

- Introduce yourself and make sure the parent understands who you are.
- Ask if the parent has a few minutes to talk.
- Be cordial.
- Try to begin with a positive statement.
- Be clear about the purpose of the call: to inform, schedule a conference, request return of forms or signed papers, ask for some action needed at home, and so on.
- Actively listen.
- Thank the parent for his or her interest and willingness to do whatever you have asked.
- Be prepared to leave a concise message that may be heard by the student and other family members.

Figure 13.4 Guidelines for parent-student-teacher conferences

1. Consider parents allies, not enemies.
2. Ask that the student attend when appropriate.
3. Arrange comfortable, nonthreatening seating, preferably around a table to increase the flow of communication.
4. Begin with positive statements about the student.
5. Present information as objectively as possible, including data when helpful.
6. Listen attentively, make eye contact, and encourage genuine interaction.
7. Avoid educational jargon.
8. Make a plan for success involving commitment and action from the student, the parents, and the teacher.
9. Keep a written record of topics, decisions, plans, and so on, and send a copy to parents.
10. Follow through and follow up.

One of the most useful forms of communication between teachers and parents occurs during parent-student-teacher conferences.

Parent-student-teacher conferences. As an educator you will inevitably have many conferences that are scheduled through the school, as well as those that are initiated by you or by parents. For many beginning teachers, as well as a fair share of experienced teachers, conference time is looked upon with dread. Rather than viewing conferences as responsibilities to be endured, you should approach them as opportunities to cultivate a partnership with parents for the sake of the students. Figure 13.4 contains guidelines for conducting conferences that are pleasant for everyone, as well as being more productive and having longer-lasting impact.

One of the most helpful ways for new teachers to become comfortable with parent-student-teacher conferences is to sit in when experienced teachers are talking with parents and students. If you are not invited to be a silent observer, ask teachers you admire if it would be possible to sit in on a conference. By doing so, you will pick up phrases, mannerisms, and strategies that will help guide your own conferences.

Involving parents in the six ways developed by Epstein et al. (Table 13.1), as well as communicating and conferencing in the ways discussed in this section, can positively impact students' learning and success in schools. However, there are barriers that prevent parents and teachers (or schools) from partnering in the education of students. As you read about some of the barriers, consider possible solutions.

Barriers to Parent and Teacher Partnering

Barriers to parental involvement in school exist on both sides of the fence; some result from the attitudes and actions of parents, and some from the attitudes and actions of teachers. James Comer (2005), speaking of what he and his team of researchers experienced, tells us, "From the beginning of our work in schools, we were struck by this mixture of parents' hesitancy to get involved and educators' subtle and even unintentional resistance to parental involvement" (p. 39).

Parental barriers. There are many legitimate barriers, such as work schedules, to parental involvement, regardless of socioeconomic status, culture, language, or educational background. However, the illegitimate barrier of apathy, or indifference, may be the most difficult to break down. Tim Mendenhall, one of our focus teachers at Rees Elementary, Utah, finds that his influence extends to the home. He has learned that one way for teachers to break through apathy is to be close to students, which leads parents to become loyal to the teacher, a phenomenon that is good for students as a partnership forms. Read what Tim has to say in In Their Own Words.

Socioeconomic Barriers. Money matters. Having it, or not having it, shapes many aspects of our lives. Some of the attitudes and actions of students and their families can be traced to their socioeconomic status, particularly when it comes to parental involvement. Families with low socioeconomic status may move more often; parents may not have ready access to transportation and may work several jobs or at odd hours. Socioeconomic barriers were discussed in more depth in Chapters 3 (pages 86–88) and 10 (see pages 296–298).

Low-income families may be mobile. If a family is renting and one of its income earners loses a job, the family may leave the house or apartment before the next rent is due. Newsletters, forms, and other communication sent through the mail may not reach these families. Families may have a phone one week, but not the next, or they may not have a phone at all. This makes phone communication very difficult. Many low-income homes do not have access to the Internet so that email is not a communication option either.

In addition, transportation may present a challenge to low-income families. They may have one car to accommodate five, six, or more family members, or they may have no vehicle at all. Some families depend entirely on public transportation, making getting to and from their students' schools very difficult. Finding or paying for child care can be difficult as well, and younger siblings may need to accompany parents to school functions.

Work can be a barrier to parental involvement at any socioeconomic level. Often in low-SES families, both parents work, perhaps at two or three jobs, and their time is extremely limited. The catch-22 is that if these parents do show up to volunteer, it probably means they lost their jobs (Bradley, 2006). At the other end of the socioeconomic spectrum, parents who are highly paid professionals may also have severe limitations on their time. In both cases, showing up at school between 8:00 A.M. and 4:00 P.M. may be virtually impossible. Even when parents do make it to school, there may be other barriers to overcome.

In Their Own Words . . .

**Tim Mendenhall
Grades 3–5 Multiage
Classroom
Rees Elementary School,
Utah**

I have found that my influence goes beyond the classroom. It overflows into the home as well. My relationships with students are built before and after school and in the hallways. Their siblings look forward to being in my classroom. I get to know parents through my students, at parent-teacher conferences, and while working with parent volunteers. I take the time to build relationships with parents. I have found that students and their families become fiercely loyal to teachers who care. It hit me when one of my student's parents said, "I feel I can come to you anytime with a problem with my student and you listen." Education is a partnership, and the more bridges we build, the more it benefits our students.

In Their Own Words . . .

**Brenda Beyal
Grades 3–5 Multiage
Classroom
Rees Elementary School,
Utah**

Tucked away in a drawer I have a note that was given to me by a parent over 10 years ago. I take it out on occasion, at times when I am having a particularly hard time with a school situation, or when I'm feeling ineffective.

I read the salutation, "Dear Respected Madam." This is one of the most gracious openings to a note that I have ever received. The note is from parents who had just migrated from India. They had asked for help with a small matter, and I was able to help solve a dilemma for them.

The words still send a surge of renewal and recommitment within me for my chosen profession—teaching. Families and parents can make emotional deposits into our teaching lives, and then some can make deep withdrawals. As a teacher, I hold onto the unintentional deposits that parents make, and, with their help, I let the withdrawals slip away from my teaching so they will not keep me from making powerful teaching and learning connections.

Cultural and Language Barriers. Children do not choose the culture in which they are born. Their families may value education, or they may consider formal education unnecessary beyond the stage of being able to read and write at survival levels.

The language of a student's family may be a major barrier to parental involvement. Chapter 3 (see pages 82–84) looked at language as a source of diversity. On this text's video in the Choosing Your Teaching Path section of MyEducationLab, you met Hector's mom, who speaks little English, and Khammany's mom, who speaks none. It is often difficult for the teachers at Rees Elementary and Roosevelt High School to meaningfully involve the families of these two students and many others for whom English is not the first language.

Brenda Beyal, one of our focus teachers at Rees Elementary, Utah, talks about "deposits" parents can make in our teaching lives in In Their Own Words. Be aware that whether or not they speak fluent English, some parents are intimidated by schools.

Educational Background Barriers. If parents were not successful in school, academically or behaviorally, they are unlikely to be enthusiastic about stepping through the doors of their children's schools. If they quit school in sixth grade, or eighth grade, or if they never graduated from high school, they may be intimidated and hesitant to talk with teachers, believing that they are incapable of helping students with anything academic.

Such barriers are difficult to overcome. Table 13.2 contains some strategies for teachers and schools as they work toward increasing parental involvement. These suggestions address specific needs. They can help resolve problems that form barriers to parental involvement. But parents aren't the only ones who put up barriers to involvement. Teachers often fail to invite parental involvement for a variety of reasons.

Teacher barriers. Teacher-generated barriers to parental involvement are less legitimate than parent-generated barriers. Teachers' failure to invite parental involvement may stem from timidity, lack of conviction that parental involvement matters, misconceptions about parents, and lack of effort.

Timidity. You may hear teachers say, "I can be up in front of my sophomores all day long, but bring in their parents, and I freeze." Some teachers become nervous when they anticipate speaking to, or with, parents. This timidity must be overcome. A skilled communicator with students can be a skilled communicator with adults. Experience makes it easier. You should jump in and make those calls, start conversations at school events, and speak confidently at conferences and meetings. A good mentor can help in this area. Ask experienced teachers how they communicate with parents or ask to be a silent observer of parental communication. Teachers may be timid not only about speaking with parents, but also about having parents help in their classrooms.

Table 13.2 Strategies to overcome barriers to parental involvement

Barrier	Strategy
Frequent address changes	Organize student families into small groups, being careful to include a family that is rooted in the community. Devise ways to help these small groups stay in touch, with the more settled family taking the lead in communicating with the teacher when families move.
Disconnected phones	Using the group idea described above, establish a phone tree as a source of class information. In this way teachers will learn about phone problems, perhaps before there is a need to call the family on a more urgent matter.
Lack of transportation	Make school events compatible with public transportation schedules. Have a teacher ride along on a route where many of the students live to serve as a welcoming guide to and from the event.
Time barriers	Schedule parent-student-teacher conferences at times that accommodate more parents. Split sessions could be 3:00–5:00 and 7:00–9:00 P.M. Provide ways for working parents to volunteer time, perhaps with weekend and evening projects that also involve students.
Child-care dilemmas	Provide child care onsite during school events and planned conference times. High school classes and organizations can be responsible for taking care of children while parents involve themselves in the life of the school.
Cultural differences	Acknowledge different perspectives and incorporate activities, artwork, celebrations, and so on, that draw families into the life of the school.
Language barriers	Find people who will serve as interpreters at events and conferences. Advertise the presence of interpreters to let parents know they will be able to communicate with teachers. Translate newsletters and forms into the languages spoken and read at home.
Limited education	Warm, friendly teachers who use jargon-free language in their communications can help encourage parental involvement. Providing after-school homework help can ease parental guilt over not knowing how to help their children with assignments.

Some teachers are uncomfortable having other adults watching and listening to them. They may be worried about facing questions and possible criticism, and find the presence of parents inhibiting and intimidating. This form of timidity can be overcome by planning excellent learning experiences for the classroom and being at your best every day with the attitude that parents are your partners. The more hands and minds the better when it comes to increasing student learning.

Parents Matter. Some teachers appear to be unconvinced that parental involvement matters. Family involvement does make a difference, especially in families with low incomes and with parents who have had little formal education (Epstein et al., 2002; Payne, 1998).

Traci Peters, our seventh grade math teacher at Cario Middle School, South Carolina, believes strongly in the value of parental involvement. See In Their Own Words to read Traci's philosophy and advice about inviting parents to be partners in education.

In Their Own Words . . .

Traci Peters
Grade 7 Math
Cario Middle School,
South Carolina

When parents send you their children, they are sending you the best ones they have. They're not keeping their brighter, better behaved children at home. They are sending you their "babies," even in middle school. They have spent years molding them and are depending on you to continue the task. In an instant, a teacher becomes the one that spends more time each day with these children than the parents. Most parents want to be informed and involved, and they want what is best for their child. Parents and teachers are on the same side—the student's side. As teachers we need to reach out. There are many benefits to parental involvement for students, teachers, and the parents themselves.

There are many ways to involve parents, from simple occasional email communication and a classroom newsletter, to more complex strategies such as home visits and family math nights. What matters is that we establish positive connections between the classroom and the homes of students. If you think of it as a give-and-take relationship, you may find very practical benefits to parent involvement. They can simplify some of your tasks by doing things such as copying and preparing materials, shopping for "fun with food" day, displaying student work in the classroom or in the halls, and so on. They will enjoy their involvement and support your efforts in the classroom!

Parents Care. Most parents love their children more than life itself. They want what is best for them, and they want their children's lives to be healthier and their futures more comfortable than their own. Most parents realize that a good education is the key to making this possible. Parents with low incomes and limited formal schooling generally want their children to succeed in school. However, these parents may need our help to show them how to support their children to make success a reality. Homes with ample incomes and well-educated parents generally know that a good education is vital. Teachers need to grasp the reality of parental concern and tenaciously find ways to involve parents.

On this text's video in the Choosing Your Teaching Path section of MyEducationLab, you have watched interviews with most of the parents of our focus students. They were all asked about their hopes and dreams for their children. To watch their interviews again on this text's video, click on a school, and then on each student's name. It is impossible to think that these parents from diverse socioeconomic, cultural, and educational backgrounds don't care about the well-being of their children when you listen to their words. How do their comments affect your determination to fulfill your responsibilities to engage parents in the life of your school? Do you anticipate having difficulty communicating with parents? If so, why? Remember that when you see a fingerprint in the margin it means that you will be asked to respond to questions and prompts based on your experiences and opinions. These questions are included in "Writing My Own Story" in Chapter 13 of the Homework and Exercises section of MyEducationLab at www.myeducationlab.com.

Your Teaching Fingerprint

Lack of Effort. The most frustrating teacher barrier to parental involvement in schools and classrooms is lack of effort. There is no legitimate reason not to make that call, write that note, or invite parents into the classroom. If you are convinced that parents are your allies in the education of students, you will draw parents into, rather than excluding or even alienating them from, the educational process.

How do you envision drawing parents into the process of educating their children? How would you overcome the barriers parents might put up? How might you overcome any reluctance you might have to make parents your partners?

Your Teaching Fingerprint

Whatever the barriers to parental involvement, teachers need to continually strive to break them down. We need to cultivate invitational attitudes that develop relationships and draw parents into the life of the school. Parents are part of the larger community. With them as active participants in the life of the school, we are reaching out into the community.

Responsibilities and opportunities regarding family/parental involvement

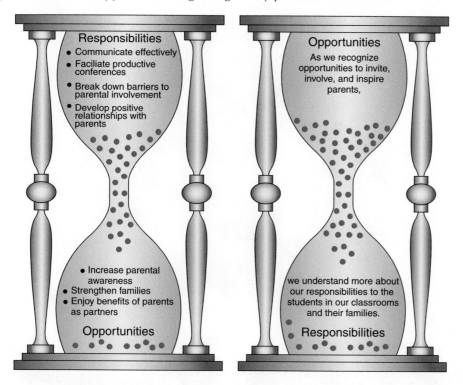

Responsibilities
- Communicate effectively
- Faciliate productive conferences
- Break down barriers to parental involvement
- Develop positive relationships with parents

- Increase parental awareness
- Strengthen families
- Enjoy benefits of parents as partners

Opportunities

Opportunities
As we recognize opportunities to invite, involve, and inspire parents,

we understand more about our responsibilities to the students in our classrooms and their families.

Responsibilities

What Are a Teacher's Responsibilities and Opportunities Regarding the Community?

Education is a public enterprise. Pick up a newspaper in almost any town or city, and you will find something in it that features, or refers to, schools and teachers. The community reads about it and hears about it, forming impressions along the way. Teachers, and those who work in and with schools, are acutely aware of how public their endeavors are. For most people in a community, what they know from the media about teachers, students, and classrooms is the sum total of their knowledge about schools. For this reason, teachers have the responsibility to be public relations agents for schools. We must put our best professional selves forward to represent education, in community groups, in church, in social gatherings, in the grocery store—everywhere we go.

The community can provide support, resources, and services that are valuable lifelines for students and their families. Individuals can volunteer their time, give money and materials, share their expertise as student mentors and guest speakers, and so on. Corporations can fund programs and events, offer employees release time to volunteer in schools, provide political support for needed policy changes, and more. Teachers should know what is available and, along with administrators and counselors, make sure families are aware of how to access community services such as health clinics, family counseling, and tutoring.

Involving community members in the life of the school is beneficial for both children and the adults who volunteer their time and energy.

Your Teaching Fingerprint

How do you envision being a community ambassador for schools? Do you think it's important to know what services are available for your students and their families? Is this part of what you imagined as the responsibilities of teaching?

When school, families, and the community work together, students receive optimum benefits, as illustrated in Figure 13.5. In another kind of community, the community that exists within the school walls, colleagues have responsibilities toward one another as well as opportunities to be enjoyed.

Figure 13.5 Optimum benefits for students

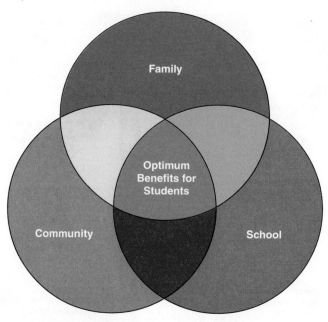

Responsibilities and opportunities regarding community

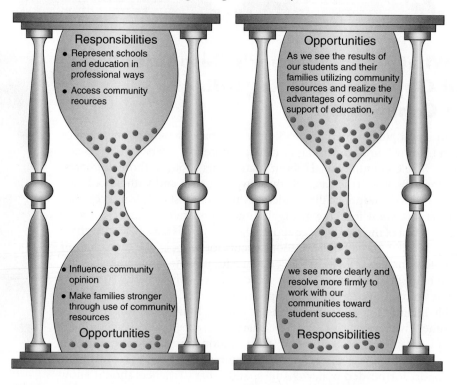

What Are a Teacher's Responsibilities and Opportunities Regarding Colleagues?

"One incontrovertible finding emerges from my career spent working in and around schools: The nature of relationships among the adults within a school has a greater influence on the character and quality of that school and on student accomplishment than anything else" (Barth, 2006, p. 9). This bold statement was made by Roland Barth, highly respected former teacher and principal and founding director of the Principals' Center at

Harvard University. He continues by saying, "In short, the relationships among the educators in a school define all relationships within the school's culture" (p. 9). These relationships include parents, families, community—the areas of responsibility and opportunity discussed so far. Is it possible that as a teacher, your relationship with a teacher down the hall affects these other relationships? Yes, according to Barth, who tells us we must find a way to confront this "elephant in the room" (p. 9): the collegial relationships that loom so large within the school but are seldom addressed.

This section examines four basic kinds of relationships among teachers. It then looks closely at the most beneficial of all relationships, the collegial relationship, and how this healthy and growth-promoting type of relationship can be established and nurtured.

Basic Relationships Among Teachers

The four basic relationships among teachers as defined by Barth (2006) are parallel play, adversarial relationships, congenial relationships, and collegial relationships.

Parallel play. Do you recall the discussion in Chapter 3 about young children engaging in parallel play (see page 72)? Children may sit on the floor just inches from one another, yet be so absorbed in their own toys and play that they never acknowledge each other's presence or offer to share their toys or play together in any way. This behavior is considered normal development for 2- and 3-year-olds. Sadly, a sort of teacher parallel play is the norm in many schools. Teachers too often close their doors, hoard their lessons and materials, and infrequently share their tools of the trade—their knowledge of curricula and repertoire of instructional strategies. This isolating approach to teaching robs the school and students of their potential for group and individual growth.

Adversarial relationships. Barth tells us that one reason so many teachers engage in a sort of parallel play is that they are attempting to avoid adversarial relationships, or those relationships characterized by blatant criticism, talking behind the backs of others, and unwarranted and destructive competition. Teachers do not look better when other teachers look worse. We should keep our eyes fixed not just on our "own" students, but on all students in everyone's classroom. We should consider all the children when asking, "And how are the children? Are they all well?"

Congenial relationships. You will no doubt develop congenial relationships with many of your colleagues. You will enjoy one another's company. People of different ages, personality types, interests, cultures, and faiths fill the ranks of public school teachers. You will find some with whom you have much in common, and others very different from yourself. Developing congenial relationships makes school more fun. Students can sense when their teachers enjoy the people around them. That's being a role model in the most practical ways. Do you recall teachers in your K–12 experience who genuinely appeared to enjoy one another's company? How could you tell?

Collegial relationships. Relationships with other teachers that promote growth through sharing of professional expertise are collegial. Roland Barth (2006) quotes famous baseball manager Casey Stengel: "Getting good players is easy. Getting 'em to play together is the hard part" (p. 11). There are lots of "good players," or competent teachers, in schools. Developing collegiality means getting them to play together. When Barth visits schools and looks for signs of collegial relationships, he looks for three components:

- Educators talking with one another about practice and sharing craft knowledge
- Educators observing one another while they are engaged in practice
- Educators rooting for one another's success

Let's put our responsibilities and opportunities regarding colleagues into context by examining each of these three indicators of collegiality.

Educators Talking with One Another About Practice and Sharing Craft Knowledge. There is a difference between congenial conversation and dialogue about

In Their Own Words . . .

Renee Ayers
Grade 2
Summit Primary School, Ohio

Many wonderful people supported and helped me during my first years of teaching: the clever curriculum director who told me about the "question chair" to stop interruptions during reading groups; the kind principal who cheered me on even when I was in tears in his office; the caring special education teacher who would come to my classroom during her planning period to tutor a special student; the 30-year-veteran teacher next door who taught me all of his "sing to learn" songs; the

school counselor who assisted me in doing hands-on science experiments with 27 second graders. I look back with such fondness as I consider the people who nurtured me.

As I grew in my career I decided I had a responsibility to pass this support on to other new teachers. In my sixth year of teaching I became a Praxis mentor with every intention of going into my protégés' classes and dishing out all my experience and advice. What I found from this experience was that by observing and supporting first-year teachers, I had created an opportunity for myself to learn. Every protégé has become a resource and friend to me. Their enthusiasm is contagious, their teaching practices are fresh, and their ability to persevere through the extreme pressure and demands of a first classroom never ceases to amaze me.

what we do as teachers. When we talk about a movie or our plans for the weekend, we are engaging in congenial conversation. This is different from talking about a challenging behavior problem and listening to suggestions from colleagues.

As discussed in Chapter 1 (see page 10), effective teachers are perpetual learners. Every day in the classroom provides learning opportunities. These learning opportunities lead us to be responsible not only to apply what we learn in our own classrooms, but also to share what we learn with other teachers. Each school has a wealth of what Barth (2006) calls "craft knowledge" (p. 10) about curriculum, instruction, assessment, classroom management, and so on, embodied in its teachers. Sharing what we know empowers all our colleagues. This can happen informally every day in conversations in the hallway and before and after school. It can also happen in a setting that invites teachers to showcase their best classroom practices in staff meetings.

Renee Ayers, our second grade focus teacher at Summit Primary School, Ohio, shares her experiences both as a new teacher and as a mentor in In Their Own Words. As you read what she has to say, think about your own receptiveness to constructive criticism. How do you respond when instructors suggest changes in your work? Do you look at suggestions as opportunities to learn? Why or why not?

Your Teaching Fingerprint

James Beane (2005) suggests **teacher study groups** as a means of building professional communities within schools. Small groups of teachers select books and journal articles to read, talk about what they have read, and discuss how it might be applied to their teaching.

One excellent way for new teachers to take advantage of experienced teachers' craft knowledge is through a mentor-mentee relationship. A teacher mentor uses experience and wisdom to answer questions and help guide new teachers. Fresh out of a teacher preparation program, most new teachers have learned lots of instructional strategies in their classes or through field experiences or student teaching that they are anxious to try. A new teacher's knowledge of theory and research may actually exceed that of more experienced colleagues. In this regard, mentors have the opportunity to learn from their mentees. However, what experienced teachers have that new teachers don't have is what Berliner (2001) calls "case knowledge." When experienced teachers face a new student, a new learning problem, or new materials, they have a memory bank of other similar situations upon which to draw. For a new teacher, having an experienced mentor to ask questions of and share descriptions of circumstances with allows ideas and suggestions to flow.

Educators Observing One Another While They Are Engaged in Practice. One of the most helpful things teachers can do is observe one another in the classroom and then describe what they see in nonevaluative, nonthreatening ways. As an observer, a teacher may be able to see dynamics between teacher and students, as well as between students and students. Observers can point out things that may be missed, and make suggestions for improvement. As teachers talk to one another and observe in colleagues' classrooms, they become more invested in one another's success.

Educators Rooting for One Another's Success. This characteristic of collegiality indicates sincere support and encouragement of teachers for one another. When teachers keep students first and want them all to succeed, then they will be rooting for each other's professional success.

One teacher who has capitalized on his concern for teachers and their ability to creatively meet the needs of their students is Charles Best, the young man featured in this chapter's In the News video. Read about him and his entrepreneurship that is benefiting teachers around the country.

Consider, too, the importance of the other adults in the school and their relationships. Chapter 12 discussed principals and assistant principals and their impact on classrooms (see pages 367–370). There are also administrative assistants, cafeteria and custodial workers, counselors, media specialists, and so on, all of whom have important roles in the life of a school. If a teacher is fortunate enough to have an assistant, this relationship also makes a significant difference in the classroom.

Relationships with Paraprofessionals

Paraprofessionals are also known as teacher aides and assistant teachers. The people who hold these positions are typically not certified teachers. Paraprofessionals are most commonly employed in early childhood and elementary settings. They may be in one classroom full-time, or they may rotate among teachers. For instance, a paraprofessional may be assigned to second grade in a school with five second grade teachers. These teachers may decide that the best use of another adult is to have the paraprofessional join the classes during the times when the children are in reading circles. Or the teachers may want extra help in their classrooms when students are working on projects that require the use of multiple materials.

Some schools are fortunate to have paraprofessionals who have worked for 20 or 30 years with multiple generations of students. They may know the community well and be valuable assets. If you are fortunate enough to have a teacher's aide or assistant in your classroom, treat this individual with respect. You have professional knowledge that may exceed that of a paraprofessional in some regards, but chances are your assistant has a lot

In the News

Charles Best: Providing a Quality Education for All Students

Charles Best believes that teaching is one of the highest callings and, as he puts it, "just plain fun." This remarkable young man has made it his mission in life to make a difference in the lives of kids through teaching—and through a web-based nonprofit organization he created called Donors Choose. This marvelous idea, to allow donors to personally choose to whom they give their money and resources and to know that what they give goes directly into the classroom, provides a satisfying experience for all involved.

To view this video, go to this text's DVD. Click on In the News, Chapter 13, and then on *Charles Best: Providing a Quality Education for All Students*. After watching the video, respond to these questions.

1. Charles describes both the student population and the staff at his school. Does the setting appeal to you? If so, why? If not, why not?

2. Charles expresses his initial concern that teachers wouldn't participate and ask for classroom resources. Why do you think he was concerned? Would you be willing to ask for donations on the Donors Choose website?

3. Why do you think Charles says he has to take complex ideas and reduce them to their essence in his classroom? What is he afraid will happen when he does this?

Responsibilities and opportunities regarding colleagues

Responsibilities
- Share craft knowledge
- Observe and learn from one another
- Root for one anothers success

Opportunities
- Learn new strategies
- Benefit from supportive relationships
- Enjoy camaraderie

Opportunities
As we enjoy and learn from collegial relationships,

our responsibilites increase to perpetuate the benefits of collegiality.

Responsibilities

of what experienced teachers have in terms of case knowledge. Learn from them even as you direct their participation in your lesson plans.

The power of teachers taking responsibility for establishing collegial relationships and availing themselves of the opportunities that come with these relationships is immeasurable. This power enables teachers to take their influence beyond their classrooms and their schools.

What Are a Teacher's Responsibilities and Opportunities Regarding Systemic Involvement?

Teachers, the people who understand much about child and adolescent development and how to meet the academic needs of their students, have a responsibility to extend their influence beyond the classroom. Extending teacher influence at the local, district, state, and national levels is what systemic involvement is all about. It is possible and desirable for teachers to become involved themselves in the systemic decision-making process. This responsibility is often both energy- and time-consuming, but the opportunities to benefit students are many. Please keep in mind that you should postpone most of the options discussed in this section until you have acquired several years of teaching experience. These are responsibilities and opportunities you can grow into with time.

Teacher Involvement in the School

Being an active participant in the collegiality of a school is a positive way to be involved. For new teachers this may mean benefiting from a strong mentor relationship with experienced teachers and maintaining a helpful, open spirit. When you become more confident in your new role, you will have opportunities to be part of committees and task forces with specific decision-making and action responsibilities, including

- planning special events
- choosing grade level or subject area curriculum materials

- selecting new books for the media center
- developing schedules
- working with business partners
- planning for future growth
- collaborating with other teacher groups (e.g., regular education with special education, core subjects with related arts)

There are opportunities to serve in official ways as teacher leaders, as discussed in Chapter 12 (see page 370). Many elementary schools have teachers designated as subject area specialists. Early childhood and elementary schools often designate grade level chairpersons who meet regularly with teachers of the same grade to determine needs and discuss their concerns. They work with other grade level chairs and the administration to meet these needs and remedy areas of concern. Middle schools that are organized into teams usually have team leaders. Junior highs and high schools are typically organized by subject area departments, each with a chairperson.

Serving on a School Improvement Council is a serious responsibility you may consider after teaching for several years. It is an opportunity to represent your colleagues in discussions and decisions that affect most aspects of the life of your school. Serving on the council requires knowledge of how your school fits within the governance of the district.

Teacher Involvement in the District

Every district functions within state guidelines and with the use of state funds, as discussed in Chapter 12 (see pages 360–363). Being informed about how your district functions begins with paying attention to who is in leadership roles and how the chain of command works. Most districts have grade level or subject area specialists, or both. It is a good idea to take advantage of specialists' expertise when opportunities arise. You may first encounter such specialists at district meetings.

Attending school district board meetings is often an eye-opening experience. You may meet district personnel and get a sense of how the board and district superintendent work together. In addition, you will get a glimpse of what's on the minds of concerned citizens. As a citizen and an educator, you have a responsibility to ask questions, voice your opinions, and serve on district committees.

District committees and task forces may form to make decisions and take action such as

- textbook selection (within state guidelines if applicable)
- curriculum planning to incorporate state standards
- recommendations for creating activities to involve parents

It is advisable to wait until at least your third or fourth year of teaching to take on district level responsibilities. For one thing, your major focus for the first few years should be on your classroom teaching responsibilities and building your knowledge of the curriculum and of instruction. In addition, a few years in a district will give you perspective on systemic issues and prepare you for even wider involvement later.

Teacher Involvement at State and National Levels

As you read in Chapter 12 (see pages 359–360), the U.S. Department of Education, the secretary of education, and the president implement programs and policies that affect the states. Curriculum standards (Chapter 4) and accountability testing (Chapter 5) are determined at the state level and serve to guide districts and their schools. There are few opportunities for classroom teachers to be involved at state and national governance levels. However, committees and task forces at the state level are occasionally convened to address issues such as

- curriculum standards revision
- textbook adoption options for districts
- program guidelines for new initiatives, such as statewide training of school math coaches (teachers specifically designated to help other teachers with math instruction)

State and national legislators need to hear from teachers because teachers are closest to the students. Writing letters and emails to those in political power can inform them about the day-to-day successes and needs of students. Derek Boucher, one of our focus teachers at Roosevelt High School, feels strongly about his responsibility to help those outside schools understand more about students and learning. Read what he has to say in In Their Own Words.

Decisions that affect students and classrooms, whether local, district, state, or national, are best made with teachers' input. Our conscientious, rational involvement will provide opportunities to influence decisions while promoting the image and respectability of the teaching profession.

In Their Own Words . . .

Derek Boucher
High School History
and Reading
Roosevelt High School,
California

In 2002 I read *Resisting Reading Mandates* by Dr. Elaine Garan. Her book exposed many of the biases and conflicts of interest that exist among those who make national policy decisions regarding K–12 reading instruction.

I was so inspired by her revealing work that I wrote an opinion editorial that was published in our local newspaper. What happened next shocked me. Attorneys from a large educational publishing company that

was implicated in Dr. Garan's book contacted me. This company stood to benefit financially from the new reading policy. They wanted to stop me from expressing my opinion and the newspaper from publishing opinions that disagreed with their position. At that moment, I realized the power and responsibility teachers have to express their opinions about what works in the classroom.

Since that time, I have submitted opinion pieces to educational journals, as well as over a dozen letters to the editor of our local newspaper. Many outside the classroom feel they know what is best for our children and classrooms. It is our responsibility as professionals on the front line, who work with children on a daily basis, to share our experience and perspective.

Responsibilities and opportunities regarding systemic involvement

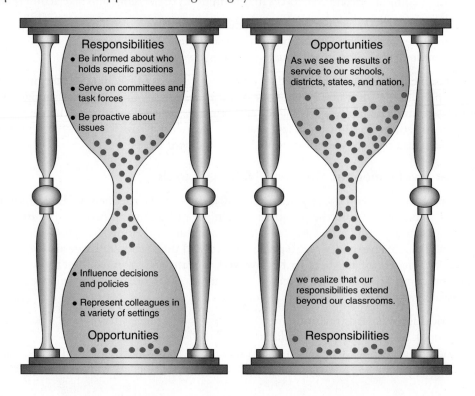

What Are a Teacher's Responsibilities and Opportunities Regarding the Teaching Profession?

Chapter 1 (see pages 14–17) discussed the teaching profession, teacher professionalism, and professional organizations. This section looks specifically at two areas of responsibility and opportunity regarding the teaching profession: involvement in professional organizations and contributions to the professional knowledge base (what we know about teaching).

Teacher Involvement in Professional Organizations

The effectiveness of any organization depends in large measure on its membership. Teachers are responsible for the effectiveness of professional teacher organizations, whether large and politically aggressive, like the National Education Association (NEA) and the American Federation of Teachers (AFT), or small, like a district social studies council with the purpose of providing resources and information for area social studies teachers. In most cases, membership in professional organizations is voluntary, although there are instances when teachers may feel pressured into joining specific groups.

Subject area organizations, such as the National Council of Teachers of English (NCTE) and the National Council of Teachers of Mathematics (NCTM), provide valuable information and resources, as discussed in Chapter 4 (see pages 116–117). Membership helps teachers do what they do better. Every teacher who belongs makes subject area organizations stronger. Most states have their own subject area organizations that are affiliates of the national subject area groups. State membership fees are generally less and their conferences are more accessible because they are within the individual states. Membership in these state organizations is a good place to begin.

It is important for teachers to take advantage of the opportunities professional organizations provide. In turn, teachers have a responsibility to join professional organizations to help build the teaching profession. You can find out more about various professional organizations by accessing their websites, listed in Figure 1.2 (see page 5).

Contributions to the Professional Knowledge Base

As teachers, we have a continuing opportunity to develop professional knowledge about teaching through numerous books, articles, and staff development sessions. It is our responsibility to read, watch, and listen to learn.

It is also our responsibility to contribute to the professional knowledge base. When a teacher tries an instructional strategy that works well with a particular topic, or with a specific group of students, sharing the experience will help other teachers. This sharing can happen in a team or grade level meeting, at a meeting of a professional organization, or in an article written for an education journal. Teachers who conduct research in their classrooms around a concept or question that captures their interest can add their findings to the teaching knowledge base. This kind of research is commonly referred to as **action research.**

Deirdre Huger-McGrew expresses her views about learning from the teaching knowledge base and giving back to the profession. Read what she has to say in In Their Own Words.

Teachers have the responsibility to represent the teaching profession in ways that demonstrate professionalism. We do so through our association with professional organizations, through the additions we make to the teaching knowledge base, and through our professional and personal behaviors and attitudes.

In Their Own Words . . .

Deirdre Huger-McGrew
Language Arts/
Social Studies
Cario Middle School,
South Carolina

Throughout my 12 years as a teacher, I've taken many courses beyond my initial teacher training. I have been involved in many teaching-related projects, most by choice and others as directed by my principal to achieve school and district goals. I have taken my professional development personally because I feel it is a part of my responsibility to nurture my growth as a teacher. It is my identity. It is who I am as a teacher. Seeking to enhance my skills makes a difference in my classroom. I take delight in embracing changing views and trying strategies that have the potential to improve my teaching.

What makes athletes, doctors, or lawyers the best in their fields? I believe it is their desire and ability to seek ways to improve what they do as professionals. This gives them an edge. Teachers should want the same. I want to continually accomplish growth-enhancing professional goals.

Responsibilities and opportunities regarding the teaching profession

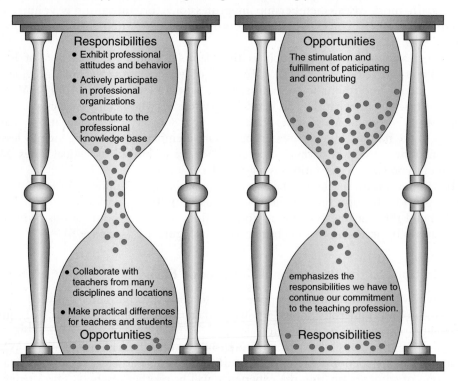

Responsibilities
- Exhibit professional attitudes and behavior
- Actively participate in professional organizations
- Contribute to the professional knowledge base
- Collaborate with teachers from many disciplines and locations
- Make practical differences for teachers and students

Opportunities

Opportunities
The stimulation and fulfillment of paticipating and contributing

emphasizes the responsibilities we have to continue our commitment to the teaching profession.

Responsibilities

What Are a Teacher's Responsibilities and Opportunities Regarding Self-Growth?

One of the eight reasons for choosing to teach described in Chapter 3 (see pages 6–10) is the opportunity for a lifetime of self-growth. This opportunity doesn't necessarily mean that teachers automatically experience professional and personal self-growth. Teachers must take the responsibility of growing both professionally and personally.

Professional Self-Growth

Professional self-growth is an absolute necessity for teacher effectiveness. There is a documented relationship between professional self-growth leading to improved teaching quality, and student achievement (Darling-Hammond & Youngs, 2002). In addition to professional opportunities to grow with help from colleagues and participation in professional organizations, there is a wealth of literature addressing the many aspects of teaching and learning discussed in the previous section. Choosing specific journals and scanning them for articles pertinent to what we teach and who we teach, and then reading them for ideas and advice, is another way for teachers to continue to grow professionally.

Advanced degrees. Teachers can continue their education by seeking advanced degrees. Combinations of on-site and distance learning often allow coursework to fit more easily into a teacher's schedule. Master's of education degrees are offered at numerous universities. Teachers also often seek advanced degrees in the subject area they teach. Not only does more in-depth study of content enrich teaching, but it also opens leadership doors, as discussed previously. Learning new content and methods is a win-win situation for us and our students.

NBPTS certification. One of the most recognized as well as state-endorsed opportunities for professional growth is certification through the National Board of Professional Teaching Standards (NBPTS). The organization was created in 1987 to emphasize what teachers should know and do to positively affect student learning. The foundation of NBPTS rests on the five core beliefs listed in Figure 13.6.

In addition to the five core propositions (beliefs), NBPTS has specific standards that must be met in each of the categories of certification. Some of these standards have been cited in the Standards Speak sections at the end of this text's chapters. There are 24 certification areas, matching the teaching assignments of over 95% of teachers. These certification areas align with the levels of school and include early childhood, middle childhood (elementary), early adolescence (middle school), and adolescence and young adulthood (high school).

As of 2006, over 47,000 teachers were certified through NBPTS. Formal certification requires teachers to

- undertake a year-long intense process involving self-reflection and assessment
- create a teaching portfolio
- complete an involved writing component
- perform successfully on a comprehensive exam

In addition to certification and recognition, some states offer widely varying incentives. In South Carolina, for instance, NBPTS certified teachers receive an additional $7,500 per year for 10 years, do not have to go through normal state certification procedures, and are reimbursed for the expenses involved in achieving certification. In Wisconsin, however, only about half of the cost of NBPTS certification is reimbursable the first year, and certified teachers receive a $2,500 stipend each of the 9 remaining years of certification. It is interesting to note that in 2005, South Carolina had 580 new NBPTS certified teachers, while Wisconsin had 71.

Besides benefiting our students and the profession in general, a sense of ongoing professional growth will contribute positively to our sense of personal self-growth.

Personal Self-Growth

We can't separate our professional and personal lives completely. However, we can nurture personal relationships and enjoy interests outside of school. Our sense of personal well-being affects every aspect of our lives, including our professional competence.

Have you considered how you might balance the personal and professional aspects of your life? You will soon need to pay attention to this balance as you begin to spend time in schools as part of your field experiences leading to teacher certification. Chapter 14 will discuss how to get the most out of all the opportunities for professional growth that are ahead of you. For now, however, think about what brings you

Your Teaching
Fingerprint

Figure 13.6 Core beliefs of the National Board for Professional Teaching Standards

Proposition 1: Teachers Are Committed to Students and Learning.

Teachers

- are dedicated to making knowledge accessible to all students. They believe all students can learn.
- treat students equitably.
- understand how students develop and learn.
- respect the cultural and family differences students bring to their classroom.
- are concerned with their students' self-concept, their motivation, and the effects of learning on peer relationships.
- are concerned with the development of character and civic responsibility.

Proposition 2: Teachers Know the Subjects They Teach and How to Teach Those Subjects to Students.

Teachers

- have mastery over the subject(s) they teach.
- have skill and experience in teaching.
- are able to use diverse instructional strategies to teach for understanding.

Proposition 3: Teachers Are Responsible for Managing and Monitoring Student Learning.

Teachers

- deliver effective instruction.
- know how to engage students to ensure a disciplined learning environment.
- know how to assess the progress of individual students as well as the class as a whole.
- use multiple methods for measuring students' growth and understanding.

Proposition 4: Teachers Think Systematically about Their Practice and Learn from Experience.

Teachers

- model what it means to be an educated person—they read, they question, they create, and they are willing to try new things.
- are familiar with learning theories and instructional strategies and stay abreast of current issues in American education.
- critically examine their practice on a regular basis to deepen knowledge, expand their repertoire of skills, and incorporate new findings into their practice.

Proposition 5: Teachers Are Members of Learning Communities.

Teachers

- collaborate with others to improve student learning.
- are leaders and actively know how to seek and build partnerships with community groups and businesses.
- work with other professionals on instructional policy, curriculum development, and staff development.
- can evaluate school progress and the allocation of resources.
- know how to work collaboratively with parents to engage them productively in the work of the school.

Source: Reprinted with permission from the National Board for Professional Teaching Standards, www.nbpts.org. All rights reserved.

personal satisfaction and pleasure. These are activities you will want to continue in order to achieve personal and professional balance.

The healthier we are professionally and personally, the better able we are to meet the needs of our students. Read In Their Own Words to see what Chris Roberts, Rees Elementary, Utah, has to say about maintaining a healthy, interesting life, and how doing so affects students.

In Their Own Words . . .

**Chris Roberts
Grades 3–5 Multiage
Classroom
Rees Elementary School,
Utah**

I heard or read somewhere that "you teach who you are." I know, after teaching 29 years, that there is a lot of truth in those five words. I've had students return to visit me years after they've been in my class, and I get invited to many of their weddings. As we catch up on the years that have passed, none of them talk about their reading or math; they tell me about me. . . . [T]heir memories don't focus on the great unit I taught on Native Americans, but rather on the time I told them about a trip I went on or a belief I have about life. I don't think you can be an excellent teacher if your own life is boring or "unexamined," as Henry David Thoreau would caution. Children will naturally be less interested in learning from someone whom they find uninteresting. Don't let the classroom, and pressures you will surely face, rule your life. Live a full life. Share with your students what you learn and experience on your amazing path.

Responsibilities and opportunities regarding self-growth

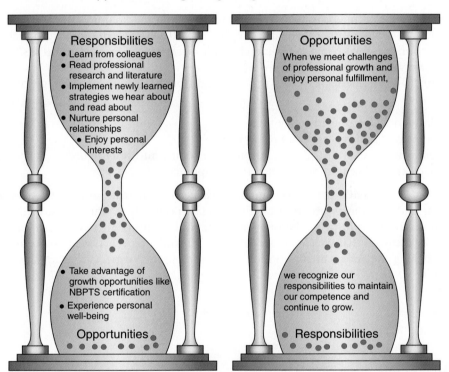

What Are a Teacher's Responsibilities and Opportunities Regarding Students?

For teachers, students are absolutely at the top of the list of responsibilities and the primary focus of opportunities. This whole text is about how to be effective teachers and how to meet student needs. When we fulfill our responsibilities and take advantage of our opportunities in the first six areas (family, community, colleagues, systemic involvement, the teaching profession, self-growth), we are doing so for the children and adolescents we affect. We are working toward being able to answer the recurring questions, "And how are the children? Are they all well?" in resoundingly positive ways. This brief section highlights some ways to keep our responsibilities and opportunities clearly focused on our students.

Taking Responsibility for Student Learning

Effective teachers take responsibility for teaching all students successfully (Zeichner, 2003). In their research, Corbett, Wilson, and Williams (2005) found that the common link among teachers who consistently reach students whom others might consider unreachable is that they take responsibility for student learning. These teachers asserted, "All students can learn," not, "All students can learn, but . . ." (p. 8). These teachers who take responsibility for student learning also stated that "they could not alter conditions outside school that impinged on student performance, but they could affect the conditions in their classrooms" (p. 12).

Teachers who take responsibility for student learning take no excuses—from students, parents, or themselves. They find ways to engage students in learning, as discussed in Chapter 7. They use instructional strategies that fit both the content and the learners, and they model respect and enthusiasm. To them, "effective teaching means giving students no other choice but success" (Corbett et al., 2005, p. 12). Read what Craig Cleveland has to say about teaching all students in an environment that promotes learning in In Their Own Words. Craig believes in unconditional teaching.

Unconditional Teaching

Alfie Kohn (2005) reminds us that "[t]eaching the whole child requires that we accept students for who they are rather than what they do" (p. 20). He calls this unconditional teaching. He continues by saying, "If some children matter more to us than others, then all children are valued only conditionally" (p. 20).

Kohn (2005) further explains that unconditional teaching involves gestures that consistently

- let kids know we're glad to see them
- demonstrate that we trust and respect them
- reveal who we truly are, that is, not just controlling authority figures
- let kids know that they are listened to and appreciated

Read what Louisa LaGrotto, 2006 Indiana Teacher of the Year, says in Teachers' Days, Delights, and Dilemmas about managing a classroom where students are given and respond positively to respect. She offers advice about creating an effective and efficiently managed classroom that welcomes and includes all students. When we practice unconditional teaching, we accept the responsibility to maintain high expectations for all students' learning.

In Their Own Words . . .

Craig Cleveland
History
Roosevelt High School,
California

Educators first teach who they are. Their disposition, view of life, and how they perceive their students is picked up on and learned by the students before the first quiz. The opportunity for excellent student performance in the classroom is directly related to how the teacher interacts with the students. I believe that teachers must be fair, have no favorites, and be liberal in providing needed help. Kindness is the fundamental rule for communication between student and teacher. Kindness is hopeful, encourages students to do better, and shows respect for others. Both Guillermo and Khamanny come from supportive families where they are loved. They thrive in a classroom environment where their ideas are listened to and respected. I believe that students are more willing to take risks in class when they know that their contribution will be appreciated.

Teachers' Days, Delights, and Dilemmas

Louisa LaGrotto 2006 Indiana Teacher of the Year

I have been called a guru of classroom management. When I find a method that works, I get very passionate and vocal about it. My classroom operates on many of the principles outlined in Harry Wong's *The First Days of School*. I have very high expectations for my students, in terms of both achievement and behavior. Here are some guidelines that may help you in your own classroom.

1. Students want to know where they fit in your room's design. So designate seating, give them a place to socialize when appropriate, and let them know the teacher-only zone.
2. Announce and post what student activities will occur each day. My students see written messages on the door, on the white board, and on their weekly agendas. A different student volunteers to publicly make announcements about our daily lesson as well.
3. Make students comfortable being leaders in your class. I offer numerous jobs for which students may volunteer. Students lead homework reviews, do warm-up questions and drills on skills, take notes for absent students, pass out and collect materials, share stories and talents, and more. Because it's the subject I teach, the students do all these things in Spanish.
4. Establish clear procedures for proper behavior, respect for others, and a smoothly operating class. Practice them.
5. Present a classroom management plan as a contract. Students and teacher read the contract, question the contract, and acknowledge the contract via student and parent signatures.

As teachers, our image matters greatly to students. They look at us all the time. So, be interesting! What you wear, what you say, what you know about their world hooks them into *your* world. Most of us can effectively manage time, materials, desks, our own moods. But students bring in *their* own moods and issues over which we have no control. So stop trying, and just model the gifts you wish to give your students: happiness, enthusiasm, a love for learning, respect for all cultures, and patience.

High Expectations

When we take responsibility for teaching all students unconditionally regardless of the circumstances, we will necessarily have high expectations for them (Gehrke, 2005). In an article entitled "They Can Because They Think They Can," Richard Vacca (2006), noted expert in the field of reading instruction, states that providing learning experiences that allow students to be successful will increase their sense of **self-efficacy.** Vacca tells us, "Self-efficacy is an 'I can' belief in oneself that leads to a sense of competence" (p. 56). Unlike sometimes empty self-esteem techniques that focus on building self-concept with words and are devoid of actual accomplishments, Vacca's concept of self-efficacy is solidly grounded in the accomplishment of a continuum of increasingly difficult challenges. As students master a concept or skill, they are encouraged to attempt even more difficult tasks. In this way, our high expectations for students lead to their own high expectations for themselves. If this sounds familiar, you are probably recalling the discussion of scaffolding in Chapter 4 (see page 126).

You have learned that there are many factors to consider when it comes to student achievement. How much responsibility do you think teachers bear for student learning? Can what a teacher does in the classroom overcome obstacles that students face outside the classroom, such as poverty, lack of family involvement, and a background deficient in content and skills? Why or why not?

Your Teaching Fingerprint

Concluding Thoughts

It's possible to spend an entire career in the position of teacher and never accept the inherent responsibilities that accompany the position. How unfortunate and sad for the individual who chooses to go through the motions, but never invests the commitment and care necessary to take advantage of opportunities to make a difference in the lives of students.

Responsibilities and opportunities regarding students

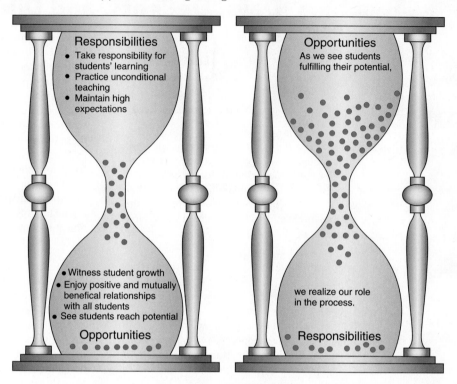

On the positive side, it is possible to spend an entire career accepting responsibilities to families, community, colleagues, the educational system, the profession, self-growth, and students. Fulfilling each responsibility brings opportunities to affect students' lives and to enjoy a career filled with challenge and satisfaction.

What Role Will Diversity Play in My Teaching Identity?

One of a teacher's most important responsibilities is to recognize diversity in its many forms and to be accountable for students as individuals. Students present themselves as they are, each with unique characteristics in terms of both strengths and needs.

Getting to know students as individuals entails getting to know their family circumstances—their ethnicity, culture, socioeconomic status, and more. Knowing that parental involvement increases academic achievement and attendance and improves students' attitudes toward school and their behavior is all the impetus teachers should need not only to know about the families of their students, but also to know the families themselves. The challenges faced by many minority families and families of low socioeconomic status affect students both in school and outside school. These are the students who benefit most from teachers' proactive efforts to involve their families in the life of the school.

Chapter in Review

What are a teacher's responsibilities and opportunities regarding family involvement?

- Most family-school interactions will be with parents.
- Parental involvement increases academic achievement and attendance rates and leads to more positive attitudes and behavior.

- There are many ways to communicate with parents about opportunities for involvement.
- Parent-student-teacher conferences provide excellent opportunities for communication and action.
- Both parents and teachers create barriers to family involvement.

What are a teacher's responsibilities and opportunities regarding the community?

- Teachers have the responsibility to be positive, productive public relations agents for their schools and education.
- The community provides valuable support and services for children and their families.
- When schools, families, and the community work together, students benefit.

What are a teacher's responsibilities and opportunities regarding colleagues?

- To be collegial requires overt efforts to create and maintain mutually beneficial relationships.
- There are tremendous opportunities for professional and personal growth through collegial relationships within a school.

What are a teacher's responsibilities and opportunities regarding systemic involvement?

- Teachers have a responsibility to extend their influence beyond the classroom.
- New teachers can become actively involved in their schools.
- With a few years of teaching experience, teachers can extend their involvement to district, state, and even national arenas.

What are a teacher's responsibilities and opportunities regarding the teaching profession?

- The teaching profession is strengthened through teacher involvement in local, statewide, and national teacher organizations.
- Teachers have many opportunities to add to the teaching knowledge base through research, writing, and participation.

What are a teacher's responsibilities and opportunities regarding self-growth?

- Professional and personal self-growth does not happen automatically.
- Reading, talking with colleagues, and other informal avenues to professional growth are available, as well as formal opportunities such as advanced degrees and National Board of Professional Teaching Standards certification.
- It is important for teachers to balance their professional and personal lives by developing interests and friendships that promote healthy lifestyles.

What are a teacher's responsibilities and opportunities regarding students?

- Teachers should develop and maintain a sense of responsibility for student learning.
- To teach unconditionally means to accept all students for who they are rather than for what they do.
- Teachers need to maintain high expectations for all students, which, in turn, help students expect more of themselves.

Professional Practice

Licensure Test Prep

What follows is a case study similar to what you will find on the Praxis™ II PLT exam. Read each component and answer multiple-choice questions 1–3 and then constructed-response items 4 and 5. It is wise to read the questions before reading the case so you will be aware of your purpose for reading.

Jonathan just got home from report card pickup night at Timberland Middle School (TMS), an urban school of about 700 students. He is disappointed, to say the least. While 32 students' family members showed up to retrieve report cards, the Trail Blazers eighth grade team has 96 students. The ones who didn't show up worry Jonathan the most. Many of the parents who came were familiar to him because they regularly volunteer at the school or were chaperones on last month's field trip. It's not that he didn't want to see them, he had just hoped that families of the students who give him reason to be concerned would have attended this first schoolwide opportunity for parents to meet the teachers.

This is Jonathan's first year of teaching, and he has discovered that he has a real affinity for relating to kids who already have a number of strikes against them when it comes to the likelihood of academic success. About 65% of the kids at TMS qualify for free or reduced-price lunch. These students are primarily African American and Hmong and live in the city-owned projects that are within walking distance of the school. The other 35% live in a revitalized part of downtown in refurbished stately homes. Their parents generally have high levels of education and work in the professional arena.

The Team

Jonathan teaches science on a five-teacher team. Kathy, the other first-year teacher on the team, teaches English language arts. She and Jonathan share a lot of the same ideas about how best to teach middle school kids. The social studies and math teachers, Gerald and Patricia, have taught for decades and often speak about retirement in glowing terms. They are still dedicated to what's best for students, but are less likely to try new instructional strategies. Tamika, the teacher who teaches all subjects to a small group of students who have already failed two grades between kindergarten and eighth grade, is a spirited advocate for "her kids."

Mrs. Parker

The principal of TMS is a veteran administrator who was specifically hired this year from out of state with the charge to make TMS a "flagship middle school where learning is engaging and students are encouraged to reach new heights." These words form the mantra of the parents who have committed to put their children back into public school after many promises from the district superintendent. Mrs. Parker knows her reputation is at stake. She is delighted with the professional families who have faith in her and who send their children to school ready to learn. She knows the challenges that confront her to create an atmosphere of high academic standards for all students. She has established heterogeneous classes in science, social studies, and related arts, with tracking in math and English language arts.

The Lab Challenge

Jonathan believes in hands-on science learning. One of the superintendent's promises was that TMS would have state-of-the-art science labs. This is one of the things that attracted Jonathan to the school. The kids who attended private schools are used to premier facilities, but before this year TMS barely had enough science rooms with water available, let alone full set-ups for extensive experimentation. Students who have been at TMS for other grade levels know the new things were added for the new "rich kids" and have never been exposed to real hands-on science. Jonathan has taken heterogeneous science classes a step further by inviting Tamika's at-risk group to join his science classes. He has purposefully assigned lab groups to include one or two of the "new" kids, two veteran TMS students, and one of Tamika's students.

1. Knowing what you do about Jonathan's team, which two kinds of relationships do you think he has with Gerald and Patricia?
   a. congenial and collegial
   b. adversarial and parallel play
   c. congenial and parallel play
   d. collegial and parallel play

2. Mrs. Parker has already received phone calls from three parents concerned that their children always have to take the lead in group lab work because the other group members either don't have a clue about how to proceed or their behavior is off task. What might Jonathan say to Mrs. Parker when she confronts him about labs to best express his motivation for grouping the way he does?
   a. All the kids deserve a chance to experience hands-on science.
   b. Young adolescents learn so much from each other. The one who teaches learns almost as much as the one who is being taught. They are also learning about relationships.
   c. Because of the grouping plan, there is a better chance that the new equipment will last.
   d. Integration doesn't happen by chance, and heterogeneous grouping within heterogeneous classes is the only way to make heterogeneous classes have full impact.

3. Jonathan is interested in determining the benefits, if any, of his lab grouping scheme. In order to do this, he will likely employ
   a. journal search techniques.
   b. action research.
   c. developmental determination.
   d. grouping pattern determination.

4. Jonathan has submitted a proposal to present at next year's NMSA national conference. He is very excited about doing research on heterogeneous science lab groups and their effect on student learning. If his proposal is accepted, he wants to invite one of his teammates to go to the conference as his co-presenter. Choose two of his teammates and justify why each might be a good choice to support what Jonathan wants to present.

5. Besides placing students in heterogeneous groups for lab, what are two other things Jonathan might do to foster academic achievement for all his students, including those who have been designated as academically gifted? Explain each.

Standards Speak

More standards are cited here than in other chapters because this chapter addresses so many aspects of the teaching profession. The first five standards speak to professional growth and collegiality. The next three standards deal with family-community-school relationships. Read the standards carefully and then respond to the questions related to them.

INTASC Principle 1, Dispositions

The teacher is committed to continuous learning and engages in professional discourse about subject matter knowledge and children's learning of the discipline.

INTASC Principle 9, Performances

The teacher draws upon professional colleagues within the school and other professional arenas as supports for reflection, problem solving, and new ideas, actively sharing experiences and seeking and giving feedback.

NBPTS, Early Adolescence Generalist, Standards XII: Collaboration with Colleagues

Accomplished generalists work with colleagues to improve schools and advance knowledge and are proactive in their field.

NMSA, Standard 7 Middle Level Professional Roles, Performance 4

Middle level teacher candidates engage in and support ongoing professional practices for self and colleagues (e.g., attend professional development activities and conferences, participate in professional organizations).

NMSA, Standard 7 Middle Level Professional Roles, Disposition 3

Middle level teacher candidates believe that their professional responsibilities extend beyond the classroom and school (e.g., advising committees, parent-teacher organizations).

INTASC Principle 10 Performances

The teacher establishes respectful and productive relationships with parents and guardians from diverse home and community situations, and seeks to develop cooperative partnerships in support of student learning and well-being.

NBPTS, Middle Childhood Generalist, Standard IX Family Involvement

Accomplished teachers initiate positive, interactive relationships with families as they participate in the education of their children.

NMSA, Standard 6 Family and Community Involvement

Middle level teacher candidates understand the major concepts, principles, theories, and research related to working collaboratively with family and community members, and they use that knowledge to maximize the learning of all young adolescents.

Respond to the following questions in your class notebook and/or discuss your responses with your classmates as directed by your instructor.

1. With all the responsibilities of teaching in your own classroom, what strategies do you think you might use to stay informed and contribute to colleagues' growth, your own growth, and the promotion of the teaching profession in time-effective ways?

2. Given the opportunity to attend a professional conference, how might you best use your time in order to take advantage of the professional and personal opportunities for growth?

3. After reading this chapter, what three techniques do you anticipate using regularly to involve families in the life of your school?

4. NBPTS Standard IX calls for "interactive relationships." This entails more than one-way communication. What techniques could you use to increase interactive communication and encounters with families?

MyEducationLab

The following interactive features may be found in Chapter 13 of MyEducationLab.

Homework and Exercises

Writing My Own Story

To write your own story by responding to some of the questions in the text accompanied by fingerprint icons, plus others, go to the "Writing My Own Story" section of the Homework and Exercises for Chapter 13 of MyEducationLab.

What's My Disposition?

To reflect on your beliefs and attitudes concerning the teaching profession, go to Chapter 13's "What's My Disposition?" feature of the Homework and Exercises section of MyEducationLab.

Exploring Schools and Classrooms

If your course involves experiences in schools, the questions and prompts in the "Exploring Schools and Classrooms" feature of Chapter 13's Homework and Exercises section of MyEducationLab will guide you as you explore local schools and classrooms.

Virtual Field Experience

To respond to questions and prompts regarding the Choosing Your Teaching Path videos that connect to specific chapter content, go to Chapter 13's Virtual Field Experience section of MyEducationLab. The questions will help you make sense of what you have read in the chapter.

Chapter 14

Charting My Teaching Course

The compass rose has appeared on charts and maps since the 1300s. The eight major points and the additional 24 bisections, for a total of 32 points, have specific names and degree designations that indicate directions on land and at sea. Those in charge of travel and navigation have learned the name and direction for each point for over seven centuries. They may have been heading south-southeast, but they understood all the other direction indicators.

As an educational tool, this chapter's compass rose will help you navigate toward your teaching identity. Notice that the four major directional points are the four levels of school you have learned about in this text, and through the video in the Choosing Your Path section of MyEducationLab at www.myeducationlab.com. The major sections of the education compass rose are bisected with an additional four points that indicate options for your consideration. A course like the one you are completing helps you find your teaching identity. You may decide to be a regular classroom teacher in one of the four major levels, or you may decide to be a related arts teacher or a special education teacher, with certification spanning all the grade levels or concentrated in just one. You may have a future goal of becoming an administrator, either at the school building level (principal, assistant principal) or at a district level (subject coordinator, superintendent, etc.). Or you may take another direction, leading toward counseling, speech therapy, or other specializations.

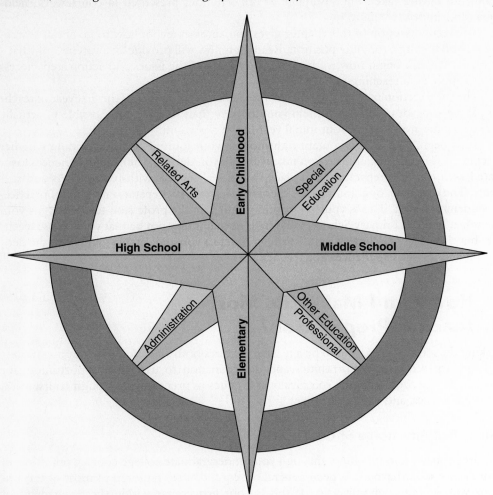

Keep in mind that a degree in education, or even one course, is useful in many ways even if you opt not to make education a career. Hopefully, your time in this course has increased your understanding of education in the United States enough to make you an informed advocate for students, teachers, and schools.

It's time to chart your teaching course. Have you decided that a teaching career is a good fit for your interests and abilities? Consider this chapter to have fingerprints throughout, all with the purpose of helping you choose your teaching path and clarify your teaching identity. Every page will help guide you. Picture the compass rose as you proceed. The chapter also includes letters filled with wisdom and advice from our focus teachers.

Here are the big questions the chapter will address. Each section includes frequently asked questions and answers.

- How can I make the most of teacher preparation?
- How can I make the most of searching for a teaching position?
- How can I thrive, not merely survive, during my first year of teaching?

Introduction

Within the next few years all of the information in this chapter will be relevant to you. The first section features information that applies to you right now. Have you ever thought after an opportunity passes, "I sure wish I had paid more attention or tried harder"? All of us have. Taking seriously the concepts in this chapter may save you from regrets later on about not having taken full advantage of opportunities presented in coursework, field-work, and student teaching.

The second section of this chapter gives you an overview of how to go about searching for and finding a teaching position. Reading it now will provide an awareness of what's to come. You can begin now to think through some of the issues and action steps necessary to apply for a teaching job.

The third section provides a glimpse of some of the challenges of the first year of teaching, along with ideas and tips to help you do more than survive. It is possible to actually thrive in some areas during your initial year in the classroom.

Let's begin with where you are right now in your journey toward deciding whether teaching is for you. The courses you take will help you decide. The field experiences associated with teacher preparation will place you in real schools with real teachers and students. The capstone, or culminating experience, in teacher preparation is clinical practice, or student teaching. This is your opportunity to try on the profession to see if it fits you. Brandi, at Summit Primary School, Ohio, tells us that it may not be that you choose teaching, but that teaching chooses you. Read her letter to you and catch a glimpse of the dedication and joy she experiences as a teacher.

How Can I Make the Most of Teacher Preparation?

Making the most of preparing to be a teacher requires both vigilance and determination—vigilance to recognize opportunities and determination to use these opportunities for growth. This section will look specifically at avenues of preparation through coursework, field experiences, and clinical practice.

Taking Full Advantage of Coursework

You are probably about halfway through your undergraduate college coursework. Most of your classes so far have likely been general, or core, courses required of most of the students who attend your university. If this is your first course within the department or

In Their Own Words . . .

Brandi Wade
Kindergarten
Summit Primary,
Ohio

Dear Teacher Candidates,

It may not so much be that you choose teaching, but that teaching chooses you. It will be in your heart and on your mind constantly. While it's never easy for more than 5 minutes at a time, teaching is the most important profession you can pursue. I am truly blessed to be a kindergarten teacher. I get to teach a different lesson, meet a different challenge, and see life from different perspectives every day in my classroom.

Laugh with the children, laugh at yourself, and never hold a grudge. Don't be afraid to say, "I'm sorry," to a child when you have done something unprofessional or hurtful. If children do hurtful things, just hug them a little more tightly and make them feel safe. Children learn best when they feel safe and loved no matter what.

I don't teach to be remembered, although it's nice to think that you'll never be completely forgotten. I teach so that I can remember. I remember their personalities and how they grow. I remember the times we struggled with learning and succeeded, as well as those times when we fell short of our goals. I remember the laughter and the tears we shared.

Some people say, "Leave school at school." The best teachers I know often lose sleep thinking about, and worrying about, their students. It's worth every toss and turn!

Sincerely,
Brandi

In Their Own Words . . .

Chris Roberts
Grades 3–5
Multiage Classroom
Rees Elementary School,
Utah

Dear Teacher Candidates,

I am so pleased you have chosen to be a teacher! Thank you for joining our ranks. The main thing I want to share with you is this quote by Ron Miller that I have hanging in my classroom: "Our work is not about a curriculum or a teaching method. It is about

nurturing the human spirit with love." I know this will never be assessed on any kind of performance review of your teaching, but it is the most important thing you will do in your daily work. The relationship you build with each individual student will determine how successful you will be with that student. This will, in turn, affect the climate of the entire classroom. One way to nurture students is to really listen to them. Few are truly listened to. Another way to nurture students involves having a healthy sense of humor and laughing with them. You've heard it before; don't take yourself too seriously!

Education should be about helping our students have joy in their lives. I hope you have an incredible, joyous career!

Best wishes!
Chris

school of education, you probably have several semesters ahead of you. Here are some questions and answers related to your college courses.

Q: Why are general education courses important in teacher preparation?

A: Teachers need to be informed, interested, and interesting. Chris at Rees Elementary, Utah, is a terrific role model for us in this regard. We have read about his adventures that make him so interesting and now, in his letter to you, he talks about nurturing students as they grow.

Teachers are responsible for facilitating student learning of content. General education courses provide a wide spectrum of information and skills that contribute to your status as a well-rounded adult, information and skills that allow you to put much of what you teach into context. Many of these courses will help you develop dispositions that determine your attitudes and the values you carry with you for life. These

Table 14.1   Importance of noneducation coursework

Course	Promotes an Understanding of . . .
Philosophy	Pursuit of truth; nature of conflict; structure of knowledge
Psychology	Nature of learning; knowledge of self; research methods; study of behavior
Sociology	Socialization; socioeconomic status; social rules and processes; human social interaction
History	Perspectives from the past; lessons of conflict; methods of problem solving
English	Communication; literacy; persuasive writing
Math	Logic; problem solving
Science	Scientific method; experimentation; cause and effect

courses should not be viewed as fillers or as experiences that must be endured until you can enroll in classes specifically designed for teacher preparation. Table 14.1 may help you see more clearly the value of noneducation coursework.

Angelica at Roosevelt High School, California, sees her teaching position as twofold. She is a history teacher as well as a Spanish speaker teaching students in bilingual classes. Her advice about filling a niche in schools may be accomplished through concentration in a subject area offered in general education coursework.

Q: What courses will I likely take in the department of education?

A: Your plan of study within a department of education has been mapped out by instructors who have given serious consideration to what you need to know and be able to do as a teacher. The names of courses will vary, but the basic content of department of education courses is fairly similar from college to college. Regardless of the level or

In Their Own Words . . .

Angelica Reynosa
World History
Roosevelt High School,
California

Dear Teacher Candidates,

I can't imagine being anywhere else professionally than in a school. My husband and I are both teachers. It is a wonderful life!

I teach in a school where minority populations are the majority. Most of my students, and indeed most of the students at Roosevelt, are Latino Americans. Some were born in America; others have been here for only a few weeks. Some have families with established careers; others have families who are undocumented workers. Regardless, they are the faces of an ever-growing Latino presence in America. Some of my students, like Hugo, have secure, loving homes headed by parents who risked their lives to come to America. Hugo will be successful. He knows it's his legacy. He attends school regularly, and he is learning English quickly.

I see my job as not only a teacher of a course for high school credit, but also as an advocate for the well-being of my students, most of whom are in bilingual classes so that they can learn their subjects while learning to be fluent in English. As a Spanish speaker, I am able to teach both history and coping skills in English communication. Find your special niche in education. You have unique talents and gifts that will be valuable to students. Search for those talents and develop them for the sake of the students.

With my very best wishes,
Angelica

Figure 14.1   Topics and concepts addressed in education coursework

Human growth and development
Exceptional learners
Educational psychology
Education and society
Education and diversity
Learning theory
Group dynamics
History of education
Legal, governance, and financial aspects of education
Educational technology
Curriculum development
Instructional strategies
Classroom management
Schools, families, and community
Arts integration
Techniques for teaching reading
Methods courses that are content or level specific

subject area you choose to teach, you will likely have courses that address the topics and concepts listed in Figure 14.1 and more. If you choose to teach in early childhood or elementary school, you may have courses such as World of the Young Child and Arts for Children. You will likely take methods courses in each of the core areas—math, English language arts, science, and social studies. These courses will focus on instructional strategies that work particularly well with the subject area curriculum and level of students.

If you are preparing to teach middle school, you may have courses such as Young Adolescent Development and Middle Level Learning Environments. Most future high school teachers major in a subject area and minor in education. Middle and high school teachers will concentrate on their chosen content area(s) and methods for teaching that content in grades 6 through 12. Special education, physical education, and other fields require specific coursework in a particular discipline or area of study leading to certification that may span early childhood through high school.

Q: **How can I take full advantage of education coursework?**

A: What you learn in your education classes sets the groundwork for your professional life. This realization should inspire you to pay attention, complete all reading assignments, participate in class group work (with enthusiasm!), keep up with assignments, and so on. Beyond these logistical aspects of the courses, you should do what is necessary for you to own the knowledge and skills. This means to internalize and reflect on what you learn through reading, lectures, and class discussions. Put more into your class assignments than required. Apply the course content to everything you know about schools and teaching.

In 2003 the Public Education Network surveyed new teachers about what they felt prepared to do as a result of teacher preparation. Consider the results, shown in Figure 14.2. Pay particular attention to what new teachers say are areas in which they are least prepared. These should be points of emphasis for you so you will enter the profession with a sense of preparedness that perhaps the survey teachers did not have. You may want to undertake extra reading, research, and observation. One of the most valuable ways to learn about actual classroom practices is through field experiences.

Taking Full Advantage of Field Experiences

One of the most valuable aspects of a teacher preparation program is the opportunity to spend time in schools. Field experiences, or practicum experiences, involve observing

Figure 14.2   Survey results of perceived preparedness

New teachers feel most prepared to
- create collaborative classroom environments
- teach all students
- develop curriculum that builds on student interests and needs
- understand how student development influences learning
- relate classroom experience to the real world

New teachers feel least prepared to
- address learning needs of English language learners
- work with families
- develop interdisciplinary curricula
- address special learning needs
- assume leadership

Source: From *The Voice of the New Teacher,* by Public Education Network, 2003.

Figure 14.3   Observing the learning environment and classroom management techniques

Name _____ Date _____ Time _____
Class observed _____ Teacher _____
School _____ Lesson topic _____

1. Describe the classroom. Include neatness, creative use of space/walls, arrangement of desks/tables, technology available, unusual features, student work displayed, etc.

2. Does the teacher have easy proximity to all the students?

3. What technique does the teacher use to get the attention of the students?

4. Is an established behavior plan in place? How can you tell?

5. Do any behavior problems become evident? If so, describe them.

6. How does the teacher handle behavior difficulties?

7. Do you sense that the classroom environment is conducive to learning? Why or why not?

and/or participating in actual classrooms. Your field experiences may be embedded in particular courses. For instance, when you take a course in classroom management, you may be required to be in schools for 10 hours, during which time you observe and complete forms similar to the one in Figure 14.3. Some colleges have separate courses devoted to field experiences that may or may not be directly tied to other coursework. For instance, you may have a 3-credit-hour field course each semester once you are admitted to a teacher education program. What you are asked to observe and the nature of your participation may be determined by each of the instructors in your other courses. Or you may have an extensive log to keep that chronicles specific observations and participation.

You may have the opportunity to have early field experiences in early childhood, elementary, middle, and high school classrooms before you are required to declare your chosen level of certification. You may also have a chance to observe in related arts classes and special education settings. Ideally you will have the opportunity to visit

Figure 14.4   Observing an individual student

Name _____ Date _____ Time _____
Student observed (first name) _____ Teacher _____
School _____ Grade _____ Lesson topic _____

1. What do you notice about this student (physical appearance, cultural background, language, social interaction, skills and abilities, motivation, attitude, self-concept, etc.)?

2. How is the student responding to the teacher's lesson?

3. Is the student interacting with other students? Describe.

4. What is the quality of the student's work?

5. Name something positive the student did during the lesson.

6. Name something negative the student did during the lesson.

7. What else did you observe about the student?

rural, suburban, and urban schools. All of these experiences will help you decide on your teaching identity. Here are some questions and answers that will help clarify what field experiences will be like.

Q: What will I do in field experiences?

A: Early field experiences will likely be devoted to structured observations. This means you will be looking for specific things and responding to prompts that purposefully call attention to aspects of the classroom. You may be asked to focus on the teacher, the students as a group, or perhaps on an individual student, using a form similar to the one in Figure 14.4.

Field experiences that are associated with, or embedded in, methods courses will likely incorporate your first teaching experiences. You may begin with 15 minutes of instruction with a small group, followed by brief lessons with an entire class, then experience teaching whole classes for an entire period. The ultimate field experience is clinical practice. The next section of the chapter discusses this experience.

Q: How can I make the most of field experiences?

A: Your field experiences will be most meaningful if you approach opportunities to be in schools with real teachers and real students positively and with enthusiasm. After all, this is your chance to preview your chosen profession. Here are some general guidelines:

1. Make sure you know your instructor's expectations.
2. Dress and behave professionally.
3. Remember that you are a guest in the school.
4. Keep a detailed log of your experiences, even if it is not required in the course.
5. Spend time after the field experience reflecting on your time in schools. Write questions that you have about what you observed.

Q: What if I see things that are contrary to what I have learned in my education courses?

A: This will inevitably happen. You are learning about what is optimum in classrooms, the theory of why teachers conduct classes and approach students and their learning in specific ways. You study this to understand what's possible. But in real classrooms, the variables are many and teachers, as human beings, do not always respond to students and opportunities in ways that are best. You won't either—at least not all the time. One of the purposes of field experiences is to let you see reality, reflect on what you see, and formulate possible solutions to the dilemmas that arise.

You will no doubt see what you consider poor instruction. You will probably hear a teacher or two scream at children or humiliate a child in front of the class. It is difficult to watch this type of behavior and say nothing. But you must remain calm. Remember guideline 3—you are the guest. It is not your place to correct a teacher or act indignant in the face of teacher behavior you view as inappropriate. Also realize that you do not know the whole picture of what takes place in the classroom. You are seeing a snapshot. The time to express your dismay or outrage is in your college class with your instructor and classmates. We learn a great deal from observing incorrect methods and behavior. Learning what not to do as a result of seeing its actual, or potential, damage is powerful.

Now is the time to determine that you will seek out teacher colleagues who will nurture you as a professional—who will share what works and who value collegiality. Brenda at Rees Elementary, Utah, has valuable advice for you about this and other aspects of teaching.

All your field experiences prepare you for the ultimate field experience—your clinical practice experience.

In Their Own Words . . .

Brenda Beyal
Grades 3–5
Multiage Classroom
Rees Elementary School,
Utah

Dear Teacher Candidates,

What a wonderful, scary, exhilarating, confusing, demanding profession you have chosen. Wonderful, because you spend it with children. Scary, because you have to teach them to become literate, capable human beings. Exhilarating, because your creative juices have a place to flourish. Confusing, when students come with baggage and with very little room for instruction, practice, and evaluation. And, finally, demanding, because it takes hard work, perseverance, and commitment. To help with your journey, I offer the following five bits of advice.

1. *Be present in your classroom. Be intellectually, emotionally, and socially present in your room. Pay attention to the students, what they are saying and doing. Keep yourself present.*
2. *Search out colleagues who will nourish you and your profession. Find the teachers who aren't protective and territorial over their teaching. Search out the ones who share, don't compete, and have a philosophy similar to yours.*
3. *Continue learning, read education journals, subscribe to a professional publication, and read for pleasure.*
4. *Focus on student learning and not on your teaching. Teach to see students grasp ideas and come up with their own ideas. You may have delivered a lesson that was outstanding, uses all the bells and whistles, the correct language you have been taught, and still not reach a child. Focus on student learning.*
5. *Live a rich life. Children need teachers who experience, explore, and discover. Take vacations, learn to knit, do it.*

Sincerely,
Brenda

Figure 14.5 Characteristics of a successful student teaching experience

- Clarity of goals, including the use of standards guiding the performances and practices to be developed
- Modeling of good practices by more expert teachers in which teachers make their thinking visible
- Frequent opportunities for practice with continuous formative feedback and coaching
- Multiple opportunities to relate classroom work to university coursework
- Graduated responsibility for all aspects of classroom teaching
- Structured opportunities to reflect on practice with an eye toward improving it

Source: From *A Good Teacher in Every Classroom* (p. 43), by the National Academy of Education, 2005, San Francisco: Jossey-Bass.

Taking Full Advantage of Clinical Practice

Clinical practice, or student teaching, is the capstone experience of your teacher preparation program. The one- or two-semester experience will allow you to use what you have learned in your courses and practiced in your other field experiences. You will get to know a group of students well as you gradually take over full teaching duties. Your student teaching experience will probably require the hardest work you've ever done.

In a report released in 2005, the National Academy of Education lists the characteristics of a successful student teaching experience. As you read the characteristics in Figure 14.5, you will begin to understand the scope and importance of this exceptionally valuable internship. The following questions and answers will help clarify the experience for you.

Q: What should the goals be for my clinical practice experience?

A: George Posner (2005), a recognized expert on field experience, gives us six broad goals of clinical practice:

1. To find out what teaching is really like
2. To see if I really like teaching
3. To see if I really can do it
4. To learn some skills and modify certain habits and characteristics
5. To develop my own approach or style
6. To apply what I've learned in college to real students and to real classrooms (p. 16)

These are simple, practical goals to adopt as your own.

Q: To whom will I be responsible when I am a clinical intern?

A: There will be two very important adults in your clinical experience. One will be your cooperating teacher. It is in this person's classroom that you will spend 10 weeks to a full school year. Some colleges have established what is known as a Professional Development School, or PDS. This is an official partnership between the college and a school, entailing mutually agreed upon responsibilities and benefits. The school benefits from the presence of clinical interns and college faculty, who often provide assistance to the school in numerous ways. The college (and you!) benefit from a school relationship that provides cooperating teachers who regularly host teacher candidates.

Other colleges do not have official partnerships with schools or districts, but rather collaborate with a number of schools that open their classrooms to clinical interns. In either case, your cooperating teacher will be your mentor, whose charge is to provide the characteristics of a successful clinical practice experience as described in Figure 14.5.

The other very important adult in your clinical practice will be your college supervisor. This instructor will visit you and your cooperating teacher numerous times. He or she will observe your lessons, consult with you about what is observed, and

The relationship between a clinical intern and cooperating teacher can be one of mutual growth.

Your college supervisor during clinical practice can be a valuable resource and confidant.

give you constructive feedback. In addition, your supervisor will probably have other clinical interns and will meet regularly with all of you as a group. These meetings will be opportunities for you to talk about your experiences in nonthreatening and empathetic circumstances.

Q: How can I make the most of my clinical practice experience?

A: As with other field experiences, there are common-sense things you can do to make the most of clinical practice. Here are some actions and attitudes that will be valuable to you.

1. *Keep a journal.* You will probably be asked to do this by your supervising instructor. But even if you're not, you will be very glad you wrote about your experiences, responses, and questions. Keeping a journal will help you reflect and learn more from your experiences. Reading your journal and considering ways to improve are professional activities that Craig at Roosevelt High School, California, advises you to do in his letter.

2. *Keep up.* You will be very busy, with more responsibility and pressure than you've ever experienced. There will be lesson plans to write, materials to gather, paperwork to complete—all this while you are learning your craft, your profession. Don't get behind. Don't put off what needs to be done. Keep up so the workload won't snowball and overwhelm you.

3. *Be positive.* We choose our attitudes. Being positive is a choice. It doesn't mean glossing over difficulties, but rather approaching each day with possibilities in focus.

4. *Be realistic.* Being realistic is not in conflict with being positive. It is acceptance that some of your lessons will not go as planned, nor are you going to solve all the problems of the students in your classroom. You are learning, and your time in the classroom is limited.

5. *Confide in someone you trust.* You will find that no one understands what you are experiencing as completely as another clinical intern. You should also confide in your supervisor.

6. *Be professional.* Dress professionally, speak professionally, be respectful of the adults and students in your school, and earn their respect.

Clinical practice is a unique opportunity to practice for your teaching career. The next step is looking for, and getting, a teaching position.

How Can I Make the Most of Searching for a Teaching Position?

The day you begin to seriously consider your first teaching position may come much more quickly than you anticipated. It will probably dawn on you right before you begin your clinical practice that the time is approaching when you will look for the position that will

In Their Own Words . . .

Craig Cleveland
History
Roosevelt High School,
California

Dear Teacher Candidates,

Much of what you need to know about effective teaching and learning is found within yourself already. The environment and circumstances in which you learned powerful and life-changing lessons may have been in school or elsewhere in life. The relevant and meaningful lessons your students learn will need to be both inside and outside the school if education is going to have the power to transform them into thoughtful, mature people.

Essential to creating a learning environment in the classroom is a researched and clearly articulated philosophy about how learning happens. When such a philosophy is in place, then teachers are able to make sound and reliable instructional decisions and refinements.

Continuing my education in a graduate program, reading professional literature, regularly reflecting on my teaching with an eye toward improvement, and having ongoing conversations with friends and colleagues help make more concrete my beliefs about how learning happens. A ninth grade student of mine made the insightful statement, "Learning is natural." I believe learning is natural when the learner has interest and a voice as a participant within the learning environment of school.

I wish you years of growth and pleasure in the teaching profession!

Sincerely,
Craig

put you in charge of a whole classroom. A bit frightening? You are not alone if the reality fills you with anxiety. At the same time, it will be exhilarating because you will be beginning a career for which you have prepared.

Before you begin searching for a position, it is advantageous to take a close look at your skills, both to determine your strengths and to make visible to you areas that are weaknesses. Table 14.2 is a self-assessment that will bring structure to a serious examination of your skills.

There are logical steps to preparing to search for a teaching position. You don't have to be ready now, but an awareness of what's ahead is beneficial. Here are some questions and answers to consider.

Q: How can I be sure I qualify for a teaching position?

A: If you graduate from a teacher preparation program, you will have opportunities to learn about what your state requires in terms of certification. Most states require some sort of test, and many require one or more of the Praxis series you have been introduced to in Professional Practice at the end of each chapter. Acquiring teacher certification or a license qualifies you for teaching in your state. Do not put off whatever paperwork or exams your college and state require. Receiving results of exams and then waiting for state department processing take time. You will want to be certified quickly once you qualify so you can begin searching for a position.

If you want to move to another state, go to www.professionalteacher.com. This comprehensive site allows you to select a state and be directed to certification offices across the country. This is a quick and easy way to get information about what you need to do to teach in any state.

Q: How can I find out about available positions?

A: There are numerous sources. Here are a few of them:

- District websites
- Your campus career center
- Job fairs conducted on your campus or in district offices

Table 14.2   Self-assessment

Concept	Ask Yourself
Communication skills	Can I express my thoughts clearly when speaking and writing?
Interpersonal skills	Do I communicate well with others? How comfortable am I speaking with people from different cultures?
Flexibility	How do I handle change? Am I receptive immediately to new ideas and situations, or do I need time to adjust?
Leadership	How do I guide and motivate others to accomplish a recognized objective?
Intelligence	How well do I retain new information? Am I a problem solver?
Ability to handle conflict	What evidence do I have that demonstrates my ability to combat stressful situations and antagonism?
Initiative	Can I identify purposeful work and take action?
Self-confidence	What examples can I provide signifying my maturity and ability to deal positively and effectively with situations and people?
Acceptance of responsibility	Do I tend to take initiative or do I generally look for direction from others?
Creativity	Would I be comfortable with trying a unique or untried approach to solve a problem? Do I like to find new ways to reach a particular goal?

Source: From *The ABC's of Job-Hunting for Teachers* (p. 62), by M. C. Clement, 2003, Indianapolis, IN: Kappa Delta Pi.

Attending job fairs is a good way to find out about positions and to let principals know about your skills.

- State websites—type in the name of the state and then "teaching jobs"
- Word of mouth while you are student teaching

Q: How do I begin to apply?

A: Do your homework. Check online or call the district that interests you and ask for an application packet. Read it thoroughly and ask if you are unsure about how to complete it. Pay particular attention to deadlines and procedures. District hiring policies vary.

Q: How do I tell principals about me?

A: There are several standard ways to tell principals who you are and entice them to call you for an interview. Here is some brief information.

- *Credential file.* Most colleges will help you develop a credential file. Typically this file consists of transcripts, a resume, and letters of reference that are prescribed by your teacher education program. Your college will send your file to whoever requests it. This saves you the time and expense of gathering materials, making copies, and sending a packet to each prospective employer.
- *Cover letter.* Just having your credential file sent to a school will not necessarily bring your skills to the attention of a principal.

You need to send or deliver a packet that includes a cover letter to introduce yourself. It should

- be brief
- be addressed to an individual, not "To whom it may concern"
- be clear about the position or type of position you are seeking
- include one or two unique aspects of your qualifications

- *Resume.* This one-page bulleted summary should be organized and easy to read. It should include
  - your name, address, phone number, email address
  - the type of position you are seeking
  - information about your certification(s)
  - your teaching experience (clinical practice, significant field experiences)
  - your education, beginning with the most recent
  - related experiences (camps, after-school programs, campus leadership positions, etc.)
  - membership in organizations and honors you have received
  - references' names and contact information

  Your resume must have no grammatical or typographical mistakes, and it should be printed on high-quality paper. There are websites that assist with resume writing that you can find by typing "teacher resume." A sample resume is provided in Figure 14.6.

- *References.* Choose your references carefully. It is wise to include your college clinical practice supervisor, your cooperating teacher, a teacher who has firsthand knowledge of your teaching skills, and perhaps even the principal where you did your clinical practice. Ask for permission to include the individuals you choose before listing them in your resume.

- *Portfolio.* You will likely create a portfolio as part of your teacher preparation program. It will probably be an electronic collection of artifacts (products that provide evidence) that show your growth as a teacher candidate. The portfolio you will use in your search for a position should have a different slant. It should serve as a showcase of your best work. Although providing a CD of your portfolio to a principal is certainly acceptable, many principals still prefer a paper portfolio. It may serve you well to provide both. Your portfolio should include
  - a table of contents
  - your resume
  - a brief philosophy of education
  - lesson plans and project outlines
  - a video of you teaching a lesson and working with students
  - pictures of students participating in your classroom
  - student work (actual or scanned)
  - documentation of collaboration with other teachers
  - a list of professional activities, memberships, and honors

  Your credential file, cover letter, resume, references, and portfolio say a lot about you. But the most personal way to express who you are professionally and personally is through an interview.

Q: What can I expect in an interview?

A: After a principal paper screens candidates, he or she will decide who to invite for interviews. An interview is something you can prepare for. Figure 14.7 lists some potential interview questions and prompts. As you consider these items, think about how best to express your responses. Clement (2006) describes a way to "teach" the interviewer what you know and can do pertaining to a question. The acronym PAR stands for *p*roblem, *a*ction, *r*esults. In a PAR response you

- describe an actual or potential problem
- tell about actions you took or would take
- report the results or potential results

Figure 14.6 Sample resume

Jesse D. White
2614 Vista Drive, Apt. 2-E
Mount Pleasant, SC 29464
843-267-4359
Jesse1084@yahoo.com

Objective: To obtain a middle level social studies teaching position

Education:

2006   B.S. in Middle Level Education
                                        College of Charleston
                                        Charleston, SC
2002   High School Diploma
                                        Wando High School
                                        Mount Pleasant, SC

Intern Experience: Clinical Practice
Spring 2006   Sedgefield Middle School
                                        Berkeley County School District
                                        Goose Creek, SC
                                        8th grade social studies
Fall 2005   Field Experience
                                        Cario Middle School
                                        Mount Pleasant, SC
                                        7th grade language arts
Spring 2005   Field Experience
                                        Brentwood Middle School
                                        North Charleston, SC
                                        6th grade—all core subjects

Work Experience:

May 2005–   Mount Pleasant Recreation Department
present   Fencing Instructor
                                        Age 10–adult classes
                                        Developed and taught fencing classes three times a
                                            week in eight-week modules, from beginner to
                                            advanced levels
June 2001–   Gameworld
April 2005   Mount Pleasant, SC
                                        Retail sales and demonstration of game technology

Extracurricular Interests and Activities:
June 2003   Selected to design and paint mural in commercial area
                                            of Isle of Palms, SC
May 2003–present   Set designer and sound technician for Isle of Palms Rya
                                            Dance Troop

Honors:
2004–2006   Member: Kappa Delta Pi Education Honor Society
October 2005   Mount Pleasant Recreation Department Employee of
                                            the Month
References: Available on Request

A sample PAR response is shown in Figure 14.8.

Q: How can I make the most of an interview opportunity?

A: There are some dos and don'ts of interviewing that will help make the experience more productive and help you portray the type of teacher you will be in a classroom. Figure 14.9 lists some of these valuable tips.

Figure 14.7 Possible interview questions and prompts

Introductory
What has drawn you to teaching?
What experiences have you had that let you know working with children or adolescents is something you would enjoy?
What was the most significant thing you learned in your student teaching experience?
Why have you chosen to seek a position in our district (school)?

Knowledge of curriculum
On what would you base the topics and skills emphasized in your classroom?
Tell me about a curriculum standard (in the field or grade level of the position) and the concepts you might highlight in a lesson.

Instructional planning
How do you approach planning for a lesson?
Tell me about an instructional strategy that you particularly like and why.
Have you planned and taught an interdisciplinary unit? Briefly tell me about it.
Tell me about a lesson you taught that didn't go as planned. What happened?
Tell me about a lesson that moved much faster than you anticipated. What did you do?
Tell me about a lesson that took much longer than you anticipated. Why did it take longer? What did you do?
Have you facilitated a group project that was particularly successful? Tell me about it.
What types of assessment do you use? How do you determine if your students have learned?
Tell me about ways you have planned for student differences.

Motivation and management
How have you motivated at-risk learners in your classroom?
What techniques have you used to challenge high-achieving or gifted and talented learners?
Tell me about a difficult student or situation and how you handled the student or situation.
What rules and expectations would you set for classroom behavior?

Growing as a professional
How do you stay current in your subject area? How do you learn more about teaching techniques?
What professional journals do you read?
Have you attended a professional conference?
Do you plan to pursue a graduate degree?

Figure 14.8 Sample PAR response to the question, "How would you encourage students to read?"

In my student teaching semester I learned that we had to build in some reading time in class, similar to the Drop Everything and Read programs in elementary schools [problem]. I discussed it with my cooperating teacher, who gave me permission to incorporate reading into my sophomore classes, and it worked well. I learned that I have to give some time in class for reading, specify tasks for students to do concerning what they read, and set realistic time limits [action]. I learned that I can't allow too much time for in-class reading, or it will discourage reading outside of class while leaving less time to cover other curriculum topics [result]. It's about finding balance.

Source: From "The Game Has Changed: Tips for Finding a New Teaching Position," by M. C. Clement, 2006, *Kappa Delta Pi Record, 42*(3), pp. 118–119.

When the job search ends with acceptance of a teaching position, the excitement is incredible. When the thrill of being hired begins to subside, the realization that you will soon make the transition from student to teacher can be sobering. Let's look at the first year, beginning with the first day.

Figure 14.9   Dos and don'ts of interviewing

Do

- Take time to think through possible responses to questions (see Figure 14.7).
- Research information about the school and district. If there's something you particularly like, say so. If you have questions, there will be time at the end of the interview to ask them.
- Locate the school or district office the day before so you will know where you are going.
- Dress professionally with few accessories.
- Arrive early (at least 15 minutes).
- Introduce yourself in a confident manner and shake hands firmly.
- Be positive and optimistic.
- Convey your experience collaborating with teams or groups of people.
- Make eye contact with those with whom you speak throughout the school visit.
- Be prepared to ask a couple of questions at the end of the interview. They can be as simple as "What professional development opportunities are available?" or "Do new teachers benefit from a mentor/mentee relationship?" or "What technology do teachers have access to?"
- Take a well-crafted cover letter, resume, and portfolio to leave with the principal.
- Thank the people in the interview and the office staff.
- Write a follow-up note expressing your interest and thanking the principal for the opportunity to visit.

Don't

- Be late.
- Be overly modest. This is your time to shine, not in a bragging sense, but in well-spoken statements about your strengths and what you have to offer the school.
- Feel hurried to answer questions. It is acceptable to say, "That's a good question. Please let me think about it for a moment."
- Tell personal stories unless they directly relate to your teaching ability.
- Talk about interviews at other schools, especially not in derogatory ways.
- Forget to smile!

■ How Can I Thrive, Not Merely Survive, During My First Year of Teaching?

Nothing compares to the anticipation first-year teachers experience as the opening of school approaches. The questions are many. The excitement and the anxiety are palpable. You have been growing toward the profession, and now it's time to grow in the profession. Let's look at a few of the questions that beginning teachers have about how to survive—as well as how to thrive—during their initial year in the classroom. But before you read these questions and answers, read what Denis Cruz, California's 2006 Teacher of the Year, has to say about teaching in Teachers' Days, Delights, and Dilemmas.

Q: Will my teacher preparation program really prepare me for my first classroom?

A: Classes, field experiences, and clinical practice lay the foundation for your work as a teacher. Your teacher preparation program prepares you to be a beginner. It prepares you with background, theory, ideas, strategies, and the language of teaching and schools. But much of the real learning is just beginning. There's no way to completely prepare you for being the one adult in charge of a classroom where you meet 15 or 115 students daily. You can thrive in this learn-on-the-job world if you stay open, learn from mistakes, and keep moving forward each day.

Q: When I begin teaching will I be highly qualified?

A: The No Child Left Behind Act of 2001 took bold steps, as discussed in numerous places in this text, to improve the learning of all children. One of the most important aspects of NCLB is the stipulation that every child be taught by highly qualified

Teachers' Days, Delights, and Dilemmas

Denis Cruz
2006 California
Teacher of the Year

Teaching is the greatest profession on the planet! America's future citizens and leaders are sitting in our classrooms today. As teachers, we have been given the unique opportunity of affecting our future by investing our time, energy, and wisdom into our students now. We have been given the privilege, responsibility, and high calling to help children grow into successful and caring adults. Not only do we help children attain academic proficiency, we must also help them grow socially, emotionally, and morally.

"You must become lifelong learners!" I passionately tell my students. I try to instill in them a belief that they *can* learn and must take responsibility to learn. I model it to them by showing them the book I'm currently reading or the recent article I've come across. I explain what new learning I am acquiring. Teachers have a unique position from which to model all aspects of education, including collaboration, respect, determination, and responsibility.

Without a doubt, I know all students can succeed. I have never, ever had a student who could not. By the time Michael came to me in sixth grade he had been in and out of foster homes and had missed over one hundred days of school. Michael was reading at the first grade level and was labeled mentally retarded. That year Michael's foster parents adopted him. We had numerous conferences and were in constant communication about Michael's progress. Michael, his new parents, and I collaboratively set up goals for him to make sure he would succeed. Two years later Michael graduated from eighth grade as an honor student. He was selected as one of eight students for special teacher recognition. I know I had a powerful impact on Michael and that he made powerful, positive choices to achieve his goal. When I think of the numerous rewards I find in teaching, I am always drawn back to my students. Children like Michael make me grateful that I am a teacher and give me hope for the future.

teachers. As with other elements in the legislation, the definition of exactly what is meant by "highly qualified" was left up to each state to define. The two essential characteristics, according to NCLB, are that "highly qualified" teachers be licensed and that they demonstrate a high level of competence in the subject(s) they teach. Each state has its own version of "highly qualified," with some attaching more stringent criteria and others taking a more lax stance. You learned in Chapter 1 (see pages 12–14) that there are numerous paths to certification, with widely varying requirements. Check with your instructor or your state to find out the criteria for highly qualified status.

Q: What do I do the first day of school?

A: Of course the answer to this question will depend on the level of school and the subject(s) you will teach. Some schools have paperwork that must be distributed and tasks that must be performed on the first day. The best way to know what is required is to ask a teacher in your grade level or subject area to explain it to you in detail. Beyond that, the students in your class(es) just want to see each other and meet you. While paperwork is important, the environment you establish the first day is crucial.

Have lessons ready to go. Set the expectation that learning is what your classroom is all about. Make the lessons engaging, and let the students know that your expectations for them are high. The old adage that teachers shouldn't smile until Christmas is not the way to approach your students. Enjoy them—and let it show.

Make your classroom inviting with interesting posters and personal touches, as suggested in the discussion in Chapter 7 about the many ways to invite students to learn. Find out as much as you can about your students before school starts. They will

Enjoy the teaching and learning process—and let your students know it.

In Their Own Words . . .

Renee Ayers
Grade 2
Summit Primary School,
Ohio

Dear Teacher Candidates,

Prepare yourself for a rewarding and challenging adventure. Let me list just some of what I think is rewarding about teaching early childhood education, and some of what I consider challenging.

Some of the rewards:

- *preparing my classroom each August*
- *savoring the first day of school excitement*
- *toothless smiles*
- *building a rapport with the children*
- *singing with the children*
- *watching children learn to enjoy books*
- *witnessing children's enthusiasm for math*
- *the "oh I get it, Mrs. Ayers" moments*
- *working with that special/challenging child you are sure to have each year*
- *helping families*
- *seeing a child's growth from the beginning to the end of the year*
- *receiving high fives, hugs, and homemade gifts*
- *and, finally, enjoying winter, spring, and summer vacation (I would be lying if I didn't include these as rewards)*

Some of the challenges:

- *preparing my classroom each August*
- *organizing the first day of school*
- *being excited about lost teeth (even though it sort of grosses me out)*
- *building a rapport with the children*
- *singing with the children (I don't have the best voice or musical talent, but I try)*
- *discovering books the children will enjoy*
- *making math fun*
- *helping children make connections in their learning*
- *working with that special/challenging child you are sure to have each year*
- *assessing growth from the beginning of the year to the end of the year*
- *helping families*
- *documenting a child's growth from the beginning to the end of the year*
- *giving lots of high fives, hugs, praise and always being excited about homemade gifts*
- *and, finally, grade cards and administrative paperwork (again, I would be lying if I didn't include these as challenges)*

Do you see a connection here? The same things that are challenging as a teacher make the profession rewarding. So, prepare yourself for a rewarding and challenging adventure!

Fondly,
Renee

recognize your extra effort. Among the rewards and challenges of teaching, according to Renee at Summit Primary, Ohio, is the first day of school. Read her letter to you and notice that the same component of teaching that is rewarding can also be challenging.

Q: What is an induction program?

A: An induction program provides information, mentoring, and continuing support for new teachers. The information comprises facts about the school, district, and state, including procedures and policies. This text has already discussed the value of a mentor in helping you adjust to your new career. The continuing support provided by your mentor and others may involve the curriculum, instruction, assessment, and time and classroom management. Many induction programs provide time for new teachers to meet together informally to support one another. Participation in an induction program will be a valuable experience.

Figure 14.10 is a list of things new teachers wished they had in their first year. Keep this list in mind, particularly if an induction program is not available to you. Ask for these things. Some simply take a little research and others, like 9, will depend on the willingness of an experienced teacher. Don't be afraid to ask. What veteran teachers do as routine will be new and unfamiliar to you.

Figure 14.10 New teachers' top 10 wish list

1. A new teacher handbook
2. A copy of the state and local instructional standards for their subject and grade level
3. A statement of their school's philosophy, goals, and values
4. A student handbook
5. A school discipline policy
6. A sample student report card
7. Forms and instructions for ordering books and supplies
8. An organizational chart describing school and district staff and related roles
9. A checklist, designed by veteran teachers, to help them know what to expect on their first day
10. A list of cultural and educational resources available in the community

Source: From *The Voice of the New Teacher*, by Public Education Network, 2003.

Figure 14.11 Teaching diverse students

- Get to know each student individually. A good relationship is key to student and teacher success and is based on open communication, trust, and respect.
- Learn about yourself and your background. Ask yourself how your background may affect your teaching style and your relationship with students.
- Learn about the racial and cultural backgrounds of your students, and get to know their parents.
- Create an environment where students can have safe dialogues on diversity, including race, culture, class, and sexual orientation.
- Help foster a school environment where staff members can have open discussions on race, culture, class, and sexual orientation.
- Master a variety of instructional strategies to reach students with different interests and strengths.

Source: From *The Voice of the New Teacher* (p. 16), by Public Education Network, 2003.

Q: What if my students are very different from me?

A: Teaching students who are different from you in terms of ethnicity, race, socioeconomic status, family structure, motivation, and other aspects will happen. As you have read What Role Will Diversity Play in My Teaching Identity? at the end of each chapter, you have no doubt been prompted to consider this question. The Public Education Network has formulated advice for teachers on how to capitalize on the diversity in their classrooms. The list in Figure 14.11 provides guidelines that are appropriate regardless of the population of students in your classroom.

Q: My instructors say that we should stay out of the teachers' lounge because negative teachers congregate there. What else can I do to combat negativity?

A: In your field experiences you will likely encounter teachers who seem to see the negative side of almost everything. Unfortunately, there are teachers who have had difficulties in the classroom. They have become discouraged and have not been able to move beyond the problems. You will notice that teachers who are negative attract one another and often spread their negativity in the one place designated as a gathering spot for teachers—the teachers' lounge. It's a good idea to spend as little time as possible wherever such teachers tend to gather. It will be evident which teachers have positive attitudes and optimistic spirits. Gravitate to them. Keeping yourself positive is the best preventive medicine to fight off negativity.

Aligning yourself with teachers who have similar interests and enthusiasm for teaching and students will help you thrive as a new teacher.

Q: Should I go to graduate school?

A: Over half of all teachers have graduate degrees. Some pursue an advanced degree for the love of learning, some to have career options within education, and some for the increase in salary that generally accompanies a master's degree. Most who seek degrees attest to their value in terms of their professionalism and effectiveness in the classroom.

Does a teacher's advanced degree really lead to increased student learning? The National Council on Teacher Quality (2006) tells us that research does not confirm increased effectiveness due to advanced degrees. Even though they report no overall benefits from teachers acquiring master's degrees, several of our focus teachers tell us in their individual cases that an advanced degree made them more effective. Read what Derek at Roosevelt High School, California, has to say in his letter to teacher candidates.

Attending graduate school is probably something that should wait until you are reasonably comfortable with yourself as a teacher and your role in the classroom. Waiting 2 or 3 years will also make the coursework and intense reflection required in graduate study more meaningful to you. You will have real experiences in the classroom that will help you relate theory to practice. In other words, what you learn will make more sense in the context of what you have experienced.

Q: What if teaching is not what I thought it would be?

A: There will be some aspects of teaching that match your expectations. But even after a full semester of clinical practice, having your own classroom may present some challenges and circumstances for which you are not prepared. There will be plenty of days

In Their Own Words . . .

**Derek Boucher
History and Reading
Roosevelt High School,
California**

Dear Teacher Candidates,

After twelve years working in an urban, public high school in the Central Valley of California, I still firmly believe that teaching is a noble profession. Allow me to share the components that have made the biggest difference in my life as a teacher.

Love your content area. Engage in reading, writing, research, discussions, and even travel in your content area. The passion these activities generate comes across to students and changes lives.

Developing a philosophy of education will serve you better than learning multiple strategies. From a rich philosophy, great strategies emerge. Strategies apart from a philosophy come and go. In 1995, my teacher education program pushed me to think deeply about my philosophy of teaching and learning. For example, I believe that curriculum should be relevant and meaningful to students as often as possible. Humans are innately curious. I believe that faith in the learner is imperative.

Go to graduate school. After five years in the profession, I enrolled in graduate school and studied in the area of Reading/Language Arts. This experience changed my life as a professional, and benefited me infinitely more than school district training has ever done. Find the most progressive graduate program around and go for it! You'll never regret it.

Wishing you professional growth,
Derek

when you will work very hard and do all you can but see no payoff in terms of student learning or personal satisfaction. Sometimes the real rewards take a while to materialize. Read what Tim at Rees Elementary, Utah, has to say about the rewards of teaching in his letter to you.

Remember that schools and teaching assignments vary. If in your first year you find teaching is not what you had hoped or envisioned, perhaps a change is in order. As Deirdre at Cario Middle School, South Carolina, tells us in her letter, teachers sometimes discover where they are most effective while teaching in a different circumstance.

If you are convinced that teaching is not for you, your teacher preparation will serve you well as training in collaboration, organization, planning, and communication, all skills that are desirable in many professions and in life.

Q: How can I burn brightly, without burning out, my first year as a teacher?

A: All of the questions and answers in this section have addressed ways not merely to survive in the classroom, but also to thrive. Traci at Cario Middle School, South Carolina,

In Their Own Words . . .

**Tim Mendenhall
Grades 3–5
Multiage Classroom
Rees Elementary School,
Utah**

Dear Teacher Candidates,
  I would first encourage you to follow your heart. Trust yourself and do what you feel needs to be done for your students. Don't follow a program just because it's been adopted. If there is something better for your students, use it, adjust it. Education is messy. You will try things and fail. That's how we learn.

Second, more than reading and math, teaching your students to be lifelong learners is your ultimate goal. Make your classroom fun. If you don't like a book or an activity, why do you think they will? Love what you are doing, and they will learn to love learning.

Finally, stay at teaching long enough to get the REAL pay. This could be a child bringing you a Cherry Coke (instead of an apple) every Friday. Or a former student running off the football field to talk with you when he is quarterback and supposed to be leading a play. Or a parent coming back and telling you that you are still their child's favorite teacher (even after all the years and they are now graduating from high school). The pay is great; you just have to wait for it sometimes.

Good Luck!

Tim

In Their Own Words . . .

**Deirdre Huger-McGrew
Language Arts/
Social Studies
Cario Middle School,
South Carolina**

Dear New Teacher,
  I would personally like to extend a warm welcome to you as you embark on an adventurous journey into the world of children and education. It's not a straight

and narrow path, but rather a diverse path based on the needs of students. The journey begins with your desire to be a teacher. Whether it's math or reading, teaching young children or adolescents, your focus will determine how you will approach teacher preparation. I began as an elementary teacher with a love for books. Today I'm a middle school teacher focusing on reading. I would never have thought that my journey would take this turn. Many of us "grow into" an area of expertise. Keep your mind open and receptive for the "I never thought of that" idea. Your journey will be unique to you. Welcome!

My best to you!
Deirdre

In Their Own Words . . .

Traci Peters
Grade 7 Math
Cario Middle School,
South Carolina

Dear Teacher Candidates,

What an exciting career you have chosen. I can assure you that your years as a teacher will be filled with memories that last a lifetime! Many things change each year as a new group of students enter your life. Yet many things must stay the same. Here are just a few things on my "have to do each year" list:

- *Love your students as if they were your own children, even the ones who know just what buttons to push. In order to love them, you have to get to know them. So talk to them about things other than the textbook!*
- *Laugh with your students. If you don't enjoy teaching, then why do it? Middle school kids are especially funny and definitely want all the attention they can get.*
- *Follow a routine every day. This doesn't mean that you have to do the same thing every day, but it does mean that kids like structure.*
- *Stay organized. It saves lots of time and frustration!*
- *Plan with your colleagues—it'll make for more exciting lessons and give you some much needed "adult time." Don't forget to ask for help when you need it!*
- *Respect your students and their parents and, in turn, they will respect you. Most important, respect yourself. A happy teacher makes a happy class!*
- *Be consistent with your discipline, from day to day and from student to student. Be sure that you don't overuse the word "no" when "yes" is sometimes more appropriate. Remember to reward good behavior, and be sure that the consequence fits the not-so-good behavior.*

Good luck to you in your first year of teaching. Be confident that you will make a difference in your students' lives and that all of your hard work does pay off!

Sincerely,
Traci

gives you some practical advice as you enter the classroom. In addition, here are some actions and attitudes to make your first year of teaching successful—as measured by both student learning and your satisfaction.

- Plan, plan, and then plan some more.
- Teach with energy and enthusiasm.
- Learn all you can about your students.
- Meet your students' families and invite them to be your partners in the education of their students.
- Establish routines and help students learn habits that will enhance your classroom.
- Capitalize on the freshness and excitement of the beginning of the school year.
- Leave your personal problems at home. Give students 100% of your attention while at school.
- Respond to students and situations, don't react. Responses are based on thought; reactions are spontaneous and impulsive.
- Repeat "I am the teacher, I am the teacher" and act it. You are the adult in the classroom and must model maturity.
- Love what you do, and show it!

Concluding Thoughts

Congratulations on completing this text and the course that made it required reading! If this is your first course in teacher preparation, you now probably have a sense of what's ahead in your college program. With each step in teacher preparation your passion for education will likely grow.

If, however, you have decided that teaching is not for you, thank you for opening your mind to what education in the United States is like and to what the needs are of the

50 million students who attend pre-K–12 schools. You are more informed than the majority of the American public. Expressing your opinion will be easier (and hopefully more valid) now that you have a greater understanding of the challenges and opportunities that lie within U.S. schools. Be an advocate for children and their futures—and thus for the future of us all. Please frequently ask, "And how are the children? Are they all well?"

For those of you who are sure that teaching is in your future, or who are still seriously considering the profession, you have quite an adventure ahead of you. Let's return for a moment to the compass rose in the opening pages of this chapter. The essence of navigation is to determine true north. For teachers, true north is a carefully crafted philosophy of our beliefs about teaching and learning. We are surrounded by magnetic fields—non-research-based fads, changing societal dilemmas, disillusionment, negativity—all with the potential to lead us off course. Our challenge is to align our chosen path on the compass rose to true north and stay focused on students.

Each page in this book is written by the hands, and from the heart, of a teacher. There is no finer way to spend a lifetime than in a classroom fulfilling our individual teaching identities. To be a teacher is to live in a world of possibility—to know that what we do matters. Join us.

What Role Will Diversity Play in My Teaching Identity?

You will no doubt have students in your classroom who differ from you in ethnicity, race, socioeconomic status, family structure, motivation, and other aspects. You will want to maximize the benefits of having these students in your classroom and increase learning for all your students. To do so, you first need to understand as much as you can about your own background and beliefs and how they may influence your teaching. Then, you want to get to know the students individually and find out as much as you can about them. You should create an atmosphere in your classroom and help foster one in your school that encourages honest dialogue about differences. Finally, you should continually learn and practice instructional strategies that address multiple differences in how students learn.

Chapter in Review

How can I make the most of teacher preparation?

- General education courses provide a wide spectrum of information and skills that help teachers put learning in context.
- Education coursework content should be internalized and utilized by teacher candidates.
- Keeping an ongoing and reflective log of observations and participation in field experiences will enhance their value.
- Learning from negative experiences is valuable.
- As the capstone of your preparation, student teaching should be approached with energy and openness to learning.

How can I make the most of searching for a teaching position?

- It is your responsibility to make sure you fulfill the requirements for licensure in the state in which you plan to teach.
- It is important to be organized and thorough when searching and applying for teaching positions.
- You can tell a principal about yourself through a credential file, resume, reference letters, a portfolio, and an interview.

How can I thrive, not merely survive, during my first year of teaching?

- After several years of growing toward the profession of teaching, it's now time to grow in the profession.
- Teacher preparation qualifies you to be a beginner in the classroom.
- The first year of teaching is generally filled with more questions than answers. It is hard work.
- There are positive guidelines to follow as a new teacher that will result not only in surviving, but also in increased student learning and personal satisfaction.

Professional Practice

Licensure Test Prep

Read the following and answer the constructed-response questions.

1. Justin Wilson attends college on a soccer scholarship. He enjoys playing on the team and faithfully attends practices. He has been told that teacher education majors can continue to be on sports teams, but it generally means a great deal of juggling of their schedules. They typically have to give up considerable free time to fulfill all the field hours required prior to student teaching.

    Justin has always wanted to be a high school coach. His degree will be in physical education with a minor in education. Justin is having a hard time understanding why he has to do all the field requirements when he is absolutely certain of what he wants to do and where he wants to do it. Attending all the practices and games plus going out to schools three mornings a week leaves little free time. What two aspects of field experience would you emphasize to Justin to help him understand why field work is vital to him? Explain each.

2. Maria Ramirez is excited about her future as an early childhood teacher. She has enjoyed her field experiences in preschool settings for 3- and 4-year-olds. Last semester she was in a first grade classroom. This semester her clinical internship is in a kindergarten class, and she thinks she has found her place in life. This is her grade level of choice.

    Although Maria loves going to school every day, she is bothered by one aspect of her clinical practice. In the first few weeks when she was observing and helping out Mrs. Lawson, her cooperating teacher, Maria found that she disagreed with many things Mrs. Lawson did and said. Maria thinks of herself as an advocate for all children, not just those who cooperate and achieve. She now has the definite impression that Mrs. Lawson pays much more attention to some students than to others. She seems to have much lower expectations for the students who show less readiness for kindergarten. These students are all from low-income homes, and most are African American or Hispanic American. As Maria begins taking over classroom duties and teaching, how should she approach her position as a clinical intern given the situation she perceives? Explain your advice to Maria.

3. There are certain conditions under which clinical practice is most effective and productive. Briefly explain three characteristics of a clinical practice experience that are likely to lead to success for the intern, cooperating teacher, and students.

Standards Speak

All of the standards cited in the first 13 chapters apply to who you are as a professional. This last chapter focuses on making the most of your teacher preparation and your first year in the classroom. Rather than responding to questions about individual standards, think about standards as a tool in goal setting and determining progress toward goals.

Use these questions to frame the response that you will write in your class notebook and/or discuss with your classmates as directed by your instructor.

1. Are standards useful for shaping actions and attitudes? If so, why and how? If not why not?

2. Standards are written by people. What qualifications do you think standards authors should have? Should an individual write standards, or should they be written by people working in collaboration?

3. Should standards be used to examine actions and attitudes? If so, why? What makes them user-friendly as assessment tools?

4. How will you use standards in your everyday work as a teacher?

MyEducationLab

The following interactive features may be found in Chapter 14 of MyEducationLab.

Homework and Exercises

Writing My Own Story
To write your own story by responding to some of the questions in the text accompanied by fingerprint icons, plus others, go to the "Writing My Own Story" section of the Homework and Exercises for Chapter 14 of MyEducationLab.

What's My Disposition?
To reflect on your beliefs and attitudes concerning the teaching profession, go to Chapter 14's "What's My Disposition?" feature of the Homework and Exercises section of MyEducationLab.

Exploring Schools and Classrooms
If your course involves experiences in schools, the questions and prompts in the "Exploring Schools and Classrooms" feature of Chapter 14's Homework and Exercises section of MyEducationLab will guide you as you explore local schools and classrooms.

Virtual Field Experience

To respond to questions and prompts regarding the Choosing Your Teaching Path videos that connect to specific chapter content, go to Chapter 14's Virtual Field Experience section of MyEducationLab. The questions will help you make sense of what you have read in the chapter.

References

Adler, M. (1982). *The Paideia Proposal: An educational manifesto.* New York: Simon & Schuster, Inc.

Alexander, W. M., & McEwin, C. K. (1989). *Schools in the middle: Status and progress.* Columbus, OH: National Middle School Association.

Alliance for Technology Access. (2006). *ATA Co-Founder Honored as Local Hero for Disability Awareness Month.* Retrieved November 8, 2006, from http://www.ataccess.org/default.html

Allington, R. L. (2002a). What I've learned about effective reading instruction. *Phi Delta Kappan, 83*(10), 740–747.

Allington, R. L. (2002b). You can't learn much from books you can't read. *Educational Leadership, 60*(3), 7–11.

American Academy of Pediatrics. (2004). Corporal punishment in schools, 2004 state legislation report. *Pediatrics, 106*(2), 343. Retrieved May 22, 2006, from http://www.mnaap.org/corp_punishment.html

American Association of Suicidology. (2003). *Youth suicide fact sheet.* Retrieved April 6, 2006, from www.suicidology.org/associations/1045/files/Youth2003.pdf

American Association of University Women. (2001). *Hostile hallways: Bullying, teasing, and sexual harassment in school.* New York: Harris Interactive 2001.

American Council for the Teaching of Foreign Language. (2005). *Standards for foreign language learning.* Retrieved July 1, 2005, from http://www.actfl.org

American Psychiatric Association. (2005a). *Let's talk facts about depression.* Retrieved April 6, 2006, from www.healthyminds.org/multimedia/depression.pdf

American Psychiatric Association. (2005b). *Let's talk facts about teen suicide.* Retrieved April 6, 2006, from www.healthyminds.org/multimedia/teensuicide/depression.pdf

American Psychological Association. (2000). *Diagnostic and statistical manual of mental disorders* (4th ed., rev.). Washington, DC: Author.

Ariza, E. N. (2002). Cultural considerations: Immigrant parents involvement. *Kappa Delta Pi Record, 38*(3), 134–137.

Association for Childhood Education International. (2005). *Program Standards for Elementary Teacher Preparation.* Retrieved July 4, 2007, from http://www.acei.org/2006Standard31.doc

Azzam, A. M. (2005). The funding gap. *Educational Leadership, 62*(5), 93.

Azzam, A. M. (2006). Digital opportunity. *Educational Leadership, 63*(4), 89–92.

Bandura, A., Barbaranelli, C., Caprara, G. V., & Pastorelli, C. (2001). Self-efficacy beliefs as shapers of children's aspirations and career trajectories. *Child Development, 72,* 187–206.

Banks, J. A. (2003). *Teaching strategies for ethnic studies* (7th ed.). Boston: Allyn & Bacon.

Banks, J. A. (Ed.). (2004). *The handbook of research on multicultural education.* San Francisco: Jossey-Bass.

Barber, B. R. (1997). Public schooling: Education for a democracy. In *The public purpose of education and schooling,* J. I. Goodlad and T. J. McMannon (Eds.), San Francisco: Jossey-Bass.

Barnett, W. S. (2003). Preschool: The most important grade. *Educational Leadership, 60*(7), 54–57.

Barth, R. S. (2001). *Learning by heart.* San Franciso: Jossey-Bass.

Barth, R. S. (2006). Improving relationships within the schoolhouse. *Educational Leadership, 63*(6), 9–13.

Beagle, D. R. (2006). *The information commons handbook.* New York: Neal-Schuman.

Beane, J. A. (2005). *A reason to teach: Creating classrooms of dignity and hope.* Portsmouth, NH: Heinemann.

Berliner, D. C. (2000). A personal response to those who bash teacher education. *Journal of Teacher Education, 51*(5), 358–371.

Berliner, D. C. (2001). Improving the quality of the teaching force: A conversation with David Berliner. *Educational Leadership, 58*(8), 6–10.

Biddle, B., & Berliner, D. (2002). Unequal school funding in the United States. *Educational Leadership, 59*(8), 48–59.

Bloom, B. S. (1956). *Taxonomy of educational objectives: Handbook I. Cognitive domain.* New York: Longman, Green.

Blum, R. W. (2005). A case for school connectedness. *Educational Leadership, 62*(7), 16–19.

Boyer, P., & Stuckey, S. (2005). *American nation in the modern era.* Austin, TX: Holt, Rinehart, and Winston.

Boynton, M., & Boynton, C. (2005). *The educator's guide to preventing and solving discipline problems.* Alexandria, VA: Association for Supervision and Curriculum Development.

Bradley, F. (2006). Answering the perplexities of parent involvement. *Education Update, 48*(6), 4.

Brameld, T. (1956). *Toward a reconstructed philosophy of education.* New York: Holt, Rinehart and Winston.

Bredekamp, S., & Copple, C. (Eds.). (1997). *Developmentally appropriate practice in early childhood programs* (3rd ed.). Washington, DC: National Association for the Education of Young Children.

Brembs, B., Lorenzetti, F. D., Reys, F. D., Baxter, D. A., & Byrne, J. H. (2002). Operant reward learning in aplysdia: Neuronal correlates and mechanisms. *Science, 296*(5573), 1706–1710.

Bridgeland, J. M., Dilulio, J. J., & Morison, K. B. (2006). *The silent epidemic: Perspectives of high school dropouts.* Retrieved April 8, 2006, from http://www.civicenterprises.net/pdfs/thesilentepidemic3-06.pdf

Brimley, V., & Garfield, R. (2004). *Financing education* (9th ed.). Boston: Allyn & Bacon.

Burns, M. (2006). Tools for the mind. *Educational Leadership, 63*(4), 48–53.

Button, W. H., & Provenzo, E. F., Jr. (1989). *History of education and culture in America.* Upper Saddle River, NJ: Prentice Hall.

California Department of Education. (2006). *Ed-Data.* Retrieved April 7, 2007, from http://www.ed-data.k12.ca.us

Campbell, A., Shirley, L., & Candy, J. (2004). A longitudinal study of gender-related cognition and behavior. *Developmental Science, 7,* 1–9.

Carnegie Corporation. (1989). *Turning points: Preparing American youth for the 21st century.* New York: Author.

Carter, G. R. (2003). *NCLB and the diverse needs of rural schools.* Retrieved September 26, 2004, from www.ascd.org/cms/index.cfm

Center for Applied Research in Educational Technology. *Questions and answers.* Retrieved July 3, 2007, from http://caret.iste.org/index.cfm?fuseaction=topics

Chartock, R. K. (2004). *Educational foundations: An anthology* (2nd ed.). Upper Saddle River, NJ: Merrill/Prentice Hall.

Child Welfare Information Gateway. (2006a). *Child abuse and neglect fatalities: Statistics and interventions.* Retrieved April 22, 2007, from http://www.childwelfare.gov/pubs/factsheets/fatality.cfm

Child Welfare Information Gateway. (2006b). *Recognizing child abuse and neglect: Signs and symptoms.* Retrieved April 22, 2007, from http://www.childwelfare.gov/pubs/factsheets/signs.cfm

Clement, M. C. (2003). *The ABC's of job-hunting for teachers.* Indianapolis, IN: Kappa Delta Pi.

Clement, M. C. (2006). The game has changed: Tips for finding a new position. *Kappa Delta Pi Record, 42*(3), 115–119.

Codell, E. R. (1999). *Educating Esme: Diary of a teacher's first year.* Chapel Hill, NC: Algonquin Books of Chapel Hill.

Cohen, S. S. (1974). *A history of colonial education, 1607–1776.* New York: Wiley.

Colin, C. (2005). No more books. *Edutopia, I*(7), 40.

Comer, J. P. (2005). The rewards of parent participation. *Educational Leadership, 62*(6), 38–42.

Corbett, D., & Wilson, B. (2002). What urban students say about good teaching. *Educational Leadership, 60*(1), 18–22.

Corbett, D., Wilson, B., & Williams, B. (2005). No choice but success. *Educational Leadership, 62*(6), 8–12.

Cornett, C. E. (2003). *Creating meaning through literature and the arts: An integration resource for classroom teachers* (2nd ed.). Upper Saddle River, NJ: Merrill/Prentice Hall.

Corporation for Public Broadcasting. (2003). *Connected to the future: A report on children's Internet use from Corporation for Public Broadcasting.* Retrieved December 27, 2005, from http://cpb.org/ed/resources/connected

Council of Chief State School Officers. (2006). *Chief state school officers method of selection.* Retrieved June 20, 2005, from http://www.ccsso.org/chief_state_school_officers/method_of_selection/index.cfm

Counts, G. (1932). *Dare the school build a new social order?* New York: John Dey.

Cradler, J. (2003). Technology's impact on teaching and learning. *Learning and Leading with Technology, 30*(7), 54–57.

Craig, G. J., & Dunn. W. L. (2007). *Understanding human development.* Upper Saddle River, NJ: Prentice Hall.

Cuban, L. (2001). *Oversold and underused.* Boston: Harvard University Press.

Cubberly, E. (1934). *Public education in the United States.* Boston: Houghton Mifflin.

Darling-Hammond, L. (1997). *The right to learn.* San Francisco: Jossey-Bass.

Darling-Hammond, L. (2003). Keeping good teachers: Why it matters, what leaders can do. *Educational Leadership, 60*(8), 7–13.

Darling-Hammond, L., & Youngs, P. (2002). Defining "highly qualified teachers": What does "scientifically-based research" tell us? *Education Researcher, 31*(9), 13–25.

DeAngelis, T. (2004). Size-based discrimination may be hardest on children. *Monitor on Psychology, 35*(1), 62.

Delgado-Gaitan, C., & Trueba, H. (1991). *Crossing cultural borders: Education for immigrant families in America.* New York: Falmer.

DeVries, R., & Zan, B. (2003). When children make rules. *Educational Leadership, 61*(1), 64–67.

Dewey, J. (1900). *The school and society.* Chicago: University of Chicago Press.

Dewey, J. (1902). *The child and the curriculum.* Chicago: University of Chicago Press.

Dewey, J. (1933). *How we think: A restatement of the relation of reflective thinking to the educative process.* Boston: D.C. Heath.

Dewey, J. (1938). *Experience and education.* New York: Macmillan/Collier.

Dewey, J. (1944). *Democracy and education.* New York: Free Press.

Dewey, J. (1956). *The child and the curriculum, and the school and society.* Chicago: University of Chicago Press.

Diversity Data. (2000). *Principal Magazine, 79*(5), 18.

Dunklee, D. R., & Shoop, R. J. (2002). *The principal's quick reference guide to school law: Reducing liability, litigation, and other potential legal tangles.* Thousand Oaks, CA: Corwin Press.

Dyck, B. A. (2004). Technology integration: Rethinking the role of the student. *Middle Ground, 8*(2), 20–23.

Education Commission of the States. (2004). *Open enrollment 50-state report.* Retrieved June 22, 2006, from http://mb2.ecs.org/reports/Report.aspx?id=268.

Education Vital Signs. (2006a). *As educators face a childhood obesity "epidemic," other indicators of well-being improve.* Retrieved March 30, 2006, from http://www.asbj.com/evs/06/studenthealth.html

Education Vital Signs. (2006b). *Graduation statistics and systemic reform spark a conversation among state leaders.* Retrieved March 30, 2006, from http://www.asbj.com/evs/06/studenthealth.html

Educational Testing Service. (2005). *One-third of a nation: Rising dropout rates and declining opportunities.* Princeton, NJ: Author.

Educational Testing Service. (2007). *Praxis II Overview.* Retrieved June 25, 2007, from www.ets.org

Eisner, E. (Ed.). (1985). *Learning and teaching the ways of knowing: The eighty-fourth yearbook of the National Society for the Study of Education.* Chicago: University of Chicago Press.

Eisner, E. (2002). *The educational imagination: On the design and evaluation of school programs* (3rd ed.). New York: Macmillan College.

Eisner, E. W. (2000). *Prospects: The quality review of comparative education.* (UNESCO Publication Vol. 30, No. 3) Paris.

Epstein, J. L., Sanders, M. G., Simon, B. S., Salinas, K. C., Jansorn, N. R., & VanVoorhis, F. L. (2002). *School, family, and community partnerships: Your handbook for action.* Thousand Oaks, CA: Corwin Press.

Erwin, J. C. (2003). Giving students what they need. *Educational Leadership, 61*(1), 19–23.

Farkas, S., Johnson, J., & Felono, T. (2000). *A sense of calling: Who teaches and why.* Washington, DC: Public Agenda.

Feistritzer, C. E. (2005). *Alternative teacher certification: An overview.* Retrieved May 25, 2005, from www.ncei.com

Feldman, R. S. (2006). *Development across the life span* (4th ed.). Upper Saddle River, NJ: Prentice Hall.

Fessenden, F., & Barbanel, J. (2005). The rise of the six-figure teacher. *The New York Times.* Retrieved May 20, 2005, from http://www.nytimes.com/2005/05/15/nyregion/15iteach.html

First Amendment Center. (2006). *Public schools and sexual orientation: A First Amendment framework for finding common ground.* Retrieved April 2, 2006, from www.firstamendmentcenter.org/pdf/sexual.orientation.guidelines.pdf

Fischer, L., Schimmel, D., & Stellman, L. (2003). *Teachers and the law* (6th ed.). Boston: Allyn & Bacon.

Focus Adolescent Services. (2006). *Youth who drop out.* Retrieved April 20, 2006, from http://www.focusas.com/Dropouts.html

Fox, M. A., Connolly, B. A., & Snyder, T. D. (2005). *Youth indicators 2005: Trends in the well-being of American youth.* Washington, DC: National Center for Education Statistics.

Franklin, B. (1931). Proposals relating to education of youth in Pennsylvania. In T. Woody (Ed.), *Educational views of Ben Franklin.* New York: McGraw-Hill.

Friere, P. (1970). *Pedagogy of the oppressed.* New York: Herder and Herder.

Gable, R. A., Hendrickson, J. M., Tonelson, S. W., & Van Acker, R. (2000). Changing disciplinary and instructional practices in the middle school to address IDEA. *The Clearing House, 73*(4), 205–208.

Gallahue, D. L., & Ozmun, J. C. (1998). *Understanding motor development: Infants, children, adolescents, adults.* Boston: McGraw-Hill.

Garbarino, J. (1999). *Lost boys: Why our sons turn violent and how we can save them.* New York: The Free Press.

Gardner, H. (1999). *The disciplined mind: What all students should understand.* New York: Simon & Schuster.

Gardner, H. (2005, May 25). *Multiple lens on the mind.* Paper presented at the ExpoGestion Conference in Bogota, Columbia. Retrieved June 30, 2007, from http://www.pz.harvard.edu/PIs/HG_Multiple_Lenses.pdf

Gathercoal, P., & Crowell, R. (2000). Judicious discipline. *Kappa Delta Pi Record, 36*(4), 173–177.

Gay, G. (2000). *Culturally responsive teaching.* New York: Teachers College Press.

Gehrke, R. S. (2005). Poor schools, poor students, successful teachers. *Kappa Delta Pi Record, 42*(1), 14–17.

George, P. (2004). Editor's notes. *Middle Ground, 8*(2), 2.

Gilligan, C. (1982). *In a different voice*. Cambridge, MA: Havard University Press.

Ginott, H. G. (1993). *Teacher and child*. New York: Collier Books/Macmillan.

Glass, T. E., Bjork, L., & Brunner, C. C. (2000). *The Study of the American Superintendency*. Arlington, VA: American Association of School Administrators.

Glasser, W. (1998). *Choice theory*. New York: Harper Collins.

Gober, D. A., & Mewborn, D. S. (2001). Promoting equity in mathematics classrooms. *Middle School Journal, 32*(3), 31–35.

Goldstein, L. (2003, April 16). Special education growth spurs cap plan in pending IDEA. *Education Week, 22*(31), 1–17.

Goleman, D. (1995). *Emotional intelligence*. New York: Bantam Books.

Gollnick, D. M., & Chinn, P. C. (2006). *Multicultural education in a pluralistic society* (7th ed.). Upper Saddle River, NJ: Merrill/Prentice Hall.

Good, H. G. (1964). *A history of American education*. New York: Macmillan.

Goodlad, J. I. (1984). *A place called school*. New York: McGraw Hill.

Goodlad, J. I. (2004). Teaching what we hold sacred. *Educational Leadership, 61*(4), 18–21.

Greene, M. (1978). *Landscape of learning*. New York: Teachers College Press.

Greene, M. (1995). What counts as philosophy of education? In W. Kohli (Ed.), *Critical conversations in philosophy of education*. New York: Routledge.

Gregoire, M. A., & Lupinetti, J. (2005). Supporting diversity through the arts. *Kappa Delta Pi Record, 41*(4), 159–163.

Gunter, M. A., Estes, T. H., & Mintz, S. L. (2007). *Instruction: A models approach* (5th ed.). Boston: Allyn & Bacon.

Gutek, G. L. (2005). *Historical and philosophical foundations of education* (4th ed.). Upper Saddle River, NJ: Merrill/Prentice Hall.

Hall, D. (2005). *Getting honest about grad rates: How states play the numbers and students lose*. The Education Trust. Retrieved January 2, 2007, from http://www2.edtrust.org/NR/rdonlyres/C5A6974D-6C04-4FB1-A9FC-05938CB0744D/0/Getting_Honest.pdf

Haskins, R., Paxson, C., & Donahue, E. (2006). *Fighting obesity in the public school*. Policy brief of The Future of Children. Retrieved April 6, 2006, from http://www. futureofchildren.princeton.edu/briefs/FOC%20policy%20brief%20spr%2006.pdf

Hasselbring, T. S., & Bausch, M. E. (2006). Assistive technologies for reading. *Educational Leadership, 63*(4), 72–75.

Haycock, K. (2003). Toward a fair distribution of teacher talent. *Educational Leadership, 60*(4), 11–15.

Haynes, C. C. (2006, March). A moral battleground, a civil discourse. *USA Today*. Retrieved March 23, 2006, from http://www.usatoday.com/news/opinion/editorials/2006-03-19-faith-edit_x.htm

Haynes, C. C., Chaltain, S., Ferguson, J. E., Hudson, D. L., & Thomas, O. (2003). *The First Amendment in schools*. Alexandria, VA: Association for Supervision and Curriculum Development.

Hess, F. M. (2002). *School boards at the dawn of the 21st century: Conditions and challenges of district governance*. Arlington, VA: National School Boards Association. Retrieved June 10, 2007, from http://www.nsba.org/site/docs/1200/1143.pdf

Heward, W. L. (2006). *Exceptional children: An introduction to special education* (8th ed.). Upper Saddle River, NJ: Merrill/Prentice Hall.

Hirsch, E. D. (1987). *Cultural literacy: What every American needs to know*. Boston: Houghton Mifflin.

Hodgkinson, H. (2001). Educational demographics: What teachers should know. *Educational Leadership, 58*(4), 6–11.

Holloway, J. H. (2000). Extracurricular activities: The path to academic success? *Educational Leadership, 57*(4), 87–88.

Holmes, M., & Weiss, B. J. (1995). *Lives of women public school teachers: Scenes from American educational history.* New York: Garland.

Howe, K. R. (1996). A conceptual basis for ethics in teacher education. *Journal of Teacher Education, 37,* 6.

Howsam, R. B., Corrigan, D. C., Denemark, G. W., & Nash, R. J. (1976). *Educating a profession.* Washington, DC: American Association of Colleges of Teacher Education.

Illich, I. (1971). *Deschooling society.* New York: Harper and Row.

Infoplease. (2004). *Teen birthrates continue to decline.* Retrieved April 7, 2006, from http://www.infoplease.com/ipa/A0193727.html

Ingersoll, R. (1997). *The status of teaching as a profession: 1990–1991.* Washington, DC: U.S. Department of Education.

International Society for Technology in Education. (2000a). *Essential conditions for teacher preparation.* Retrieved July 4, 2007, from http://cnets.iste.org/teachers/t_stands.html

International Society for Technology in Education. (2000b). *Profiles for technology literate students.* Retrieved July 3, 2007, from http://cnets.iste.org/students/s_profiles.html

International Society for Technology in Education (2002). *Profiles for technology literate students.* Eugene, OR: Author. Retrieved April 15, 2007, from http://cnets.iste.org/students/s_profiles.html

International Society for Technology in Education. (2005). *Educational technology standards and performance indicators for all teachers.* Retrieved April 14, 2007, from http://cnets.iste.org/teachers/t_stands.html

International Society for Technology in Education. (2005). *Mission statement.* Retrieved July 1, 2005, from http://www.iste.org

International Society for Technology in Education. (2005a). *National educational technology standards for teachers: Preparing teachers to use technology.* Eugene, OR: Author. Retrieved April 14, 2007, from http://cnets.iste.org/teachers/

International Society for Technology in Education. (2005b). *Technology foundation standards for all students,* 2005. Retrieved April 14, 2007, from http://cnets.iste.org/students/s_stands.html

International Society for Technology in Education. (2007). *National educational technology standards for students* (2nd ed.). Retrieved July 5, 2007, from http://cnets.iste.org/students/

Jackson, R., & Harper, K. (2002). *Teacher planning and the universal design for learning.* Wakefield, MA: National Center on Accessing the General Curriculum.

Jacobsen, D. A. (2003). *Philosophy in classroom teaching: Bridging the gap* (2nd ed.). Upper Saddle River, NJ: Merrill/Prentice Hall.

Jenkins, H. (2005). Getting into the game. *Educational Leadership, 62*(7), 48–51.

Jerald, C. (2003). Beyond the rock and the hard place. *Educational Leadership, 61*(3), 12–16.

Johnson, D. W., & Johnson, R. T. (1999). *Learning together and alone: Cooperative, competitive, and individualistic learning.* Boston: Allyn & Bacon.

Johnson, J., & Duffett, A. (2003). *Where we are now: 12 things you need to know about public opinion and public schools.* New York: Public Agenda. Retrieved April 11, 2007, from http://www.publicagenda.org/research/PDFs/where_we_are_now.pdf

Johnson, J. A., Musial, D., Hall, G. E., Golnick, D. M., & Dupuis, V. L. (2005). *Introduction to the foundations of American education.* Boston: Allyn & Bacon.

Johnson, S. M., & Kardos, S. M. (2005). Bridging the generation gap. *Educational Leadership, 62*(8), 8–14.

Johnston, L. D., O'Malley, P. M., Bachman, J. G., & Schulenberg, J. E. (2005). *Monitoring the future: National results on adolescent drug use.* Retrieved April 15, 2006, from http://monitoringthefuture.org/pubs/monographs/overview2005.pdf

Kaufman, P., Alt, M. N., & Chapman, C. (2001). *Dropout rates in the United States: 2000.* Washington, DC: National Center for Education Statistics.

Klem, A. M., & Connell, J. P. (2004). Relationships matter: Linking teacher support to student engagement and achievement. *Journal of School Health, 74*(7), 262–273.

Kneller, G. F. (1971). *Introduction to the philosophy of education.* New York: Wiley.

Kohlberg, L. (1984). *The psychology of moral development: Essays on moral development* (Vol. 2). San Francisco: Harper & Row.

Kohn, A. (2000, September 27). Standardized testing and its victims. *Education Week,* pp. 60, 46–47.

Kohn, A. (2002). The 500-pound gorilla. *Phi Delta Kappan, 84*(2), 113–119.

Kohn, A. (2005). Unconditional teaching. *Educational Leadership, 63*(1), 20–24.

Kostelnik, M. J., Soderman, A. K., & Whiren, A. P. (2004). *Developmentally appropriate curriculum: Best practices in early childhood education* (3rd ed.). Upper Saddle River, NJ: Merrill/Prentice Hall.

Kounin, J. S. (1970). *Discipline and group management in classrooms.* New York: Holt, Rinehart, & Winston.

Kozol, J. (1991). *Savage inequalities: Children in America's schools.* New York: Crown.

Krashen, S. (2002). Whole language and the great plummet of 1987–1992. *Phi Delta Kappan, 83*(10), 748–753.

Lambert, L. (2003). *Leadership capacity for lasting school improvement.* Alexandria, VA: Association for Supervision and Curriculum Development.

LaMorte, M. W. (2005). *School law: Cases and concepts* (7th ed.). Boston: Allyn & Bacon.

Landsman, J. (2006). Bearers of hope. *Educational Leadership, 63*(5), 26–32.

Lazarus, W., Wainer, A., & Lipper, L. (2005). *Measuring digital opportunity for America's children: Where we stand and where we go from here.* Santa Monica, CA: The Children's Partnership.

Leinwand, D. (2006, April). Fewer teens using drugs. *USA Today.* Retrieved April 10, 2006, from http://www.usatoday.com/news/nation/2006-04-06-drug-use_x.htm

Lemlech, J. K. (2004). Knowledge alive. *Educational Leadership, 62*(1), 14–18.

Lemlech, J. K. (2004). *Teaching in elementary and secondary classrooms.* Upper Saddle River, NJ: Merrill/Prentice Hall.

Levine, M. (2003). Celebrating diverse minds. *Educational Leadership, 61*(2), 12–18.

Lewis-Charp, H. (2003). Breaking the silence: White students' perspectives on race in multiracial schools. *Phi Delta Kappan, 85*(4), 279–285.

Lezotte, L. W. (1991). *Correlates of effective schools: The first and second generation.* Okemos, MI: Effective Schools Products, Ltd.

Lightfoot, S. L. (1978). *Worlds apart: Relationships between families and schools.* New York: Basic Books.

Lincoln, E., & Meltzer, M. (1968). *A pictorial history of the Negro in America* (3rd ed.). New York: Crown.

Little, C. (2001). What matters to students. *Educational Leadership, 59*(2), 61–64.

Loeper, J. L. (1973). *Going to School in 1776.* New York: Macmillan.

Lounsbury, J. H. (1991). *As I see it.* Columbus, OH: National Middle School Association.

Lumpkin, A. (2007). Caring teachers: The key to student learning. *Kappa Delta Pi Record, 43*(4), 158–160.

MacDonald, G. J. (2004, October 19). Schools lay tender trap for truants. *Christian Science Monitor.* Retrieved April 6, 2006, from http://www.csmonitor.com/2004/1019/plls02-legn.html

Magid, L. (2005). *Kids' rules for online safety.* National Center for Missing and Exploited Children. Retrieved December 28, 2006, from http://www.safekids.com/kidsrules.htm

Maine Learning Technology Initiative. (2005). Retrieved January 15, 2006, from http://www.state.me.us/mlti

Mann, H. (1891). *Annual reports.* Boston: Lee and Shepard Publications.

Manning, M. L., & Bucher, K. T. (2003). *Classroom management: Models, applications, and cases.* Upper Saddle River, NJ: Merrill/Prentice Hall.

March, T. (2006). The new whatever, whenever, and wherever. *Educational Leadership, 63*(4), 14–19.

Marzano, R. J. (2000). *Transforming classroom grading.* Alexandria, VA: Association for Supervision and Curriculum Development.

Marzano, R. J. (2003a). *Classroom management that works: Research-based strategies for every teacher.* Alexandria, VA: Association for Supervision and Curriculum Development.

Marzano, R. J. (2003b). *What works in schools: Translating research into action.* Alexandria, VA: Association for Supervision and Curriculum Development.

Marzano, R. J., Pickering, D. J., & Pollock, J. R. (2001). *Classroom instruction that works.* Alexandria, VA: Association for Supervision and Curriculum Development.

Maslow, A. H. (1999). *Toward a psychology of being* (3rd ed.). New York: Wiley.

McCloud, S. (2005). From chaos to consistency. *Educational Leadership, 62*(5), 46–49.

McDevitt, T. M., & Ormrod, J. E. (2004). *Child development: Educating and working with children and adolescents.* Upper Saddle River, NJ: Merrill/Prentice Hall.

McHugh, J. (2005). Synching up with the kids. *Edutopia, 1*(7), 32–35.

McNeil, J. D. (1995). *Curriculum: The teacher's initiative.* Upper Saddle River, NJ: Prentice Hall.

McNergney, R. F., & McNergney, J. M. (2007). *Education: The practice and profession of teaching.* Boston: Allyn & Bacon.

Merrow, J. (2004). Meeting superman. *Phi Delta Kappan, 85*(6), 455–460.

Miller, P. C., & Endo, H. (2004). Understanding and meeting the needs of ESL students. *Phi Delta Kappan, 85*(10), 786–791.

Moats, L. C. (2001). When older students can't read. *Educational Leadership, 58*(6).

Montessori, M. (1967). *The discovery of the child.* Notre Dame, IN: Fides Publications.

Morrison, G. R., & Lowther, D. L. (2005). *Integrating computer technology into the classroom* (2nd ed.). Upper Saddle River, NJ: Merrill/Prentice Hall.

Morrison, G. S. (2003). *Fundamentals of early childhood education* (3rd ed.). Upper Saddle River, NJ: Merrill/Prentice Hall.

Mothers Against Drunk Driving. (2004). *Fatalities and alcohol-related fatalities among 15–20 year olds—2003 v. 2002.* Retrieved May 26, 2006, from http://www.madd.org/stats/9659

Mukhopadhyay, C., & Henze, R. C. (2003). How real is race? Using anthropology to make sense of human diversity. *Phi Delta Kappan, 84*(9), 669–678.

Mursell, J. L. (1946). *Successful teaching.* New York: McGraw-Hill.

National Academy of Education. (2005). *A good teacher in every classroom.* San Francisco: Jossey-Bass.

National Association for the Education of Young Children. (2001). *NAEYC standards for early childhood professional preparation: Initial licensure programs.* Retrieved July 4, 2007, from http://www.naeyc.org/faculty/pdf/2001.pdf

National Association of State Boards of Education. (2005). *State education governance at-a-glance.* Retrieved June 20, 2006, from http://www.nasbe.org/Educational_Issues/Governance/Governance_chart.pdf

National Board of Professional Teaching Standards. (2006). *The five core propositions.* Retrieved August 3, 2006, from http://www.nbpts.org/the_standards/the_five_core_propositions

National Center for Education Statistics. (2001a). *Characteristics of school principals.* Washington, DC: U.S. Department of Education. Retrieved July 8, 2006, from http://www.nces.ed.gov

National Center for Education Statistics. (2001b). *Statistics of state school systems: Revenues and expenditures for public elementary and secondary education.* Washington, DC: U.S. Department of Education. Retrieved August 2, 2006, from http://www.nces.ed.gov

National Center for Education Statistics. (2002). *Statistics of state school systems: Revenues and expenditures for public elementary and secondary education.* Washington, DC: U.S. Department of Education.

National Center for Education Statistics. (2003). *Common core of data surveys 2003.* Retrieved May 15, 2005, from http://www.nces.ed.gov/programs/projections

National Center for Education Statistics. (2003). *National elementary and secondary school enrollment model.* Retrieved August 2, 2005 from http://www.nces.ed.gov/pubs2003

National Center for Education Statistics. (2004). *Children born in 2001: First results from the base year of the early childhood longitudinal study, birth cohort (ECLS-B).* Washington, DC. Retrieved March 5, 2007, from http://nces.ed.gov/pubsearch/pubsinfo.asp?pubid=2005036.

National Center for Education Statistics. (2004). *National household education survey.* Retrieved March 16, 2007, from http://nces.ed.gov/quicktables/result.asp?SrchKeyword=national+household+education+survey&topic=All&Year=2004

National Center for Education Statistics. (2005). *Common core of data.* Washington, DC: Retrieved July 22, 2006, from http://nces.ed.gov/pubs2005/2005314.pdf

National Center for Education Statistics. (2005). *Digest of education statistics tables and figures.* Retrieved June 24, 2007, from http://nces.ed.gov/programs/digest/d05/tables/dt05.005.asp

National Center for Education Statistics. (2005). *Digest of education statistics: 2005.* Retrieved March 25, 2007, from http://nces.ed.gov/programs/digest/d05/tables/dt05_063.asp

National Center for Education Statistics. (2005). *Indicators of school crime and safety.* Washington, DC: Author. Retrieved March 22, 2006, from http://nces.ed.gov/pubs2005/2005002.pdf

National Center for Education Statistics. (2005). *Trends in international mathematics and science study.* Retrieved April 10, 2007, from http://nces.ed.gov/timss/ index.asp.

National Center for Education Statistics. (2005a). *Overview of public elementary and secondary students, staff, schools, school districts, revenues, and expenditures: School year 2004–2005 and fiscal year 2004* (Common Core of Data). Washington, DC: U.S Department of Education. Retrieved January 7, 2007, from http://www.nces.ed.gov

National Center for Education Statistics. (2005b). *Projections of Education Statistics to 2014.* Washington, DC: U.S. Department of Education. Retrieved May 21, 2007 from http://nces.ed.gov/pubs2007/2005074.pdf

National Center for Education Statistics. (2006). *Public elementary/secondary school universe survey, 2003–04,* and *State nonfiscal survey of public elementary/secondary education, 2003–2004.*

National Center for Education Statistics. (2006). *The nation's report card.* Retrieved April 10, 2007, from http://nces.ed.gov/nationsreportcard/.

National Center for Education Statistics. Fast Response Survey System. (2005). *Survey on advanced telecommunications in U.S. public schools, K–12.* Retrieved January 3, 2007, from http://nces.gov/surveys/frss/publications/2005015/

National Council for Teachers of English. (1996). *Standards for English language arts.* Retrieved April 1, 2007, from www.ncte.org

National Council for the Social Studies. (2005). *Curriculum standards for social studies: Executive summary.* Retrieved July 1, 2005, from http://www.socialstudies.org/standards/execsummary/

National Council of Teachers of Mathematics. (1995). *Assessment standards for school mathematics.* Reston, VA: Author.

National Council of Teachers of Mathematics. (2000). *Principles and standards for school mathematics.* Reston, VA: Author.

National Council on Teacher Quality. (2006). *Increasing the odds: How policies can yield better teachers.* Retrieved November 24, 2006, from http://www.nctq.org/nctq/images/nctq_io.pdf

National Education Association. (2001). *Attracting and keeping quality teachers.* Washington, DC: Author. Retrieved May 15, 2005, from http://nea.org/teachershortage.index

National Education Association. (2003). *Status of the American public school teacher 2000–2001.* Washington, DC: Author. Retrieved May 15, 2005, from http://www.nea.org/edstats/images/status.pdf

National Education Association. (2005). *About NEA*. Retrieved May 27, 2005, from http://www.nea.org/aboutnea

National Education Association. (2005). *Rankings and estimates: Estimates of school statistics* 2005. Washington, DC: Author.

National Governors Association. (2006). *Clearinghouse on educational policy issues*. Retrieved June 20, 2006, from http://www.nga.org

National Middle School Association. (2002). *Initial teacher preparation standards*. Westerville, OH: Author. Retrieved November 24, 2006, from www.nmsa.org/professionalpreparation/NMSAStandards

National Middle School Association. (2002). *NMSA performance-based standards for initial middle level teacher preparation*. Retrieved June 14, 2005, from http://www.nmsa.org

National Middle School Association (2003). *This we believe: Successful schools for young adolescents*. Westerville, OH: Author.

National School Boards Association. (2005). *Educational vital signs*. Arlington, VA: Author.

National Science Teachers Association. (2005). *National Science Education Standards*. Retrieved July 1, 2005, from http://books.nap.edu/html/nses/6a.html

Neill, A. S. (1960). *Summerhill: A radical approach to child rearing*. New York: Hart.

Nelson, J. L., Carlson, K., & Palonsky, S. B. (2000). *Critical issues in education: A dialectic approach* (4th ed.). New York: McGraw-Hill.

Neuman, S. B. (1999). Books make a difference: A study of access to literacy. *Reading Research Quarterly, 34*(3), 286–311.

Neuman, S. B. (2003). From rhetoric to reality: The case for high-quality compensatory prekindergarten programs. *Phi Delta Kappan, 84*(4), 286–291.

Nieto, S. M. (2003). Profoundly multicultural questions. *Educational Leadership, 60*(4), 6–10.

Niguidula, D. (2005). Documenting learning with digital portfolios. *Educational Leadership, 63*(3), 44–47.

Noddings, N. (1992). *The challenge to care in schools: An alternative approach to education*. New York: Teachers College Press.

Norris, C., Sullivan, T., Poirot, J., & Soloway, E. (2003). No access, no use, no impact: Snapshot surveys of educational technology in K–12. *Journal of Research on Technology in Education, 36*(1), 15–27.

North American Association of State and Provincial Lotteries. (2006). *Member lotteries*. Retrieved August 15, 2006, from http://www.naspl.org

O'Bannon, B. W., & Puckett, K. (2007). *Preparing to use technology: A practical guide to curriculum integration*. Boston: Allyn & Bacon.

O'Connor, K. (2002). *How to grade for learning*. Arlington Heights, IL: Skylight Professional Development, Pearson Education, Inc.

Ohanion, S. (2003). Capitalism, calculus, and conscience. *Phi Delta Kappan, 84*(10), 736–747.

Ophelia Project. (2005). *Bullies, broken hearts . . . and the harsh reality of relational aggression*. Retrieved April 9, 2006, from www.opheliaproject.org

Ornstein, A. C. (2003). *Pushing the envelope: Critical issues in education*. Upper Saddle River, NJ: Merrill/Prentice Hall.

Ornstein, A. C., & Levine, D. U. (2006). *Foundations of education* (9th ed.). Boston: Houghton Mifflin.

Ozmon, H., & Craver, S. (2008). *Philosophical foundations of education* (8th ed.). Upper Saddle River, NJ: Merrill/Prentice Hall.

Pauken, P. D. (2006). Student rights. In C. Russo (Ed.), *Key legal issues for schools: The ultimate resource for school business officials*. Lanham, MD: Rowman & Littlefield Education.

Paulson, A. (2006, March 3). Dropout rates high, but fixes underway. *Christian Science Monitor*. Retrieved April 18, 2006, from http://www.csmonitor.com/2006/0303/p01s02-legn.html

Paxson, C., Donahue, E., Orleans, C. T., & Grisso, J. A. (2006). Introducing the issue. *The Future of Children, 16*(1), 3–15.

Payne, R. K. (1998). *A framework for understanding poverty.* Highlands, TX: RFT Publishing.

Payne, R. K. (2003). *A framework for understanding poverty* (3rd rev. ed.). Highlands, TX: RFT Publishing.

Payne, R. K. (2005). *A framework for understanding poverty.* (4th rev. ed.). Highlands, TX: RFT Publishing.

Perkins-Gough, D. (2005). Fixing high schools. *Educational Leadership, 62*(7), 88–89.

Perrone, V. (1991). *A letter to teachers: Reflections on schooling and the art of teaching.* San Francisco: Jossey-Bass.

Phelps, P.H. (2003). Teacher professionalism. *Kappa Delta Pi Record, 40*(1), 10–11.

Piaget, J. (1970). Piaget's theory. In P. Mussen (Ed.), *Carmichael's manual of child psychology.* New York: Wiley.

Pianta, R. C., & LaParo, K. (2003). Improving early school success. *Educational Leadership, 60*(7), 24–29.

Polite, L., & Saenger, E. B. (2003). A pernicious silence: Confronting race in the elementary classroom. *Phi Delta Kappan, 85*(4), 274–278.

Popham, W. J. (2001). *The truth about testing: An educator's call to action.* Alexandria, VA: Association for Supervision and Curriculum Development.

Posner, G. J. (2005). *Field experience: A guide to reflective teaching.* Boston: Allyn & Bacon.

Powell, S. D. (2005). *Introduction to middle school.* Upper Saddle River, NJ: Merrill/Prentice Hall.

Prensky, M. (2006). Listen to the natives. *Educational Leadership, 63*(4), 8–13.

Public Education Network. (2003). *The voice of the new teacher.* Washington, DC: Author.

Pulliam, J., & Van Patten, J. (2007). *History of education in America* (9th ed.). Upper Saddle River, NJ: Merrill/Prentice Hall.

Ravitch, D. (2000). *Left back: A century of failed school reforms.* New York: Simon & Schuster.

Ray, R. D. (2006). *Research facts on homeschooling.* National Home Education Research Institute. Retrieved June 25, 2007, from http://www.nheri.org/content/view/199

Reeves, D. B. (2004). *Accountability for learning: How teachers and school leaders can take charge.* Alexandria, VA: Association for Supervision and Curriculum Development.

Renard, L. (2005). Teaching the DIG generation. *Educational Leadership, 62*(7), 44–47.

Renzulli, J. S., Gentry, M., & Reis, S. M. (2004). A time and place for authentic learning. *Educational Leadership, 62*(1), 73–77.

Richardson, R. C., & Norman, K. I. (2000). Intrinsic goodness: Facilitating character development. *Kappa Delta Pi Record, 36*(4), 168–172.

Richardson, W. (2006). The educator's guide to the read/write Web. *Educational Leadership, 63*(4), 24–27.

Riley, R. W. (1998). *Secretary's statement on religious expression.* Retrieved November 12, 2006, from www.ed.gov/inits/religionandschools

Ringstaff, C., & Kelley, L. (2002). *The learning return on our technology investment: A review of findings from research.* San Francisco: WestEd RTEC. Available from http://www.wsetedrtec.org

Rippa, S. A. (1997). *Education in a free society: An American history* (8th ed.). New York: Longman.

Roberts, P. L., Kellough, R. D., & Moore, K. (2006). *A resource guide for elementary school teachers* (6th ed.). Upper Saddle River, NJ: Merrill/Prentice Hall.

Roblyer, M. D. (2006). *Integrating educational technology into teaching.* Upper Saddle River, NJ: Merrill/Prentice Hall.

Roschelle, J., Penuel, W. R., & Abrahamson, L. (2004). The networked classroom. *Educational Leadership, 61*(5), 50–53.

Rosenberg, M. S., O'Shea, L. J., & O'Shea, D. J. (2006). *Student teacher to master teacher: A practical guide for educating students with special needs.* Upper Saddle River, NJ: Merrill/Prentice Hall.

Rosenshine, B. (1971). *Teaching behaviors and student achievement*. London: National Foundation for Educational Research.

Rowan, B. (1994). Comparing teachers' work with work in other occupations: Notes on the professional status of teaching. *Educational Researcher, 23*(6), 4–17, 21.

Scherer, M. (2001). Perspectives. *Educational Leadership, 58*(8), 5.

Schlozman, S. C. (2002). Why "just say no" isn't enough. *Educational Leadership, 59*(7), 87–89.

School Choice Wisconsin. (2004). *Milwaukee's public schools in an era of choice*. Retrieved July 22, 2006, from www.schoolchoicewi.org/data/research

Scriven, M. (1990). Can research-based teacher evaluation be saved? *Journal of Personnel Evaluation in Education, 4*(1), 19–32.

Sergiovani, T. J. (2001). *The principalship: A reflective practice perspective* (4th ed.). Boston: Allyn & Bacon.

Shelley, G. B., Cashman, T. J., Gunter, R. E., & Gunter, G. A. (2006). *Integrating technology in the classroom* (4th ed.). Boston: Thomson.

Silver, H. F., Strong, R. W., & Perini, M. J. (2000). *So each may learn: Integrating learning styles and multiple intelligences*. Alexandria, VA: Association for Supervision and Curriculum Development.

Simmons, R. (2002). *Odd girl out: The hidden culture of aggression in girls*. Orlando, FL: Harcourt.

Simon, A., & Boyer, E. (1968*). Mirrors for behavior: An anthology of classroom observation instrument*s. Philadelphia: Research for Better Schools.

Sizer, T. R. (1985). *Horace's compromise*. Boston: Houghton Mifflin.

Stanford News Service. (1994). *Ralph Tyler, one of the century's foremost educators, dies at 91*. Retrieved March 1, 2006, from Stanford University News Service website: http://www.stanford.edu/dept/news/pr/94/940228Arc4425.html

Sternberg, R., & Horvath, J. (1995). A prototype view of expert teaching. *Educational Researcher, 24*(6), 9–17.

Sternberg R. J. (2007). Who are the bright children? The cultural context of being and acting intelligent. *Educational Researcher, 36*(3), 148–155.

Stevenson, C. (2002). *Teaching ten to fourteen year olds* (3rd ed.). New York: Longman.

Stiggins, R. J. (2001). Building a productive assessment future. *National Association of Secondary School Principals, 85*(621), 2–4.

Story, M., Kaphingst, K. M., & French, S. (2006). The role of schools in obesity prevention. *The Future of Children, 16*(1), 109–131.

Stronge, J. H. (2002). *Qualities of effective teachers*. Alexandria, VA: Association for Supervision and Curriculum Development.

Sullivan, A. (2006). *White House pushes more schools to drug-test students*. Retrieved April 1, 2006, from http://www.infoshop.org/inews/article.php?story=20060320104929207&mode=print

Swanson, C. B. (2004). *The real truth about low graduation rates*. Washington, DC: Urban Institute. Retrieved April 14, 2006, from www.urban.org/publications/411050.html

Swanson, C. B. (2006). Tracking U.S. trends. *Education Week, 25*(35). Retrieved January 3, 2007, from http://www.edweek.org

Symonds, P. M. (1934). *Mental hygiene of the school child*. New York: Macmillan.

Takaki, R. (1993). *A different mirror: A history of multicultural America*. New York: Little, Brown.

Teach for America. (2006). *Record number of top graduates to lead classrooms in low-income communities nationwide*. Retrieved April 4, 2007, from http://www.teachforamerica.org/newsroom/documents/TeachForAmerica_News_20060907.html

Technology Counts 2002. (2002, May). Education Week. Retrieved December 17, 2005, from http://www.edweek.org/sreports/tc02

Tehie, J. B. (2007). *Historical foundations of education*. Upper Saddle River, NJ: Merrill/Prentice Hall.

Tell, C. (2001). Who's in our classrooms: Teachers speak for themselves. *Educational Leadership, 58*(8), 18–23.

Tenneyson Center for Children. (2006). *The numbers are alarming . . . and growing.* Retrieved April 18, 2006, from http://www.childabuse.org/abuse%20stats.html

Thompson, M., & Grace, C. O. (2001). *Best friends, worst enemies: Understanding the social lives of children.* New York: Ballantine.

Thornburgh, N. (2006, April 17). Dropout nation. *Time,* pp. 30–40.

Tienken, C. (2003, winter). Tech-mix learning. *New Teacher Advocate, 11*(2).

Tomlinson, C. S. (1999). *The differentiated classroom. Responding to the needs of all learners.* Alexandria, VA: Association for Supervision and Curriculum Development.

Tough, P. (2006, November 26). What it takes to make a student. *New York Times Magazine.* Retrieved June 17, 2007, from http://www.nytimes.com/2006/11/26/magazine/26tough.html

Traina, R. (1999). What makes a teacher good? *Education Week, 18*(19), 34.

Turnbull, R., Turnbull, A., & Wehmeyer, M. (2007). Exceptional lives: Special education in today's schools (5th ed.). Upper Saddle River, NJ: Merrill/Prentice Hall.

Tyler, R. (1949). *Basic principles of curriculum and instruction.* Chicago: University of Chicago Press.

U.S. Census Bureau. (2002). *Current population survey, 1960–2002 annual demographic supplements.* Retrieved April 28, 2005, from www.census.gov/prod/2002pubs/p60–219.pdf

U.S. Census Bureau. (2006). *Public Education Finances 2004.* Washington, DC: Author.

U.S. Census Bureau with U.S. Department of Education. (2006). *Income, poverty, and health insurance coverage in the United States: 2005.* Retrieved April 6, 2006, from http://www.census.gov/prod/2006pubs/p60-231.pdf

U.S. Department of Education. (1999). *Teacher's guide to religion in public schools.* Washington, DC: Author.

U.S. Department of Education. (2005). *Key policy letters signed by the education secretary or deputy secretary.* Retrieved March 18, 2007, from http://www.ed.gov/policy/elsec/guid/secletter/051021.html

U.S. Department of Education. (2006). *The federal role in education.* Retrieved July 27, 2006, from www.ed.gov/about/overview/fed/role.html

U.S. Department of Health, Education, and Welfare. (1966). *Equality of educational opportunity: Summary report* (The Coleman report). Washington, DC: U.S. Government Printing Office.

U.S. Department of Health and Human Services. (2005). *Child maltreatment 2005.* Author. Retrieved April 22, 2007, from http://www.acf.dhhs.gov/programs/cb/pubs/cm05/index.htm

U.S. Department of Justice (2003). *School crime supplement to the National Crime Victimization Survey, 2003.* Washington, DC: Author.

U.S. Department of Justice. (2005). *Indicators of school crime and safety: 2005.* Washington, DC: Author.

U.S. General Accounting Office. (2002). *School finance: Per-pupil spending differences between selected inner city and suburban schools varied by metropolitan area.* Washington, DC: Author.

Underwood, J., & Webb, L. D. (2006). *School law for teachers: Concepts and applications.* Upper Saddle River, NJ: Merrill/Prentice Hall.

Underwood, M. (2003). *Social aggression among girls.* New York: Guilford.

Urban Institute. (2005). *High concentration of limited-English students challenges implementation of No Child Left Behind.* Retrieved November 5, 2006, from http://www.fcd-us.org/news/challengesnochildact.html

Urban Schools: Executive Summary. (2000). *Urban schools: The challenge of location and poverty.* Retrieved May 14, 2006, from http://nces.ed.gov/pubs/96184ex.html

Vacca, R. T. (2002). From efficient decoders to strategic readers. *Educational Leadership, 60*(3), 7–11.

Vacca, R. T. (2006). They can because they think they can. *Educational Leadership, 63*(5), 56–59.

Vermeer, H. J., Boekaerts, M., & Seeger, G. (2000). Motivational and gender differences: Sixth-grade students' mathematical problem-solving behavior. *Journal of Educational Psychology, 92,* 308–315.

Vygotsky, L. S. (1978). *Mind in society: The development of higher psychological processes.* Cambridge, MA: Harvard University Press.

Warhaftig, A. (2005). A costly gift. *Teacher Magazine, 17*(2), 61.

Webb, L., Metha, A., & Jordan, K. F. (2007). *Foundations of American education* (5th ed.). Upper Saddle River, NJ: Merrill/Prentice Hall.

Wenglinsky, H. (2005). *Using technology wisely: The keys to success in schools.* New York: Teachers College Press.

Westbrook, R. B. (1996). Public schooling and American democracy. In R. Soder (ed.), *Democracy, education, and the schools.* San Francisco: Jossey-Bass.

White, J. L., & Cones, J. H. (1999). *Black men emerging: Facing the past and seizing a future in America.* New York: W. H. Freeman.

White-Hood, M. (2006). Targeting the school bully. *Middle Ground, 9*(4) 30–32.

Why computers fail as teachers [cover]. (2000, September 25). *U.S. News and World Report.*

Wiener, R., & Pristoop, E. (2006). How states shortchange the districts that need the most help. In *The Educational Trust Funding Gap 2006.* Retrieved June 28, 2007, from http://www2.edtrust.org/NR/rdonlyres/CDEF9403-5A75-437E-93FF-EBF1174181FB/0/FundingGap2006.pdf

Wiggins, G. P., & McTighe, J. (2005). *Understanding by design* (2nd ed.). Alexandria, VA: Association for Supervision and Curriculum Development.

Wolfram, W., Adger, C., & Christian, D. (1999). *Dialects in schools and communities.* Mahwah, NJ: Erlbaum.

Wolk, S. (2003). Hearts and minds. *Educational Leadership, 61*(1), 14–18.

Wolk, S. (2007). Why go to school? *Phi Delta Kappan, 88*(9), 648–658.

Zeichner, K. M. (2003). The adequacies and inadequacies of three current strategies to recruit, prepare, and retain the best teachers for all students. *Teacher College Record, 105*(3), 490–519.

Zull, J. E. (2004). The art of changing the brain. *Educational Leadership, 62*(1), 68–72.

Glossary

A

Academic freedom. A form of expression that allows teachers to use their judgment in making decisions about what to discuss, what to assign as readings, what teaching strategies to use, etc.

Academic rigor. The content of what we teach is meaningful, and our expectations of the learning of that content are demanding.

Academies. Early secondary schools designed to teach content intended to prepare students to participate in business and trade.

Accountability. Holding a person or program responsible for an outcome.

Achievement gap. Disparity among students, with some excelling while others languish with respect to learning and academic success.

Action research. Research conducted by teachers in their classrooms around a concept or question that captures their interest; results of research may be added to the teaching knowledge base.

Adequate Yearly Progress. School report that consists of a number of elements determined by each individual state with guidance from No Child Left Behind requirements. AYP data are kept by race, socioeconomic status, and gender. Typical components of the AYP report include graduation rate, attendance, math scores, reading/language arts achievement data, and other indicators of student progress.

Advocate for students. Support and defend students, always putting their needs first.

Aesthetics. The determination of what is beautiful and artistic.

Alternative school. School designed for students who are not successful in a traditional school setting.

American Federation of Teachers (AFT). America's second largest professional association for teachers.

Analytic rubric. Specifies separate parts of an assessment task, product, or performance and the characteristics of various levels of success for each.

Assessment. Gathering evidence of student learning.

Assistive technology. Devices and services that benefit students with disabilities by helping them communicate, increasing their mobility, and aiding in multiple ways that enhance their capacity to learn.

Association for Childhood Education International (ACEI). Organization that provides standards for the preparation of elementary teachers.

Associative play. Children begin to share toys and verbally communicate.

At-risk students. Those who are in serious danger of not completing school and/or who may be heading toward nonproductive or counterproductive lifestyles.

Attention deficit/hyperactivity disorder (AD/HD). A learning disability in which students demonstrate three defining characteristics—inattention, hyperactivity, and impulsivity—in persistent patterns that are more severe than in others of the same age.

Authentic teaching. Teaching what's needed, when it's needed, and doing so appropriately.

Axiology. Branch of philosophy that addresses values, both in ethics and aesthetics. Ethics is the determination of what's right and what's wrong. Aesthetics is the determination of what is beautiful and artistic.

B

Backward design. An approach to planning for teaching and learning that starts with deciding on the desired learning results (curriculum), then identifies how to collect the evidence necessary to know if the results have been achieved (assessment), and then proceeds to choosing how to help students acquire the desired knowledge and skills (instruction).

Benchmarks. Statements of what students should know and be able to do at specific developmental stages.

Bilingual education. The delivery of instruction in two languages.

Bilingual Education Act of 1968. Provided funds to assist non-English-speaking students (mostly Hispanic) who were dropping out of high school at a rate of about 70%.

Black Codes. Prior to the Civil War, Black Codes were enacted, predominantly in the South, that prohibited the education of slaves.

Black Law. A law that specifically forbade a school from educating African Americans from other states without the permission of local authorities.

Block grants. Grants that provide funding with few restrictions for its use, allowing states and school districts the freedom to use the money in ways that meet their specific needs.

Block schedule. A schedule allowing for longer class periods; a block schedule may be comprised of a wide variety of schedule options.

Blogs. A way to share content and perspectives using the Internet as a communication tool.

Bond referendum. Allows school districts to borrow money stipulated for specific projects. The school board asks voters in the district to approve the borrowing of the money (the bond) that will be repaid over a period of time.

Brain-based learning. Looking at learning through study of the brain and then using what is discovered to guide teaching and learning techniques.

Breach of contract. Contracts are binding on both parties. If a person signs one and then backs out or takes a different job, or if the district backs out, the person or the district may be sued for damages.

Brown v. Board of Education. In 1954 Chief Justice Earl Warren declared that segregating children based solely on race was wrong and illegal. Some schools integrated peacefully, while others did not.

Buckley Amendment. Also known as the Family Educational Rights and Privacy Act (FERPA) of 1974. Allows parents and guardians access to their students' academic records and requires written parental permission for the records to be shared with anyone else. When students turn 18, they have control over who sees their records.

Bullying. Relationally aggressive behavior; a type of emotional or physical violence where individuals use relationships to harm others.

C

Case law. Based on the doctrine of *stare decisis*, a Latin phrase meaning "let the decision stand;" once a decision is made in a court of law, that decision sets a precedent for future cases of a similar nature until challenged or overturned.

Categorical grants. Money that is allocated or funds that are earmarked for specific purposes.

Center for Applied Research in Educational Technology (CARET). A project funded through the International Society for Technology in Education (ISTE). In CARET's continuing study, conditions have been identified for effectively integrating technology into curriculum and instruction. CARET also provides reasons for using technology in schools.

Charter school. A public school that is freed in specific ways from typical regulations required of other public schools.

Child abuse. Any act that results in death, serious harm, or exploitation of children.

Child neglect. A form of abuse resulting from the failure to act in the best interest of children.

Civil Rights Act of 1964. Stipulates that if schools discriminate based on race, color, or national origin, they are not eligible for federal funding.

Classroom assessment. Encompasses every deliberate method of gathering information about the quantity and quality of learning.

Classroom climate. The everyday environment of teachers and students working together.

Classroom community. A classroom where students and teacher tend to be like-minded and have common beliefs, understandings, and aims.

Classroom management. The establishment and enforcement of rules and disciplinary actions; teacher strategies to ensure an orderly classroom environment.

Clinical internship. Also known as student teaching or clinical practice; involves extended fieldwork in which teacher candidates teach lessons and, for a designated period of time, take over all classroom duties.

Coleman Report. Report written in 1966 that concluded that family and community factors such as poverty and parental levels of education prevented some children from learning, that no matter what schools did, some children would not be successful in school.

Collective bargaining. Act of negotiating with employers and/or states to gain additional benefits for members of the bargaining group; a right practiced in most states by teacher associations and unions. States often allow unions to negotiate with school boards concerning elements of teacher contracts and working conditions.

Common schools. Community-supported elementary schools for all children established in response to many economic, social, and political factors.

Community. The neighborhood, town, city, and/or county in which a person lives.

Comprehensive high school. High schools that attempt to meet the educational needs of all adolescents on a single campus.

Compulsory education law. Requires children to attend school until a specified age.

Computer-assisted instruction (CAI). Involves instructional software that is self-contained and self-paced; allows individual students, including students with special needs, English language learners, and those in advanced placement courses, to work on skills they need in ways that don't depend on other students or require a great deal of teacher time.

Computer-enhanced instruction (CEI). Interactive simulation software may be used in inquiry-based lessons where students control much of the input and teachers guide the discovery process.

Computer-managed instruction (CMI). Instruction that uses tutorial or problem-solving software or any computer program that diagnoses student progress and adjusts accordingly.

Consequences. Implies more natural ramifications for wrongdoing than the word *punishment,* which can be arbitrary.

Constructivism. A way of approaching instruction that builds on progressivism as students are challenged to construct, or discover, knowledge about their environments. Process is valued in progressivism, often more than product. The theory is that students who learn through the processes of construction, discovery, and problem solving will be better able to adapt to a changing world.

Content. Knowledge and skills that are taught.

Content standards. Specific knowledge students should have and skills they should be able to do.

Contract. An agreement between parties that includes the rights and responsibilities of each. When teachers begin jobs in schools they sign initial contracts.

Cooperating teacher. A classroom teacher who serves as the host and mentor during clinical practice.

Cooperative learning. Loosely defined, any instance of students working together in small groups.

Cooperative play. Children actively coordinate ways to keep interaction going.

Copyright laws. Federal laws that protect the rights of a creator or author to own intellectual property and to prevent others from copying or distributing it without permission. Intellectual property includes written material, original audio and visual work, and computer programs. Copyright laws also provide guidelines for authorized use of someone else's intellectual property.

Core subjects. Generally considered language arts, math, science, and social studies.

Corporal punishment. Physical punishment practiced in some school settings.

Council for Exceptional Children (CEC). National organization that represents the needs of students with exceptionalities and fosters appropriate education for them.

Criterion-referenced test. Student scores indicate levels of mastery of a subject and are not dependent on how other students perform.

Cultural identity. Results from the interactions of many factors, including language, religion, gender, income level, age, values, beliefs, race, and ethnicity.

Culturally responsive teaching. What teachers do to make multicultural education a reality.

Culture. A composite of social values, cognitive codes, behavioral standards, worldviews, and beliefs that characterize a group of people.

Curriculum. The educational term for what students experience in schools.

Cybercheating. A variety of ways students may be dishonest through the use of technology, including plagiarism involving students using what they find on the Internet as their own.

D

Dame schools. In colonial days, dames were respected women who, usually without formal schooling, had learned to read and write and who turned their homes into schools where parents paid to have their children educated.

Deductive reasoning. A process that begins with a general statement from which more specific statements are assumed to be true.

Democratic classroom. A classroom setting that promotes choice, community, authentic learning, and a relevant, creative curriculum; students participate in the establishment of behavioral expectations.

Departmentalization. School organizational pattern in which teachers teach their own subjects and meet occasionally with other teachers who teach the same subject.

Depression. Mental illness characterized by a deep sense of sadness and a loss of interest or pleasure in activities.

Developmental appropriateness. Teaching and learning that matches students' physical, cognitive, social, emotional, and character development.

Diagnostic assessment. Assesses student knowledge and skill levels before beginning a unit of study; commonly referred to as pretesting.

Dialects. Deviations from standard language rules used by identifiable groups of people.

Differentiation of instruction. Varying instruction based on the needs of students.

Digital divide. Inequities in technology access and use that exist among students; socioeconomic status and minority designation have widely been considered the biggest roadblocks to educational access.

Digital media. All elements in a project are in electronic format.

Digital portfolio. Multimedia collection of a student's work that is stored and reviewed in electronic format.

Direct instruction. A general lesson model that includes a distinct opening, presentation of information, practice, and teacher feedback and review.

Dispositions. Attitudes and beliefs that guide and determine behavior.

Distance learning. Involves the acquisition of knowledge and skills through instruction delivered using technology.

District school board. Governing body composed of elected citizens responsible for setting policies that affect the operation of schools.

Due process. The steps a district must take to pursue the charges when a tenured teacher is threatened with dismissal; important principle that requires guidelines to be followed to ensure that individuals are protected from arbitrary or capricious treatment by those in authority.

E

Early childhood education. The care and education of the youngest students in the United States, typically considered birth through age 8.

Ebonics. Black English, one of the best-known and most controversial dialects in the United States.

Education for All Handicapped Children Act (Public Law 94-142). Federal law passed in 1975 that guaranteed a free and appropriate education to all children with disabilities in the least restrictive environment; renamed Individual with Disabilities Education Act in 1990.

Education Maintenance Organization (EMO). An organization contracted to take over the management of a public school for profit.

Educational technology. Any technology that assists teachers in teaching and students in learning.

Effective schools. Schools that meet the learning needs of the students who attend them.

Effective Schools Movement. Originated in the 1970s to develop research pertaining to the assertion that all children can learn; purpose was to find schools deemed effective for all children and identify common characteristics.

Elementary and Secondary Education Act. Enacted during the presidency of Lyndon B. Johnson to provide extra funding, called Title I funding, for schools with high numbers of children from low-income homes.

Emotional intelligence quotient (EQ). A set of skills that accompany the expression, evaluation, and regulation of emotions. A high-level EQ indicates a person's ability to understand others' as well as his or her own feelings, respond appropriately to them, and, in general, get along.

Encore courses. Also known as related arts or exploratory courses; all courses other than what are considered the core courses of math, English language arts, social studies, and science.

English as a second language (ESL). Students receive individualized assistance; unlike bilingual education, ESL services are delivered only in English; little or no emphasis is placed on preserving native language or culture; and ESL teachers do not need to speak another language.

English language learners (ELL). Non-English speakers and students with limited English proficiency.

Entitlements. Grants given to certain segments of the population that have specific needs; the federal government deems these individuals entitled to extra assistance.

Epistemology. Branch of philosophy that addresses the dilemma of determining truth and ways of acquiring knowledge.

Essentialism. A philosophy of education based on the belief that there is a core curriculum that everyone in the United States should learn. This core can shift in response to societal changes, but should always be basic, organized, and rigorous.

Ethics. Standards of conduct based on moral judgments; the determination of what's right and what's wrong.

Ethnicity. An individual's country of origin and ancestry.

Evaluation. Judgments about, and the assigning of values to, the *results* of assessments.

Existentialism. Primary emphasis is on the individual. As a philosophy of education, existentialism contends that teachers teach the whole person, not just math, reading, science, or any other particular subject. Each student searches for personal meaning and personal understanding. If learning about a subject area increases a student's sense of self, then it's worthwhile.

Expectations. A word with positive connotations that may be used in place of *rules*, a word with negative connotations.

Expenditure per pupil. The average amount of money spent from federal, state, and local sources on an individual student.

Exploratory courses. Also known as related arts or encore courses, all courses other than math, English language arts, social studies, and science; may include art, music, physical education, industrial arts, languages, drama, computer education, and others.

Expulsion. Semipermanent or permanent dismissal from school for a semester or for an indefinite period.

Extracurriculum. Includes the organized experiences students have that are beyond the formal curriculum.

Extrinsic incentives. Incentives that are imposed, or originate outside the individual.

F

Fair use. Specific limitations on the use of copyrighted materials.

Family Educational Rights and Privacy Act (FERPA) of 1974. Commonly called the Buckley Amendment, allows parents and guardians access to their students' academic records and requires written parental permission for the records to be shared with anyone else. When students turn 18, they have control over who sees their records.

Feeder system. Configuration of schools in a district; typically in one feeder system of schools early childhood/elementary schools feed into middle schools that feed into a particular high school.

Formal curriculum. Encompasses what is intentionally taught, what is stated as the goals of student learning.

Formative assessment. A series of assessments in a variety of formats that help monitor student progress.

For-profit schools. Schools that are operated by private companies for profit.

Full-service school. A public school that provides a comprehensive program of education and includes student and community services such as after-school and family education programs.

Functional behavioral assessment (FBA). A management plan through a team of educators utilizing a process that looks for events and actions that may lead to misbehavior and devises strategies to help students abide by classroom expectations.

G

Gender. The sense of being male or female, as opposed to sex, which refers to anatomical differences.

Gender bias. The favoring of one gender over the other in specific circumstances.

Gender equity. The fair and balanced treatment of males and females.

Gender stereotyping. Occurs when perceived gender differences are assumed for all people.

Gifted and talented. Exceptional learners who demonstrate high levels of intelligence, creativity, and achievement.

Grade. Judgment of assessment quality (evaluation) with a number attached to it.

Grant. Funds provided by a source to pay for equipment or services requested by teachers and others.

Great Books. The writings of those considered to be the great thinkers throughout the history of Western civilization, such as Homer, Shakespeare, Melville, Einstein, and many others.

Grievance. A formal complaint filed by an individual teacher or group of teachers against a district.

H

Head Start. The largest provider of government-funded preschool education, employing one of every five U.S. preschool teachers.

Hierarchy of needs. Maslow's (1908–1970) theory that all human beings experience the same needs.

High school completion rate. As defined by the U.S. Department of Education, the "percentage of students, measured from the beginning of high school, who graduate from a high school with a regular diploma in the standard number of years"; also known as graduation rate.

High schools. Schools that most often encompass grades 9–12.

High/Scope. An approach to early childhood education built on consistency and few transitions during the day.

High-stakes tests. Standardized tests that have far-reaching consequences.

Highly qualified. Those who meet government guidelines for teacher quality in public schools.

Holistic rubric. A grading instrument that uses one scale for an entire project.

Homeschooled. Refers to students who receive most of their academic instruction in their homes.

Hypermedia. Advanced form of multimedia with all the sources of media hyperlinked to other documents.

I

Idealism. A philosophy based on the belief that ideas are the only reliable form of reality. Idealists believe that the physical world changes continually, and ideas are what should be taught.

Incentives. A word that may be used in place of the overused and value-laden word *rewards*.

Inclusion. Students attend their home school with their age- and grade-appropriate peers, participate in extracurricular activities, and receive special education and support services to the maximum extent possible in the general education classroom.

Individualized educational program (IEP). A plan developed for a student by educators, the family, and others as appropriate, involving details of how to reach specific goals. A student's IEP must be revisited annually and student progress evaluated.

Individuals with Disabilities Education Act (IDEA). Also referred to as PL94-142 (and the revised version of the Education for All Handicapped Children Act of 1975), this act made special education services a right, not a privilege, because it required schools to place students in least-restrictive environments within public schools.

Individuals with Disabilities Education Improvement Act. Reauthorization of IDEA in 2004 that compiled all U.S. laws that affect children with disabilities into one statute.

Inductive reasoning. Given specific statements, a general conclusion may be logically assumed.

Informal curriculum. What students learn that isn't written in a lesson plan or necessarily intentionally transmitted to students.

In loco parentis. Serving in place of parents.

Inquiry learning. When students pursue answers to questions posed by others or developed on their own, they are involved in inquiry learning. Observation, questioning, hypothesizing, and predicting are all part of inquiry-based learning.

Instruction. Encompasses the strategies used to convey the curriculum with the desired end result of student learning.

Instructional software. Software designed specifically for student use to learn about concepts and/or practice skills related to a subject area.

Instrumental aggression. Aggression based on attempting to meet a specific goal, such as grabbing a particular toy or establishing dominance in an activity; most common among boys.

Integrated curriculum. Involves making connections among subject areas through the use of a unifying topic or theme.

Integration literacy. Using technology in meaningful ways for both delivery of instruction and problem solving within the curriculum.

Intelligence. The capacity for knowing and learning.

Intelligence quotient (IQ). The results of a test that affixes a number to intelligence.

Interdisciplinary. Term often used to describe curricular links or connections among subjects.

Interdisciplinary team. The preferred organizational structure for middle level education, involving a team of teachers (2–5) working with a distinct group of students for an entire year.

Intermediate grades. Typically grades 4 and 5 in an elementary setting.

Internet. Computer network that allows people around the world to search for information, share resources, and communicate.

Interstate New Teacher Assessment and Support Consortium (INTASC). Organization that sets standards for what new teachers should know and be able to do.

Intrinsic incentives. Incentives that come from within and result from students' natural drives.

J

Junior high. Schools developed in 1909 to be a bridge between elementary and high school; typically grades 7–9.

K

Kalamazoo Case. Established that the legislature could tax for support of both common and secondary schools, propelling public high schools into school systems in every state.

Kindergarten. German for "children's garden," the school year that precedes first grade.

L

Language. Primary means of communication; transmits knowledge and passes on culture.

Latin grammar school. First established in 1635 in Boston for boys whose families could afford to send them on for more education beyond the dame school; considered the forerunner of modern high schools and specifically prepared boys to attend Harvard University, established in 1636.

Learning. A complex and dynamic process involving thinking, perception, experience, and memory.

Learning disabled (LD). A general category of students with disorders involving problems understanding or using language that results in significant differences between learning potential and achievement.

Learning modalities. Auditory (hearing), visual (seeing), tactile (touch), and kinesthetic (movement); all four are used in the process of learning, but individuals tend to favor one or two over the others.

Learning styles. Ways in which individuals learn most effectively and efficiently.

Least restrictive environment (LRE). The setting within which students with disabilities can function at capacity; generally the setting with students who do not have disabilities that also meets the educational needs of the students with disabilities.

Liable. To be responsible for; liability is what teaching is all about—accepting responsibility for students while they are under our supervision.

Limited English proficiency (LEP). Students with LEP may speak and understand some English, but not enough to be successful in classes taught in English without additional assistance.

Logic. Reasoning that attempts to avoid vagueness and contradictions. To use logic simply means to think clearly to understand a situation, solve a problem, or draw a conclusion. There are two basic kinds of reasoning, or logic, commonly addressed in school. One is **deductive reasoning,** a process that begins with a general statement from which more specific statements are assumed to be true. Another kind of logic, **inductive reasoning,** works the other way: given some specific statements, a general conclusion may be assumed.

Looping. School practice that keeps a teacher with a particular group of students for more than 1 year.

M

Magnet school. A public school with a specific emphasis or theme and curriculum and instructional programs tailored with unique opportunities that attract certain students.

Massachusetts Act of 1642. First compulsory education law in the New World; required all White children to attend school.

Meta-analysis. A research technique involving the analysis of multiple studies.

Metaphysics. Branch of philosophy that addresses the search for reality and purpose. The word *metaphysics* means "beyond the material or the physical." Those who study metaphysics look for answers that go beyond scientific experiments.

Micromanagement. Managing to a level of detail that is inappropriate for a particular position. For instance, when school board members go beyond policy making into what is considered day-to-day operations, they may be seen as micromanaging.

Middle school. Schools for young adolescents with a distinct philosophy that embraces both academic rigor and developmental appropriateness; may include any combination of grades 5–9.

Montessori. An approach to early childhood education with mixed-age grouping and self-pacing.

Morrill Act. In 1862 the government granted states 30,000 acres of land for every senator and representative in Congress in 1860. The income the state generated from this land was to be used to support at least one college.

Multiage classroom. Classroom where children in two, three, or more grade levels learn together.

Multicultural curriculum. Curriculum that purposefully includes contributions and viewpoints from the perspectives of different cultures, ethnicities, races, genders, and socioeconomic levels.

Multicultural education. An instructional approach that celebrates diversity and promotes equal educational opportunities.

Multimedia. Using more than one medium to communicate information.

Multiple intelligences theory (MI). A theory developed by Howard Gardner that intelligence is multidimensional, that individual brains work in ways that give each of us our own personal intelligences; includes eight intelligences.

N

A Nation at Risk: The Imperative for Educational Reform. Report commissioned by President Reagan in 1983 that referred to U.S. public education as a "rising tide of mediocrity." In response, various proposals for reform and improvement surfaced.

National Assessment of Educational Progress (NAEP). Only standardized test systematically administered to a sampling of students across the United States. The NAEP is administered to fourth, eighth, and twelfth graders in math, reading, writing, science, history, economics, geography, civics, foreign language, and a variety of the arts; often called the nation's report card.

National Association for the Education of Young Children (NAEYP). Organization with the mission of leading and consolidating the efforts of individuals and groups that work to achieve healthy development and constructive education for all young children; provides teacher preparation standards for pre-K–third grade teachers.

National Board of Professional Teaching Standards (NBPTS). Board that sets standards, establishes policies, and issues certificates designating teachers with skills to perform effectively.

National Council for the Accreditation of Teacher Education (NCATE). Agency that scrutinizes university teacher education programs. About two thirds of states require university teacher education programs to be accredited (authorized to prepare teachers) through NCATE.

National Defense Education Act of 1958. Called for strengthening of science, math, and foreign language programs; teachers were given training in the use of new methods and materials in hopes of bringing American student learning up to, and beyond, the levels of learning in other countries.

National Education Association (NEA). The largest professional education association in the United States, with a total of over 5 million members including teachers, administrators, professors, counselors, and other educators.

National Middle School Association (NMSA). Organization that provides standards for the preparation of teachers for grades 5–9, and advocates for the needs and education of young adolescents.

Nature. Refers to the genetically inherited influences on who we are.

New England Primer. First published in 1690 for children in upper elementary and secondary levels. Published for over 150 years with few substantial changes over its lifetime, the *New England Primer* included a spelling guide based on the alphabet denoted in brief rhymes and pictures, the Lord's Prayer, the Apostles' Creed, the Ten Commandments, a list of the books of the Bible, the Puritan catechism, and numbers 1–100.

No Child Left Behind Act of 2001 (NCLB). Federal law that holds schools accountable for student learning, regardless of student diversity. States are required to test all students in grades 3–8 annually to determine progress.

Norm referenced. Tests used to compare students; administered to a group of students selected because they represent a cross section of U.S. students (norm group).

Normal schools. Publicly funded secondary schools specifically designed to prepare teachers for the classroom.

Norms. Expectations that are foundational, including physical norms for preserving the health and safety of students, moral norms pertaining to respect for others, and societal norms for politeness and individual responsibility.

Northwest Land Ordinance of 1787. Divided federally owned land in the wilderness into townships and required that schools be built.

Null curriculum. What is not taught in school.

Nurture. Refers to the influence of the environment, including everything that happens except for what can be accounted for genetically.

O

Obesity. Extreme overweight as indicated by body mass index (BMI), a measure of how much a person weighs relative to height.

Old Deluder Satan Act. Because education was considered the best way to fight the devil, the act (also known as the Massachusetts Act of 1647) established that every town of 50 or more households must provide a school.

Open enrollment. A plan that allows students to choose from among virtually all the schools in a school district.

Overlapping. A teacher's ability to multitask, to take care of several things at once.

P

Pacing guide. A document that dictates the timing of content coverage; helps assure that all grade level standards are part of the curriculum.

Parallel play. Children agreeably sharing the same space, but not communicating.

Paraprofessional. A teacher aide or assistant teacher; typically not a certified teacher.

Parochial schools. Schools affiliated with religious organizations.

Pedagogy. The combining of curriculum and instruction to foster learning.

Perennialism. A philosophy of education based on a core curriculum with themes and questions that endure, that are everlasting; as life changes and times change, the real substance and truths of life remain the same.

Performance standards. Designated levels of the knowledge or skills that are considered acceptable at a particular grade level.

Philosophy. *Philo* means "love," and *sophos* means "wisdom." Philosophy, then, means "love of wisdom." This love of wisdom, or philosophy, becomes a means of answering fundamental questions.

Philosophy of education. The *love of wisdom* regarding teaching that expresses itself in attitudes and actions every day in the classroom.

Podcast. Similar to a radio program distributed on the Web; examples of podcasts include museum tours, weekly classroom reports, oral histories, and interviews.

Portfolio. Assessment tool for which either students or teachers assemble a cohesive package of representative evidence of student learning.

Postmodernism. Grew out of a sense that those in power control those who don't have power. This control, postmodernists believe, is manifested through major institutions like schools.

PowerPoint. Presentation program used by teachers to deliver instruction and by students to demonstrate skills and display project products.

Pragmatism. A philosophy that says that student-centered perspectives integrated with firsthand experiences are most effective.

Praxis Series. Battery of tests published by the Educational Testing Service (ETS) that may be used to determine the qualifications of individuals to be licensed or certified to teach in a variety of disciplines and grade levels.

Preschool. A semistructured environment for 3- and 4-year-olds housed in a school setting; care is enhanced by exposure to basic educational concepts.

Primary grades. Typically grades K–3.

Principal. Oversees every aspect of school life and answers to the district for all that occurs at the school. The principal's role involves administrative tasks such as facility maintenance, attendance, discipline, parent/community relationships and communication, transportation, and all manner of paperwork. Principals are also instructional leaders with knowledge of, and experience with, the teaching and learning process.

Private schools. The two elements that make schools public—public funding and public accountability—are both absent in private schools.

Privilege gap. Gap between the haves and the have-nots.

Problem-based learning (PBL). Focusing student attention and effort on a real-life problem that has more than one solution path or product.

Process standards. Processes that support content learning by explaining how the content might be best learned and how to use the content once it is acquired.

Processing. Sending a student out of the classroom with the purpose of reflection and planning for better choices.

Profession. An occupation that meets certain criteria, including (1) extensive training to enter, (2) inclusion of a code of ethics, and (3) service as the primary product.

Professionalism. A way of being involving attitudes and actions that convey respect, uphold high standards, and demonstrate commitment to those served.

Progressive education. In 1896 John Dewey established a method of involving students in their own learning through cooperative groups, which grew into a major movement with far-reaching implications; interests guide what is learned about traditional subjects.

Progressivism. A student-centered philosophy of education that focuses on curriculum that is of interest to students. Progressivists view education as more than preparation for the future; it is life itself. The progressive philosophy of education endorses experiential learning full of opportunities for student discovery and opportunities to solve problems.

Property taxes. Values of property are determined, and a small percentage of the assessed amount (usually less than 1%) is collected annually and used for local services.

Proximity. The accessibility of teacher to students.

Public domain. A work is in the public domain if it is more than 75 years old or is published by a government agency; work in the public domain is not protected by copyright.

Public Law 94-142 (PL94-142). Common way of referring to the Individuals with Disabilities Education Act (IDEA), an act that made special education services a right, rather than a privilege.

Public schools. Public schools are funded through some form of taxation and are accountable to the community through elected or governmental officials who have policy and oversight responsibilities.

R

Race. Term used to classify people according to their physical characteristics that are nature given. Race classifies people at birth.

Racism. A form of prejudice that may be perpetuated by individuals or governments stemming from a belief that one race is superior to another.

Realism. Based on the belief that some facts are absolutes no matter who recognizes them. Realists contend that the only way to know these absolutes is to study the material world.

Reduction in force. Occurs in schools when there are fewer students, budget cuts, or the cancellation of a program. Reduction in force (rif) may also apply to tenured teachers. The general rule of "riffing" is that the last hired are the first to go if it becomes necessary.

Reflection. Thinking about what is done, how it's done, and the consequences of actions or inactions, all with the goal of being a better teacher.

Reflective practitioner. A teacher who thinks critically about teaching and the consequences of actions or inactions, all with the goal of being more effective with students.

Reggio Emilia. An approach to early childhood education for ages 3 months to 6 years based on relationships among children, families, and teachers.

Related arts courses. Also known as exploratory courses or encore courses; all courses other than math, English language arts, social studies, and science; may include art, music, physical education, industrial arts, languages, drama, computer education, etc.

Relational aggression. Subtle actions that may hurt emotionally rather than physically; may include name-calling, gossiping, or saying mean things just to be hurtful; most common among girls.

Reliability. The degree to which an assessment yields a pattern of results that is repeatable and consistent over time.

Resource teacher. A special education teacher who helps students develop strategies for school success.

Ripple effect. An effect that occurs when one action directly affects another.

Romanticism. A philosophy of education that contends that the needs of the individual are more important than the needs of society; also known as naturalism.

Routine. An expected action that occurs in a given circumstance to accomplish a task efficiently.

Rubric. Assessment tool that makes explicit what is being assessed, lists characteristics of degrees of quality, and provides a rating scale to differentiate among these degrees.

Rural. Indicates an area with fewer than 2,500 people and a minimum of retail stores and services.

S

Scaffolding. The support given to children to help them move through progressive levels of learning.

School choice. Method of letting parents decide which schools their students attend.

School connectedness. Student bonding and engagement in the school experience.

School culture. The prevailing atmosphere of a school that provides the context of learning experiences; as places where people work together and learn together, schools function according to their cultures.

School district. An organizational structure of local schools defined by geographic boundaries.

School-to-Work. Federal government program initiated to bring real-world, work-related skills and understanding to students through courses and experiences that introduce them to career possibilities.

School venues. The variety of ways Americans "do school" in the over 120,000 schools in the United States. The most prominent venues are public schools and private schools.

Self-contained classroom. An organizational structure involving one teacher and a group of students for whom the teacher is accountable much of the school day.

Self-efficacy. An "I can" belief in oneself that leads to a sense of competence; the concept of self-efficacy is solidly grounded in the accomplishment of a continuum of increasingly difficult challenges.

Settlement houses. Established by early American reformers to confront the problem of urban poverty; community service centers that provided educational opportunities, skills training, and cultural events.

Sexual harassment. Behavior with sexual implications that is neither wanted nor welcome; may include obvious looks with lewd intent, taunts with sexual innuendo, touching, kissing, groping, and any behavior that has sexual connotations.

Sexual orientation. The sex to which a person is romantically or socially attracted is considered a person's sexual orientation.

Single gender. All male or all female.

Site-based management. Public school management structure in which governance is in the hands of those closest to it, generally teachers, administrators, and parents.

Social cognition. Process of relating to others and thinking about them and oneself.

Social reconstructionism. A philosophy of education that looks to education to change society, rather than just teach about it. Social reconstructionism as an education philosophy calls on schools to educate students in ways that will help society move beyond all forms of discrimination to the benefit of everyone worldwide.

Software. Computer programs that are written to perform specific applications; application software and instructional software are two basic types used in schools.

Special education services. Services provided by schools to help students with disabilities function and learn in ways optimal to each.

Special education students. Students with disabilities that require services enabling them to function and learn in ways optimal to each individual.

Stages of cognitive development. Jean Piaget (1896–1980) recognized distinct differences in children's and adolescents' responses to questions that directly correlated to their chronological ages and categorized these differences into stages.

Stages of moral reasoning. Noted developmental psychologist Lawrence Kohlberg contends that people pass through distinct stages as they develop morally.

Standard English. A composite of the language spoken by educated, middle-class people in the United States.

Standardized test. Test given to multiple groups of students, designed for specific grade levels, and typically repeated annually. These tests are administered and scored under controlled conditions, and their exact content is unknown to everyone except the test makers before they are administered.

Standards. Expectations for what individuals should know and be able to do.

Standards-based test. Test written using the content of a specific set of standards.

State board of education. Volunteers who are either elected or appointed by the governor; state legislatures give state boards oversight authority; boards act in regulatory and advisory capacities.

State department of education. Operates under the guidance of the governor, legislature, and state board of education; also known as state office of education or perhaps department of public instruction.

State superintendent. The one person given responsibility for managing the state department of education; also known as chief state education officer or commissioner of education.

Streaming video. Video that is either stored on a site or is live as it downloads on the computer.

Student self-monitoring. Students assume control of their own behavior as they develop a sense of ownership for that behavior.

Student teaching. Also known as clinical internship or clinical practice; involves extended fieldwork in which teacher candidates teach lessons and, for a designated period of time, take over all classroom duties.

Students with exceptionalities. Learners with abilities or disabilities that set them apart from other learners.

Substance abuse. A pattern of alcohol or drug use that can lead to detrimental and habitual consumption, impaired functioning at school and work, and legal difficulties.

Suburban. Indicates neighborhoods and small-to-medium-size towns that are located on the fringe of cities or are their own distinct locations.

Summative assessment. A formal assessment involving judgments about the success of a process or product; most often occurs at the end of a unit of study.

Superintendent. A school district's chief executive officer; hired by the district school board; advises the board and carries out board policies.

Suspension. Time out of school that may range from 1 day to less than a semester, but is usually for 10 days or less.

Special-interest group. A group of people who join together with a common mission and work to have an impact.

T

Tableau. Freeze-frame role-playing with students choosing a book passage, striking a pose that depicts the passage, and holding the pose while a narrator reads the passage.

Tax cap. An upper limit to taxation.

Teach for America. Most widely known of all alternative licensing programs; TFA recruits individuals who are college seniors or recent graduates who agree to teach in high-needs rural or urban schools for at least 2 years.

Teacher think-aloud. An instructional strategy in which teachers think out loud about how to approach a problem, make sense of new information, use self-restraint in volatile situations, consider options, discard what doesn't work, and begin to refine what makes sense.

Tenure. Continuing contract status; a teacher with tenure is entitled to a contract each year unless the district has reason to not renew it or the teacher decides to go elsewhere. In most states tenure doesn't guarantee a particular position in a particular school, but it does guarantee employment in the district.

Thinking skills. Skills that aid in processing information.

Title I funding. Federal compensatory funds provided through the Elementary and Secondary Education Act given to public schools where more than 50% of the students qualify for free or reduced-price meals; used to supplement regular school funding in schools with high numbers of students from low-income settings.

Title IX of the Education Amendments Act of 1972. Prohibits government money from being used for anything that discriminates on the basis of gender.

Token economy. A system of giving symbolic rewards for appropriate behavior and withholding or taking away rewards for inappropriate behavior.

Town schools. Early American schools established for whole communities; while some schools still limited curriculum to reading, writing, and the classics, specialized schools in the form of academies became popular.

Traditional public schools. Schools that have no admission criteria, other than perhaps residency in a particular attendance zone.

Transition. When students change activities or locations, they are in transition; generally a time when most classroom disruptions happen.

Trends in International Mathematics and Science Study (TIMSS). International tests that compare students worldwide; administered every 4 years since 1995.

Truancy. Nonattendance during compulsory education, not including excused absences generally granted for health reasons.

Tyler Rationale. Ralph Tyler developed four questions that should be asked throughout the stages of curriculum development.

U

Understand. To make sense of what one knows and to have the ability to use it in various situations and contexts.

Unfunded mandate. A legally enforceable law without monetary support provided.

Unit of study. Organizes curriculum, instruction, and assessment around a major theme or distinct body of content; provides planned cohesion.

Urban. Indicates cities with large downtowns and dense populations.

V

Validity. The degree to which an assessment measures what it is supposed to measure.

Virtual schools. Schools that deliver instruction only through distance learning.

Vocational Education Act of 1963. Quadrupled the amount of money allocated for vocational education.

Voucher. Government-issued piece of paper that represents part of a state's financial contribution for the education of a student; parents choose a school and present the voucher, and the government allocates funding to the school accordingly.

W

Wayside teaching. Teaching that occurs inside and outside the classroom through attitudes, values, habits, interests, and classroom climate.

WebQuest. Inquiry projects in which most or all of the information is obtained through the Internet. Instructions for a WebQuest typically call for it to include information that introduces a topic, a description of the task to be completed, suggested sources to be explored, guidance about the project product, and directions for a closing.

Wiki. Website serving as an information source that anyone can edit at any time; an online encyclopedia with more than 500,000 entries; entries are altered by contributors who add information as needed or desired; not valid as a legitimate source.

Withitness. Refers to a teacher's awareness of what's going on in the whole classroom, enabling the teacher to step in when needed to keep the environment positive; originated with Jacob Kounin.

Y

Young adolescents. Students between ages 10 and 15.

Z

Zero tolerance. School-imposed nonnegotiable consequences for certain infractions. For instance, the consequence for fighting may be automatic suspension for 3 days.

Zone of proximal development. The level at which a child can almost, but not completely, grasp a concept or perform a task successfully; theory proposed by Lev Vygotsky.

Name Index

Abrahamson, L., 180
Adams, T., 327
Addams, J., 253
Adger, C., 82
Adler, M., 260, 262, 274–275, 276–277
Ahlbrecht, R., 187–188
Albano, G., 61
Allington, R. L., 131
Alt, M. N., 316
Ayers, R., 23, 32, 50, 133, 143, 186–187, 211n, 402, 438
Azzam, A. M., 192, 376n

Bachman, J. G., 306n
Bacon, F., 240
Bandura, A., 77
Banks, J. A., 80, 119, 262
Barbanel, J., 9
Barbaranelli, C., 77
Barber, B. R., 39
Barnett, W. S., 50
Barth, R. S., 38, 400–401, 402
Bartlett, C., 54
Bausch, M. E., 169, 182
Baxter, D. A., 112–113
Beagle, D. R., 197
Beane, J. A., 63–64, 402
Beecher, C., 251
Berliner, D. C., 20, 262, 402
Best, C., 403
Bethune, M. M., 256, 257
Beyal, B., 24, 25, 38, 52, 133, 134, 188, 189, 200, 206, 211, 269, 282–283, 357, 396, 428
Bjork, L., 370n
Black, H., 341
Blandon, J., 354
Bloom, B. S., 124, 126, 145, 258, 259
Blum, R. W., 122
Boekaerts, M., 77
Boucher, D., 10, 29, 33, 55, 135, 190, 206, 212, 227, 278, 323, 325, 406, 440
Boyd, D., 368
Boyer, P., 244, 253, 257n, 259
Boynton, C., 210, 219, 221, 222n, 228
Boynton, M., 210, 219, 221, 222n, 228
Bradley, F., 395
Brameld, T., 279
Bredekamp, S., 70n, 72n, 73n, 75n, 76n
Brembs, B., 112–113
Bridgeland, J. M., 313, 316
Brimley, V., 375, 377
Brown, K., 298, 299
Brunner, C. C., 370n
Bucher, K. T., 223n
Burns, M., 194, 197
Bush, G. W., 18, 359
Bush, J., 156
Button, W. H., 246
Byrne, J. H., 112–113

Calvin, J., 240
Campbell, A., 74
Candy, J., 74

Canter, , 223
Caprara, G. V., 77
Cario, C. B., 369
Carlson, K., 273
Carter, G. R., 56
Carter, J. E., 260
Cashman, T. J., 178
Chaltain, S., 328
Chapman, C., 316
Chartock, R. K., 250, 251, 253, 256, 277, 279, 282
Chinn, P. C., 79, 80, 82, 299, 319
Christian, D., 82
Clausen, J., 230–232
Clement, M. C., 432n, 433, 435n
Cleveland, C., 28, 55, 67, 82, 135–136, 190–191, 200, 212, 227, 412, 430, 431
Clinton, W., 260, 348, 359
Codell, E. R., 20
Cohen, S. S., 242, 246
Colin, C., 196
Collins, M., 262
Comenius, 240
Comer, J. P., 262, 391, 394–395
Cones, J. H., 303
Connell, J. P., 122
Connolly, B. A., 304n
Copple, C., 70n, 72n, 73n, 75n, 76n
Corbett, D., 19, 412
Cornett, C. E., 119
Corrigan, D. C., 14n
Counts, G., 279
Cradler, J., 179
Craig, G. J., 308n
Crandall, P., 252
Craver, S., 282
Crowell, R., 74
Cruz, D., 436, 437
Cuban, L., 197, 262
Curwin, 223

Darling-Hammond, L., 19, 207, 262, 408–409
DeAngelis, T., 308
Delgado-Gaitan, C., 79
Delpit, L., 224
Denemark, G. W., 14n
DeVries, R., 214
Dewey, J., 10, 112, 113–114, 145, 205, 207, 208, 254, 256, 278
Dilulio, J. J., 313, 316
Donahue, E., 307, 308, 309n
Douangsavanh, K., 103
DuBois, W. E. B., 256, 257
Duffett, A., 161
Dunklee, D. R., 220, 335n, 337n, 348n
Dunn, W. L., 308n
Dyck, B. A., 182

Edelman, M. W., 262
Edmonds, R., 60
Eisner, E., 122, 259n, 271
Endo, H., 82
Epstein, J. L., 390, 391, 392n, 394, 397

Erasmus, D., 240
Erwin, J. C., 216, 218n
Escalante, J., 262

Farkas, S., 6
Feistritzer, C. E., 13
Feldman, R. S., 70, 71, 72n, 73n, 75n, 76n
Felono, T., 6
Ferguson, J. E., 328
Fessenden, F., 9
Fischer, L., 335n, 336, 337n, 338n, 340, 346, 348n, 350, 351n
Fogelman, C., 138–139
Ford, G., 60
Ford, J., 101
Fox, M. A., 304n
Francis, S., 100
Franklin, B., 244
Freire, P., 262, 279
French, S., 308
Froebel, F., 250

Gable, R. A., 224
Gallahue, D. L., 70n, 72n, 73n, 75n, 76n
Gallaudet, T., 251
Garbarino, J., 292–293
Gardner, H., 89, 262
Garfield, R., 375, 377
Gathercoal, P., 74, 223
Gay, G., 79
Gehrke, R. S., 413
Gentry, M., 126, 163
George, P., 170
Gilligan, C., 74
Ginott, H. G., 12, 208
Glass, T. E., 370n
Glasser, W., 218, 223, 262
Gober, D. A., 77
Goldstein, L., 93
Goleman, D., 72, 73n
Gollnick, D. M., 79, 80, 82, 299, 319
Good, H. G., 243, 246, 251n, 256
Goodlad, J. I., 40, 136, 262
Gordon, , 223
Gorman, P., 377
Grace, C. O., 312
Greene, M., 262, 280–281
Gregoire, M. A., 119
Gren, J., 87
Griner, D., 56, 57
Grisso, J. A., 308, 309n
Gunter, G. A., 178
Gunter, R. E., 178
Gutek, G. L., 246n, 253, 278

Hall, D., 256, 315
Hamilton, B. E., 307n
Harper, K., 94
Harris, D., 329
Haskins, R., 307
Hasselbring, T. S., 169, 182
Haycock, K., 19, 60
Haynes, C. C., 306, 328
Heath, K., 271

Hendrickson, J. M., 224
Henze, R. C., 79, 299
Hess, F. M., 364, 365
Heward, W. L., 92–93, 94, 95n, 96
Hill, L., 57, 369
Hirsch, E. D., 262, 274
Hodgkinson, H., 80
Holloway, J. H., 122
Holmes, M., 251
Howe, K. R., 324, 325n
Howe, S., 251
Howsam, R. B., 14n
Hudson, D. L., 328
Huger-McGrew, D., 26, 27, 33, 54,
    134–135, 149, 169, 190, 205, 211,
    407, 408, 441

Illich, I., 262, 279
Ingersoll, R., 14n

Jackson, A., 247
Jackson, R., 94
Jacobsen, D. A., 270, 279
Jansorn, N. R., 392n
Jefferson, T., 104, 244
Jenkins, H., 180
Jerald, C., 162
Johnson, D. W., 126
Johnson, J., 6, 161
Johnson, L. B., 60, 259
Johnson, R. T., 126
Johnson, S. M., 4, 20
Johnston, L. D., 306n
Jordan, K., 14n, 240, 274

Kaphingst, K. M., 308
Kardos, S. M., 4, 20
Kaufman, P., 316
Kelley, L., 193–194
Kellough, R. D., 52
Kennedy, J. F., 258–259
Klem, A. M., 122
Kneller, G. F., 254n
Koeneke, K., 160
Kohl, H., 262
Kohlberg, L., 74, 75n
Kohn, A., 45, 156–157, 224, 412
Koppel, T., 42
Kostelnik, M. J., 50
Kounin, J. S., 205, 208, 209, 223, 262
Kozol, J., 58, 224, 262
Krashen, S., 132
Kutcher, S., 99
Kutcher, T., 98, 99, 102

Lael, J., 122
LaGrotto, L., 412, 413
Lambdin, D. V., 113
Lambert, L., 367, 368n
LaMorte, M. W., 330, 333, 335n, 337n,
    338, 340, 341, 346, 348n
Landsman, J., 298, 299, 300n, 301
LaParo, K., 50
Larsen, Mike, 52, 188, 369
Lazarus, W., 192
Leinwand, D., 304
Lemlech, J. K., 112, 126, 207, 209
Levine, M., 97
Lewis, A., 156
Lewis-Charp, H., 300
Lezotte, L. W., 60, 61n
Lightfoot, S. L., 390
Lincoln, A., 253

Lindquist, M. M., 113
Lipper, L., 192
Little, C., 121
Locke, J., 240
Loeper, J. L., 220n, 244n
Lorenzetti, F. D., 112–113
Lounsbury, J. H., 121
Lowther, D. L., 179, 180, 183
Lumpkin, A., 207
Lupinetti, J., 119
Luther, M., 240

MacDonald, G. J., 314
Magid, L., 193n
Mancia, H., 101
Mann, H., 247, 249, 250, 251
Manning, M. L., 223n
Marshall, T., 334
Martin, M., 42
Martinez, H., 103, 106
Marx, K., 279
Marzano, R. J., 127, 128n, 149, 153, 208,
    220, 222, 391
Maslow, A. H., 69, 299
Matthews, T. J., 307n
McBeath, D., 102
McCloud, S., 216
McDevitt, T. M., 70n, 71n, 72n, 73n,
    75n, 76n
McGuffey, W. H., 249–250
McHugh, J., 170
McNeil, J. D., 259n
McNergney, J. M., 250n, 253, 351n
McNergney, R. F., 250n, 253, 351n
McTighe, J., 144–145, 146n, 151, 262
Mendenhall, T., 24, 25, 33, 38, 52, 133,
    134, 165, 188, 203, 206, 211, 225,
    226, 395, 441
Mendler, , 223
Merrow, J., 61
Metha, A., 14n, 240, 274
Mewborn, D. S., 77
Miller, P. C., 82
Moats, L. C., 131
Montessori, M., 256
Moore, K., 52
Morison, K. B., 313, 316
Morrison, G. R., 179, 180, 183
Morrison, G. S., 49, 50
Mukhopadhyay, C., 79, 299
Mursell, J. L., 137

Nash, R. J., 14n
Neill, A. S., 280
Nelson, J. L., 273
Neuman, S. B., 86, 298n
Niederberger, M., 344
Nieto, S. M., 80, 262
Niguidula, D., 196
Nix, S., 354
Nixon, R. M., 259
Noddings, N., 207, 262
Norman, K. I., 76n
Norris, C., 195, 197

O'Bannon, B. W., 178
O'Connor, K., 153
Ohanion, S., 156, 158–159
O'Malley, P. M., 306n
Orleans, C. T., 308, 309n
Ormrod, J. E., 70n, 71n, 72n, 73n, 75n,
    76n
Ornstein, A. C., 243, 250, 252, 270–271

O'Shea, D. J., 96
O'Shea, L. J., 96
Ozmon, H., 282
Ozmun, J. C., 70n, 72n, 73n, 75n, 76n

Palonsky, S. B., 273
Pastorelli, C., 77
Pauken, P. D., 346
Paulson, A., 316
Paxson, C., 307, 308, 309n
Payne, R. K., 86, 87–88, 224, 298n,
    397
Penuel, W. R., 180
Perez, S. A., 224
Perini, M. J., 90, 91n
Perkins-Gough, D., 54
Perrone, V., 288
Perryman, D., 303
Pestalozzi, J., 250
Peters, T., 3, 27, 54, 134–135, 164, 175,
    189–190, 206, 212, 225, 397, 398,
    441–442
Phelps, P. H., 15–17
Piaget, J., 70–71, 126
Pickering, D. J., 127, 128n
Planta, R. C., 50
Poirot, J., 195
Polite, L., 300
Pollock, J. R., 127, 128n
Popham, W. J., 155, 156
Posner, G. J., 429
Powell, S. D., 76n, 92n, 125n, 153
Prensky, M., 172, 180, 197, 198
Provenzo, E. F., Jr., 246
Puckett, K., 178
Pulliam, J., 277

Rank, Kathy S., 131
Ravitch, D., 274
Ray, R. D., 44
Reagan, R., 260, 359, 374
Reeves, D. B., 155, 163
Reis, S. M., 126, 163
Renard, L., 170, 177
Renzulli, J. S., 126, 163
Reyes, M., 102
Reynosa, A., 29, 55, 106, 135, 190, 212,
    227, 237, 424
Reys, F. D., 112–113
Reys, R. E., 113
Richardson, R. C., 76n
Richardson, W., 196
Riley, R. W., 348, 349n
Ringstaff, C., 193–194
Rippa, S. A., 256
Roberts, C., 24, 25, 38, 52, 111, 133,
    134, 188, 206–207, 211, 213, 225,
    357, 411, 423
Roberts, P. L., 52
Roblyer, M. D., 175, 176n, 182n, 185n,
    192, 197
Romero, M., 55, 369
Roschelle, J., 180
Rosenberg, M. S., 96
Rowan, B., 14n
Russell, T. D., 158

Sadker, D., 156
Saenger, E. B., 300
Salinas, K. C., 392n
Sanders, M. G., 392n
Sawatsky, J., 29
Saxon, B., 258

Schimmel, D., 335*n*, 336, 337*n*, 338*n*, 351*n*
Schlozman, S. C., 304
Schulenberg, J. E., 306*n*
Schwab, N., 344
Seeger, G., 77
Sergiovani, T. J., 367
Shelley, G. B., 178, 180, 184
Sherry, A., 157
Shirley, L., 74
Shoop, R. J., 220, 335*n*, 337*n*, 348*n*
Silver, H. F., 90, 91*n*
Simon, B. S., 392*n*
Sirleaf, E. J., 119
Sizer, T. R., 262, 274
Skinner, B. F., 223
Slavin, R., 262
Smith, N. L., 113
Snyder, T. D., 304*n*
Soderman, A. K., 50
Soloway, E., 195
Stellman, L., 335*n*, 336, 337*n*, 338*n*, 351*n*
Sternberg, R. J., 79
Stevenson, C., 221
Stiggins, R. J., 155, 156
Story, M., 308
Stroman, J., 334
Strong, R. W., 90, 91*n*
Stronge, J. H., 19
Stuckey, S., 244, 253, 257*n*, 259
Sullivan, A., 305
Sullivan, T., 195
Sutton, P., 101

Suydam, M. N., 113
Swanson, C., 179, 316
Symonds, P. M., 212

Takaki, R., 253
Tehie, J. B., 241
Tell, C., 29
Thomas, K. H., 214
Thomas, O., 328
Thompson, M., 312
Thornburgh, N., 316, 317
Tienken, C., 180
Todd, D., 100
Toliver, K., 262
Tomlinson, C. A., 262
Tomlinson, C. S., 127
Tonelson, S. W., 224
Toscano, G., 103
Tough, P., 61
Trueba, H., 79
Turnbull, R., 93, 94, 95*n*, 96
Tyler, R., 114, 145, 257, 259

Underwood, J., 336, 339, 350, 351
Underwood, M., 77

Vacca, R. T., 131, 413
Van Acker, R., 224
Van Patten, J., 243, 250, 252, 277
Vanvoorhis, F. L., 392*n*
Ventura, S. J., 307*n*
Vermeer, H. J., 77
Vygotsky, L., 71, 126

Wade, B., 23, 37, 50, 133, 186, 206, 224–225, 291, 422, 423
Wainer, A., 192
Warhaftig, A., 194
Warren, E., 257
Washington, B. T., 253, 256
Webb, L. D., 14*n*, 240, 246, 250, 251*n*, 260, 274, 336, 339, 350, 351
Webster, N., 246
Wehmeyer, M., 93
Weiss, B. J., 251
Westbrook, R. B., 40
Whiren, A. P., 50
White, J. L., 303
White-Hood, M., 311
Whittle, C., 174
Wiggins, G. P., 144–145, 146*n*, 151, 262
Wiley, A., 100
Willard, E., 251
Williams, B., 412
Williams, R., 240
Wilson, B., 19, 412
Winburn, L., 6, 7
Wolfram, W., 82
Wolk, S., 123, 213
Wong, H., 413
Woods, T., 80

Youngs, P., 408–409

Zan, B., 214
Zeichner, K. M., 412
Zull, J. E., 112, 113

Subject Index

AAHE (American Association for Health Education), 117

AAHPERD (American Alliance for Health, Physical Education, Recreation and Dance), 16

AAUW (American Association of University Women), 343, 345

Abuse. *See* Child abuse

Academic freedom, 334–335

Academic magnet school, 55

Academic rigor, 12, 112

Academies, 244, 246, 249, 250

Accelerated Reader (AR) program, 190

Accidents, liability for, 337–339

Accountability, 160–163, 164
  challenges of, 161–163
  defined, 144
  law on, 161, 260–261
  of parents and families, 161
  of school districts and school boards, 161
  of state and federal governments, 161
  of students, 160–161
  of teachers, 161, 162
  technology and, 193

ACEI (Association for Childhood Education International), 16, 24, 31, 34, 171

Achievement
  evaluating, 148, 150–153, 164
  gender and, 77

Achievement gap, 8, 61, 77, 376

ACTFL (American Council for the Teaching of Foreign Language), 16, 117

Action research, 407

Adequate Yearly Progress (AYP) reports, 47, 161–162

Advanced degrees, 409

Adversarial relationships among teachers, 401

Advocate for students, 11, 12

Aesthetics, 273

Affiliations, of private schools, 43

Africa, children in, 4

African Americans
  achievement gap and, 61
  leaders of, 256–257
  nineteenth-century education of, 252–253
  separate but equal doctrine and, 252–253
  standardized testing and, 157, 158, 160
  teachers among, 5
  twentieth-century education of, 256–257
  violence among, 312–313

AFT (American Federation of Teachers), 15, 16, 333, 407

Aggression
  instrumental, 77
  relational, 77

AIDS, 306, 307

Alabama, Tuskegee Institute in, 253

Alaska, rural schools in, 56

Alcohol abuse, 304–306

Alliance for Technology Access (ATA), 182

Alternative high schools, 55

Alternative schools, 41–42, 43, 55

American Alliance for Health, Physical Education, Recreation and Dance (AAHPERD), 16

American Association for Health Education (AAHE), 117

American Association of Suicidology, 309

American Association of University Women (AAUW), 343, 345

American Council for the Teaching of Foreign Language (ACTFL), 16, 117

American Federation of Teachers (AFT), 15, 16, 333, 407

American Psychiatric Association, 309–310

American Psychological Association, 94

American Spelling Book, 246

"Amish exception," 350

Analytic rubric, 151, 152

Anecdotal records, 143

AR (Accelerated Reader) program, 190

Arts, 117–118

Arts-infused curriculum, 118, 119

ASCD (Association for Supervision and Curriculum Development), 15, 16, 327

Asian Americans, violence among, 312–313

Assault, 313

Assessment, 143–160
  classroom, 144, 147–150, 164
  criterion-referenced, 147
  curriculum and, 150, 162
  diagnostic, 147
  formal, 143
  formative, 148
  forms of, 149–150
  informal, 143
  instruction and, 148, 150, 162
  purposes of, 147–149
  rubric and, 151–152
  self-assessment, 143, 149, 432
  summative, 148

Assistant principals, 369–370, 371

Assistive technology, 96, 182

Association for Childhood Education International (ACEI), 16, 24, 31, 34, 171

Association for Supervision and Curriculum Development (ASCD), 15, 16, 327

Associations, professional, 15, 16. *See also specific associations*

Associative play, 73

ATA (Alliance for Technology Access), 182

At risk students, 41–42
  dropping out, 313, 315–317, 318
  matching technology resources to needs of, 182
  truancy and, 313–314, 318

Attention, of students, 209

Attention deficit/hyperactivity disorder (AD/HD), 94

Audiences, authentic, 196

Auditory learners, 91, 92

Authentic audiences, 196

Authentic teaching, 112

Authority, knowing based on, 273

Autism, 93

Axiology, 273, 275, 286

AYP (Adequate Yearly Progress) reports, 47, 161–162

Bachelor's degree, 13

Backward design, 144–147, 164
  defined, 144–145
  stages of, 145

Balanced Treatment Act (Louisiana), 351

Behavioral expectations, 213–215, 230

Behavior improvement room (BIR), 219

Benchmarks, 114

Best Friends, Worst Enemies: Understanding the Social Lives of Children (Thompson & Grace), 312

Bethel School District No. 403 v. Fraser (1986), 342, 348

Bias, gender, 76

Bilingual education, 84, 252, 360

Bilingual Education Act of 1968, 252, 360

BIR (behavior improvement room), 219

Birth rate, teen, 306, 307

Black Codes, 252–253

Black Law, 252

Blind students, 93, 251

Block grants, 374

Block schedule, 53, 55

Blogs, 196

Bloom's taxonomy, 124, 125

Boards of education, state, 362

Body mass index (BMI), 308

Bolinas-Stinson Elementary School (California), 59

Bond referendum, 377

Boston English High School, 250

Boys
  in crisis, 78
  gender differences among, 74, 76–79, 104
  instrumental aggression among, 77
  rationale for success and failure of, 77

Brain, and learning process, 112–113, 137

Brain-based learning, 112

Brain injury, traumatic, 93

Brainstorming, 129

Breach of contract, 331

Brown University, 246

Brown v. Board of Education (1954), 257, 329–330

Buckley Amendment (1974), 347
Bullying, 310, 311–312, 318
Businesses, in public school governance, 372, 383

CAI (computer-assisted instruction), 183
California, Proposition 13 in, 375
California Achievement Tests (CAT), 155
California Department of Education, 88
Camera, digital, 186
Career courses, 118
Caring classroom, 207–208
Cario Middle School (South Carolina), 26–27, 53, 54, 169, 189–190, 205, 206–207, 211–212, 225, 226
Carnegie Council on Adolescent Development, 260
Case law. See also specific cases
    on freedom of expression, 335
    on religion in schools, 351
    on student rights, 348
    Supreme Court and, 329–330
    on teacher liability, 338
    on teachers' personal lives, 337
Categorical grants, 374
CEC (Council for Exceptional Children), 15, 16, 96
CEI (computer-enhanced instruction), 183
Center for Applied Research in Educational Technology (CARET), 179–180
Center for Social Organization of Schools (Johns Hopkins University), 314
Certification. See also Licensure
    by National Board of Professional Teaching Standards, 409
    state requirements for, 12–13, 14
Chalkboards, 174
Channel One, 174
Character development, 74
Character traits, 74
Charleston Education Network (CEN), 372
Charlotte-Mecklenburg Schools (CMS), 377, 378
Charter schools, 41, 42, 43, 48
Cherry Elementary School (Kentucky), 216
Child abuse
    defined, 294
    emotional, 296
    physical, 295
    prevalence of, 294
    recognizing, 295–296
    reporting, 294, 295, 340
    sexual, 296, 340
Child and the Curriculum, The (Dewey), 114
Child neglect
    defined, 294
    reporting, 340
    signs of, 296
Child Nutrition Reauthorization Act of 2004, 308–309
Children's Partnership, 192
Child Welfare Information Gateway, 294, 295, 296n
Church of England, 238
Civil Rights Act of 1964, 259, 260, 328
Class discussion
    as instructional strategy, 128
    in middle school education, 52

Classroom. See also Learning environment
    caring, 207–208
    democratic, 213
    multiage, 24–25, 269, 357
    organization of, 206
    seating arrangement in, 206, 291
    self-contained, 24
Classroom assessment, 147–150, 164
    defined, 144
    forms of, 149–150
    purposes of, 147–149
Classroom climate, 12, 208
Classroom community, 207–208
Classroom management, 212–222
    components of, 228
    consequences and, 218–222, 230
    developmental appropriateness of, 224–227
    in early childhood education, 224–225
    in elementary education, 225
    expectations and, 213–215, 230
    general guidelines for, 228–229
    in high schools, 225–227
    incentives and, 215–218, 230
    in middle school education, 225
    observing techniques used in, 426
    plan for, 222–229, 230
    prominent theories of, 222–223
    societal context of, 224
    student needs and, 223–224
Classroom networks, 176
Clinical internship, 13
Clinical practice, taking full advantage of, 429–430
CMI (computer-managed instruction), 183
Coalition of Essential Schools, 276
Cochlear implants, 182
Code of Conduct, 227
Code of Ethics, 325, 326
Cognitive development, 70–71
Coleman Report, 60
Colleagues, teacher responsibilities regarding, 400–404, 415
Collective bargaining, 15, 333
Colleges and universities
    for African Americans, 252–253
    in colonial America, 246
    in nineteenth century, 252–254
    in public school governance, 372, 383
Colonial America
    colleges in, 246
    education in, 238–247
    original colonies in, 241–243
    religion in, 238, 240, 242, 246
    schools in, 240–243, 244–247
    teachers in, 243, 244
    textbooks in, 242
Colorado Student Assessment Program (CSAP), 156, 157, 158, 160
Columbine High School tragedy, 311, 341
Common schools, 249–250
Communication
    electronic, 393
    with family, 221–222, 392–394
    on Internet, 196
    technology for, 179
    telecommunications, 187–188
Communication skills, 116
Community
    accountability of, 161
    classroom, 207–208
    defined, 297

impact on students, 297, 318
    teacher responsibilities regarding, 399, 400, 415
Compass rose, 421
Competition, school choice and, 46, 49
Comprehensive high schools, 27, 55
Comprehensive Tests of Basic Skills (CTBS), 155
Compulsory education, religion and, 348, 350
Compulsory education law, 242
Computer-assisted instruction (CAI), 183
Computer-enhanced instruction (CEI), 183
Computer-managed instruction (CMI), 183
Computer(s), 175. See also Technology
    for all students, 195
    hand-held, 176
    instruction and, 183
    as teachers, 197
Concrete operations, 71
Congress, influence on public education, 359
Consequences, 218–222, 230
    constructive correcting of, 220–221, 222
    defined, 212
    matching to misbehavior, 219
    serious, 220, 227
    teacher-prescribed, 219–220
Constructivism, 126, 273, 277
Content, 112, 127, 323
Content priorities, 145–147
Content standards, 114
Contracts, teaching contracts, 331, 332, 335
Controversy, curriculum and, 120, 122
Cooperating teachers, 13
Cooperative group, 127
Cooperative learning, 126
Cooperative play, 73
Copyright laws, 339–340
Core subjects, 24
Corporal punishment, 220, 221, 346–347. See also Classroom management; Consequences
Corporation for Public Broadcasting, 191
Council for Exceptional Children (CEC), 15, 16, 96
Council of Chief State School Officers, 362
Count Me In program, 314
Coursework, taking full advantage of, 422–425
Courts, and public education, 359, 362. See also Supreme Court
Crime, 312–313, 314, 318
Criterion-referenced assessment, 147
CSAP (Colorado Student Assessment Program), 156, 157, 158, 160
CTBS (Comprehensive Tests of Basic Skills), 155
Cultural diversity, 79–82, 105
Cultural identity, 79
Cultural Literacy: What Every American Needs to Know (Hirsch), 276
Culturally responsive teaching, 81
Culture(s)
    as barrier to parental involvement, 396
    changing, 39
    characteristics of, 79
    ethnic component of culture, 80

Culture(s) *(continued)*
   racial component of culture, 79–80
   school, 38–39, 62
Curriculum, 113–123, 137
   arts-infused, 118, 119
   assessment and, 150, 162
   controversy and, 120, 122
   defined, 112, 113
   developing, 114
   extracurriculum, 113, 122
   formal, 113–120, 137
   informal, 111, 113, 120–122
   integrated, 118
   kinds of, 111–112, 113
   multicultural, 118, 119
   needs of society and, 113
   needs of students and, 113, 114, 213, 214
   needs of subject and, 113
   null, 113, 122–123
   religion and, 120, 351–352
Cybercheating, 194

Dame schools, 241, 247
Dance, 119
DARE (Drug Abuse Resistance Education), 305
Dare the School Build a New Social Order? (Counts), 279
Dartmouth College, 246
Davis v. Monroe County Board of Education (1999), 345, 348
Deaf-blindness, 93, 251
Decision makers, 12
Deductive reasoning, 274
Democratic classroom, 213
Demonstration, 128–129
Departmentalization, 53
Depression, 309
Deschooling Society (Illich), 279
Detention, 219
Development, 69–74
   character, 74, 76
   cognitive, 70–71
   emotional, 71–72, 73
   physical, 69–70
   social, 72–74, 75
Developmental appropriateness, 12, 112, 224–227
Developmental delay, 93
Diagnostic assessment, 147
Dialects, 82
Differentiation of instruction, 127
Digital camera, 186
Digital divide, 191–192
Digital media, 177
Digital portfolios, 195–196
Direct instruction, 124–125
Disabilities, students with, 93–96, 105
   categories of disabilities, 93
   history of education of, 251
   inclusion of, 95–96
   individualized educational programs (IEPs) for, 94–95, 223
   legal support for, 94
   principles for educating, 95
   technology and, 179, 182
Disciplinary action, 346–347
Discipline. *See* Classroom management; Consequences
Discrimination, 300–301
Dismissal, of teachers, 331–332
Distance learning, 196–197

District school boards, 364–366, 383
   accountability of, 161
   defined, 364
   duties of, 365
   election of, 364–365
   profile of members of, 365
   public and, 365–366
District superintendents, 366
Divergent questions, 129
Diversity, 78–97
   among students, 61, 439
   among teachers, 6, 30
   cultural, 79–82, 105
   in family structure, 85, 105
   gender and, 78
   of intellectual ability, 88–92, 105
   of language, 82–84, 105
   of religion, 85–86, 105
   socioeconomic, 86–88, 89, 105
   teaching identity and, 61, 104, 136, 163, 198, 229, 261, 317, 382, 414
Diversity Data, 80
Divine revelation, knowing based on, 273
Donations, private, 377
Drama, 119
Dress codes, 341–342, 349
Drill and practice, 129
Dropping out, 313, 315–317, 318
Drug abuse, 304–306
Drug Abuse Resistance Education (DARE), 305
Drug testing, 343
Due process, 328, 332–333

Early childhood
   character development in, 76
   cognitive development in, 72
   emotional development in, 73
   physical development in, 70
   social development in, 75, 77
Early childhood education
   classroom management in, 224–225
   differences in teaching, 22–24, 31
   history of, 250
   in kindergarten, 50, 51, 291
   matching instruction to school levels, 133
   in preschool, 49–50
   in primary grades, 50–51
   routines in, 210
   structure and organization of, 49–51
   technology use in, 185–187
   in twentieth century, 256
Eckmann v. Board of Education (1986), 336, 337
Edison Schools, 45, 174
Educating Esme: Diary of a Teacher's First Year (Codell), 20
Education. *See also* History of education; Philosophy of education; Societal context of education
   as a priority, 246–247
   bilingual, 84, 252, 360
   compulsory, 348, 350
   progressive, 254
   special, 93, 94
   of teachers, 4, 13, 250–251, 422–425
   value of, 8
   of women, 241, 246
Educational technology, 170. *See also* Technology
Educational Testing Service (ETS), 13, 20, 32, 315

Education Amendments Act of 1972, Title IX, 44, 76, 259, 328
Education Commission of the States, 46
Education for All Handicapped Children Act of 1975, 94, 259–260, 360
Education Maintenance Organizations (EMOs), 45
Education Trust, 19
Education Vital Statistics (EVS), 306, 317, 380*n*
Education Week, 179
Effective schools, 59–61, 63
   characteristics of, 60
   correlates of, 61
Effective Schools Movement, 60
ELA (English language arts), 116, 118
Elementary and Secondary Education Act, 60, 259, 260–261
Elementary education
   classroom management in, 225
   differences in teaching, 24–26, 31, 33
   matching instruction to school levels, 133–134
   routines in, 211
   sample schedules for, 52, 53, 211
   structure and organization of, 51–53
   technology use in, 187–189
Elementary school students
   character development in, 76
   cognitive development in, 72
   comfortable settings for reading, 132
   emotional development in, 73
   physical development in, 70
   social development in, 75
ELL (English language learners), 82–84, 190
Elvin v. City of Waterville (1990), 337
EMOs (Education Maintenance Organizations), 45
Emotional abuse, 296
Emotional development, 71–72, 73
Emotional disturbance, 93
Emotional Intelligence (Goleman), 72
Emotional intelligence quotient (EQ), 72
Employment rights, of teachers, 331–333
Encore subjects, 115
English, standard, 82
English as a second language (ESL) programs, 84
English Classical School, 250
English language arts (ELA), 116, 118
English language learners (ELL), 82–84, 190
Entitlements, 374
Environment. *See also* Learning environment
   least restrictive, 95
Epistemology, 272–273, 275, 286
E. Pluribus Unum, 253
Equal Educational Opportunity Survey (1966), 60
Equity
   gender equity, 78
   technology and, 191–192
Era of standards, 114
ESL (English as a second language) programs, 84
Essay tests, 149
Essentialism, 275–276, 277, 285, 287
Ethics, 273, 324–325, 352–353
Ethnicity
   as component of culture, 80
   defined, 80
   discrimination and, 300–301

graduation rates and, 316
in nineteenth-century education, 251–253
in public schools by state, 81
racism and, 299–304, 318
standardized testing and, 157, 158, 160
of teachers, 5, 6, 30, 300–301, 302
technology use and, 192
Evaluation
defined, 150
of programs, 148–149
of student achievement, 148, 150–153, 164
Exceptional students, 92–97, 105
gifted and talented students, 96–97
students with disabilities, 93–96
Exclusionary punishment, 346–347
Existentialism, 275, 280–281, 285, 287
Expectations
behavioral, 213–215, 230
defined, 213
discrimination and, 300–301
sample list of, 215
of teachers for students, 413
Expenditure per pupil, 378–381
Expenditures, on schools, 377–382
Experience, knowing based on, 273
Exploratory arts, 53
Expression, freedom of. See Freedom of expression
Expulsion, 346
Extracurriculum, 113, 122
Extrinsic incentives, 216–217

Fair use, 339
Families
accountability of, 161
communication with, 221–222, 392–394
impact on students, 294–296, 318
teacher responsibilities involving, 390–398, 414–415
of teachers, 8
Family diversity, 85, 105
Family Educational Rights and Privacy Act (FERPA) of 1974 (Buckley Amendment), 347
Federal government
accountability of, 161
education funding from, 373–374, 384
influence on public education, 359–360, 383
Feedback
formative assessment and, 148
standardized tests and, 155
Feeder system of school, 363
FERPA (Family Educational Rights and Privacy Act) of 1974 (Buckley Amendment), 347
Field experiences, taking full advantage of, 425–428
Fifth Amendment, 332
Fifth-year program, 13
Finance. See Funding
First Amendment Center, 307
First Amendment to the Constitution, 327–328, 350
First day of school, 437–438
First Steps to School Readiness Initiative (South Carolina), 50
Focus Adolescent Services, 314
Folkloria program, 119
Forced-choice forms of assessment, 149

Foreign language, 117
Formal assessment, 143
Formal curriculum, 113–120, 137
arts-infused, 118, 119
defined, 113
integrated, 118
multicultural, 118, 119
subjects of, 115–118
Formal operations, 71
Formative assessment, 148
For-profit private schools, 44–45
Fourteenth Amendment, 328, 332
Fourth Amendment, 328, 342–343
Fourth grade, sample schedule for, 53
Franklin Academy, 244
Freedman's Bureau, 253
Freedom, academic, 334–335
Freedom of expression
of students, 340–342
of teachers, 333–334, 335
Freedom of speech
of students, 342
of teachers, 327–328
Freedom of the press, 342
Fresh start, 221
Fresno Unified School District (California), 88
Full service schools, 40, 43
Functional behavioral assessment (FBA), 224
Functional illiteracy, 131
Funding, 373–382, 384
allocation of, 381–382
federal, 373–374, 384
law on, 60
local, 375–377, 384
lottery-based, 375
from private donations, 377
sources of, 373–377, 384
spending of, 377–382, 384
state, 374–375, 384
for technology, 193–194
Title I, 60
Funding gap, 376

Gangs, 313
Gender
achievement and, 77
defined, 74
education and, 241, 246
generalizations about, 77
sexual orientation and, 78
single-gender private schools, 44, 45
social aspects of, 77
of teachers, 5, 6, 30
Gender bias, 76
Gender differences, 74, 76–79, 104
Gender diversity, 78
Gender equity, 78
Gender stereotyping, 76
Geographic isolation, 56
GI Bill, 359–360
Gifted students, 96–97
Girls
gender differences among, 74, 76–79, 104
rationale for success and failure of, 77
relational aggression among, 77
Goals 2000, 260, 359
Good Beginnings Alliance (Hawaii), 50
Good News Club v. Milford Central School (2001), 350, 351
Goss v. Lopez (1975), 346, 348
Governance. See Public school governance

Governors, role in public education, 360–361
Governor's Early Childhood Initiative (Kentucky), 50
Grade, 152
Grade levels
differences in teaching, 21–29, 31
matching instruction to, 133–136, 137
technology use by, 184
Grading
guidelines for, 153
reasons for, 153, 164
of schools, 47
of students, 152–153, 164
Graduate school, 440
Graduation rates, 315–316
Grants
block, 374
categorical, 374
Graphic organizers, 129–130
Great Books, 276, 277
Grievances, 333

Hampton Institute, 253
Hand-held computers, 176
Hawaii
Good Beginnings Alliance in, 50
school district in, 363
Hazelwood School District v. Kuhlmeier (1988), 342, 348
Head Start, 50, 259, 360
Health issues, 304–310, 318
childhood obesity, 307–309, 318
sexuality-related concerns, 306–307, 318
substance abuse, 304–306, 318
suicide, 309–310, 318
of teachers, 336
Hearing impairments, 93
Herdahl v. Pontotoc County School District (1996), 351
Hierarchy of needs, 69
Higher education
for African Americans, 252–253
in colonial America, 246
in nineteenth century, 252–254
High school completion, 315
High school education
classroom management in, 225–227
comprehensive high schools, 27, 55
history of, 250
matching instruction to school levels, 135–136
routines in, 211–212
schedule for, 55
structure and organization of, 54–56
teachers and, 27–28, 31, 33, 54–55
technology use in, 190–191
types of high schools, 55
High school students
character development in, 76
cognitive development in, 72
emotional development in, 73
identity development in, 71
physical development in, 70
social development in, 72
High/Scope approach to early childhood education, 49–50
High-stakes tests, 154, 155
Hispanic Americans
nineteenth-century education of, 252
teachers among, 5
violence among, 312–313

History of education, 236–264
  awareness of history in the making, 261–263, 264
  colleges in, 246
  education as a priority in, 246–247
  in eighteenth century, 243–247, 263–264
  ethnic groups in, 251–253
  immigrants in, 253
  in nineteenth century, 247–254, 264
  separate but equal doctrine in, 252–253
  in seventeenth century, 238–243, 263
  of students with disabilities, 251
  in twentieth century and beyond, 254–261, 264
HIV/AIDS, 306, 307
Holidays, religious, 350–351
Holistic rubric, 151, 152
Homeschooling, 44, 45, 350
Homework hotline, 392
Homosexuality, 78, 306–307, 318, 336
Household chores, and gender differences, 74, 76
Hull House (Chicago), 253
Hunger, 299
Hurricane Katrina, 325
Hypermedia, 177–178

ICT (Information and Communications Technology), 192
IDEA (Individuals with Disabilities Education Act), 94, 224, 251, 328
Idealism, 281
Identity
  cultural, 79
  development of, 71
  teaching, 61, 104, 136, 163, 198, 229, 261, 317, 382, 414
IEPs (individualized educational programs), 94–95, 223
Illiteracy, functional, 131
Immigrants
  classroom success of, 301–303
  education of, 253, 301–303
Incentives
  defined, 212
  extrinsic, 216–217
  intrinsic, 216, 217–218
  in learning environment, 215–218, 230
Inclusion, 95–96
Individualized educational programs (IEPs), 94–95, 223
Individuals with Disabilities Education Act (IDEA), 94, 224, 251, 328
Induction program, 438
Inductive reasoning, 274
Infoplease, 306, 307n
Informal assessment, 143
Informal curriculum, 111, 113, 120–122
Information and Communications Technology (ICT), 192
Information Commons Handbook, The (Beagle), 197
Ingraham v. Wright (1977), 346, 348
In loco parentis, 337–338, 339
Inquiry-based instruction, 125–126
Inquiry learning, 125
Instruction
  assessment and, 148, 150, 162
  big ideas of, 123–127
  computers and, 183
  constructivist, 126, 273, 277
  cooperative learning and, 126

defined, 112
  differentiation of, 127
  direct, 124–125
  implementing, 123–130
  inquiry-based, 125–126
  interdisciplinary, 126
  matching to school levels, 133–136, 137
  student-centered, 275, 277–281, 285, 287
  teacher-centered, 275–278, 285, 287
  teaching thinking skills and, 124
Instructional software, 175, 176
Instructional strategies, 128–130
Instrumental aggression, 77
INTASC. *See* Interstate New Teacher Assessment and Support Consortium (INTASC)
Integrated curriculum, 118
Integration literacy, 184
Intellectual ability, differences in, 88–92, 105
Intellectual development, 70–71
Intelligence
  culture and, 79
  emotional intelligence, 72
  multiple intelligences, 89–90, 91
  sensorimotor intelligence, 71
  views of, 90
Intelligence quotient (IQ), 88
Interdisciplinary instruction, 126
Interdisciplinary team, 53, 54
Interest centers, 206
Intermediate grades, 24
International Reading Association (IRA), 16, 116
International Society for Technology in Education (ISTE), 117, 170, 184, 185, 186, 187–191, 199–200
  standards and performance indicators for students, 173, 186, 188, 191
  standards for teachers, 172
Internet, 176–177, 178, 184, 192
  cheating and, 194
  communication on, 196
  copyright laws and, 340
Interruptions, responding to, 209
Interstate New Teacher Assessment and Support Consortium (INTASC)
  knowledge principles of, 107–108, 200, 232, 288, 320, 355, 386, 417–418
  standards of, 17, 33, 140, 166, 266
Interventions, unobtrusive, 219
Interview, job, 433–436
Intrinsic incentives, 216, 217–218
Intuition, knowing based on, 273
Iowa Tests of Basic Skills (ITBS), 155
IQ (intelligence quotient), 88
IRA (International Reading Association), 16, 116
Isaacs v. Board of Education of Howard County (1999), 348
ISTE. *See* International Society for Technology in Education (ISTE)
ITBS (Iowa Tests of Basic Skills), 155

Jamestown, Virginia, 238
Jigsaw instructional strategy, 130
Jim Crow laws, 136
Job, student, 210
Job fairs, 432
Job interviews, 433–436
Job performance, of teachers, 335–336

Job search, 430–436, 443
Job security, 8–9
Journal, of student teacher, 430
JROTC (Junior Reserve Officer Training Corp), 123
Junior high schools, 256. *See also* Middle school education
Junior Reserve Officer Training Corp (JROTC), 123

Kalamazoo case, 250
Kappa Delta Pi (KDP), 15–16
Kaufman v. City of New York (1961), 338
Keefe v. Geanakos (1969), 334, 335
Kentucky, Governor's Early Childhood Initiative in, 50
Kids' Rules for Online Safety, 192–193
Kindergarten
  early childhood education in, 50, 51, 291
  making changes in, 291
  in nineteenth century, 250
  sample half-day schedule for, 51
Kinesthetic learners, 91, 92
Kingsville Independent School District v. Cooper (1980), 335
Knowing, sources of, 273
Krizek v. Cicero-Stickney Township High School (1989), 335

Labor unions, 333. *See also specific unions*
Language
  as barrier to parental involvement, 396
  defined, 82
  dialects of, 82
Language arts. *See* English language arts (ELA)
Language diversity, 82–84, 105
Language impairments, 93
Latin grammar school, 241, 250
Law(s), 325–353. *See also* Case law; *and names of specific laws*
  on bilingual education, 252, 360
  on bullying and harassment, 312
  case, 329–330, 335, 337, 338
  on civil rights, 259, 260, 328
  on compulsory education, 242
  on copyright, 339–340
  on education of African Americans, 252–253
  on education of low-income children, 259
  on equal educational opportunity, 60
  federal, 328–329
  on funding for education, 60
  on gender bias, 76
  on health of students, 308–309
  on higher education, 253–254
  Jim Crow, 136
  local, 329
  on relationship between school and religion, 348–352, 353
  on responsibilities of teachers, 337–340, 353
  on rights of students, 340–348, 353
  on rights of teachers, 330–337, 353
  schools and, 44, 325–330, 353
  on search and seizure, 328, 342–343
  on segregation in schools, 257, 329–330
  on single-gender schools, 44
  state, 329
  on students with disabilities, 94, 224, 251, 259–260

U.S. Constitution and, 324, 327–328, 329, 330, 366
on vocational education, 259
LCS (Local School Council), 371
LD (learning disabled), 93–94
Leadership capacity, building, 368
Learning
brain and, 112–113, 137
brain-based, 112
cooperative, 126
defined, 112
distance, 196–197
inquiry, 125
motivation and, 112–113, 180
problem-based (PBL), 126–127
taking responsibility for student learning, 412
teachers as facilitators of, 11–12, 183
technology and, 179–182, 198
Learning disabled (LD), 93–94
Learning environment, 203–230. See also Environment
building community in, 207–208
consequences in, 218–222, 230
creating, 205–209, 229–230
establishing expectations in, 213–215, 230
as home away from home, 205
incentives in, 215–218, 230
interest centers in, 206
observing, 426
physical space in, 205
proximity in, 206
routines and, 209–212, 230
seating arrangement in, 206, 291
wall space in, 206–207
Learning modalities, 90
Learning styles, 90–92
Lease-purchase option, 377
Least restrictive environment (LRE), 95
Lecture, 128
Legislation. See Law(s); and names of specific laws
Legislatures, state, 361
LEP (limited English proficiency), 82–84
Lesson planning, technology tools for, 178
Letter to the Editor features
on Colorado Student Assessment Program, 156, 157, 158
on corporal punishment, 221
on Maine Learning Technology Initiative (MLTI), 180–181
on minority teachers, 302
on school decisions made by students, 379
on school vouchers, 48
scoring guide for, 20
on sexual harassment of students, 345
on students of low socioeconomic status, 89
in support of teachers, 21
on teaching the origin of human beings, 120
Liability, of teachers, 337–339
Licensure, state requirements for, 12–13
Licensure Test Prep, 32–33, 63–64, 106, 138–139, 164–165, 199–200, 230–232, 265–266, 287–288, 319, 354, 384–385, 416–417, 444
Limited English proficiency (LEP), 82–84
Listening, in English language arts, 116
Literacy, integration, 184
Local funding, 375–377, 384
Local School Council (LSC), 371

Lockers, search of, 343
Logic
defined, 274
knowing based on, 273
philosophy of education and, 274, 275, 286
Looping, 51–52
Lottery-based funding, 375
Louisiana, Balanced Treatment Act in, 351
LRE (least restrictive environment), 95

MADD (Mothers Against Drunk Driving), 305
Magnetic resonating imaging (MRI), 112
Magnet schools, 41, 43, 55
Maine Learning Technology Initiative (MLTI), 180–181
Maltreatment, 294–296
Management. See also Classroom management
of individual schools, 367–371, 383
micromanagement, 366
site-based, 367–368
Mancha v. Field Museum of Natural History (1971), 338
Manipulatives, 174, 175
Maslow's hierarchy of needs, 69
Massachusetts Act of 1642, 242
Massachusetts Act of 1647, 242
Massachusetts Bay Colony
religion in, 240
schools in, 241
Master of arts in teaching (MAT) degree, 13
Mathematics, 116
Math manipulatives, 174, 175
MAT (Metropolitan Achievement Tests), 155
McGuffey readers, 250
McREL (Midcontinent Research for Education and Learning), 127, 149
Measuring Digital Opportunity for America's Children (Lazarus, Wainer, & Lipper), 192
Mental retardation, 93
Mentor-mentee relationship, 402
Metaphysics, 272, 275, 286
Metropolitan Achievement Tests (MAT), 155
Mexican Americans, nineteenth-century education of, 252
Michigan, Kalamazoo case in, 250
Micromanagement, 366
Microphones, 182
Midcontinent Research for Education and Learning (McREL), 127, 149
Middle school education
class discussion in, 52
classroom management in, 225
departmentalized, 53
matching instruction to school levels, 134–135
routines in, 211–212
schedule for, 53–54
structure and organization of, 53–54
subjects in, 53
teachers and, 26–27, 31, 33
technology use in, 189–190
in twentieth century, 256
Middle school students
character development in, 76
cognitive development in, 72

emotional development in, 73
physical development in, 70
social development in, 75
Milwaukee Parental Choice Program (MPCP), 48
Misbehavior. See also Behavioral expectations
consequences of, 218–222, 230
matching consequences to, 219
Montana, rural schools in, 56
Montessori approach to early childhood education, 49, 256
Moral reasoning, stages of, 74, 75
Morrill Act (1862), 253–254
Morrison v. State Board of Education (1969), 335–336, 337
Mothers Against Drunk Driving (MADD), 305
Motivation
extrinsic, 216–217
intrinsic, 216, 217–218
learning and, 112–113, 180
technology and, 180
MRI (magnetic resonating imaging), 112
MTNA (Music Teachers National Association), 16
Multiage classroom, 24–25, 269, 357
Multicultural curriculum, 118, 119
Multicultural education, 80–81
Multicultural Education in a Pluralistic Society (Gollnick & Chin), 319
Multimedia, 177, 178
Multiple intelligences (MI) theory, 89–90, 91
Murray v. Pittsburgh Board of Education (1996), 334, 335
Music, 119
Music Teachers National Association (MTNA), 16

NAACP (National Association for the Advancement of Colored People), 257
NAASPL (North American Association of State and Provincial Lotteries), 375
NAEA (National Art Education Association), 16
NAEP (National Assessment of Educational Progress), 154–155, 179, 180, 261
NAEYC (National Association for the Education of Young Children), 16, 22, 31, 34, 171, 386
NAGC (National Association for Gifted Children), 16
Name-calling, 312
NASPE (National Association for Sport and Physical Education), 117
NATIE (National Association for Trade and Industrial Education), 16
National Academy of Education, 429
National Art Education Association (NAEA), 16
National Assessment of Educational Progress (NAEP), 154–155, 179, 180, 261
National Association for Gifted Children (NAGC), 16
National Association for Sport and Physical Education (NASPE), 117
National Association for the Advancement of Colored People (NAACP), 257
National Association for the Education of Young Children (NAEYC), 16, 22, 31, 34, 171, 386

National Association for Trade and Industrial Education (NATIE), 16

National Association of State Boards of Education, 362, 365

National Board of Professional Teaching Standards (NBPTS), 18, 33, 34, 64, 107, 140, 166, 201, 232, 266, 288, 320, 355, 386, 409, 410n, 418

National Business Education Association (NBEA), 16

National Center for Education Statistics (NCES), 4, 5n, 39, 42, 44, 68, 81n, 82, 85, 154, 306, 310, 313, 363, 370n, 374n, 381n

National Center for Health Statistics, 307n

National Child Abuse and Neglect Data System (NCANDS), 294

National Council for Teachers of English (NCTE), 16, 116, 170, 171n, 407

National Council for Teachers of Mathematics (NCTM), 16, 114, 147, 170, 171n, 180, 407

National Council for the Accreditation of Teacher Education (NCATE), 13, 33, 107, 140, 166, 201, 320

National Council for the Social Studies (NCSS), 16, 116–117, 171

National Council of Education Statistics, 58n

National Council on Teacher Quality, 440

National Defense Education Act of 1958, 257

National Educational Technology Standards for Teachers (NETS for Teachers), 172

National Education Association (NEA), 4, 5n, 6, 7n, 8, 9n, 15, 16, 325, 326, 333, 343n, 407
  Code of Ethics of, 325, 326

National Education Technology Standards, 184

National Governors Association (NGA), 360–361

National Honor Society, 77

National Middle School Association (NMSA), 16, 31, 260
  standards for family and community involvement, 418
  standards for teachers, 26, 33, 34, 64, 140, 166, 232, 418
  standards for technology, 171

National School Boards Association, 365, 380n

National School Lunch Program, 360

National Science Teachers Association (NSTA), 16, 116, 170–171

National Standards for Arts Education, 117

National Vital Statistics Report, 307n

Nation at Risk, A, 160, 260, 276, 373

Native Americans, nineteenth-century education of, 251–252

Nature vs. nurture, 68

NBEA (National Business Education Association), 16

NBPTS. *See* National Board of Professional Teaching Standards (NBPTS)

NCANDS (National Child Abuse and Neglect Data System), 294

NCATE (National Council for the Accreditation of Teacher Education), 13, 33, 107, 140, 166, 201, 320

NCES. *See* National Center for Education Statistics (NCES)

NCLB Act. *See* No Child Left Behind (NCLB) Act of 2001

NCSS (National Council for the Social Studies), 16, 116–117, 171

NCTE (National Council for Teachers of English), 16, 116, 170, 171n, 407

NCTM (National Council for Teachers of Mathematics), 16, 114, 147, 170, 171n, 180, 407

NEA. *See* National Education Association (NEA)

Needs. *See also* Student needs
  basic, 69, 218
  hierarchy of, 69

Negativity, 439

Neglect. *See* Child neglect

Neighborhood schools, 48

Networks, classroom, 176

New England Primer, 242

New Jersey, graduation rate in, 315

New Jersey v. T.L.O. (1985), 343, 348

Newsletter, classroom, 392

Newspapers, school, 342

NGA (National Governors Association), 360–361

NMSA. *See* National Middle School Association (NMSA)

No Child Left Behind (NCLB) Act of 2001
  on accountability, 161, 260–261
  achievement gap and, 61
  controversy concerning, 329
  on education funding, 374
  impact of, 328–329, 359, 360
  on minimum requirements for new teachers, 18
  on school choice, 47
  on standardized testing, 155
  state government and, 363
  on teacher qualifications, 436–437
  technology and, 193

Nondiscrimination, right to, 347

Nonparticipation, student right of, 347

Nonreligious private schools, 45

Nonverbal interventions, 219

Norm-referenced tests, 155

Norms, defined, 214

North American Association of State and Provincial Lotteries (NAASPL), 375

Northwest Land Ordinance of 1787, 246

Note taking, as instructional strategy, 129

NSTA (National Science Teachers Association), 16, 116, 170–171

Null curriculum, 113, 122–123

Nurture vs. nature, 68

Obesity, 307–309, 318

Observation
  assessment and, 149
  of individual student, 427
  of learning environment and classroom management techniques, 426

Odd Girl Out: The Hidden Culture of Aggression in Girls (Simmons), 312

Old Deluder Satan Act, 242

Online plagiarism, 194

Open enrollment, 46, 48

Ophelia Project, 311

Oral reports, 149

Organization
  of early childhood education, 49–51
  of elementary education, 51–53

of high school education, 54–56
of learning environment, 206
of middle school education, 53–54

Orthopedic impairments, 93

Overhead projectors, 174, 175, 186, 190

Overlapping, 208

Owasso Independent School District v. Falso (2002), 347

Pacing guide, 162

Paideia Proposal, The (Adler), 260, 276–277

Palmetto Achievement Challenge Test (PACT), 190

Parallel play, 73, 401

Paraprofessionals, teacher relationships with, 403–404

Parental involvement
  barriers to, 394–398
  importance of, 391, 397
  student performances and, 391
  teacher responsibilities involving, 390–398, 414–415
  types of, 392
  ways to achieve, 391–394

Parent(s)
  accountability of, 161
  caring of, 398
  communication with, 221–222, 392–394
  educational background of, 396
  phone calls with, 392–393, 394
  in public school governance, 371, 383
  reasons for homeschooling, 44, 350
  recognizing child abuse by, 295
  right to school choice, 48–49
  volunteer opportunities for, 391

Parent-student-teacher conferences, 394

Parent-student-teacher events, 391

Parent Teacher Association (PTA), 371

Parochial (religious) private schools, 43, 45

PBL (problem-based learning), 126–127

Pedagogy, 123

Pedagogy of the Oppressed (Friere), 279

Perennialism, 275, 276–277, 278, 285, 287

Performance standards (benchmarks), 114

Performance tasks, in assessment, 149

Perkins School for the Blind, 251

Personal conduct, of teachers, 335–336, 337

Personal lives, of teachers, 335–337

Personal self-growth, 409–410

Phi Delta Kappa (PDK), 16

Philosophy of education, 268–287
  affect on teaching and learning, 274–282
  axiology, 273, 275, 286
  branches of, 272–274, 286
  defined, 270, 286
  developing, 282–285, 287
  epistemology, 272–273, 275, 286
  essentialism, 275–276, 277, 285, 287
  existentialism, 275, 280–281, 285, 287
  idealism, 281
  importance of, 270–271
  logic, 274, 275, 286
  metaphysics, 272, 275, 286
  perennialism, 275, 276–277, 278, 285, 287
  postmodernism, 281–282
  progressivism, 275, 277–278, 279, 285, 287

realism, 281
romanticism, 281
sample questions and philosophical responses, 285
social reconstructionism, 275, 278–280, 285, 287
Philosophy trees, 277, 278, 279, 280, 281, 282–283, 284
Physical abuse, 295
Physical development, 69–70
Physical education, 117
Pickering v. Board of Education (1968), 334, 335
Pierce v. Society of Sisters (1925), 348, 350
Plagiarism, online, 194
Play
associative, 73
cooperative, 73
parallel, 73, 401
Pocket chart schedule, 211
Podcast, 196
Portfolios
for assessment, 150
digital, 195–196
for job search, 433
Postmodernism, 281–282
Power of the Neighborhood School, The, 377, 379
PowerPoint software, 175, 187
Pragmatism, 277
Praise, 216–217
Praxis™ II Principles of Learning and Teaching (PLT) Test, 32
Prayer, in school, 349, 350
Preoperational thought, 71
Preschools, structure and organization of, 49–50
President, influence on public education, 359
Press, freedom of, 342
Pretesting, 147
Primary grades
early childhood education in, 50–51
sample schedules for, 51, 52, 53
teachers and, 24, 31, 33
Principals
assistant, 369–370, 371
profile of, 370
of schools, 367–369, 370
Privacy
of student records, 347
technology and, 192
Private schools, 42–45
admittance to, 47
affiliations of, 43
for-profit, 44–45
homeschooling, 44, 45, 350
nonreligious, 45
parochial (religious), 43, 45
religious, 43, 45
religious diversity in, 85
single-gender, 44, 45
vouchers and, 47, 48
Privilege gap, 86, 298
Problem-based learning (PBL), 126–127
Problem-solving skills, 180
Process, 127
Processing, 219–220
Process standards, 114
Product, 127
Profession, characteristics of, 14–15
Professional associations, 15, 16. *See also specific associations*
Professional development, 179, 194–195

Professional ethics, 325
Professionalism
defined, 14
of teachers, 14–17, 30, 323
Professional knowledge base, contributions to, 407
Professional organizations, teacher involvement in, 407. *See also specific organizations*
Professional Practice, 31–32
Professional self-growth, 408–409
Programs, evaluating, 148–149
Progressive education, 254
Progressivism, 275, 277–278, 279, 285, 287
Progress monitoring, 147–148. *See also* Assessment
Project Head Start, 50, 259, 360
Projectors, overhead, 174, 175, 186, 190
Property taxes, 375–376
Proposals Relating to the Youth of Pennsylvania (Franklin), 244
Protection, students' right to, 342–348
Proximal development, zone of, 71
Proximity, 206
PTA (Parent Teacher Association), 371
Public domain, 339, 340
Public Education Network, 372, 425, 426*n*, 439
Public Law 94–142, 60, 94
Public school governance, 356–372
businesses in, 372, 383
federal government in, 359–360, 383
management structure of individual schools, 367–371, 383
overview of, 358
parents in, 371, 383
school districts in, 363–366, 383
special interest groups in, 372, 383
state government in, 360–363, 383
universities in, 372, 383
Public school(s), 39–42
alternative, 41–42, 43
charter, 41, 42, 43, 48
ethnicity in, 81
full service, 40, 43
funding of. *See* Funding
magnet, 41, 43, 55
open enrollment and, 46, 48
principal settings of, 56–59, 62
purpose of, 40
rural, 56–58
school choice and, 46
traditional, 40, 43
"Public Schools and Sexual Orientation: A First Amendment Framework for Finding Common Ground," 307
Punishment. *See also* Classroom management; Consequences
corporal, 220, 221, 346–347
exclusionary, 346–347
Purdue University, 254
Puritans, 238, 240, 242

Quakers, 242, 243, 246
Questioning, 129
Question(s), divergent, 129

Race, as component of culture, 79–80
Racism, 299–304
defined, 299
immigrants and, 301–303
societal context of education and, 299–300, 318

Rape, 313
READ 180 program, 169, 175, 190
Reading, teaching, 130–132, 137
Reading Is Fundamental (RIF), 16
Realism, 281
Reasoning
deductive, 274
inductive, 274
knowing based on, 273
stages of moral reasoning, 74, 75
Reason to Teach: Creating Classrooms of Dignity and Hope (Beane), 63
Reconstructionism, 275, 278–280, 285, 287
Record-keeping software, 179
Records
access and privacy of, 347
anecdotal, 143
Reduction in force, 332
Rees Elementary School (Utah), 24–25, 38, 50, 52, 111, 119, 134, 188–189, 203, 211, 213, 225, 269, 282, 357, 395, 423–424
References, professional, 433
Reflection, 10
Reflective practitioners, 10
Reggio Emilia approach to early childhood education, 50
Related arts, 53
Relational aggression, 77
Reliability, of tests, 155
Religion
in colonial America, 238, 240, 242, 246
compulsory education and, 348, 350
curriculum and, 120, 351–352
in nineteenth-century schools, 249
relationship between school and, 348–352, 353
Religious diversity, 85–86, 105
Religious holidays, 350–351
Religious private schools, 43, 45
Research, action, 407
Resource teacher, 94
Respect, 215, 229
Responsibilities of teachers. *See* Teacher responsibilities
Resume, 433, 434
Rhode Island, colonial religion in, 240
"Riffing" rule, 332
RIF (Reading Is Fundamental), 16
Rights
civil, 259, 260, 328
of students, 340–348, 353
of teachers, 330–337, 353
Ripple effect, 209
Roberts v. City of Boston (1849), 252
Role-playing, 130
Romanticism, 281
Roosevelt High School (California), 28, 33, 55, 67, 79, 82, 88, 119, 135–136, 190–191, 206, 212, 227, 237, 278, 323, 424
Routines
defined, 209
in early childhood education, 210
in elementary education, 211
in high school education, 211–212
learning environment and, 209–212, 230
in middle school education, 211–212
practicing, 209–210
Rubric, 151–152
Rural schools, 56–58

SADD (Students Against Drunk Driving), 305

Safe and Drug Free Schools Act of 2004, 312

Safekids.com, 192

Safe School Initiative, 311

Safety, technology and, 192–193

Salaries, 9

Santa Fe Independent School District v. Doe (2000), 350, 351

Savage Inequalities (Kozol), 58

Scaffolding, 71

Schedule
  block, 53, 55
  for elementary education, 52, 53, 211
  for high school education, 55
  for kindergarten, 51
  for middle school education, 53–54
  pocket chart, 211

School administrators, 367–371

School and Society (Dewey), 114

School boards. *See* District school boards

School choice, 46–49
  advocates of, 48–49
  competition and, 46, 49
  critics of, 48–49
  No Child Left Behind Act on, 47
  public-to-public, 46
  vouchers for, 47–48

School Choice Wisconsin, 48

School connectedness, 122

School districts, 363–366, 383
  accountability of, 161
  defined, 363
  district school boards in, 161, 364–366, 383
  district superintendent and, 366
  feeder system of schools in, 363
  size of, 363
  teacher involvement in, 405

School Improvement Council (SIC), 371

School(s), 36–63
  academies, 244, 246, 249, 250
  alternative, 41–42, 43, 55
  assistant principals of, 369–370, 371
  charter, 41, 42, 43, 48
  common, 249–250
  culture of, 38–39, 62
  dame, 241, 247
  at different levels, 49–56, 62
  effective, 59–61, 63
  in eighteenth century, 244–247, 263–264
  expenditures on, 377–382
  feeder system of, 363
  for-profit, 44–45
  full service, 40, 43
  future of technology in, 195–197, 198, 199
  grading of, 47
  Latin grammar, 241, 250
  law and, 44, 325–330, 353
  lease-purchase option for, 377
  magnet, 41, 43, 55
  management structure of, 367–371, 383
  neighborhood, 48
  in nineteenth century, 247–250, 264
  open enrollment and, 46, 48
  principals of, 367–369, 370
  private, 42–45, 85, 350
  public, 39–42, 43, 56–59, 62, 81
  purpose of, 40

relationship between religion and, 348–352, 353
  rural, 56–58
  secondary, 250
  segregation in, 257, 329–330
  in seventeenth century, 240–243, 263
  suburban, 56, 57–58
  teacher involvement in, 404–406
  teacher leaders of, 370–371
  town, 246
  traditional, 40, 43
  urban, 58–59
  virtual, 197

School-to-work program, 118

School venues, 39–45, 62

Science, 116

Science manipulatives, 174

Scopes Monkey Trial (1925), 351

Scoring guide for Letter to the Editor features, 20

Search and seizure, law on, 328, 342–343

Seating arrangement, 206, 291

Secondary schools, 250. *See also* High school education

Second grade, sample schedule for, 52

Second Morrill Act (1890), 254

Segregation, 257, 329–330

Self-assessment, 143, 149, 432

Self-contained classroom, 24

Self-growth
  personal, 409–410
  professional, 408–409
  of teachers, 10, 408–411, 415

Self-monitoring, student, 217

Sensorimotor intelligence, 71

Separate but equal doctrine, 252–253

September 11 terrorist attacks, 40

Serviceman's Readjustment Act (GI Bill), 359–360

SES. *See* Socioeconomic status (SES)

Settlement houses, 253

Sexual abuse, 296, 340

Sexual harassment, 343–345

Sexuality-related health concerns, 306–307, 318

Sexually transmitted diseases (STDs), 306, 307

Sexual orientation, 78

Sheehan v. St. Peter's Catholic School (1971), 338

Shoplifting, 314

Single-gender private schools, 44, 45

Site-based management, 41, 367–368

Social cognition, 73, 74

Social development, 72–74, 75

Social reconstructionism, 275, 278–280, 285, 287

Social Studies, 116–117

Social studies teaching aids, 174

Societal context of education, 290–318
  bullying, 310, 311–312, 318
  community, 297, 318
  dropping out, 313, 315–317, 318
  family, 294–296, 318
  health issues, 304–310, 318, 336
  racism, 299–300, 318
  society, 297, 318
  socioeconomic status, 298–299, 318
  theft, 312–313, 318
  truancy, 313–314, 318
  violence, 312–313, 318

Society, impact on students, 297, 318

Socioeconomic status (SES)
  affect on students, 298–299, 318
  as barrier to parental involvement, 395
  digital divide and, 191–192
  diversity in, 86–88, 89, 105
  hunger and, 299
  low, 298–299

Software, 175, 195

South Carolina
  graduation rate in, 315
  public-private partnership boards in, 50
  standards-based test in, 190

Special education services, 93, 94

Special interest groups, 372, 383

Speech, freedom of. *See* Freedom of speech

Speech Communication Association (SCA), 16

Speech impairments, 93

Spending, 377–382

Stages of cognitive development, 71

Stages of moral reasoning, 74, 75

Standard English, 82

Standardized tests, 153–160, 164
  defined, 153
  general, 155
  high-stakes, 154, 155
  norm-referenced, 155
  pros and cons of, 156–160
  reliability of, 155
  standards-based tests vs., 153–154
  state standards-based, 155–156
  types of, 154–156
  validity of, 155

Standard(s), 114–115, 137
  content, 114
  defined, 114
  era of, 114
  performance, 114
  process, 114
  technology and, 170–172, 193

Standards-based tests, 153–154, 155–156

Stanford Achievement Tests (SAT), 155

Stanford News Service, 259*n*

Stare decisis doctrine, 329

State boards of education, 362

State courts, role in public education, 362

State departments of education, 362–363

State governments
  accountability of, 161
  education funding from, 374–375, 384
  role in public education, 360–363, 383

State legislatures, role in public education, 361

State standards-based tests, 155–156

State superintendents of education, 362

Station v. Travelers Insurance Co. (1974), 338

STDs (sexually transmitted diseases), 306, 307

Stereotyping, by gender, 76

Stone v. Grabam (1980), 351

Strategies, instructional, 128–130

Streaming video, 175

Stroman v. Colleton County School District (1992), 334, 335

Structure
  for early childhood education, 49–51
  for elementary education, 51–53
  for high school education, 54–56
  management structure of schools, 367–371, 383

for middle school education, 53–54
Student-centered instruction
existentialism, 275, 280–281, 285, 287
progressivism, 275, 277–278, 279, 285, 287
social reconstructionism, 275, 278–280, 285, 287
Student needs
basic, 69, 218
classroom management and, 223–224
curriculum and, 113, 114, 213, 214
intrinsic motivation and, 218
technology and, 182
Student(s), 66–105
accountability of, 160–161
development of, 69–74, 75, 76
with disabilities, 93–96, 105, 179, 182, 223, 251
diversity of, 61, 439
dress codes and, 341–342, 349
drug testing of, 343
on effective teachers, 19
with exceptionalities, 92–97, 105
freedom of expression and, 340–342
getting attention of, 209
grading, 152–153, 164
health of, 304–310, 318
hunger and, 299
law and, 44, 325–330, 340–348, 353
misconduct of teachers with, 336
monitoring progress of, 147–148
observing, 427
privacy of records of, 347
right of nonparticipation, 347
rights of, 340–348, 353
right to be protected, 342–348
at risk, 41–42, 182, 313–317, 318
sexual harassment of, 343–345
similarities among, 68–74, 104
teacher's responsibilities regarding, 411–413, 415
ways to develop relationships with teachers, 208
Students Against Drunk Driving (SADD), 305
Student self-monitoring, 217
Student teaching, 13, 429–430
Subject(s)
core, 24
encore, 115
of formal curriculum, 115–118
in middle school education, 53
teacher's interest in, 8
Substance abuse, 304–306, 318
Suburban schools, 56, 57–58
Suicide, 309–310, 318
Summative assessment, 148
Summit Primary School (Ohio), 23, 37, 47, 50, 143, 185–187, 210, 224–225, 402
Superintendents
district, 366
state, 362
Supreme Court. *See also specific cases*
case law and, 329–330
on legal rights of students, 341, 343, 346, 347
on legal rights of teachers, 334
on religion in schools, 350, 351
Suspension, 225, 227

Tactile learners, 91, 92
Talented students, 96–97

Tardif v. Quinn (1976), 336, 337
Taxes, property, 375–376
Teacher-centered instruction
essentialism and, 275–276, 277, 285, 287
perennialism and, 275, 276–277, 278, 285, 287
Teacher leaders, 370–371
Teacher mentor, 402
Teacher responsibilities
law on, 337–340, 353
regarding colleagues, 400–404, 415
regarding community, 399, 400, 415
regarding family involvement, 390–398, 414–415
regarding self-growth, 408–411, 415
regarding students, 411–413, 415
regarding systemic involvement, 404–406, 415
regarding teaching profession, 407–408, 415
Teacher(s), 2–31
academic freedom of, 334–335
accountability of, 161, 162
advanced degrees for, 409
as advocates for students, 11, 12
age of, 5
as barrier to parental involvement, 396–398
basic relationships among, 401–403
characteristics of, 17–21, 31
classroom climate and, 12, 208
in Colonial America, 243, 244
cooperating, 13
as decision makers, 12
dismissal of, 331–332
diversity of, 6, 30
diversity of students and, 439
due process rights of, 332–333
in early childhood education, 22–24, 31
education of, 4, 13, 250–251, 422–425
at elementary school level, 24–26, 31, 33
employment rights of, 331–333
ethics for, 324–325
ethnicity of, 5, 6, 30, 300–301, 302
as facilitator of learning, 11–12, 183
family of, 8
first year of, 436–442, 444
freedom of expression and, 333–334, 335
gender of, 5, 6, 30
grievances of, 333
highly qualified, 18
at high school level, 27–28, 31, 33, 54–55
influence of, 8
job search of, 430–436, 443
job security of, 8–9
law and, 44, 325–337, 353
legal rights of, 330–337, 353
liability of, 337–339
marital status of, 4, 5
at middle school level, 26–27, 31, 33
misconduct with students, 336
negativity in, 439
number of, 4, 5
ongoing study by, 14
on-the-job training of, 14
personal conduct and job performance of, 335–336, 337

personal lives of, 335–337
preparation of, 12–14, 30, 250–251, 422–430, 443
professionalism of, 14–17, 30, 323
professional organizations and, 407
qualifications of, 12–13
reasons for becoming, 6–10
relationships with paraprofessionals, 403–404
resource, 94
resume of, 433, 434
roles of, 10–12, 30, 183
salaries of, 9
school culture and, 38–39
self-growth of, 10, 408–411, 415
teaching contracts of, 331, 332, 335
technology tools for, 178–179
tenure of, 331
timid, 396–397
in United States, 4–6, 30
ways to develop relationships with students, 208
Teachers' Days, Delights, and Dilemmas features, 6, 7, 57, 87, 131, 160, 187, 214, 258, 271, 303, 327, 368, 413, 437
Teacher's Mission, A, 298, 299
Teachers of English to Speakers of Other Languages (TESOL), 16
Teachers of the Year, 6, 7
Teacher study groups, 402
Teacher think-aloud, 129
Teach for America, 14
Teaching
authentic, 112
culturally responsive, 81
first year of, 436–442, 444
reading, 130–132, 137
student, 13, 429–430
unconditional, 412
wayside, 121
writing, 132–133, 137
Teaching contracts, 331, 332, 335
Teaching position, searching for, 430–436, 443
Teaching profession, teacher's responsibilities and opportunities regarding, 407–408, 415
Teaching teams, 53, 54, 125
Teams. *See* Teaching teams
Technology, 168–199
assistive, 96, 182
defined, 170
in early childhood education, 185–187
educational, 170
in elementary education, 187–189
equity and, 191–192
funding for, 193–194
future of, in schools, 195–197, 198, 199
in high school education, 190–191
high-tech teaching tools, 175–178
integrating, 184, 185, 193
issues surrounding and affecting use of, 191–195, 199
low-tech teaching tools, 172–175
matching to needs of at risk students, 182
in middle school education, 189–190
privacy and, 192
professional development and, 179, 194–195
reasons for using, 179–182

Technology (continued)
    research on impact of, 179
    safety and, 192–193
    standards and, 170–172, 193
    student learning and, 179–182, 198
    students with disabilities and, 179, 182
    as subject of formal curriculum, 117
    for teachers, 178–179
    use by grade level, 184
    using in classrooms, 183–191, 199
    wireless, 195
Tech-prep courses, 118
Teen birth rate, 306, 307
Telecommunications, 187–188
Television, as technology tool, 174
Tenneyson Center for Children, 294
Tenure, 331
TESOL (Teachers of English to Speakers
    of Other Languages), 16
Test(s). *See also* Standardized tests
    high-stakes, 154, 155
    norm-referenced, 155
    preparation for, 162–163
    standards-based, 153–154, 155–156
Test-taking skills, 162–163
Texas, school districts in, 363
Texas A&M, 254
Textbooks, 115, 196
    McGuffey readers, 250
    New England Primer, 242
Theater, 119
Theft, 312–313, 318
Think-aloud, teacher, 129
Thinking skills, 124
Think-pair-share, 130
Thompson v. Southwest District (1980), 337
Threats, 229
Time-out, 219
TIMSS (Trends in International
    Mathematics and Science Study), 154
Tinker Doctrine, 341
*Tinker v. Des Moines Independent
    Community School District* (1969),
    340–341, 348
Title I funding, 60
Title IX of the Education Amendments
    Act of 1972, 44, 76, 259, 328

Token economy, 216
Town schools, 246
Traditional public schools, 40, 43
Transitions, 210
Traumatic brain injury, 93
Trees, philosophy, 277, 278, 279, 280,
    281, 282–283, 284
Trends in International Mathematics and
    Science Study (TIMSS), 154
Troy Female Seminary, 251
Truancy, 313–314, 318
*Turning Points: Preparing American Youth
    for the 21st Century* (Carnegie Council
    on Adolescent Development), 260
Tuskegee Institute (Alabama), 253
Tyler Rationale, 114

Unconditional teaching, 412
Understanding
    defined, 145
    facets of, 146
Understanding by Design (Wiggins &
    McTighe), 145
Unfunded mandate, 242–243
Uniforms, 341–342
Unions, 333. *See also specific unions*
Unit of study, 147
University of California, 254
University of Chicago, 277
University of Illinois, 254
University of Maine, 254
University of Pennsylvania, 246
Urban Institute, 301
Urban schools, 58–59
Urban Schools (2000), 58
U.S. Census Bureau, 56, 68, 85, 86, 382n
U.S. Constitution, 324, 327–328, 329,
    330, 366
U.S. Department of Education, 78, 81n,
    93n, 315, 359, 360, 373
U.S. Department of Health and Human
    Services (DHHS), 294, 304, 305
U.S. Department of Justice, 312, 313
U.S. General Accounting Office, 58
U.S. News and World Report, 197

U.S. Substance Abuse and Mental Health
    Services Administration, 304

Validity, of tests, 155
Verbal interventions, 219
Victimization, 310–313
Videos
    in high school education, 190
    streaming, 175
Violence, 312–313, 318
Virginia Bill for the More General
    Diffusion of Knowledge, 246
Virtual High School, Inc. (VHS), 197
Virtual schools, 197
Visual arts, 119, 269
Visual impairments, 93
Visual learners, 91, 92
Vocational Education Act of 1963, 259
Vocational high school, 55
Vouchers, 47–48

Ware v. Morgan County School District
    (1988), 337
Wayside teaching, 121
Weapons, possession of, 313
WebQuests, 177
Weight issues, 307–309
Welcome letter, 392, 393
Wells High School (California), 59
White boards, 174
"Wide-awakeness," 280
Wiki, 196
Wireless technology, 195
Wisconsin v. Yoder (1972), 350, 351
Withitness, 208
Women
    education of, 241, 246
    as teachers, 251, 252
Writing, teaching, 132–133, 137

Yale University, 246
Young adolescents, defined, 26

Zero tolerance policies, 313
Zone of proximal development, 71